Essentials of Marketing

4e

Charles W. Lamb, Jr.

M.J. Neeley Professor of Marketing
M.J. Neeley School of Business
Texas Christian University

Joseph F. Hair, Jr.

Alvin C. Copeland Endowed Chair
of Franchising and Director,
Entrepreneurship Institute
Louisiana State University

Carl McDaniel

Chair, Department of Marketing
College of Business Administration
University of Texas at Arlington

THOMSON

SOUTH-WESTERN

Australia · Canada · Mexico · Singapore · Spain · United Kingdom · United States

THOMSON

SOUTH-WESTERN

Essentials of Marketing, 4e
Charles W. Lamb, Joseph F. Hair, and Carl McDaniel

VP/Editorial Director:
Jack Calhoun

VP Editor-in-Chief:
Michael P. Roche

Senior Publisher
Melissa Acuña

Acquisitions Editor:
Steve Hazelwood

Developmental Editor:
Jamie Gleich Bryant

Marketing Manager:
Nicole Moore

Production Editor:
Amy McGuire

Media Developmental Editor:
Peggy Buskey

Media Production Editor:
Pam Wallace

Manufacturing Coordinator:
Diane Lohman

Compositor:
Pre-Press Company, Inc.

Printer:
Quebecor World Dubuque
Dubuque, IA

Design Project Manager:
Ann Marie Rekow

Internal Designer:
Christy Carr

Cover Designer:
Anne Marie Rekow

Photography Manager:
Deanna Ettinger

Photo Researcher:
Charlotte Goldman

For permission to use material from this text or product, contact us by
Tel (800) 730-2214
Fax (800) 730-2215
http://www.thomsonrights.com

For more information
contact South-Western,
5191 Natorp Boulevard,
Mason, Ohio 45040.
Or you can visit our Internet site at:
http://www.swlearning.com

To my grandsons, Cameron and Chandler Stock.

—*Charles W. Lamb, Jr.*

To my loving and supportive wife Dale, and my son Joe, III, and his wife Kerrie.

—*Joseph F. Hair, Jr.*

To Ann and Billy Boswell—
The finest sister and brother-in-law a person could have.

—*Carl McDaniel*

Brief Contents

Your Guide to Features
(by Part)

Your Guide to Features
(by Part)

Contents

PART 4

Promotion and Pricing
  Decisions 399

ABOUT THIS EDITION

You are holding a textbook that has experienced a dramatic increase with each edition in the number of colleges and university student-users. We are very grateful to the hundreds of professors that have selected our text to give college students their first exposure to the dynamic world of marketing. We are honored that a vast majority of professors stay with our text edition after edition. Our research gives us an indication why this is true. *Students find* Essentials of Marketing, *by Lamb, Hair, and McDaniel, the most exciting, readable, and enjoyable text of their college career.*

OUTLINE

So What's New . . .
- Brand New Content
- Opening Vignettes
- Global Perspective Boxes
- Ethics in Marketing
- Review-It
- Think About It: Ethics Exercise
- Try It: Entrepreneurship Case
- Watch It
- Flip It, Click It, Spin It
- Marketing Miscues
- Critical Thinking Cases

What Makes *Essentials of Marketing 4e* so Popular with Students?
- We Grab Their Attention
- It's Easy to Learn
- We Integrate Technology in a Meaningful Way
  - Xtra!
  - Fresh Internet Activities and Real-Time Examples
  - Technology Exercises that Reinforce the Chapter Concepts
  - New Internet Marketing Chapter
  - Who Wants to Be a Marketer
- We Offer a Robust, Comprehensive Web Site

What Makes *Essentials of Marketing 4e* so Popular with Instructors?
- Our Integrated Learning System
- Our Text Pedagogy Excites and Reinforces Learning

Innovative and Valuable Instructor Supplements
- Instructor Resource CD-ROM
- PowerPoint™ CD-ROM with Integrated Video Examples
- Triple Option Video Package
- A Value-Based Instructor's Manual Like No Other, the Core of Our Integrated Learning System
- Comprehensive Test Bank and Windows Testing Software
- WebTutor™ Advantage
- Other Outstanding Supplements

Innovative and Valuable Student Supplements
- The Grademaker Study Guide and Workbook
- Xtra!
- Video CD-ROM
- Cadotte: Experience Marketing at the Marketplace

So What's New...

If you are already familiar with *Essentials of Marketing*, you may be asking, "So what's new?" The answer is quite a bit. In addition to the dozens of new examples in each chapter, we have added new content and revised and updated existing material throughout the book.

BRAND NEW CONTENT

PART 1   A new Chapter 2 (Ethics, Social Responsibility, and the Marketing Environment) has a new section on American values and new content on demographics, including material and an exhibit on women as principal economic decision makers. We have revised the section on older consumers and included a completely new section on multicultural marketing. Chapter 3 (Developing a Global Vision) has been greatly revised to reflect constant changes in the global marketplace. We have updated the section on the impact of globalization on trade and added new content on the U.S. Commercial Service which includes a new exhibit on how the service helps companies that want to go global. There is updated information on direct foreign investment, new sections on the Free Trade Agreement of the Americas (FTAA), the Association of South East Asian Nations (ASEAN), and the Asia-Pacific Economic Cooperation (APEC), plus a map that depicts the member countries of the trade agreements discussed in the chapter.

PART 2   Chapter 4 (Consumer Decision Making) has new material on trends in gender marketing, and Chapter 5 (Business Marketing) has a completely revised section on business marketing on the Internet. Chapter 6 (Segmenting and Targeting Markets) now includes updated information based on the 2000 census, plus a thoroughly revised section on bases for segmenting business markets.

PART 3   Part 3 begins with Chapter 8 (Product and Services Concepts), which has a new section on global brands. Chapter 9 (Developing and Managing Products) follows with new exhibits on the history of new product introductions and the diffusion process, plus a completely new section on on-line test marketing. Distribution concepts can be difficult, so we have revised Chapter 10 (Supply Chain Management) to give students an introduction to supply chain management that sticks to the basics. We have condensed the chapter in several areas to make it more readable.

PART 4   Chapter 12 (Marketing Communications and Personal Selling). Chapter 14 (Internet Marketing) is completely revised for every edition of *Essentials of Marketing* to reflect the constantly evolving world of Internet marketing and e-commerce. We have thoroughly revised the chapter, which now includes more information on security and privacy issues, the best ways to measure Internet marketing success, and how to apply Porter's Five Industry Forces to on-line marketing efforts. Chapter 15 (Pricing Concepts) opens with more examples of elastic and inelastic demand, a thoroughly revised and expanded section on the impact of Internet and extranets on pricing, and a revised section on Internet auctions. Expanded discussions of choosing a pricing strategy, predatory pricing, and bundling and services follows. The chapter also has a new section on the implications of zero-percent financing and a revised section on value pricing, with a new section on dangers of pricing products too low.

OPENING VIGNETTES

Each chapter begins with a new, current, real-world story about a marketing decision or situation facing a company. These vignettes have been carefully prepared to stimulate student interest in the topics to come in the chapter and can be used to begin class discussion. A special section before the chapter summary called **Connect It** answers the teaser questions posed in the opening vignette and helps illustrate how the chapter material relates to the real world of marketing. In the Fourth Edition, you'll read about companies like Soapworks, Coleman, *Maxim*, Red Bull, and Universal Studios.

13

It's after midnight and the dance clubs are jumping—music is pulsating, lights are flashing, people are dancing, and the bar is littered with little silver and blue cans. Yes, Red Bull is in the house—and has absolutely no intention of leaving the party.

Red Bull, exported from Austria, has created and dominated the energy drink category with marketing savvy, guerrilla tactics, and unusual distribution methods. Dietrich Mateschitz, the owner of Red Bull International, created the caffeine-charged beverage in 1987, based on a popular health tonic he discovered in Thailand. After spreading into neighboring countries including Hungary, Slovenia, Germany, and Switzerland, Red Bull charged into the U.S. market, virtually creating the energy drink market and taking it by the horns.

Initially, Red Bull was the drink of choice for extreme athletes and all-night ravers, but the taurine-based energy drink has gained a larger following and can now be found on supermarket shelves in almost every state. According to Red Bull's Web site at (**http://www. redbull.com**), "Taurine is a conditionally essential amino acid, which naturally occurs in the body. But in times of extreme physical exertion, the body no longer produces the required amounts and a relative deficiency results." Hence, a need is identified and Red Bull races to fill it.

In less than three years, Red Bull has spawned a hot new beverage category and boosted sales from a base of $12 mil-

in 1999, according to Beverage Marketing Corporation. Now Coke, Anheuser-Busch, and Pepsi are looking to get a piece of the action, and some predict that sales of energy drinks in the United States could top $500 million in the next few years.

But with 70 percent of the market share, Red Bull executives feel confident that they can continue leading the category by employing the same marketing techniques that put them on the map in the first place.

The company's consistent strategy has been to "open up" a market by securing unusual distribution channels. Red Bull initially began its U.S. charge in Santa Monica, California, by piggybacking with established distributors that deliver a number of brands. As the drink became more popular, Red Bull narrowed its distribution methods by contacting smaller distributors and insisting that they sell only Red Bull. Otherwise, Red Bull sets up warehouses and hires college students to deliver its product. Results have been incredible—in a new market, Red Bull generally breaks even within the first three months and shows a profit after six.

Another tactic that Red Bull employs is hiring local hipsters "who embody the spirit of Red Bull" in target areas around in a Red Bull logoed ca... samples, and educate consum... the product.

Sales teams also visit target accounts—trendy nightclubs a...

Red Bull supplies the bar with a bran... cooler and other POP (Point-of-Pur- chase) items. The sales teams also... to get the drink into convenience sto... near colleges, gyms, health-food sto... and supermarkets.

While Red Bull relies heavily on s... pling events at bars and nightclubs,... native sports have proved to be a na... fit for the product. Red Bull underwri... number of extreme sports competiti... and sponsors about three dozen ath... like kayaker Tao Berman, who set a... world record by paddling over a 98-... waterfall. Another unique event Red... sponsors is a DJ Academy. The late... one, held in New York City and taugh... such mix masters as MJ Cole and... Shadow Boy, was offered to sixty as... ing DJs from around the world.

Once established in a market, Re... employs more traditional advertising... rent ads portray an animated bull ch... ter and carry the tag "Red Bull Gives... Wings." The ads run on late-night T... on popular alternative radio shows. ...

How do marketers like Red Bull d... cide what type of advertising messa... should be conveyed to prospective... sumers? How do marketers decide... which media to use? How do public... tions and publicity benefit a markete...

CONNECT IT

As you finish reading this chapter, think back to the opening story about how Red Bull created and continues to dominate the energy drink category with marketing savvy, guerrilla tactics, and unusual distribution methods. To advertise its products, Red Bull's promotional team went through the same creative steps as other marketers—from determining what appeal to use to choosing the appropriate executional style. Great effort was also expended in deciding which medium would best reach the desired target market. Public relations and publicity also played a significant role in the success Red Bull has achieved.

GLOBAL PERSPECTIVE BOXES

GLOBAL PERSPECTIVES

Powering into Europe

Coca-Cola Company sees the fragmented and fast-growing European sports-drink market as an important opportunity, which is why the company is investing $40 million to $50 million to launch Powerade in Europe. It is Coke's biggest marketing push in Europe in six years. "There is an open field in Europe. It's not like the United States," says Keith Pardy, director of strategic marketing for Coca-Cola West Europe.

Sports drinks command an even higher premium in Europe than in the United States, where the market is well established. A 500-milliliter bottle of a sports drink costs between 90 pence and £1 ($1.31–$1.45) in Britain, for example, compared with about 75 pence for the same size bottle of Coke or Pepsi.

Moreover, Coke believes Europeans aged 13 to 29, the target market for Powerade, increasingly are making sports a bigger part of their lives. Coke says its new Powerade drink increases endurance during exercise by combining the benefits of a sports drink with the energy boost of drinks such as Red Bull, made by a closely held Austrian company. The formula in Europe is the same as in the new vitamin-B-enhanced U.S. Powerade, but the taste is slightly different because of certain European regulations on ingredients, Mr. Pardy says. The look is the same as in the United States, with a futuristic letter "P" logo.

As in the United States, Coke is marketing Powerade to the likes of surfers and skateboarders. Posters to be placed in gyms across Europe as part of the advertising campaign for Powerade will allude to "extreme sports" challenges, for example. But the company hopes the drink will eventually transcend its original use, and that European youths will begin drinking sports beverages more generally, as youths do in the United States.

"We want to grow the market in Europe to the point where you'll use it whenever you need en- durance, beyond sports occasions," Mr. Pardy says.

Powerade will be launched in Britain, Ireland, France, Germany, Spain, Sweden, Turkey, Italy, Poland, Hungary, and Greece. The drink, which will be sold in citrus, orange, and vivid-blueberry flavor, will be distributed first through vending machines in gyms, sports centers, and soccer stadiums before moving to convenience stores and supermarkets.

Advertising for the drink will span billboards, television commercials, sponsorships with sports figures, the Internet, and direct mail. Most of the advertising will be directed at a male audience, as the sports-drink market is generally skewed more toward men in Europe.[28]

Describe Coke's target market strategy for Powerade in Europe. Explain the marketing mix that the company plans to employ.

Today most businesses compete not only locally and nationally, but globally as well. Companies that have never given a thought to exporting now face competition from abroad. Thinking globally should be a part of every manager's tactical and strategic planning. Accordingly, we address this topic in detail early in Chapter 3. We have also integrated numerous global examples within the body of the text and identified them with the icon shown in the margin.

Global marketing is fully integrated throughout the book, cases, and videos, as well. Our **Global Perspectives** boxes, which appear in most chapters, provide expanded global examples of the marketing issues facing companies in countries from Asia to Africa to Europe. Each box concludes with thought-provoking questions carefully prepared to stimulate class discussion. You'll read about the Chinese supply chain, marketing beverages in developing nations, and exporting marketing savvy, among others.

ETHICS IN MARKETING

In this edition we continue our emphasis on ethics. The **Ethics in Marketing** boxes, complete with questions focusing on ethical decision making, have been revised in each chapter. This feature offers provocative examples of how ethics comes into play in many marketing decisions. Is it ethical to target teens at school? What about using sex as an advertising appeal? Or conducting racial profiling at retail stores? Students will consider these and many other hotly debated ethical questions.

REVIEW IT

In order to make our **Integrated Learning System** even more effective, we have distributed the end-of-chapter discussion and writing questions within the chapter summary in a **Review It** section. Questions are numbered according to the learning objective to which they correspond. For example, the summary point for learning objective 5 in Chapter 13 has four related questions. They are numbered 5.1, 5.2, 5.3, and 5.4. This reorganization helps students identify questions pertinent to the learning objective they are studying, allowing each chapter to function as a series of modules that can be read over multiple study sessions.

THINK ABOUT IT

In today's business environment, ethics are extremely important. In recent years, there have been numerous scandals and trials that stem from a lack of ethical judgment. In 2002, over 150 companies revised their earnings forecasts, signaling that perhaps their accounting methods were questionable. And who can forget the scandals linked to Adelphia, Tyco, ImClone, WorldCom, and of course Enron and Arthur Andersen?

Although some might say that these occurances are the work of a few bad apples spoiling the bunch, it is clear that ethical decision making plays a very important role in a company's success and prosperity. **Think About It** is a new ethics exercise appearing in every chapter. A brief scenario presents students with a situation in which the right thing to do may or may not be crystal clear. To help students make appropriate ethical decisions, we always refer students back to the AMA's Code of Ethics, found on-line at **http://www.marketingpower.com**. This gives students a resource for the exercise and also helps reinforce the ethical standards that marketers should uphold.

SO WHAT'S NEW...

TRY IT: ENTREPRENEURSHIP CASE

Entrepreneurship, whether in the newest dot com or in America's largest corporations, is what fueled the greatest period of expansion in American history. Nine chapters have new entrepreneurship cases highlighting the challenges facing entrepreneurs in the 21st century. **Try It** cases focus on a wide variety of companies, like Look-Look (a marketing research company specializing in cool spotting), Identix (maker of optical identification systems based on a person's biological features, such as eye patterns or fingerprints), Global Lightwave (an Israeli optics company), IslanderISP (an Internet service provider started by high-school students on Seattle's exclusive Mercer Island suburb), and Noodé (a skin care company and product line for Generations X and Y).

But we also recognize that entrepreneurial activities take place across the Fortune 500, so we profile industry giants like W. W. Grainger, which offers over 600,000 maintenance, repair, and operating items, and Valvoline. Both have used a highly entrepreneurial approach in various parts of their business. Your students will find these cases an exciting and challenging aspect of each chapter. But our coverage of small business issues doesn't stop there.

Many students will either work for a small business or strike out on their own to form an organization. For this reason, we continue to include **Apply It: Application for Entrepreneurs** at the end of each chapter. **Try It** cases apply general marketing concepts to the world of start-ups and small business. The **Apply It** exercises are scenarios that require students to apply the material in the chapter to a small business marketing situation. In addition, small business examples throughout each chapter are identified by the icon in the margin.

WATCH IT

Video is a valuable teaching tool, so this edition has a completely new video package that combines short, medium, and long segments. **Watch It** gives students a brief description of segments relating to that chapter. For instance, in Chapter 8 (Product and Services Concepts), the short segments are ads for Kenmore, Chrysler, Radio Shack, and AOL with WebMD; the medium segment is about organic labeling; and the long segment is about Fluker Cricket Farms in Baton Rouge, Louisiana. Students are prepared for video viewing in or out of class by reading the **Watch It** at the end of the chapter.

Because we offer a comprehensive set of learning resources, students may not know what is available to help them study. The Fourth Edition adds two brief new sections at the end of each chapter to help students identify the study aids that are right for them. **Flip It** describes learning opportunities in the Grademaker Study Guide and Workbook. **Click It** reminds students of the many resources at their disposal at **http://lamb. swlearning.com**, and lists the materials for review on Xtra!

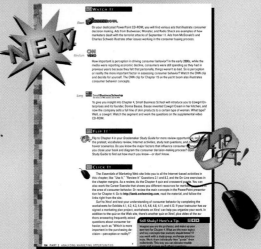

MARKETING MISCUES

Mistakes can have tough consequences, but they also offer a great lesson. This is especially true in marketing. At the end of each part you will find new cases that describe good and bad ideas that couldn't make it in the rough and tumble marketplace. Often amusing and always interesting, these cases about Kmart, Metricom, Jeremy's Microbatch Ice Cream, and Duracell will help your students avoid the same mistakes made by these well-known companies.

CRITICAL THINKING CASES

Making smart decisions is at the heart of successful marketing. **Critical Thinking Cases** at the end of each part put your students in the role of decision maker. They will evaluate the marketing plans of well known organizations like Hewlett-Packard, Square Two Golf, Segway, and iTunes.

WHAT MAKES *ESSENTIALS OF MARKETING 4E* SO POPULAR WITH STUDENTS?

WE GRAB THEIR ATTENTION

We have done extensive research to provide a comprehensive, up-to-the-minute introduction to the field of marketing. Because we weave hundreds of real-world examples into our discussions, our text is called lively and interesting. You should know that this never means superficial or shallow. The latest concepts are covered in detail in a lucid manner with numerous illustrations. For example, in Chapter 2 on the marketing environment, you'll read this passage.

> In recent years there have been explosive population increases among African Americans, Hispanics, and Asians, with those groups now accounting for 79 million out of 281 million Americans. Collectively, they represent an estimated $1 trillion in annual spending power. Hispanics are the fastest growing segment of the population. The diversity of the U.S. population is projected to stabilize around 2023, as the birthrate of minorities levels off.

Is this straightforward information that students need to know? Absolutely. Does that mean that students find this and the other concepts and research-based facts presented in their book very compelling, let alone interesting? Maybe, maybe not. But what we do is combine this information with examples of how real companies are using that information to their benefit (or not using them, to their detriment). The passage below is also in Chapter 2, and it shows how Procter & Gamble, one of the largest global consumer products companies, is using demographic statistics (like those above) in its Multicultural Market Development Organization.

> Procter & Gamble has created a new "Multicultural Market Development Organization" to reach minority markets. Now, every six months, the firm sends out 4.5 million copies of its promotional magazine "Avanzando con tu Familia," or "Getting Ahead with your family." That's one copy for every two Hispanic households. Marketers have reworked the Spanish slogan for Cover Girl makeup, and product developers are creating new Secret deodorant scent names that they hope will appeal to Hispanic consumers. In addition, P&G's new line of Pampers diapers with a "cloth-like backside" come in boxes written in both English and Spanish.

This is just one example of how we have illustrated the principles and concepts in this book with literally hundreds of fresh, new examples.

IT'S EASY TO LEARN

Since the First Edition, one of the hallmarks of *Essentials of Marketing* has been its **Integrated Learning System.** Many of today's students are not only students–many work, commute, and some even have families of their own. This can make it hard to read a chapter in a single sitting. In fact, it can take anywhere from two to five sittings to completely read through a chapter once. With all the starting and stopping of studying, it can be hard to retain the chapter concepts.

Our unique **Integrated Learning System** breaks each chapter into modules organized around the learning objectives, which are placed in the margin throughout the chapter. Students know exactly where a learning objective begins and where it ends. And in the Fourth Edition, we have separated the review questions at the end of each chapter and placed them after the appropriate summary point. Students can answer the questions that relate to the material they have just read. Likewise, the Grademaker Study Guide and Workbook is organized by learning objective, with different types of review questions for each objective. Students can divide the material in each chapter into manageable chunks, read it, review it, and practice it—without losing it!

WE INTEGRATE TECHNOLOGY IN A MEANINGFUL WAY

From the beginning, we have integrated new technologies into our **Integrated Learning System** in a meaningful way. The Fourth Edition continues this tradition by adding new and exciting content to our technology materials. We have also enhanced and refined popular media supplements to bring concepts alive in the classroom.

XTRA!

Our new Xtra! is like no other. We have included extra content modules on competitive intelligence and multicultural marketing. In a brand new video feature, each chapter has an "Ask the Author" segment in which one of the authors responds to frequently asked questions about the marketing topics discussed in the given chapter. For Xtra!, we have revised the Marketing Planning Worksheets to make them easier to use, plus we have created new exhibit worksheets for the tables and diagrams in the text. Students can print out the worksheets, and following the instructions on the sheet, fill in the diagram or table. They can then check their recall of important topics using the actual text exhibit. Other self-assessment tools include a quiz for each chapter that contains questions similar to what they will see on exams and in the Grademaker Study Guide and Workbook. And lastly, Xtra! features a copy of the PowerPoint™ presentation.

FRESH INTERNET ACTIVITIES AND REAL-TIME EXAMPLES

Despite the technology bust of 2000, the Internet is here to stay and continues to be a powerful resource for teaching and learning. Each chapter of *Essentials of Marketing* contains numerous examples of the Internet's role in marketing, designated throughout the text by the icon in the margin. In addition, we regularly offer opportunities for students to use the Internet to further their study of chapter content. On Line activities with URLs appear in the margins throughout each chapter and are tied to either organizations mentioned in the text or the concepts being discussed. For example, in Chapter 4, students will read about how gender marketing is influencing the video game industry, which is beginning to develop new games based on popular female characters like Barbie and Nancy Drew aimed at capturing female customers. The On Line activity below allows students to explore this trend in greater detail.

Because each activity calls for student effort and feedback, you can use these mini-exercises as additional assignments or quizzing opportunities. We have kept the best exercises from the Third Edition and added ninety new ones. Knowing how fast the Internet changes, we have a made a concerted effort to create exercises and direct students to sites that have staying power and that will not become obsolete by the end of the semester.

> **GameGirlz**
>
> What kind of games are available at the Game-Girlz Web site? How do the games "for" girls differ from the games "for" boys at GameSpot?
>
> **http://www.gamegirlz.com**
>
> **http://www.gamespot.com**
>
> **On Line**

Links to all URLs in the book are located on the text's Internet site at **http://lamb.swlearning.com.**

WHAT MAKES ESSENTIALS OF *MARKETING* 4E SO POPULAR WITH STUDENTS?

Nearly every chapter has multiple technology assignments in the **Review It** section. Questions that contain a technology component are identified with the on-line icon. For example, after reviewing the factors that affect the promotional mix in Chapter 12, students are sent to the Web for the following activities:

7.2 **INFOTRAC COLLEGE EDITION** **WRITING** Choose two companies, one a consumer-products company and the other an on-line retailer. Conduct some research on these two companies in terms of their promotional practices by observation (such as looking in magazines, the newspaper, television, Web site, etc.) and searching at your campus library. You may also use InfoTrac (**http://www.infotrac-college.com**) to locate any articles written on the promotional activities of the companies you select. Describe some of the types of promotions that these companies have engaged in during the last year—for example, ran television ads, sponsored an event, held a sweepstakes, or expanded sales force. To the best of your abilities, determine the objective of each promotion in relation to the AIDA model. For example, the objective of a magazine ad might be to gain attention or to create interest, while the objective of a coupon might be to stimulate the action of purchase. Also note if the companies' promotions are integrated or not.

7.3 **ON-LINE** Visit **http://www.teenresearch.com**. What research can this company offer about the size and growth of the teen market, the buying power of teenagers, and their buying habits? Why might these statistics be important to a company targeting teenagers in terms of marketing communications and promotion strategy?

In addition to the numerous Internet assignments throughout the book, we continue to offer students access to the InfoTrac database maintained by the Gale Research Group. InfoTrac contains over 14 million articles from over 3,800 sources dating back to 1980. Students can use InfoTrac to connect with the real world of marketing through refereed academic journals, business and popular magazines and newspapers, and a vast array of government publications.

With so many articles and publications at the students' disposal, they could get lost in research. So we have created guided exercises to help them develop their research and critical reading skills. For instance, in Chapter 15, after students review the government regulations that affect pricing, they can do the following exercise:

InfoTrac exercises like this one can be found throughout the text to either guide an original research project or provide structured reading exercise.

8.1 **INFOTRAC COLLEGE EDITION** What kind of factors can push a respectable firm to enter a price-fixing arrangement with a competitor? Using InfoTrac (**http://www.infotrac-college.com**), read about the price-fixing scandals that rocked the art auction industry or the Hollywood movie studios and Blockbuster Video during 2001 and 2002. If there are more current scandals, read a selection of articles on a particular industry. Then compile a list of business practices and pricing issues that are present in the reports of each scandal. Is each scandal unique, or are there overlapping characteristics? What conclusion can you draw about price fixing from the articles you read? How does the federal government deal with price fixing?

E-commerce changes at the speed of light. We completely rewrite Chapter 14, Internet Marketing, with each edition to keep pace with the dynamic world of e-commerce. The latest marketing innovations, technology shifts, and dot com successes and failures are covered like no other text. We don't neglect the traditional companies but explain how many of these firms are morphing to "bricks and clicks." Our Internet Marketing chapter is located at the text's Web site at **http://lamb.swlearning.com** and contains all of the features of our print chapters with the added bonus of direct links to company examples and sources of information.

When we debuted **Who Wants to Be a Marketer?** with the Third Edition, we did not anticipate how popular it would become. Developed by John Drea of Western Illinois University, this exciting supplement to the Fourth Edition of *Essentials of Marketing* by Lamb, Hair, and McDaniel is an in-class, computer-based game. **Who Wants to Be a Marketer?** is a fun and exciting way to review terminology and concepts with students. This easy-to-use game only requires Microsoft PowerPoint™ and a method to display the screen to the entire class (such as a data projector). **Who Wants to Be a Marketer?** has two rounds of fifty original questions per each chapter, for a total of 1,500 questions! **Who Wants to Be a Marketer?** is only available for adopters of *Essentials of Marketing* by Lamb, Hair, and McDaniel.

WE OFFER A ROBUST, COMPREHENSIVE WEB SITE

Lamb, Hair, and McDaniel's Web site contains a wide array of supplementary products for instructors to use to enhance their course material and presentations, and for guiding students down the path to a clear understanding of the concepts presented within the text. It also offers Web pages dedicated to students' needs and geared toward helping them succeed. The instructor's site includes: the entire Test Bank, the entire Instructor Manual, "Great Ideas in Teaching Marketing," the entire PowerPoint™ presentation with hyperlinks in viewable and printable formats, case updates for all the end-of-chapter and end-of-part cases (one update per case per semester), and "Who Wants to Be a Marketer?" The abundant student materials include:

- The **Interactive Study Center** contains materials for every chapter of *Essentials of Marketing, 4e:* crossword puzzles of marketing terminology; Internet Applications which contain **On Line** margin activities plus **Use It** and **Review It** items from the text that have an Internet component; and interactive quizzes with a self-assessment for each chapter.

- A downloadable set of **PowerPoint™ slides** and the order form for the Grademaker Study Guide and Workbook, plus an abridged sample chapter from the study guide can be found on the Student Resources page.

- **Chapter 14** on Internet Marketing.

- The **Marketing Plan Project** features a new small business every semester. Students can read the case and develop a marketing plan for a real company struggling with various marketing issues. In conjunction with questions keyed to every chapter, instructors can use the **Marketing Plan Project** as a comprehensive case. Without the questions, the case provides the basis for a student project, which can be submitted at its completion to the profiled company via the publisher as part of the **Marketing Plan Project** Contest. Guidelines and contest rules appear on the **Marketing Plan Project** page at **http://lamb.swlearning.com**.

- To help students get started in the field of marketing, the Lamb, Hair, and McDaniel Web site features **Your Marketing Career**. This valuable tool presents information on a variety of marketing careers and includes helpful advice and a multitude of resources for starting a marketing career. A self-assessment tool, career listings with compensation ranges, a features-advantages-benefits model to help students determine job fit, a list of resources for job prospecting, information on how to write a résumé, and a pre-interview checklist are only some of the many career materials available at **Your Marketing Career**.

- **Career Exersites** are unique Internet activities designed to help students use the Web as a career research tool. Developed specifically for each chapter, the exersites give students resources for researching a marketing career in a field related to the chapter content. For example, the exersite for Chapter 7 (Decision Support Systems and Marketing Research) lists useful Web sites for exploring a career in marketing research with an activity to help build career skills.

- **Net News** allows students to read marketing news without having to cull through the plethora of business periodicals to find it. Each article consists of current news relating to the chapter topics. Discussion questions follow the article to help students apply what they know to the situation presented.

OUR INTEGRATED LEARNING SYSTEM™

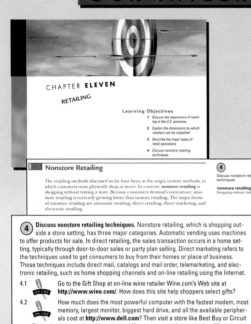

All of our new and exciting content is anchored by the cornerstone of our text, our fully **Integrated Learning System**. The text and all major supplements are organized around the learning objectives that appear at the beginning of each chapter, so *Essentials of Marketing 4e* is both easy to teach from and to learn.

A numbered icon like the one shown in the margin identifies each objective in each chapter and appears next to its related material throughout the text, Instructor's Manual, Test Bank, and Study Guide. In other words, every learning objective links the text, Study Guide, Test Bank, and all components of the Instructor's Manual.

Chapter learning objectives are the linchpin of the **Integrated Learning System**. They provide a structure for your lesson plans– everything you need to assure complete coverage of each objective icon. Do you want to stress more on learning objective 4, Chapter 11, "Discuss nonstore retailing techniques?" No problem. Go to the Instructor's Manual, objective 4, Chapter 11, and you'll find supplemental material. Do you want to emphasize the same objective on an exam? In every chapter in the Test Bank, questions are organized by type and level of difficulty. Now you can test on objective 4 by type of question and degree of difficulty. This value-driven system for you, the instructor, delivers what it promises–full integration.

The integrated system also delivers value for students as they prepare for exams. The learning objective icons identify all the material in the text and Study Guide that relate to each specific learning objective. Students can easily check their grasp of each objective by reading the text sections, reviewing the corresponding summary section, answering the Study Guide questions for that objective, and returning to the appropriate text sections for further review when they have difficulty with any of the questions. Students can quickly identify all material relating to an objective by simply looking for the learning objective icon. And every chapter still concludes with a detailed study tip to help students master marketing concepts.

OUR TEXT PEDAGOGY EXCITES AND REINFORCES LEARNING

Pedagogical features are meant to reinforce learning, but that doesn't mean that they have to be boring. We have created teaching tools within the text itself that will excite student interest as well as teach.

◉ **Cross-Functional Connections:** No marketer is an island. Marketing professionals work with every functional area of the company. The **Cross-Functional Connections** that open every part explore the give and take between marketing and all other business functions. Solutions to the topical questions are provided at the end of each part so that students can test their understanding of how marketing is integrated with the other functions of business.

@ **Opening Vignettes, Revisited at Chapter Conclusions:** Each chapter begins with a new, current, real-world story about a marketing decision or situation facing a company. A special section before the Review It chapter summary called Connect It answers the teaser questions posed in the opening vignette and helps illustrate how the chapter material relates to the real world of marketing.

@ **Use It:** Students are often heard to comment, "Yes, I can use this information when I graduate and get into my career, but what take-away value can I get right now?" Use It addresses this concern by covering a topic related to the chapter that the student can put to work today. For example, in Chapter 3 (Developing a Global Vision), Use It tells students how to find a job overseas and also offers tips on changing money abroad.

@ **Define It:** Key terms appear in boldface in the text, with definitions in the margins, making it easy for students to check their understanding of key definitions. A complete alphabetical list of key terms appears at the end of each chapter as a study checklist called Define It, with page citations for easy reference.

@ **Review It:** Each chapter ends with Review It, a summary that distills the main points of the chapter. Chapter summaries are organized around the learning objectives so that students can use them as a quick check of their understanding of chapter concepts. Discussion questions and activities are under the learning objective to which they pertain.

@ **Writing Questions:** To help students improve their writing skills, we have included writing exercises with the Review It questions at the end of each chapter. These exercises are marked with the icon shown here. The writing questions are designed to be brief so that students can accomplish writing assignments in a short time and grading time is minimized.

@ **End of Chapter Team Activities:** The ability to work collaboratively is key to success in today's business world. End-of-chapter team activities, identified by the icon shown here, give students opportunities to learn to work together by engaging in consensus building and problem solving.

@ **Apply It–Application for Entrepreneurs:** These short scenarios prompt students to apply marketing concepts to small business and entrepreneurial settings. Each scenario ends with provocative questions to aid student analysis and comprehension.

@ **Think About It—Ethics Exercise:** Short ethical dilemmas help students practice doing the right thing. Questions following each scenario prompt students to make an ethical decision and refer them to the AMA Code of Ethics.

@ **Try It–Entrepreneurship Case:** All chapters contain Try It, an entrepreneurship case with questions to help work through problems facing real small business companies today.

All components of our comprehensive support package have been developed to help you prepare lectures and tests as quickly and easily as possible. We provide a wealth of information and activities beyond the text to supplement your lectures, as well as teaching aids in a variety of formats to fit your own teaching style.

INNOVATIVE AND VALUABLE INSTRUCTOR SUPPLEMENTS

INSTRUCTOR RESOURCE CD-ROM

Managing your classroom resources is now easier than ever. The new Instructor Resource CD-ROM contains all key instructor supplements–Instructor's Manual, Test Bank, and PowerPoint™.

POWERPOINT™ CD-ROM

To take full advantage of the new features of the *Essentials of Marketing 4e* PowerPoint™ presentation, you'll want to use the customizable PowerPoint™ CD-ROM. Many of the hundreds of full-color images provided with *Essentials of Marketing 4e*, contain valuable teaching notes to help guide you through your lecture. In addition, hyperlinks to the On Line activities in the chapter margins are embedded in each chapter of slides so that you can maximize your use of these activities during class time, and short thirty-second television ads from recent Super Bowl broadcasts are embedded in the slide presentation and only viewable through the PowerPoint™ CD-ROM. All you need is Windows to run the PowerPoint™ viewer and an LCD panel for classroom display.

TRIPLE OPTION VIDEO PACKAGE

The video package to accompany *Essentials of Marketing 4e* is the most comprehensive in our history. We provide you with three options for video use: Each chapter has a combination of thirty-second clips (short) embedded in the instructor's PowerPoint™ CD-ROM presentation, two- to four-minute clips (medium) for classroom viewing, and a ten- to fifteen-minute clip (long) for both classroom viewing and home viewing via the new video CD-ROM. There are fifty-two short clips, seventeen medium clips, and thirteen long segments.

The short clips consist of television ads that were originally broadcast during the Super Bowl games. The medium clips have been pulled from CNN's news footage archives and show how marketing principles operate in the world of big business. And the long clips are excerpted footage from various episodes of the thirty-minute Small Business School (SBS) program broadcast nationwide on PBS.

Each chapter has a designated SBS segment as the lead segment for that chapter, but because the SBS programs cover all aspects of business, SBS segments raise more issues than just those presented in the assigned chapter. For example, the lead segment for Chapter 1 is on Wahoo's Fish Taco, a uniquely Californian restaurant, but the content in the Wahoo's Fish Taco segment also relates to material in Chapter 4 (Consumer Decision Making), Chapter 6 (Segmenting and Targeting Markets), Chapter 11 (Retailing), and Chapter 13 (Advertising, Sales Promotion, and Public Relations). The rich SBS videos will help reinforce learning by showing people who are doing marketing every day–and not according to thematic units. The multifaceted SBS videos give you maximum flexibility in how you use the videos, and combined with the short and medium option videos, the possibilities are endless!

A VALUE-BASED INSTRUCTOR'S MANUAL LIKE NO OTHER, THE CORE OF OUR INTEGRATED LEARNING SYSTEM™

Our Instructor's Manual is the core of our **Integrated Learning System**. For the Fourth Edition of *Essentials of Marketing*, we have made our popular Instructor's Manual even more valuable for new and experienced instructors alike. Here is a list of the new features that will reduce class preparation time:

◎ Suggested syllabi for twelve- and sixteen-week terms.

◎ A pedagogy grid for each chapter briefly laying out 1) all the options the professor has in the chapter and 2) what key points in the chapter each feature addresses. The features included on the grid are the opening vignette, the boxed features, **Use It**, **Apply It**, **Try It**, and each video option.

◎ Three suggested lesson plans for each chapter: a lecture lesson plan, a small-group-work lesson plan, and a video lesson plan.

We have retained the proven features like the detailed chapter outline, lists of support material, supplemental articles, additional class activities, and solutions for all **Review It**, **Apply It**, and **Try It** and part cases in the book. Our manual is truly "one-stop shopping" for instructors teaching any size of marketing course.

COMPREHENSIVE TEST BANK AND WINDOWS TESTING SOFTWARE

To complete the **Integrated Learning System**, our enhanced Test Bank is organized around the learning objectives. It is available in print and new Windows software formats (ExamView testing software).

With ExamView, you can choose to prepare tests that cover all learning objectives or emphasize those you feel are most important. This updated Test Bank is one of the most comprehensive on the market, with over 3,000 true/false, multiple-choice, scenario, and essay questions. Our testing database, combined with the ease of ExamView, takes the pain out of exam preparation.

WEBTUTOR™ ADVANTAGE

WebTutor™ Advantage puts you ahead of the game in providing on-line course management for instructors and on-line learning for students. It contains all of the interactive study guide components that you could ever want and many valuable technology-oriented additions you never thought you'd get! **WebTutor™ Advantage** also contains e-lectures—this valuable student resource combines the robust PowerPoint™ presentation with narration. **WebTutor™ Advantage** also contains the Small Business School digitized videos and pedagogy, "Ask the Authors" video segments, and the "Who Wants to Be a Marketer?" game.

WebTUTOR™ Advantage

OTHER OUTSTANDING SUPPLEMENTS

⊚ **Transparency Acetates:** To supplement the PowerPoint™ presentation, 250 transparency acetates are available. They include figures and diagrams from the *Essentials of Marketing* parent text, *Marketing 7e,* as well as synopses of important text content. Because the acetate package is from the parent text, many of the transparencies supplement the content in *Essentials of Marketing 4e.* Images are tied to the **Integrated Learning System** through the Instructor's Manual lecture outlines. Transparencies and their discussion prompts appear within the learning objective content where they apply. In addition, if you need more acetates than the 250 in our package, our PowerPoint™ presentation is available in printable format on the instructor and student resource pages of the Lamb, Hair, and McDaniel Web site (**http://lamb.swlearning.com**). View the slides and create your own acetates tailored to your particular course needs.

⊚ **Handbook for New Instructors:** This helpful booklet was specifically designed for instructors preparing to teach their first course in principles of marketing. It provides helpful hints on developing a course outline, lecturing, testing, giving feedback, and assigning projects.

⊚ **Great Ideas in Teaching Marketing:** We have moved **Great Ideas** to our instructor's resource page on the Lamb, Hair, and McDaniel Web site. In this way, we can regularly add to our collection of teaching ideas without having to wait for the next edition of *Essentials of Marketing.* Submissions will be collected, organized, and presented on-line to keep Great Ideas a dynamic and up-to-date teaching resource. For Great Ideas, go to **http://lamb.swlearning.com.**

INNOVATIVE AND VALUABLE STUDENT SUPPLEMENTS

Essentials of Marketing 4e provides an excellent vehicle for learning the fundamentals. For students to gain a true understanding of marketing, however, it's best if they can apply the principles they are learning in the classroom. And it's best if they have study aids that address their particular learning style. Our student supplements meet the needs of a variety of learning styles from visual to auditory, from hands-on to abstract conceptualization.

THE GRADEMAKER STUDY GUIDE AND WORKBOOK

The **Grademaker Study Guide and Workbook** has been greatly updated for the Fourth Edition. As part of the **Integrated Learning System**, the study guide questions are linked to the learning objectives by numbered icons. A student having difficulty with the material found in Chapter 5, Learning Objective 2, can quickly go to this Learning Objective in the Grademaker and find numerous questions and aids to master that material. Every chapter includes application questions in a variety of formats to help students to master concepts. Study guide questions are designed to be similar in type and difficulty level to the Test Bank questions. By careful review of the Grademaker, students can dramatically improve their test scores. Each Grademaker chapter opens with a self-assessment pre-test to help students identify areas where they need the most review, followed by chapter outlines with definitions, vocabulary practice, true/false, multiple choice, agree/disagree, and essay questions. Two new sections have been created for this edition of the Grademaker: marketing scenarios and marketing applications. Each scenario presents a marketing situation and is followed by a series of questions that ask students to evaluate the situation presented. The new applications require students to put marketing concepts to work, such as in the creation of a print advertisement for the chapter on Advertising, Sales Promotion, and Public Relations (Chapter 13).

XTRA!

As described above, **Xtra!** is like no other interactive content that has ever accompanied *Essentials of Marketing*. Videos, exhibit worksheets, supplemental content modules, quizzes, and PowerPoint™ slides are the powerful Xtra! study tools we have created especially for this edition. Xtra! is the most powerful electronic learning tool created for *Essentials of Marketing*.

VIDEO CD-ROM

Video brings marketing concepts alive like no other format. Unfortunately, today's time-pressed instructors and students rarely have the space in the tightly-packed syllabus to dedicate to watching lengthy videos. Our video CD-ROM contains all thirteen of the **Small Business School** videos (the long segments described in the **Watch It** at the end of each chapter) and can be packaged with *Essentials of Marketing*. Pedagogy created specifically for each video segment helps students experience how marketing concepts are in use in some of the country's most successful small businesses.

CADOTTE: EXPERIENCE MARKETING AT THE MARKETPLACE

This simulation will challenge students to make tough marketing decisions in a competitive, fast-paced market where the customers are demanding and the competition is working hard to increase market share. Theory comes alive as students learn to manage a new business venture, increase profit, improve customer satisfaction, and capture dominant market share.

ACKNOWLEDGEMENTS

This book could not have been written and published without the generous expert assistance of many people. First we wish to thank Julie Baker, Texas Christian University, for her contributions to several chapters. J.D. Mosley-Matchett did an excellent job in updating the Internet chapter. We would also like to recognize and thank Vicky Crittenden, Boston College, and Bill Crittenden, Northeastern University, for contributing the Cross-Functional Connections that open each part. Vicky also did and excellent job on the Critical Thinking cases and Marketing Miscues. We must also thank Jeffrey Gleich for contributing all of the new Entrepreneurship cases.

We also wish to thank each of the following persons for their work on the best supplement package that is available today. Our gratitude goes out to: Susan Peterson of Scottsdale Community College for her tremendous revision of the Instructor Manual and her detailed update of the Study Guide; Thomas and Betty Pritchett of Kennesaw State University for revising our comprehensive Test Bank and for writing the quizzes that appear in other parts of the package; Deborah Baker of Texas Christian University, who revised the PowerPoint™ presentation and added the wonderful teaching notes, hyperlinks, and videos to her already complete slide presentation; James Hess of Ivy Tech State College, who narrated our interactive lectures; Jeffrey Gleich for the excellent video teaching notes; and John Drea of Western Illinois University, who created the fun classroom review game, "Who Wants to Be a Marketer?"

Our secretaries and assistants, Fran Eller at TCU, RoseAnn Reddick at UTA, and Jessica Rupp at University of North Texas typed the manuscript, provided important quality control, and helped keep the project (and us) on schedule. Their dedication, hard work, and support were exemplary.

Our deepest gratitude goes to the team at Thomson Learning that has made this text a market leader. Jamie Gleich Bryant, our developmental editor, and Amy McGuire, our production editor, made this text a reality. A special thanks goes to Steve Hazelwood, our acquisitions editor, and Melissa Acuña, our Publisher, for their suggestions and support.

Finally, we are particularly indebted to our reviewers:

BARRY ASHMEN
Bucks County Community College

THOMAS S. BENNETT
Gaston Community College

KEN BELL
Ellsworth Community College

LARRY BORGEN
Normandale Community College

P.J. FORREST
Mississippi College

DANIEL J. GOEBEL
University of Southern Mississippi

MARK GREEN
Simpson College

RICHARD A. HALBERG
Houghton College

DOROTHY R. HARPOOL
Wichita State University

THOMAS J. LANG
University of Miami

RONALD E. MICHAELS
University of Central Florida

MONICA PERRY
University of North Carolina, Charlotte

WILLIAM RECH
Bucks County Community College

DICK ROSE
University of Phoenix (deceased)

JAMES V. SPIERS
Arizona State University

JEFFREY SCHMIDT
University of Illinois

WAYNE ALEXANDER
Moorhead State University

LINDA ANGLIN
Mankato State University

THOMAS S. BENNETT
Gaston Community College

JAMES C. BOESPFLUG
Arapahoe Community College

VICTORIA BUSH
University of Mississippi

JOSEPH E. CANTRELL
DeAnza College

G. L. CARR
University of Alaska, Anchorage

DEBORAH CHIVIGES CALHOUN
College of Notre Dame of Maryland

JOHN ALAN DAVIS
Mohave Community College

WILLIAM M. DIAMOND
SUNY–Albany

JACQUELINE K. EASTMAN
Valdosta State University

KEVIN M. ELLIOTT
Mankato State University

KAREN A. EVANS
Herkimer County Community College

RANDALL S. HANSEN
Stetson University

HARI S. HARIHARAN
University of Wisconsin, Madison

TIMOTHY S. HATTEN
Black Hills State University

JAMES E. HAZELTINE
Northeastern Illinois University

PATRICIA M. HOPKINS
California State Polytechnic

KENNETH R. LAWRENCE
New Jersey Institute of Technology

J. GORDON LONG
Georgia College

LARRY MAES
Davenport University

KARL MANN
Tennessee Tech University

CATHY L. MARTIN
Northeast Louisiana University

IRVING MASON
Herkimer County Community College

ANIL M. PANDYA
Northeastern Illinois University

MICHAEL M. PEARSON
Loyola University, New Orleans

CONSTANTINE G. PETRIDES
Borough of Manhattan Community College

PETER A. SCHNEIDER
Seton Hall University

DONALD R. SELF
Auburn University at Montgomery

MARK T. SPENCE
Southern Connecticut State College

JAMES E. STODDARD
University of New Hampshire

RANDY STUART
Kennesaw State University

ALBERT J. TAYLOR
Austin Peay State University

JANICE E. TAYLOR
Miami University of Ohio

RONALD D. TAYLOR
Mississippi State University

SANDRA T. VERNON
Fayetteville Technical Community College

CHARLES R. VITASKA
Metro State College, Denver

JAMES F. WENTHE
Georgia College

LINDA BERNS WRIGHT
Mississippi State University

WILLIAM R. WYND
Eastern Washington University

MEET THE AUTHORS

CHARLES W. LAMB, JR.
TEXAS CHRISTIAN UNIVERSITY

Charles W. Lamb, Jr., is the M.J. Neeley Professor of Marketing, M.J. Neeley School of Business, Texas Christian University. He served as chair of the department of marketing from 1982 to 1988 and again from 1997 to 2003. He is currently chair of the Department of Information Systems and Supply Chain Management and president-elect of the Academy of Marketing Science.

Lamb has authored or co-authored more than a dozen books and anthologies on marketing topics and over 150 articles that have appeared in academic journals and conference proceedings.

In 1997, he was awarded the prestigious Chancellor's Award for Distinguished Research and Creative Activity at TCU. This is the highest honor that the university bestows on its faculty. Other key honors he has received include the M.J. Neeley School of Business Research Award, selection as a Distinguished Fellow of the Academy of Marketing Science and a Fellow of the Southwestern Marketing Association.

Lamb earned an associate degree from Sinclair Community College, a bachelor's degree from Miami University, an MBA from Wright State University, and a doctorate from Kent State University. He previously served as assistant and associate professor of marketing at Texas A & M University.

JOSEPH F. HAIR, JR.
LOUISIANA STATE UNIVERSITY

Joseph Hair is Alvin C. Copeland Endowed Chair of Franchising and Director, Entrepreneurship Institute, Louisiana State University. Previously, Hair held the Phil B. Hardin Chair of Marketing at the University of Mississippi. He has taught graduate and undergraduate marketing and marketing research courses.

Hair has authored 27 books, monographs, and cases and over 60 articles in scholarly journals. He also has participated on many university committees and has chaired numerous departmental task forces. He serves on the editorial review boards of several journals.

He is a member of the American Marketing Association, Academy of Marketing Science, Southern Marketing Association, and Southwestern Marketing Association.

Hair holds a bachelor's degree in economics, a master's degree in marketing, and a doctorate in marketing, all from the University of Florida. He also serves as a marketing consultant to businesses in a variety of industries, ranging from food and retailing to financial services, health care, electronics, and the U.S. Departments of Agriculture and Interior.

CARL MCDANIEL
UNIVERSITY OF TEXAS, ARLINGTON

Carl McDaniel is a professor of marketing at the University of Texas–Arlington, where he has been chairman of the marketing department since 1976. He has been an instructor for more than 20 years and is the recipient of several awards for outstanding teaching. McDaniel has also been a district sales manager for Southwestern Bell Telephone Company. Currently, he serves as a board member of the North Texas Higher Education Authority.

In addition to Marketing, McDaniel also has co-authored numerous textbooks in marketing and business. McDaniel's research has appeared in such publications as the *Journal of Marketing, Journal of Business Research, Journal of the Academy of Marketing Science*, and *California Management Review.*

McDaniel is a member of the American Marketing Association, Academy of Marketing Science, Southern Marketing Association, Southwestern Marketing Association, and Western Marketing Association.

Besides his academic experience, McDaniel has business experience as the co-owner of a marketing research firm. Recently, McDaniel served as senior consultant to the International Trade Centre (ITC), Geneva, Switzerland. The ITC's mission is to help developing nations increase their exports. He has a bachelor's degree from the University of Arkansas and his master's degree and doctorate from Arizona State University.

PART 1

The World of Marketing

CROSS-FUNCTIONAL BUSINESS SYSTEMS: PUTTING THE CUSTOMER AT THE CENTER

Businesses today are faced with many changes and expectations. Technology has become a driving force in all decisions. Technological innovations force companies to adapt very quickly to a new way of doing business. The speed of change in today's business world has empowered functional-level managers to make decisions that will help give their firms a competitive edge in a rapidly evolving, digitized marketplace.

In this environment, it is imperative that all departments have a customer focus. This focus needs to be reflected in the daily activities of all employees, regardless of the area in which they work—accounting, finance, manufacturing, human resources, or marketing. A customer focus that permeates every facet of the organization does not come easily, however, nor has it always been implemented successfully.

Historically, three levels formed a "hierarchy of strategy" within a company: corporate strategy, business strategy, and functional strategy. The corporate- and business-level strategies were supported by the individual functional strategies that united the various activities necessary to gain competitive advantage. Traditionally, each functional area performs specialized portions of the organization's tasks. For example, the functional-level *marketing* strategy resolves questions concerning what products deliver customer satisfaction and value, what price to charge, how to distribute products, and what type of marketing communication activities will produce the desired impact. On the other hand, the functional-level *manufacturing* strategy decides what products should be manufactured and at what production rate, and how to make the products. Since such functional activities require expertise in only one functional area, managers have traditionally been trained to manage "vertically."

Vertical activities have led to the creation of corporate silos in business. Employees working in a silo generally do not understand the importance of their processes in providing the final product or service to the customer. Silos have resulted in departments comprised of functional specialists who have tended to talk only with each other. For example, marketers talk to other marketing folks, operational discussions take place on the shop floor among manufacturing engineers, development team members talk within their R&D groups, and financial analysts and accountants talk with one another.

Individual functional-level strategies can result in intraorganizational conflict. For example, conflict between the marketing group and the production schedule is common. Marketing wants output increased or decreased immediately, but the production schedule, once made, is often seen as very inflexible.

For a customer-focused strategy to be effective, however, functional groups must work in partnership with one another. Crossing functional boundaries is referred to as managing "horizontally" and requires significant coordination among business functions. For example, marketing managers must take a keen interest in financial issues and operational managers should better understand the firm's customers.

Today's business environment has put considerable pressure on functional groups to work together more harmoniously. In the twenty-first century, we see a dramatic rush to get products to the marketplace at a much faster rate than ever before. At the same time, customers are much more demanding about what they want in these products. The bottom line: Customers want customized products delivered immediately. Companies such as General Electric, Hewlett-Packard, and Ford have dedicated considerable time and resources to understanding and implementing high levels of cross-functional integration (often referred to as *internal partnering*).

In GE's entry-level Financial Management Program, trainees work in various jobs throughout the world during the first two years of employment. Members of this program change jobs every six months. Each change generally brings a new geographic location and a new cross-functional perspective on GE's businesses. Unfortunately, successful cross-functional interactions in most companies do not come easy and are often mired in conflict. Reasons for conflict between and among functional areas include divergent personalities, physical separation, data differences, and suboptimal reward systems.

Marketing people tend to be extroverted and interact easily with others, while R&D and manufacturing people are frequently introverted and known to work well with individual work processes and output. In addition to being distinct by their personalities, marketers and their product management colleagues in R&D and manufacturing are often housed in different locations. This is surprising when you think about the overlapping impact all three groups have on a company's product.

The marketing department is typically located in the company's headquarters—which may be in the heart of a major business district, with sales located strategically close to customers. Manufacturing is often located in low-wage areas, low-rent districts, and close to suppliers or even in a different country. It becomes too easy for each department to "do its own thing," particularly if the groups are separated by language differences as well as time zones.

Another major source of conflict between marketing and its R&D and manufacturing counterparts is the type of data collected and used in decision making. Technical specialists in R&D and manufacturing have a difficult time understanding the attitudinal data that marketers work with. For example, marketing's forecasts are rarely 100 percent accurate, but manufacturing can determine the precise costs associated with production processes.

Not surprisingly, marketing's reward system based on increased sales is often in direct conflict with manufacturing and R&D's reward systems that are driven by cost reduction. Marketing's ability to increase sales may mean offering consumers depth in the product line. Unfortunately, increased depth leads to more changeover in the production lines, which in turn drives up the cost of production.

A major challenge for marketers has been reducing conflict between the marketing department and other business functions. Closer working relationships among human resources and information technology professionals have resulted in two major facilitating mechanisms: cross-functional teams and an information technology infrastructure.

Hewlett-Packard's team approach to its product development illustrates this functional integration. From concept to market entry, teams of engineers, marketers, manufacturers, financiers, and accountants weave functional-level information into a cohesive program for product introduction. All information is shared across functional groups, and reports on cross-functional activities are prepared regularly.

Recognizing the customer's role in the organization and empowering employees are both necessary for success in today's business environment. Rapidly changing technology has made the cross-functional communication process much easier. This is good news since cross-functional integration is as good for the customer as it is for business.

Questions for Discussion

1. What is the overlap among marketing, manufacturing, finance, accounting, and human resources? What does each of these functions do that results in this overlap?

2. Why is cross-functional coordination necessary to have a customer-oriented firm?

3. What roles do teamwork and technology play in cross-functional coordination?

Check It Out

For articles and exercises on the material in this part, and for other great study aids, visit the *Essentials of Marketing* Web site at **http://lamb.swlearning.com.**

CHAPTER **ONE**
AN OVERVIEW OF MARKETING

Learning Objectives

1 *Define the term* marketing

2 *Describe four marketing management philosophies*

3 *Explain how firms implement the marketing concept*

4 *Describe the marketing process and identify the variables that make up the marketing mix*

5 *Describe several reasons for studying marketing*

In 1994, Amilya Antonetti began to talk seriously about breaking into the $4.7 billion U.S. laundry-detergent market. Industry veterans told her she had to be joking. "They all laughed hysterically," Antonetti recalls. "They'd say, 'Honey, have you ever heard of Clorox? Have you ever heard of Tide? There's no place for you here.'"

Time and again, buyers for grocery stores told Antonetti that none of *their* customers would be interested in the hypoallergenic cleansing products she began developing after learning that her infant son's health problems were aggravated by the chemicals in standard brands. After one such conversation, Antonetti came close to admitting defeat. Then she did an about-face, marched right back into the guy's office, and declared, "I have one more thing to say to you: I *am* your customer."

Convinced that there were others out there like her, Antonetti did her own market research by haunting grocery-store aisles. She spent hours talking with female shoppers, she says, "Asking and asking and asking, What is it here that's missing?" She persuaded a retired soap buyer for Safeway to put her in touch with formulators. Then in late 1995, she and her lawyer husband, Dennis Karp, sold their home, secured $120,000 in loans from the Small Business Administration, and set up shop as SoapWorks in northern California's San Leandro.

It was a long haul, but five years later, grocery-store buyers were no longer laughing. And now Antonetti has shelf space in 2,500 stores from California to Florida. She generated revenues of $5 million in 1999. And she owes her success to the very customers that grocery-store buyers claimed did not exist. "There was very clearly a niche that was not being served," says Antonetti, who

has boldly enlisted would-be customers in her sales effort. "If a mom comes in here and asks, 'Why are you not at my store?' I tell her, 'Look, your store already knows about me. I've already talked with every major chain. If you want us to be in your store, you need to talk to your store manager.'"

That's just what happened with Joellen Sutterfield, a fashion-industry executive who credits SoapWorks products with reducing the skin rashes she has suffered all her life. Sutterfield boasts that she hectored Safeway store managers for more than a year before they finally placed their first $50,000 SoapWorks order. "Now," Sutterfield says, "I'm working on the manager at the Whole Foods Market in San Ramon."

At Trader Joe's, SoapWorks has found a "cult following," says product manager Annette Davidson. A SoapWorks customer herself, Davidson says store managers at the 131-store chain reported such "huge demand" from customers that she decided to stock an expanded product line. Indeed, Antonetti's customers have become such apostles for SoapWorks, it's as if she's mixed a marketing ingredient into her formula.

But the secret to SoapWorks' customer-driven marketing scheme isn't solely in the suds. What really makes it work is Antonetti's demonstrated allegiance to her customers, who are smitten as much by what SoapWorks stands for as by what's inside the bottle.

"Our customers fit into a niche that was not being served by Tide and Cheer and All," says Antonetti. A black binder chock-full of customers' letters and e-mail messages attests to that. A few gripes do jump out from the correspondence: laundry powder left undissolved and weak grease-cutting agents. But most of the missives read like this: "After meeting you in Children's Hospital, we began using the products you gave us, and they are wonderful. We no longer need to leave the house after cleaning, and we all breathe much easier." Another writer credits SoapWorks laundry and bar soap with ridding them all of "painful, dry, flaky skin." Then there are those who simply seem smitten with Antonetti: "Thank you for caring about me and my children."

Now that she's gained a foothold in the market, Antonetti is more aggressively taking on the mainstream competition. She has a new label with a much bigger brand name and bold-colored bubbles. She's also formulating a more upscale product line based on cold-processed whole-leaf aloe.[1]

Amilya's initial motivation to go into the laundry-detergent business was based on her infant son's health needs. Describe her philosophy of business.

On Line ▮ ◀ ▶

SoapWorks

How does SoapWorks use its Web site to connect with its market? What indications do you have that this is a customer-oriented company?

http://www.soapworks.com

What Is Marketing?

1

Define the term *marketing*

What does the term *marketing* mean to you? Many people think it means the same as personal selling. Others think marketing is the same as personal selling and advertising. Still others believe marketing has something to do with making products available in stores, arranging displays, and maintaining inventories of products for future sales. Actually, marketing includes all of these activities and more.

Marketing has two facets. First, it is a philosophy, an attitude, a perspective, or a management orientation that stresses customer satisfaction. Second, marketing is a set of activities used to implement this philosophy. The American Marketing Association's definition encompasses both perspectives: "**Marketing** is the process of planning and executing the conception, pricing, promotion, and distribution of ideas, goods, and services to create exchanges that satisfy individual and organizational goals."[2]

marketing
The process of planning and executing the conception, pricing, promotion, and distribution of ideas, goods, and services to create exchanges that satisfy individual and organizational goals.

The Concept of Exchange

exchange
The idea that people give up something to receive something they would rather have.

Exchange is the key term in the definition of marketing. The concept of **exchange** is quite simple. It means that people give up something to receive something they would rather have. Normally, we think of money as the medium of exchange. We "give up" money to "get" the goods and services we want. Exchange does not require money, however. Two persons may barter or trade such items as baseball cards or oil paintings.

An exchange can take place only if the following five conditions exist:

1. There must be at least two parties.
2. Each party has something that might be of value to the other party.
3. Each party is capable of communication and delivery.
4. Each party is free to accept or reject the exchange offer.
5. Each party believes it is appropriate or desirable to deal with the other party.[3]

Exchange will not necessarily take place even if all these conditions exist. They are, however, necessary for exchange to be possible. For example, you may place an advertisement in your local newspaper stating that your used automobile is for sale at a certain price. Several people may call you to ask about the car, some may test-drive it, and one or more may even make you an offer. All five conditions are necessary for an exchange to exist. But unless you reach an agreement with a buyer and actually sell the car, an exchange will not take place. Notice that marketing can occur even if an exchange does not occur. In the example just discussed, you would have engaged in marketing even if no one bought your used automobile.

Marketing Management Philosophies

2

Describe four marketing management philosophies

Four competing philosophies strongly influence an organization's marketing activities. These philosophies are commonly referred to as production, sales, market, and societal marketing orientations.

Production Orientation

production orientation
A philosophy that focuses on the internal capabilities of the firm rather than on the desires and needs of the marketplace.

A **production orientation** is a philosophy that focuses on the internal capabilities of the firm rather than on the desires and needs of the marketplace. A production orientation means that management assesses its resources and asks these questions: "What can we do best?" "What can our engineers design?" "What is easy to produce, given our equipment?" In the case of a service organization, managers ask, "What services are most convenient for the firm to offer?" and "Where do our talents lie?" Some have referred to this orientation as a *Field of Dreams* orientation, referring to the movie line, "If we build it, they will come." The furniture industry is infamous for its disregard of customers and for its slow cycle times. This has always been a production-oriented industry.

There is nothing wrong with assessing a firm's capabilities; in fact, such assessments are major considerations in strategic marketing planning. A production orientation falls short because it does not consider whether the goods and services that the firm produces most efficiently also meet the needs of the marketplace. Sometimes what a firm can best produce is exactly what the market wants. For example, the research and development department of 3M's commercial tape division developed and patented the adhesive component of Post-it Notes a year before a commercial application was identified. In other situations, as when competition is weak or demand exceeds supply, a production-oriented firm can survive and even prosper. More often, however, firms that succeed in competitive markets have a clear understanding that they must first determine what customers want and then produce it, rather than focus on what company management thinks should be produced.

Sales Orientation

A **sales orientation** is based on the ideas that people will buy more goods and services if aggressive sales techniques are used and that high sales result in high profits. Not only are sales to the final buyer emphasized but intermediaries are also encouraged to push manufacturers' products more aggressively. To sales-oriented firms, marketing means selling things and collecting money.

The fundamental problem with a sales orientation, as with a production orientation, is a lack of understanding of the needs and wants of the marketplace. Sales-oriented companies often find that, despite the quality of their sales force, they cannot convince people to buy goods or services that are neither wanted nor needed.

Some sales-oriented firms simply lack understanding of what is important to their customers. Many so-called dot-com businesses that came into existence in the late 1990s are no longer around. Some experts have predicted that 95 to 98 percent of the dot-coms will go out of business.[4] Most of those that did focused on the technology rather than the customer.

Kimberly Knickle couldn't have been happier when she signed up with online grocer Streamline.com. With two kids and a job, the $30 a month extra was worth it. Streamline installed a refrigerator in her garage to make deliveries when she wasn't home, picked up the dry cleaning, delivered stamps, and dropped off parcel shipments. The best part was the customer service. When something went wrong, Streamline instantly credited her account. She could always get someone on the phone. As the company gained a larger customer base, however, Knickle's enthusiasm turned sour. The deliveries became inconsistent, telephone customer service put her on hold more often, and the company overcharged her several times. The big blow came when it revamped its Web site: In the past, she could place an order for thirty items quickly, but the company switched to a new system that checked inventory in real time,

sales orientation
The idea that people will buy more goods and services if aggressive sales techniques are used and that high sales result in high profits.

AP/WIDE WORLD PHOTOS

Workers prepare registration forms for bidders atop front lobby tables, which themselves were available for purchase, at the liquidation of on-line grocer Webvan Group. After churning through $830 million in two years, the company was forced into bankruptcy. Despite having mastered its supply chain and supplying great service, Webvan was not able to generate enough revenue to stay in business.

slowing down the interface tremendously. "The grocery store is two minutes away," Knickle says. "In 25 minutes, I could get two-thirds of my shopping done at the store. This was supposed to make my life easier."[5]

Market Orientation

marketing concept
The idea that the social and economic justification for an organization's existence is the satisfaction of customer wants and needs while meeting organizational objectives.

The **marketing concept** is a simple and intuitively appealing philosophy. It states that the social and economic justification for an organization's existence is the satisfaction of customer wants and needs while meeting organizational objectives. It is based on an understanding that a sale does not depend on an aggressive sales force, but rather on a customer's decision to purchase a product. What a business thinks it produces is not of primary importance to its success. Instead, what customers think they are buying—the perceived value—defines a business. The marketing concept includes the following:

- Focusing on customer wants and needs so that the organization can distinguish its product(s) from competitors' offerings

- Integrating all the organization's activities, including production, to satisfy these wants

- Achieving long-term goals for the organization by satisfying customer wants and needs legally and responsibly

The marketing concept recognizes that there is no reason why customers should buy one organization's offerings unless they are in some way better at serving the customers' wants and needs than those offered by competing organizations.

Customers have higher expectations and more choices than ever before. This means that marketers have to listen more closely than ever before.[6] They also have to anticipate needs, to solve problems before they start, to provide service that wows, and to offer responses to mistakes that more than make up for the original error.[7] For example, Netpulse Communications provides Internet connections to health clubs allowing exercisers to surf the Web or check their e-mail while they are working out. Netpulse uses a monitoring system to diagnose problems remotely. So, if a janitor accidentally disconnects a power cord, a service representative can call the club and ask them to plug the machine back in. Nine times out of ten Netpulse reports a problem to the club before anyone there is even aware of it.[8]

A market-oriented organization recognizes that customer groups and their wants vary, so it creates products and services to address these differences. *Grace* magazine embodies the full-fashioned lifestyle with features and columns that highlight relevant fashion, beauty, and style tips for larger women. But while fashion features are definitely geared to the 68 percent of American women size twelve and up, the rest of the magazine is far more general interest.

Firms that adopt and implement the marketing concept are said to be market oriented. Achieving a **market orientation** involves obtaining information about customers, competitors, and markets; examining the information from a total business perspective; determining how to deliver superior customer value; and implementing actions to provide value to customers.[9] It also entails establishing and maintaining mutually rewarding relationships with customers.

market orientation
A philosophy that assumes that a sale does not depend on an aggressive sales force but rather on a customer's decision to purchase a product.

Today, companies of all types are adopting a market orientation. Bill Marriott, Marriott International's CEO, logs an average of 150,000 travel miles each year visiting the company's hotels, inspecting them, and talking to employees at all levels in the organization. Burton Snowboards became the best-known brand in one of the world's fastest-growing sports by identifying its most important customers, figuring out the product that those customers want, and then designing it. Almost every day Burton staffers visit with some of the 300 professional riders worldwide who advise the company. These conversations take place on the slopes and on the phone. If one of them has a suggestion or a problem, a Burton employee calls back within twenty-four hours. Riders help develop virtually every Burton product.[10]

Understanding your competitive arena and competitors' strengths and weaknesses is a critical component of market orientation. This includes assessing what existing or potential competitors might be intending to do tomorrow as well as what they are doing today. Western Union failed to define its competitive arena as telecommunications, concentrating instead on telegraph services, and was eventually outflanked by fax technology. Had Western Union been a market-oriented company, its management might have better understood the changes taking place, seen the competitive threat, and developed strategies to counter the threat.[11]

Western Union

Has Western Union rebounded from its failure to define its competitive arena as telecommunications? Evaluate the company's Web site to find out. Against whom does Western Union seem to be competing in the twenty-first century?

http://www.westernunion.com

On Line

Societal Marketing Orientation

One reason a market-oriented organization may choose not to deliver the benefits sought by customers is that these benefits may not be good for individuals or society. This philosophy, called a **societal marketing orientation**, states that an organization exists not only to satisfy customer wants and needs and to meet organizational objectives but also to preserve or enhance individuals' and society's long-term best interests. Marketing products and containers that are less toxic than normal, are more durable, contain reusable materials, or are made of recyclable materials is consistent with a societal marketing orientation. Duracell and Eveready battery companies have reduced the levels of mercury in their batteries and will eventually market mercury-free products. Turtle Wax car wash products and detergents are biodegradable and can be "digested" by waste treatment plants. The company's plastic containers are made of recyclable plastic, and its spray products do not use propellants that damage the ozone layer in the earth's upper atmosphere.

societal marketing orientation
The idea that an organization exists not only to satisfy customer wants and needs and to meet organizational objectives but also to preserve or enhance individuals' and society's long-term best interests.

Implementation of the Marketing Concept

In an established organization, changing to a customer-driven corporate culture must occur gradually. Furthermore, middle managers alone cannot effect a change in corporate culture; they must have the total support of the CEO and other top executives.

The success of Nordstrom, the Seattle-based retailer, illustrates the results of strong management support for customer-oriented service. Employees can do almost anything to satisfy shoppers. One story, which the company doesn't deny, tells of a customer who got his money back on a tire, even though Nordstrom doesn't sell tires. Nordstrom, like many other successful marketers, understands that key issues in developing competitive advantage today include creating customer value, maintaining customer satisfaction, and building long-term relationships.

3
Explain how firms implement the marketing concept

customer value
The ratio of benefits to the sacrifice necessary to obtain those benefits.

Customer Value and Customer Satisfaction

Customer value is the ratio of benefits to the sacrifice necessary to obtain those benefits. The automobile industry illustrates the importance of creating customer value. To penetrate the fiercely competitive luxury automobile market, Lexus adopted a customer-driven approach, with particular emphasis on service. Lexus stresses product quality with a standard of zero defects in manufacturing. The service quality goal is to

Although Turtle Wax is not founded upon a societal marketing orientation in the same way as, say, the Sierra Club, the company still communicates to its customers that it is concerned about the environment. This placement on the Turtle Wax Web site reminds customers that the company includes societal concerns in its corporate philosophy.

COURTESY OF TURTLE WAX, INC.

Zane's Cycles

What evidence of a market orientation do you see on Zane's Cycles' Web site? How does the company demonstrate its commitment to the customer?

http://www.zanescycles.com

 On Line

treat each customer as one would treat a guest in one's home, to pursue the perfect person-to-person relationship, and to strive to improve continually. This pursuit has enabled Lexus to establish a clear quality image and capture a significant share of the luxury car market.

Customer value is not simply a matter of high quality. A high-quality product that is available only at a high price will not be perceived as a good value, nor will bare-bones service or low-quality goods selling for a low price. Instead, customers value goods and services that are of the quality they expect and that are sold at prices they are willing to pay. Value can be used to sell a Mercedes Benz as well as a $3 Tyson frozen chicken dinner.

ON LINE Value also stretches beyond quality and price to include customized options and fast delivery. Dell Computer Corporation encourages shoppers to customize products to their liking on its Web sites. By one count, customers can choose from among more than 25,000 different computer configurations. General Motors has introduced a build-to-order system that allows customers to custom design cars on-line for delivery in as few as four days.[12]

Marketers interested in customer value

- *Offer products that perform:* This is the bare minimum requirement. Consumers have lost patience with shoddy merchandise.

- *Give consumers more than they expect:* Christopher Zane, owner of Zane's Cycles, one of the ten largest bicycle shops in the United States, suggests removing the bar rather than raising it. Zane's Cycles offers lifetime free service, lifetime parts warranties, and ninety-day price protection. The price protection plan is important to demonstrate to customers that they are getting free lifetime parts and services along with the lowest price available for the brands and models that they buy.[13]

- *ON LINE* *Avoid unrealistic pricing:* E-marketers are leveraging Internet technology to redefine how prices are set and negotiated. With lower costs, e-marketers can often offer lower prices than their brick-and-mortar counterparts. The enormous popularity of auction sites such as eBay and Amazon.com and the customer-bid model used by Priceline illustrate that on-line customers are interested in bargain prices. Many are not willing to pay a premium for the convenience of examining the merchandise and taking it home with them.

- *ON LINE* *Give the buyer facts:* Today's sophisticated consumer wants informative advertising and knowledgeable salespeople. A study by Andersen Consulting (now Accenture) revealed that Web sites that don't provide enough information are among the top ten things that "irk" Internet shoppers most.[14]

- *Offer organization-wide commitment in service and after-sales support:* People fly Southwest Airlines because the airline offers superior value. Although passengers do not get assigned seats or meals (just peanuts or crackers) when they use the airline, its service is reliable and friendly and costs less than most major airlines. All Southwest employees are involved in the effort to satisfy customers. Pilots tend to the boarding gate when their help is needed and ticket agents help move luggage. One reservation agent flew from Dallas to Tulsa with a frail, elderly woman whose son was afraid she couldn't handle the change of planes by herself on her way to St. Louis.

customer satisfaction
The feeling that a product has met or exceeded the customer's expectations.

Customer satisfaction is the feeling that a product has met or exceeded the customer's expectations. Keeping current customers satisfied is just as important as attracting new ones and a lot less expensive. Firms that have a reputation for delivering high levels of customer satisfaction do things differently from their competitors. Top management is obsessed with customer satisfaction, and employees throughout the organization understand the link between their job and satisfied customers. The culture of the organization is to focus on delighting customers rather than on selling products. John Chambers, chief executive of Cisco Systems, advises managers to "make your customers the center of your culture."[15] One way that Cisco does this is by directly linking employee compensation programs to customer satisfaction study results.[16]

Staples, the office supply retailer, offers great prices on its paper, pens, fax machines, and other office supplies, but its main strategy is to grow by providing customers with the best solutions to their problems. Its approach is to emulate customer-intimate companies like Home Depot and Airborne Express. These companies do not pursue one-time transactions: They cultivate relationships.

Volvo

How does Volvo use its Web site to maintain customer relations? Do you think Volvo has a sales or a market orientation? What evidence do you have to support your conclusion?

http://www.volvocars.com

On Line

Building Relationships

Attracting new customers to a business is only the beginning. The best companies view new customer attraction as the launching point for developing and enhancing a long-term relationship. Companies can expand market share in three ways: attracting new customers, increasing business with existing customers, and retaining current customers. Building relationships with existing customers directly addresses two of the three possibilities and indirectly addresses the other.

Relationship marketing is a strategy that entails forging long-term partnerships with customers. It begins with developing a clear understanding of who your customers are, what they value, what they want to buy, and how they prefer to interact with you and be served by you.[17] Companies then build relationships with customers by offering value and providing customer satisfaction. They are rewarded with repeat sales and referrals that lead to increases in sales, market share, and profits. Costs also fall because serving existing customers is less expensive than attracting new ones.

Lee Iacocca, former president of both Ford and Chrysler, says that if you "take care of your customers, everything else will fall into place. You have to understand your customers, and you have to follow them. You have to change as your customers' lives change."[18]

The Internet is an effective tool for generating relationships with customers because of its ability to interact with the customer. With the Internet, companies can use e-mail for fast customer service, discussion groups for building a sense of community, and database tracking of buying habits for customizing products.[19]

Customers also benefit from stable relationships with suppliers. Business buyers have found that partnerships with their suppliers are essential to producing high-quality products while cutting costs. Customers remain loyal to firms that provide them greater value and satisfaction than they expect from competing firms.

AP/WIDE WORLD PHOTOS

Customer-intimate companies achieve great success by building longtime relationships with their customers. Home Depot is an industry benchmark in customer satisfaction. Here, employee Juan Cruz loads plywood for a customer preparing her home against an impending hurricane.

relationship marketing
A strategy that entails forging long-term partnerships with customers.

Most successful relationship marketing strategies depend on customer-oriented personnel, effective training programs, employees with authority to make decisions and solve problems, and teamwork.

- *Customer-oriented personnel:* For an organization to be focused on building relationships with customers, employees' attitudes and actions must be customer oriented. An employee may be the only contact a particular customer has with the firm. In that customer's eyes, the employee is the firm. Any person, department, or division that is not customer oriented weakens the positive image of the entire organization. For example, a potential customer who is greeted discourteously may well assume that the employee's attitude represents the whole firm.

- *The role of training:* Leading marketers recognize the role of employee training in customer service and relationship building. Of *Fortune*'s 100 best companies to work for, fifty-three offer on-site university courses and ninety-one have tuition reimbursement programs.[20] It is no coincidence that the public companies on this list such as Southwest Airlines and Cisco Systems perform much better than other firms in their respective industries. All new employees at Disneyland and Walt Disney World must attend Disney University, a special training program for Disney employees. They must first pass Traditions 1, a daylong course focusing on the Disney philosophy and operational procedures. Then they go on to specialized training. Similarly, McDonald's has Hamburger University. At American Express's Quality University, line employees and managers learn how to treat customers. There is an extra payoff for companies such as Disney and McDonald's that train their employees to be customer oriented. When employees make their customers happy, the employees are more likely to derive satisfaction from their jobs. Having contented workers who are committed to their jobs leads to better customer service and greater employee retention.

empowerment
Delegation of authority to solve customers' problems quickly—usually by the first person that the customer notifies regarding a problem.

- *Empowerment:* In addition to training, many marketing-oriented firms are giving employees more authority to solve customer problems on the spot. The term used to describe this delegation of authority is **empowerment**. Employees develop ownership attitudes when they are treated like part-owners of the business and are expected to act the part. These employees manage themselves, are more likely to work hard, account for their own performance and the company's, and take prudent risks to build a stronger business and sustain the company's success. FedEx customer service representatives are trained and empowered to resolve customer problems. Although the average FedEx transaction costs only $16, the customer service representatives are empowered to spend up to $100 to resolve a customer problem.

  After John Yokoyama, owner of Pike Place Fish in Seattle's historic Farmer's Market, committed to empowering his employees, his cost of doing business dropped from 77 percent to 54 percent—a 43 percent increase in gross profit. Yokoyama attributes this success to each individual in the company taking personal responsibility for company profitability. "They like to win. They take it personally. They set new records nearly every month."[21]

  Empowerment gives customers the feeling that their concerns are being addressed and gives employees the feeling that their expertise matters. The result is greater satisfaction for both customers and employees.

teamwork
Collaborative efforts of people to accomplish common objectives.

- *Teamwork:* Many organizations, such as Southwest Airlines and Walt Disney World, that are frequently noted for delivering superior customer value and providing high levels of customer satisfaction assign employees to teams and teach them team-building skills. **Teamwork** entails collaborative efforts of people to accomplish common objectives. Job performance, company performance, product value, and customer satisfaction all improve when people in the same department or work group begin supporting and assisting each other and emphasize cooperation instead of competition. Performance is also enhanced when people in different areas of responsibility such as production and sales or sales and service practice teamwork, with the ultimate goal of delivering superior customer value and satisfaction.

The Marketing Process

Earlier in this chapter, *marketing* was defined as the process of planning and executing the conception, pricing, promotion, and distribution of ideas, goods, and services to create exchanges that satisfy individual and organizational objectives. Marketing, therefore, includes the following activities:

Describe the marketing process and identify the variables that make up the marketing mix

- Gathering, analyzing, and interpreting information about the environment (*environmental scanning*).
- Understanding the organization's mission and the role marketing plays in fulfilling this vision.
- Finding out what benefits people want the organization to deliver and what wants they want the organization to satisfy (*market opportunity analysis*).
- Developing a marketing strategy by deciding exactly which wants, and whose wants, the organization will try to satisfy (*target market strategy*); by setting marketing objectives; and by developing appropriate marketing activities (the *marketing mix*) to satisfy the desires of selected target markets.
- Implementing the strategy.
- Periodically evaluating marketing efforts and making changes if needed.

These activities and their relationships, shown in Exhibit 1.1, form the foundation on which most of the rest of this book is based.

Environmental Scanning

Environmental scanning is the collection and interpretation of information about forces, events, and relationships that may affect the organization. It helps identify market opportunities and threats and provides guidelines for the marketing strategy.

Chapter 2 examines the following six categories of uncontrollable environmental influences that affect marketing decisions:

environmental scanning
The collection and interpretation of information about forces, events, and relationships that may affect the future of an organization.

- *Social forces* such as the values of potential customers and the changing roles of families and women working outside the home.
- *Demographic forces* such as the ages, birth and death rates, and locations of various groups of people.
- *Economic forces* such as changing incomes, inflation, and recession.
- *Technological forces* such as advanced communications and data retrieval capabilities.
- *Political and legal forces* such as changes in laws and regulatory agency activities.
- *Competitive forces* from domestic and foreign-based firms.

Organization Mission

One of top management's most important responsibilities is to formulate the organization's basic statements of purpose and mission. An organization's mission statement answers the question, "What is this firm's business?" Mission statements

| Exhibit 1.1 | The Marketing Process

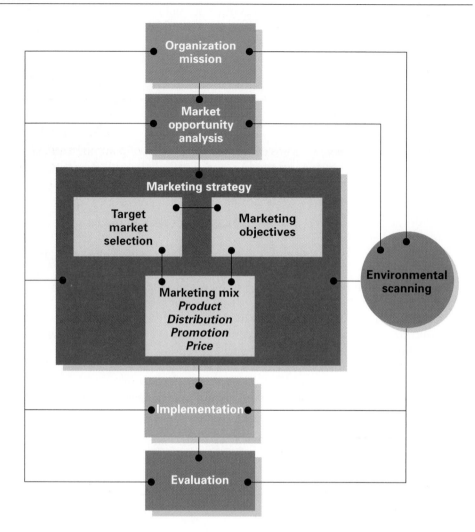

are based on a careful analysis of the benefits sought by present and potential customers, as well as existing and anticipated environmental conditions. This long-term vision of what the organization is or is striving to become establishes the boundaries within which objectives, strategies, and actions must be developed.

market opportunity analysis
A description and estimation of the size and sales potential of market segments of interest to a firm and assessment of key competitors in these market segments.

Marketing Opportunity Analysis

A market segment is a group of individuals or organizations that shares one or more characteristics. It therefore has relatively similar product needs. A **market opportunity analysis** describes market segments of interest to the firm, estimates their size and sales potential, and assesses key competitors in these market segments.

marketing strategy
A plan that involves selecting one or more target markets, setting marketing objectives, and developing and maintaining a marketing mix that will produce mutually satisfying exchanges with target markets.

marketing mix
A unique blend of product, distribution, promotion, and pricing strategies designed to produce mutually satisfying exchanges with a target market.

Marketing Strategy

As Exhibit 1.1 illustrates, **marketing strategy** involves three activities: selecting one or more target markets, setting marketing objectives, and developing and maintaining a **marketing mix** (product, distribution, promotion, and pricing) that will produce mutually satisfying exchanges with target markets.

Target Market Strategy

The three general strategies for selecting target markets are to try to appeal to the entire market with a single marketing mix, to concentrate on only one segment of the market, or to attempt to appeal to multiple market segments using multiple marketing mixes. The characteristics, advantages, and disadvantages of each strategic option are examined in Chapter 6.

Marketing Objectives

A **marketing objective** is a statement of what is to be accomplished through marketing activities—for example, getting 100 people to test-drive a new car during the month of November or getting 2,000 passengers to fly on a new commuter airline during the first week in June. Marketing objectives should be consistent with organizational objectives, should be measurable, and should specify the timeframe during which they are to be achieved.

Carefully specifying marketing objectives offers two major benefits. First, when the objectives are attainable and challenging, they motivate those charged with achieving the objectives. They also serve as standards by which everyone in the organization can gauge their performance. Second, the process of writing specific marketing objectives forces executives to sharpen and clarify their thinking. Written objectives also allow marketing efforts to be integrated and pointed in a consistent direction.

marketing objective
A statement of what is to be accomplished through marketing activities.

GLOBAL PERSPECTIVES

Powering into Europe

Coca-Cola Company sees the fragmented and fast-growing European sports-drink market as an important opportunity, which is why the company is investing $40 million to $50 million to launch Powerade in Europe. It is Coke's biggest marketing push in Europe in six years. "There is an open field in Europe. It's not like the United States," says Keith Pardy, director of strategic marketing for Coca-Cola West Europe.

Sports drinks command an even higher premium in Europe than in the United States, where the market is well established. A 500-milliliter bottle of a sports drink costs between 90 pence and £1 ($1.31–$1.45) in Britain, for example, compared with about 75 pence for the same size bottle of Coke or Pepsi.

Moreover, Coke believes Europeans aged 13 to 29, the target market for Powerade, increasingly are making sports a bigger part of their lives. Coke says its new Powerade drink increases endurance

during exercise by combining the benefits of a sports drink with the energy boost of drinks such as Red Bull, made by a closely held Austrian company. The formula in Europe is the same as in the new vitamin-B–enhanced U.S. Powerade, but the taste is slightly different because of certain European regulations on ingredients, Mr. Pardy says. The look is the same as in the United States, with a futuristic letter "P" logo.

As in the United States, Coke is marketing Powerade to the likes of surfers and skateboarders. Posters to be placed in gyms across Europe as part of the advertising campaign for Powerade will allude to "extreme sports" challenges, for example. But the company hopes the drink will eventually transcend its original use, and that European youths will begin drinking sports beverages more generally, as youths do in the United States.

"We want to grow the market in Europe to the point where you'll use it whenever you need en-

durance, beyond sports occasions," Mr. Pardy says.

Powerade will be launched in Britain, Ireland, France, Germany, Spain, Sweden, Turkey, Italy, Poland, Hungary, and Greece. The drink, which will be sold in citrus, orange, and vivid-blueberry flavor, will be distributed first through vending machines in gyms, sports centers, and soccer stadiums before moving to convenience stores and supermarkets.

Advertising for the drink will span billboards, television commercials, sponsorships with sports figures, the Internet, and direct mail. Most of the advertising will be directed at a male audience, as the sports-drink market is generally skewed more toward men in Europe.[22]

Describe Coke's target market strategy for Powerade in Europe. Explain the marketing mix that the company plans to employ.

Marketing Mix

As noted earlier, the term *marketing mix* refers to a unique blend of product, distribution (place), promotion, and pricing strategies (the **four Ps**) designed to produce mutually satisfying exchanges with a target market. The marketing manager can control each component of the marketing mix, but the strategies for all four components must be blended to achieve optimal results. Any mix is only as good as its weakest component. For example, an excellent product with a poor distribution system will likely fail.

Successful marketing mixes have been carefully tailored to satisfy target markets. At first glance, McDonald's and Wendy's may appear to have roughly identical marketing mixes. After all, they are both in the fast-food business. However, McDonald's targets parents with young children. It has Ronald McDonald, special children's Happy Meals, and playgrounds. Wendy's generally targets the adult crowd. Wendy's doesn't have a playground, but it does have carpeting (for a more adult atmosphere), and it pioneered fast-food salad bars.

Variations in marketing mixes do not occur by chance. They represent fundamental marketing strategies devised by astute marketing managers attempting to gain advantages over competitors and to achieve competitive success.

Product Strategies

Typically, the marketing mix starts with the product "P." The heart of the marketing mix, the starting point, is the product offering and product strategy. It is hard to design a distribution strategy, decide on a promotion campaign, or set a price without knowing the product to be marketed.

The product includes not only the physical unit but also its package, warranty, after-sale service, brand name, company image, value, and many other factors. A Godiva chocolate has many product elements: the chocolate itself, a fancy gold wrapper, a customer satisfaction guarantee, and the prestige of the Godiva brand name. We buy things not only for what they do (benefits) but also for what they mean to us (status, quality, or reputation).

Products can be tangible goods such as computers, ideas like those offered by a consultant, or services such as medical care. Products should also offer customer value. Product and service decisions are covered in Chapters 8 and 9.

Distribution (Place) Strategies

Distribution strategies are concerned with making products available when and where customers want them. Would you rather buy a kiwi fruit at the twenty-four-hour grocery store within walking distance or fly to Australia to pick your own? A part of this place "P" is physical distribution, which involves all the business activities concerned with storing and transporting raw materials or finished products. The goal of distribution is to make sure products arrive in usable condition at designated places when needed. Distribution strategies are covered in Chapters 10 and 11.

COURTESY OF WENDY'S INTERNATIONAL, INC.

Although competing in the saturated fast-food industry, Wendy's does an excellent job of differentiating itself through its product mix. Rather than cater to families with young children, Wendy's tailors its offerings to meet the needs and wants of the adult lunch crowd. Its salad offerings are part of this strategy.

Promotion Strategies

Promotion includes personal selling, advertising, sales promotion, and public relations. Promotion's role in the marketing mix is to bring about mutually satisfying exchanges with target markets by informing, educating, persuading, and reminding them of the benefits of an organization or a product. A good promotion strategy, like using the Dilbert character in a national promotion strategy for Office

Depot, can dramatically increase sales. Good promotion strategies do not guarantee success, however. Despite massive promotional campaigns, the movies *Titan A.E.* and *Pearl Harbor* had disappointing box-office returns. Each element of the promotion "P" is coordinated and managed with the others to create a promotional blend or mix. These integrated marketing communications activities are described in Chapters 12 and 13. Technology-driven aspects of promotional marketing are covered in Chapter 14.

Pricing Strategies

Price is what a buyer must give up to obtain a product. It is often the most flexible of the four marketing mix elements—the quickest element to change. Marketers can raise or lower prices more frequently and easily than they can change other marketing mix variables. Price is an important competitive weapon and is very important to the organization because price multiplied by the number of units sold equals total revenue for the firm. Pricing decisions are covered in Chapter 15.

Implementation

Implementation is the process that turns marketing plans into action assignments and ensures that these assignments are executed in a way that accomplishes the plans' objectives. Implementation activities may involve detailed job assignments, activity descriptions, timelines, budgets, and lots of communication. Although implementation is essentially "doing what you said you were going to do," many organizations repeatedly experience failures in strategy implementation. Brilliant marketing plans are doomed to fail if they are not properly implemented. These detailed communications may or may not be part of the written marketing plan. If they are not part of the plan, they should be specified elsewhere as soon as the plan has been communicated.

implementation
The process that turns marketing plans into action assignments and ensures that these assignments are executed in a way that accomplishes the plans' objectives.

Evaluation

After a marketing plan is implemented, it should be evaluated. **Evaluation** entails gauging the extent to which marketing objectives have been achieved during the specified time period. Four common reasons for failing to achieve a marketing objective are unrealistic marketing objectives, inappropriate marketing strategies in the plan, poor implementation, and changes in the environment after the objective was specified and the strategy was implemented.

evaluation
Gauging the extent to which the marketing objectives have been achieved during the specified time period.

Why Study Marketing?

Now that you understand the meaning of the term *marketing*, why it is important to adopt a marketing orientation, and how organizations implement this philosophy, you may be asking, "What's in it for me?" or "Why should I study marketing?" These are important questions, whether you are majoring in a business field other than marketing (such as accounting, finance, or management information systems) or a nonbusiness field (such as journalism, economics, or agriculture). There are several important reasons to study marketing: Marketing plays an important role in society, marketing is important to businesses, marketing offers outstanding career opportunities, and marketing affects your life every day.

Describe several reasons for studying marketing

Marketing Plays an Important Role in Society

The total population of the United States exceeds 280 million people. Think about how many transactions are needed each day to feed, clothe, and shelter a population of this size. The number is huge. And yet it all works quite well, partly because the well-developed U.S. economic system efficiently distributes the output of farms and factories. A typical U.S. family, for example, consumes 2.5 tons of food a year. Marketing makes food available when we want it, in desired quantities, at accessible locations, and in sanitary and convenient packages and forms (such as instant and frozen foods).

Marketing Is Important to Businesses

The fundamental objectives of most businesses are survival, profits, and growth. Marketing contributes directly to achieving these objectives. Marketing includes the following activities, which are vital to business organizations: assessing the wants and satisfactions of present and potential customers, designing and managing product offerings, determining prices and pricing policies, developing distribution strategies, and communicating with present and potential customers.

ETHICS IN MARKETING

A Red Light for Green Marketing?

After a decade of designing products to appeal to environmentally friendly sensibilities, many companies have concluded that "green" sales pitches don't sell. Some 41 percent of consumers say they don't buy green products because they fear the products won't work as well, according to market researchers RoperASW, which conducts an annual "Green Gauge" consumer-marketing poll.

Shoppers will pay for convenience far more readily than for ideology. In June 2001, after 70 percent of baby-food shoppers said they would prefer the convenience of plastic jars, Gerber Products Company switched from glass to No. 7 plastic, which can't be recycled. Few complained about environmental effects.

These days, bottles of water, disposable mops and heavy-duty plastic plates—all items that end up in landfills—are top sellers. Recycling rates for plastic soda bottles are about a third of what they were in 1995, while the number of single-serve bottles on the shelves more than doubled to 18 billion in 2000. New York Mayor Michael Bloomberg knows the environment is so far off voters' radar screens that he proposed to cut out all metal, glass, and plastic recycling service in the city to save $57 million.

These days, only 29 percent of shoppers have recently bought a product because advertising on the label claimed it was environmentally safe or biodegradable, according to polls by RoperASW. Those who do tend to be younger and wealthier, but their ranks appear to be shrinking. Marketers have seen it coming ever since Ben & Jerry's discontinued "Rainforest Crunch" in 1997, citing slumping sales. The ice cream flavor had been introduced nationwide on Earth Day in 1990, touting conservation and nuts from rainforest trees.

Some marketers still successfully sell environmentally-friendly products, but increasingly they are doing so by playing down or skirting the green message. Personal "wellness" and safety is today's marketing fashion. Seventh Generation, a brand of natural household products, recently changed its slogan from "products for a healthy planet" to "safer for you and the environment."

"If talking about product safety is the path to get into a conversation with customers about the environment, then we haven't lost the authenticity of our mission," says Jeffrey Hollender, Seventh Generation's president.

Some environmentalists blame consumers' waning demand for green products on confusion engendered by inconsistent eco-labeling. The "chasing arrows" recycling logo, for example, appears on the bottom of foam coffee cups, even though consumers can't readily recycle them anywhere in the United States.

The "Energy Star" labeling program launched by the Environmental Protection Agency (EPA) has been considerably more successful, says green-marketing consultant Jacquelyn Ottman. The EPA and industry together tightly control which products can carry the Energy Star logo, which signals energy efficiency. And, even though some Energy Star products carry a higher price tag, the program pitches energy cost savings over the long haul. "Customers will pay the premium when the benefits justify the price," says Ms. Ottman.[23]

Why do you think that consumers have lost interest in environmentally-friendly or "green" products? Do you agree with Gerber Products Company's decision to switch from glass to plastic? Explain your reasons.

All businesspeople, regardless of specialization or area of responsibility, need to be familiar with the terminology and fundamentals of accounting, finance, management, and marketing. People in all business areas need to be able to communicate with specialists in other areas. Furthermore, marketing is not just a job done by people in a marketing department. Marketing is not a department so much as a companywide orientation. It is a part of the job of everyone in the organization, and therefore, a basic understanding of marketing is important to all businesspeople.

Marketing Offers Outstanding Career Opportunities

Between a fourth and a third of the entire civilian workforce in the United States performs marketing activities. Marketing offers great career opportunities in such areas as professional selling, marketing research, advertising, retail buying, distribution management, product management, product development, and wholesaling. Marketing career opportunities also exist in a variety of nonbusiness organizations, including hospitals, museums, universities, the armed forces, and various government and social service agencies.

As the global marketplace becomes more challenging, companies all over the world and of all sizes are going to have to become better marketers. For a comprehensive look at career opportunities in marketing and a variety of other useful information about careers, please visit our Web site at **http://lamb.swlearning.com**.

Marketing Affects Your Life Every Day

Marketing plays a major role in your everyday life. You participate in the marketing process as a consumer of goods and services. About half of every dollar you spend pays for marketing costs, such as marketing research, product development, packaging, transportation, storage, advertising, and sales expenses. By developing a better understanding of marketing, you will become a better-informed consumer. You will better understand the buying process and be able to negotiate more effectively with sellers. Moreover, you will be better prepared to demand satisfaction when the goods and services you buy do not meet the standards promised by the manufacturer or the marketer.

Businesses are not the only entities that conduct marketing activities. Not-for-profit organizations like the Pequot Museum and Research Center provide career opportunities in marketing as well.

Looking Ahead

This book is divided into fifteen chapters organized into four major parts. The chapters are written from the marketing manager's perspective. Each chapter begins with a brief list of learning objectives followed by a brief story about a marketing situation faced by a firm or industry. At the end of each of these opening vignettes, thought-provoking questions link the story to the subject addressed in the chapter. Your instructor may wish to begin chapter discussions by asking members of your class to share their views about the questions.

GLOBAL   The examples of global marketing in most chapters will help you understand that marketing takes place all over the world, between buyers and sellers in different countries. These global marketing examples throughout the book, marked with the icon shown in the margin, are intended to help you develop a global perspective on marketing.

Marketing ethics is another important topic selected for special treatment throughout the book. Chapters include highlighted stories about firms or industries that have faced ethical dilemmas or have engaged in practices that some consider unethical. Questions are posed to focus your thinking on the key ethical issues raised in each story.

Entrepreneurial insights are highlighted with icons. Every chapter also includes an application case related to small business. This material illustrates how entrepreneurs and small businesses can use the principles and concepts discussed in the book.

End-of-chapter materials begin with a final comment on the chapter-opening vignette called "Connect It." This is followed by a summary of the major topics ("Review It"), with discussion and writing questions (writing questions are identified with the icon in the margin) related to the topics. The questions include specific Internet and team activities, which are identified by appropriate icons. The on-line icon is also placed throughout the text to identify examples relating to technology. Another section, "Apply It," with discussion questions, is next, followed by a detailed ethics exercise called "Think About It." Then comes "Try It," a longer entrepreneurship case, and "Watch It," a section describing the different videos that supplement the chapter. Immediately following "Watch It" are the sections "Flip It" and "Click It," which let you know what additional learning opportunities are available in your study guide, on the *Essentials of Marketing* Web site, and on Xtra!

Essentials of Marketing 4e is also supported by InfoTrac College Edition. Several chapters throughout the book will give you the opportunity to refine your research skills through exercises specifically designed for InfoTrac. These exercises will be flagged by the icon at the left. All these features are intended to help you develop a more thorough understanding of marketing and enjoy the learning process.

The remaining chapters in Part 1 introduce you to the activities involved in developing a marketing plan, the dynamic environment in which marketing decisions must be made, ethics and social responsibility, and global marketing. Part 2 covers consumer decision making and buyer behavior; business marketing; the concepts of positioning, market segmentation, and targeting; and the nature and uses of marketing research and decision support systems. Parts 3 and 4 examine the elements of the marketing mix—product, distribution, promotion, and pricing—as well as Internet marketing.

CONNECT IT

Look back at the story at the beginning of this chapter about Amilya Antonetti's company SoapWorks. You should now find the assignment at the end of the story fairly easy. Amilya's initial motivation to enter the laundry-detergent market was based on her need to find a hypoallergenic product that would not aggravate her son's condition. She was unable to find such a product on the market and began developing her own. She tried to sell these products to grocery-store buyers but was rejected. At this point, we would describe Amilya's philosophy as sales oriented. "I need the product so others must need it. My job is to convince people to buy." But then Amilya began doing marketing research asking shoppers, "What is it here that's missing?" This reflects a market orientation. Amilya wanted to find out if other mothers wanted hypoallergenic laundry detergents. She also recognized that her products were not for everybody, but rather for specific groups of people (or market segments) with unique needs. Her success is directly related to identifying an unfulfilled need in the marketplace and developing products to satisfy that need.

Lisa Imm, age 25, an assistant marketing manager at Commtouch, Inc., a global provider of Web-based e-mail, was looking to change fields—from database marketing to Internet marketing. But she had no idea how her current skills would transfer. Bottom line: She needed to network, and fast.

ON LINE She didn't hit the party circuit or attend career fairs. Instead, she joined the e-mail list for Silicon Valley Web Grrls (www.webgrrls.com), a networking group for women who work in the technology sector. "I instantly had access to more than 1,000 people without physically having to meet them," Imm says. "The list is my virtual Rolodex."

Imm used the network not only to tap into what jobs were available but also to get valuable advice when she was considering offers: "People wrote back saying, 'I wouldn't work for that company, and this is why.' It was like having 100 personal recruiters and career counselors." A month after gathering information from the Web Grrls community and other sources, Imm landed her job.

What's her advice for others looking to take advantage of the power of a cyber-schmooze? First, be sure to join a group with credentials: "You can refer to the group on your résumé. Many times in an interview people will say, 'Wow! I've used that group too!' It's a great conversation starter." Also, give as generously as you receive. "If you don't respond to people when you've got the advice that they need, then you won't get much out of it."[24]

REVIEW IT

① **Define the term _marketing_.** The ultimate goal of all marketing activity is to facilitate mutually satisfying exchanges between parties. The activities of marketing include the conception, pricing, promotion, and distribution of ideas, goods, and services.

1.1 **ON LINE** What is the AMA? What does it do? How do its services benefit marketers?
http://www.marketingpower.com

1.2 **INFOTRAC COLLEGE EDITION** Log on to InfoTrac at **http://www.infotrac-college.com** and conduct a keyword search for "marketing." Read a couple of the articles. Based on what you have learned in this chapter, how do these articles describe or relate to marketing?

② **Describe four marketing management philosophies.** The role of marketing and the character of marketing activities within an organization are strongly influenced by its philosophy and orientation. A production-oriented organization focuses on the internal capabilities of the firm rather than on the desires and needs of the marketplace. A sales orientation is based on the beliefs that people will buy more products if aggressive sales techniques are used and that high sales volumes produce high profits. A market-oriented organization focuses on satisfying customer wants and needs while meeting organizational objectives. A societal marketing orientation goes beyond a market orientation to include the preservation or enhancement of individuals' and society's long-term best interests.

2.1 **WRITING** Your company president has decided to restructure the firm to make it more market oriented. She is going to announce the changes at an upcoming meeting. She has asked you to prepare a short speech outlining the general reasons for the new company orientation.

2.2 Donald E. Petersen, former chairman of the board of Ford Motor Company, remarked, "If we aren't customer driven, our cars won't be either." Explain how this statement reflects the marketing concept.

2.3 Give an example of a company that might be successfully following a production orientation. Why might a firm in this industry be successful following such an orientation?

3 **Explain how firms implement the marketing concept.** To implement the marketing concept successfully, management must embrace and endorse the concept and encourage its spread throughout the organization. Changing from a production or sales orientation to a marketing orientation often requires changes in authority and responsibility as well as front-line experience for management.

3.1   A friend of yours agrees with the adage "People don't know what they want—they only want what they know." Write your friend a letter expressing the extent to which you think marketers shape consumer wants.

3.2   Your local supermarket's slogan is "It's your store." However, when you asked one of the stock people to help you find a bag of chips, he told you it was not his job and that you should look a littler harder. On your way out, you noticed a sign with an address for complaints. Draft a letter explaining why the supermarket's slogan will never be credible unless the employees carry it out.

4 **Describe the marketing process and identify the variables that make up the marketing mix.** The marketing process includes understanding the organization's mission and the role marketing plays in fulfilling that mission, setting marketing objectives, scanning the environment, developing a marketing strategy by selecting a target market strategy, developing and implementing a marketing mix, implementing the strategy, designing performance measures, and evaluating marketing efforts and making changes if needed. The marketing mix combines product, distribution (place), promotion, and pricing strategies in a way that creates exchanges satisfying to individual organizational objectives.

4.1   Form a small group of three or four members. Suppose you and your colleagues all work for an up-and-coming gourmet coffee company that has several stores, mostly in large cities across the United States. Your team has been assigned the task of assessing whether the company should begin marketing on the Internet. Each member has been assigned to visit three or four Internet sites for ideas. Some possibilities are:

- Toys 'R' Us at **http://www.toysrus.com**
- Wal-Mart at **http://www.walmart.com**
- Godiva chocolates at **http://www.godiva.com**
- Levi Strauss at **http://www.levi.com**

Use your imagination and look up others. As you can see, many companies are easy to find, as long as you can spell their names. Typically, you would use the following: **http://www.companyname.com**

Has Internet marketing helped the companies whose sites you visited? If so, how? What factors should your company consider before committing to Internet activity? Prepare a three- to five-minute presentation to give to your class.

5 **Describe several reasons for studying marketing.** First, marketing affects the allocation of goods and services that influence a nation's economy and standard of living. Second, an understanding of marketing is crucial to understanding most businesses. Third, career opportunities in marketing are diverse, profitable, and expected to increase significantly during the coming decade. Fourth, understanding marketing makes consumers more informed.

5.1   Write a letter to a friend or family member explaining why you think that a course in marketing will help you in your career in some field other than marketing.

DEFINE IT

APPLY IT

Application for Entrepreneurs

Lisa King enjoyed working as a camp counselor during the summer. She started about the time she entered high school and continued through college. She even took a job at a camp the summer after graduating from college. She rationalized that this "internship," developing the camp yearbook, would help prepare her for a job in advertising.

As the summer passed, Lisa spent more time thinking about "what she was going to do when she grew up," as she liked to put it. Her thoughts always seemed to return to camping.

Lisa finally decided that she would like to open a small retail store specializing in camping supplies. The more she thought about it, the better she liked the idea.

She finally got up enough nerve to call her father, Tom, to discuss the idea. Tom's first response was, "Have you prepared a written plan?"

Lisa remembered preparing a marketing plan in her first class in marketing at the University of Miami. She asked her father to FedEx the text to her.

With financial backing from Tom, Lisa and her sister Jill opened Santorini Camping Supply the following fall. They picked the name Santorini because it was their favorite place in the Greek isles and, as Jill put it, "We just like the name."

On the first day the store was open, a customer asked Lisa if Santorini's guaranteed the products it sold. Lisa proudly replied, "Every product that is purchased from Santorini Camping Supply has a lifetime guarantee. If at any time you are not satisfied with one of our products, you can return it to the store for a full refund or exchange."

Questions

1. What marketing management philosophy is Santorini's expressing? Why have you reached this conclusion?

2. Do you think a lifetime guarantee for this kind of product is too generous? Why or why not?

3. Do you think this policy will contribute to success or to bankruptcy?

4. Suggest other customer service policies that might be appropriate for Santorini Camping Supply.

THINK ABOUT IT

In today's business environment, ethics are extremely important. In recent years, there have been numerous scandals and trials that stem from a lack of ethical judgment. For example, Adelphia Communications Corporation, which was the fourth largest cable television provider in the United States, declared bankruptcy, was under federal scrutiny for inflating numbers and making undisclosed loans to its major shareholders, and saw its principals arrested for fraud. The former CEO of Tyco International was charged with tax evasion and making secret deals with underlings. In 2002, over 150 firms revised their earnings reports, signaling that perhaps

Still Shaky? Here's a Tip.

Use your textbook more like a notebook and less like a reference book. The margins are a great place for writing questions on content you don't understand, highlighting important concepts, and adding examples to help you remember the material. Writing in your book makes it a more comprehensive resource for marketing and a better study tool.

their accounting methods were questionable. And who can forget the catastrophic collapse of Enron and the guilty verdict against the most venerated accounting firm in the United States, Arthur Andersen, LLP?

Although some might say that these occurrences are the work of a few bad apples spoiling the bunch, it is clear that ethical decision making plays a very important role in a company's success and prosperity. For this reason, we are including an ethical exercise in every chapter. A brief scenario will present you with a situation in which the right thing to do may or may not be crystal clear, and you will need to decide the ethical way out of the dilemma. To help you with these decisions, we will always refer you back to the AMA's Code of Ethics, found on-line at **http://www.marketingpower.com**. This will give you a resource for the exercise and will also help reinforce the ethical standards that marketers should uphold.

Ethics Exercise

Abercrombie & Fitch, a retail clothing chain based in New Albany, Ohio, launched a line of thong underwear for pre-teen girls. Words like "eye candy" and "wink wink" were printed on the front of the skimpy underwear that some argued would fit girls aged five to ten. Abercrombie is known for its provocative ads and sexually oriented catalogs. Supporters of the strategy claim that producing thong-style underwear for the age ten to sixteen crowd is a good move; critics think that the line is tasteless and that marketing it to young girls is contemptuous.

Questions

1. Is marketing adult-styled undergarments to a younger audience unethical?

2. Would Abercrombie have been in the spotlight had the sexy words been omitted from the product?

3. What does the AMA Code of Ethics have to say about using sex to market products to adult consumers? To younger consumers? Read the code at **http://www. marketingpower.com** and then write a brief paragraph on how the code relates to this situation.

 TRY IT

Entrepreneurship Case
A Noodé for a New Generation

When Seth Ratner launched Noodé (pronounced "newday") in spring 2001, it was with a very clearly articulated marketing strategy—and a hefty first-year sales goal of $1.7 million. Nine months after rollout, Ratner's plan seems to be working quite well: His skin care company and product line has already topped the $1 million mark and shows no signs of slowing.

Formerly of Zirh Skin Nutrition, a male skin care line that was acquired by Shiseido in 2000, Ratner recognized an underserved market in young people ages fifteen to twenty-nine, a group he named "Generation Me." A combination of Generation X and Generation Y, Generation Me had long been ignored by the more-recognized skin care companies, which tended to make products to help older consumers fight wrinkles and recondition aging skin. No serious conservatively priced, high-end skin care solutions existed for young skin problems, such as oily skin, combination skin, and acne. That is, until Noodé.

Noodé's twelve-product line was developed by a group of dermatologists focusing on prevention and maintenance rather than repair. Although the products are serious skin care, their names all tie into the Generation Me market: Clean Me face wash, Scrub Me Gently facial scrub, Make Me Soft facial moisturizer, Help Me acne cream, Renew Me face peel, Make Me Moist body lotion, Rub Me massage oil, Wash Me Everywhere body wash, Scrub Me Harder body scrub, Heal and Protect Me face and body cream for calming and reducing redness, and the newest product, Shield Me sunscreen gel with SPF 15. Noodé intends to focus exclusively on skin care—and not branch out into cosmetics—in order to avoid losing the message of serious skin care.

NOODÉ SKINCARE LLC. 1-888-972-3477

So with only eleven products when the line was launched (Shield Me was added in spring 2002), how did Noodé ring up so many sales in such a short period of time? The starting point was zeroing in on the Generation Me market. Ratner wanted to identify what fifteen- to twenty-nine-year-olds wanted. He found that they are consumers concerned about "me" and want products exclusively for "me." Once the target market was clearly identified, Ratner built a product line to meet its needs and wants. That is why none of the flagship products contained sun protection. Generation Me likes to look tan, and Noodé products are geared toward a youthful market. The new Shield Me product seems to send a conflicting message, but the SPF 15 gives only enough protection not to burn during daily activities. Also appealing to the target market is the product packaging. Colorful products packaged in clear bottles with funky writing attract interest. Creamier products are sold in an innovative style of packaging referred to as a "tottle," which is a tube and a bottle combined, which prevents accidental discharge of the product.

Once the market and product were ready, Noodé introduced them in high-end retailers like Henri Bendel, Bloomingdale's, Fred Segal, and Nordstrom. The idea was to build relationships with stores, train store personnel, and make brochures, literature, and samples available to store customers. Noodé cosponsored a Teen Appreciation Day at Bloomingdale's during the 2001 back-to-school season with Ralph fragrances, Tony & Tina cosmetics, and *Lucky* magazine. Teens received free facials and makeovers during the event, which generated a month's worth of sales for Noodé in a single day. The cost of sponsorship was minimal.

Keeping promotion costs minimal has been a key tactic for Ratner. Rather than roll out his new product and company with a pricey national advertising campaign, he chose to use catalog inserts, postcards, in-store support combined with a heavy sampling program, and store events like the Teen Appreciation Day. Low promotion costs help Noodé make the most of its pricing strategy. Price points range from $15 for the Rub Me and Scrub Me products to $20 for the Help Me acne product.

In a market full of high-priced products aimed at older consumers, Noodé is certainly poised to be a long-term success. Noodé brings together a fun, cool skin care line (that's still serious and effective) with the niche market it's designed to serve.

Questions

1. Which marketing philosophy is Noodé following? Explain.

2. How is Noodé implementing the marketing process?

3. How is Noodé using the elements of the marketing mix to meet the needs and wants of Generation Me?

WATCH IT

At the end of every chapter, "Watch It" will tell you about the different video options that accompany the text and support the chapter content. Each chapter will have a combination of thirty-second clips (short) embedded in the instructor's PowerPoint presentation, two- to four-minute clips (medium) for classroom viewing, and a ten- to fifteen-minute clip (long) for classroom viewing and available on a separate video CD-ROM. The short clips contain television ads that were originally broadcasted during Super Bowl games. The medium clips include CNN's news footage showing how marketing principles operate in the world of business. And the long clips are excerpts from various episodes of the thirty-minute Small Business School (SBS) program nationally broadcasted on PBS.

Because the SBS program covers all aspects of business, SBS segments raise more issues that just those presented in a single chapter. For example, the lead segment for Chapter 1 about Wahoo's Fish Taco, a uniquely Californian restaurant, also relates to material in Chapter 4 (Consumer Decision Making), Chapter 6 (Segmenting and Targeting Markets), Chapter 11 (Retailing), and Chapter 12 (Advertising, Public Relations, and Sales Promotion). The rich SBS videos will help reinforce what you've learned by introducing you to people who are doing marketing every day—and not according to thematic units.

Read the descriptions and get ready to watch it!

Short

How can an advertisement convey a company's marketing focus? Watch the 30-second television spots on Lipton, OfficeDepot, and Dodge that are embedded in the Chapter 1 PowerPoint presentation found on your PowerPoint CD-ROM. Evaluate each ad based on the overview of marketing you just read.

Medium

Smaller banks are maximizing their marketing orientation through innovative customer service, and as a result, they are enjoying higher stock valuations on Wall Street. Watch the CNN clip for Chapter 1 and make a list of the ways that Commerce Bank is implementing the marketing concept.

Long

To give you insight into Chapter 1, Small Business School will introduce you to a company that shows the marketing concept in action. You'll meet two men who are building a chain of surfer food joints called Wahoo's Fish Taco. The restaurant, started by three brothers, Wing Lam, Ed Lee, and Ming Lee, has won numerous awards and has a return-on-investment that is off the charts. Step into the master class to see how the marketing concept is thriving in small business.

FLIP IT

 To learn more about the study opportunities available in your Study Guide, read the "Flip It" section at the end of each chapter. Each Study Guide chapter includes vocabulary review, study test questions, Internet activities, marketing applications and scenarios, and more. To help you determine the concepts you most need to review, you can perform a self-assessment by completing the pretest at the beginning of each Study Guide chapter. Can you explain the four marketing management philosophies? What about listing the steps in the marketing process? Check out your *Grademaker Study Guide* and find out.

CLICK IT

 The *Essentials of Marketing* Web site is rich with materials to help you review and master marketing concepts. Check your knowledge with the free quizzes, practice key terms using the crossword puzzles, or review key concepts using the PowerPoint slides. The "Use It" about Web Grrls and "Review It" questions 1.1, 1.2, and 4.1 are loaded in the *Essentials of Marketing* Web site's Chapter 1 content. Go to **http://lamb.swlearning.com**, read the material, and follow the convenient links.

Xtra! is available optionally to accompany *Essentials of Marketing, 4e* and is loaded with review opportunities and supplemental material. In addition to the quiz on the Web site, there's another quiz on Xtra! You can also quiz yourself using the worksheet for Exhibit 1.1 and see the videos of the authors answering frequently asked questions about marketing management philosophies such as "Are production firms ever successful?" Surf to Xtra! and log on with your access code (in the front of every new copy of this book) to find out.

CHAPTER **TWO**
ETHICS, SOCIAL RESPONSIBILITY, AND THE MARKETING ENVIRONMENT

Learning Objectives

1 Describe the role of ethics and ethical decisions in business

2 Discuss corporate social responsibility

3 Discuss the external environment of marketing, and explain how it affects a firm

4 Describe the social factors that affect marketing

5 Explain the importance to marketing managers of current demographic trends

6 Explain the importance to marketing managers of multiculturalism and growing ethnic markets

7 Identify consumer and marketer reactions to the state of the economy

8 Identify the impact of technology on a firm

9 Discuss the political and legal environment of marketing

10 Explain the basics of foreign and domestic competition

Some things go out of fashion. That has been a hard lesson for Levi Strauss & Co., a company whose 501 blue jeans became famous in 1984 when a hunky model stripped them off in a laundromat for millions of admiring young women in Levi's television ads of the time.

"In the mid-80s, Levi's transformed the denim sector with that ad," says Sean Pillot de Chenecey, a youth-trend specialist at forecasting firm Captain Crikey in London. "But Levi's then committed the cardinal sin of becoming self-referential" by focusing too much on the 501 and not paying attention to changing tastes in threads. And while Levi's was stagnating, competitors such as Earl Jean and Diesel crowded the market with new products that seemed hipper to a generation stricken with chronic brand-attention-deficit disorder.

A sales decline at the closely held apparel maker began after a peak in 1996, when Levi's reported global sales of $7.1 billion, and has persisted ever since. Now the San Francisco-based company speaks of "slowing the decline" rather than boosting sales.

Levi's management readily admits it has made some mistakes. And instead of sloughing off the blame on a decline in the denim market, Levi's delivers a mea culpa: "We weren't selling in stores where young people shop. We weren't making the products they were interested in. We weren't branding our products in a famous way, and we weren't serving our customers well," says Robert Hanson, president of the Levi's brand in Europe, ticking off the four main reasons for Levi's recent hard times in Europe.

"We were responsible for the decline in the denim market," he adds.

Levi's is indeed the classic jeans maker, but some industry executives aren't as hard on the company and doubt it single-handedly brought on a decline in demand for denim. "Sometimes your products go out of fashion," says Alex Batchelor, managing director for Interbrand UK, a brand consultancy that is part of Omnicom Group.

But Levi's is making a concerted effort to come back. In the midst of a massive restructuring in which the company laid off thousands of workers and closed plants in the United States and Europe, Levi's is trying to put its best feet forward with new products and promotions.

In Levi's latest ad campaign in Europe, it promotes its "engineered" jeans, those with twisted seams designed to ergonomically fit both men and women.

After pushing the 501 for years, Levi's has developed a range of jeans in a bid to create a trickle-down effect: The company produces several high-end products, known as its red line and vintage lines, and also manufactures more basic models for mass consumption.

The company's retail plans mirror its product diversification in Europe. In what the company calls its "Icon" stores, the Levi's brand name is nowhere to be seen. Instead, the stores sell expensive vintage Levi's products alongside secondhand

books, vinyl albums, and custom-made shoes designed by local artisans.

In contrast, the company's heavily branded flagship stores offer themselves to the middle market and often adopt a more youthful approach. In department stores, Levi's introduced what it calls the advanced retail concept, which drapes jeans like spaghetti and displays Levi's products like fresh pasta and produce in a grocery store.

"Some we hang like spaghetti, others lie down like lasagna," Mr. Hanson says. He hopes the new presentation will have the jeans selling—as in the brand's glory days—like hot cakes.[1]

Changing tastes, fashion trends, and demographics all represent threats and/or opportunities to marketing managers. These are only a few factors in the external environment that can have an impact on a firm. Does the external environment affect the marketing mix of most companies? What other uncontrollable factors in the external environment might affect Levi's?

Ethical Behavior in Business

1

Describe the role of ethics and ethical decisions in business

ethics
The moral principles or values that generally govern the conduct of an individual.

morals
The rules people develop as a result of cultural values and norms.

Regardless of the intensity of the competition or the shifting external environment, firms must compete in an ethical manner. **Ethics** refers to the moral principles or values that generally govern the conduct of an individual or a group. Ethics can also be viewed as the standard of behavior by which conduct is judged. Standards that are legal may not always be ethical, and vice versa. Laws are the values and standards enforceable by the courts. Ethics consists of personal moral principles and values rather than societal prescriptions.

Defining the boundaries of ethicality and legality can be difficult. Often, judgment is needed to determine whether an action that may be legal is indeed ethical. For example, advertising liquor, tobacco, and X-rated movies in college newspapers is not illegal in many states, but is it ethical?

Morals are the rules people develop as a result of cultural values and norms. Culture is a socializing force that dictates what is right and wrong. Moral standards may also reflect the laws and regulations that affect social and economic behavior. Thus, morals can be considered a foundation of ethical behavior.

Morals are usually characterized as good or bad. "Good" and "bad" have different connotations, including "effective" and "ineffective." A good salesperson makes or exceeds the assigned quota. If the salesperson sells a new stereo or television set to a disadvantaged consumer—knowing full well that the person can't keep up the monthly payments—is the salesperson still a good one? What if the sale enables the salesperson to exceed his or her quota?

Another set of connotations for "good" and "bad" are "conforming" and "deviant" behaviors. A doctor who runs large ads for discounts on open-heart surgery would be considered bad, or unprofessional, in the sense of not conforming to the norms of the medical profession. "Bad" and "good" are also used to express the distinction between criminal and law-abiding behavior. And finally, the terms "good" and "bad" as defined by different religions differ markedly. A Muslim who eats pork would be considered bad, as would a fundamentalist Christian who drinks whiskey.

Morality and Business Ethics

Today's business ethics actually consists of a subset of major life values learned since birth. The values businesspeople use to make decisions have been acquired through family, educational, and religious institutions.

Ethical values are situation specific and time oriented. Nevertheless, everyone must have an ethical base that applies to conduct in the business world and in personal life. One approach to developing a personal set of ethics is to examine the consequences of a particular act. Who is helped or hurt? How long lasting are the consequences? What actions produce the greatest good for the greatest number of people? A second approach stresses the importance of rules. Rules come in the form of customs, laws, professional standards, and common sense. Consider these examples of rules:

- Always treat others as you would like to be treated.

- Copying copyrighted computer software is against the law.

- It is wrong to lie, bribe, or exploit.

The last approach emphasizes the development of moral character within individuals. Ethical development can be thought of as having three levels:[2]

- *Preconventional morality*, the most basic level, is childlike. It is calculating, self-centered, and even selfish, based on what will be immediately punished or rewarded. Fortunately, most businesspeople have progressed beyond the self-centered and manipulative actions of preconventional morality.

- *Conventional morality* moves from an egocentric viewpoint toward the expectations of society. Loyalty and obedience to the organization (or society) become paramount. At the level of conventional morality, an ethical marketing decision would be concerned only with whether it is legal and how it will be viewed by others. This type of morality could be likened to the adage "When in Rome, do as the Romans do."

- *Postconventional morality* represents the morality of the mature adult. At this level, people are less concerned about how others might see them and more concerned about how they see and judge themselves over the long run. A marketing decision maker who has attained a postconventional level of morality might ask, "Even though it is legal and will increase company profits, is it right in the long run? Might it do more harm than good in the end?"

Ethical Decision Making

How do businesspeople make ethical decisions? There is no cut-and-dried answer. Some of the ethical issues managers face are shown in Exhibit 2.1. Studies show that the following factors tend to influence ethical decision making and judgments:[3]

- *Extent of ethical problems within the organization:* Marketing professionals who perceive fewer ethical problems in their organizations tend to disapprove more strongly of "unethical" or questionable practices than those who perceive more ethical problems. Apparently, the healthier the ethical environment, the greater is the likelihood that marketers will take a strong stand against questionable practices.

- *Top-management actions on ethics:* Top managers can influence the behavior of marketing professionals by encouraging ethical behavior and discouraging unethical behavior.

- *Potential magnitude of the consequences:* The greater the harm done to victims, the more likely it is that marketing professionals will recognize a problem as unethical.

- *Social consensus:* The greater the degree of agreement among managerial peers that an action is harmful, the more likely it is that marketers will recognize a problem as ethical.

- *Probability of a harmful outcome:* The greater the likelihood that an action will result in a harmful outcome, the more likely it is that marketers will recognize a problem as unethical.

- *Length of time between the decision and the onset of consequences:* The shorter the length of time between the action and the onset of negative consequences, the more likely it is that marketers will perceive a problem as unethical.

- *Number of people to be affected:* The greater the number of persons affected by a negative outcome, the more likely it is that marketers will recognize a problem as unethical.

Perhaps the most egregious example of unethical business practices in recent memory was the Enron scandal that extended to the company's auditing firm, the venerable Arthur Andersen. Thousands of employees were negatively—even detrimentally—affected by the scandal.

Ethical Guidelines

Many organizations have become more interested in ethical issues. One sign of this interest is the increase in the number of large companies that appoint ethics officers—from virtually none five years ago to

Exhibit 2.1

Unethical Practices Marketing
Managers May Have to Deal With

- Entertainment and gift giving
- False or misleading advertising
- Misrepresentation of goods, services, and company capabilities
- Lies told customers in order to get the sale
- Manipulation of data (falsifying or misusing statistics or information)
- Misleading product or service warranties
- Unfair manipulation of customers
- Exploitation of children and/or disadvantaged groups
- Stereotypical portrayals of women, minority groups, and senior citizens

- Invasion of customer privacy
- Sex-oriented advertising appeals
- Product or service deception
- Unsafe products or services
- Price deception
- Price discrimination
- Unfair remarks and inaccurate statements about competitors
- Smaller amounts of product in the same-size packages

code of ethics
A guideline to help marketing managers and other employees make better decisions.

almost 25 percent of large corporations now. In addition, many companies of various sizes have developed a **code of ethics** as a guideline to help marketing managers and other employees make better decisions. In fact, a national study found that 60 percent of the companies maintained a code of ethics, 33 percent offered ethics training, and 33 percent employed an ethics officer.[4] Some of the most highly praised codes of ethics are those of Boeing, Hewlett-Packard, Johnson & Johnson, and Norton Company.

Creating ethics guidelines has several advantages:

- It helps employees identify what their firm recognizes as acceptable business practices.

- A code of ethics can be an effective internal control on behavior, which is more desirable than external controls like government regulation.

- A written code helps employees avoid confusion when determining whether their decisions are ethical.

- The process of formulating the code of ethics facilitates discussion among employees about what is right and wrong and ultimately leads to better decisions.

Businesses, however, must be careful not to make their code of ethics too vague or too detailed. Codes that are too vague give little or no guidance to employees in their day-to-day activities. Codes that are too detailed encourage employees to substitute rules for judgment. For instance, if employees are involved in questionable behavior, they may use the absence of a written rule as a reason to continue behaving that way, even though their conscience may be saying no. The checklist in Exhibit 2.2 is an example of a simple but helpful set of ethical guidelines. Following the checklist will not guarantee the "rightness" of a decision, but it will improve the chances that the decision will be ethical.

Although many companies have issued policies on ethical behavior, marketing managers must still put the policies into effect. They must address the classic "matter of degree" issue. For example, marketing researchers must often resort to deception to obtain unbiased answers to their research questions. Asking for a few minutes of a respondent's time is dishonest if the researcher knows the interview will last forty-five minutes. Not only must management post a code of ethics, but it must also give examples of what is ethical and unethical for each item in the code. Moreover, top management must stress to all employees the importance of adhering to the company's code of ethics. Without a detailed code of ethics and top management's support, creating ethical guidelines becomes an empty exercise. A recent survey of 2,300 employees of large corporations found that 75 percent had observed violations of the law or company standards in the previous twelve months.

Among other things, workers noted sexual harassment, conflicts of interest, employment discrimination, deceptive sales practices, unsafe working conditions, and environmental breaches. "People are not reporting misconduct because they are not encouraged to do so," says Richard Girgenti, a KPMG executive. The study found that nearly 75 percent of workers believed cynicism, low morale, and indifference were to blame for misconduct.[5] Many of these concerns have been addressed by the Professional Standards Committee of the American Marketing Association. The American Marketing Association's code of ethics is included on its Web site at **http://www.marketingpower.com.**

ON LINE

University of British Columbia Centre for Applied Ethics

Research corporate codes of ethics through the Applied Ethics Resources page. Compare the codes of three companies. What common themes do you find?

http://www.ethics.ubc.ca/resources/business

On Line

Corporate Social Responsibility

Ethics and social responsibility are closely intertwined. Besides questioning tobacco companies' ethics, one might ask whether they are acting in a socially responsible manner when they promote tobacco. Are companies that produce low-cost handguns socially responsible in light of the fact that these guns are used in the majority of inner-city crimes? **Corporate social responsibility** is a business's concern for society's welfare. This concern is demonstrated by managers who consider both the long-range best interests of the company and the company's relationship to the society within which it operates.

One theorist suggests that total corporate social responsibility has four components: economic, legal, ethical, and philanthropic.[6] The **pyramid of corporate social responsibility**, shown in Exhibit 2.3, portrays economic performance as the foundation for the other three responsibilities. At the same time that it pursues profits (economic responsibility), however, a business is expected to obey the law (legal responsibility); to do what is right, just, and fair (ethical responsibilities); and to be a good corporate citizen (philanthropic responsibility). These four components are distinct but together constitute the whole. Still, if the company doesn't make a profit, then the other three responsibilities are moot.

Many companies are already working to make the world a better place to live. Consider these examples:

- Fetzer Vineyards of California has eliminated 91 percent of its waste since 1991 while sales have doubled. The winery grows grapes organically, relying on natural pest control.[7]

- Ben & Jerry's Ice Cream uses unbleached paper in its cartons and purchases only steroid-free milk.[8]

(2)

Discuss corporate social responsibility

corporate social responsibility
Business's concern for society's welfare.

pyramid of corporate social responsibility
A model that suggests corporate social responsibility is composed of economic, legal, ethical, and philanthropic responsibilities and that the firm's economic performance supports the entire structure.

Exhibit 2.2

Ethics Checklist

- Does the decision benefit one person or group but hurt or not benefit other individuals or groups? In other words, is my decision fair to all concerned?

- Would individuals or groups, particularly customers, be upset if they knew about my decision?

- Has important information been overlooked because my decision was made without input from other knowledgeable individuals or groups?

- Does my decision presume that my company is an exception to a common practice in this industry and that I therefore have the authority to break a rule?

- Would my decision offend or upset qualified job applicants?

- Will my decision create conflict between individuals or groups within the company?

- Will I have to pull rank or use coercion to implement my decision?

- Would I prefer to avoid the consequences of my decision?

- Did I avoid truthfully answering any of the above questions by telling myself that the risks of getting caught are low or that I could get away with the potentially unethical behavior?

- The Entrepreneurs' Foundation, in Menlo Park, California, has sixty-one member companies that have each donated roughly $100,000 worth of stock for the purpose of addressing the needs of people in their community.[9]

- Abbott Laboratories funds free hearing examinations for the elderly at EarCare Clinics.[10]

- Target Stores gives 5 percent of its pretax earnings to charity.[11]

A current study ranked (in order) Home Depot, Johnson & Johnson, DaimlerChrysler, Anheuser-Busch, and McDonald's as having the highest level of social responsibility in America.[12] Yet, does being socially responsible create additional demand for the company's goods and services? The answer is quite complex. In some cases, it is "yes," and in others, "no." For example, one factor is the issue on which the company focuses, such as health, education, or charitable giving and how this is perceived by the target market. Other factors are product/service quality and how the target market perceives the importance of social responsibility.[13]

The External Marketing Environment

Discuss the external environment of marketing, and explain how it affects a firm

target market
A defined group most likely to buy a firm's product.

Whereas ethical culture guides the firm's marketing strategy from the inside, the firm also considers numerous external factors in building and refining its marketing mix. As you learned in Chapter 1, managers create a marketing mix by uniquely combining product, distribution, promotion, and price strategies. The marketing mix is, of course, under the firm's control and is designed to appeal to a specific group of potential buyers. A **target market** is a defined group that managers feel is most likely to buy a firm's product.

Over time, managers must alter the marketing mix because of changes in the environment in which consumers live, work, and make purchasing decisions. Also, as markets mature, some new consumers become part of the target market; others drop out. Those who remain may have different tastes, needs, incomes, lifestyles, and buying habits than the original target consumers.

☐ Exhibit 2.3

Pyramid of Corporate Social Responsibility

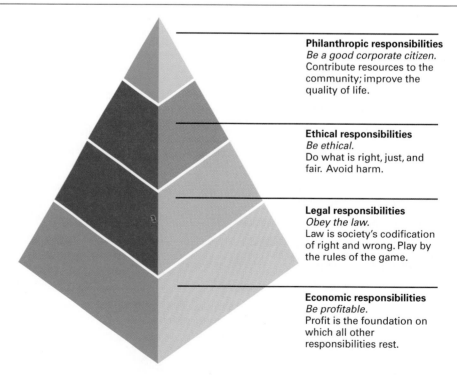

Philanthropic responsibilities
Be a good corporate citizen.
Contribute resources to the community; improve the quality of life.

Ethical responsibilities
Be ethical.
Do what is right, just, and fair. Avoid harm.

Legal responsibilities
Obey the law.
Law is society's codification of right and wrong. Play by the rules of the game.

Economic responsibilities
Be profitable.
Profit is the foundation on which all other responsibilities rest.

Although managers can control the marketing mix, they cannot control elements in the external environment that continually mold and reshape the target market. Exhibit 2.4 shows the controllable and uncontrollable variables that affect the target market, whether it consists of consumers or business purchasers. The uncontrollable elements in the center of the diagram continually evolve and create changes in the target market. In contrast, managers can shape and reshape the marketing mix, depicted on the left side of the exhibit, to influence the target market.

Understanding the External Environment

Unless marketing managers understand the external environment, the firm cannot intelligently plan for the future. Thus, many organizations assemble a team of specialists to continually collect and evaluate environmental information, a process called environmental scanning. The goal in gathering the environmental data is to identify future market opportunities and threats.

For example, as technology continues to blur the line between personal computers, television, and compact disc players, a company like Sony may find itself competing against a company like Dell. Research shows that children would like to find more games bundled with computer software, while adults are more likely to desire various word-processing and business-related software. Is this information an opportunity or a threat to Dell marketing managers?

Environmental Management

 No one business is large or powerful enough to create major change in the external environment. Thus, marketing managers are basically adapters rather than agents of change. For example, despite the huge size of General Motors and Ford, these companies are continually challenged to meet the competitive push by the Japanese for an ever-growing share of the U.S. automobile market. Competition is basically an uncontrollable element in the external environment.

 A firm is not always completely at the mercy of the external environment, however. Sometimes a firm can influence external events. For example, extensive lobbying by FedEx enabled it to acquire virtually all of the Japanese routes that it has sought. Japan had originally opposed new cargo routes for FedEx. The favorable decision was based on months of lobbying by FedEx at the White House, at several agencies, and in Congress for help in overcoming Japanese resistance. When a company

Bob Nardelli, CEO of The Home Depot, working with associates on Habitat for Humanity build, Atlanta 2002

"Roll Up Your Sleeves and Join Me"

Volunteerism is something all of us at The Home Depot understand and embrace. It's been a part of our culture from the beginning. Collectively and individually, we have always returned to our communities a fair measure of what we have earned. We are 250,000 strong. We know we can make a difference. So can you. Volunteer in your community today.

Bob

Bob Nardelli

TEAMDEPOT
Building Better Communities

© 2002. Homer TLC. Inc

Corporate social responsibility has become a part of American expectations. Bob Nardelli's Home Depot was ranked as having the highest level of social responsibility. Nardelli is pictured here working on a Habitat for Humanity house with Home Depot associates in Atlanta.

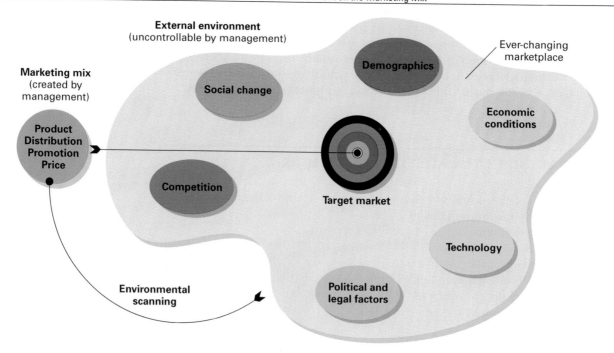

External environment
(uncontrollable by management)

Marketing mix
(created by
management)

Social change

Demographics

Ever-changing
marketplace

Economic
conditions

Product
Distribution
Promotion
Price

Competition

Target market

Technology

Environmental
scanning

Political and
legal factors

environmental management
When a company implements
strategies that attempt to shape
the external environment within
which it operates.

implements strategies that attempt to shape the external environment within which it operates, it is engaging in **environmental management**.

The factors within the external environment that are important to marketing managers can be classified as social, demographic, economic, technological, political and legal, and competitive.

Social Factors

4

Describe the social factors that affect marketing

Social change is perhaps the most difficult external variable for marketing managers to forecast, influence, or integrate into marketing plans. Social factors include our attitudes, values, and lifestyles. Social factors influence the products people buy, the prices paid for products, the effectiveness of specific promotions, and how, where, and when people expect to purchase products.

American Values

A *value* is a strongly held and enduring belief. During the United States' first 200 years, four basic values strongly influenced attitudes and lifestyles:

- *Self-sufficiency:* Every person should stand on his or her own two feet.

- *Upward mobility:* Success would come to anyone who got an education, worked hard, and played by the rules.

- *Work ethic:* Hard work, dedication to family, and frugality were moral and right.

- *Conformity:* No one should expect to be treated differently from everybody else.

These core values still hold for a majority of Americans today. A person's values are key determinants of what is important and not important, what actions to take or not to take, and how one behaves in social situations.

A person's values are typically formed through interaction with family, friends, and other influencers such as teachers, religious leaders, and politicians. The environment can also play a key role in shaping one's values. For example, people born during the Great Depression tend to be very conservative with money. People who came of age in the "hippie revolution" of the 1960s tend to be much less conservative with money.[14]

Values also influence our buying habits. Today's consumers are demanding, inquisitive, and discriminating. No longer willing to tolerate products that break down, they are insisting on high-quality goods that save time, energy, and often calories. U.S. consumers rank the characteristics of product quality as (1) reliability, (2) durability, (3) easy maintenance, (4) ease of use, (5) a trusted brand name, and (6) a low price. Shoppers are also concerned about nutrition and want to know what's in their food, and most are also environmentalists.

The Poverty of Time

Today, fewer consumers say that expensive cars, designer clothes, pleasure trips, and "platinum" credit cards are necessary components of a happy life. Instead, they put value on nonmaterial accomplishments, such as having control of their lives and being able to take a day off when they want.[15] Dual-career families have a **poverty of time**, with few hours to do anything but work and commute to work, handle family situations, do housework, shop, sleep, and eat. Of the people who say they don't have enough time, only 33 percent said that they were very happy with their lives.[16]

A poverty of time means that people will decrease the amount of time spent doing things they dislike. That means doing less housework and home maintenance, and doing more dining out. It also means paying more attention to brand names—not in search of status, but to make buying decisions quicker and easier. Consumers on a constrained time budget will likely favor small shops over large ones, spend less time comparing prices, use technology to reduce transaction time, and patronize businesses that make life easier.[17]

No company has learned this better than Kinko's, the copy-shop empire. A few years ago, Kinko's noticed that busy customers in its stores didn't just want to do their photocopying and head home. They wanted to pop into a store, create a computer document, print it out, staple it, glue it, hole-punch it, and put it in a three-ring binder. In response, Kinko's has added computer workstations to many of its stores, along with sophisticated technical support and basic supplies that turn each of its copy centers into home offices away from home.

PHOTO COURTESY OF KINKO'S INC.

Today, 39 percent of Americans often spend leisure time getting ready for work.[18] Casual Fridays and home offices seem to be further blurring the boundaries between work and leisure. A recent survey noted that the leisure activity done most often was to spend time with the family.[19] There is little doubt that the value employees place on time versus money will continue to shift in favor of time. More employers will offer time off as an incentive. Aladdin Equipment, a Sarasota, Florida, maker of pool and spa replacement parts, achieved a 50 percent reduction in absenteeism and a 10 percent increase in productivity after it launched a four-and-one-half-day-a-week production schedule.[20] Perhaps the 7 percent annual growth in home-based self-employment is a backlash against the lack of quality of family time.[21]

The Growth of Component Lifestyles

People in the United States today are piecing together **component lifestyles**. A lifestyle is a mode of living; it is the way people decide to live their lives. In other

poverty of time
A lack of time to do anything but work, commute to work, handle family situations, do housework, shop, sleep, and eat.

Time-pressed individuals represent a tremendous marketing opportunity. Kinko's has made the most of opportunities to serve customers by transforming from a corner copy shop into a network of locations featuring additional services such as rental computers and sign and banner departments.

component lifestyles
The practice of choosing goods and services that meet one's diverse needs and interests rather than conforming to a single, traditional lifestyle.

words, they are choosing products and services that meet diverse needs and interests rather than conforming to traditional stereotypes.

In the past, a person's profession—for instance, banker—defined his or her lifestyle. Today, a person can be a banker and also a gourmet, fitness enthusiast, dedicated single parent, and Internet guru. Each of these lifestyles is associated with different goods and services and represents a target audience. For example, for the gourmet, marketers offer cooking utensils, wines, and exotic foods through magazines like *Bon Appetit* and *Gourmet*. The fitness enthusiast buys Adidas equipment and special jogging outfits and reads *Runner* magazine. Component lifestyles increase the complexity of consumers' buying habits. The banker may own a BMW but change the oil himself or herself. He or she may buy fast food for lunch but French wine for dinner, own sophisticated photographic equipment and a low-priced home stereo, and shop for socks at Kmart or Wal-Mart and suits or dresses at Brooks Brothers.

The unique lifestyles of every consumer can require a different marketing mix. Sometimes blending products for a single target market can result in failure. To the bright young founders of WebTV, it looked like a home run: hook televisions up to the Net and tap into the vast market of couch potatoes curious about the World Wide Web. After burning through an estimated $50 million to advertise the new service, however, WebTV and partners Sony and Philips Electronics counted a disappointing fifty thousand subscribers. The problem was the wrong marketing message. Couch potatoes want to be better entertained, whereas computer users are content to explore the Internet using small PC screens.

The Changing Role of Families and Working Women

Component lifestyles have evolved because consumers can choose from a growing number of goods and services, and most have the money to exercise more options. The growth of dual-income families has resulted in increased purchasing power. Approximately 58 percent of all females between sixteen and sixty-five years old are now in the workforce, and female participation in the labor force is expected to grow to 63 percent by 2005.[22] Today, more than 9 million women-owned businesses in the United States generate $3.6 trillion in revenues.[23] The phenomenon of working women has probably had a greater effect on marketing than has any other social change.

As women's earnings grow, so do their levels of expertise, experience, and authority. Working-age women are not the same group businesses targeted thirty years ago. They expect different things in life—from their jobs, from their spouses, and from the products and services they buy.

The automotive industry has finally begun to realize the power of women in vehicle purchase decisions. Women are the principal buyers for 45 percent of all cars and trucks sold in the United States.[24] Saturn's advertising aims not only to attract women as customers, but also to woo them into the business. In an industry with a woefully small representation of women in sales, 16 percent of Saturn's sales staff are women, compared with 7 percent industry-wide. This has had a visible impact on sales to women. Even though about half of all automotive purchases are made by women, Saturn claims that women buy 64 percent of its cars.[25]

The growth in the number of working women has meant an increase in dual-career families. Although dual-career families typically have greater household incomes, they have less time for family activities (poverty of time). Their purchasing roles (which define the items traditionally bought by the man or the woman) are changing, as are their purchasing patterns.

In a recent survey, two-thirds to three-quarters of women said they are making many major economic decisions either independently or equally with a spouse. Few of the women said they left important marketplace decisions to others.[26]

Most importantly, as Exhibit 2.2 shows, cost is more prominent in decisions made by women, whereas quality is relatively more important to men. This

Exhibit 2.5

Understanding Who Holds the Purse Strings

What's Important When You Shop	Women (%)	Men (%)
The quality of a product matters more than cost or other factors	48	54
The cost of an item is very critical to me	23	18

Women As Principal Decision Makers	All Women (%)
Set up, follow budget	64
Arrange travel	62
Purchase appliances	61
Purchase insurance	56
Invest in stocks, funds	50
Make a will	46
Buy a home	37

SOURCE: Christy Harvey, "A Guide to Who Holds the Purse Strings," *Wall Street Journal*, June 22, 2000, A14.

knowledge has important ramifications for managers creating a new marketing mix. Exhibit 2.5 also reveals where women act as principal decision makers.

When it comes to big-ticket, long-term items, women remain active in the decision-making process, though a plurality say they are more likely to make these decisions with a spouse. Life experience is an important factor in women's independence in long-term planning; married women over age fifty-five are more likely to make these decisions on their own than their younger counterparts are. Single women, of course, make more of their own decisions.[27]

More working women has meant an ever-increasing demand for time-saving devices and products, particularly for the kitchen. An increasingly popular way to preserve foods is irradiation. Irradiation, however, evokes the notion of nuclear weapons in the minds of some consumers. The "Ethics in Marketing" box explores how this new technology is being promoted in the marketplace.

Demographic Factors

Another uncontrollable variable in the external environment—also extremely important to marketing managers—is **demography**, the study of people's vital statistics, such as their age, race and ethnicity, and location. Demographics are significant because the basis for any market is people. Demographic characteristics are strongly related to consumer buyer behavior in the marketplace. The vast wealth of America, and the resulting consumption of products and services, is reflected in the demographics of the United States versus the rest of the world (see Exhibit 2.6). This exhibit tells marketers many things. For example, the United States is growing much slower than the rest of the world. Faster growth, if it is coupled with rising incomes, means expanding markets. The longer life span of Americans suggests a growing market for products and services targeted toward the elderly. Read through the table and determine other implications for marketers.

We turn our attention now to a closer look at age groups, their impact, and the opportunities they present for marketers. The cohorts have been given the names of Generation Y, Generation X, and baby boomers. You will find that each cohort group has its own needs, values, and consumption patterns.

Explain the importance to marketing managers of current demographic trends

demography
The study of people's vital statistics, such as their age, race and ethnicity, and location.

Irradiated Food by Any Other Name Might Be a Winner

The scene in the television commercial is straight out of Norman Rockwell, with a gray-haired woman pedaling her bicycle through quaint, sun-streaked streets.

This could be a spot for aspirin, or for orange juice. But as the woman makes her way home, to a barbecue with elderly friends and children, it becomes apparent that she isn't pushing a specific product. "SureBeam is much like milk pasteurization," says a homey voice-over. "It makes foods safer by helping to eliminate harmful bacteria."

And what is SureBeam? It happens to be one company's patented method of food irradiation. The thirty-second advertisement asks viewers to look for packages with the SureBeam seal. The "i" word is never mentioned—deliberately.

Irradiation involves exposing foods to controlled levels of ionizing radiation, such as gamma rays, electron beams, and X-rays. The decades-old process kills most pathogens, including potentially deadly strains of E. coli bacteria. Currently, the technology is approved by the Food and Drug Administration for use on some foodstuffs like spices, fresh fruits, and vegetables as well as certain fresh meats. The agency is expected to broaden its approval to cover packaged foods like hot dogs.

But despite the FDA's blessing and the fact that the process might prevent some of the 5,000-plus food-safety-related deaths each year, many Americans frown upon the technology.

Irradiated foods are not radioactive. Still, consumer groups are divided on their safety. The National Consumers League, for instance, lauds irradiation as a valuable safety net; Public Citizen, on the other hand, contends that health-related issues loom. In any case, the amount of irradiated food on the shelves of U.S. grocery stores today is small.

SureBeam Corporation's ads are sure to fuel the debate. The company is based in San Diego. Its clients include Omaha Steaks and Huisken Meats, and it is working with food giant Kraft Foods Inc., which currently has no irradiated food on the market. (A Kraft spokeswoman says the company is doing research with SureBeam "that could further enable us to improve the quality of our products.")

SureBeam has used the euphemism "electronic pasteurization" as part of its corporate logo and makes only scant reference to irradiation on its Web site and in other marketing materials. "There's no label that says, 'this product has been fumigated,' " says Andrew Hyncik, SureBeam's marketing director. "Why should we have to call attention to the fact that we've been irradiated?" A SureBeam spokesman says that "disinfestations" best describes the company's process for treating fruits and vegetables.[28]

Would you mind eating irradiated foods? Why or why not? Do you think that SureBeam's promotional campaign is deceptive? Should foods that have been irradiated be conspicuously labeled as such? What about fumigated veggies?

Exhibit 2.6

The Demographic Facts of Life*

United States		Planet Earth
283.5 million	Population	6.1 billion
3,717,796	Area, in square miles	51,789,516
15	Births per 1,000	22
9	Deaths per 1,000	9
120	Doubling time in years at current rate	51
337.8 million	Projected population, 2025	7.8 billion
7	Infant deaths per 1,000 live births	57
74 (male), 79 (female)	Life expectancy	64 (male), 68 (female)
21	Percent of population under age 15	31
13	Percent of population over age 65	7
74	Population per square mile	117
75	Percent urban	45
635 species	Endangered/threatened animals	5,205 species
447 species	Endangered/threatened plants	33,798 species
1,512 gallons	Daily water use per capita	465 gallons
59.4 barrels of oil equivalent	Energy use per capita	9.5 barrels of oil equivalent
1.3	Persons per motor vehicle	9
3	Percent of labor force in agriculture	49
19	Percent of labor force in industry	20
78	Percent of labor force in services	31
806	Televisions per 1,000 people	225

SOURCE: Zero Population Growth (www.zpg.org).   *Data are for 2001.

Generation Y

Those designated by demographics as **Generation Y** were born between 1979 and
1994. They are about sixty million strong, more than three times as large as Generation X. If this group of consumers does not like the mature brands of the baby
boomers or Generation X, then marketers will be in trouble. Why? Simply because
of the size of the Gen Y market. For example, baby boomers are into Lexus, Estee
Lauder, L. L. Bean, and Coke. Gen Y-ers like Jeep Wrangler, Hard Candy, The
North Face, and Mountain Dew.

Gen Y-ers, having grown up in an even more media-saturated, brand-conscious
world than their parents, respond to ads differently and prefer to encounter those
ads in different places. The marketers that capture Gen Y's attention do so by
bringing their messages to the places these kids congregate, whether it's the Internet, a snowboarding tournament, or cable TV. The ads may be funny or disarm-
ingly direct. What they don't do is suggest that the advertiser knows Gen Y better
than these savvy consumers know themselves.

Generation Y is already driving the educational software and snowboard industries and soon will drive many others. Hawaiian Tropic, the nation's number
three suntan lotion company, has dramatically increased its spring break promotions to Gen Y-ers at Panama City Beach, South Padre Island, and Daytona Beach.

For Generation Y, anyone can be a star. Everyone deserves to have his or her
say. For young people, getting heard and becoming well known are not only easy,
they seem natural. You can create your own Web site; make a movie with your own
webcam or digital camera; post your thoughts, pictures, and writings on-line; even
be on television. Part of the draw of reality TV shows like *Survivor* is that "real people" can become stars.[29]

Generation Y also loves customized products and services. Research found that
85 percent of those aged eighteen to twenty-four said they wished more products
were customized to their unique tastes and needs. Only 62 percent of those sixty-
five and older expressed similar feelings. The product categories in which Generation Y consumers wanted customized goods and services were (in rank order)
clothes, shoes, travel planning, and computers and electronics.[30]

Companies are learning that they have to provide something unique and
deeply personal to win loyalty. Winning consumer loyalty and repeat business is exactly what Wyndham Hotels seems to be doing with its mass customized guest
recognition program, Wyndham By Request. Guests can join the free program by
filling out a detailed preference form: Do you prefer foam or feather pillows? Sweet
or salty snacks? A glass of Merlot or a cold Bud in the minifridge? Requests are automatically filled each time a customer reserves a room at any Wyndham property.

Generation X

Generation X—people born between 1965 and 1978—consists of 40 million consumers. It is the first generation of latchkey children—products of dual-career
households or, in roughly half of the cases, of divorced or separated parents.
Generation X began entering the workforce in the era of downsizing and downturn, so its members are likelier than the previous generation to be unemployed,

Generation Y
People born between 1979 and
1994.

Generation X
People born between 1965 and
1978.

bored
maddy's board room

www.madelineshoes.com

Madeline
mad about shoes

Generation X is not nearly as large as either Generation Y or the baby boom generation. Still, it represents a lucrative market, since its members spend a larger-than-average share of their incomes on restaurant meals, clothing, and electronics.

baby boomers
People born between 1946 and 1964.

underemployed, and living at home with Mom and Dad. Yet, as a generation that's been bombarded by multiple media since their cradle days, Gen X-ers are savvy and cynical consumers.

The members of Generation X don't mind indulging themselves. Among the young women of Generation X, 38 percent go to the movies in a given month, compared with 19 percent of the women who are now forty-five and older. The members of Generation X devote a larger-than-average share of their spending dollars to restaurant meals, alcoholic beverages, clothing, and electronic items such as televisions and stereos. They are more materialistic than past generations but have less hope of achieving their goals.

Travel companies, such as hotels, airlines, and car rental companies, that have spent the last thirty years marketing to baby boomers have discovered that Gen X-ers have vastly different preferences and interests from the older generation. To woo them, travel companies are creating unusual perks and unconventional gags in TV commercials. They're taping airfare promos to pizza boxes, teaching kickboxing classes in hotel fitness centers, and replacing buttoned-down restaurants with sweatshirt-casual bistros.

Starwood created an entire hotel chain for those customers, giving it the name W. Each hotel, where rooms go for about $300 a night, features contemporary designs, hip bars, and whimsical amenities such as gumball machines with Hot Tamale candies that make them magnets for young travelers, Starwood's vice president Guy Hensley says. And if they outgrow W's, Starwood hopes they'll switch to its more traditional Sheratons and Westins. "If we catch hold of the Generation X crowd now, they'll stay with us forever," says Hensley.[31]

Another example of creating a product specifically for Gen X-ers comes from Harley-Davidson. Harley-Davidson/Buell targeted the Buell "Blast" directly to Gen X-ers. This new model is a smaller, lighter, easier-handling, one-cylinder motorcycle, selling for under $4,500, and it was designed specifically for the male or female new rider or novice rider who is not yet ready for the traditionally heavier Harley-Davidson cruising or touring bikes.[32]

Baby Boomers: America's Mass Market

Almost 78 million **baby boomers** were born in the United States between 1946 and 1964, which created a huge market. The oldest are now over fifty-five, but they cling to their youth. One study found that baby boomers see themselves as continuing to be very active after they turn fifty. They won't even think of themselves as being senior citizens until after they turn sixty (39 percent) or seventy (42 percent).[33]

This group cherishes convenience, which has resulted in a growing demand for home delivery of items like large appliances, furniture, and groceries. In addition, the spreading culture of convenience explains the tremendous appeal of prepared take-out foods and the necessity of VCRs and cell phones.

Baby boomers' parents raised their children to think for and of themselves. Studies of child-rearing practices show that parents of the 1950s and 1960s consistently ranked "to think for themselves" as the number one trait they wanted to instill in their children.[34] Postwar affluence also allowed parents to indulge their children as never before. They invested in their children's skills by sending them to college. They encouraged their children to succeed in a job market that rewarded competitive drive more than cooperative spirit and individual skills more than teamwork.

In turn, the sheer size of the generation encouraged businesses to promote the emerging individuality of baby boomers. Even before the oldest baby boomers started earning their own living more than three decades ago, astute businesspeople saw the profits that come from giving millions of young people what they want.

Businesses offered individualistic baby boomers a growing array of customized products and services—houses, cars, furniture, appliances, clothes, vacations, jobs, leisure time, and even beliefs.

The importance of individualism among baby boomers led to a **personalized economy**—a system that delivers customized goods and services at a good value on demand. Successful businesses in a personalized economy give customers what they want when they want it. To do this, they must know their customers extremely well. In fact, the intimacy between producer and consumer is exactly what makes an economy personalized.

As the age of today's average consumer moves toward forty, average consumption patterns are also changing. People in their early forties tend to focus on their families and finances. As this group grows in number, its members will buy more furniture from manufacturers like Lazy Boy, American Martindale, Baker, and Drexel-Heritage to replace the furniture they bought early in their marriages. The demand for family counselors and wellness programs should also increase. Additionally, discount investment brokers like Charles Schwab and E-trade and mutual funds like Fidelity and Dreyfus should profit. Because middle-aged consumers buy more reading materials than any other age group, the market for books and magazines should remain strong throughout the late 2000s. Women ages forty to sixty-four will be the largest age demographic group by the year 2010.[35] *More* magazine has been created to target this market. *More* promises features about fashion, beauty, and health, as well as pieces on married life after three decades. And all the models in *More*'s editorial pages are forty-plus.

Baby boomers are now in the nesting stage of their lives. Secure in their careers and generally stable, boomers are in their low-migration years. The fact that boomers are becoming homebodies, while other segments of the population are moving, means that boomers are not relocating to many of the nation's new economic "hot spots" (the Sunbelt states) that are attracting other segments of the population, such as newly arrived immigrants and Gen X-ers. Rather, boomers are returning to more "mature" (and often more pricey) regions of the country that they lived in when they were younger, such as New England and the eastern seaboard, the upper Midwest, the upper Rocky Mountains West and the Pacific Northwest.[36]

Grand Circle Travel
Maupintour

How does Grand Circle Travel dispel the stereotypes about seniors on its Web page? Compare it to Maupintour's site. Given that both companies target seniors, which company does this more effectively? Why do you think this is so?

http://www.gct.com/

http://www.maupintour.com/

On Line

personalized economy
Delivering customized goods and services at a good value on demand.

Older Consumers: Not Just Grandparents

As mentioned above, the oldest baby boomers have already crossed the fifty-five threshold that many demographers use to define the "mature market." Today's mature consumers are wealthier, healthier, and better educated than those of earlier generations. By 2005, 115 million consumers will be fifty years of age or older, making up 40 percent of the population.[37] Consumers in the mature market keep up with the times, are quite definite about their wants and needs, and have a series of unique behavior patterns. To summarize:

- They take frequent vacations.

- They eat out often—in both high-end and fast-food restaurants.

- They have specific needs with regard to banking and investment services, with definite differences between boomers and older consumers (those over sixty years old).

- They own computers, and they utilize them for a broad range of purposes.

- They are heavily into the Internet, including on-line shopping.

- They are somewhat light viewers of television (watching the major networks for news and entertainment, cable for education).[38]

Mature consumers are not happy with the way they are treated by marketers and advertisers. For the most part, they believe marketers and advertisers do not have their interests or needs in mind when developing products, designing packaging, and preparing advertising.

- More than half feel marketers do only a fair to poor job in considering their needs when they develop new products.

- Two out of five say marketers do only a fair to poor job in considering their needs when they develop packaging (as opposed to the 4 percent who feel they do an excellent job).

- And, most damaging to advertisers, almost half of boomers feel advertisers and their agencies ignore them in preparing their campaigns (4 percent are satisfied).[39]

Marketers who want to actively pursue the mature market must understand it. Aging consumers create some obvious opportunities. JCPenney's Easy Dressing clothes feature Velcro-fastened clothing for women with arthritis or other ailments who may have difficulty with zippers or buttons. Sales from the first Easy Dressing catalog were three times higher than expected. Chicago-based Cadaco offers a line of games with easy-to-read big print and larger game pieces. The series focuses on nostalgia by including Michigan rummy, hearts, poker, and bingo. Trivia buffs more familiar with Mitch Miller than Guns 'n' Roses can play Parker Brothers' "The Vintage Years" edition of *Trivial Pursuit*. The game, aimed at the sixty-plus crowd, poses questions covering the era from Charles Lindbergh to Dwight D. Eisenhower.

To persuade active retirees to move, the housing industry first renamed retirement developments, now often called "active-adult communities." Now, builders are also piling on amenities. Miami-based homebuilder Lennar Corporation has souped up its clubhouses in the past five years, adding restaurants, concierge services, computer labs, and gyms. In collaboration with a local university, Del Webb Corporation is building a several-thousand-square-foot educational center at Sun City Grand in Phoenix, where the company is based, that has classrooms, a lecture hall, a library, and a Starbucks.[40]

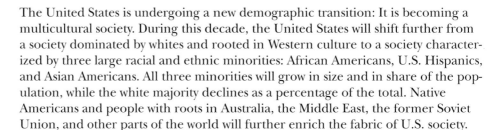

Growing Ethnic Markets

6

Explain the importance to marketing managers of multiculturalism and growing ethnic markets

Read more about multicultural marketing in the supplemental module on Xtra!

The United States is undergoing a new demographic transition: It is becoming a multicultural society. During this decade, the United States will shift further from a society dominated by whites and rooted in Western culture to a society characterized by three large racial and ethnic minorities: African Americans, U.S. Hispanics, and Asian Americans. All three minorities will grow in size and in share of the population, while the white majority declines as a percentage of the total. Native Americans and people with roots in Australia, the Middle East, the former Soviet Union, and other parts of the world will further enrich the fabric of U.S. society.

The labor force of the past was dominated by white men who are now retiring. Today's senior workers are equal parts women and men, and still overwhelmingly white. But in the entry-level jobs, a multicultural labor force is emerging. The proportion of non-Hispanic whites in the workforce in 2005 is estimated to be 74 percent, down from 77 percent in 1998.

Because so many white men are retiring, the non-Hispanic white labor force is growing slowly—by only 8 percent between 1994 and 2005. The number of Hispanic workers is growing much faster—by 36 percent—due to the continued immigration of young adults, higher birthrates, and relatively few retirees. These forces are also boosting the number of Asian workers—by 39 percent. The number of black workers is increasing too—by 15 percent, a rate slightly slower than the rate of growth of black adults in general (16.5 percent).[41]

Ethnic and Cultural Diversity

multiculturalism
When all major ethnic groups in an area—such as a city, county, or census tract—are roughly equally represented.

Multiculturalism occurs when all major ethnic groups in an area—such as a city, county, or census tract—are roughly equally represented. Because of its current demographic transition, the trend in the United States is toward greater multiculturalism.

San Francisco County is the most diverse county in the nation. The proportions of major ethnic groups are closer to being equal there than anywhere else. People of many ancestries have long been attracted to the area. Elsewhere, however, a careful examination of the statistics from the latest U.S. Census Bureau reveals that the nation's minority groups, especially Hispanics and Asians, are heavily clustered in selected regions and markets. Rather than witnessing the formation of a homogeneous national melting pot, we are seeing the creation of numerous mini-melting pots, while the rest of America remains much less diverse.[42]

In a broad swath of the country, the minority presence is still quite limited. As Exhibit 2.7 makes clear, America's racial and ethnic patterns have taken on distinctly regional dimensions. Hispanics dominate large portions of counties in a span of states stretching from California to Texas. Blacks are strongly represented in counties of the South as well as selected urban areas in the Northeast and Midwest. The Asian presence is relatively small and highly concentrated in a few scattered counties, largely in the West. And Native Americans are concentrated in select pockets in Oklahoma, the Southeast, the upper Midwest, and the West. Multiethnic counties are most prominent in California and the Southwest, with mixes of Asians and Hispanics, or Hispanics and Native Americans.[43]

Marketing Implications of Multiculturalism

In recent years the number of blacks, Hispanics, and Asians has grown explosively, and those groups now account for 79 million out of 284 million Americans. Collectively, they represent an estimated $1 trillion in annual spending power.[44] Hispanics are the fastest growing segment of the population. The diversity of the U.S. population is projected to stabilize around 2023, as the birthrates among minorities level off.

The marketer's task is more challenging in a diverse society because of differences in educational level and demand for goods and services. What's more, ethnic

Exhibit 2.7

Micro Multiculturalism

LEGEND
White
Black
Hispanic
Asian
Native American
Multiethnic

SOURCE: William Frey, "Micro Melting Pots," *American Demographics*, June 2001, 20–21.

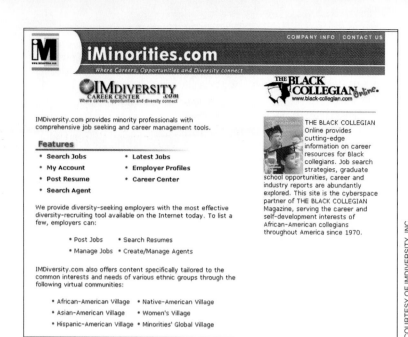

Multicultural marketing has found great success on the Internet. Numerous sites, like iMinorities.com, provide information and services targeted toward a variety of minority groups.

markets are not homogeneous. There is not an African American market or a Hispanic market, any more than there is a white market. Instead, there are many niches within ethnic markets that require micromarketing strategies. For example, African Eye, which offers women's designer fashions from Africa, attracted a thousand women to a fashion show at Prince Georges Plaza near Washington, D.C. The show featured the latest creations by Alfadi, a high-fashion Nigerian designer, who also hosted the show. African Eye's dresses and outfits blend African and Western influences and are priced at $50 to $600. Says Mozella Perry Ademiluyi, the president and cofounder of African Eye: "Our customer is professional, 30 to 65, has an income level of $30,000-plus and often is well-traveled. They don't just want to wear something that is African. They want something that is well-tailored, unique, and creative as well."[45]

Procter & Gamble has created a new "Multicultural Market Development Organization" to reach minority markets. Now, every six months, the firm sends out 4.5 million copies of its promotional magazine *Avanzando con tu Familia* (Getting Ahead with Your Family). That's one copy for every two Hispanic households. Marketers have reworked the Spanish slogan for Cover Girl makeup, and product developers are creating new Secret deodorant scent names that they hope will appeal to Hispanic consumers. In addition, P&G's new line of Pampers diapers with "cloth-like backside" comes in boxes labeled in both English and Spanish.

Procter & Gamble isn't new to the Hispanic market. Cover Girl, which started using Latina models in 1993, added makeup shades aimed at Hispanic women a few years ago: darker shades for foundation and powder, and brighter colors for lipsticks and nail polish. P&G was also one of the first sponsors of *Sabado Gigante,* a Saturday variety show that has run on Spanish-language TV for fourteen years. P&G has been the top spender for Spanish advertising for many years.[46]

Another large company that has increased its emphasis on multicultural marketing is Sears, Roebuck and Company. Sears has around thirty stores nationwide located in urban areas with large Asian populations. Recently, the company recognized an opportunity to boost fall sales in those stores by forging a connection with the Asian Moon Festival.

The September holiday is a harvest-time celebration, similar to Thanksgiving, that is celebrated in many Asian countries. It coincides with the kickoff of retail's fall selling season (when Sears would be staging promotions, anyway), so a Moon Festival tie-in made sense. "We've had great success with it," says Gilbert Davila, Sears' vice president of multicultural and relationship marketing. "It's a good way for us to connect with the community."[47] Sears also does promotions tied to Black History Month in February and Mexican Independence Day in September.

For the Moon Festival, in addition to offering a free gift with any purchase over $10, the stores host a number of cultural events, such as performances by local dance troupes. The performances typically involve people dancing with— or in—large puppets representing animals or mythological creatures, as puppets are a traditional element in Asian culture.

The Asian market is a particular challenge for marketers because of the many different languages. Depending on the makeup of the surrounding communities, Sears advertises the Moon Festival in Mandarin, Cantonese, Vietnamese, or Korean; there are seven or eight stores in each language group, most of them in California. The programs staged in the stores are conducted in English, however. The ads run mainly in local Asian-language newspapers.

To learn more about multicultural marketing, read the supplemental module on Xtra!.

The Internet Goes Multicultural

 Since 1995, non-English-speaking Internet users have gone from less than 10 percent to as high as 50 percent, according to researcher Wired Digital. African Americans outpace all other segments—including the general market—for on-line adoption, according to Forrester Research.[48]

Today, approximately 40 percent of all African American households, 43 percent of Hispanic Americans, and 71 percent of Asian Americans are on-line.[49] During the holiday season in 2000, the average African American household spent $225 on on-line purchases, while Latino households spent $254—the same as white households. And Asian Americans outspent all other groups, with an average of $331 on e-commerce purchases during the same period.[50] In 2004, minorities are expected to spend an estimated $24.5 billion on-line.[51]

The huge growth in the multicultural on-line market has resulted in a proliferation of Web sites targeted to specific ethnic groups. Examples include AsianAvenue.com, a site for Asian Americans; StarMedia Network, which focuses on Latinos inside and outside the United States; and iMinorities, a job site for minorities. One of the more popular sites for African Americans is BlackPlanet.com, which averages 300 million page views per month.

African American portal BET.com recently partnered with Fannie Mae, the nation's largest source of funds to lenders for residential mortgages. The partnership is Fannie Mae's first major on-line marketing effort targeting minorities, even though Fannie Mae is very active in the on-line mortgage market. The multiyear partnership includes a newly created HomeCenter minisite on BET.com that's intended to simplify the home mortgage process. The HomeCenter offers practical tips, such as explaining the implications of different interest rates, and suggestions on how to evaluate, manage, and protect one's credit history. The information is geared to address concerns specific to African Americans.[52]

Black Entertainment Television
How rich is the Home Center content on BET's Web site? What concerns does Fannie Mae address that seem to be specific to African Americans? What general concerns are explained?
http://www.bet.com

On Line

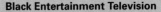

Economic Factors

In addition to social and demographic factors, marketing managers must understand and react to the economic environment. The three economic areas of greatest concern to most marketers are the distribution of consumer income, inflation, and recession.

⑦
Identify consumer and marketer reactions to the state of the economy

Rising Incomes

As disposable (or after-tax) incomes rise, more families and individuals can afford the "good life." Fortunately, U.S. incomes have continued to rise, although at a rather slow pace. After adjustment for inflation, median incomes in the United States rose less than 4 percent between 1980 and 2000.

Today, about two-thirds of all U.S. households earn a "middle-class" income. The rough boundaries for a middle-class income are $18,000, above poverty, to about $75,000, just short of wealth.[53] In 2001, almost half the households were in the upper end of the $18,000 to $75,000 range, as opposed to only a quarter in 1980. More than 10 percent of households now earn above $75,000.[54] As a result, Americans are buying more goods and services than ever before. For example, in raising a child to age seventeen, a middle-class family will spend over $124,000 in 2001 dollars. This new level of affluence is not limited to professionals or even individuals within specific age or education brackets. Rather, it cuts across all household types, well beyond what businesses traditionally consider to be markets for high-priced goods and services. This rising affluence stems primarily from the increasing number of dual-income families.

During the 2000s, many marketing managers are focusing on families with incomes over $35,000, because this group has the most discretionary income. The average American household has over $12,000 in discretionary income each year. Some marketers are concentrating their efforts on higher quality, higher priced goods and services. The Lexus automobile and American Airlines' "international class" service for business-class seats on transcontinental flights are examples of this trend.

Inflation

Inflation is a general rise in prices without a corresponding increase in wages, which results in decreased purchasing power. Fortunately, the United States has had a low rate of inflation for over a decade. The late 1990s and early 2000s have been marked by an inflation rate under 4 percent. The low rate of inflation is due to the tremendous productivity of the high-tech sector of the economy and the stability of the price of services. Both education and healthcare costs are rising much more slowly than in the past. The other good news is that the American economy grew at an annual rate of over 4 percent from 1997 to 2000.[55] These economic conditions benefit marketers, because real wages, and hence purchasing power, go up when inflation stays down. A significant increase in inflation almost always depresses real wages and the ability to buy more goods and services.

In times of low inflation, businesses seeking to increase their profit margins can do so only by increasing their efficiency. If they significantly increase prices, no one will purchase their goods or services.

In more inflationary times, marketers use a number of pricing strategies to cope. (See Chapter 15 for more on these strategies.) But in general, marketers must be aware that inflation causes consumers to either build up or diminish their brand loyalty. In one research session, a consumer panelist noted, "I used to use just Betty Crocker mixes, but now I think of either Betty Crocker or Duncan Hines, depending on which is on sale." Another participant said, "Pennies count now, and so I look at the whole shelf, and I read the ingredients. I don't really understand, but I can tell if it's exactly the same. So now I use this cheaper brand, and honestly, it works just as well." Inflation pressures consumers to make more economical purchases. Nevertheless, most consumers try hard to maintain their standard of living.

In creating marketing strategies to cope with inflation, managers must realize that, despite what happens to the seller's cost, the buyer is not going to pay more for a product than the subjective value he or she places on it. No matter how compelling the justification might be for a 10 percent price increase, marketers must always examine its impact on demand. Many marketers try to hold prices level as long as is practical.

Recession

A **recession** is a period of economic activity when income, production, and employment tend to fall—all of which reduce demand for goods and services. The slowdown in the high-tech sector, overextended consumer credit, and the terrorist attacks on America resulted in the economy slipping into a recession in 2001. The problems of inflation and recession go hand in hand, yet recession requires different marketing strategies:

- *Improve existing products and introduce new ones:* The goal is to reduce production hours, waste, and the cost of materials. Recessions increase the demand for goods and services that are economical and efficient, offer value, help organizations streamline practices and procedures, and improve customer service.

- *Maintain and expand customer services:* In a recession, many organizations postpone the purchase of new equipment and materials. Sales of replacement parts and other services may become an important source of income.

- *Emphasize top-of-the-line products and promote product value:* Customers with less to spend will seek demonstrated quality, durability, satisfaction, and capacity to save time and money. High-priced, high-value items consistently fare well during recessions.

Technological and Resource Factors

Sometimes new technology is an effective weapon against inflation and recession. New machines that reduce production costs can be one of a firm's most valuable assets. The power of a personal-computer microchip doubles about every eighteen months. The Pentium Pro, for example, introduced in 1995, contains 5.3 million transistors and performs three hundred million instructions per second (MIPS). The 886 chip, introduced in 2000, has fifteen million transistors and performs one thousand MIPS. Our ability, as a nation, to maintain and build wealth depends in large part on the speed and effectiveness with which we invent and adopt machines that lift productivity. For example, coal mining is typically thought of as unskilled, backbreaking labor. But visit Cyprus Amax Mineral Company's Twenty-mile Mine near Oak Creek, Colorado, and you will find workers with push-button controls who walk along massive machines that shear thirty-inch slices from an 850-foot coal wall. Laptop computers help miners track equipment breakdowns and water quality.

The United States excels at both basic and applied research. **Basic research** (or *pure research*) attempts to expand the frontiers of knowledge but is not aimed at a specific, pragmatic problem. Basic research aims to confirm an existing theory or to learn more about a concept or phenomenon. For example, basic research might focus on high-energy physics. **Applied research**, in contrast, attempts to develop new or improved products. The United States has dramatically improved its track record in applied research. For example, the United States leads the world in applying basic research to aircraft design and propulsion systems.

The huge investment in information technology has helped America hold down inflation, maintain economic growth, and effectively compete in world markets. Business purchases of information technology have been rising by 25 percent a year since the 1970s. MIT economics professor Erik Brynjolfsson says that hard-to-quantify innovations in the way companies do business are actually far more valuable than the hardware and software they've purchased. "More than $1 trillion in those intangibles has been built up over the past ten years."[56]

Information technology and the Internet have been the innovations driving increased productivity for the past decade. They will continue to do so in the foreseeable future. When Oracle wanted to boost operating margins, it automated such functions as office supply purchasing. That helped keep the workforce stable at 41,000 even as sales soared 30 percent. The company saved about $1 billion, and margins jumped from 20 percent to 33 percent.[57] Dell uses WebMethods software to act as a type of translator enabling instant communication between Dell's order management system and customers' procurement systems. By making it easier for corporate customers to use the Internet to place orders, Dell has dramatically reduced procurement errors and shaved approximately $5 million a year off its costs. Dell also uses TradeMatrix software to run its plants. This system allows Dell to see deep inside suppliers' business processes and vice versa. It tells suppliers which parts to get to which plant and when. TradeMatrix has saved Dell millions of dollars and has become a major competitive advantage. Dell's inventory averages one-tenth the average level of its rivals.[58] For more examples of how information technology and the Internet are boosting productivity, see Exhibit 2.8.

Sometimes, even though new technology is available, its effective utilization can be stymied by the external environment. Our "Global Perspectives" box details

8
Identify the impact of technology on a firm

basic research
Pure research that aims to confirm an existing theory or to learn more about a concept or phenomenon.

applied research
An attempt to develop new or improved products.

Exhibit 2.8

How Companies Are Using the
Internet and Information Technology
to Boost Productivity throughout
the Organization

Process	Example	Payoff
Innovation	Royal Dutch/Shell's "Game-Changer" teams use the Net to generate new business ideas.	New "Light Touch" oil discovery method found 30 million barrels
Collaboration	Ocean Spray's extranet assesses cranberry quality immediately and helps growers get better prices.	Growers get higher profits; Ocean Spray cuts waste and boosts productivity
Design	Honeywell uses the Net to help fashion a customized prototype of anything from a fan blade to a golf club head.	Design time cut from 6 months to 24 hours
Purchasing	Ford's AutoXchange creates massive on-line trading bazaar for its 30,000 suppliers.	Could save as much as $8 billion in first few years
Manufacturing	BP Amoco, using Net technology from Honeywell, can quickly identify plant inefficiencies.	Stems 2% per day productivity loss in Grangemouth, Scotland, refinery
Logistics	Cement maker Cemex uses Net-based truck dispatch system to speed deliveries to customers.	Cement delivered within 20 minutes, down from 3 hours
Marketing	Weyerhaeuser uses the Net to weed out its least valuable customers at Marshfield, Wisconsin, door plant.	Boosted the plant's return on net assets from −2% to 27% in a five-year period.
Service	GE Power Systems lets customers use the Net to compare the performance of its turbines against other GE turbines in the market.	Turbine productivity expected to rise by 1% to 2% annually.

SOURCE: "Working the Web," *Business Week*, February 14, 2000, 116.

how culture and tradition in Japan have slowed the use of the Internet and information technology.

Political and Legal Factors

9

Discuss the political and legal environment of marketing

Business needs government regulation to protect innovators of new technology, the interests of society in general, one business from another, and consumers. In turn, government needs business, because the marketplace generates taxes that support public efforts to educate our youth, protect our shores, and so on. The private sector also serves as a counterweight to government. The decentralization of power inherent in a private-enterprise system supplies the limitation on government essential for the survival of a democracy.

Every aspect of the marketing mix is subject to laws and restrictions. It is the duty of marketing managers or their legal assistants to understand these laws and conform to them, because failure to comply with regulations can have major consequences for a firm. Sometimes just sensing trends and taking corrective action before a government agency acts can help

The Internet Runs Headlong into Japan's Cultural Traditions

Japan's electronics manufacturers are rushing to capitalize on the popularity of the Internet, rolling out everything from Internet music players to digital cameras to Web-friendly computers. There's just one problem: Very little of the gear can be bought on-line in Japan.

The few exceptions come mostly from Sony Corporation. When it launched its PlayStation 2 video-game machine in Japan, enthusiastic buyers not only lined up for blocks in Akihabara, Tokyo's electronics district, they mobbed Sony's Web site. The site sold 380,000 PlayStation 2 units—nearly 40 percent of the total.

In the United States, electronic goods are readily sold on-line: Dell Computer Corporation says its dell.com Web site generates nearly 50 percent of its total sales, an average of $40 million a day as of year-end 1999. But it is going to be harder in Japan. That's partly for cultural reasons, industry insiders say: The Japanese tend to be pickier about what they buy and are reluctant to deal with merchants at a distance.

An even bigger obstacle is a major fortress of Old Japan: Each of the top electronics makers has a nationwide network of exclusive

dealers, usually mom-and-pop stores long on the personal touch but short on information about up-to-date products.

Take a look at a typical store on Tokyo's Shinobazu Avenue, an outlet that is part of the 22,000-member Panasonic/National retail network. The dusty shelves are filled with 1950s hits—AM radios, space heaters. Asked about Will PC, a heavily advertised Panasonic computer, the aged owner says: "I'm sorry, is that a new product? I don't know anything about computers, since we don't stock any."

Manufacturers are reluctant to compete with these merchants, with whom they have long relationships. And small stores and big discounters would object to price cutting on direct sales via the Net.

All this explains an apparent paradox: Many electronics executives, who stand to win big on sales of Web-related products, dismiss Internet sales as a nonstarter. "We can't do it," says Akiyoshi Takano, president of Sanyo Electric Company's multimedia company, which sells such popular Web-related products as digital cameras.

But what about the success of PlayStation 2 on the Internet? Skeptics note that game fans knew

all about the new PlayStation from advance publicity, so they had no need to test it out in the store. Still, many retailers are worried. "This sort of thing would have been unthinkable before now," says Takeo Higashikawa, the manager of a Sony-affiliated store. He thinks Sony was too "dry" and "American" in elbowing aside longtime retailers in favor of Internet sales. "What about the people who worked so hard over the years selling Sony's?" he wonders. Koichiro Katsurayama, a spokesman for Sony Computer Entertainment, says Sony gave retailers and its Web site equal treatment.

Many Japanese retailers are hoping the Internet will end up as a vehicle for only such specialty items. But a Sony managing director, Sunobu Horigome, says that's wishful thinking.[59]

Do you think e-commerce will ever be as popular in Japan as in the United States? What might Japanese manufacturers do to avoid clashes with Japanese retailers? Can you think of other countries where culture and tradition might hinder the development of e-commerce? What about in the United States?

---

avoid regulation. This didn't happen in the case of the tobacco industry. As a result, Joe Camel and the Marlboro Man are fading into the sunset along with other strategies used to promote tobacco products.

The challenge is not simply to keep the marketing department out of trouble, however, but to help it implement creative new programs to accomplish marketing objectives. It is all too easy for a marketing manager or sometimes a lawyer to say no to a marketing innovation that actually entails little risk. For example, an overly cautious lawyer could hold up sales of a desirable new product by warning that the package design could prompt a copyright infringement suit. Thus, it is important to have a thorough understanding of the laws established by the federal government, state governments, and regulatory agencies to control marketing-related issues.

Federal Legislation

Federal laws that affect marketing fall into several categories. First, the Sherman Act, the Clayton Act, the Federal Trade Commission Act, the Celler-Kefauver Antimerger Act, and the Hart-Scott-Rodino Act were passed to regulate the competitive environment. Second, the Robinson-Patman Act was designed to regulate pricing practices. Third, the Wheeler-Lea Act was created to control false advertising. These key pieces of legislation are summarized in Exhibit 2.9.

Primary U.S. Laws That Affect
Marketing

Legislation	Impact on Marketing
Sherman Act of 1890	Makes trusts and conspiracies in restraint of trade illegal; makes monopolies and attempts to monopolize a misdemeanor.
Clayton Act of 1914	Outlaws discrimination in prices to different buyers; prohibits tying contracts (which require the buyer of one product to also buy another item in the line); makes illegal the combining of two or more competing corporations by pooling ownership of stock.
Federal Trade Commission Act of 1914	Creates the Federal Trade Commission to deal with antitrust matters; outlaws unfair methods of competition.
Robinson-Patman Act of 1936	Prohibits charging different prices to different buyers of merchandise of like grade and quantity; requires sellers to make any supplementary services or allowances available to all purchasers on a proportionately equal basis.
Wheeler-Lea Amendments to the FTC Act of 1938	Broadens the Federal Trade Commission's power to prohibit practices that might injure the public without affecting competition; outlaws false and deceptive advertising.
Lanham Act of 1946	Establishes protection for trademarks.
Celler-Kefauver Antimerger Act of 1950	Strengthens the Clayton Act to prevent corporate acquisitions that reduce competition.
Hart-Scott-Rodino Act of 1976	Requires large companies to notify the government of their intent to merge.

State Laws

State legislation that affects marketing varies. Oregon, for example, limits utility advertising to 0.5 percent of the company's net income. California has forced industry to improve consumer products and has also enacted legislation to lower the energy consumption of refrigerators, freezers, and air conditioners. Several states, including New Mexico and Kansas, are considering levying a tax on all in-state commercial advertising.

Regulatory Agencies

Although some state regulatory bodies more actively pursue violations of their marketing statutes, federal regulators generally have the greatest clout. The Consumer Product Safety Commission, the Federal Trade Commission, and the Food and Drug Administration are the three federal agencies most directly and actively involved in marketing affairs. These agencies, plus others, are discussed throughout the book, but a brief introduction is in order at this point.

Consumer Product Safety Commission (CPSC)
A federal agency established to protect the health and safety of consumers in and around their homes.

The sole purpose of the **Consumer Product Safety Commission (CPSC)** is to protect the health and safety of consumers in and around their homes. The CPSC has the power to set mandatory safety standards for almost all products that consumers use (about fifteen thousand items). The CPSC consists of a five-member committee and about eleven hundred staff members, including technicians, lawyers, and administrative help. The commission can fine offending firms up to

$500,000 and sentence their officers to up to a year in prison. It can also ban dangerous products from the marketplace.

The **Federal Trade Commission (FTC)** also consists of five members, each holding office for seven years. The FTC is empowered to prevent persons or corporations from using unfair methods of competition in commerce. It is authorized to investigate the practices of business combinations and to conduct hearings on antitrust matters and deceptive advertising. The FTC has a vast array of regulatory powers (see Exhibit 2.10). Nevertheless, it is not invincible. For example, the FTC had proposed to ban all advertising to children under age eight, to ban all advertising of the sugared products that are most likely to cause tooth decay to children under age twelve, and to require dental health and nutritional advertisements to be paid for by industry. Business reacted by lobbying to reduce the FTC's power. The two-year lobbying effort resulted in passage of the FTC Improvement Act of 1980. The major provisions of the act are as follows:

> It bans the use of unfairness as a standard for industrywide rules against advertising. All the proposals concerning children's advertising were therefore suspended, because they were based almost entirely on the unfairness standard. It requires oversight hearings on the FTC every six months. This congressional review is designed to keep the commission accountable. Moreover, it keeps Congress aware of one of the many regulatory agencies it has created and is responsible for monitoring.

Businesses rarely band together to create change in the legal environment as they did to pass the FTC Improvement Act. Generally, marketing managers only react to legislation, regulation, and edicts. It is usually less costly to stay attuned to the regulatory environment than to fight the government. If marketers had toned down their hard-hitting advertisements to children, they might have avoided an FTC inquiry altogether. The FTC also regulates advertising on the Internet as well

Federal Trade Commission

As a marketing manager, how would you use the FTC Web site in designing a new marketing campaign?

http://www.ftc.gov

On Line

Federal Trade Commission (FTC)
A federal agency empowered to prevent persons or corporations from using unfair methods of competition in commerce.

Exhibit 2.10

Powers of the Federal Trade Commission

Remedy	Procedure
Cease-and-Desist Order	A final order is issued to cease an illegal practice—and is often challenged in the courts.
Consent Decree	A business consents to stop the questionable practice without admitting its illegality.
Affirmative Disclosure	An advertiser is required to provide additional information about products in advertisements.
Corrective Advertising	An advertiser is required to correct the past effects of misleading advertising. (For example, 25 percent of a firm's media budget must be spent on FTC-approved advertisements or FTC-specified advertising.)
Restitution	Refunds are required to be given to consumers misled by deceptive advertising. According to a 1975 court-of-appeals decision, this remedy cannot be used except for practices carried out after the issuance of a cease-and-desist order.
Counteradvertising	The FTC proposed that the Federal Communications Commission permit advertisements in broadcast media to counteract advertising claims (also that free time be provided under certain conditions).

as Internet abuses of consumer privacy (discussed in Chapter 7). The **Food and Drug Administration (FDA)**, another powerful agency, is charged with enforcing regulations against selling and distributing adulterated, misbranded, or hazardous food and drug products. In the last decade it took a very aggressive stance against tobacco products and may be turning its attention to the fast food industry.

Competitive Factors

(10)

Explain the basics of foreign and domestic competition

Food and Drug Administration (FDA)
A federal agency charged with enforcing regulations against selling and distributing adulterated, misbranded, or hazardous food and drug products.

The competitive environment encompasses the number of competitors a firm must face, the relative size of the competitors, and the degree of interdependence within the industry. Management has little control over the competitive environment confronting a firm.

Competition for Market Share and Profits

As U.S. population growth slows, costs rise, and available resources tighten, firms find that they must work harder to maintain their profits and market share regardless of the form of the competitive market. Take, for example, the competition among airlines. To stop start-up Legend Airlines from starting operations at Dallas's Love Field, American Airlines sued the city of Dallas, the federal government, and the new airline itself. It also lobbied Congress, beseeched its frequent fliers, posted billboards around the city, and secretly paid for radio advertising from a "concerned citizens" group protesting expanded use of Dallas's close-in airport, Love Field. When none of that worked, American's parent, AMR Corporation, leased an asbestos-laden, abandoned terminal at Love Field—an airport it didn't even serve—just as the start-up, Legend Airlines, was negotiating for the same space. AMR said it needed more "office space"—fifteen miles from its headquarters. Legend nevertheless prevailed and in March 2000 began flying fifty-six-seat jets to Los Angeles and Washington, offering exclusively first-class seating, gourmet meals, and satellite TV, all for regular coach fare. Nevertheless, aggressive competition from American soon spelled the demise of Legend. A bankruptcy auction offered everything from leather seats to Styrofoam cups.

One of the greatest competitive battles in America is occurring in consumer package goods, and the two giants going toe-to-toe are Procter & Gamble and Unilever. Between 1996 and 2001, $52 billion Unilever and $40 billion P&G have been living in a parallel slow-growth universe. Since 1996, Unilever's sales have declined an average of 3.6 percent a year. P&G's have inched up 3.6 percent a year. Every market they compete in is barely growing, flat, or declining.

In this kind of environment, "it's a death struggle to incrementally gain share," says Burt Flickinger, a former P&G brand manager who now works as a consumer products consultant. P&G and Unilever have to slog it out for every fraction of every share in every category in every market where they compete. And that's a lot of slogging. Both companies own hundreds of the world's best-known brands—Crest, Pampers, Ivory (Procter & Gamble); Dove, Vaseline, Lipton (Unilever)—competing in some 140 countries. But perhaps the fiercest competition is taking place in the U.S. market for laundry detergent, where P&G's Tide and Unilever's Wisk have been locked in battle for more than thirty-five years.

In recent years, nobody has played this game better than Tide. While the rest of the industry stagnated, Tide's sales climbed by 41 percent, to $1.8 billion over the past five years. It now owns 40 percent of the market. Its strategy? First, Tide spends more than $100 million a year promoting its brand name by advertising on

TV, billboards, subways, buses, magazines, and the Internet. It sponsors a NASCAR race car and youth soccer leagues. It holds nationwide publicity stunts, such as its recent Dirtiest Kid in America contest. Tide has made itself an American brand icon—right up there with Coke and McDonald's.

But the real genius of Tide's strategy is its relentless stream of new and improved products. Each year P&G spends close to $2 billion on R&D, a large portion of which goes toward developing new formulations of Tide. There's Tide With Bleach, Tide Free (which has no fragrance), Tide WearCare (which purports to keep fabrics vibrant longer), and Tide Kick (whose package includes a nozzle to rub detergent directly into fabrics). In all, Tide has spawned more than sixty variations of itself.[60]

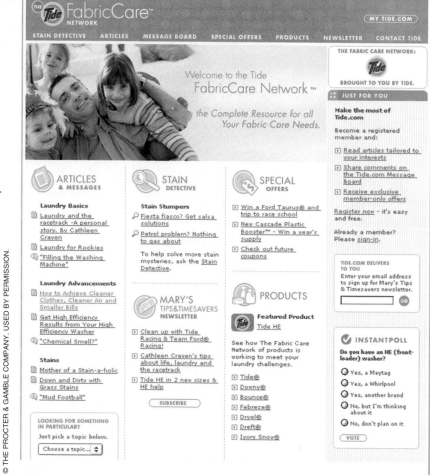

Competition is a driving force in the marketing environment, including laundry. Tide has become one of America's brand icons, in part by continually improving its product and increasing its market share. How competitive is the world of detergent? The formula for Tide is covered by 44 patents.

© THE PROCTER & GAMBLE COMPANY. USED BY PERMISSION.

Global Competition

American Airlines, Unilever, and Procter & Gamble are savvy international competitors conducting business throughout the world. Many foreign competitors also consider the United States to be a ripe target market. Thus, a U.S. marketing manager can no longer worry about only domestic competitors. In automobiles, textiles, watches, televisions, steel, and many other areas, foreign competition has been strong. In the past, foreign firms penetrated U.S. markets by concentrating on price, but today the emphasis has switched to product quality. Nestlé, Sony, Rolls Royce, and Sandoz Pharmaceuticals are noted for quality, not cheap prices.

Global competition is discussed in much more detail in Chapter 3.

CONNECT IT

Look back at the story about Levi's. You should now understand that the external environment affects all firms and their marketing mixes. All of the other external variables, besides demographics and social factors, can influence Levi's sales. Political and legal factors may block the importation of Levi's into some countries. Changing labor laws can increase production costs. Boom periods and recessions can also affect sales.

Are you at the preconventional, conventional, or postconventional stage of ethical development? If you determine that you are at the preconventional level, you should begin striving for a more mature ethical outlook. This may mean taking an ethics course, reading a book on ethics, or engaging in a lot of introspection about yourself and your values. A person with preconventional ethics will probably have a difficult time succeeding in today's business world.

Ethics: A Part of Everyday Life

Realize that ethics plays a part in our lives every day. We all must answer questions such as these:

How do I balance the time and energy obligations of my work and my family?
How much should I pay my employees?
What should I do with the child of my husband's first marriage who is disrupting our new family?
How am I spending my money?
Should I "borrow" a copy of my friend's software?
If I know my employee is having troubles at home, should I treat her differently?
What should I do if I know a neighbor's child is getting into serious trouble?
How do I react to a sexist or racist joke?

Too many people make decisions about everyday questions without considering the underlying moral and ethical framework of the problems. They are simply swept along by the need to get through the day. Our challenge to you is to always think about the ethical consequences of your actions. Make doing so a habit.

Waiting for dramatic events before consciously tackling ethical considerations is like playing a sport only on the weekend. Just as a weekend warrior often ends up with pulled muscles and poor performance, people who seldom consider the ethical implications of daily activities won't have the coordination to work through the more difficult times in their lives. Don't let this happen to you.

Know Your Ethical Values

To get a better idea of your own level of ethical development, take an ethics test. Go to **http://www.worldbank.org/wbi/corpgov/eastasia/m5/m5selftest.htm**. Check your responses against those of others and read their comments. This test will give you better insight into yourself. A short discussion is provided after each question.

Work for a Socially Responsible Firm

When you enter the job market, make certain that you are going to work for a socially responsible organization. Ask a prospective employer how the company gives back to society. If you plan to work for a large company, check out Fortune's current list of America's most admired corporations. (It appears around March 1.)

If you plan to work for a multinational firm, examine *Fortune*'s list of the most globally admired corporations, which appears in October. The list is broken down by industry and includes ten to fifteen companies in each industry. Working for an ethical, socially responsible organization will make you proud of the place where you work.

REVIEW IT

1 **Describe the role of ethics and ethical decisions in business.** Business ethics may be viewed as a subset of the values of society as a whole. The ethical conduct of businesspeople is shaped by societal elements, including family, education, religion, and social movements. As members of society, businesspeople are morally obligated to consider the ethical implications of their decisions.

Ethical decision making is approached in three basic ways. The first approach examines the consequences of decisions. The second approach relies on rules and laws to guide decision making. The third approach is based on a theory of moral development that places individuals or groups in one of three developmental stages: preconventional morality, conventional morality, or postconventional morality.

Many companies develop a code of ethics to help their employees make ethical decisions. A code of ethics can help employees identify acceptable business practices, can be an effective internal control on behavior, can help employees avoid confusion when determining whether decisions are ethical, and can facilitate discussion about what is right and wrong.

1.1 **WRITING** Write a paragraph discussing the ethical dilemma in the following situation and identifying possible solutions: An insurance agent forgets to get the required signature from one of her clients who is buying an automobile insurance policy. The client acknowledges the purchase by giving the agent a signed personal check for the full amount. To avoid embarrassment and inconvenience, the agent forges the client's signature on the insurance application and sends it to the insurance company for processing.

② **Discuss corporate social responsibility.** Social responsibility in business refers to a firm's concern for the way its decisions affect society. Social responsibility has four components: economic, legal, ethical, and philanthropic. These are intertwined, yet the most fundamental is earning a profit. If a firm does not earn a profit, the other three responsibilities are moot. Most businesspeople believe they should do more than pursue profits. Although a company must consider its economic needs first, it must also operate within the law, do what is ethical and fair, and be a good corporate citizen.

2.1 Describe at least three situations in which you would not purchase the products of a firm even though it is very socially responsible.

2.2 A firm's only responsibility to society is to earn a fair profit. Comment.

③ **Discuss the external environment of marketing and explain how it affects a firm.** The external marketing environment consists of social, demographic, economic, technological, political and legal, and competitive variables. Marketers generally cannot control the elements of the external environment. Instead, they must understand how the external environment is changing and the impact of change on the target market. Then marketing managers can create a marketing mix to effectively meet the needs of target customers.

3.1 What is the purpose of environmental scanning? Give an example.

3.2 **TEAM** Form six teams and make each one responsible for one of the uncontrollable elements in the marketing environment. Your boss, the company president, has asked each team to provide a one-year and a five-year forecast of the major trends the firm will face. The firm is in the telecommunications equipment industry. It has no plans to become a telecommunications service provider like, for example, MCI and AT&T. Each team should use the library, the Internet, and other data sources to make its forecasts. Each team member should examine a minimum of one data source. The team should then pool its data and prepare its recommendation. A spokesperson for each team should present the findings to the class.

④ **Describe the social factors that affect marketing.** Within the external environment, social factors are perhaps the most difficult for marketers to anticipate. Several major social trends are currently shaping marketing strategies. First, people of all ages have a broader range of interests, defying traditional consumer profiles. Second, changing gender roles are bringing more women into the workforce and increasing the number of men who shop. Third, a greater number of dual-career families has led to a poverty of time, creating a demand for timesaving goods and services.

4.1 Every country has a set of core values and beliefs. These values may vary somewhat from region to region of the nation. Identify five core values for your area of the country. Clip magazine advertisements that reflect these values and bring them to class.

⑤ **Explain the importance to marketing managers of current demographic trends.** Today, several basic demographic patterns are influencing marketing mixes. Because the U.S. population is growing at a slower rate, marketers can no longer rely on profits from generally expanding markets. Marketers are also faced with increasingly experienced consumers among the younger generations, many of whom are "turned off" by traditional marketing mixes. And because the population is also growing older, marketers are offering more products that appeal to middle-aged and elderly markets.

5.1 Baby boomers in America are aging. Describe how this might affect the marketing mix for the following:

a. Bally's Health Clubs
b. McDonald's
c. Whirlpool Corporation
d. The state of Florida
e. Target Stores

5.2 **WRITING** You have been asked to address a local Chamber of Commerce on the subject of "Generation Y." Prepare an outline for your talk.

5.3 How should Ford Motor Company market differently to Generation Y, Generation X, and baby boomers?

6 **Explain the importance to marketing managers of multiculturalism and growing ethnic markets.** Multiculturalism occurs when all major ethnic groups in an area are roughly equally represented. Growing multiculturalism makes the marketer's task more challenging. America is not a melting pot but numerous mini-melting pots. Hispanics are the fastest growing segment of the population followed by African Americans. Many companies are now creating departments and committees to effectively target multicultural market segments. The heavy use of the Internet by minorities has resulted in the creation of many Web sites and portals tailored specifically for the needs of each group.

6.1 Explain how the Internet is having an impact on multicultural marketing.

6.2 **WRITING** Go to the library and look up a minority market such as the Hispanic market. Write a memo to your boss that details the many submarkets within this segment.

7 **Identify consumer and marketer reactions to the state of the economy.** Marketers are currently targeting the increasing number of consumers with higher discretionary income by offering higher quality, higher priced goods and services. During a time of inflation, marketers generally attempt to maintain level pricing to avoid losing customer brand loyalty. During times of recession, many marketers maintain or reduce prices to counter the effects of decreased demand; they also concentrate on increasing production efficiency and improving customer service.

7.1 Explain how consumers' buying habits may change during a recessionary period.

7.2 **WRITING** Periods of inflation require firms to alter their marketing mix. Suppose a recent economic forecast expects inflation to be almost 10 percent during the next eighteen months. Your company manufactures hand tools for the home gardener. Write a memo to the company president explaining how the firm may have to alter its marketing mix.

8 **Identify the impact of technology on a firm.** Monitoring new technology is essential to keeping up with competitors in today's marketing environment. The United States excels in basic research and, in recent years, has dramatically improved its track record in applied research. Information technology and the Internet have been driving increased U.S. productivity for the past decade. Without innovation, U.S. companies can't compete in global markets.

8.1 Give three examples of how technology has benefited marketers. Also, give several examples of how firms have been hurt by not keeping up with technological changes.

9 **Discuss the political and legal environment of marketing.** All marketing activities are subject to state and federal laws and the rulings of regulatory agencies. Marketers are responsible for remaining aware of and abiding by such regulations. Some key federal laws that affect marketing are the Sherman Act, Clayton Act, Federal Trade Commission Act, Robinson-Patman Act, Wheeler-Lea Amendments to the FTC Act, Lanham Act, Celler-Kefauver Antimerger Act, and Hart-Scott-Rodino Act. The Consumer Product Safety Commission, the Federal Trade Commission, and the Food and Drug Administration are the three federal agencies most involved in regulating marketing activities.

9.1 The Federal Trade Commission and other governmental agencies have been both praised and criticized for their regulation of marketing activities. To what degree do you think the government should regulate marketing? Explain your position.

(10) **Explain the basics of foreign and domestic competition.** The competitive environment encompasses the number of competitors a firm must face, the relative size of the competitors, and the degree of interdependence within the industry. Declining population growth, rising costs, and shortages of resources have heightened domestic competition. Yet small firms that have an effective marketing mix continue to be able to compete with the giants. Meanwhile, dwindling international barriers are bringing in more foreign competitors and offering expanding opportunities for U.S. companies abroad.

10.1 Explain how the nature of competition is changing in America.

10.2 Might there be times when a company becomes too competitive? If so, what could be the consequences?

DEFINE IT

applied research 49
baby boomers 42
basic research 49
code of ethics 32
component lifestyles 37
Consumer Product Safety
   Commission (CPSC) 52
corporate social responsibility 33
demography 39

environmental management
   35
ethics 30
Federal Trade Commission
   (FTC) 53
Food and Drug Administra-
   tion (FDA) 54
Generation X 41
Generation Y 41
inflation 48

morals 30
multiculturalism 44
personalized economy 43
poverty of time 37
pyramid of corporate social
   responsibility 33
recession 48
target market 34

APPLY IT

Application for Entrepreneurs

Jeanette and Jeff Horowitz just inherited $175,000 from Jeanette's late Polish uncle, David Forski. The couple had always wanted to own a franchise and, after some initial investigation, have narrowed their choices down to two. The first is FASTSIGNS, the original retail sign franchise that has hundreds of locations and is found in virtually every state. Its advantages are business customers; standard business hours; a clean, attractive retail environment; national advertising support; and operational and marketing support.

Jeanette and Jeff's other opportunity is a Subway sandwich franchise, a highly rated sandwich system with over 13,000 restaurants. Its key advantages are a simple system with no cooking, low initial investment, quality products, and complete training and support.

Questions

1. What are some of the threats in the external environment that Jeanette and Jeff may face?

2. What factors in the external environment may create an opportunity for Jeff and Jeanette?

3. Go to **http://www.subway.com** and **http://www.fastsigns.com** and determine which franchise is more appealing to you. Why?

Ethics Exercise

Jane Barksdale has designed a line of clothing targeted toward Hispanic Americans. The items are sold only by catalog and on the Internet. She thinks that she can increase sales by publicizing that the firm is owned by a Hispanic American and all the employees are Hispanic Americans. She is not Hispanic American nor are most of the employees. She needs a high level of sales to pay her bank loan and remain in business.

Questions

1. Should she claim that she is Hispanic American?

2. Does the AMA Code of Ethics address this issue? Go to **http://www.marketingpower. com** and review the code. Then, write a brief paragraph on what the AMA Code of Ethics contains that relates to Jane Barksdale's dilemma.

TRY IT

Entrepreneurship Case

Identix: Shedding Light on Modern Security

Prior to the 2001 terrorist attacks against the United States, the high-tech field of biometrics—optical identification systems based on a person's biological features, such as eye patterns or fingerprints—probably seemed like something reserved for science fiction movies and top-secret government facilities. In fact, several companies were hard at work before the attacks developing biometrics applications for banking, travel, and civic identification validation. Chief among them is Identix (previously Visionics).

Formed in 1994 by Joseph Atick and other scientists and engineers, Identix was the first company to discover the proper algorithms for facial recognition. In 2001, Identix took in over $30 million of the $200 million market for biometrics technology in the United States. The total market value is expected to grow to $1 billion by 2004, and most predict Identix will lead the development of this nascent industry.

Sales of its most popular product, a facial recognition technology used in surveillance equipment called FaceIt, grew by 69 percent in 2001. The product is used in video surveillance and can scan for and authenticate specific faces within a crowd. The software that powers it can also improve the quality of a captured image, cut extraneous faces from a picture's background, and track a particular facial image over time.

Other Identix products are in hot demand as well—two from its Live Scan division, the TENPRINTER and FingerPrinter CMS, have been installed at forty-four airports, including those in Los Angeles, Boston, and Cincinnati. Orders are rising and should be boosted further by an FAA grant of $45 million to fund installation of biometrics products in U.S. airports. The company's products were also used at the 2002 Winter Olympic Games in Salt Lake City, Utah, and a recent deal with Honeywell will give its products vastly improved distribution potential, market visibility, and credibility.

Identix's products are also penetrating markets for use in systems used for involuntary identification in law enforcement. The U.S. Army uses a wearable, mobile version of FaceIt (it has a micro camera attached to an eyeglass) for its Digital Military Police program. Several civic police departments use another product, IBIS—an identification based information system—to photograph and scan fingerprints of subjects in the field. The IBIS remote data terminal can then verify identification information within minutes using a remote central database via wireless communication networks.

Though the advantages of increased security are apparent in times of crisis, many wonder if the increased proliferation of biometrics technology will lead to a compromise of personal privacy in the future, as the emotional aftershocks of the September 11th tragedies subside. Joseph Atick is on the record as saying that he is not working to create a national ID system, and that scanned images that don't match those on existing watch lists are immediately deleted from Identix's and Identix's customers' databases.

Americans' fear of privacy on the Internet is already a major social and economic concern, and concerns for privacy under conditions of surveillance or identification validation can only be expected to meet or exceed these already intense levels. In the latter case, however, the issue is one of concern for civil liberties more than one of techno phobia. Identix, therefore, needs to educate and address its customers, the government, and the public with regards to those concerns, or the market it has worked so hard to develop and lead might just disappear before its fiber-optic eyes.

Questions

1. Describe the technological, social, and political factors that are shaping the biometrics market.

2. How is Identix reacting to the above environmental conditions?

3. Does Identix appear to be acting in an ethical manner? Why or why not?

4. Explain why you support or oppose the implementation of biometrics-based security measures.

 WATCH IT

Short

The ad for GMC in Chapter 2's PowerPoint presentation on the PowerPoint CD-ROM illustrates how issues related to competition find their way into advertising. Consider the impact of demographic trends as you watch the three ads for Cadillac.

Medium  **VIDEO**

As you learned in the chapter, the political environment shapes the marketing environment in numerous ways. Riceland Farms had a large contract to sell rice to Iran, and on the point of shipment, the U.S. government placed an embargo on Iran. Find out how Riceland Farms emerged from what could have been a devastating (even bankrupting) trade embargo. Other CNN clips that address the issues in Chapter 2 are the clips for Chapter 3 (on trade agreements), Chapter 5 (on coffee purchasing), Chapter 10 (on a Palestinian brewery), and Chapter 14 (on Internet gambling).

Long  SmallBusinessSchool ▫
the Series on PBS stations and the Web

To give you insight into Chapter 2, Small Business School will introduce you to Record Technologies, a company that blossomed just as its product was seemingly made obsolete. How could a company that makes vinyl LPs succeed in a digital world? By rigorously scanning its environment. Watch the segment and work the questions on the supplemental video CD-ROM.

 FLIP IT

 Flip to Chapter 2 in your *Grademaker Study Guide* for more review opportunities, including the pretest, vocabulary review, study test questions, marketing applications and scenarios, and more. Can you draw the marketing environment? Can you close your book and list the uncontrollable factors in the external environment? Open your Study Guide to find out how much you know—or don't know.

CLICK IT

The *Essentials of Marketing* Web site links you to all the Internet-based activities in this chapter, such as "Use It," "Apply It," and the On-line exercises in the chapter margins. As a review, do the Chapter 2 quiz and crossword puzzle. You can also work the Career Exercise that shows you what kind of marketing careers are available at the Food and Drug Administration (FDA) and Federal Trade Commission (FTC), federal agencies responsible for monitoring diverse marketing practices. Go to **http://lamb.swlearning.com**, read the material, and follow the links right from the site.

Surf to Xtra! to find the supplemental content module on multicultural marketing. You can also test your understanding with the worksheets for Exhibits 2.1, 2.2, 2.3, 2.4, 2.7, 2.8, 2.9, and 2.10. In addition to the quiz on the Web site, there's another quiz on Xtra!, plus video of the authors answering frequently asked questions about the marketing environment. Isn't it true that if you have a really great product, there is no need to worry about the external environment? Is it really that important for firms to be socially responsible? Surf to Xtra! and find out.

Still Shaky? Here's a Tip.

Create your own diagram of the marketing environment and compare it to the example in the chapter. Read a selection of business articles and list the factors at play in each of the articles you read. Visit the *Essentials of Marketing* Web site at **http://lamb.swlearning.com** for a wealth of review and mastery activities.

CHAPTER **THREE**

DEVELOPING A GLOBAL VISION

Learning Objectives

1 *Discuss the importance of global marketing*

2 *Discuss the impact of multi-national firms on the world economy*

3 *Describe the external environment facing global marketers*

4 *Identify the various ways of entering the global marketplace*

5 *List the basic elements involved in developing a global marketing mix*

6 *Discover how the Internet is affecting global marketing*

In brainstorming attractions for its new theme park in Japan, Universal Studios' American designers dreamed up a beast especially for the Japanese: a huge, primeval octopus purportedly hailing from the nearby harbor. Of course, they also envisioned the usual cast of characters from the Hollywood movie studio: E.T., Beetlejuice, and the Terminator. But the ambitious goal Universal set for its first theme park overseas was to rival the phenomenal success of Tokyo Disneyland, the best-attended theme park in the world. To do that, Universal knew it would have to match Disney's knack for making Americana palatable to the Japanese.

And that proved trickier than it sounds.

Descending from a line of silver-screen monsters that began with the Japanese-invented Godzilla, the "Octosaurus" would be a sure hit, Universal's park planners thought. Not so.

To the Japanese, monsters like Godzilla seem dated. Besides, octopuses are friendly, and also tasty. And why would a giant, primeval one be living in their hometown harbor? In the end, the sea monster was dumped, along with several samurai warriers and geisha dancers that had been inserted into entertainment scripts.

In its effort to replicate Disney's magic, Universal's team set into motion one of the most exhaustive attempts ever to mimic what the Japanese have done with everything from Buddhism to American baseball: subtly altering a foreign creation to make it uniquely their own.

"Tokyo Disneyland isn't an American experience. It's a totally Japanese experience," says Norman Elder, another member of the original Disney team in Japan and now head of Universal's marketing efforts here. "Ultimately, they have to embrace the park as their own."

It was in the United States, actually, that the Japanization of Universal began. By surveying Japanese visitors at Universal parks in Orlando and Los Angeles, Universal gradually drew a picture of what the Japanese did and didn't like about the U.S. parks. For example, cramped in their small homes, they swooned at expansive space. But accustomed to modest portions of food, many were turned off by the mountainous servings in the United States.

By mid-1999, a marketing survey in Japan had cataloged Japanese expectations for every aspect of Universal Studios Japan, from bathrooms to souvenir sales. One theme was clear, if a bit contradictory: Japanese wanted an authentic American experience, while expecting the park to cater to their own cultural preferences.

Searching for the right formula required painstaking attention to detail. Universal set up a test kitchen in Japan, where ten Japanese and U.S. chefs tested four thousand recipes to develop U.S.-style dishes with a touch of Japanese flavor. A seafood pizza and gumbo-style soup made the cut. A fried-shrimp concoction with colored rice crackers didn't. American tasters liked it. Japanese simply found it gross.

Julie Appelt, who was born and raised in Japan, and studied theater in the United States, was hired to ensure the shows and skits anchoring the park's entertainment didn't run afoul of Japanese sensibilities. American writers drafted scripts that were then translated into Japanese and given to a Japanese creative staff. There, cultural references and puns that Japanese wouldn't understand were stripped out.

In the final performances, English is used whenever possible. In a musical number based on the *Beetlejuice* movie, the main character banters away in Japanese while his sidekicks speak and sing in English. Snippets of Japanese and a Japanese stuntman were injected into a Wild West show to make the gunfight story more understandable to Japanese without ruining the effect of the U.S. performers.

Other features are uniquely Japanese. The nation's penchant for buying edible souvenirs inspired a 6,000-square-foot confection shop packed with Japanese sweets like dinosaur-shaped bean cakes. Restrooms include Japanese-style squat toilets. Even the park layout caters to the tendency of Japanese crowds to flow clockwise in an orderly manner, contrary to more-chaotic U.S. crowds that steer right.

And on the Jurassic Park water slide, millions of dollars were spent to widen the landing pond, redesign boat hulls, and install underwater wave-damping panels to reduce spray. Why? Many fastidious Japanese don't like to get wet, even on what's billed as one of the world's biggest water slides.[1]

Global marketers often face problems in the external environment that domestic marketers never encounter. Vastly different cultural values and ideas, for example, can present unique challenges as shown above. What are some other variables in the international external environment that can affect global marketers? Is it possible to market products the same way all over the world? Is globalization the wave of the future in international marketing?

Rewards of Global Marketing

global marketing
Marketing that targets markets throughout the world.

global vision
Recognizing and reacting to international marketing opportunities, being aware of threats from foreign competitors in all markets, and effectively using international distribution networks.

Today, global revolutions are under way in many areas of our lives: management, politics, communications, technology. The word *global* has assumed a new meaning, referring to a boundless mobility and competition in social, business, and intellectual arenas. No longer just an option, **global marketing**—marketing that targets markets throughout the world—has become an imperative for business.

U.S. managers must develop a global vision not only to recognize and react to international marketing opportunities but also to remain competitive at home. Often a U.S. firm's toughest domestic competition comes from foreign companies. Moreover, a global vision enables a manager to understand that customer and distribution networks operate worldwide, blurring geographic and political barriers and making them increasingly irrelevant to business decisions. In summary, having a **global vision** means recognizing and reacting to international marketing opportunities, being aware of threats from foreign competitors in all markets, and effectively using international distribution networks.

Over the past two decades, world trade has climbed from $200 billion a year to over $7 trillion. Countries and companies that were never considered major players in global marketing are now important, some of them showing great skill.

Today, marketers face many challenges to their customary practices. Product development costs are rising, the life of products is getting shorter, and new technology is spreading around the world faster than ever. But marketing winners relish the pace of change instead of fearing it.

An example of a young company with a global vision that has capitalized on new technology is Ashtech in Sunnyvale, California. Ashtech makes equipment to capture and convert satellite signals from the U.S. government's Global Positioning System. Ashtech's chief engineer and his team of ten torture and test everything built by Ashtech—expensive black boxes of chips and circuits that use satellite signals to tell surveyors, farmers, mining machine operators, and others where they are with great accuracy. Over half of Ashtech's output is exported. Its biggest customer is Japan.

Adopting a global vision can be very lucrative for a company. Gillette, for example, gets about two-thirds of its revenue from its international division. About 70 percent of General Motors' profits come from operations outside the United States. Although Cheetos and Ruffles haven't done very well in Japan, the potato chip has been quite successful. PepsiCo's (owner of Frito-Lay) overseas snack business brings in more than $3.25 billion annually.

Another company with a global vision is Pillsbury. The Pillsbury Doughboy is used in India to sell a product that the company had just about abandoned in America: flour. Pillsbury (owned by General Mills) has many higher margin products such as microwave pizzas in other parts of the world, but it discovered that in this tradition-bound market, it needed to push the basics.

Even so, selling packaged flour in India has been almost revolutionary, because most Indian housewives still buy raw wheat in bulk, clean it by hand, store it in huge metal hampers, and, every week, carry some to a neighborhood mill, or *chakki*, where it is ground between two stones.

To help reach those housewives, the Doughboy himself has gotten a makeover. In TV advertising, he presses his palms together and bows in the traditional Indian greeting. He speaks six regional languages.

Pillsbury is exploiting a potentially huge business. India consumes about sixty-nine million tons of wheat a year, second only to China. (The United States consumes about twenty-six million tons.) Much of India's wheat ends up as *roti*, a flat bread prepared on a griddle that accompanies almost every meal. In a nation where people traditionally eat with their hands, *roti* is the spoon. The blue Pillsbury

Pillsbury is reaping the rewards of having a global marketing strategy in India. Although wheat is still ground by hand at home in the vast majority of cases, Pillsbury is already the market leader in packaged flour.

DINODIA PICTURE AGENCY

flour package, which features the Doughboy hoisting a *roti,* has become the market leader in Bombay.

Global marketing is not a one-way street, whereby only U.S. companies sell their wares and services throughout the world. Foreign competition in the domestic market used to be relatively rare but now is found in almost every industry. In fact, in many industries the United States has lost significant market share to imported products. In electronics, cameras, automobiles, fine china, tractors, leather goods, and a host of other consumer and industrial products, U.S. companies have struggled at home to maintain their market shares against foreign competitors.

For the past two decades, U.S. companies often appeared to have difficulty competing with foreign rivals. Today, however, America has embarked on a new productivity boom. The United States has the highest productivity among all industrialized countries. The United States is the low-cost producer among industrialized nations, with unit labor costs rising more slowly than in either Japan or Germany. The value of goods manufactured annually by America's 380,000 manufacturing companies is more than 50 percent greater than what's turned out in Japan and a third larger than the combined output of France, Germany, and Britain.[2] Since the early 1990s, no major industrial nation's output has grown faster. American business is fully prepared to compete in the global marketplace.

Importance of Global Marketing to the United States

Many countries depend more on international commerce than the United States does. For example, France, Britain, and Germany all derive more than 19 percent of their gross domestic product from world trade, compared to about 12 percent for the United States. Nevertheless, the impact of international business on the U.S. economy is still impressive:

- The United States exports about a fifth of its industrial production and a third of its farm products.[3]
- One of every sixteen jobs in the United States is directly or indirectly supported by exports.
- U.S. businesses export over $500 billion in goods to foreign countries every year, and almost a third of U.S. corporate profits is derived from international trade and foreign investment.[4]
- Exports account for 20 percent of America's growth in economic activity.[5]
- The United States is the world's leading exporter of grain, selling more than $12 billion of this product a year to foreign countries, or about one-third of all agricultural exports.[6]
- Chemicals, office machinery and computers, automobiles, aircraft, and electrical and industrial machinery make up almost half of all nonagricultural exports.

These statistics might seem to imply that practically every business in the United States is selling its wares throughout the world, but nothing could be further from the truth. About 85 percent of all U.S. exports of manufactured goods are shipped by 250 companies; less than 10 percent of all manufacturing businesses, or around 25,000 companies, export their goods on a regular basis.[7] Most small- and medium-sized firms are essentially nonparticipants in global trade and marketing. Only the very large multinational companies have seriously attempted to compete worldwide. Fortunately, more of the smaller companies are now aggressively pursuing international markets.

The Fear of Trade and Globalization

The protests in Seattle and Genoa during meetings of the World Trade Organization and the protests in New York during the convocation of the World Bank and the International Monetary Fund (the three organizations are discussed later in the chapter) showed that many people fear world trade and globalization. What do they fear? The negatives of global trade are as follows:

- Millions of Americans have lost jobs due to imports or production shifts abroad. Most find new jobs—that pay less.

- Millions of others fear losing their jobs, especially at those companies operating under competitive pressure.

- Employers often threaten to export jobs if workers do not accept pay cuts.

- Service and white-collar jobs are increasingly vulnerable to operations moving offshore.[8]

AP/WIDE WORLD PHOTOS

Successful global marketers have discovered that the path to profitability is through tailoring products to various tastes and desires. A Japanese salesclerk displays a package of flounder and spinach stew, a jar of white bait porridge, and a wild duck cream stew, all produced by America's leading baby-food maker, Gerber. The Japanese baby-food market has tripled in the past fifteen years, and more than four hundred infant entries jostle for spots on Japan's jam-packed supermarket shelves.

Mike Dolan, deputy director of Public Citizens' Global Trade Watch, speaks of a phenomenon he calls "downward harmonization"—the term is a takeoff on "harmonization," which refers to efforts by business to create global products and regulatory policies that make it easier to move production anywhere in the world and to create jobs in developing countries. But those jobs, Dolan says, often go to countries with the weakest laws governing labor, health and safety, and the environment—countries where corporations can pay substandard wages to employ workers in sweatshop conditions. Dolan's group has documented how the movement of jobs across borders compromises living standards for workers in industrialized countries, and how pressure from international regulators and from big companies has hurt efforts to regulate dangerous technologies and hazardous products in developing countries. Even human rights issues suffer—getting pushed off the agenda in favor of business-driven rights like copyright protection. "It's a lowering of consumer protection globally," says Dolan.[9]

Dolan and others are concerned that globalization is destroying national cultures, as when McDonald's changes the world's eating habits; that it is destroying the environment; and that poor countries are not participating in the new wealth globalization creates. These are the grievances voiced at protests when global organizations convene.

Benefits of Globalization

A closer look, however, reveals that globalization has been the engine that creates jobs and wealth. Benefits of global trade include:

- In China and the rest of East Asia, more people rose out of poverty between 1990 and 2000 than the entire population of the United States. The main reason was global trade.[10]

- In Africa, with its many developing economies, per capita income rose 3.6 percent per year during the 1990s, double the 1.8 percent of developed countries, and trade was the single biggest reason.[11]

- Productivity grows more quickly when countries produce goods and services in which they have a comparative advantage (discussed later in the chapter). Living standards can go up faster.

- Global competition and cheap imports keep down prices, so inflation is less likely to arrest economic growth.

- An open economy spurs innovation with fresh ideas from abroad.

- Export jobs often pay more than other jobs.[12]

- Relatively few American workers are in direct competition with workers from poorer countries. Most U.S. workers produce goods and services for industries that face little cross-border competition such as healthcare and construction. Immigration has a much more direct impact on American wages than trade does.[13]

The Globalization Track Record

International trade now accounts for almost 20 percent of global gross domestic product, up from just 10 percent a decade ago.[14] Nations such as Hungary, Malaysia, and even China have made the leap into high-end manufacturing—improving living standards and offering better careers for many workers.

Other nations have not fared as well. The key to success is a government that makes the best use of inflows of foreign investment and know-how. That requires a track record of business-friendly policies to lure multinationals and domestic entrepreneurs alike to train workers, invest in modern technology, and nurture local suppliers and managers.

It also means paying more attention to basics such as solid governmental policies, good public education, a legal system that protects property rights, and a society where prosperity is widely shared. These are the kind of pro-growth policies that most of East Asia employed to develop from sweatshops in the 1960s and 1970s to industrial powers.[15]

The old Soviet bloc demonstrates how competition is dividing Eastern Europe into winners and losers. Hungary and Poland are thriving, while Romania, Bulgaria, and, to some extent, the Czech Republic are lagging. Different approaches to privatization help explain this divergence. The Czech Republic and Romania essentially issued shares in local factories to their citizens—a policy that seemed like a fair way to benefit the public. But that approach put insiders in charge of their enterprises. Hungary, instead, sold factories to both local businesspeople and multinationals. That accelerated the restructuring of the manufacturing sector.[16]

The Impact of Terrorism on Global Trade

The terrorist attacks on America on September 11, 2001, changed forever the way the world conducts business. The immediate impact was a shrinkage of global trade. Globalization will continue because the world's major markets are too vitally integrated for globalization to stop. Nevertheless, the process will be slower and costlier.

Companies are paying more for insurance and to provide security for overseas staff and property. Heightened border inspections slow movements of cargo, forcing companies to stock more inventory. Tighter immigration policies curtail the liberal inflows of skilled and blue-collar workers that allowed companies to expand while keeping wages in check. Meanwhile, greater concern about political risk is causing companies to greatly narrow their horizons when making new investments.[17] The impact of terrorism will lessen over time, but multinational firms will always, now, be on guard.

Multinational Firms

The United States has a number of large companies that are global marketers. Many of them have been very successful. A company that is heavily engaged in international trade, beyond exporting and importing, is called a **multinational corporation**. Multinational corporations move resources, goods, services, and skills across national boundaries without regard to the country in which the headquarters is located. The leading multinational firms in the world are listed in Exhibit 3.1.

A multinational corporation is more than a business entity, as the following paragraph explains:

Discuss the impact of multinational firms on the world economy

multinational corporation
A company that is heavily engaged in international trade, beyond exporting and importing.

Exhibit 3.1

Rank	Company Name	Country	Revenues ($ Millions)	Number of Employees
1	Wal-Mart Stores	U.S.	246,525.0	1,300,000
2	General Motors	U.S.	186,763.0	315,000
3	ExxonMobil	U.S.	182,466.0	92,500
4	Royal Dutch/Shell Group	Brit./Neth.	179,431.0	116,000
5	BP	Britain	178,721.0	115,250
6	Ford Motor	U.S.	163,871.0	350,321
7	DaimlerChrysler	Germany	141,421.1	365,571
8	Toyota Motor	Japan	131,754.2	264,096
9	General Electric	U.S.	131,698.4	350,000
10	Mitsubishi	Japan	109,386.1	47,370
11	Mitsui	Japan	109,630.7	37,734
12	Allianz	Germany	101,930.2	181,651
13	Citigroup	U.S.	100,789.0	252,500
14	Total	France	96,944.9	121,469
15	ChevronTexaco	U.S.	92,043.0	53,014
16	Nippon Telegraph & Telephone	Japan	89,644.0	207,400
17	ING Group	Netherlands	88,102.3	115,000
18	Itochu	Japan	85,856.4	39,109
19	International Business Machines	U.S.	83,132.0	315,889
20	Volkswagen	Germany	82,203.7	324,892
21	Siemens	Germany	77,205.2	426,000
22	Sumitomo	Japan	75,745.2	31,589
23	Marubeni	Japan	72,164.8	27,000
24	Verizon Communications	U.S.	67,625.0	229,497
25	American International Group	U.S.	67,482.0	80,000

SOURCE: "The World's Largest Corporations," *Fortune,* July 21, 2003, 106.

The multinational corporation is, among other things, a private "government," often richer in assets and more populous in stockholders and employees than are some of the nation-states in which it carries on business. It is simultaneously a "citizen" of several nation-states, owing obedience to their laws and paying them taxes, yet having its own objectives and being responsive to a management located in a foreign nation. Small wonder that some critics see in it an irresponsible instrument of private economic power or of economic "imperialism" by its home country. Others view it as an international carrier of advanced management science and technology, an agent for the global transmission of cultures bringing closer the day when a common set of ideals will unite mankind.[18]

Many multinational corporations are enormous. For example, the sales of both ExxonMobil and General Motors are larger than the gross domestic product of all but twenty-two nations in the world. A multinational company may have several worldwide headquarters, depending on where certain markets or technologies are. Britain's APV, a maker of food-processing equipment, has a different headquarters for each of its worldwide businesses. ABB Asea Brown Boveri, the European electrical engineering giant based in Zurich, Switzerland, groups its thousands of products and services into fifty or so business areas. Each is run by a leadership team that crafts global business strategy, sets product development priorities, and decides where to make its products. None of the teams work out of Zurich headquarters;

they are scattered around the world. Leadership for power transformers is based in Germany, electric drives in Finland, and process automation in the United States.

Multinational Advantage

Large multinationals have several advantages over other companies. For instance, multinationals can often overcome trade problems. Taiwan and South Korea have long had an embargo against Japanese cars for political reasons and to help domestic carmakers. Yet Honda USA, a Japanese-owned company based in the United States, sends Accords to Taiwan and Korea. Another example is Germany's BASF, a major chemical and drug manufacturer. Its biotechnology research at home is challenged by the environmentally conscious Green movement. So BASF moved its cancer and immune-system research to Cambridge, Massachusetts.

Another advantage for multinationals is their ability to sidestep regulatory problems. When U.S. drugmaker SmithKline (now GlaxoSmithKline) and Britain's Beecham decided to merge, it was in part so they could avoid licensing and regulatory hassles in their largest markets. The merged company can say it's an insider in both Europe and the United States. "When we go to Brussels, we're a member state [of the European Union]," one executive explains. "And when we go to Washington, we're an American company."[19]

Multinationals can also shift production from one plant to another as market conditions change. When European demand for a certain solvent declined, Dow Chemical instructed its German plant to switch to manufacturing a chemical that had been imported from Louisiana and Texas. Computer models help Dow make decisions like these so it can run its plants more efficiently and keep costs down.

Multinationals can take a great idea in one part of their empire and leverage it around the world. Managers at chipmaker ST Microelectronics' Malaysian plant recently figured out a way to radically compress the assembly time for certain chips, from five days to five hours. Now the company plans to transfer the technique to its Moroccan plant.[20]

Finally, multinationals can often save a lot in labor costs, even in highly unionized countries. For example, Xerox started moving copier-rebuilding work to Mexico, where wages are much lower. Its union in Rochester, New York, objected because it saw that members' jobs were at risk. Eventually, the union agreed to change work styles and to improve productivity to keep the jobs at home.

Global Marketing Standardization

Traditionally, marketing-oriented multinational corporations have operated somewhat differently in each country. They use a strategy of providing different product features, packaging, advertising, and so on. However, Ted Levitt, a Harvard professor, described a trend toward what he referred to as "global marketing," with a slightly different meaning.[21] He contended that communication and technology have made the world smaller so that almost everyone everywhere wants all the things they have heard about, seen, or experienced. Thus, he saw the emergence of global markets for standardized consumer products on a huge scale, as opposed to segmented foreign markets with different products. In this book, global marketing is defined as individuals and organizations using a global vision to effectively market goods and services across national boundaries. To make the distinction, we can refer to Levitt's notion as **global marketing standardization**.

Global marketing standardization presumes that the markets throughout the world are becoming more alike. Firms practicing global marketing standardization produce "globally standardized products" to be sold the same way all over the world. Uniform production should enable companies to lower production and marketing costs and increase profits. However, research indicates that superior sales and profits do not necessarily follow from global standardization.[22]

Levitt cited Coca-Cola, Colgate-Palmolive, and McDonald's as successful global marketers. His critics point out, however, that the success of these three companies is really based on variation, not on offering the same product everywhere.

global marketing standardization
Production of uniform products that can be sold the same way all over the world.

Coca-Cola Company

How does Coca-Cola's mission statement reflect its commitment to global markets? Does the site as a whole reflect this commitment?

http://www.cocacola.com/

Colgate-Palmolive

Compare the Colgate-Palmolive site with the Coca-Cola site. Which more strongly conveys a global image?

http://www.colgate.com/

McDonald's, for example, changes its salad dressings and provides self-serve espresso for French tastes. It sells bulgogi burgers in South Korea and falafel burgers in Egypt. It also offers different products to suit tastes in Germany (where it offers beer) and Japan (where it offers sake). Further, the fact that Coca-Cola and Colgate-Palmolive sell some of their products in more than 160 countries does not signify that they have adopted a high degree of standardization for all their products globally. Only three Coca-Cola brands are standardized, and one of them, Sprite, has a different formulation in Japan. Some Colgate-Palmolive products are marketed in just a few countries. Axion paste dishwashing detergent, for example, was formulated for developing countries, and La Croix Plus detergent was custom made for the French market. Colgate toothpaste is marketed the same way globally, although its advanced Gum Protection Formula is used in only twenty-seven nations.

Nevertheless, some multinational corporations are moving toward a degree of global marketing standardization. Eastman Kodak has launched a world brand of blank tapes for videocassette recorders. Procter & Gamble (P&G) calls its new philosophy "global planning." The idea is to determine which product modifications are necessary from country to country while trying to minimize those modifications. P&G has at least four products that are marketed similarly in most parts of the world: Camay soap, Crest toothpaste, Head and Shoulders shampoo, and Pampers diapers. However, the smell of Camay, the flavor of Crest, and the formula of Head and Shoulders, as well as the advertising, vary from country to country.

External Environment Facing Global Marketers

Describe the external environment facing global marketers

A global marketer or a firm considering global marketing faces problems, often due to the external environment, as many of the same environmental factors that operate in the domestic market also exist internationally. These factors include culture, economic and technological development, political structure and actions, demographic makeup, and natural resources.

Culture

Central to any society is the common set of values shared by its citizens that determine what is socially acceptable. Culture underlies the family, the educational system, religion, and the social class system. The network of social organizations generates overlapping roles and status positions. These values and roles have a tremendous effect on people's preferences and thus on marketers' options. Inca Kola, a fruity, greenish-yellow carbonated drink, is the largest-selling soft drink in Peru. Despite being compared to "liquid bubble gum,"

AP/WORLD WIDE PHOTOS

Culture is a major factor marketers face when marketing products globally. Inca Kola, the largest selling soft drink in Peru, is a symbol of national heritage. Here a firefighter is delivering a case of the beverage to police engaged in a hostage stand-off.

the drink has become a symbol of national pride and heritage. The drink was invented in Peru and contains only fruit indigenous to the country. A local consumer of about a six-pack per day says, "I drink Inca Kola because it makes me feel like a Peruvian." He tells his young daughter, "This is our drink, not something invented overseas. It is named for your ancestors, the great Inca warriors."[23]

Culture may influence product preferences as in Inca Kola or influence the marketing mix in other ways. A U.S. luggage manufacturer found out that culture also affects thinking and perception. The company designed a new Middle East advertising campaign around the image of its luggage being carried on a magic flying carpet. A substantial part of a group in a marketing research study thought they were seeing advertising for Samsonite *carpets*. Green Giant learned that it could not use its Jolly Green Giant in parts of Asia where a green hat worn by a man signifies that he has an unfaithful wife.[24]

Business gift giving is common throughout the world. Yet culture can result in different interpretations of business gifts:

- Flowers are a well-recognized and appreciated gift in the United States, but in China, flowers can be interpreted as a symbol of death.

- A professional travel alarm clock is perfect for a U.S. businessperson who constantly travels. In China, however, clocks symbolize a severing of ties.

- In the United States, wrapping gifts with black or white paper is natural for fortieth birthdays and wedding celebrations. Although gifts in Japan should always be wrapped attractively in paper, black or white wrapping paper is used only for funerals.

- U.S. souvenirs such as electronic gadgets bearing a company logo are highly appreciated in the Middle East. It is important to understand, however, that gifts for wives are unacceptable in the Middle East, although gifts for children are allowed.

- While some alcohol-related corporate gifts are considered inappropriate in the United States, a good bottle of cognac is a much-appreciated business gift in Switzerland.

- In Argentina, business associates do not offer gifts to each other until a fairly close relationship has developed. Once it has, however, scarves, books, and music, in accordance with the recipient's tastes, are readily accepted.[25]

Language is another important aspect of culture. Marketers must take care in translating product names, slogans, production instructions, and promotional messages so as not to convey the wrong meaning. For example, Mitsubishi Motors had to rename its Pajero model in Spanish-speaking countries because the term describes a sexual activity. Toyota Motors' MR2 model dropped the number 2 in France because the combination sounds like a French swearword. The literal translation of Coca-Cola in Chinese characters means "bite the wax tadpole."

Each country has its own customs and traditions that determine business practices and influence negotiations with foreign customers. In many countries, personal relationships are more important than financial considerations. For instance, skipping social engagements in Mexico may lead to lost sales. Negotiations in Japan often include long evenings of dining, drinking, and entertaining, and only after a close personal relationship has been formed do business negotiations begin. The Japanese go through a very elaborate ritual when exchanging business cards. An American businesswoman was unaware of this important cultural tradition. She came into a meeting and tossed some of her business cards across the table at a group of stunned Japanese executives. One of them turned his back on her and walked out. The deal never went through.

Making successful sales presentations abroad requires a thorough understanding of the country's culture. Germans, for example, don't like risk and need strong reassurance. A successful presentation to a German client will emphasize three points: the bottom-line benefits of the product or service, that there will be strong service support, and that the product is guaranteed.[26] In southern Europe,

United Nations

How does the United Nations talk about economic development? Visit the Economic and Social Council's Web page to find out how the UN is involved in helping developing nations prosper.

http://www.un.org/esa

 On Line

it is an insult to show a price list. Without negotiating, you will not close the sale. The English want plenty of documentation for product claims and are less likely to simply accept the word of the sales representative. Scandinavian and Dutch companies are more likely to approach business transactions as Americans do than are companies in any other country.[27]

Fortunately, some habits and customs seem to be the same throughout much of the world. A study of 37,743 consumers from forty different countries found that 95 percent brushed their teeth daily.[28] Other activities that majorities worldwide engage in include reading a newspaper, listening to the radio, taking a shower, and washing their hair.

Economic and Technological Development

A second major factor in the external environment facing the global marketer is the level of economic development in the countries where it operates. In general, complex and sophisticated industries are found in developed countries, and more basic industries are found in less developed nations. Higher average family incomes are common in the more developed countries compared to the less developed markets. Larger incomes mean greater purchasing power and demand not only for consumer goods and services but also for the machinery and workers required to produce consumer goods.

To appreciate marketing opportunities (or lack of them), it is helpful to examine the five stages of economic growth and technological development: traditional society, preindustrial society, takeoff economy, industrializing society, and fully industrialized society.

The Traditional Society

traditional society
A society in the earliest stages of economic development, largely agricultural, with a social structure and value system that provide little opportunity for upward mobility.

Countries in the traditional stage are in the earliest phase of development. A **traditional society** is largely agricultural, with a social structure and value system that provide little opportunity for upward mobility. The culture may be highly stable, and economic growth may not get started without a powerful disruptive force. Therefore, introducing single units of technology into such a country is probably wasted effort. In Ghana, for instance, a tollway sixteen miles long and six lanes wide, intended to modernize distribution, does not connect to any city or village or other road.

The Preindustrial Society

preindustrial society
A society in the second stage of economic development, involving economic and social change and the emergence of a middle class with an entrepreneurial spirit.

The second stage of economic development, the **preindustrial society**, involves economic and social change and the emergence of a middle class with an entrepreneurial spirit. Nationalism may begin to rise, along with restrictions on multinational organizations. Countries like Madagascar and Uganda are in this stage. Effective marketing in these countries is very difficult because they lack the modern distribution and communication systems that U.S. marketers often take for granted. Peru, for example, did not establish a television network until 1975.

The Takeoff Economy

takeoff economy
A society in the third stage of economic development, involving a period of transition from a developing to a developed nation.

The **takeoff economy** is the period of transition from a developing to a developed nation. New industries arise and a generally healthy social and political climate emerges. Kenya and Vietnam have entered the takeoff stage. Although the political situation in Kenya is not considered particularly healthy, there are significant areas of economic growth. Oil exploration is increasing and Kenya is set to become the world's largest exporter of tea. In an effort to develop its economy, Vietnam now offers large tax breaks to foreign investors that promise jobs. Gold Medal Footware, headquartered in Taiwan, now employs five hundred young workers in Danang and hopes to increase the number to twenty-five hundred.

The Industrializing Society

The fourth phase of economic development is the **industrializing society**. During this era, technology spreads from sectors of the economy that powered the takeoff to the rest of the nation. Mexico, China, India, and Brazil are among the nations in this phase of development.

Countries in the industrializing stage begin to produce capital goods and consumer durable products. These industries also foster economic growth. As a result, a large middle class begins to emerge, and the demand for luxuries and services grows.

One of the fastest growing economies in the world today (about 7–8 percent per year) is China. This has resulted in per capita incomes quadrupling in only the last decade and a half. A population of 1.2 billion is producing a gross domestic product of over $1.4 trillion a year. This new industrial giant will be the world's largest manufacturing zone, the largest market for such key industries as telecommunications and aerospace, and one of the largest users of capital.

Rapidly growing large markets like China create enormous opportunities for American global marketers. One tempting market, for example, is the twenty-one million babies born in China each year. One-child families are the rule, so parents spare few expenses bringing up the baby. The Walt Disney Company is in department stores in a dozen or so Chinese cities with the Disney Babies line of T-shirts, rattles, and crib linens—all emblazoned with likenesses of baby Mickey Mouses and other characters.

industrializing society
A society in the fourth stage of economic development, when technology spreads from sectors of the economy that powered the takeoff to the rest of the nation.

The Fully Industrialized Society

The **fully industrialized society**, the fifth stage of economic development, is an exporter of manufactured products, many of which are based on advanced technology. Examples include automobiles, computers, airplanes, oil exploration equipment, and telecommunications gear. Britain, Japan, Germany, France, Canada, and the United States fall into this category.

The wealth of the industrialized nations creates tremendous market potential. Therefore, industrialized countries trade extensively. Also, industrialized nations usually ship manufactured goods to developing countries in exchange for raw materials like petroleum, precious metals, and bauxite.

fully industrialized society
A society in the fifth stage of economic development, a system based on the export of manufactured products, many of which are based on advanced technology.

Political Structure and Actions

Political structure is a third important variable facing global marketers. Government policies run the gamut from no private ownership and minimal individual freedom to little central government and maximum personal freedom. As rights of private property increase, government-owned industries and centralized planning tend to decrease. But rarely will a political environment be at one extreme or the other. India, for instance, is a republic with elements of socialism, monopoly capitalism, and competitive capitalism in its political ideology. Each year the Heritage Foundation publishes a ranking of countries according to their level of economic freedom. The Foundation considers fifty economic variables including banking and finance, trade policy, and regulation. The freest economies in order are Hong Kong, Singapore, Ireland, New Zealand, Luxembourg, the United States, the Netherlands, and Australia. The most repressed is North Korea.[29]

Many countries have changed from a centrally planned economy to a market-oriented one. Eastern European nations like Hungary and Poland have also been moving quickly with market reforms. Many of the reforms have increased foreign trade and investment. For example, in Poland, foreigners are now allowed to invest in all areas of industry, including agriculture, manufacturing, and trade. Poland even gives companies that invest in certain sectors some tax advantages.

Changes leading to market-oriented economies are not restricted to Eastern Europe and Russia. Many countries within Latin America are also attempting market reforms. Countries like Brazil and Mexico are reducing government control over many sectors of the economy. They are also selling state-owned companies to foreign and domestic investors and removing trade barriers that have protected their markets against foreign competition. Brazil has now overtaken Italy and Mexico to become the tenth largest automobile manufacturer in the world. India has recently opened up its market of nine hundred million consumers. Although India's per capita average income is quite low ($330), an estimated 250 million+ Indians have enough income to be considered middle class.

Actions by governments can either help or hinder competitors. Unfortunately, governments often do the latter. In a very unusual move, the government of Thailand has decided to launch a chain of more than three thousand Thai restaurants worldwide over the next five years, with the largest number, more than a thousand, slated for the United States. The restaurants, which will go by the names Elephant Jump for the fast-food branches, Cool Basil for the mid-priced restaurants, and Golden Leaf for the upscale eateries, are believed to be the first ever launched by a government.[30] These restaurants will compete with private restaurants around the world.

Another potential cloud on the horizon for some types of companies doing business abroad is the threat of nationalization, whereby a government takes over the ownership of certain industries or companies, such as airlines in Italy and Bull Computer in France, to infuse more capital into their development. Industries are also nationalized to allow domestic corporations to sell vital goods below cost. For example, for many years France has been supplying coal to users at a loss.

Legal Considerations

Closely related to and often intertwined with the political environment are legal considerations. Nationalistic sentiments of the French led to a law that requires pop music stations to play at least 40 percent of their songs in French (even though French teenagers love American and English rock and roll).

Many legal structures are designed to either encourage or limit trade. Here are some examples:

- *Tariff: a tax levied on the goods entering a country.* For example, the United States imposed a stiff tariff on steel imports in an effort to protect about five thousand U.S. jobs.

- *Quota: a limit on the amount of a specific product that can enter a country.* The United States has strict quotas for imported textiles, sugar, and many dairy products. Several U.S. companies have sought quotas as a means of protection from foreign competition. For example, Harley-Davidson convinced the U.S. government to place quotas on large motorcycles imported to the United States. These quotas gave the company the opportunity to improve its quality and compete with Japanese motorcycles.

- *Boycott: the exclusion of all products from certain countries or companies.* Governments use boycotts to exclude companies from countries with which they have a political dispute. Several Arab nations boycotted Coca-Cola because it maintained distributors in Israel.

- *Exchange control: a law compelling a company earning foreign exchange from its exports to sell it to a control agency, usually a central bank.* A company wishing to buy goods abroad must first obtain foreign currency exchange from the control agency. Generally, exchange controls limit the importation of luxuries. For instance, Avon Products drastically cut back new production lines and products in the Philippines because exchange controls prevented the company from converting pesos to dollars to ship back to the home office. The pesos had to be used in the Philippines. China restricts the amount of foreign currency each Chinese company is allowed to keep from its exports. Therefore, Chinese companies must usually get the government's approval to release funds before they can buy products from foreign companies.

- *Market grouping: also known as a common trade alliance; occurs when several countries agree to work together to form a common trade area that enhances trade opportunities.* The best-known market grouping is the European Union (EU), whose members are Austria, Belgium, Denmark, Finland, France, Germany, Greece, Ireland, Italy, Luxembourg, the Netherlands, Portugal, Spain, Sweden, and the United Kingdom. The EU, which was known as the European Community before 1994, has been evolving for more than four decades, yet until recently, many trade barriers existed among member nations.

- *Trade agreement: an agreement to stimulate international trade.* Not all government efforts are meant to stifle imports or investment by foreign corporations. The Uruguay Round of trade negotiations is an example of this. Likewise, China's most favored nation (MFN) status is considered a trade agreement. The largest Latin American trade agreement is **Mercosur,** which includes Brazil, Argentina, Chile, Bolivia, Uruguay, and Paraguay. The elimination of most tariffs among the trading partners has resulted in trade revenues of over $16 billion annually. The economic boom created by Mercosur will undoubtedly cause other nations to seek trade agreements on their own or enter Mercosur. The European Union, discussed on pages 79–80, hopes to have a free-trade pact with Mercosur in the future.

Mercosur
The largest Latin American trade agreement, which includes Brazil, Argentina, Chile, Bolivia, Uruguay, and Paraguay.

Uruguay Round

The **Uruguay Round** is an agreement to dramatically lower trade barriers worldwide. Adopted in 1994, the agreement has been signed by 142 nations.[31] It is the most ambitious global trade agreement ever negotiated. The agreement has reduced tariffs by one-third worldwide. This, in turn, should raise global income by $235 billion annually. Perhaps most notable is the recognition of the new global realities. For the first time an agreement covers services, intellectual property rights, and trade-related investment measures such as exchange controls.

Uruguay Round
An agreement to dramatically lower trade barriers worldwide; created the World Trade Organization.

The Uruguay Round made several major changes in world trading practices:

- *Entertainment, pharmaceuticals, integrated circuits, and software:* The rules protect patents, copyrights, and trademarks for twenty years. Computer programs receive fifty years' protection and semiconductor chips receive ten years'. But many developing nations have a decade to phase in patent protection for drugs. France, which limits the number of U.S. movies and TV shows that can be shown, refused to liberalize market access for the U.S. entertainment industry.

- *Financial, legal, and accounting services:* Services came under international trading rules for the first time, creating a vast opportunity for these competitive U.S. industries. Now it is easier for managers and key personnel to be admitted to a country. Licensing standards for professionals, such as doctors, cannot discriminate against foreign applicants. That is, foreign applicants cannot be held to higher standards than domestic practitioners.

- *Agriculture:* Europe is gradually reducing farm subsidies, opening new opportunities for such U.S. farm exports as wheat and corn. Japan and Korea are beginning to import rice. But U.S. growers of sugar and citrus fruit have had their subsidies trimmed.

- *Textiles and apparel:* Strict quotas limiting imports from developing countries are being phased out, causing further job losses in the U.S. clothing trade. But retailers and consumers are the big winners, because quotas have added $15 billion a year to clothing prices.

- *A new trade organization:* The **World Trade Organization (WTO)** replaced the old **General Agreement on Tariffs and Trade (GATT)**, which was created in 1948. The old GATT contained extensive loopholes that enabled countries to avoid the trade-barrier reduction agreements—a situation similar to obeying the law only if you want to! Today, all WTO members must fully comply with all agreements under the Uruguay Round. The WTO also has an effective dispute settlement procedure with strict time limits to resolve disputes.

The service agreement under the Uruguay Round requires member countries to create adequate penalties against counterfeiting and piracy. China, which

World Trade Organization (WTO)
A trade organization that replaced the old General Agreement on Tariffs and Trade (GATT).

General Agreement on Tariffs and Trade (GATT)
Provided loopholes that enabled countries to avoid trade-barrier reduction agreements.

is joining the WTO, has done little to control its rampant piracy problems. The Chinese government estimates that counterfeit products with a total value of $16 billion are sold in the country each year.[32] Gillette estimates that a minimum of 25 percent of the firm's razor blades and Duracell batteries sold each year in China are fake. Procter & Gamble estimates that 20 percent of its products in China are fakes. The company has found products it doesn't even produce such as Head and Shoulders soap and Safeguard shampoo! Japan estimates that seven million of the eleven million motorcycles sold in China each year are fake Yamaha, Honda, and Suzuki machines.[33] The Chinese government is beginning to move more aggressively against counterfeiting with its admission to the WTO.

The trend toward globalization has brought to the fore several specific examples of the influence of political structures and legal considerations: the North American Free Trade Agreement, the Free Trade Agreement of the Americas, the Association of Southeast Asian Nations, the Asia-Pacific Economic Cooperation, and the European Union.

North American Free Trade Agreement

North American Free Trade Agreement (NAFTA)
An agreement between Canada, the United States, and Mexico that created the world's largest free-trade zone.

At the time it was instituted, the **North American Free Trade Agreement (NAFTA)** created the world's largest free-trade zone. Ratified by the U.S. Congress in 1993, the agreement includes Canada, the United States, and Mexico, with a combined population of 360 million and economy of $6 trillion.

Canada, the largest U.S. trading partner, entered a free-trade agreement with the United States in 1988. Thus, most of the new long-run opportunities for U.S. business under NAFTA have been in Mexico, America's third largest trading partner. Tariffs on Mexican exports to the United States averaged just 4 percent before the treaty was signed, and most goods entered the United States duty-free. Therefore, the main impact of NAFTA was to open the Mexican market to U.S. companies. When the treaty went into effect, tariffs on about half the items traded across the Rio Grande disappeared. The pact removed a web of Mexican licensing requirements, quotas, and tariffs that limited transactions in U.S. goods and services. For instance, the pact allowed U.S. and Canadian financial-services companies to own subsidiaries in Mexico for the first time in fifty years.

The real test of NAFTA is whether it can deliver rising prosperity on both sides of the Rio Grande. For Mexicans, NAFTA must provide rising wages, better benefits, and an expanding middle class with enough purchasing power to keep buying goods from the United States and Canada. As of 2001, that scenario was working. Between 1993 and 2001, U.S. exports to Mexico rose 170 percent, far above the 68 percent for overall U.S. exports. Mexican exports to the United States grew 241 percent during the same period.[34]

NAFTA, to date, has been very successful, displacing some workers but creating far more jobs than have been lost. For more information about NAFTA, see the Office of NAFTA & Inter-American Affairs at **http://www.mac.doc.gov/nafta**.

Free Trade Area of the Americas

Free Trade Area of the Americas (FTAA)
A regional trade agreement that, when signed, will create a regional trading zone encompassing 36 countries in North and South America.

The goal of **Free Trade Area of the Americas (FTAA)**, is to establish a free-trade zone similar to NAFTA throughout the Western Hemisphere. If created, FTAA would likely supplant Mercosur, a free-trade agreement between Brazil, Argentina, Uruguay and Paraguay. If ratified by all member nations, FTAA would become the largest trading zone in the world, consisting of 800 million people in thirty-four countries in both North and South America with a combined gross domestic product of $11 trillion![35] Similar to NAFTA, FTAA pledges to support trade "without barriers, without subsidies, without unfair practices, and with an increasing stream of productive investments."[36] Leaders from each of the thirty-four countries have agreed to finish FTAA negotiations by 2005. If that occurs, over the next decade nontariff barriers would be removed, tariffs would gradually be reduced to zero, rules for investing and financial markets would be standardized, and a process would be established to handle trade disputes.[37] For more information about FTAA, see **www.ftaa-alca.org**. For more information about Mercosur, see **http://www.mercosur.org/english/default.htm**.

Association of Southeast Asian Nations

The **Association of Southeast Asian Nations** (**ASEAN**) and the **Asia-Pacific Economic Cooperation** (**APEC**) are the two largest and most important regional trading groups in Asia. ASEAN is a trade agreement between Brunei Darussalam, Cambodia, Indonesia, Laos, Malaysia, Myanmar, the Philippines, Singapore, Thailand, and Vietnam. Together, these countries form a market of more than 330 million people. U.S. trade with ASEAN countries is sizable, exceeding $75 billion a year. In fact, the United States is ASEAN's largest trading partner, while the member nations of ASEAN are the United States' fifth largest trade group. ASEAN member countries have agreed to create an ASEAN free-trade area beginning in 2015 for the six original countries (Brunei Darussalam, Indonesia, Malaysia, the Philippines, Singapore, and Thailand) and in 2018 for newer member countries (Cambodia, Laos, Myanmar, and Vietnam).[38] For more information about ASEAN, see **http://www.aseansec.org**.

Association of Southeast Asian Nations (ASEAN)
A trade agreement among ten Asian nations.

Asia-Pacific Economic Cooperation (APEC)
A trade agreement that includes most ASEAN countries plus eleven other nations.

Asia-Pacific Economic Cooperation

The Asia-Pacific Economic Cooperation (APEC) is a broader agreement between Australia, Canada, Chile, People's Republic of China, Hong Kong, China, Japan, Korea, Mexico, New Zealand, Papua New Guinea, Peru, Russia, the United States, and all the members of ASEAN, except Cambodia, Laos, and Myanmar.[39] APEC's twenty-one member countries contain 2.5 billion people, account for 47 percent of all global trade, and have a combined gross domestic product of over $18 trillion. APEC countries agreed to begin reducing trade barriers in the year 2000, though it will take until 2020 for all trade barrier reductions to be completely phased in. For more information about APEC, see **http://www.apecsec.org.sg**.

European Union

In 1993, all twelve member countries of the European Community (EC) ratified the **Maastricht Treaty**. The treaty, named after the Dutch town where it was developed, set forth a plan to take the EC further toward economic, monetary, and political union. Officially called the Treaty on European Union, the document outlined plans for tightening bonds among the member states and creating a single market. The European Commission, which drafted the treaty, notes that Maastricht has created over two million new jobs.

Maastricht Treaty
An agreement among twelve countries of the European Community to pursue economic, monetary, and political union.

Although the heart of the treaty deals with developing a unified European market, Maastricht was also intended to increase integration among the European Union members in areas much closer to the core of national sovereignty. The treaty created a common currency and an independent central bank in 1999. The European Monetary Union (EMU) was launched on January 1, 1999, with Austria, Belgium, Finland, France, Germany, Ireland, Italy, Luxembourg, the Netherlands, Portugal, and Spain as members. Britain, Sweden, and Denmark chose not to join at the outset. Greece, which was too far from the EMU's stringent fiscal requirement to join at the start, joined later. A new European Central Bank was

In 2002, the euro became the currency of the EMU. The currency board pictured here shows the currencies of the EMU countries in euros.

© AFP/CORBIS

also created along with an EMU currency called the euro. Together, the members of the EMU have a $6.4 trillion economy, the second largest in the world.

Common foreign, security, and defense policies are also goals, as well as European citizenship—whereby any European Union citizen can live, work, vote, and run for office anywhere in the member countries. The treaty standardized trade rules and coordinated health and safety standards. Duties, customs procedures, and taxes were also standardized. A driver hauling cargo from Amsterdam to Lisbon can now clear four border crossings by showing a single piece of paper. Before the Maastricht Treaty, the same driver would have carried two pounds of paper to cross the same borders. The overall goal is to end the need for a special product for each country—for example, a different Braun electric razor for Italy, Germany, France, and so forth. Goods marked GEC (goods for EC) can be traded freely, without being retested at each border. For more information about the Maastricht Treaty and the European Union, go to **http://europa.eu.int/index-en.htm**.

American businesses have recently been stung by aggressive antitrust actions taken by the European Commission, the European Union's executive branch. By EU law, the Commission must review any merger or acquisition involving any companies with significant revenues in the European Union. Thus, the Commission threatened to block AOL's acquisition of Time Warner unless Virgin Records was sold first. It was. The biggest action to date was denying the merger of General Electric with Honeywell, both U.S. firms. Even Jack Welch, the legendary General Electric CEO, could not persuade the European Commission to let the merger go through.[40]

Some economists have called the European Union the "United States of Europe." It is an attractive market, with 320 million consumers and purchasing power almost equal to that of the United States. But the European Union will probably never be a United States of Europe. For one thing, even in a united Europe, marketers will not be able to produce a single Europroduct for a generic Euroconsumer. With twelve different languages and individual national customs, Europe will always be far more diverse than the United States. Thus, product differences will continue. It will be a long time, for instance, before the French begin drinking the instant coffee that Britons enjoy. Preferences for washing machines also differ: British homemakers want front-loaders, and the French want top-loaders; Germans like lots of settings and high spin speeds; Italians like lower speeds. Even European companies that think they understand Euroconsumers often have difficulties producing "the right product." Atag Holdings NV, a diversified Dutch company whose main business is kitchen appliances, was confident it could cater to both the "potato" and "spaghetti" belts—marketers' terms for consumer preferences in northern and southern Europe. But Atag quickly discovered that preferences vary much more than that. For example, on its ovens, burner shape and size, knob and clock placement, temperature range, and colors vary greatly from country to country. Although Atag's kitchenware unit has lifted foreign sales to 25 percent of its total from 4 percent in the mid-1980s, it now believes that its range of designs and speed in delivering them, rather than the magic bullet of a Euro-product, will keep it competitive.[41]

An entirely different type of problem facing global marketers is the possibility of a protectionist movement by the European Union against outsiders. For example, European automakers have proposed holding Japanese imports at roughly their current 10 percent market share. The Irish, Danes, and Dutch don't make cars and have unrestricted home markets; they would be unhappy about limited imports of Toyotas and Datsuns. But France has a strict quota on Japanese cars to protect Renault and Peugeot. These local carmakers could be hurt if the quota is raised at all.

Interestingly, a number of big U.S. companies are already considered more "European" than many European companies. Coca-Cola and Kellogg's are considered classic European brand names. Ford and General Motors compete for the largest share of auto sales on the continent. IBM and Dell Computer dominate their markets. General Electric and AT&T are already strong all over Europe and have invested heavily in new manufacturing facilities throughout the continent.

Although many U.S. firms are well prepared to contend with European competition, the rivalry is perhaps more intense there than anywhere else in the world.

In the long run, it is questionable whether Europe has room for eight mass-market automakers, including Ford and GM, when the United States sustains just three. Similarly, an integrated Europe probably doesn't need twelve national airlines.

A global map of the regional trade agreements discussed in the preceding sections is depicted in Exhibit 3.2.

Demographic Makeup

The three most densely populated nations in the world are China, India, and Indonesia. But that fact alone is not particularly useful to marketers. They also need to know whether the population is mostly urban or rural, because marketers may not have easy access to rural consumers. In Belgium about 90 percent of the population lives in an urban setting, whereas in Kenya almost 80 percent of the population lives in a rural setting. Belgium is thus the more attractive market.

Just as important as population is personal income within a country. The wealthiest countries in the world include Japan, the United States, Switzerland, Sweden, Canada, Germany, and several of the Arab oil-producing nations. At the other extreme are countries like Mali and Bangladesh, with a fraction of the per capita purchasing power of the United States. However, a low per capita income is not in itself enough reason to avoid a country. In countries with low per capita incomes, wealth is not evenly distributed. There are pockets of upper- and middle-class consumers in just about every country of the world. In some countries, such as India, the number of consumers is surprisingly large.

The most significant global economic news of the past decade is the rise of a global middle class. From Shekou, China, to Mexico City and countless cities in between, there are traffic jams, bustling bulldozers, and people hawking tickets to

Global Map of Regional Trade Agreements **Exhibit 3.2**

Maastricht Treaty of Europe Austria, Belgium, Denmark, Finland, France, Germany, Greece, Italy, Ireland, Luxembourg, The Netherlands, Portugal, Spain, Sweden, and the United Kingdom.

ASEAN Brunei Darussalam, Cambodia, Indonesia, Laos, Malaysia, Myanmar, the Philippines, Singapore, Thailand, and Vietnam.

APEC Australia, Canada, Chile, China, Hong Kong, Japan, Korea, Mexico, New Zealand, Papua New Guinea, Peru, Russia, the United States, and all members of ASEAN except Cambodia, Laos, and Myanmar.

NAFTA (North American Free Trade Agreement) United States, Canada, and Mexico.

FTAA (Free Trade Area of the Americas) United States, Canada, Mexico, and all the countries in Central America and South America.

various events. These are all signs of a growing middle class. In China, per capita incomes are rising rapidly. Developing countries, excluding Eastern Europe and the republics of the former Soviet Union, should grow about 4 percent annually over the next decade.

Growing economies demand professionals. In Asia, accountants, stock analysts, bankers, and even middle managers are in short supply. Rising affluence also creates demand for consumer durables such as refrigerators, VCRs, and automobiles. Companies like Procter & Gamble and Gillette offer an array of products at different price points to attract and keep customers as they move up the income scale. The percentage of the world's population that lives in industrialized nations has been declining since 1960, because industrialized nations have grown slowly and developing nations have grown rapidly. In this decade, more than 90 percent of the world's population growth will occur in developing countries and only 10 percent in the industrialized nations. The United Nations reports that in 2000, 79 percent of the world's population resided in developing countries—for example, Guinea, Bolivia, and Pakistan.

Natural Resources

A final factor in the external environment that has become more evident in the past decade is the shortage of natural resources. For example, petroleum shortages have created huge amounts of wealth for oil-producing countries such as Norway, Saudi Arabia, and the United Arab Emirates. Both consumer and industrial markets have blossomed in these countries. Other countries—such as Indonesia, Mexico, and Venezuela—were able to borrow heavily against oil reserves in order to develop more rapidly. On the other hand, industrial countries like Japan, the United States, and much of Western Europe experienced rampant inflation in the 1970s and an enormous transfer of wealth to the petroleum-rich nations. But during much of the 1990s, when the price of oil fell, the petroleum-rich nations suffered. Many were not able to service their foreign debts when their oil revenues were sharply reduced. The U.S. dependence on foreign oil will likely remain high.

Petroleum is not the only natural resource that affects international marketing. Warm climate and lack of water mean that many of Africa's countries will remain importers of foodstuffs. The United States, on the other hand, must rely on Africa for many precious metals. Japan depends heavily on the United States for timber and logs. A Minnesota company manufactures and sells a million pairs of disposable chopsticks to Japan each year. The list could go on, but the point is clear. Vast differences in natural resources create international dependencies, huge shifts of wealth, inflation and recession, export opportunities for countries with abundant resources, and even a stimulus for military intervention.

Global Marketing by the Individual Firm

Identify the various ways of entering the global marketplace

A company should consider entering the global marketplace only after its management has a solid grasp of the global environment. Some relevant questions are "What are our options in selling abroad?" "How difficult is global marketing?" and "What are the potential risks and returns?" Concrete answers to these questions would probably encourage the many U.S. firms not selling overseas to venture into the international arena. Foreign sales could be an important source of profits.

Companies decide to "go global" for a number of reasons. Perhaps the most stimulating reason is to earn additional profits. Managers may feel that international sales will result in higher profit margins or more added-on profits. A second stimulus is that a firm may have a unique product or technological advantage not available to other international competitors. Such advantages should result in major business successes abroad. In other situations, management may have exclusive

Exhibit 3.3

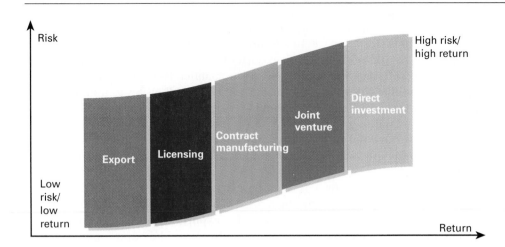

market information about foreign customers, marketplaces, or market situations not known to others. While exclusivity can provide an initial motivation for international marketing, managers must realize that competitors can be expected to catch up with the information advantage of the firm. Finally, saturated domestic markets, excess capacity, and potential for economies of scale can also be motivators to "go global." Economies of scale mean that average per-unit production costs fall as output is increased.

Many firms form multinational partnerships—called strategic alliances—to assist them in penetrating global markets; strategic alliances are examined in Chapter 5. Five other methods of entering the global marketplace are, in order of risk, export, licensing, contract manufacturing, joint venture, and direct investment. (See Exhibit 3.3.)

Export

When a company decides to enter the global market, exporting is usually the least complicated and least risky alternative. **Exporting** is selling domestically produced products to buyers in another country. A company, for example, can sell directly to foreign importers or buyers. Exporting is not limited to huge corporations such as General Motors or 3M. Indeed, small companies account for 96 percent of all U.S. exporters, but only 30 percent of the export volume. The United States is the world's largest exporter. Many small businesses claim that they lack the money, time, or knowledge of foreign markets that exporting requires. The U.S. Department of Commerce is trying to make it easier for small businesses to begin exporting. The department has created a pilot program in which it has hired a private company to represent up to fifty small businesses at specific international trade fairs. For example, FTS, Inc., was hired to represent small firms at a trade show in Italy. The company handed out company brochures and other sales information to interested prospective Italian clients. Also, after the show was over, FTS gave each participating American company a list of potential Italian distributors for their products. Each American firm paid only $2,500 to be represented at the trade fair. For companies interested in exporting, the U.S. government stands ready to help in a variety of ways.

The U.S. Commercial Service within the Department of Commerce promotes itself as "Your Global Business Partner." It offers trade specialists in more than a hundred U.S. cities and eighty countries to help beginning exporters, as well as those already engaged in global marketing, increase their business. The primary services offered by the U.S. Commercial Service are marketing research, trade events, locating qualified buyers and partners, and global business consulting. These services are explained in more detail in Exhibit 3.4.

exporting
Selling domestically produced products to buyers in another country.

On Line

Recently, the U.S. Commercial Service launched a joint venture with IBM called BuyUSA.com. The Internet service offers one-on-one export counseling provided by the U.S. Commercial Service. In addition, the site provides Web-based sales leads to exporters. A U.S. exporter fills out a questionnaire on its product offerings and receives access to qualified foreign buyers. We suggest that you go to the Web site and take the BuyUSA tour and demo to learn more about how the U.S. Commercial Service aids American firms wanting to "go global." For those interested in international business, a nongovernmental Web site that offers links to hundreds of useful sites is available from the International Federation of International Trade Associations (**http://fita.org**).

Instead of selling directly to foreign buyers, a company may decide to sell to intermediaries located in its domestic market. The most common intermediary is the export merchant, also known as a **buyer for export**, which is usually treated like a domestic customer by the domestic manufacturer. The buyer for export assumes all risks and sells internationally for its own account. The domestic firm is involved only to the extent that its products are bought in foreign markets.

A second type of intermediary is the **export broker**, who plays the traditional broker's role by bringing buyer and seller together. The manufacturer still retains title and assumes all the risks. Export brokers operate primarily in agriculture and raw materials.

Export agents, a third type of intermediary, are foreign sales agents-distributors who live in the foreign country and perform the same functions as domestic manufacturers' agents, helping with international financing, shipping, and so on. The U.S. Department of Commerce has an agent-distributor service that helps about five thousand U.S. companies a year find an agent or distributor in virtually any country of the world. A second category of agents resides in the manufacturer's country but represents foreign buyers. This type of agent acts as a hired purchasing agent for foreign customers operating in the exporter's home market.

buyer for export
An intermediary in the global market that assumes all ownership risks and sells globally for its own account.

export broker
An intermediary who plays the traditional broker's role by bringing buyer and seller together.

export agent
An intermediary who acts like a manufacturer's agent for the exporter. The export agent lives in the foreign market.

Licensing

Another effective way for a firm to move into the global arena with relatively little risk is to sell a license to manufacture its product to someone in a foreign country. **Licensing** is the legal process whereby a licensor allows another firm to use its manufacturing process, trademarks, patents, trade secrets, or other proprietary knowledge. The licensee, in turn, pays the licensor a royalty or fee agreed on by both parties.

Because licensing has many advantages, U.S. companies have eagerly embraced the concept. For instance, Marvel Enterprises granted 4Kids Entertainment international licensing rights for X-Men-the-Movie, X-Men classic, Spider Man classic, the Fantastic Four, Silver Surfer, the Incredible Hulk, Avengers, Captain America, Iron Man, and Daredevil.

A licensor must make sure it can exercise the control over the licensee's activities needed to ensure proper quality, pricing, distribution, and so on. Licensing may also create a new competitor in the long run, if the licensee decides to void the license agreement. International law is often ineffective in stopping such actions. Two common ways of maintaining effective control over licensees are shipping one or more critical components from the United States or locally registering patents and trademarks to the U.S. firm, not to the licensee. Garment companies maintain control by delivering only so many labels per day; they also supply their own fabric and collect the scraps, and do accurate unit counts.

Franchising is a form of licensing that has grown rapidly in recent years. More than 350 U.S. franchisors operate more than thirty-two thousand outlets in foreign countries, bringing in sales of over $6 billion.[42] Over half of the international franchises are for fast-food restaurants and business services. New Horizons Computer Learning Centers has been franchising internationally since 1992. It now has

licensing
The legal process whereby a licensor agrees to let another firm use its manufacturing process, trademarks, patents, trade secrets, or other proprietary knowledge.

Exhibit 3.4

Assistance Provided by the U.S.
Commercial Service

Marketing Research

COUNTRY COMMERCIAL GUIDES
provide overviews for doing business in more than 120 countries with information on market conditions, best export prospects, financing, finding distributors, and legal and cultural issues.

INDUSTRY SECTOR ANALYSES
offer succinct international market information on specific industries that can help determine market potential, market size, and competitors for a firm's products and services.

INTERNATIONAL MARKET INSIGHTS
report on current conditions in specific country markets and identify upcoming opportunities for generating sales.

WEBCASTS
present market opportunities and insights on how to do business in specific countries. They are available on **http://www.usatrade.gov**.

FLEXIBLE MARKET RESEARCH
provides timely, customized, reliable answers to a company's inquiries about a market and its receptivity to its products and services.

Locating Qualified Buyers and Partners

MATCHMAKER TRADE DELEGATIONS
let managers meet face-to-face with qualified business prospects in two to four promising export markets. The program includes comprehensive country briefings, logistical support, and follow-up counseling.

INTERNATIONAL PARTNER SEARCHES
deliver detailed company information on up to five prescreened potential partners that have expressed an interest in a company's products and services.

GOLD KEY
arranges one-on-one appointments with carefully selected potential business partners in a targeted export market.

INTERNATIONAL COMPANY PROFILES
provide affordable, fast credit checks and background information on potential international buyers and other business partners.

TRADE OPPORTUNITY PROGRAM
provides daily worldwide trade leads from companies seeking to purchase or represent a firm's products or services. These leads are reviewed by trade specialists and commercial officers.

GOLD KEY USA
helps international buyers locate the best U.S. suppliers. Counseling before and after business meetings is part of this service.

VIRTUAL MATCHMAKERS
give sales managers the opportunity to meet with groups of prescreened international business prospects and get answers to market questions in an interactive video conference focusing on a specific industry.

VIDEO GOLD KEY
enables sales managers to meet with individual potential business partners throughout the world without leaving the United States. Available now in more than 100 U.S. and international locations.

Trade Events

COMMERCIAL NEWS USA
promotes a firm's products and services to more than 400,000 international buyers. A great way to reach a targeted audience eager to buy U.S. products and services, this magazine has a proven track record of high response rates and sales results.

SHOW TIME
provides in-depth counseling at major trade shows from a team of market and industry specialists who know the local and regional markets.

CATALOG EXHIBITIONS
showcase a firm's product and service literature in fast-growing export markets around the world.

SINGLE COMPANY PROMOTIONS
provide meeting space and carefully screened invitation lists to help a company present successful seminars featuring its products and services.

INTERNATIONAL BUYER PROGRAM
recruits and brings more than 125,000 international end-users and distributors to visit top U.S. trade shows. The Commercial Service helps organize meetings and provide matchmaking services and business counseling to help generate sales.

U.S. PAVILIONS
put companies in the best international trade shows with access to thousands of buyers. One-on-one matching at the show with potential buyers arranged by the commercial service's team of market and industry specialists can help generate sales and long-term business relationships at these high-volume shows.

Consulting

- Determine the best markets for a firm's products and services.

- Develop an effective export strategy.

- Evaluate international competitors.

- Identify and comply with legal and regulatory issues.

- Locate export financing.

- Settle disputes.

- Win contract bids.

- Learn about cultural and business protocol.

SOURCE: U.S. Commercial Service.

locations in forty-five countries. Most of the inquiries New Horizons receives about franchise opportunities come through the U.S. Commercial Service's Gold Key program (see Exhibit 3.4).[43]

Contract Manufacturing

contract manufacturing
Private-label manufacturing by a foreign company.

Firms that do not want to become involved in licensing or to become heavily involved in global marketing may engage in **contract manufacturing**, which is private-label manufacturing by a foreign company. The foreign company produces a certain volume of products to specification, with the domestic firm's brand name on the goods. The domestic company usually handles the marketing. Thus, the domestic firm can broaden its global marketing base without investing in overseas plants and equipment. After establishing a solid base, the domestic firm may switch to a joint venture or direct investment.

Joint Venture

joint venture
When a domestic firm buys part of a foreign company or joins with a foreign company to create a new entity.

Joint ventures are similar to licensing agreements. In a **joint venture**, the domestic firm buys part of a foreign company or joins with a foreign company to create a new entity. A joint venture is a quick and relatively inexpensive way to go global and to gain needed expertise.[44] For example, Robert Mondavi Wineries entered into a joint venture with Baron Philippe de Rothschild, owner of Bordeaux's First Growth chateau, Mouton-Rothschild. They created a wine in California called Opus One. It was immediately established as the American vanguard of quality and price. Mondavi has entered other joint ventures with the Frescobaldi family in Tuscany and with Errazuriz in Chile. "We're doing these wines from around the world because they're going to come here anyway," he said. "The industry is going global, so we're going global, too."[45]

Robert Mondavi Winery has a very aggressive joint venture strategy. Opus One is the result of pairing with the premier French vintner Baron Philippe de Rothschild. The brand has been well received by American wine drinkers and hailed for its high quality.

COURTESY OF OPUS ONE

Recently, General Motors entered into a joint venture with Avtovaz, a Soviet-era auto manufacturer in Russia, to produce a car to be called the Chevrolet Niva. Russia is expected to be one of the top ten growth markets for cars during the first decade of the 2000s, and GM wants to be a player. The assembly and engineering will be done at low cost in Russia. GM is providing $333 million and technology. Avtovaz offers skilled workers and a distribution system.[46]

Joint ventures can be very risky. Many fail; others fall victim to a takeover, in which one partner buys out the other. In a survey of 150 companies involved in joint ventures that ended, three-quarters were found to have been taken over by Japanese partners. Gary Hamel, a professor at the London Business School, regards joint ventures as a race to learn: The partner that learns fastest comes to dominate the relationship and can then rewrite its terms.[47] Thus, a joint venture becomes a new form of competition.

Sometimes joint venture partners simply can't agree on management strategies and policies. For example, Procter & Gamble and its Vietnamese partner can't agree on what to do next in their unprofitable joint venture. Consumer-products giant P&G wants to inject more cash into the business; but because Phuong Dong Soap & Detergent, its state-owned partner, has said it's unable to provide the cash to match it, P&G has offered to buy out the Vietnamese stake. So far Phuong Dong has flatly refused to sell, and Ministry of Planning and Investment officials have described such an option as "impossible."[48]

In a successful joint venture, both parties gain valuable skills from the alliance. In the General Motors–Suzuki joint venture in Canada, for example, both parties have contributed and gained. The alliance, CAMI Automotive, was formed to manufacture low-end cars for the U.S. market. The plant, run by Suzuki management, produces the Geo Metro/Suzuki Swift—the smallest, highest-gas-mileage GM car sold in North America—as well as the Geo Tracker/Suzuki Sidekick sport utility vehicle. Through CAMI, Suzuki has gained access to GM's dealer network and an expanded market for parts and components. GM avoided the cost of developing low-end cars and obtained models it needed to revitalize the lower end of its product line and its average fuel-economy rating. The CAMI factory may be one of the most productive plants in North America. There GM has learned how Japanese carmakers use work teams, run flexible assembly lines, and manage quality control.

Direct Investment

Active ownership of a foreign company or of overseas manufacturing or marketing facilities is **direct foreign investment**. Direct foreign investment by U.S. manufacturers is currently about $50 billion annually. Direct investors have either a controlling interest or a large minority interest in the firm. Thus, they have the greatest potential reward and the greatest potential risk.

Wal-Mart has now made direct investments in nine countries with more than 1,100 stores. International sales now top $32 billion.[49] Not all of its global investments have been successful. In Germany, Wal-Mart bought the twenty-one store Wertkauf hypermarket chain in 1997 and then seventy-four unprofitable and often decrepit Interspar stores in 1998. Problems in integrating and upgrading the stores resulted in at least $200 million in losses. Like all other German stores, Wal-Mart stores in Germany are required by law to close at 8 P.M. on weekdays and 4 P.M. on Saturdays, and they cannot open at all on Sundays. And costs are astronomical. Derek Rowe, an American brought over to supervise the $5 million renovation of the Dortmund store, estimated that construction costs in Germany are five times what they are in the United States.[50]

Now Wal-Mart seems to be turning the corner on its international operations. It is pushing operational authority down to country managers in order to respond better to local cultures. Wal-Mart enforces certain core principles such as "everyday low prices," but country managers handle their own buying, logistics, building design, and other operational decisions.

Direct investment by American companies in China has mushroomed. Today, direct investment there amounts to more than $8 billion, up from less than $200 million in 1989.[51] U.S. firms that have recently built manufacturing facilities in China include LaCrosse Footwear (winter boots), Lexmark (printers), Motorola (cell phones), Rubbermaid (cookware and storage products), Raleigh (bicycles), Cooper Tools (wrenches), Mattel Murray (Barbie doll playhouses), and Samsonite (luggage). These firms intend to sell not only to the 1.2 billion Chinese population but also to U.S. customers and the global market.

Sometimes firms make direct investments because they can find no suitable local partners. Also, direct investments avoid the communication problems and conflicts of interest that can arise with joint ventures. Other firms simply don't want to share their technology, which they fear may be stolen or ultimately used against them by creating a new competitor. Texas Instruments (TI) has historically been one of the latter companies. "TI was a technology company that hated to share anything," said Akira Ishikawa, senior vice president of TI's semiconductor group. "It wasn't in the culture to share or teach the most advanced semiconductor technologies. It was taboo. If you talked about that, you might be fired immediately."[52] Now TI has changed its attitude and entered into five Asian joint ventures. The reason was primarily to spread its financial risk.

A firm may make a direct foreign investment by acquiring an interest in an existing company or by building new facilities. It might do so because it has trouble transferring some resource to a foreign operation or getting that resource locally. One important resource is personnel, especially managers. If the local labor market is tight, the firm may buy an entire foreign firm and retain all its employees instead of paying higher salaries than competitors.

The United States is a popular place for direct investment by foreign companies. In 2002, the value of foreign-owned businesses in the United States was more than $475 billion.

The Global Marketing Mix

To succeed, firms seeking to enter into foreign trade must still adhere to the principles of the marketing mix. Information gathered on foreign markets through research is the basis for the four Ps of global marketing strategy: product, place (distribution), promotion, and price. Marketing managers who understand the advantages and disadvantages of different ways of entering the global market and the effect of the external environment on the firm's marketing mix have a better chance of reaching their goals.

The first step in creating a marketing mix is developing a thorough understanding of the global target market. Often this knowledge can be obtained through the same types of marketing research used in the domestic market (see Chapter 7). However, global marketing research is conducted in vastly different environments. Conducting a survey can be difficult in developing countries, where telephone ownership is rare and mail delivery slow or sporadic. Drawing samples based on known population parameters is often difficult because of the lack of data. In some cities in South America, Mexico, and Asia, street maps are unavailable, streets are unidentified, and houses are unnumbered. Moreover, the questions a marketer can ask may differ in other cultures. In some cultures, people tend to be more private than in the United States and do not like to respond to personal questions on surveys. For instance, in France, questions about one's age and income are considered especially rude.

Product and Promotion

With the proper information, a good marketing mix can be developed. One important decision is whether to alter the product or the promotion for the global marketplace. Other options are to radically change the product or to adjust either the promotional message or the product to suit local conditions.

One Product, One Message

The strategy of global marketing standardization, which was discussed earlier, means developing a single product for all markets and promoting it the same way all over the world. For instance, Procter & Gamble uses the same product and promotional themes for Head and Shoulders in China as it does in the United States. The advertising draws attention to a person's dandruff problem, which stands out in a nation of black-haired people. Head and Shoulders is now the best-selling shampoo in China despite costing over 300 percent more than local brands. Buoyed by its success with Head and Shoulders, Procter & Gamble is using the same product and same promotion strategy with Tide detergent in China. It also used another common promotion tactic that it has found to be successful in the United States. The company spent half a million dollars to reach agreements with local washing machine manufacturers, which now include a free box of Tide with every new washer.

Metabolife International has devised five herbal medicine products for both the Chinese and the American markets. Both markets have a huge demand for herbal products, but their vastly different concepts of medicine have stymied companies that want to unlock both markets with one product. Until now, most dietary-supplement companies in the United States have hawked just one Chinese herb at a time. In China, however, herbs are almost always mixed together in formulas that are sold in a dizzying number of combinations depending on specific symptoms. A typical Chinese pharmacy, for example, offers dozens of herbal cold formulas depending on symptoms.

Metabolife selected five ailments—the common cold, arthritis, headache, premenstrual syndrome, and upset stomach—and asked a team of Chinese doctors to come up with one formula for each. Next, Metabolife researchers analyzed the formulas, identified the active ingredients, and put them in pill form. The result is a form of Chinese medicine called Chinac, which offers U.S. consumers a mixture of herbs similar to that found in medicine sold in China but without the variety found in a Chinese pharmacy. For example, the cold pill, called Immune Health Formula, is a mix of herbs aimed at relieving a typical winter flu.

But Metabolife figures Americans and Chinese are becoming more similar in their approach to herbal medicine. For Americans, Chinac offers a quick and easy entrée into what is for most consumers an unfamiliar field of medicine. For Chinese consumers, Metabolife may offer a welcome change to the confusing choices they face in a Chinese pharmacy.[53]

Global media—especially satellite and cable TV networks like CNN International, MTV Networks, and British Sky Broadcasting—make it possible to beam advertising to audiences unreachable a few years ago. "Eighteen-year-olds in Paris have more in common with eighteen-year-olds in New York than with their own parents," says William Roedy, director of MTV Europe. Almost all of MTV's advertisers run unified, English-language campaigns in the twenty-eight nations the firm reaches. The audiences "buy the same products, go to the same movies, listen to the same music, sip the same colas. Global advertising merely works on that premise."[54] Although teens throughout the world prefer movies above all other forms of television programming, they are closely followed by music videos, stand-up comedy, and then sports.

Even a one-product, one-message strategy may call for some changes to suit local needs, such as variations in the product's measurement units, package sizes, and labeling. Pillsbury, for example, changed the measurement unit for its cake mixes because adding "cups of" has no meaning in many developing countries. Also, in emerging economies, such as India, many people still buy a single cigarette rather than a package and one egg rather than a dozen. Hindustan Lever, a subsidiary of giant Lever Brothers, flooded the market with small packets of shampoo called sackets instead of bottles. The firm also markets toothpaste the same way. Now shampoo in sackets outsells traditional bottles. Hindustan now commands more than 70 percent of the market.[55]

Unchanged products may fail simply because of cultural factors. The game *Trivial Pursuit* failed in Japan. It seems that getting the answers wrong can be seen as a loss of face. Any type of war game tends to do very poorly in Germany, even though Germany is by far the world's biggest game-playing nation. A successful game in Germany has plenty of details and thick rulebooks. *Monopoly* remains the world's favorite

© GILLES BASSIGNAC/GETTY IMAGES/GETTY NEWS SERVICES

board game; it seems to overcome all cultural barriers. The game is available in twenty-five languages, including Russian, Croatian, and Hebrew.

Product Invention

In the context of global marketing, product invention can be taken to mean either creating a new product for a market or drastically changing an existing product.

Mattel, Scrabble
Hasbro, Monopoly

Visit Mattel's Scrabble site and Hasbro's Monopoly site. Which game has more of an international presence on the Internet? Does this surprise you? Why?

http://www.mattelscrabble.com
http://www.monopoly.com

On Line

A one-product, one-message strategy does not work for all products. Parker Brothers' *Monopoly*, however, uses this strategy very successfully. A French Riviera version of the popular game debuted at the 2000 Cannes film festival. Depicted here is the Russian gameboard.

For the Japanese market, Nabisco had to remove the cream filling from its Oreo cookies because Japanese children thought they were too sweet. Ford thinks it can save billions on its product development costs by developing a single small-car chassis and then altering its styling to suit different countries. Campbell Soup invented a watercress and duck gizzard soup that is now selling well in China. It is also considering a cream of snake soup. Frito-Lay's most popular potato chip in Thailand is shrimp flavored. Dormont Manufacturing Company makes a simple gas hose that hooks up to deep-fat fryers and similar appliances. Sounds like something that could be sold globally, right? Wrong—in Europe differing national standards means that a different hose is required for each country. Minutiae such as the color of the plastic coating or how the end pieces should be attached to the rest of the hose and the couplings themselves create a myriad of design problems for Dormont Manufacturing.

Coca Cola's Thums Up cola outsells Coke by a four-to-one margin in India. In Turkey, Coke sells a pear-flavored drink, while in Germany it offers a berry drink. Now, Coke is developing soft drinks for tastes around the world.

Consumers in different countries use products differently. For example, in many countries, clothing is worn much longer between washings than in the United States, so a more durable fabric must be produced and marketed. For Peru, Goodyear developed a tire that contains a higher percentage of natural rubber and has better treads than tires manufactured elsewhere in order to handle the tough Peruvian driving conditions. Rubbermaid has sold millions of open-top wastebaskets in America; Europeans, picky about garbage peeking out of bins, wanted bins with tight lids that snap into place.

Product Adaptation

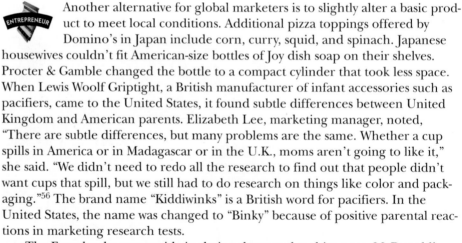

Another alternative for global marketers is to slightly alter a basic product to meet local conditions. Additional pizza toppings offered by Domino's in Japan include corn, curry, squid, and spinach. Japanese housewives couldn't fit American-size bottles of Joy dish soap on their shelves. Procter & Gamble changed the bottle to a compact cylinder that took less space. When Lewis Woolf Griptight, a British manufacturer of infant accessories such as pacifiers, came to the United States, it found subtle differences between United Kingdom and American parents. Elizabeth Lee, marketing manager, noted, "There are subtle differences, but many problems are the same. Whether a cup spills in America or in Madagascar or in the U.K., moms aren't going to like it," she said. "We didn't need to redo all the research to find out that people didn't want cups that spill, but we still had to do research on things like color and packaging."[56] The brand name "Kiddiwinks" is a British word for pacifiers. In the United States, the name was changed to "Binky" because of positive parental reactions in marketing research tests.

The French take great pride in their culture and architecture. McDonald's has become the focal point of French fears of economic globalization and the infringement of American pop culture on their Gallic traditions. McDonald's French branch claims that it is not global or American, but part of the French reality. Etienne Aussedat, McDonald's communications director in France, states, "Our restaurants are franchises and they are run by French businessmen. We buy our potatoes from farms in northern France, our beef from western France and our lettuces from Perpignan in southern France."[57] The concrete box restaurant design is being replaced by "de chez nous." Wooden structures made with trees from the Vosges Mountains in eastern France and façades that reflect traditional brasseries are now being built. The burgers feature "sauce à la moutarde," cantal cheese, and buns made by "La Boulangarie Française."

When products are defective, the way a corporation handles the situation varies from country to country. Consider the tainted milk story in the "Ethics in Marketing" box.

Pouring on the Apologies

Even in a country where apologies are an art form, Yumi Ito was taken aback by the gymnastics that two businessmen performed in her living room one Sunday.

Dressed in dark blue suits, the two men—employees of Japan's largest milk maker—literally prostrated themselves before her. Their heads touched the floor as they bowed over and over again to express remorse. The problem: Their company had produced a bad batch of milk that sickened Ms. Ito's one-and-a-half-year-old daughter. Their performance "was painful to watch," Ms. Ito said afterward, her recovered daughter jumping around beside her.

In a quintessentially Japanese show of corporate damage control, Snow Brand Milk Products Company put 2,000 employees into the streets—fully 13 percent of its workforce—to personally bow, scrape, apologize, and pay cash compensation to each of more than 14,000

people sickened by tainted milk from its factory in Osaka. About 180 victims were hospitalized.

The effort is remarkable even for Japan, where companies such as Snow Brand often send out employees to apologize for product flaws that in other countries might rate a replacement and a form letter. Yet Snow Brand executives say the crisis—heightened by criticism that senior officials were responding inadequately—demands extraordinary countermeasures. At stake was the fate of a conglomerate with $12.1 billion in annual sales of dairy products, wine, frozen pizzas, and other goods.

Noriaki Okuyama, a burly manager who plans ice-cream-sales strategy for eastern Japan, earnestly briefed the Snow Brand employees. His instructions: apologize first, then ask about the victim's health. After that, face the delicate issue of compensation. If possible, get a receipt for the

health-related expenses the customers are claiming. If that isn't possible, or if they get mad, back off and pay them anyway, he said. How much? "It's your judgment call," said Mr. Okuyama, sweat streaming down his brow. "If the amount is within 30,000 yen ($280), it should be OK." And don't talk back, no matter how angry the customer gets, Mr. Okuyama warned.

Then came questions: "What about pets?" asked a grizzled man in a gray suit. "Pets are the same as people," Mr. Okuyama replied. "We have to bear expenses for their sickness, too."[58]

Do you think that Snow Brand took the proper action? Can you imagine a U.S. manufacturer doing the same? Why or why not? Lawyers file thousands of product liability lawsuits in America each year. If U.S. companies followed the lead of Japanese firms in apologizing for defective products, might there be fewer lawsuits?

Only two years after the contaminated milk scandal that rocked Japan's Milk Products Company, company executives were forced to bow to the press again. This time the company was charged with allegedly passing off imported Australian beef as domestic in order to benefit from a government scheme to buy up homegrown beef as a precaution against mad cow disease.

AP/WORLD WIDE PHOTOS

Message Adaptation

Another global marketing strategy is to maintain the same basic product but alter the promotional strategy. Bicycles are mainly pleasure vehicles in the United States. In many parts of the world, however, they are a family's main mode of transportation. Thus, promotion in these countries should stress durability and efficiency. In contrast, U.S. advertising may emphasize escaping and having fun.

Harley-Davidson decided that its American promotion theme, "One steady constant in an increasingly screwed-up world," wouldn't appeal to the Japanese market. The Japanese ads combine American images with traditional Japanese ones: American riders passing a geisha in a rickshaw, Japanese ponies nibbling at a Harley motorcycle. Waiting lists for Harleys in Japan are now six months long.

A new campaign for ExxonMobil offers a fresh twist on message adaptation. The company wants the ads to carry the same look and feel regardless of the country in which they appear. To do this, ExxonMobil has produced five hours of commercial footage to be used as a library by local markets. As many as six different casts act out essentially the same story lines, with local markets picking which vignettes they want to use in their region. The company will use the footage to advertise its brands in a hundred countries. The campaign, which carries the tagline "We are drivers too," was tweaked to account for cultural differences. For example, the advertising agency asked actors to alternate using their right and left hands in scenes where they were eating food. In some regions, food is customarily eaten using only the right hand. ExxonMobil spent $150 million on the campaign.[59]

Global marketers find that promotion is a daunting task in some countries. For example, commercial television time is readily available in Canada but severely restricted in Germany. Until recently, marketers in Indonesia had only one subscription TV channel with few viewers (120,000 out of a nation of more than 200 million people). Because of this limited television audience, several marketers, such as the country's main Toyota dealer, had to develop direct-mail campaigns to reach their target markets.

Some cultures view a product as having less value if it has to be advertised. In other nations, claims that seem exaggerated by U.S. standards are commonplace. On the other hand, Germany does not permit advertisers to state that their products are "best" or "better" than those of competitors, a description commonly used in U.S. advertising. The hard-sell tactics and sexual themes so common in U.S. advertising are taboo in many countries. Procter & Gamble's advertisements for Cheer detergents were voted least popular in Japan because they used hard-sell testimonials. The negative reaction forced P&G to withdraw Cheer from the Japanese market. In the Middle East, pictures of women in print advertisements have been covered with censors' ink.

Language barriers, translation problems, and cultural differences have generated numerous headaches for international marketing managers. Consider these examples:

- A toothpaste claiming to give users white teeth was especially inappropriate in many areas of Southeast Asia, where the well-to-do chew betel nuts and black teeth are a sign of higher social status.

- Procter & Gamble's Japanese advertising for Camay soap nearly devastated the product. In one commercial, a man meeting a woman for the first time immediately compared her skin to that of a fine porcelain doll. Although the ad had worked in other Asian countries, the man came across as rude and disrespectful in Japan.

Pricing

Once marketing managers have determined a global product and promotion strategy, they can select the remainder of the marketing mix. Pricing presents some unique problems in the global sphere. Exporters must not only cover their production costs but also consider transportation costs, insurance, taxes, and tariffs. When deciding on a final price, marketers must also determine what customers are willing to spend on a particular product. Marketers also need to ensure that their foreign buyers will pay them. Because developing nations lack mass purchasing power, selling to them often poses special pricing problems. Sometimes a product can be simplified in order to lower the price. The firm must not assume that low-income countries are willing to accept lower quality, however. Although the nomads of the Sahara are very poor, they still buy expensive fabrics to make their clothing. Their survival in harsh conditions and extreme temperatures requires this expense. Additionally, certain expensive luxury items can be sold almost anywhere.

Companies must also be careful not to be so enthusiastic about entering a market that they use poor pricing strategies. Sales of Compaq computers have been growing very rapidly in China, but partially because the company (now owned by Hewlett-Packard) has been giving away computers against its will. Recently, a Chinese distributor failed to repay $32 million for computers that Compaq had extended on credit. Analysts say Compaq is now owed over $100 million by delinquent dealers and distributors in China.

Also, money-back guarantees don't always work well in developing nations. Amway in China told customers that if they were not satisfied, they could bring the product (soap) back for a full refund, no questions asked—even if the bottles were empty. Some enterprising third parties began repackaging the soap and returning the empty bottles. Others just scoured empty bottles out of trash cans to seek refunds. When refunds mounted to $100,000 per day, Amway rescinded the policy, only to face angry distributors who marched into offices to complain. They felt they were entitled to the refunds. Amway offers the same guarantee worldwide—with very different results—so it was surprised by the Chinese reaction.[60]

Dumping

Dumping is generally considered to be the sale of an exported product at a price lower than that charged for the same or a like product in the "home" market of the exporter. This practice is regarded as a form of price discrimination that can potentially harm the importing nation's competing industries. Dumping may occur as a result of exporter business strategies that include (1) trying to increase an overseas market share, (2) temporarily distributing products in overseas markets to offset slack demand in the home market, (3) lowering unit costs by exploiting large-scale production, and (4) attempting to maintain stable prices during periods of exchange rate fluctuations.

Historically, the dumping of goods has presented serious problems in international trade. As a result, dumping has led to significant disagreements among countries and diverse views about its harmfulness. Some trade economists view dumping as harmful only when it involves the use of "predatory" practices that intentionally try to eliminate competition and gain monopoly power in a market. They believe that predatory dumping rarely occurs and that antidumping enforcement is a protectionist tool whose cost to consumers and import-using industries exceeds the benefits to the industries receiving protection.

The Uruguay Round rewrote the international law on dumping. Now, under the agreement:

1. Dumping disputes are resolved by the World Trade Organization.

2. Dumping terms are specifically defined. For example, the "dumped price" must be at least 5 percent below the home market price before it is considered dumping.

3. At least 25 percent of the members of an industry must support its government filing a dumping complaint with the World Trade Organization. In other words, a government can't file a complaint if only one or two firms complain (unless they make up 25 percent of the industry).

Countertrade

Global trade does not always involve cash. Countertrade is a fast-growing way to conduct global business. In **countertrade**, all or part of the payment for goods or services is in the form of other goods or services. Countertrade is thus a form of barter (swapping goods for goods), an age-old practice whose origins have been traced back to cave dwellers. The U.S. Department of Commerce says that roughly 30 percent of all global trade is countertrade. In fact, both India and China have made billion-dollar government purchasing lists, with most of the goods to be paid for by countertrade.

One common type of countertrade is straight barter. For example, PepsiCo sends Pepsi syrup to Russian bottling plants and in payment gets Stolichnaya vodka, which is then marketed in the West. Another form of countertrade is the compensation agreement. Typically, a company provides technology and equipment for a

dumping
The sale of an exported product at a price lower than that charged for the same or a like product in the "home" market of the exporter.

countertrade
A form of trade in which all or part of the payment for goods or services is in the form of other goods or services.

plant in a developing nation and agrees to take full or partial payment in goods produced by that plant. For example, General Tire Company supplied equipment and know-how for a Romanian truck tire plant. In turn, General Tire sold the tires it received from the plant in the United States under the Victoria brand name. Pierre Cardin gives technical advice to China in exchange for silk and cashmere. In these cases, both sides benefit even though they don't use cash.

Atwood Richards is the world's largest company specializing in countertrade. When companies turn over unsold products to Atwood, they receive trade credits. The credits can be used to obtain other products and services Atwood has acquired—everything from hotel rooms and airline tickets to television advertising time, forklift trucks, carpeting, pulp, envelopes, steel castings, or satellite tracking systems.

Distribution

Solving promotional, price, and product problems does not guarantee global marketing success. The product still has to get adequate distribution. For example, Europeans don't play sports as much as Americans do, so they don't visit sporting-goods stores as often. Realizing this, Reebok started selling its shoes in about eight hundred traditional shoe stores in France. In one year, the company doubled its French sales. Harley-Davidson had to open two company-owned stores in Japan to get distribution for its Harley clothing and clothing accessories.

The Japanese distribution system is considered the most complicated in the world. Imported goods wind their way through layers of agents, wholesalers, and retailers. For example, a bottle of ninety-six aspirins costs about $20 because the bottle passes through at least six wholesalers, each of whom increases the selling price. As a result, the Japanese consumer pays the world's most exorbitant prices. These distribution channels seem to be based on historical and traditional patterns of socially arranged trade-offs, which Japanese officials claim are very hard for the government to change. Today, however, the system seems to be changing because of pressure from the Japanese consumer. Japanese shoppers are now placing low prices ahead of quality in their purchasing decisions. The retailer who can cut distribution costs and therefore the retail price gets the sale. For example, Kojima, a Japanese electronics superstore chain like the U.S. chains Circuit City and Best Buy, had to bypass General Electric's Japanese distribution partner Toshiba to import its merchandise at a good price. Toshiba's distribution system required refrigerators to pass through too many hands before they reached the retailer. Kojima went directly to GE headquarters in the United States and persuaded the company to sell it refrigerators, which were then shipped directly to Kojima. It is now selling GE refrigerators for about $800—half the price of a typical Japanese model.

Retail institutions in other countries also may differ from what a company is used to in its domestic market. The terms *department store* and *supermarket* may refer to types of retail outlets that are very different from those found in the United States. Japanese supermarkets, for example, are large multistory buildings that sell not only food but also clothing, furniture, and home appliances. Department stores are even larger outlets, but unlike their U.S. counterparts, they emphasize foodstuffs and operate a restaurant on the premises. For a variety of reasons, U.S.-type retail outlets do not exist or are impractical in developing countries. For instance, consumers may not have the storage space to keep food for several days. Refrigerators, when available, are usually small and do not allow for bulk storage. Attempting to build new retail outlets can be a frustrating battle. In Germany's Ruhr Valley, the discounter All Kauf SB-Warenhaus GmbH has struggled to build a store for fifteen years on land that it owns. Local authorities are blocking construction because they are afraid the store will hurt local retailers.

Europe's freight-rail system is a throwback to another era. No two countries use the same signaling systems or electric current for their trains. Trains in France and Britain run on the left side of dual-track lines, while those in the rest of Europe run on the right. Because France and Spain use two different gauges of track, trains crossing their shared border must stop to let each car be lifted so that its wheels can be changed.

In many developing nations, channels of distribution and the physical infrastructure are inadequate. To combat these problems, companies are using creative strategies. Colgate-Palmolive has introduced villagers in India to the concept of brushing teeth by rolling into villages with video vans that show half-hour infomercials on the benefits of toothpaste. The company received more than half of its revenue in that nation from rural areas in 2003. Until recently, the rural market was virtually invisible, due to a lack of distribution.

Certainly, not all global distribution is inefficient or primitive. United Parcel Service, through its wholly owned UPS Logistics Group, is embarking on an ambitious plan to dominate Asia's logistics business. UPS's new master plan envisions "superhubs" that will serve as single nodes for all incoming and outgoing goods.[61]

UPS Logistics recently opened a warehouse in Singapore, a joint venture with National Semiconductor Corporation. Every night at ten o'clock, the same unmarked truck goes past the tropical beaches of Malaysia on a two-hour journey south to the new warehouse. The cargo is also always the same: some of the most sophisticated semiconductors on earth, manufactured in a massive National Semiconductor plant outside Melaka. Most of the chips have a drop-dead delivery date of two or three days to factories throughout Asia, North America, and Europe, where they will eventually find their way into all manner of technology—from U.S. military aircraft to Japanese office equipment.

What distinguishes the 98,000-square-foot warehouse from others in the region is the invisible hand of custom-built software. In less than an hour, the incoming chips are bar coded, repackaged, and put aboard ships and planes. If an employee misdirects a box, the software shuts down a part of the system until the box is put in the correct slot or on the right conveyor belt.

The Impact of the Internet

In many respects "going global" is easier than it has ever been before. Opening an e-commerce site on the Internet immediately puts a company in the international marketplace. Sophisticated language translation software can make any site accessible to persons around the world. Global shippers such as UPS, FedEx, and DHL help solve international e-commerce distribution complexities. E4X, Inc., offers software to ease currency conversions. Sites that use E4X's software can post prices in U.S. dollars, then ask their customers what currency they wish to use for payment. If the answer is anything but dollars, E4X takes over the transaction and translates the price into any of twenty-two currencies, collects the payment from the customer, and pays the site in dollars, just as though it were any other transaction. Customers never realize they're dealing with a third party.[62]

6

Discover how the Internet is affecting global marketing

Nevertheless, the promise of "borderless commerce" and the new "Internet economy" are still being restrained by the old brick-and-mortar rules, regulations, and habits. For example, Americans spend an average of $6,500 per year by credit card whereas Japanese spend less than $2,000. Many Japanese don't even have a credit card. So how do they pay for e-commerce purchases? 7-Eleven Japan, with over eight thousand convenience stores, has come to the rescue. eS-Books, the Japanese Web site partner of Yahoo! Japan, lets shoppers buy books and videos on the Internet, then specify to which 7-Eleven the merchandise is to be shipped. The buyer goes to that specific store and pays cash for the e-purchase.[63]

In Germany it is typically cheaper to buy books from Amazon.com in the United Kingdom rather than the local site. Why? Germany, France, and several

other European states allow publishing cartels through which groups
of book publishers can legally dictate retail prices to booksellers—both
on-line and on the ground. *Galileo's Daughter,* a biography by Dava So-
bel, for example, sells at the list price of 50.24 marks ($26.99) on Ger-
many's Amazon.de; at Amazon.co.uk, it costs 40 percent less.[64]

The e-commerce site for the American clothing retailer Lands' End
in Germany is not allowed to mention its unconditional refund policy
because German retailers, which normally do not allow returns after
fourteen days, sued and won a court ruling blocking mention of it.

Scandinavians, like the Japanese, are reluctant to use credit cards, the currency of the Internet, and the French have an *horreur* of revealing the private information that Net retailers ask for. French Web sites tend to be decidedly French.
For example, FNAC, the largest French video, book, and music retailer, offers a
daily "cultural newspaper" at its site.[65] A trendy Web site in France will have a black
background, while bright colors and a geometrical layout give a site a German
feel. Dutch surfers are keen on video downloads, and Scandinavians seem to have
a soft spot for images of nature.[66]

Whatever their preferences in Web design, Europeans have shown themselves interested in saving money through Internet shopping. One of the hot
test e-commerce sites in Europe, LetsBuyIt.com in Sweden, is about nothing but
bargains.

CONNECT IT

Look back at the story about Universal Studios in
Japan. Besides cultural factors, other uncontrollable
variables in the global external environment include
economic and technological, political, and demographic variables as well as natural resources.

Most products cannot be marketed exactly the
same way all over the world. Different cultures, lan-

guages, levels of economic development, and distribution channels in global markets usually require
either new products or modified products. Pricing,
promotion, and distribution strategies must often
be altered as well. There is no doubt that international markets will become even more important in
the future.

USE IT

Study the Role of a Global Manager

As business becomes more global,
chances are that you may become a global
manager. Start learning right now what this means
and if it's right for you. The life of a global manager
can be hectic. One way to see if you might be cut out
to be a global manager is to spend some time
abroad. The ideal situation is to find a job overseas
during the summer months. This experience will
help you decide if you want to be a global manager.
Also, it will look good on your résumé. One source
of international jobs information is **http://www.
internationaljobs.org/**.

Travel Abroad

Dene Harrington, senior relationship manager at
Visa International in London, says: "We find that
employers [worldwide] look favorably on people
who have taken time out for traveling. They've
shown that they're able to organize a trip, look after
their security and finances. Experience of different
cultures, confidence in meeting people, and self-
reliance are very important skills in their future
career, whatever that may be."[67]

STA Travel (**http://www.statravel.com**) with
three hundred branches worldwide, specializes in
student and youth travel. Students and those under

age twenty-six with certain youth identification cards get discounts of up to a third off the published prices of airfares, hotels, city tours, around-the-world tickets, and overland tours.

Busabout (**http://www.busabout.com**) is a novel way for young travelers to explore Europe by road. Buses link seventy cities with service every one to two days in each direction allowing you the freedom to stop off for as long as you like along the way. The buses are nonsmoking and air-conditioned with an on-board guide to book your travel selections and accommodations as you go.

Hostels or budget hotels range from $12 to $22 a night. You decide when and where to start, stop off, or end the trip. Thus, you might buy a cheap "open-jaw" ticket (flying in to one city, departing from another). Arrive in Athens, for example, and return from London, or fly to Madrid and leave from Rome.

You can buy two types of passes at a 10 percent discount for students or those under twenty-six. A Consecutive Pass allows unlimited travel in the Busabout network, from two weeks to seven months. A Flexipass allows you to choose the number of traveling days within a time frame, ranging from ten days in two months to thirty days in four months.

A rail pass is another great way to get around Europe. Go to **http://railpass.com** for more information.

Changing Money Abroad

If you travel, work, or study abroad, you are going to need to change U.S. dollars into foreign currency. Making mistakes when changing money can cost you 10 to 20 percent of your bankroll. Here are a few tips about changing money abroad.

1. Know the exchange rate between U.S. dollars and the currencies of the countries you plan to visit before you go. Go to **http://www.cnnfn. com/markets/currencies** for the latest quotations. Keep up with the changing rates by reading *USA Today International* or the *International Herald Tribune* every day.

2. Avoid changing money at airports, train stations, and hotels. These places usually have the worst rates. Ask local people where they change money. Locals know where the best rates are.

3. Try to bargain with the clerk. Sometimes you can do better than the posted rate simply by asking.

4. Rather than making several small transactions, make one large exchange. This will often get you a better rate.

5. Don't change more than you will need. You'll pay another fee to change the foreign currency back to U.S. dollars.

6. Use a credit card. Typically, any major credit card will give you a better rate than a change booth or bank. Sometimes the spread is substantial, so minimize cash and use credit.

7. Traveler's checks usually have a worse exchange rate than cash. In other words, a $100 American Express traveler's check will give you less in exchange than a $100 bill. If your traveler's checks are lost or stolen, however, they will be replaced, so the peace of mind is usually worth the added expense.

8. Use your American ATM card to withdraw cash at foreign money machines. If your card is part of a global network, such as Cirrus or Plus, you may be able to withdraw money for a nominal fee at a reasonable exchange rate.

REVIEW IT

(1) **Discuss the importance of global marketing.** Businesspeople who adopt a global vision are better able to identify global marketing opportunities, understand the nature of global networks, and compete against foreign competition in domestic markets.

    1.1 What is meant by "having a global vision"? Why is it important?

    1.2 Isolationists have suggested that America would be much better off economically and politically if we just "built a wall" around the country and didn't deal with outsiders. Do you agree? Why or why not?

(2) **Discuss the impact of multinational firms on the world economy.** Multinational corporations are international traders that regularly operate across national borders. Because of their vast size and financial, technological, and material resources, multinational corporations have a great influence on the world economy. They have the ability to overcome trade problems, save on labor costs, and tap new technology.

2.1 Rubbermaid, the U.S. manufacturer of kitchen products and other household items, is considering moving to global marketing standardization. What are the pros and cons of this strategy?

2.2 Do you believe that multinationals are beneficial or harmful to developing nations? Why? What could foreign governments do to make them more beneficial?

(3) **Describe the external environment facing global marketers.** Global marketers face the same environmental factors as they do domestically: culture, economic and technological development, political structure and actions, demography, and natural resources. Cultural considerations include societal values, attitudes and beliefs, language, and customary business practices. A country's economic and technological status depends on its stage of industrial development: traditional society, preindustrial society, takeoff economy, industrializing society, or fully industrialized society. The political structure is shaped by political ideology and such policies as tariffs, quotas, boycotts, exchange controls, trade agreements, and market groupings. Demographic variables include population, income distribution, and growth rate.

3.1 Many marketers now believe that teenagers in the developed countries are becoming "global consumers." That is, they all want and buy the same goods and services. Do you think this is true? If so, what has caused the phenomenon?

3.2 Renault and Peugeot dominate the French market but have no presence in the U.S. market. Why do you think that this is true?

3.3 **WRITING** Suppose that you are the marketing manager for a consumer-products firm that is about to undertake its first expansion abroad. Write a memo for your staff reminding them of the role culture will play in the new venture. Give examples.

3.4 **WRITING** Suppose that your state senator has asked you to contribute a brief article to her constituents' newsletter that answers the question, "Will there ever be a 'United States of Europe'?" Write a draft of your article, and include reasons why or why not.

3.5 **TEAM** Divide into six teams. Each team will be responsible for one of the following industries: entertainment; pharmaceuticals; computers and software; financial, legal, or accounting services; agriculture; and textiles and apparel. Interview one or more executives in each of these industries to determine how the Uruguay Round and NAFTA have affected and will affect their organizations. If a local firm cannot be contacted in your industry, use the library and the Internet to prepare your report.

3.6 What are the major barriers to international trade? Explain how government policies may be used to either restrict or stimulate global marketing.

3.7 Explain the impact of the Uruguay Round.

(4) **Identify the various ways of entering the global marketplace.** Firms use the following strategies to enter global markets, in descending order of risk and profit: direct investment, joint venture, contract manufacturing, licensing, and export.

4.1 Candartel, an upscale manufacturer of lamps and lampshades in America, has decided to "go global." Top management is having trouble deciding how to develop the market. What are some market entry options for the firm?

4.2 Explain how the U.S. Commercial Service can help companies wanting to enter the international market.

4.3 What are some of the advantages and potential disadvantages of entering a joint venture?

5 **List the basic elements involved in developing a global marketing mix.** A firm's major consideration is how much it will adjust the four Ps—product, promotion, place (distribution), and price—within each country. One strategy is to use one product and one promotion message worldwide. A second strategy is to create new products for global markets. A third strategy is to keep the product basically the same but alter the promotional message. A fourth strategy is to slightly alter the product to meet local conditions.

5.1 The sale of cigarettes in many developed countries either has peaked or is declining. However, the developing markets represent major growth markets. Should U.S. tobacco companies capitalize on this opportunity?

5.2 Describe at least three situations where an American company might want to keep the product the same but alter the promotion. Also, give three examples where the product must be altered.

6 **Discover how the Internet is affecting global marketing.** Simply opening a Web site can open the door for international sales. International carriers, like UPS, can help solve logistics problems. Language translation software can help an e-commerce business become multilingual. Yet cultural differences and old-line rules, regulations, and taxes hinder rapid development of e-commerce in many countries.

6.1 Describe how "going global" via the Internet presents opportunities and challenges.

6.2 Give several examples of how culture may hinder "going global" via the Internet.

DEFINE IT

Asia-Pacific Economic
  Cooperation (APEC) 79
Association of Southeast
  Asian Nations (ASEAN)
  79
buyer for export 84
contract manufacturing 86
countertrade 93
direct foreign investment
  87
dumping 93
export agent 84
export broker 84

exporting 83
Free Trade Area of the
  Americas (FTAA) 78
fully industrialized society
  75
General Agreement on Tar-
  iffs and Trade (GATT) 77
global marketing 66
global marketing standardization 71
global vision 66
industrializing society 75
joint venture 86

licensing 84
Maastricht Treaty 79
Mercosur 77
multinational corporation
  69
North American Free Trade
  Agreement (NAFTA) 78
preindustrial society 74
takeoff economy 74
traditional society 74
Uruguay Round 77
World Trade Organization
  (WTO) 77

APPLY IT

Application for Entrepreneurs

Larry and Laurie Walther own a shop in Taos, New Mexico, that sells fine rugs crafted by Native Americans. They have expanded their business beyond Taos via direct mail. In fact, they have discovered a growing market in the United Kingdom. It seems that Europeans, particularly the English, French, and Germans, have an ongoing love affair with Native American culture. Larry and Laurie are now considering a direct-mail campaign to Germany. The typical American receives about 350 direct-mail pieces per year, whereas a German household gets fewer than 70. Also, Germany has 40 percent more people than the United Kingdom.

Yet, marketing to Germans by direct mail is different. Most buyers don't use credit cards when purchasing by mail. One German law dictates the size of free samples that can be distributed; another says that advertising mail cannot be camouflaged as a personal letter. Privacy laws restrict the preparation of finely targeted U.S.-style mailing lists. Mail carriers have to obey "no advertising" stickers that many Germans affix to their mailboxes.

Questions

1. Should Larry and Laurie attempt to enter the German market? Why or why not?

2. What can be done to overcome the credit card problem?

THINK ABOUT IT

Ethics Exercise

Moore Electronics sells automated lighting for airport runways. The government of an Eastern European country has offered Moore a contract to provide equipment for the fifteen major airports in the country. The official in charge of awarding the contract, however, is demanding a 5 percent kickback. He told Moore to build this into the contract price so that there would be no cost to Moore. Without the kickback, Moore loses the contract. Such kickbacks are considered a normal way of doing business in this country.

Questions

1. What should Moore do?

2. Does the AMA Code of Ethics address this issue? Go to **http://www.marketingpower .com** and review the code. Then write a brief paragraph on what the AMA Code of Ethics contains that relates to Moore's dilemma.

TRY IT

Entrepreneurship Case

Israel: A Ray of Light in the Global Optics Industry

 Though it's some 20,000 miles away from Silicon Valley, Israel has managed to produce its own version of the high-tech wonderland. The Internet revolution, biotechnology, and, yes, optics are driving the economy of this tiny country of just 6.4 million people. Today, there are some 50 optical start-ups around Israel. On a per capita basis, that would equate to about 2,200 optical companies in the United States.

Three major factors drive this growth: an inherent entrepreneurial attitude bred in Israel, world-class research universities, and funding through the venture capital community. The result has been a set of research-intensive companies that give a glimpse of how optical systems may be shaped over the next few years. The ultimate hope of many is to produce an Israeli-based optical powerhouse—a goal that so far has eluded many Israeli entrepreneurs.

The optical market here has all of the key ingredients for long-term growth—research and development, funding, and experience. There are more engineers per capita in Israel than anywhere else in the world. Israel, for example, has about 140 engineers per 10,000 employees versus roughly 70 engineers within the United States.

Many of those engineers and doctoral students are doing their research in Israel's world-class universities. Israel has been able to develop renowned research institutions like the Technion, Ben Gurion University, and Tel Aviv University. Homegrown talent is particularly important because of the strong connection between optical research and commercial optical products.

Most new optical companies are looking to leverage Israel's R&D skills to develop components or subsystems. Carriers currently are less willing to risk their networks on a start-up than they might have been in 2001—particularly a start-up that might be long on R&D but short on marketing and selling to a traditional telco (telecom company). For a carrier to purchase a system from an Israeli start-up takes "some guts," says Doron Nevo, a principal with an optics company called Kilolambda.

Ron Shilon certainly knows what Nevo is talking about. The CEO of Flexlight Networks, a supplier of passive-optical-network (PON) subsystems, has a simple explanation of why Flexlight is going after the subsystem market. "It's just too difficult for small start-ups, located 10,000 miles away, to pitch the carriers directly," he says.

And if past record is any indication of the future, many of the companies will look to cash out early, a problem that Tzvi Marom, president and CEO of BATM, a manufacturer of optical switches, laments. "We have not been able to build an optical industry here as much as we've built a collection of individual companies," says Marom, "Behind someone who sells products from Japan, for example, are zillions of companies supporting them." In Israel, Marom says, entrepreneurs have become so infatuated with the fast exit that there is no opportunity to craft those larger companies.

Instead, Israel has become a sort of start-up production line, generating high-tech start-ups that are subsequently acquired by the Nortels, Ciscos, and Lucents of the world. Then again, that may not be such a bad position after all.

Questions

1. Why have Israeli firms turned to the global marketplace to sell their products? Describe the global visions, and the responses to them, that drive that decision.

2. How have Israeli firms used their strengths to capture opportunities in the global marketplace for their optics products? What elements of the internal environment drive the development of their globally oriented optics industry?

3. What method of entering the global marketplace have the Israeli optics firms chosen? Do you think their choice makes the most sense? Why or why not?

WATCH IT

Short

To see how global marketing influences advertising, watch the Jumpman, Levi's, and Nike ads on the *Essentials of Marketing* PowerPoint CD-ROM. When watching the ads, think about what makes them suitable or unsuitable for global marketing, and what global strategy they could support.

Medium **VIDEO**

Trade agreements are proliferating around the world, but still some regions are having difficulty competing in certain regions. For example, because Europe does not have a trade agreement with Latin American countries, it is unable to secure coffee at as competitive a price as the United States, which does have a trade agreement with Latin America. Watch the CNN clip for this chapter to see how trade agreements translate into competitive advantage.

Long
Small**BusinessSchool**
the Series on PBS stations and the Web

To give you insight into Chapter 3, Small Business School will introduce you to Automated Food Systems, maker of the machinery that produces 95 percent of the 2.5 billion corn dogs consumed in the United States each year. In fact, this quintessentially American food is consumed throughout the world, and foreign companies that sell corn-dog type foods also produce them on Automated Food machines. Watch the segment and work the questions on the supplemental video CD-ROM.

 FLIP IT

 Flip to Chapter 3 in your *Grademaker Study Guide* for more review opportunities, including the pretest, vocabulary review, study test questions, marketing applications, and much, much more. Do you know the major trade agreements? Can you close your book and list the ways a firm can enter the global marketplace? Open your Study Guide to find out how much you know—or don't know.

CLICK IT

The *Essentials of Marketing* Web site links you to all the Internet-based activities in this chapter, like "Use It" and the On-Line exercises in the chapter margins. As a review, do the Chapter 3 quiz and crossword puzzle. You can also work the Career Exersite that shows you different types of global marketing careers. Or, review the main concepts in the PowerPoint presentation for Chapter 3. Go to **http://lamb.swlearning.com**, read the material, and follow the links right from the site.

Surf to Xtra! to test your understanding of global marketing by completing the worksheets for Exhibits 3.2, 3.3, and 3.4. If your instructor has assigned a marketing plan project, worksheets on Xtra! can help you organize your work. In addition to the quiz on the Web site, there's another quiz on Xtra!, plus video of the authors answering frequently asked questions about global marketing, such as "Is global marketing only important to large multinational corporations?" and "What is the best way to enter global marketing?" Surf to Xtra! and find out.

Still Shaky? Here's a Tip.

Work out any Discussion and Writing Questions that your professor didn't assign as homework. Visit your professor or TA during office hours to check your answers.

MARKETING MISCUES

Kmart's Blue Lights Are in the Red, and There's Nothing Special about It

Is there anything special about Kmart anymore? Do consumers know what Kmart and its brands stand for? Does Kmart have an image in the retail marketplace? Answers to these questions were crucial to Kmart's long-term survival as the company entered into Chapter 11 bankruptcy proceedings in early 2002. Kmart's case was the largest retail bankruptcy filing in U.S. history, as well as the sixth-largest bankruptcy case in U.S. history.

More than a hundred years ago, Sebastian Kresge opened his first five-and-dime store in Michigan. This store was the first of what would come to be known as the S. S. Kresge Company. The company's business philosophy was to offer products that consumers needed at prices they could afford. In doing so, management expected that customers would keep returning. The company thought it had found the key to customer loyalty.

Unfortunately for Kresge, another retailing guru would soon enter the picture. In 1962, when Kresge launched the Kmart concept, Sam Walton was setting in motion the debut of Wal-Mart. Kmart never expected that the retailing showdown with Wal-Mart would ultimately result in Kmart's appearance in bankruptcy court. For forty years, it battled Wal-Mart, and in the end, Kmart had lost. What went wrong?

According to market analysts, Kmart made a series of strategic and tactical blunders. Strategically, Kmart failed to differentiate itself as a retailer. Instead of carving a niche for itself in the retail industry, it became boxed in between two different, yet similar, discount retailers—Wal-Mart and Target Corporation. Wal-Mart, with its "always low prices," solidly established itself as the low-price leader. With reasonably low prices, but not as low as Wal-Mart, Target became known as the trendy discounter by focusing on fashionable merchandise. Tactically, Kmart's blunders left shoppers with less than pleasant shopping experiences. Customers cited in-store concerns such as poor customer service, long checkout lines, inconsistent price marking, dingy stores, empty shelves, and old merchandise as issues that led to Kmart's downfall.

Some would say that this downfall should not have come as a surprise to Kmart management, employees, and customers. Kmart appeared to have focused solely on its competition and what they were doing rather than focusing on its customers and what they wanted. In the end, Kmart could not differentiate itself from Wal-Mart because it could not price below it. Nor could Kmart sway Target customers because it appeared unable to provide the in-store experience that made customers feel chic as they purchased discounted clothing.

At the time of its bankruptcy filing, Kmart was the third largest retailer in the United States, with 2,100 stores across the United States and Puerto Rico. While Kmart was filing Chapter 11, Wal-Mart boasted sales of $200 billion, with growth rates of 15 to 20 percent, and Target's 1,055 stores posted record sales revenue of $37 billion. With competition like this, there was doubt as to whether Kmart could rectify its past strategic missteps and differentiate itself in the retail marketplace. Could Kmart devise a unique and compelling strategy that would leave the company's fractured image behind? Or, should Kmart's blue lights be turned off forever?

Questions

1. Is this an example of poor strategy formulation or poor strategy implementation?

2. Describe Kmart's marketing mix in the years leading up to 2002.

3. Describe Kmart's marketing management philosophy.

Hewlett-Packard's CoolTown Puts Everyone and Everything on the Web

While the business world has focused on the merger between Hewlett-Packard Company (**http://www.hp. com**) and Compaq Computer Corporation, techno wizards at Hewlett-Packard Laboratories in Palo Alto, California, are spending their time conducting a living experiment. Dubbed "CoolTown," the experiment attempts to bridge the physical and virtual worlds and showcases HP's product offerings in building this bridge. Given HP's complex product line that has led to an unclear image in the marketplace, the jury is still out as to whether CoolTown will be successful at conveying the company's vision for the future in this wireless era.

The Company

Hewlett-Packard Company was founded in 1939 by Bill Hewlett and Dave Packard. Hewlett and Packard believed that HP existed to invent the "useful and significant." To them, the term *useful* meant contributions that would free businesses and consumers to focus on what mattered most to them. The term *significant* was indicative of HP's vow not only to make a profit but to also make a difference. The bottom line is that HP will help create a world where technology works for the consumer and not vice versa. Consistent with this vision is the set of corporate objectives, referred to as "The HP Way." The company's objectives focus on seven major areas: profit, customers, fields of interest, growth, company people, management, and citizenship.

At the beginning of the twenty-first century, HP is listed in the top twenty of the *Fortune* 500. Carly Fiorina is CEO, the company has almost ninety thousand employees, and company revenue is around $45 billion. Product offerings include printers, personal computers, servers, wireless devices, software, and consulting services. The company refers to its vision as service-centric computing, meaning that information technologies are delivered, managed, and purchased as services. To fulfill this vision, HP's strategy focuses on three key areas of invention: (1) enabling intelligent, connected devices and environment, (2) enabling an always-on Internet infrastructure, and (3) enabling a new generation of applications delivered as e-services.

When Fiorina took the helm in 1999, she envisioned a reinvention of HP. At that time, HP had a major market niche with its printers but was lackluster in the remainder of its markets. Many felt that the company was not only old-fashioned but also resistant to change. In a major move to reinvent HP, Fiorina spearheaded the merger with Compaq Computer. The merger could be a major step toward HP becoming a technology solutions provider.

Marketing Deficiencies

Although the merger between HP and Compaq may take the company in the technology solutions direction, some are concerned about the longer term implications of HP's weak marketing. HP is not known for its ability to tell a compelling story in the marketplace. Its image as a stodgy, old company is not expected to fare well in the new age economy. While boasting a strong product line, the company has not been able to excite the marketplace. With expectations of 45 percent annual growth and market share of $80 billion by 2004, the company will have to rectify its marketing deficiencies to remain competitive and meet its goals.

CoolTown

In June 2001, HP launched CoolTown. This project, which was developed at HP Laboratories, is a mock city that allows users to experience life in a technological environment. The goal of CoolTown is to make this futuristic environment transparent to the user. CoolTown visitors can experience how wireless technologies will change their lives.

Four components work in sync to make CoolTown functional: the Internet, handheld electronics, wireless networks, and computer intelligence. Combining these ingredients, users can see what a typical wireless day would be like. Examples include a CoolTown bookstore that recognizes customers and recommends new books, a CoolTown bus line that pinpoints bus location so that the rider does not get to the bus stop too early or too late, a CoolTown conference room where the speaker can control the projector remotely, and the CoolTown museum where a visitor can purchase products on-line as they are being viewed at the exhibit. Basically, CoolTown allows smart devices to link to other smart devices that are using the same language.

Of course, all of the technology employed in CoolTown is HP technology. The Coolbase Appliance Server is an embedded server from HP, Coolkit enables developers to build applications to run on

Cool-base, E-Squirt allows mobile phones or PDAs to direct e-services to other devices, and Beacons are handheld devices that broadcast to other wireless units (for example, PDAs and phones). Naturally, when HP customers are touring the CoolTown show-room, HP's Jornada handheld computers are used to navigate through the experience.

CoolTown, in conjunction with HP's Mobile E-Services Bazaar, has allowed HP to tap into new markets. Rather than focus on internal uses for CoolTown products, HP now can partner with wireless application engineers who can use HP products when they develop e-services for their customers. Additionally, the hope is that the CoolTown experience will interest customers in purchasing HP's consulting services to help with the wireless integration process.

HP as Net Innovator

While the Hewlett-Packard Company of the twenty-first century sees itself as an innovator, this image is very different from the stodgy company it became during the late twentieth century. It is unlikely that to-day's marketplace would identify HP on its short list of Internet innovators. Can HP compete with the likes of Microsoft, Oracle, and Sun Microsystems? How can HP merge its engineering expertise with a marketing message that will change its image in the customer's mindset?

Questions

1. What is HP's core business? How did the company build on this core business?

2. Does HP's success depend on its engineering prowess or its marketing expertise?

3. Describe the component parts of CoolTown and explain how these integrated parts could be used in everyday life. How does CoolTown help HP change its image in the marketplace?

4. Is the "new" HP consistent with the company's original reason for being in existence (to invent the "useful and significant")? Why or why not?

MARKETING PLANNING ACTIVITIES

Throughout the rest of this book, these end-of-part marketing planning activities will help you build a strategic marketing plan for a company of your choosing. To help you complete your plan, use the Marketing Planning Worksheets on Xtra! If you need a company for the basis of your work, follow the "Marketing Plan Project" link on the *Essentials of Marketing* Web site (**http://lamb.swlearning.com**).

The World of Marketing

In the world of marketing, many different types of goods and services are offered to many different markets. Throughout this text, you will construct a marketing plan for your chosen company. Writing a marketing plan will give you a full depth of under-standing for your company, its customers, and its marketing mix elements. The company you choose should be one that interests you, such as the manu-facturer of your favorite product, a local business where you would like to work, or even a business you would like to start yourself to satisfy an unmet need or want. Despite recent troubles in the dot-com sector, you may also consider the Internet portion of marketing. Most firms have two options for imple-menting Internet marketing: starting an Internet busi-ness that is wholly operated in the e-marketing world or creating an Internet component of a marketing plan for a traditional, existing business. Both Internet opportunities require careful strategic marketing planning in order for the venture to succeed.

For electronic sources of information, search on the Electric Library at **http://www.elibrary.com** or the Internet Public Library at **http://www.ipl.org**. Another excellent source of information is the Sales and Marketing Executives Marketing Library at **http://www.smei.org**.

For some general help on business plans and marketing plans, visit **http://www.bplans.com** or **http://www.businessplans.org**. Another very useful site is **http://www.emarketer.com**.

The first part of strategic planning deals with the world of marketing and involves stating your business mission with a marketing orientation, set-ting objectives, finding a differential advantage, and performing an assessment of strengths, weaknesses, opportunities, and threats. Use the following exer-cises to guide you through the first part of your strategic marketing plan:

1. Describe your chosen company. How long has it been in business, or when will it start business? Who are the key players? Is the company small or large? Does it offer a good or service? What are the strengths and weaknesses of this com-pany? What are the orientation and organiza-tional culture? List all the ways that your company follows the marketing concept. Can your company satisfy the needs and wants of customers and still be profitable, legal, and so-cially responsible?

2. What should be the business mission of your company? Write the mission statement, keeping in mind the benefits offered to customers rather than the product or service sold. If you are start-

ing the on-line arm of a traditional store, should you make any changes to the company's overall mission statement? For fun, visit the mission statement generator at **http://unitedmedia.com/comics/dilbert/games/index.html**, which may help illustrate how *not* to write your business mission statement.

3. Set marketing objectives for your chosen company. Make sure the objectives fit the criteria for good objectives. List at least three specific, measurable objectives for your company. Be sure these objectives relate to the mission statement and include a time frame.

4. Scan the marketing environment. Identify opportunities and threats to your chosen company in areas such as technology, the economy, the political and legal environment, and competition. Is your competition foreign, domestic, or both? Also, identify opportunities and threats based on possible market targets, including social factors, demographic factors, and multicultural issues.

5. Assume your company is or will be marketing globally. How should your company enter the global marketplace? How will international issues affect your firm?

6. Does your chosen business have a differential or competitive advantage? If it does not, there is no point in marketing the product. Can you create a sustainable advantage with skills, resources, or elements of the marketing mix? Assess your company's strength by asking, "What is the key differential or competitive advantage of my firm?" If you have an Internet offering, consider what advantages are gained by operating in the Internet space. What are other keys to the potential success of your company? What other strengths can your firm capitalize on?

7. Continue by taking an honest look at the weaknesses of your firm. What are the disadvantages to operating in the Internet space? How can you overcome them? You might want to enlist the help of a friend to act as a consultant who can give an unbiased opinion. Are there any ethical problems in the organization?

8. Identify any ethical issues that could affect your chosen firm. What steps should be taken to handle these issues? How should your company integrate corporate social responsibility into the plan? Describe how your company will handle privacy concerns. In addition to suggestions for philanthropic responsibilities, write up a brief code of ethics for your firm. To see other codes of ethics, go to **http://www.iit.edu/departments/csep/PublicWWW/codes/**.

9. The last part of your analysis should identify opportunities and threats in the external marketing environment. You'll do this by scanning the environment.

a. To learn more about demographic, ethnic, and social trends that could affect your firm, investigate data from the U.S. Census Bureau at **http://www.census.gov**.

b. To learn more about economic factors that could influence the strategies of your firm, visit the U.S. Economic and Statistics Administration at **http://www.esa.doc.gov** or the Bureau of Economic Analysis at **http://www.bea.doc.gov**.

c. Be sure to look for computer and Internet usage statistics and think about whether they are a positive indicator for the target market you have selected. The resources at **http://cyberatlas.internet.com** and **http://acnielsen.com/products/reports/netwatch** can help. Determine which emerging technologies will have an impact on your company. Are these technological developments opportunities or threats?

d. Understand how political and legal factors may influence your marketing decisions at **http://www.lawguru.com**. You may also wish to investigate the Web sites of federal government agencies that regulate your firm and industry. The Federal Trade Commission is at **http://www.ftc.gov**. The Federal Communications Commission is at **http://www.fcc.gov**. The Food and Drug Administration is at **http://www.fda.gov**. The Consumer Product Safety Commission is at **http://www.cpsc.gov**. The Better Business Bureau is at **http://www.bbb.org**. The Internal Revenue Service is at **http://www.irs.gov**. From here you can download all kinds of required and helpful forms.

e. Identify your key competitors. A simple "yellow pages" (**http://bigbook.com**) listing of firms in the same business category can start your search. For on-line competitors, try **http://www.bizrate.com**. For more specific information on a competitor, investigate **http://www.companiesonline.com**.

f. Competition often comes from companies that are working on the same exact market as yours. That is especially true in the Internet space. After you search for your direct competition, look for and think about what other companies are positioned to execute a similar business strategy for your target market. Determine if there are any players who might be able to develop technology more quickly or reach your target customers more effectively than you.

g. If you choose an Internet presence, your product or service will be visible to a global community. Therefore, it is important to assess the international marketplace as well. A listing of international chambers of commerce is at **http://www.worldchambers.com** and the CIA World Factbook is at **http://www.cia.gov/cia/publications/factbook/**.

CROSS-FUNCTIONAL CONNECTIONS SOLUTIONS

**Cross-Functional Business Systems:
Putting the Customer at the Center**

Questions

1. What is the overlap among marketing, manufacturing, finance, accounting, and human resources? What does each of these functions do that results in this overlap?

   The overlap among all functional areas within a firm lies in providing the final product or service to the consumer. Each functional area contributes in different ways to delivering the desired product to the end customer. Marketing, manufacturing, finance, accounting, and human resources work from the idea that the customer is most important and that the goal is to produce a product that meets the changing needs of consumers. Marketing and manufacturing tend to come into direct contact with the company's customers and products. Finance, accounting, and human resources tend to work on the periphery and may never come into contact with the physical aspects of the product and may never meet the end-user of the product or service. However, working together and utilizing each area's expertise and knowledge result in an integrated production process that aims to satisfy the customer.

2. Why is cross-functional coordination necessary in order to have a customer-oriented firm?

   Historically, everyone assumed that the customer belonged to the marketing department. We know now that this is not true. Everyone in the organization must understand the customer's wants and needs in order to satisfy these needs. Without the customer, there would be no need for an organization. For example, no customers would mean no products to develop or manufacture, no accounts receivable, and no need for employees. From the customer's perspective, good or bad products belong to the entire company—not just one particular function. Customers will not keep coming back if the company produces only low-quality merchandise—even if the marketing group has some of the best marketers in the world. Likewise, a high-quality product will not be successful in the marketplace if the product is positioned inaccurately, advertised inappropriately, priced too high or too low, or not available in the right outlets. Therefore, it is imperative that the business functions work together to send the same message to the marketplace.

3. What roles do teamwork and technology play in cross-functional coordination?

   Technology has created a digitized marketplace in which business decisions have to be made quickly in order for the firm to remain competitive. Customer demands increase in this fast-paced market, making it necessary for all functional areas to work together to deliver products to a market quickly. In working as a team, functional areas partner in the production/delivery process, sharing relevant information with one another, as well as eliminating wasted time spent when working independently in departments.

Suggested Readings

Bryant Avey, "Building a People-Center Culture in the D-Age," *Chief Executive,* September 1999, 10.

Charles H. Noble, "Building the Strategy Implementation Network," *Business Horizons,* November–December 1999, 19–28.

Analyzing Marketing Opportunities

PART 2

INFORMATION INTEGRATION TO SATISFY CUSTOMER WANTS AND NEEDS

Understanding customers is at the heart of the information-gathering process. Information is the key to success in determining individual buying behavior, sharpening the company's target marketing skills, or understanding competitive actions. The traditional perception of information gathering is that it is the "job" of the marketing department. However, many companies now realize that marketing belongs to the entire company. It is everyone's responsibility to understand the marketplace.

Kellogg USA has focused extensively on improving its research efforts. The company's strategy involves better cross-functional acquisition and dissemination of market research information. The ultimate goal is to use the information to help move new and improved products into the marketplace much more quickly. In its attempt to increase company profits, Kellogg's has moved its traditional product development process out of marketing. Now, the company uses cross-functional teams comprised of business functional areas, food technologists, and engineers to develop new products. Kellogg's marketers no longer take sole responsibility for the collection and use of information. Kellogg is proactive in this regard, but the historical debate surrounding type of data continues in many companies.

The information debate between marketing and other business functions centers on the qualitative versus the quantitative format of functional data. The qualitative data collected by marketers are perceived to be abstract compared to the quantitative data used by other functional areas. It has been difficult to get engineers and accountants to understand that marketing data provide statistically valid information that is important in making company-wide decisions.

Aside from the need for a general cross-functional sharing of data, there are five major areas in which information gathering and dissemination processes need to be formally integrated across functions: benchmarking studies, customer teaming, customer satisfaction studies, data-mining, and forecasting.

Benchmarking is the process of comparing a firm's performance with the performance of other companies in various areas. A benchmarking study could focus upon cross-company comparisons of purchasing processes, inventory management, product development cycles, or even hiring practices. Gathering information on a firm's competitors during a benchmarking study involves an extensive amount of secondary research. Recently, cross-functional "shadow teams" have been formed to assist in better benchmarking of competitive activities. Shadow teams integrate internal information with all externally available information on specific competitors.

The Ford Motor Company was an early pioneer of the use of benchmarking. In the early 1980s, the company was at a competitive disadvantage compared to many foreign automobile manufacturers. Ford executives recognized that remaining competitive would require a steep reduction in costs. One benchmarking study focused upon reducing the number of employees in the accounts payable department. Using information gained in a benchmarking study of its competitors, Ford was able to decrease its accounts payable staff by more than one-half. Similarly, many of the creative aspects (e.g., Six Sigma, Workout) of Jack Welch's tenure at General Electric were the result of benchmarking studies of competing and noncompeting companies.

Many companies are now *teaming* employees with customers in an attempt to bring the customer into the organization. Site visits are one popular way of understanding customer needs and/or watching how a finished product is utilized in the business process. These visits involve team members from across various functions. Tellabs, a telecommunications company that develops voice and data transmission products, teams its marketers and research and development engineers with customers in an attempt to reduce the risks inherent in new product development. To better understand how customers use its film, Kodak sends manufacturing employees to visit professional users of its film products. Kodak depends upon accurate market information to understand both the customers' buying processes and their actual usage of their Kodak products.

Customer satisfaction is driven by issues related to the firm's operational functions (e.g., inventory management) and its operational capabilities (e,g., technology), as well as its product mix. Therefore, a valid *customer satisfaction study* should gather information that can be shared with manufacturing (regarding satisfaction with speed of delivery), research and development (regarding satisfaction with product quality), human resources (regarding satisfaction with complaint handling), and finance/accounting (regarding satisfaction with credit policies). As such, all of these functional areas need to have input into the design of such studies.

The digital age has led to considerable *data-mining*. E-commerce capabilities have allowed companies to gather and analyze customer information in a matter of minutes, rather than having to wait for results from months-long data-gathering processes. This use of technology is where considerable cross-functional interactions must occur. Companies such as DoubleClick, Kozmo, and AltaVista gather and store a wealth of consumer information—information that has to be effectively disseminated to the appropriate individuals.

Forecasting crosses the boundaries of multiple business functions. For example, marketing may offer a discount on a particular price. The impact of this price discount is felt simultaneously in many functional areas including manufacturing. The production plan will have to accommodate the expected increase in product sales and the oftentimes below-average product sales immediately after the discount period. While price is easy for marketers to change, manufacturing's plans cannot be changed overnight. A price change may affect the company's production schedule, finished goods inventory, and the availability of raw materials. Unfortunately, marketing's ability to make price changes quickly has been the cause of much conflict between marketing and manufacturing.

Much of a firm's financial planning is driven by the company's sales forecast. Marketing has historically had a reputation of being too optimistic in its projections. As a result, financial planners have been known to take the sales forecast with "a grain of salt," and planning has often evolved around a lower than predicted level of sales. Marketing, then, looks at financial planners as too conservative and as basing their plans on internal data that are not driven by the marketplace.

Predicting worldwide demand has become a forecasting challenge for many companies. Some cross-functional teams are using software programs to help predict demand across their supply chains. Precise real-time forecasts disseminated over their corporate intranets enable the synchronization of production and inventory with customer demand.

Marketplace information is a key driver in all decisions made by a company, so all functional areas must participate in the gathering and dissemination of information. The importance of information is reflected in a new executive position, chief knowledge officer, that is now being staffed in many companies.

Questions for Discussion

1. Why has information historically been perceived as "owned" by the marketing department?
2. What data differences exist across functions?
3. What is the job of a chief knowledge officer?

CHAPTER **FOUR**
CONSUMER DECISION MAKING

Learning Objectives

1   Explain why marketing managers should understand consumer behavior

2   Analyze the components of the consumer decision-making process

3   Explain the consumer's post-purchase evaluation process

4   Identify the types of consumer buying decisions and discuss the significance of consumer involvement

5   Identify and understand the cultural factors that affect consumer buying decisions

6   Identify and understand the social factors that affect consumer buying decisions

7   Identify and understand the individual factors that affect consumer buying decisions

8   Identify and understand the psychological factors that affect consumer buying decisions

Observing changes in consumer behavior is often a risky task involving picking up on a small blip on a marketer's radar that over time becomes more and more obvious. But in the wake of the terrorist attacks on September 11, 2001, consumer behavior in the United States changed, if only briefly, sending marketers scrambling overnight to adjust marketing campaigns.

In the days following the terrorist attacks, American consumers became less motivated by the need for prestige and self-expression. Instead consumers became focused on security, protection, friends, and family. For example, wealthy Americans who normally could be expected to purchase a luxury automobile were purchasing bulletproof and bomb-resistant SUVs. Wal-Mart customers bought guns, ammunition, gas cans, and televisions. Survival companies saw sales of gas masks and bomb shelters surge. And long-distance phone calls increased 100 percent as Americans checked in with loved ones.

In addition, Americans put materialism aside as a wave of volunteerism and patriotism swept the nation. During the first week after the attacks, Americans from all walks of life donated more than $325 million and 500,000 units of blood to relief efforts. Red, white, and blue became a fashion statement overnight as retailers struggled to meet the surging demand for U.S. flags. And firefighters and police officers replaced business tycoons as our national heroes.

Marketers had tough decisions to make. How do you promote products in the wake of a national tragedy? When will consumers be ready to think about new cars, computers, or movies? Should we take advantage of the nation's patriotic zeal, or will it be seen as opportunistic? Without the luxury of time to study consumer behavior, marketers waded in slowly with mixed results.

In the beginning, many companies simply chose to run sentimental ads honoring the victims and their families or encouraging Americans to get back to normal by shopping and dining out. Hollywood decided to err on the side of caution and pulled several war films scheduled for fall release. Automobile manufacturers, unable to afford slow sales, began running commercials designed to appeal to the nation's sense of patriotic duty. Microsoft decided to stick with plans to launch Windows XP in New York City with enthusiasm after changing the product's marketing slogan from "You Can Fly" to "Yes You Can."

During this time, manufacturers saw an increase in demand for U.S.-made products. The greeting card industry saw a surge in sales. Parents purchased cap guns and GI Joe dolls for their children. Consumers bought comfort food like Campbell's soup and read magazines like *Real Simple* and *Country Living*.[1]

Then Americans began to return to a sense of normalcy. And as they did, marketers began trying to understand what the new normal would be. What do you think? Did the events of September 11, 2001, change American culture, or did they just cause a dramatic blip in consumer behavior? What motivates consumers today? What factors affect their buying decisions? Questions like these will be considered as you read this chapter on the consumer decision-making process and its influences.

The Importance of Understanding Consumer Behavior

Explain why marketing managers should understand consumer behavior

consumer behavior
Processes a consumer uses to make purchase decisions, as well as to use and dispose of purchased goods or services; also includes factors that influence purchase decisions and product use.

Consumers' product and service preferences are constantly changing. In order to address this constant state of flux and to create a proper marketing mix for a well-defined market, marketing managers must have a thorough knowledge of consumer behavior. **Consumer behavior** describes how consumers make purchase decisions and how they use and dispose of the purchased goods or services. The study of consumer behavior also includes an analysis of factors that influence purchase decisions and product use.

Understanding how consumers make purchase decisions can help marketing managers in several ways. For example, if a manager knows through research that gas mileage is the most important attribute for a certain target market, the manufacturer can redesign the product to meet that criterion. If the firm cannot change the design in the short run, it can use promotion in an effort to change consumers' decision-making criteria. For example, an automobile manufacturer can advertise a car's maintenance-free features and sporty European style while downplaying gas mileage.

The Consumer Decision-Making Process

Analyze the components of the consumer decision-making process

consumer decision-making process
A five-step process used by consumers when buying goods or services.

When buying products, consumers generally follow the **consumer decision-making process** shown in Exhibit 4.1: (1) need recognition, (2) information search, (3) evaluation of alternatives, (4) purchase, and (5) postpurchase behavior. These five steps represent a general process that moves the consumer from recognition of a product or service need to the evaluation of a purchase. This process is a guideline for studying how consumers make decisions. It is important to note that this guideline does not assume that consumers' decisions will proceed in order through all of the steps of the process. In fact, the consumer may end the process at any time; he or she may not even make a purchase. Explanations as to why a consumer's progression through these steps may vary are offered at the end of the chapter in the section on the types of consumer buying decisions. Before addressing this issue, we will describe each step in the process in greater detail.

Need Recognition

need recognition
Result of an imbalance between actual and desired states.

The first stage in the consumer decision-making process is need recognition. **Need recognition** occurs when consumers are faced with an imbalance between actual and desired states. For example, do you often feel thirsty after strenuous exercise? Has a television commercial for a new sports car ever made you wish you could buy it? Need recognition is triggered when a consumer is exposed to either an internal or an external **stimulus**. Hunger and thirst are *internal stimuli;* the color of an automobile, the design of a package, a brand name mentioned by a friend, an advertisement on television, or cologne worn by a stranger are considered *external stimuli.*

stimulus
Any unit of input affecting one or more of the five senses: sight, smell, taste, touch, hearing.

A marketing manager's objective is to get consumers to recognize an imbalance between their present status and their preferred state. Advertising and sales promotion often provide this stimulus. Surveying buyer preferences provides marketers with information about consumer wants and needs that can be used to tailor products and services. For example, Procter & Gamble frequently surveys consumers regarding their wants and needs. P&G used the Internet to test market its Crest Whitestrips home-bleaching kit. The test revealed that 80 percent of potential buyers were women between the ages of thirty-five and fifty-four, identifying the best target market for the product. The company was then able to fine-tune its marketing plan before launching the product nationwide.[2] In

Exhibit 4.1

Consumer Decision-Making Process

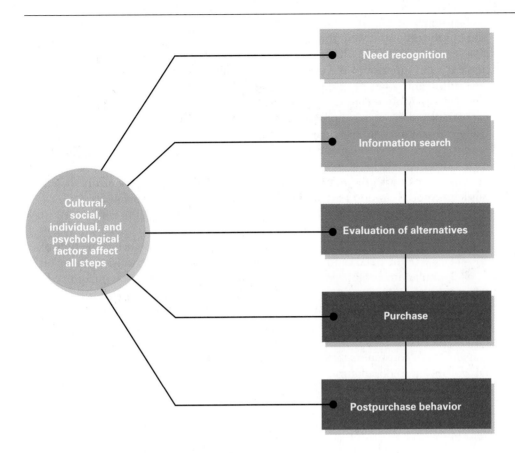

another example of how far P&G will go to learn about market trends, the company recently began videotaping consumers at home in its own version of reality TV to learn things about them that surveys do not reveal.[3]

Marketing managers can create wants on the part of the consumer. A **want** exists when someone has an unfulfilled need and has determined that a particular good or service will satisfy it. Young children may want toys, video games, and baseball equipment to meet their innate need to play and learn new skills. Teenagers may want compact discs, fashionable sneakers, and wide-leg jeans to fulfill their need of belonging. A want can be for a specific product or it can be for a certain attribute or feature of a product. For instance, adults may want ready-to-eat meals, drive-through dry cleaning service, and catalog shopping to fulfill their need for convenience. Older consumers may want goods and services that offer convenience, comfort, and security. Remote-controlled appliances, home deliveries, speaker phones, and motorized carts are all designed for comfort and convenience. A personal transmitter that can signal an ambulance or the police in an emergency offers security for older consumers.

Another way that marketers create new products and services is by observing trends in the marketplace. For example, as baby boomers become grandparents, marketers have created a whole industry around fulfilling their need to be involved in the lives of their grandchildren. Today, hospitals offer grandparenting classes to explain the theory behind new approaches to child care and to teach grandparents how to help parents while avoiding conflicts. Retailers encourage new grandparents to register so that their friends can plan baby showers to help them stock up on grandparenting essentials. And travel agents have packages specifically designed for grandparents wanting to vacation with their grandchildren including new camps and resorts that cater to children and grandparents.[4]

want
Recognition of an unfulfilled need and a product that will satisfy it.

Consumers recognize unfulfilled wants in various ways. The two most common occur when a current product isn't performing properly and when the consumer is about to run out of something that is generally kept on hand. Consumers may also recognize unfulfilled wants if they become aware of a product whose features make it seem superior to the one currently used. Such wants are usually created by advertising and other promotional activities. For example, Dockers recently created the new Mobile Pant that offers professional men seven invisible pockets to carry their wallet, keys, cellphone, and PDA (personal digital assistant). The advertising campaign for the new pants is designed to create a need among professional men for a better way to carry their business paraphernalia without giving up their casual style.[5] Similarly, aware of the popularity of MP3s and consumers' desire to take their music with them, more than a dozen car stereo manufacturers such as Sonicblue and Kenwood have added MP3 capabilities to their products. Other companies are also hoping to fulfill consumer needs with small portable MP3 players such as the iPod by Apple Computers.[6]

GLOBAL Marketers selling their products in global markets must carefully observe the needs and wants of consumers in various regions. Unilever hit on an unrecognized need of European consumers when it introduced Persil Tablets, premeasured laundry detergent in tablet form. Though the tablets are more expensive than regular laundry detergents, Unilever found that European consumers considered laundry a chore and wanted the process as simple and uncomplicated as possible. Unilever launched the tablets as less messy and more convenient to consumers tackling the pile of dirty clothes on wash day. The laundry tablets proved so popular in the United Kingdom that Unilever's Persil brand edged ahead of rival Procter & Gamble's best-selling Ariel powder detergent.[7]

Information Search

After recognizing a need or want, consumers search for information about the various alternatives available to satisfy it. An information search can occur internally, externally, or both. An **internal information search** is the process of recalling information stored in the memory. This stored information stems largely from previous experience with a product. For instance, while traveling you encounter a restaurant belonging to a chain that you tried somewhere else. By searching your memory, you can probably remember whether the food was good and in your price range.

In contrast, an **external information search** seeks information in the outside environment. There are two basic types of external information sources: nonmarketing-controlled and marketing-controlled. A **nonmarketing-controlled information source** is not associated with marketers promoting a product. A friend might recommend an IBM personal computer because he or she bought one and likes it. Nonmarketing-controlled information sources include personal experience (trying or observing a new product); personal sources (family, friends, acquaintances, and coworkers); and public sources, such as Underwriters Laboratories, *Consumer Reports*, and other rating organizations. For instance, consumers rely heavily on doctor and pharmacist recommendations when buying over-the-counter medications, and many consumers buy an OTC drug for the first time because their pharmacist recommends it. A recent survey on new car purchases by Generation Y found these car buyers were almost twice as likely as older buyers to get information about new cars from friends and relatives. Car manufacturers would therefore be likely to focus their marketing strategy on generating enthusiasm for their models via word of mouth.[8]

internal information search
The process of recalling past information stored in the memory.

external information search
The process of seeking information in the outside environment.

nonmarketing-controlled information source
A product information source that is not associated with advertising or promotion.

Consumers rely on external nonmarketing controlled information when buying a variety of products. For example, consumers rely heavily on the recommendations of doctors and pharmacists before buying an over-the-counter medication.

On the other hand, a **marketing-controlled information source**, is biased toward a specific product, because it originates with marketers promoting that product. Marketing-controlled information sources include mass-media advertising (radio, newspaper, television, and magazine advertising), sales promotion (contests, displays, premiums, and so forth), salespeople, product labels and packaging, and the Internet. Many consumers, however, are wary about the information they receive from marketing-controlled sources, arguing that most marketing campaigns stress the attributes of the product and don't mention the faults. These sentiments tend to be stronger among better educated and higher income consumers. For instance, in spite of extensive advertising highlighting its philanthropic activities, Philip Morris Companies continues to have a poor reputation among consumers. In fact, after a recent survey revealed that an extensive image campaign had not changed consumer opinion about the company, Philip Morris decided to change its corporate name to Altria to shift the focus away from the Philip Morris brand and onto the company's other brands like Kraft Foods and Miller Beer. In another example, surveys showed that consumers were skeptical about quality assurance advertisements made by Bridgestone's Firestone Tires in the wake of the company's massive tire recall.[9]

The extent to which an individual conducts an external search depends on his or her perceived risk, knowledge, prior experience, and level of interest in the good or service. Generally, as the perceived risk of the purchase increases, the consumer enlarges the search and considers more alternative brands. For instance, assume you want to buy a digital camera. The decision is a relatively risky one due to the expense and the technical nature of the camera's features, so you are motivated to search for information about models, options, and capabilities. You may decide to compare attributes of many cameras because the value of the time expended in finding data will be less than the cost of buying the wrong camera.[10] In contrast, more than 60 percent of bar patrons don't know what they will drink until seconds before they place their order, challenging the marketers of alcoholic beverages to find ways of "educating" potential customers on the spot.[11]

A consumer's knowledge about the product or service will also affect the extent of an external information search. If the consumer is knowledgeable and well informed about a potential purchase, he or she is less likely to search for additional information. In addition, the more knowledgeable the consumer is, the more efficiently he or she will conduct the search process, thereby requiring less time to search.

Another closely related factor that affects the extent of a consumer's external search is confidence in one's decision-making ability. A confident consumer not only has sufficient stored information about the product but also feels self-assured about making the right decision. People lacking this confidence will continue an information search even when they know a great deal about the product. Consumers with prior experience in buying a certain product will have less perceived risk than inexperienced consumers. Therefore, they will spend less time searching and limit the number of products that they consider.

A third factor influencing the external information search is product experience. Consumers who have had a positive prior experience with a product are more likely to limit their search to only those items related to the positive experience. For example, many consumers are loyal to Honda automobiles, which enjoy low repair rates and consequently high customer satisfaction, and they often own more than one.

Product experience can also play a major role in a consumer's decision to make a high-risk purchase. For example, TiVo, the maker of personal video recorders, found that due to the expensive and complex nature of its product, advertising was only moderately effective in generating sales. Instead, personal experience is the most important factor in the decision to purchase a PVR.[12]

Finally, the extent of the search undertaken is positively related to the amount of interest a consumer has in a product. A consumer who is more interested in a product will spend more time searching for information and alternatives. For

marketing-controlled information source
A product information source that originates with marketers promoting the product.

example, suppose you are a dedicated runner who reads jogging and fitness magazines and catalogs. In searching for a new pair of running shoes, you may enjoy reading about the new brands available and spend more time and effort than other buyers in deciding on the right shoe.

The consumer's information search should yield a group of brands, sometimes called the buyer's **evoked set** (or **consideration set**), which are the consumer's most preferred alternatives. From this set, the buyer will further evaluate the alternatives and make a choice. Consumers do not consider all the brands available in a product category, but they do seriously consider a much smaller set. For example, there are dozens of brands of shampoos and close to two hundred types of automobiles available in the United States, yet most consumers seriously contemplate only about four shampoos and no more than five automobiles when faced with a purchase decision. Having too many choices can, in fact, confuse consumers and affect their decision to buy. In a recent survey, only 3 percent of customers who were presented with thirty varieties of jam made the decision to purchase. In contrast, 30 percent of shoppers who had only six choices made a purchase.[13]

Evaluation of Alternatives and Purchase

After getting information and constructing an evoked set of alternative products, the consumer is ready to make a decision. A consumer will use the information stored in memory and obtained from outside sources to develop a set of criteria. These standards help the consumer evaluate and compare alternatives. One way to begin narrowing the number of choices in the evoked set is to pick a product attribute and then exclude all products in the set that don't have that attribute. For instance, assume that John is thinking about buying a new notebook computer to replace his current desktop machine. He is interested in one with a large color active-matrix display, CD-RW drive, and a processor speed of at least 1.2 gigahertz, so he excludes all notebooks without these features.

Another way to narrow the number of choices is to use cutoffs, or minimum or maximum levels of an attribute that an alternative must pass to be considered. Suppose John still must choose from a wide array of notebook computers that have active-matrix screens, CD-RW drives, and 1.2-plus processor speeds. He then names another product attribute: price. Given the amount of money he has set aside for a new computer, John decides he cannot spend more than $2,500. Therefore, he can exclude all notebook computers priced above $2,500. A final way to narrow the choices is to rank the attributes under consideration in order of importance and evaluate the products based on how well they perform on the most important attributes. To reach a final decision, John would pick the most important attributes, such as processor speed and active display, weigh the merits of each, and then evaluate alternative notebook computers on those criteria.

If new brands are added to an evoked set, the consumer's evaluation of the existing brands in that set changes. As a result, certain brands in the original set may become more desirable. Suppose John sees two notebook computers priced at $1,999 and $2,199. At the time, he may judge the $2,199 notebook computer as too expensive and choose not to purchase it. However, if he then adds to his list of alternatives another notebook computer that is priced at $2,499, he may view the $2,199 one as less expensive and decide to purchase it.

The goal of the marketing manager is to determine which attributes have the most influence on a consumer's choice. Several attributes may collectively affect a consumer's evaluation of products. A single attribute, such as price, may not adequately explain how consumers form their evoked set. Moreover, attributes that the marketer thinks are important may not be very important to the consumer. For example, if you are buying a new car, you will first have to determine which cars are in your price range. But then you would also likely consider size, styling, and the reputation of the car manufacturer before making a final decision.

A brand name can also have a significant impact on a consumer's ultimate choice. In a recent on-line survey, Johnson & Johnson was found to have the best corporate reputation among American companies, benefiting from its heritage as the premier maker of baby powder and shampoo. Respondents uniformly cited the familiarity and comfort they feel in using J&J products on their children. When faced with dozens of products on the drugstore shelf, consumers naturally gravitate toward J&J products. By providing consumers with a certain set of promises, brands in essence simplify the consumer decision-making process so consumers do not have to rethink their options every time they need something.[14]

Following the evaluation of alternatives, the consumer decides which product to buy or decides not to buy a product at all. If he or she decides to make a purchase, the next step in the process is an evaluation of the product after the purchase.

Postpurchase Behavior

When buying products, consumers expect certain outcomes from the purchase. How well these expectations are met determines whether the consumer is satisfied or dissatisfied with the purchase. For example, a person buys a used car with somewhat low expectations for the car's actual performance. Surprisingly, the car turns out to be one of the best cars she has ever owned. Thus, the buyer's satisfaction is high, because her fairly low expectations were exceeded. On the other hand, a consumer who buys a brand-new car would expect it to perform especially well. But if the car turns out to be a lemon, she will be very dissatisfied because her high expectations have not been met. Price often creates high expectations.

For the marketer, an important element of any postpurchase evaluation is reducing any lingering doubts that the decision was sound. This is particularly important because 75 percent of all consumers say they had a bad experience in the last year with a product or service they purchased.[15] When people recognize inconsistency between their values or opinions and their behavior, they tend to feel an inner tension called **cognitive dissonance**. For example, suppose a consumer spends half his monthly salary on a new TV entertainment system. If he stops to think how much he has spent, he will probably feel dissonance. Dissonance occurs because the person knows the purchased product has some disadvantages as well as some advantages. In the case of the entertainment system, the disadvantage of cost battles the advantage of technological superiority.

Consumers try to reduce dissonance by justifying their decision. They might seek new information that reinforces positive ideas about the purchase, avoid information that contradicts their decision, or revoke the original decision by returning the product. People who have just bought a new car often read more advertisements for the newly purchased car than for other cars in order to reduce dissonance. In some instances, people deliberately seek contrary information in order to refute it and reduce dissonance. Dissatisfied customers sometimes rely on word of mouth to reduce cognitive dissonance, by letting friends and family know they are displeased.

Marketing managers can help reduce dissonance through effective communication with purchasers. For example, a customer service manager may slip a note inside the package congratulating the buyer on making a wise decision. Postpurchase letters sent by manufacturers and dissonance-reducing statements in instruction booklets may help customers feel at ease with their purchase. Advertising that displays the product's superiority over competing brands or guarantees can also help relieve the possible

3

Explain the consumer's postpurchase evaluation process

cognitive dissonance
Inner tension that a consumer experiences after recognizing an inconsistency between behavior and values or opinions.

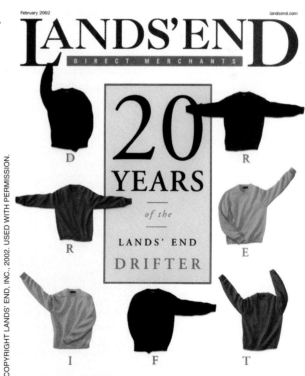

dissonance of someone who has already bought the product. Catalog merchant Lands' End, for example, offers consumers a no-questions-asked guarantee: If a product purchased through a Lands' End catalog does not work out, no matter what the reason, the company will provide a prompt, no-hassle refund or exchange. Hyundai Motor Company promotes its "Hyundai Advantage" warranty, which includes ten-year engine and transmission coverage, bumper-to-bumper coverage for five years or sixty-thousand miles, and five years of unlimited roadside assistance. Hyundai even promises limited reimbursement of lodging expenses incurred as a result of a breakdown.[16]

Types of Consumer Buying Decisions and Consumer Involvement

Identify the types of consumer buying decisions and discuss the significance of consumer involvement

involvement
The amount of time and effort a buyer invests in the search, evaluation, and decision processes of consumer behavior.

routine response behavior
The type of decision making exhibited by consumers buying frequently purchased, low-cost goods and services; requires little search and decision time.

All consumer buying decisions generally fall along a continuum of three broad categories: routine response behavior, limited decision making, and extensive decision making (see Exhibit 4.2). Goods and services in these three categories can best be described in terms of five factors: level of consumer involvement, length of time to make a decision, cost of the good or service, degree of information search, and the number of alternatives considered. The level of consumer involvement is perhaps the most significant determinant in classifying buying decisions. **Involvement** is the amount of time and effort a buyer invests in the search, evaluation, and decision processes of consumer behavior.

Frequently purchased, low-cost goods and services are generally associated with **routine response behavior**. These goods and services can also be called low-involvement products because consumers spend little time on search and decision before making the purchase. Usually, buyers are familiar with several different brands in the product category but stick with one brand. Consumers engaged in routine response behavior normally don't experience need recognition until they are exposed to advertising or see the product displayed on a store shelf. Consumers buy first and evaluate later, whereas the reverse is true for extensive decision making. A parent, for example, will not stand at the cereal shelf in the grocery store for twenty minutes thinking about which brand of cereal to buy

Exhibit 4.2

Continuum of Consumer Buying Decisions

	Routine	Limited	Extensive
Involvement	low	low to moderate	high
Time	short	short to moderate	long
Cost	low	low to moderate	high
Information Search	internal only	mostly internal	internal and external
Number of Alternatives	one	few	many

for the children. Instead, he or she will walk by the shelf, find the family's usual brand, and put it into the cart.

Limited decision making typically occurs when a consumer has previous product experience but is unfamiliar with the current brands available. Limited decision making is also associated with lower levels of involvement (although higher than routine decisions) because consumers do expend moderate effort in searching for information or in considering various alternatives. Suppose the children's usual brand of cereal, Kellogg's Corn Flakes, is unavailable in the grocery store. Completely out of cereal at home, the parent now must select another brand. Before making a final selection, he or she may pull from the shelf several brands similar to Kellogg's Corn Flakes, such as Corn Chex and Cheerios, to compare their nutritional value and calories and to decide whether the children will like the new cereal.

Consumers practice **extensive decision making** when buying an unfamiliar, expensive product or an infrequently bought item. This process is the most complex type of consumer buying decision and is associated with high involvement on the part of the consumer. This process resembles the model outlined in Exhibit 4.1. These consumers want to make the right decision, so they want to know as much as they can about the product category and available brands. People usually experience cognitive dissonance only when buying high-involvement products. Buyers use several criteria for evaluating their options and spend much time seeking information. Buying a home or a car, for example, requires extensive decision making.

The type of decision making that consumers use to purchase a product does not necessarily remain constant. For instance, if a routinely purchased product no longer satisfies, consumers may practice limited or extensive decision making to switch to another brand. And people who first use extensive decision making may then use limited or routine decision making for future purchases. For example, a new mother may first extensively evaluate several brands of disposable diapers before selecting one. Subsequent purchases of diapers will then become routine.

Factors Determining the Level of Consumer Involvement

The level of involvement in the purchase depends on five factors: previous experience, interest, perceived risk, situation, and social visibility.

- *Previous experience:* When consumers have had previous experience with a good or service, the level of involvement typically decreases. After repeated product trials, consumers learn to make quick choices. Because consumers are familiar with the product and know whether it will satisfy their needs, they become less involved in the purchase. For example, consumers with pollen allergies typically buy the sinus medicine that has relieved their symptoms in the past.

- *Interest:* Involvement is directly related to consumer interests, as in cars, music, movies, bicycling, or electronics. Naturally, these areas of interest vary from one individual to another. Although some people have little interest in nursing homes, a person with elderly parents in poor health may be highly interested.

- *Perceived risk of negative consequences:* As the perceived risk in purchasing a product increases, so does a consumer's level of involvement. The types of risks that concern consumers include financial risk, social risk, and psychological risk. First, financial risk is exposure to loss of wealth or purchasing power. Because high risk is associated with high-priced purchases, consumers tend to become extremely involved. Therefore, price and involvement are usually directly related: As price increases, so does the level of involvement. For example, someone who is thinking of buying a home will normally spend much time and effort to find the right one. Second, consumers take social risks when they buy products that can affect people's social opinions of them (for example, driving an old, beat-up car or wearing unstylish clothes). Third, buyers undergo psychological risk if they feel that making the wrong decision might cause some concern or anxiety. For example, should a working parent hire a baby-sitter or enroll the child in a day-care center?

- *Situation:* The circumstances of a purchase may temporarily transform a low-involvement decision into a high-involvement one. High involvement comes into play when the consumer perceives risk in a specific situation. For example, an individual might routinely buy low-priced brands of liquor and wine. When the boss visits, however, the consumer might make a high-involvement decision and buy more prestigious brands.

- *Social visibility:* Involvement also increases as the social visibility of a product increases. Products often on social display include clothing (especially designer labels), jewelry, cars, and furniture. All these items make a statement about the purchaser and, therefore, carry a social risk.

Marketing Implications of Involvement

Marketing strategy varies according to the level of involvement associated with the product. For high-involvement product purchases, marketing managers have several responsibilities. First, promotion to the target market should be extensive and informative. A good ad gives consumers the information they need for making the purchase decision, as well as specifying the benefits and unique advantages of owning the product. For example, manufacturers of high-tech computers and peripheral equipment like scanners, printers, and modems run lengthy ads that detail technical information about such attributes as performance, resolution, and speed. To make the purchase decision easier, major automobile manufacturers now enable their customers to use virtual reality to test different combinations of colors, fabrics, hubcaps, and so forth. Customers can see the effect of different options using a touch screen to generate an image of the car after making their selections. They can even hear different configurations of stereo sound systems to select the one they like best.

Purchasing on-line involves added risk for many consumers, even in limited decision-making situations. To overcome the challenges of getting shoppers to complete purchases on-line, Lands-end.com created a virtual three-dimensional model that customers can use to try on clothes. It also offers an on-line "personal shopper" to help customers identify items they might like. Purchase rates have been 26 percent higher among on-line shoppers who use the model and 80 percent higher among customers who use the personal shopper.[17]

For low-involvement product purchases, consumers may not recognize their wants until they are in the store. Therefore, in-store promotion is an important tool when promoting low-involvement products. Marketing managers have to focus on package design so the product will be eye-catching and easily recognized on the shelf. Examples of products that take this approach are Campbell's soups, Tide detergent, Velveeta cheese, and Heinz ketchup. In-store displays also stimulate sales of low-involvement products. A good display can explain the product's purpose and prompt recognition of a want. Displays of health and beauty aid items in supermarkets have been known to increase sales many times above normal. Coupons, cents-off deals, and two-for-one offers also effectively promote low-involvement items.

Linking a product to a higher-involvement issue is another tactic that marketing managers can use to increase the sales of a low-involvement product. For example, many food products are no longer just nutritious but also low in fat or cholesterol. Although packaged food may normally be a low-involvement product, reference to health issues raises the involvement level. To take advantage of aging baby boomers' interest in healthier foods, a recent advertisement from H.J. Heinz Company linked its ketchup with a growing body of research that suggests lycopene, an antioxidant found in tomatoes, can reduce the risk of prostate

Although food products are generally considered low-involvement purchases, marketers can increase sales by linking high-involvement issues to their products. In this ad for Stonyfield Farm organic yogurts, the issue of children's health and welfare is elicited by the tag line "Earth to Mom."

COURTESY OF STONYFIELD FARM

and cervical cancer.[18] Similarly, food products, such as Silk soy milk and Gardenburger meatless burgers, both of which contain soy protein, tout their health benefits in reducing the risk of coronary heart disease, preventing certain cancers, and reducing the symptoms of menopause. Soy-based products, long shunned in the United States for their taste, have seen their sales skyrocket as a result of these health claims.[19]

Gardenburger

Does the Gardenburger Web site seem more health oriented or taste oriented? What makes you think so? Is the emphasis what you expected it would be?

http://www.gardenburger.com

On Line

Factors Influencing Consumer Buying Decisions

The consumer decision-making process does not occur in a vacuum. On the contrary, underlying cultural, social, individual, and psychological factors strongly influence the decision process. They have an effect from the time a consumer perceives a stimulus through postpurchase behavior. Cultural factors, which include culture and values, subculture, and social class, exert the broadest influence over consumer decision making. Social factors sum up the social interactions between a consumer and influential groups of people, such as reference groups, opinion leaders, and family members. Individual factors, which include gender, age, family life-cycle stage, personality, self-concept, and lifestyle, are unique to each individual and play a major role in the type of products and services consumers want. Psychological factors determine how consumers perceive and interact with their environments and influence the ultimate decisions consumers make. They include perception, motivation, learning, beliefs, and attitudes. Exhibit 4.3 summarizes these influences.

Cultural Influences on Consumer Buying Decisions

The first major group of factors that influence consumer decision making are cultural factors. Cultural factors exert the broadest and deepest influence over a person's consumer behavior and decision making. Marketers must understand the way a people's culture and its accompanying values, as well as their subculture and social class, influence their buying behavior.

Identify and understand the cultural factors that affect consumer buying decisions

Culture and Values

Culture is the essential character of a society that distinguishes it from other cultural groups. The underlying elements of every culture are the values, language, myths, customs, rituals, and laws that shape the behavior of the culture, as well as the material artifacts, or products, of that behavior as they are transmitted from one generation to the next. Exhibit 4.4 lists some defining components of American culture.

Culture is pervasive. Cultural values and influences are the ocean in which individuals swim, and yet most are completely unaware that it is there. What people eat, how they dress, what they think and feel, and what language they speak are all dimensions of culture. It encompasses all the things consumers do without conscious choice because their culture's values, customs, and rituals are ingrained in their daily habits.

Culture is functional. Human interaction creates values and prescribes acceptable behavior for each culture. By establishing common expectations, culture gives order to society. Sometimes these expectations are coded into laws. For example, drivers in our culture must stop at a red light. Other times these expectations are

culture
The set of values, norms, attitudes, and other meaningful symbols that shape human behavior and the artifacts, or products, of that behavior as they are transmitted from one generation to the next.

Exhibit 4.3

Factors That Affect the Consumer
Decision-Making Process

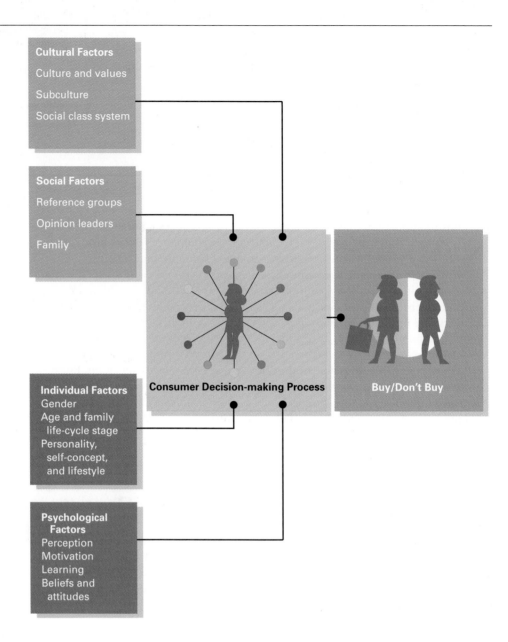

Cultural Factors

Culture and values

Subculture

Social class system

Social Factors

Reference groups

Opinion leaders

Family

Individual Factors
Gender
Age and family
    life-cycle stage
Personality,
    self-concept,
    and lifestyle

**Psychological
    Factors**
Perception
Motivation
Learning
Beliefs and
    attitudes

Consumer Decision-making Process

Buy/Don't Buy

taken for granted. For example, grocery stores and hospitals are open twenty-four hours whereas bank lobbies are open only during bankers' hours.

Culture is learned. Consumers are not born knowing the values and norms of their society. Instead, they must learn what is acceptable from family and friends. Children learn the values that will govern their behavior from parents, teachers, and peers. As members of our society, they learn to shake hands when they greet someone, to drive on the right-hand side of the road, and to eat pizza and drink Coca-Cola.

Culture is dynamic. It adapts to changing needs and an evolving environment. The rapid growth of technology in today's world has accelerated the rate of cultural change. Television has changed entertainment patterns and family communication and has heightened public awareness of political and other news events. Automation has increased the amount of leisure time we have and, in some ways, has changed the traditional work ethic. Cultural norms will continue to evolve because of our need for social patterns that solve problems.

Exhibit 4.4

Components of American Culture

Component	Examples
Values	Success through hard work Emphasis on personal freedom
Language	English as the dominant language
Myths	Santa Claus delivers presents to good boys and girls on Christmas Eve. Abraham Lincoln walked a mile to return a penny.
Customs	Bathing daily Shaking hands when greeting new people Standard gratuity of 15 percent at restaurants
Rituals	Thanksgiving Day dinner Singing the "Star Spangled Banner" before baseball games Going to religious services on the appropriate day
Laws	Child labor laws Sherman Anti-Trust Act guarantees competition.
Material artifacts	Diamond engagement rings Beanie Babies

SOURCE: Adapted from *Consumer Behavior* by William D. Wells and David Prensky. Copyright © 1996 by John Wiley & Sons, Inc. Reprinted by permission of John Wiley & Sons, Inc. All Rights Reserved.

In the United States, rapid changes in diversity are causing major shifts in culture. For example, the growth of the Hispanic community is influencing American food, music, clothing, and entertainment. Additionally, African American culture has been embraced by the mainstream. In fact, when DaimlerChrysler wanted to update its image, the company began using actors with dark hair and brown skin whose ethnic background was hard to guess as a way to give the vehicles a more hip, urban image. The company's research found that all consumers, including whites, perceived multicultural actors as cool.[20]

The most defining element of a culture is its **values**—the enduring beliefs shared by a society that a specific mode of conduct is personally or socially preferable to another mode of conduct. People's value systems have a great effect on their consumer behavior. Consumers with similar value systems tend to react alike to prices and other marketing-related inducements. Values also correspond to consumption patterns. For example, Americans place a high value on convenience. This value has created lucrative markets for products such as breakfast bars, energy bars, and nutrition bars that allow consumers to eat on the go.[21] Values can also influence consumers' TV viewing habits or the magazines they read. For instance, people who strongly object to violence avoid crime shows, and those who oppose pornography do not buy *Hustler*. Core American values—those considered central to the American way of life—are presented in Exhibit 4.5.

The personal values of target consumers have important implications for marketing managers. When marketers understand the core values that underlie the attitudes that shape the buying patterns of America's consumers and how these values were molded by experiences, they can target their message more effectively. For example, the personal value systems of matures, baby boomers, Generation

value

The enduring belief that a specific mode of conduct is personally or socially preferable to another mode of conduct.

Exhibit 4.5

Core American Values

Success	Americans admire hard work, entrepreneurship, achievement, and success. Those achieving success in American society are rewarded with money, status, and prestige. For example, Bill Gates, once a nerdy computer buff, built Microsoft Computers into an internationally known giant. Gates is now one of the richest people in the world today.
Materialism	Americans value owning tangible goods. American society encourages consumption, ownership, and possession. Americans judge others based on their material possessions; for example, the type of car they own, where they live, and what type of clothes they wear.
Freedom	The American culture was founded on the principle of religious and political freedom. The U.S. Constitution and the Bill of Rights assure American citizens the right to life, liberty, and the pursuit of happiness. These freedoms are fundamental to the legal system and the moral fiber of American culture. The Internet, for example, is built on the principle of the right to free speech. Lawmakers who have attempted to limit the material available on the Internet have met with tough free-speech opponents.
Progress	Technological advances, as well as advances in medicine, science, health, and the quality of products and services, are important to Americans. Each year, for example, more than 25,000 new or improved consumer products are introduced on America's supermarket shelves.*
Youth	Americans are obsessed with youth and spend a good deal of time on products and procedures that make them feel and look younger. Americans spend millions each year on health and beauty aids, health clubs, and healthy foods. Media and advertising encourage the quest for youth by using young, attractive, slim models, such as those in ads from fashion designer Calvin Klein.
Capitalism	Americans believe in a free enterprise system characterized by competition and the chance for monetary success. Capitalism creates choices, quality, and value for Americans. Laws prohibit monopolistic control of a market and regulate free trade. Americans encourage small business success, such as that found by Apple Computer, Wal-Mart, and McDonald's, all of which started as small enterprises with a better idea that toppled the competition.

*Data obtained from the New Products Showcase and Learning Center, Ithaca, New York, Web site at http://www.newproductworks.com, 1998.
SOURCE: From *Consumer Behavior* by William D. Wells and David Prensky. Copyright © 1996 John Wiley & Sons, Inc. Reprinted by permission of John Wiley & Sons, Inc. All Rights Reserved.

X-ers, and Generation Y-ers are quite different. The key to understanding *matures*, or everyone born before 1945, is recognizing the impact of the Great Depression and World War II on their lives. Facing these two immense challenges shaped a generation characterized by discipline, self-denial, financial and social conservatism, and a sense of obligation. Boomers, those individuals nurtured in the bountiful postwar period between 1945 and 1964, believe they are entitled to the wealth and opportunity that seemed endless in their youth. Generation X-ers are very accepting of diversity and individuality. They are also a very entrepreneurial-driven generation, ready to tackle life's challenges for themselves rather than as part of a crowd.[22] Gen Y-ers are more serious and socially conscious than Gen X-ers. Some of the defining events of their lives include Columbine, the O. J. Simpson trial, the Clinton impeachment, and the 2000 presidential election. They grew up with cable television, computers, debit cards, and cellphones, making them the most well connected generation to date—a fact that has important implications for word-of-mouth influence.[23]

Values represent what is most important in people's lives. Therefore, marketers watch carefully for shifts in consumers' values over time. For example, millions of Americans have acquired a passion for spirituality, as evidenced by the soaring sales of books with religious or spiritual themes and the popularity of television shows with similar themes. Similarly, after the September 11 terrorist attacks, when many people were fearful and concerned about self-protection, gun sales soared as did the sale of drugs to cure anthrax.

Understanding Culture Differences

GLOBAL Underlying core values can vary across cultures. Most Americans are more concerned about their health than their weight. But for many Brazilian women, being thin is more important than being healthy. In fact, a recent survey found that 75 percent of Brazilian women over the age of twenty who wanted to lose weight had taken prescription diet drugs for obesity even though less than one-third of the women were obese and the drugs presented the risk of side effects such as heart and lung damage. In contrast, most Chinese women do not place a high value on thinness and show little concern about being overweight.[24]

GLOBAL Without understanding a culture, a firm has little chance of selling products in it. Like people, products have cultural values and rules that influence their perception and use. Culture, therefore, must be understood before the behavior of individuals within the cultural context can be understood. Colors, for example, may have different meanings in global markets than they do at home. In China, white is the color of mourning and brides wear red. In the United States, black is for mourning and brides wear white. Recall from Chapter 3 that American designers at Universal Studios found they had much to learn about Japanese culture when planning a new theme park for Japan. Surveys showed that many of their original ideas to create Japanese attractions would not appeal to Japanese consumers who were hoping for an authentic American theme park that catered to their cultural differences. After extensive surveying and product testing, the result was a Universal Studios theme park with a more orderly clockwise layout, Japanese-style American food, and a Jurassic Park water slide designed to prevent riders from getting wet.[25]

GLOBAL Language is another important aspect of culture that global marketers must deal with. They must take care in translating product names, slogans, and promotional messages into foreign languages so as not to convey the wrong message. Consider the following examples of blunders made by marketers when delivering their message to Spanish-speaking consumers: General Motors discovered too late that Nova (the name of an economical car) literally means "doesn't go" in Spanish; Coors encouraged its English-speaking customers to "Turn it loose," but the phrase in Spanish means "Suffer from diarrhea"; and when Frank Perdue said, "It takes a tough man to make a tender chicken," Spanish speakers heard "It takes a sexually stimulated man to make a chicken affectionate."

As more companies expand their operations globally, the need to understand the cultures of foreign countries becomes more important. While marketers expanding into global markets generally adapt their products and business formats to the local culture, some fear that increasing globalization, as well as the proliferation of the Internet, will result in a homogeneous world culture of the future. U.S. companies in particular, they fear, are Americanizing the world by exporting bastions of American culture, such as McDonald's fast-food restaurants, Starbucks coffeehouses, Microsoft software, and American movies and entertainment. Read more about this issue in the "Global Perspectives" box.

McDonald's has responded to cultural differences like no other company. Its Web site boasts: "If meeting the demands of local culture means adding to our regular menu, we'll do it." In Japan, the company introduced the Teriyaki McBurger, and in India, McDonald's serves meatless sandwiches.

Will Cultural Differences Survive a Global Economy?

Over 150 years ago, Karl Marx and Friedrich Engels described the present day phenomenon of *globalization* when they wrote that people would "find new wants requiring for their satisfaction the products of distant lands and climes." Indeed, as Marx and Engels postulated, "modern industry has established the world market." Thirty years ago, most Chinese did not own televisions, refrigerators, or washing machines. But as economic reforms allowed more Western companies to offer their goods in China, ordinary people demanded these products. Today, 97 percent of Chinese in cities have televisions, and 88 percent have refrigerators and washing machines.

Globalization is not a new concept. Humans have been weaving commercial and cultural connections since the beginning of civilization. Today, computers, the Internet, cellular phones, cable television, and cheaper air transportation have accelerated and complicated these connections. Yet the basic dynamic remains the same: As people cross borders and oceans moving goods and services, their ideas move with them. And cultures change. The difference today is the speed at which these changes take place. Case in point: It took television thirteen years to acquire fifty million users; it took the Internet only five.

Everywhere, it seems, people are experiencing the fusion of cultures. London coffeehouses sell Italian espresso served by Algerian waiters while strains of the Beach Boys singing "I wish they all could be California girls . . ." can be heard in the background. The classic American Barbie doll, once only available as a blond, now comes in some thirty national varieties, including, most recently, Austrian and Moroccan. At Hollywood High

School in Los Angeles, the student body represents thirty-two different languages. Computer games fanatics in the United States play mah-jongg, an ancient Chinese game of strategy and luck, over the Internet against players from all over the world. *Cosmopolitan* magazine, the racy American fashion publication, is read by some 260,000 Chinese women every month. Adventurous diners in the midst of south Louisiana savor authentic Japanese sushi and join in karaoke singing. For about 100 rupees a month—about $2.34—slum-dwelling families in Mumbai (formerly Bombay) can surf more than fifty cable channels including Western imports such as TNT, MTV, CNN, and ESPN. McDonald's now has some twenty-five thousand restaurants worldwide, making the golden arches perhaps the most widely recognized trademark on the globe.

Not everyone is happy about the blending of cultures. Sociologists and anthropologists fear cultural cloning will result from what they regard as the "cultural assault" of ubiquitous Western multinationals such as McDonald's, Coca-Cola, Disney, Nike, MTV, and even the English language itself. Globalization has become a worrisome issue for many cultures. France worries about American films and television elbowing out French entertainment. Indians agonize that American junk food, television, films, blue jeans, pornography, and Christian missionaries will ruin traditional Indian values. Australians, in particular, have been phobically fearful of what they refer to as the remorseless march of American "cultural imperialism." In China, a recent book entitled *China Can Say No* became a best seller by admonishing Chinese who believe blindly in anything foreign. Critics of globalization are convinced that Western,

especially American, influences will pervade every culture, producing, as one observer terms it, one big "McWorld."

But not everyone is paranoid about cultural cloning. Proponents of globalization feel cultural change is inevitable and part of national evolution. For the most part, they contend, cultures take what they want from other cultures and adapt it to their needs. Tom Freston, CEO of MTV, contends that "kids today, outside of the U.S. in particular, travel with two passports. They have the international passport . . . that plugs them into what is going on with their peers around the world. So when you talk about action movies, sports stars, certain music stars like a Mariah Carey, certain kinds of clothing and styles, there is a homogeneity. But while that trend is going on, they have their other passport that is about their local world, which increasingly is more important to them." Hence, multinationals consistently adapt products and services to meet the needs of peoples in other lands. MTV tailors its music offerings in different countries to include local stars who sing in their own language. McDonald's outlets in India, where there are more than four hundred local languages and several very strict religions, serve mutton instead of beef and offer vegetarian menus acceptable to orthodox Hindus. Similarly, Revlon adapted the color palette and composition of its cosmetics to suit the Indian skin and climate.

Cultural change, supporters say, is a reality, not a choice. They believe that cultures won't become more uniform, but instead both old and new will tend to transform each other. Globalization won't mean just more television sets or Nike shoes, but rather a common destiny shaped by humanity.[26]

Subculture

subculture
A homogeneous group of people who share elements of the overall culture as well as unique elements of their own group.

A culture can be divided into subcultures on the basis of demographic characteristics, geographic regions, national and ethnic background, political beliefs, and religious beliefs. A **subculture** is a homogeneous group of people who share elements of the overall culture as well as cultural elements unique to their own group. Within subcultures, people's attitudes, values, and purchase decisions are even more similar than they are within the broader culture. Subcultural differences may result in considerable variation within a culture in what, how, when, and where people buy goods and services.

In the United States alone, countless subcultures can be identified. Many are concentrated geographically. People belonging to the Mormon religion, for example, are clustered mainly in Utah; Cajuns are located in the bayou regions of southern Louisiana. Hispanics are more predominant in those states that border Mexico, whereas the majority of Chinese, Japanese, and Koreans are found in the Pacific region of the United States.

Other subcultures are geographically dispersed. For example, computer hackers, people who are hearing or visually impaired, Harley-Davidson bikers, military families, university professors, and gays may be found throughout the country. Yet they have identifiable attitudes, values, and needs that distinguish them from the larger culture. For instance, Nokia Corporation sells phones that flash or vibrate for people with hearing problems while other companies, such as Nike and Pfizer, have aired commercials featuring people with various disabilities.[27] Similarly, Burger King has had good results in Chicago targeting people who work unusual hours and crave dinner-type food in the morning by advertising and offering burgers in the morning instead of waiting until 10:30 A.M. like most of its competitors.[28]

If marketers can identify subcultures, they can then design special marketing programs to serve their needs. According to the U.S. Census Bureau, the Hispanic population is the largest and fastest growing subculture, increasing at a rate of four times that of the general population. To tap into this large and growing segment, marketers have been spending a larger percentage of their marketing budgets advertising to Hispanics. Companies like Procter & Gamble, Anheuser-Busch, Hershey Foods, and Chuck E. Cheese all have Hispanic marketing campaigns, as do major league sports teams like the Texas Rangers and the Dallas Mavericks. The campaigns often feature both English and Spanish advertising and appeal to cultural pride.[29]

Other companies have been successful in targeting much smaller subcultures that are often overlooked. For example, Shaklee Corporation, a multilevel marketing company, has targeted subcultures such as the Amish, Mennonites, and Hasidic Jews. To recruit salespeople in these subcultures, Shaklee caters to their special needs. For example, Amish and Mennonite salespeople can earn a "bonus buggy" instead of the more traditional new car. To accommodate Hasidic customers, Shaklee toughened standards on their kosher products.[30]

Social Class

The United States, like other societies, does have a social class system. A **social class** is a group of people who are considered nearly equal in status or community esteem, who regularly socialize among themselves both formally and informally, and who share behavioral norms.

A number of techniques have been used to measure social class, and a number of criteria have been used to define it. One view of contemporary U.S. status structure is shown in Exhibit 4.6.

social class
A group of people in a society who are considered nearly equal in status or community esteem, who regularly socialize among themselves both formally and informally, and who share behavioral norms.

As you can see from Exhibit 4.6, the upper and upper middle classes comprise the small segment of affluent and wealthy Americans. The upper social classes are more likely than other classes to contribute something to society—for example, by volunteer work or active participation in civic affairs. In terms of consumer buying patterns, the affluent are more likely to own their own home and purchase new cars and trucks and are less likely to smoke. The very rich flex their financial muscles by spending more on owned vacation homes, vacations and cruises, and housekeeping and gardening services. The most affluent consumers are more likely to attend art auctions and galleries, dance performances, operas, the theater, museums, concerts, and sporting events.[31]

The majority of Americans today define themselves as middle class, regardless of their actual income or educational attainment. This phenomenon is most likely due to the fact that working-class Americans tend to aspire to the middle-class lifestyle while some of those who do achieve affluence may downwardly aspire to respectable middle-class status as a matter of principle.[32] Attaining goals and achieving status and prestige are important to middle-class consumers. People falling into the middle class live in the gap between the haves and the have-nots. They aspire to the lifestyle of the more affluent but are constrained by the economic realities and cautious attitudes they share with the working class.

The working class is a distinct subset of the middle class. Interest in organized labor is one of the attributes most common among the working class. This group is more likely to rate job security as the most important reason for taking a job.[33] The working-class person depends heavily on relatives and the community for economic and emotional support. The emphasis on family ties is one sign of the group's intensely local view of the world. They like the local news far more than do middle-class audiences who favor national and world coverage. They are also more likely to vacation closer to home.

Lifestyle distinctions between the social classes are greater than the distinctions within a given class. The most significant separation between the classes is the one between the middle and lower classes. It is here that the major shift in lifestyles appears. Members of the lower class typically fall at or below the poverty level in terms of income. This social class has the highest unemployment rate, and

Exhibit 4.6

U.S. Social Class

Upper Classes		
Capitalist class	1%	People whose investment decisions shape the national economy; income mostly from assets, earned or inherited; university connections
Upper middle class	14%	Upper-level managers, professionals, owners of medium-sized businesses; college-educated; family income nearly twice national average
Middle Classes		
Middle class	33%	Middle-level white-collar, top-level blue-collar; education past high school typical; income somewhat above national average
Working class	32%	Middle-level blue-collar, lower-level white-collar; income slightly below national average
Lower Classes		
Working poor	11–12%	Low-paid service workers and operatives; some high school education; below mainstream in living standard but above poverty line
Underclass	8–9%	People who are not regularly employed and who depend primarily on the welfare system for sustenance; little schooling; living standard below poverty line

SOURCE: Adapted from Richard P. Coleman, "The Continuing Significance of Social Class to Marketing," *Journal of Consumer Research*, December 1983, p. 267; Dennis Gilbert and Joseph A. Kahl, *The American Class Structure: A Synthesis* (Homewood, IL: Dorsey Press, 1982), ch. 11.

Exhibit 4.7

Social Class and Education

Percentage of adults in self-identified social classes who have a bachelor's degree or higher

Social Class	Percent
Lower	8
Working	12
Middle	34
Upper	61

SOURCE: "The New Working Class," *American Demographics*, January 1998, 51–55.

many individuals or families are subsidized through the welfare system. Many are illiterate, with little formal education. Compared to more affluent consumers, lower-class consumers have poorer diets and typically purchase much different types of foods when they shop.

Social class is typically measured as a combination of occupation, income, education, wealth, and other variables. For instance, affluent upper-class consumers are more likely to be salaried executives or self-employed professionals with at least an undergraduate degree. Working-class or middle-class consumers are more likely to be hourly service workers or blue-collar employees with only a high school education. Educational attainment, however, seems to be the most reliable indicator of a person's social and economic status (see Exhibit 4.7). Those with college degrees or graduate degrees are more likely to fall into the upper classes, while those people with some college experience but no degree fall closest to traditional concepts of the middle class.

Marketers are interested in social class for two main reasons. First, social class often indicates which medium to use for advertising. Suppose an insurance company seeks to sell its policies to middle-class families. It might advertise during the local evening news because middle-class families tend to watch more television than other classes do. If the company wants to sell more policies to upscale individuals, it might place a print ad in a business publication like the *Wall Street Journal*. The Internet, long the domain of more educated and affluent families, is becoming an important advertising outlet for advertisers hoping to reach blue-collar workers and homemakers. As the middle class rapidly adopts the medium, marketers are having to do more research to find out which Web sites will reach their audience.[34]

Second, knowing what products appeal to which social classes can help marketers determine where to best distribute their products. For example, a survey of consumer spending in the Washington, D.C. area reveals a stark contrast between Brie-eaters and Velveeta-eaters. The buyers of Brie, the soft and savory French cheese, are concentrated in the upscale neighborhoods of Northwest D.C. and the western suburbs of Montgomery County, Maryland, and Fairfax County, Virginia, where most residents are executives, white-collar professionals, or politicians. Brie fans tend to be college-educated professionals with six-figure incomes and an activist spirit. In contrast, aficionados of Velveeta, processed cheese marketed by Kraft, are concentrated in the middle-class, family-filled suburbs of Prince George's County and the predominantly black D.C. neighborhoods. Velveeta buyers tend to be married with children, high school educated, and employed at modestly paying service and blue-collar jobs.[35]

Social Influences on Consumer Buying Decisions

Identify and understand the social factors that affect consumer buying decisions

Most consumers are likely to seek out the opinions of others to reduce their search and evaluation effort or uncertainty, especially as the perceived risk of the decision increases. Consumers may also seek out others' opinions for guidance on new products or services, products with image-related attributes, or products where attribute information is lacking or uninformative. Specifically, consumers interact socially with reference groups, opinion leaders, and family members to obtain product information and decision approval.

Reference Groups

All the formal and informal groups that influence the buying behavior of an individual are that person's **reference groups**. Consumers may use products or brands to identify with or become a member of a group. They learn from observing how members of their reference groups consume, and they use the same criteria to make their own consumer decisions.

Reference groups can be categorized very broadly as either direct or indirect (see Exhibit 4.8). Direct reference groups are face-to-face membership groups that touch people's lives directly. They can be either primary or secondary. **Primary membership groups** include all groups with which people interact regularly in an informal, face-to-face manner, such as family, friends, and coworkers. In contrast, people associate with **secondary membership groups** less consistently and more formally. These groups might include clubs, professional groups, and religious groups.

Consumers also are influenced by many indirect, nonmembership reference groups that they do not belong to. **Aspirational reference groups** are those that a person would like to join. To join an aspirational group, a person must at least conform to the norms of that group. (**Norms** are the values and attitudes deemed acceptable by the group.) Thus, a person who wants to be elected to public office may begin to dress more conservatively, as other politicians do. He or she may go to many of the restaurants and social engagements that city and business leaders attend and try to play a role that is acceptable to voters and other influential people. Similarly, teenagers today may dye their hair, experiment with body piercing and tattoos, and carry around copies of "in" books so that their peers will perceive them as well read.[36]

Nonaspirational reference groups, or dissociative groups, influence our behavior when we try to maintain distance from them. A consumer may avoid buying some types of clothing or car, going to certain restaurants or stores, or even buying a home in a certain neighborhood in order to avoid being associated with a particular group.

reference group
A group in society that influences an individual's purchasing behavior.

primary membership group
A reference group with which people interact regularly in an informal, face-to-face manner, such as family, friends, or fellow employees.

secondary membership group
A reference group with which people associate less consistently and more formally than a primary membership group, such as a club, professional group, or religious group.

aspirational reference group
A group that someone would like to join.

norm
A value or attitude deemed acceptable by a group.

nonaspirational reference group
A group with which an individual does not want to associate.

Exhibit 4.8

Types of Reference Groups

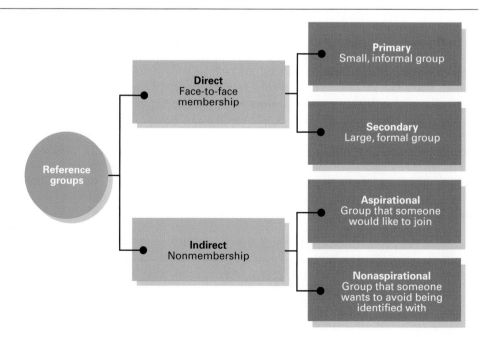

The activities, values, and goals of reference groups directly influence consumer behavior. For marketers, reference groups have three important implications: (1) they serve as information sources and influence perceptions; (2) they affect an individual's aspiration levels; and (3) their norms either constrain or stimulate consumer behavior. For example, Teenage Research Unlimited, an Illinois research firm devoted to uncovering what's cool in the teen market, recently identified four loose groups of today's teens based on their interests in clothes, music, and activities. Tracking these groups reveals how products become cool and how groups influence the adoption of cool products by other groups. According to Teenage Research Unlimited, a trend or fad often starts with "Edge" teens who have the most innovative tastes. These teens are on the cutting edge of fashion and music, and they wear their attitude all over their bodies in the form of tattoos, body piercing, studded jewelry, or colored tresses. Certain fads embraced by Edgers will spark an interest in the small group of teens called "Influencers," who project the look other teens covet. Influencers also create their own trends like rap music, baggy jeans, and pro sports clothes. Once a fad is embraced and adopted by Influencers, the look becomes cool and desirable. "Conformers" and "Passives" comprise the majority of the teen population, but they will not embrace a fad until it gets its seal of approval from the Influencers.[37]

Understanding the effect of reference groups on a product is important for marketers as they track the life cycle of their products. Retailer Abercrombie & Fitch noticed it was beginning to lose its target audience of college students when its stores began attracting large numbers of high school students trying to be more like the college students. To solve the problem, A&F created its Hollister store chain specifically for high school students.[38]

GLOBAL In Japan, companies have long relied on the nation's high school girls to give them advice during product testing. Fads that catch on among teenage girls often become big trends throughout the country and among Japanese consumers in general. Food manufacturers frequently recruit Tokyo schoolgirls to sample potato chip recipes or chocolate bars. Television networks survey high school girls to fine-tune story lines for higher ratings on prime-time shows. Other companies pay girls to keep diaries of what they buy. In 1995, Warner-Lambert hired high school girls to help choose a new gum flavor. After extensive chewing and comparing, the girls settled on a flavor that became Trickle, now Japan's best-selling bubble gum.[39]

© PETER M. WILSON/CORBIS

Japanese teenage girls have long provided the marketing litmus test companies need before launching new products. Perhaps their success in this area is due to the fact that they are caught in a pivotal clash between a tradition of collectivism and a growing sense of individualism.

Opinion Leaders

Reference groups frequently include individuals known as group leaders, or **opinion leaders**—those who influence others. Obviously, it is important for marketing managers to persuade such people to purchase their goods or services. Many products and services that are integral parts of Americans' lives today got their initial boost from opinion leaders. For example, VCRs and sport utility vehicles were embraced by opinion leaders well ahead of the general public. Exhibit 4.9 lists some products and services for which individuals often seek the advice of an opinion leader before purchasing.

Opinion leaders are often the first to try new products and services out of pure curiosity. They are typically self-indulgent, making them more likely to explore unproven but intriguing products and services. Technology companies have found that teenagers, because of their willingness to experiment, are key opinion leaders for the success of new technologies. For example, text messaging, which had its beginning with teenagers, has gained widespread appeal. Thus, many technology companies see creating a buzz among teens as a critical part of their marketing programs.[40]

opinion leader
An individual who influences the opinions of others.

Exhibit 4.9

Words of Wisdom: Opinion Leaders'
Consumer Clout Extends Far Beyond
Their Own Purchases

	Average Number of People to Whom Opinion Leaders Recommended Products* in the Past Year	Millions of Recommendations Made
Restaurant	5.0	70
Vacation destination	5.1	44
TV Show	4.9	45
Car	4.1	29
Retail store	4.7	29
Clothing	4.5	24
Consumer electronics	4.5	16
Office equipment	5.8	12
Stock, mutual fund, CD, etc.	3.4	12

*Among those who recommended the product at all
SOURCE: Roper Starch Worldwide, Inc., New York, NY. Adapted from "Maximizing the Market with Influentials,"
American Demographics, July 1995, p. 42.

Opinion leadership is a casual, face-to-face phenomenon and usually inconspicuous, so locating opinion leaders can be a challenge. Thus, marketers often try to create opinion leaders. They may use high school cheerleaders to model new fall fashions or civic leaders to promote insurance, new cars, and other merchandise. Revatex, the maker of JNCO jeans, sponsors extreme-sports athletes who appeal to the teen market. It also gives free clothes to trendsetters among teens in the hopes they will influence others to purchase the brand. JNCO outfits big-name DJs in the rave scene, as well as members of hip, alternative bands favored by the teen crowd. Similarly, the Web site of New York retailer Alloy Online (**www.alloyonline.com**) offers style tips, quizzes on topics like "What is your ideal guy type?" and gossip about teen idols like Britney Spears; it encourages teens to offer feedback about their likes and dislikes in a section called "Dig or Dis."[41] The "Ethics in Marketing" box questions how much marketers should target teenagers.

On a national level, companies sometimes use movie stars, sports figures, and other celebrities to promote products, hoping they are appropriate opinion leaders. Nike, for example, signed golf superstar Tiger Woods as a spokesperson for its products. The company hopes that consumers will see an affinity between the values that Woods represents and the values that Nike represents—earned success, discipline, hard work, achievement, and integrity. Nike also believes that the quality of Woods's golf game will be associated with the quality and value of its products. One year after Woods began appearing in ads and on the fairway with Nike's new line of golf balls, the company's market share tripled.[43]

Targeting Teens at School

As we have discussed in this chapter, marketers study consumers, identify unmet needs, develop products and services to meet those needs, and find a way to sell the products to those consumers. That sounds simple, but the process is not always without critics.

For example, soft drink manufacturers know that teenagers are the biggest consumers of their products. They also know that most soft drink consumers develop brand loyalty in their teen years, so it is critical to the manufacturers' long-term success to convince teens to choose their brand. Therefore, Coca-Cola and PepsiCo spend millions of dollars marketing their products to teens. To this point, the behavior of Coca-Cola and PepsiCo is no different from that of any other successful marketing company.

But what happens when soft drink companies target high schools for product distribution? Given the amount of time teens spend at schools, that is a logical choice. But parents, teachers, and legislators are becoming increasingly concerned over the practice.

Here are a few reason why. First, according to new statistics from the Centers for Disease Control, American high school students are three times as likely to be overweight than they were twenty years ago. Looking to explain the increase, some people point to the greater availability of soft drinks and junk foods on school campuses. Others say the increase cannot be blamed on soft drinks and junk food alone and that the increased consumption of all types of food and the decline in exercise are to blame. Still other critics blame soft drinks for tooth decay, and one study even linked soft drink consumption to fractured bones in high school girls.

Second, other critics are concerned about the commercialization of our schools. In most cases, soft drinks are sold in schools through exclusive agreements, which give the soft drink company high visibility. In return, the schools are able to use profits from a percentage of the sales to fund student programs. Because so many schools need the funding, critics say, the schools are unable to turn down the offers and, in some cases, feel the need to promote soft drink sales in spite of health concerns.

In response to criticism, the Coca-Cola Company recently announced that it would no longer encourage the exclusive agreements and would look for less commercial ways to benefit the schools. But the contracts are made not by the Coca-Cola Company, but by its bottlers, many of which have continued the practice in spite of Coca-Cola's announcement because they are proud of their relationships with the schools and because of increased competition from PepsiCo. PepsiCo says it doesn't encourage the practice of exclusive contracts but that it will bid on them when asked.[42]

So what do you think? Should Coca-Cola and PepsiCo be able to target teens at school? What if the companies reduced the number of soft drinks in machines and added more water and juice options since both companies offer those products? What are the advantages and disadvantages of targeting teens in school? We will continue to explore the controversial topic of marketing in schools in the "Ethics in Marketing" box in Chapter 8 (see page 273).

The effectiveness of celebrity endorsements depends largely on how credible and attractive the spokesperson is and how familiar people are with him or her. Endorsements are most likely to succeed if an association between the spokesperson and the product can be reasonably established. For example, comedian Bill Cosby failed as an endorser for financial products but succeeded with such products as Kodak cameras and Jell-O gelatin. Consumers could not mentally link Bill Cosby with serious investment decisions but could associate him with leisure activities and everyday consumption. Additionally, in the selection of a celebrity endorser, marketers must consider the broader meanings associated with the endorser. Although the endorser may have certain attributes that are desirable for endorsing the product, he or she may also have other attributes that are inappropriate.

A marketing manager can also try to use opinion leaders through group sanctioning or referrals. For example, some companies sell products endorsed by the American Heart Association or the American Cancer Society. The Arthritis Foundation and McNeil Consumer Products formed an alliance to launch the Arthritis Foundation line of pain relievers, which quickly jumped to the number one selling position in the over-the-counter arthritis segment. Marketers also seek endorsements from schools, churches, cities, the military, and fraternal organizations as a form of group opinion leadership. Salespeople often ask to use opinion leaders' names as a means of achieving greater personal influence in a sales presentation.

Family

The family is the most important social institution for many consumers, strongly influencing values, attitudes, self-concept—and buying behavior. For example, a family that strongly values good health will have a grocery list distinctly different from that of a family that views every dinner as a gourmet event. Moreover, the family is responsible for the **socialization process**, the passing down of cultural values and norms to children. Children learn by observing their parents' consumption patterns, and so they will tend to shop in a similar pattern.

Decision-making roles among family members tend to vary significantly, depending on the type of item purchased. Family members assume a variety of roles in the purchase process. *Initiators* are the ones who suggest, initiate, or plant the seed for the purchase process. The initiator can be any member of the family. For example, Sister might initiate the product search by asking for a new bicycle as a birthday present. *Influencers* are those members of the family whose opinions are valued. In our example, Mom might function as a price-range watchdog, an influencer whose main role is to veto or approve price ranges. Brother may give his opinion on certain makes of bicycles. The *decision maker* is the member of the family who actually makes the decision to buy or not to buy. For example, Dad or Mom is likely to choose the final brand and model of bicycle to buy after seeking further information from Sister about cosmetic features such as color and imposing additional criteria of his or her own, such as durability and safety. The *purchaser* (probably Dad or Mom) is the one who actually exchanges money for the product. Finally, the *consumer* is the actual user—Sister, in the case of the bicycle.

Marketers should consider family purchase situations along with the distribution of consumer and decision-maker roles among family members. Ordinary marketing views the individual as both decision maker and consumer. Family marketing adds several other possibilities: Sometimes more than one family member or all family members are involved in the decision; sometimes only children are involved in the decision; sometimes more than one consumer is involved; and sometimes the decision maker and the consumer are different people. Exhibit 4.10 represents the patterns of family purchasing relationships that are possible.

Children can have great influence over the purchase decisions of their parents. In many families, with both parents working and short on time, children are encouraged to participate. In addition, children in single-parent households become more involved in family decisions at an earlier age. Children are especially

socialization process
How cultural values and norms are passed down to children.

☐ **Exhibit 4.10**

Relationships among Purchasers and Consumers in the Family

		Purchase Decision Maker		
		Parent(s) Only	Child/Children Only	Some or All Family Members
Consumer	Parent(s)	golf clubs cosmetics wine	Mother's Day card	Christmas gifts minivan
	Child/ Children	diapers breakfast cereal	candy small toys	bicycle
	Some Family Members	videos long-distance phone service	children's movies	computers sports events
	All Family Members	clothing life insurance	fast-food restaurant	swim club membership vacations

SOURCE: From "Pulling the Family's Strings" by Robert Boutillier, *American Demographics,* August 1993. ©1993 PRIMEDIA Intertec, Stamford, CT. Reprinted with permission.

influential in decisions about food and eating out. Therefore, food companies listen closely to what children want. Children also are more interested in entertainment than food. Therefore, McDonald's and Burger King spend about $4 billion annually on toys for their kid meals; Quaker Oatmeal now features hidden treasures; Heinz ketchup is available in funky purple; and Parkay margarine comes in shocking pink and electric blue. Both the ketchup and the margarine come in squeezable bottles designed to allow small hands to design pictures. Promotions for food products aimed at children include a Web site that illustrates how to build a fort with french fries and books that teach children to count using Cheerios, M&Ms, and Oreos.[44] Children influence purchase decisions for many more products and services than food. Even though they are usually not the actual purchasers of such items, children often participate in decisions about toys, clothes, vacations, recreation, automobiles, and many other products.

GameGirlz

What kind of games are available at the Game-Girlz Web site? How do the games "for" girls differ from the games "for" boys at GameSpot?

http://www.gamegirlz.com
http://www.gamespot.com

On Line

Individual Influences on Consumer Buying Decisions

A person's buying decisions are also influenced by personal characteristics that are unique to each individual, such as gender; age and life-cycle stage; and personality, self-concept, and lifestyle. Individual characteristics are generally stable over the course of one's life. For instance, most people do not change their gender, and the act of changing personality or lifestyle requires a complete reorientation of one's life. In the case of age and life-cycle stage, these changes occur gradually over time.

(7) Identify and understand the individual factors that affect consumer buying decisions

Gender

Physiological differences between men and women result in different needs, such as health and beauty products. Just as important are the distinct cultural, social, and economic roles played by men and women and the effects that these have on their decision-making processes. For instance, when asked what features they would want on their next vehicle, Generation Y men yearn for more gadget and performance-oriented options, such as turbo-diesel or turbo-charged gas engines, run-flat tires, and high-intensity headlights. Generation Y women, on the other hand, prefer features that provide organization, practicality, and convenience, such as a wet storage area, power rear seats, cargo area dividers, and heated/cooled cup holders.[45]

 Men and women also shop differently. Studies show that men and women share similar motivations in terms of where to shop—that is, seeking reasonable prices, merchandise quality, and a friendly, low-pressure environment—but they don't necessarily feel the same about shopping in general. Most women enjoy shopping; their male counterparts claim to dislike the experience and shop only out of necessity. Further, men desire simple shopping experiences, stores with less variety, and convenience. Stores that are easy to shop in, are near home or office, or have knowledgeable personnel appeal more to men than to women.[46] The Internet appeals to men who find its ease of use a more enjoyable way to shop for clothing and gifts. Many Internet retailers are designing their sites to attract male gift buyers. Banana Republic's Web site prompts customers purchasing gifts to choose a price range. The site then returns five to six different suggestions. To help out its male shoppers, intimate apparel retailer Victoria's Secret lets women create password-protected wish lists and then zap them to their significant others to ensure there's no mistaking colors or sizes.[47]

Trends in gender marketing are influenced by the changing roles of men and women in society. For instance, as women around the world are working and earning

AP/WIDE WORLD PHOTOS

As the proportion of children in the U.S. population swells, this market segment is becoming increasingly important to marketers wanting to influence the kids that influence their parents' purchasing habits. Heinz's colored ketchups in the E-Z Squirt bottles are designed to do just that.

more, many industries are attracting new customers by marketing to women. The video game industry, which has traditionally targeted eighteen- to twenty-two-year-old men with games featuring guns and explosions, is beginning to develop new games based on popular female characters like Barbie and Nancy Drew aimed at capturing female customers. In South Korea, major credit card companies are now targeting working women by offering credit card benefits attractive to women such as discounts at department and bridal stores and disfigurement insurance for plastic surgery.[48]

The changing roles of women are also forcing companies that have traditionally targeted women to develop new strategies. Revlon stopped using glamorous supermodels to promote its products because it felt traditional "Cindy Crawford" ads "conveyed a man's view of women, not a woman's."[49] The company attempted to modernize its image by using new unknown models in ads highlighting universal truths about being a woman, such as a woman checking her reflection in the frozen food section of the grocery store. But the campaign did not work, and after seven months Revlon began using well-known models again with the new positioning statement "Be Unforgettable." The focus of the new campaign was on product benefits and promoting the Revlon brand name. It is often difficult for marketers to know how to respond as gender roles evolve and change.

Age and Family Life-Cycle Stage

The age and family life-cycle stage of a consumer can have a significant impact on consumer behavior. How old a consumer is generally indicates what products he or she may be interested in purchasing. Consumer tastes in food, clothing, cars, furniture, and recreation are often age related; for example, the favorite magazines for preteens aged eight to twelve include *Sports Illustrated for Kids*, *Nickelodeon*, and *Ranger Rick*. But as these consumers become teenagers their tastes in magazines diverge in favor of sports titles for boys and fashion/lifestyle titles for girls.[50]

Related to a person's age is his or her place in the family life cycle. As Chapter 6 explains in more detail, the *family life cycle* is an orderly series of stages through which consumers' attitudes and behavioral tendencies evolve through maturity, experience, and changing income and status. Marketers often define their target markets in terms of family life cycle, such as "young singles," "young married with children," and "middle-aged married without children." For instance, young singles spend more than average on alcoholic beverages, education, and entertainment. New parents typically increase their spending on health care, clothing, housing, and food and decrease their spending on alcohol, education, and transportation. Households with older children spend more on food, entertainment, personal care products, and education, as well as cars and gasoline. After their children leave home, spending by older couples on vehicles, women's clothing, health care, and long-distance calls typically increases. For instance, the presence of children in the home is the most significant determinant of the type of vehicle that's driven off the new car lot. Parents are the ultimate need-driven car consumers, requiring larger cars and trucks to haul their children and all their belongings. It comes as no surprise then that for all households with children, sport utility vehicles rank either first or second among new-vehicle purchases followed by minivans.[51]

Marketers should also be aware of the many nontraditional life-cycle paths that are common today and provide insights into the needs and wants of such consumers as divorced parents, lifelong singles, and childless couples. Three decades ago, traditional families comprised of married couples with children under eighteen accounted for nearly a majority of U.S. households. Today, traditional families make up only 23 percent of all households, while people living alone or with nonfamily members represent more than 30 percent. Furthermore, according to the U.S. Census Bureau, the number of single-mother households grew by 25 percent over the last decade. The shift toward more single-parent households is part of a broader societal change that has put more women on the career track. Although many marketers continue to be wary of targeting nontraditional families, Charles Schwab targeted single mothers in a recent advertising campaign featuring Sarah

Ferguson, the Duchess of York and a divorced mom; the idea was to appeal to single mothers' heightened awareness of the need for financial self-sufficiency.[52]

Personality, Self-Concept, and Lifestyle

Each consumer has a unique personality. **Personality** is a broad concept that can be thought of as a way of organizing and grouping how an individual typically reacts to situations. Thus, personality combines psychological makeup and environmental forces. It includes people's underlying dispositions, especially their most dominant characteristics. Although personality is one of the least useful concepts in the study of consumer behavior, some marketers believe that personality influences the types and brands of products purchased. For instance, the type of car, clothes, or jewelry a consumer buys may reflect one or more personality traits. Personality traits like those listed in Exhibit 4.11 may be used to describe a consumer's personality.

Self-concept, or self-perception, is how consumers perceive themselves. Self-concept includes attitudes, perceptions, beliefs, and self-evaluations. Although self-concept may change, the change is often gradual. Through self-concept, people define their identity, which in turn provides for consistent and coherent behavior.

Self-concept combines the **ideal self-image** (the way an individual would like to be) and the **real self-image** (how an individual actually perceives himself or herself). Generally, we try to raise our real self-image toward our ideal (or at least narrow the gap). Consumers seldom buy products that jeopardize their self-image. For example, someone who sees herself as a trendsetter wouldn't buy clothing that doesn't project a contemporary image.

Human behavior depends largely on self-concept. Because consumers want to protect their identity as individuals, the products they buy, the stores they patronize, and the credit cards they carry support their self-image. No other product quite reflects a person's self-image as much as the car he or she drives. For example, in a consumer survey conducted by Nissan, many consumers expressed dislike for family sedans like the Honda Accord and Toyota Camry, stating that, "they would buy one for their mothers, but not for themselves."[53] Likewise, Mitsubishi found that car buyers did not want to sacrifice a youthful image of themselves just because they have new responsibilities in life. Thus, advertising for the Montero sport utility vehicle and the Eclipse Spyder positions these vehicles as "spirited cars for spirited people" and encourages would-be car buyers to experience the exhilaration of driving stylish, exciting cars.

By influencing the degree to which consumers perceive a good or service to be self-relevant, marketers can affect consumers' motivation to learn about, shop for, and buy a certain brand. Marketers also consider self-concept important because it helps explain the relationship between individuals' perceptions of themselves and their consumer behavior.

An important component of self-concept is *body image*, the perception of the attractiveness of one's own physical features. For example, individuals who have

personality
A way of organizing and grouping the consistencies of an individual's reactions to situations.

self-concept
How consumers perceive themselves in terms of attitudes, perceptions, beliefs, and self-evaluations.

ideal self-image
The way an individual would like to be.

real self-image
The way an individual actually perceives himself or herself.

Exhibit 4.11

Some Common Personality Traits

- Adaptability
- Need for affiliation
- Aggressiveness
- Need for achievement
- Ascendancy
- Autonomy
- Dominance
- Deference
- Defensiveness
- Emotionalism
- Orderliness
- Sociability
- Stability
- Self-confidence

Although fitness is categorized most closely as a physiological need, it can also be considered a self-esteem need, particularly the prestigious health club memberships that it often entails. Even during recession, members will not sacrifice expensive memberships because to do so would be a subtle admission of financial difficulties.

© GETTY IMAGES/PHOTODISC

cosmetic surgery often experience significant improvement in their overall body image and self-concept. Moreover, a person's perception of body image can be a stronger reason for weight loss than either good health or other social factors.[54] With the median age of Americans rising, many companies are introducing products and services aimed at aging baby boomers who are concerned about their age and physical appearance. Sales of hair-coloring products for men, for instance, have more than doubled over the last decade, and television and print advertisements aimed at getting men to dye the gray out of their hair have tripled. Similarly, many companies including PepsiCo with Tropicana juices and Pfizer with its Viagra product are repositioning their products to focus on lifestyle. Bank of America is featuring Harley-riding seniors in its advertisements for its private-bank marketing campaign, and high-end anti-aging creams are flying off department store shelves. Finally marketers are also seeing boomers respond to products aimed at younger audiences. For instance, new Starwood "W" Hotels, designed and advertised to attract a young, hip crowd, are attracting large numbers of boomers.[55]

lifestyle
A mode of living as identified by a person's activities, interests, and opinions.

Personality and self-concept are reflected in lifestyle. A **lifestyle** is a mode of living, as identified by a person's activities, interests, and opinions. *Psychographics* is the analytical technique used to examine consumer lifestyles and to categorize consumers. Unlike personality characteristics, which are hard to describe and measure, lifestyle characteristics are useful in segmenting and targeting consumers. Lifestyle and psychographic analysis explicitly addresses the way consumers outwardly express their inner selves in their social and cultural environment.

Many companies now use psychographics to better understand their market segments. For many years, marketers selling products to mothers conveniently assumed that all moms were fairly homogeneous and concerned about the same things—the health and well-being of their children—and that they could all be reached with a similar message. But recent lifestyle research has shown that there are traditional, blended, and nontraditional moms, and companies like Procter & Gamble and Pillsbury are using strategies to reach these different types of mothers. Psychographics is also effective with other segments. Hyundai Motors targets customers it calls "Kids & Cul-De-Sacs." These consumers are up-scale, suburban families with a median household income of $68,900 who tend to shop on-line and visit Disney theme parks. Another major target for Hyundai is "Bohemian Mix," professionals aged twenty-five to forty-four with a median income of $38,500 who are likely to shop at the Gap, watch *Face the Nation*, and read *Elle* magazine.[56] Psychographics and lifestyle segmentation are discussed in more detail in Chapter 6.

Psychological Influences on Consumer Buying Decisions

Identify and understand the psychological factors that affect consumer buying decisions

An individual's buying decisions are further influenced by psychological factors: perception, motivation, learning, and beliefs and attitudes. These factors are what consumers use to interact with their world. They are the tools consumers use to recognize their feelings, gather and analyze information, formulate thoughts and opinions, and take action. Unlike the other three influences on consumer behavior, psychological influences can be affected by a person's environment because they are applied on specific occasions. For example, you will perceive different stimuli and process these stimuli in different ways depending on whether you are sitting in class concentrating on the instructor, sitting outside of class talking to friends, or sitting in your dorm room watching television.

Perception

The world is full of stimuli. A stimulus is any unit of input affecting one or more of the five senses: sight, smell, taste, touch, hearing. The process by which we select, organize, and interpret these stimuli into a meaningful and coherent picture is called **perception**. In essence, perception is how we see the world around us and how we recognize that we need some help in making a purchasing decision.

People cannot perceive every stimulus in their environment. Therefore, they use **selective exposure** to decide which stimuli to notice and which to ignore. A typical consumer is exposed to more than 250 advertising messages a day but notices only between eleven and twenty.

The familiarity of an object, contrast, movement, intensity (such as increased volume), and smell are cues that influence perception. Consumers use these cues to identify and define products and brands. The shape of a product's packaging, such as Coca-Cola's signature contour bottle, for instance, can influence perception. Color is another cue, and it plays a key role in consumers' perceptions. Packaged foods manufacturers use color to trigger unconscious associations for grocery shoppers who typically make their shopping decisions in the blink of an eye. Red, for instance, used on packages of Campbell's soups and SunMaid raisins, is associated with prolonged and increased eating. Green is associated with environmental goodness and healthy, low-fat foods. Healthy Choice entrées and Snack-Wells cookies use green. Premium products, like Sheba cat food and Ben & Jerry's ice cream, use black and gold on their packaging to convey their use of superior ingredients.[57] The shape and look of a product's packaging can also influence perception. Ivory Soap recently began packaging about one-third of its product in special packaging based on the original late nineteenth-century design. The company hopes to take advantage of a consumer trend toward simplifying life by emphasizing the brand's heritage and image of purity.[58]

What is perceived by consumers may also depend on the stimuli's vividness or shock value. Graphic warnings of the hazards associated with a product's use are perceived more readily and remembered more accurately than less vivid warnings or warnings that are written in text. "Sexier" ads excel at attracting the attention of younger consumers. Companies like Calvin Klein and Guess use sensuous ads to "cut through the clutter" of competing ads and other stimuli to capture the attention of the target audience. Similarly, Benetton ads use shock value by portraying taboo social issues, from racism to homosexuality.

Two other concepts closely related to selective exposure are selective distortion and selective retention. **Selective distortion** occurs when consumers change or distort information that conflicts with their feelings or beliefs. For example, suppose a consumer buys a Chrysler. After the purchase, if the consumer receives new information about a close alternative brand, such as a Ford, he or she may distort the information to make it more consistent with the prior view that the Chrysler is better than the Ford. Business travelers who fly often may distort or discount information about airline crashes because they must use air travel constantly in their jobs. People who smoke and have no plans to quit may distort information from medical reports and the Surgeon General about the link between cigarettes and lung cancer.

Selective retention is remembering only information that supports personal feelings or beliefs. The consumer forgets all information that may be inconsistent. After reading a pamphlet that contradicts one's political beliefs, for instance, a person may forget many of the points outlined in it.

Which stimuli will be perceived often depends on the individual. People can be exposed to the same stimuli under identical conditions but perceive them very

perception
The process by which people select, organize, and interpret stimuli into a meaningful and coherent picture.

selective exposure
The process whereby a consumer notices certain stimuli and ignores others.

selective distortion
A process whereby a consumer changes or distorts information that conflicts with his or her feelings or beliefs.

selective retention
A process whereby a consumer remembers only that information that supports his or her personal beliefs.

differently. For example, two people viewing a TV commercial may have different interpretations of the advertising message. One person may be thoroughly engrossed by the message and become highly motivated to buy the product. Thirty seconds after the ad ends, the second person may not be able to recall the content of the message or even the product advertised.

Marketing Implications of Perception

Marketers must recognize the importance of cues, or signals, in consumers' perception of products. Marketing managers first identify the important attributes, such as price or quality, that the targeted consumers want in a product and then design signals to communicate these attributes. For example, consumers will pay more for candy wrapped in expensive-looking foil packages. But shiny labels on wine bottles signify less expensive wines; dull labels indicate more expensive wines. Marketers also often use price as a signal to consumers that the product is of higher quality than competing products. Gibson Guitar Corporation briefly cut prices on many of its guitars to compete with Japanese rivals Yamaha and Ibanez but found instead that it sold more guitars when it charged more for them. Consumers perceived that the higher price indicated a better quality instrument.[59]

Of course, brand names send signals to consumers. The brand names of Close-Up toothpaste, DieHard batteries, and Caress moisturizing soap, for example, identify important product qualities. Names chosen for search engines and sites on the Internet, such as Yahoo!, Amazon.com, CDNow, and Excite, are intended to convey excitement, intensity, and vastness. Companies might even change their names to send a message to consumers. As today's electric utility companies increasingly enter nonregulated markets to sell power, natural gas, and other energy-related products and services, they are finding their old company names may hold some negative perceptions with consumers. Consequently, many are shaking their stodgy "Power & Light & Electric" names in favor of those that let consumers know they are not just about electricity anymore, such as Reliant Energy, Entergy, and Cinergy.

Consumers also associate quality and reliability with certain brand names. Companies watch their brand identity closely, in large part because a strong link has been established between perceived brand value and customer loyalty. Brand names that consistently enjoy high perceived value from consumers include Kodak, Disney, National Geographic, Mercedes-Benz, and Fisher-Price. Naming a product after a place can also add perceived value by association. Brand names using the words Santa Fe, Dakota, or Texas convey a sense of openness, freedom, and youth, but products named after other locations might conjure up images of pollution and crime.

Marketing managers are also interested in the *threshold level of perception:* the minimum difference in a stimulus that the consumer will notice. This concept is sometimes referred to as the "just-noticeable difference." For example, how much would Sony have to drop the price of a VCR before consumers recognized it as a bargain—$25? $50? or more? One study found that the just-noticeable difference in a stimulus is about a 20 percent change. For example, consumers will likely notice a 20 percent price decrease more quickly than a 15 percent decrease. This marketing principle can be applied to other marketing variables as well, such as package size or loudness of a broadcast advertisement.[60]

Another study showed that the bargain-price threshold for a name brand is lower than that for a store brand. In other words, consumers perceive a bargain more readily when stores offer a small discount on a name-brand item than when they offer the same discount on a store brand; a larger discount is needed to achieve a similar effect for a store brand.[61] Researchers also found that for low-cost grocery items, consumers typically do not see past the second digit in the price. For instance, consumers do not perceive any real difference between two comparable cans of tuna, one priced at $1.52 and the other at $1.59, because they ignore the last digit.[62]

Besides changing such stimuli as price, package size, and volume, marketers can change the product or attempt to reposition its image. Realtors, for example, have changed a property's address to enhance its image. In fact, one San Francisco real estate company almost lost a major deal when one of its potential clients refused to move into an office whose address was 444 Market Street because of the association of the number four with death in the Chinese community. The company saved the deal by renovating the lobby to include a new entrance and changing the building's address to One Front Street.[63] But marketers must be careful when adding features. How many new services will discounter Target Stores need to add before consumers perceive it as a full-service department store? How many sporty features will General Motors have to add to a basic two-door sedan before consumers start perceiving it as a sports car?

Marketing managers who intend to do business in global markets should be aware of how foreign consumers perceive their products. For instance, in Japan, product labels are often written in English or French, even though they may not translate into anything meaningful. But many Japanese associate foreign words on product labels with the exotic, the expensive, and high quality.

Marketers have often been suspected of sending advertising messages subconsciously to consumers in what is known as *subliminal perception*. The controversy began in 1957 when a researcher claimed to have increased popcorn and Coca-Cola sales at a movie theater after flashing "Eat popcorn" and "Drink Coca-Cola" on the screen every five seconds for 1/300th of a second, although the audience did not consciously recognize the messages. Almost immediately consumer protection groups became concerned that advertisers were brainwashing consumers, and this practice was pronounced illegal in California and Canada. Although the researcher later admitted to making up the data and scientists have been unable to replicate the study since, consumers are still wary of hidden messages that advertisers may be sending.

Motivation

By studying motivation, marketers can analyze the major forces influencing consumers to buy or not buy products. When you buy a product, you usually do so to fulfill some kind of need. These needs become motives when aroused sufficiently. For instance, suppose this morning you were so hungry before class that you needed to eat something. In response to that need, you stopped at McDonald's for an Egg McMuffin. In other words, you were motivated by hunger to stop at McDonald's. **Motives** are the driving forces that cause a person to take action to satisfy specific needs.

Why are people driven by particular needs at particular times? One popular theory is **Maslow's hierarchy of needs**, shown in Exhibit 4.12, which arranges needs in ascending order of importance: physiological, safety, social, esteem, and self-actualization. As a person fulfills one need, a higher level need becomes more important.

The most basic human needs are *physiological*—that is the needs for food, water, and shelter. Because they are essential to survival, these needs must be satisfied first. Ads showing a juicy hamburger or a runner gulping down Gatorade after a marathon are examples of appeals to satisfy the physiological needs of hunger and thirst.

Safety needs include security and freedom from pain and discomfort. Marketers often exploit consumers' fears and anxieties about safety to sell their products. For example, aware of the aging population's health fears, the retail medical imaging centers AmeriScan and HealthScreen America advertise that they offer consumers a full body scan for early detection of health problems such as coronary disease and cancer.[64] On the other hand, some companies or industries advertise to allay consumer fears. For example, in the wake of the September 11 terrorist attacks, the airline industry found itself having to conduct an image campaign to reassure consumers about the safety of air travel.[65]

After physiological and safety needs have been fulfilled, *social needs*—especially love and a sense of belonging—become the focus. Love includes acceptance by one's peers, as well as sex and romantic love. Marketing managers probably appeal more to

motive
A driving force that causes a person to take action to satisfy specific needs.

Maslow's hierarchy of needs
A method of classifying human needs and motivations into five categories in ascending order of importance: physiological, safety, social, esteem, and self-actualization.

Exhibit 4.12

Maslow's Hierarchy of Needs

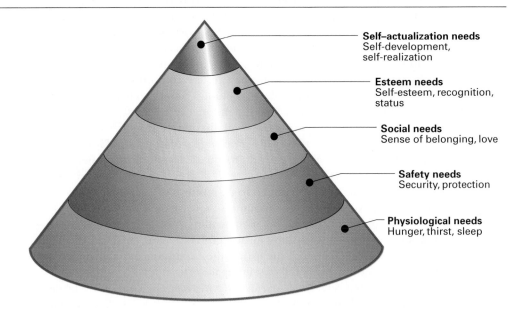

Self–actualization needs
Self-development,
self-realization

Esteem needs
Self-esteem, recognition,
status

Social needs
Sense of belonging, love

Safety needs
Security, protection

Physiological needs
Hunger, thirst, sleep

this need than to any other. Ads for clothes, cosmetics, and vacation packages suggest that buying the product can bring love. The need to belong is also a favorite of marketers, especially those marketing products to teens. Shoes and clothing brands such as Nike, adidas, Tommy Hilfiger, Gap, JNCO, and Abercrombie & Fitch score high with teenagers as "cool" brands. Teens who wear these labels feel and look like they belong to the in-crowd.

Love is acceptance without regard to one's contribution. Esteem is acceptance based on one's contribution to the group. *Self-esteem needs* include self-respect and a sense of accomplishment. Esteem needs also include prestige, fame, and recognition of one's accomplishments. Mont Blanc pens, Mercedes-Benz automobiles, and Neiman-Marcus stores all appeal to esteem needs. Most high-end spas and health clubs appeal to consumers' self-esteem needs. Like exclusive country clubs, clubs such as Chicago's East Bank Club are designed to make members feel proud of their commitment to fitness while also giving them a sense of social accomplishment. In fact, the clubs can be so effective that even during an economic recession, patrons will not give up their membership because to do so would be a public admission of financial problems.[66]

Asian consumers, in particular, are strongly motivated by status and appearance. Asians are always conscious of their place in a group, institution, or society as a whole. The importance of gaining social recognition turns Asians into some of the most image-conscious consumers in the world. Status-conscious Asians will not hesitate to spend freely on premium brands, such as BMW, Mercedes-Benz, and the best Scotch whiskey and French cognac. Indeed, marketers of luxury products such as Gucci, Louis Vuitton, and Prada find that demand for their products is so strong among image-conscious consumers that their sales are generally unaffected by economic downturns. In some cases, companies have been able to make up for sluggish European and U.S. sales by raising prices and volume in Asia.[67]

The highest human need is *self-actualization*. It refers to finding self-fulfillment and self-expression, reaching the point in life at which "people are what they feel they should be." Maslow felt that very few people ever attain this level. Even so, advertisements may focus on this type of need. For example, American Express ads convey the message that acquiring its card is one of the highest attainments in life. Similarly, Microsoft appealed to consumers' needs for self-actualization when it chose "Yes, You Can" as the Windows XP slogan.[68] And the U.S. Armed Forces' slogan urges young people to "Be all that you can be."

Even children must satisfy more than just the basic physiological and safety needs. Mattel's Barbie doll, for instance, fulfills a fundamental need that all girls share by playing out what it might be like in the grown-up world. Through Barbie, girls dream of achievement, glamour, romance, adventure, and nurturing. These dreams touch on many timeless needs, ranging from pride and success to belonging and love. Mattel zeros in on these core needs and addresses them with different Barbie products. Over the years, Barbie has been a teacher, a fashion model, a girlfriend, a dentist, an astronaut, a sister, and a veterinarian, to name a few.[69]

Learning

Almost all consumer behavior results from **learning**, which is the process that creates changes in behavior through experience and practice. It is not possible to observe learning directly, but we can infer when it has occurred by a person's actions. For example, suppose you see an advertisement for a new and improved cold medicine. If you go to the store that day and buy that remedy, we infer that you have learned something about the cold medicine.

There are two types of learning: experiential and conceptual. *Experiential learning* occurs when an experience changes your behavior. For example, if you try the new cold medicine when you get home and it does not relieve your symptoms, you may not buy that brand again. *Conceptual learning,* which is not learned through direct experience, is the second type of learning. Assume, for example, that you are standing at a soft drink machine and notice a new diet flavor with an artificial sweetener. Because someone has told you that diet beverages leave an aftertaste, you choose a different drink. You have learned that you would not like this new diet drink without ever trying it.

Reinforcement and repetition boost learning. Reinforcement can be positive or negative. If you see a vendor selling frozen yogurt (stimulus), buy it (response), and find the yogurt to be quite refreshing (reward), your behavior has been positively reinforced. On the other hand, if you buy a new flavor of yogurt and it does not taste good (negative reinforcement), you will not buy that flavor of yogurt again (response). Without positive or negative reinforcement, a person will not be motivated to repeat the behavior pattern or to avoid it. Thus, if a new brand evokes neutral feelings, some marketing activity, such as a price change or an increase in promotion, may be required to induce further consumption. Learning theory is helpful in reminding marketers that concrete and timely actions are what reinforce desired consumer behavior.

Repetition is a key strategy in promotional campaigns because it can lead to increased learning. Most marketers use repetitious advertising so that consumers will learn what their unique advantage is over the competition. Generally, to heighten learning, advertising messages should be spread over time rather than clustered together.

A related learning concept useful to marketing managers is stimulus generalization. In theory, **stimulus generalization** occurs when one response is extended to a second stimulus similar to the first. Marketers often use a successful, well-known brand name for a family of products because it gives consumers familiarity with and knowledge about each product in the family. Such brand-name families spur the introduction of new products and facilitate the sale of existing items. Jell-O frozen pudding pops rely on the familiarity of Jell-O gelatin; Clorox laundry detergent relies on familiarity with Clorox bleach; and Ivory shampoo relies on familiarity with Ivory soap. Microsoft recently entered the video game industry, hoping that the Microsoft brand would guarantee sales for the Xbox. Initial response to the Xbox has been strong based on Microsoft's reputation, but the company will have to work hard to make real progress in an industry dominated by other brand giants Sony and Nintendo.[70] Branding is examined in more detail in Chapter 8.

Another form of stimulus generalization occurs when retailers or wholesalers design their packages to resemble well-known manufacturers' brands.

learning
A process that creates changes in behavior, immediate or expected, through experience and practice.

stimulus generalization
A form of learning that occurs when one response is extended to a second stimulus similar to the first.

stimulus discrimination
A learned ability to differentiate
among similar products.

 Such imitation often confuses consumers, who buy the imitator thinking it's the original. U.S. manufacturers in foreign markets have sometimes found little, if any, brand
protection. In South Korea, Procter & Gamble's Ivory soap competes
head-on with the Korean brand Bory, which has an almost identical
logo on the package. Consumers dissatisfied with Bory may attribute
their dissatisfaction to Ivory, never realizing that Bory is an imitator.
Counterfeit products are also produced to look exactly like the original. For example, counterfeit Levi's jeans made in China are hot
items in Europe, where Levi Strauss has had trouble keeping up with
demand. The knockoffs look so much like the real thing that unsus-
pecting consumers don't know the difference—until after a few washes, when
the belt loops fall off and the rivets begin to rust.

The opposite of stimulus generalization is **stimulus discrimination**, which
means learning to differentiate among similar products. Consumers usually prefer
one product as more rewarding or stimulating. For example, some consumers prefer Coca-Cola and others prefer Pepsi; many insist they can taste a difference between the two brands.

With some types of products—such as aspirin, gasoline, bleach, paper towels—
marketers rely on promotion to point out brand differences that consumers would
otherwise not recognize. This process, called *product differentiation,* is discussed in
more detail in Chapter 6. Usually, product differentiation is based on superficial
differences. For example, Bayer tells consumers that it's the aspirin "doctors recommend most."

Beliefs and Attitudes

belief
An organized pattern of knowledge that an individual holds as
true about his or her world.

Beliefs and attitudes are closely linked to values. A **belief** is an organized pattern
of knowledge that an individual holds as true about his or her world. A consumer may believe that Sony's camcorder makes the best home videos, tolerates
hard use, and is reasonably priced. These beliefs may be based on knowledge,
faith, or hearsay. Consumers tend to develop a set of beliefs about a product's attributes and then, through these beliefs, form a *brand image*—a set of beliefs
about a particular brand. In turn, the brand image shapes consumers' attitudes
toward the product.

attitude
A learned tendency to respond
consistently toward a given object.

An **attitude** is a learned tendency to respond consistently toward a given
object, such as a brand. Attitudes rest on an individual's value system, which
represents personal standards of good and bad, right and wrong, and so forth;
therefore, attitudes tend to be more enduring and complex than beliefs.

For an example of the nature of attitudes, consider the differing attitudes of consumers around the world toward the practice of purchasing
on credit. Americans have long been enthusiastic about charging goods
and services and are willing to pay high interest rates for the privilege of postpon-
ing payment. To many European consumers, doing what amounts to taking out a
loan—even a small one—to pay for anything seems absurd. Germans especially are
reluctant to buy on credit. Italy has a sophisticated credit and banking system well
suited to handling credit cards, but Italians prefer to carry cash, often huge wads of
it. Although most Japanese consumers have credit cards, card purchases amount to
less than 1 percent of all consumer transactions. The Japanese have long looked
down on credit purchases but acquire cards to use while traveling abroad.[71]

If a good or service is meeting its profit goals, positive attitudes toward the
product merely need to be reinforced. If the brand is not succeeding, however, the
marketing manager must strive to change target consumers' attitudes toward it.
Changes in attitude tend to grow out of an individual's attempt to reconcile long-
held values with a constant stream of new information. This change can be accomplished in three ways: changing beliefs about the brand's attributes, changing the
relative importance of these beliefs, and adding new beliefs.

Changing Beliefs about Attributes

The first technique is to turn neutral or negative beliefs about product attributes into positive ones. For example, many consumers believe that it is easier and cheaper to take traditional film to be developed than it is to print their own digital photos. To change this belief, Sony Corporation has begun setting up kiosks in retail outlets that let consumers print their digital photos. The kiosks eliminate the need for consumers to purchase their own high-quality printer. Eastman Kodak and Hewlett-Packard are also developing special printers to allow retailers to offer photo printing as well.[72] Similarly, companies like Sageport and It's Never 2 Late are trying to change senior citizens' belief that computers are too complicated for them to learn. Sageport offers seniors an appliance that gives them Internet access without the confusion of operating a PC, and It's Never 2 Late is adapting software and hardware with larger type, fewer options, and more graphics to make it easier for seniors to use a PC.[73]

Changing beliefs about a service can be more difficult because service attributes are intangible. Convincing consumers to switch hairstylists or lawyers or to go to a mall dental clinic can be much more difficult than getting them to change brands of razor blades. Image, which is also largely intangible, significantly determines service patronage. For example, Tomra, a Norwegian recycling giant, hopes to increase the number of Americans who recycle by changing their perception that recycling is an unsavory chore. By building new rePlanet recycling kiosks in communities as an alternative to neighborhood recycling centers, Tomra is offering Americans a clean, convenient, service-oriented way to be responsible citizens.[74]

COURTESY OF WHITE WAVE

How did you know you liked water before you tried it?

Lactose free, high in protein, with a surprisingly good taste. *Don't be so stubborn.*

In order to increase sales, a company must change negative attitudes about its product held by those who are not buying it. One way to accomplish this is to change the beliefs about the product's attributes, such as taste. This ad for Silk soy milk does just that with its catchy question, and the follow up, "Don't be so stubborn."

Changing the Importance of Beliefs

The second approach to modifying attitudes is to change the relative importance of beliefs about an attribute. For years, consumers have known that bran cereals are high in natural fiber. The primary belief associated with this attribute is that the fiber tends to act as a mild, natural laxative. Today, however, cereal marketers promote the high fiber content of bran cereals as a possible factor in preventing certain types of cancer, vastly increasing the importance of this attribute in the minds of consumers. Similarly, the makers of Xenical, a weight-loss prescription drug, recently began marketing the medication in China, the world's second most obese nation. Most Chinese consumers place little importance on weight loss because they believe the problem is cosmetic. Therefore, to be successful in China, marketers will have to convince the Chinese and their doctors that obesity is a serious health issue that requires a medical solution.[75] You will read more about this topic in Chapter 6's "Global Perspectives" box.

Marketers can also emphasize the importance of some beliefs over others. For example, DaimlerChrysler's Jeep unit positions it as being rugged but promotes its luxury features. The newest Grand Cherokees have even more off-road capability, but very few owners ever take them off-road. Luxury features include a climate-control system with infrared beams that track drivers' and passengers' skin temperature to automatically adjust air conditioning and heat, his and her key rings that remember settings for power seats and mirrors, a system to reprogram radio stations for different drivers, and many other comforts.

Adding New Beliefs

The third approach to transforming attitudes is to add new beliefs. Although changes in consumption patterns often come slowly, cereal marketers are betting that consumers will eventually warm up to the idea of cereal as a snack. A print ad for Ralston Purina's Cookie-Crisp cereal features a boy popping the sugary nuggets into his mouth while he does his homework. Boxes of Kellogg's Cracklin' Oat Bran boast that the cereal tastes like oatmeal cookies and makes "a great snack . . . anytime." Similarly, commercials for Quaker Oats 100% Natural cereal promote eating it straight from the box. James River Corporation, the manufacturer of Dixie paper products, is also attempting to add new beliefs about the uses of its paper plates and cups with an advertising campaign aimed at positioning its product as a "home cleanup replacement." New commercials pitch Dixie paper plates as an alternative to washing dishes after everyday meals.[76]

U.S. companies attempting to market their goods overseas may need to help consumers add new beliefs about a product in general. Coca-Cola and PepsiCo have both found it challenging to sell their diet cola brands to consumers in India partly because diet foods of any kind are a new concept there, a country where malnutrition was widespread not too many years ago. Indians also have deep-rooted attitudes that anything labeled "diet" is meant for a sick person, such as a diabetic. As a general rule, most Indians are not diet-conscious, preferring food prepared in the traditional manner that tastes good. Indians are also suspicious of the artificial sweeteners used in diet colas. India's Health Ministry has required warning labels on cans and bottles of Diet Coke and Diet Pepsi saying "Not Recommended for Children."[77]

CONNECT IT

Reflecting on the chapter material, you should now be able to see how cultural, social, individual, and psychological factors affect the consumer decision-making process. Purchase decisions are influenced by many factors, from opinion leaders to peer groups. Individuals have unique values and opinions based upon the environment in which they have grown up. Marketers hoping to reach different segments must understand each segment's needs and wants, as well as the influnces that shape them, vary. Consumer behavior is a fascinating and often intricate process. An appreciation of consumer behavior and the factors that influence it will help you identify target markets and design effective marketing mixes.

USE IT

Find Product Ratings

Consumer Reports Online (**http://www.consumerreports.org**) is your one-stop source for information on hundreds of products you might be interested in purchasing, such as cars and trucks, appliances, electronics, household products, home office equipment, money and investing, health and food products, personal products, and leisure activities. The section on cars and trucks, for instance, offers a wealth of advice for those thinking of buying a new or used car, or seeking safety and maintenance tips. The site includes comparison ratings, reliability reports, negotiation advice, a personal car selector, information on car equipment and accessories, as well as exclusive ratings on auto-buying Web sites. Consumers Union, publisher of *Consumer Reports,* is a nonprofit consumer advocacy group with over sixty years of product testing. The group doesn't accept any outside advertising or support from product manufacturers, so the information you find is as unbiased as possible, but you have to pay for it as a subscriber.

REVIEW IT

1 **Explain why marketing managers should understand consumer behavior.** Consumer behavior describes how consumers make purchase decisions and how they use and dispose of the products they buy. An understanding of consumer behavior reduces marketing managers' uncertainty when they are defining a target market and designing a marketing mix.

1.1 The type of decision making a consumer uses for a product does not necessarily remain constant. Why? Support your answer with an example from your own experience.

2 **Analyze the components of the consumer decision-making process.** The consumer decision-making process begins with need recognition, when stimuli trigger awareness of an unfulfilled want. If additional information is required to make a purchase decision, the consumer may engage in an internal or external information search. The consumer then evaluates the additional information and establishes purchase guidelines. Finally, a purchase decision is made.

2.1 Visit Carpoint's Web site at **http://carpoint.ninemsn.com.au/Home/HomePage.asp.** How does the site assist consumers in the evaluation stage of choosing a new car? Develop your own hypothetical evoked set of three or four car models and present your comparisons. Which vehicle attributes would be most important in your purchase decision?

3 **Explain the consumer's postpurchase evaluation process.** Consumer postpurchase evaluation is influenced by prepurchase expectations, the prepurchase information search, and the consumer's general level of self-confidence. Cognitive dissonance is the inner tension that a consumer experiences after recognizing a purchased product's disadvantages. When a purchase creates cognitive dissonance, consumers tend to react by seeking positive reinforcement for the purchase decision, avoiding negative information about the purchase decision, or revoking the purchase decision by returning the product.

3.1 Recall an occasion when you experienced cognitive dissonance about a purchase. In a letter to a friend, describe the event and explain what you did about it.

4 **Identify the types of consumer buying decisions and discuss the significance of consumer involvement.** Consumer decision making falls into three broad categories. First, consumers exhibit routine response behavior for frequently purchased, low-cost items that require very little decision effort; routine response behavior is typically characterized by brand loyalty. Second, consumers engage in limited decision making for occasional purchases or for unfamiliar brands in familiar product categories. Third, consumers practice extensive decision making when making unfamiliar, expensive, or infrequent purchases. High-involvement decisions usually include an extensive information search and a thorough evaluation of alternatives. In contrast, low-involvement decisions are characterized by brand loyalty and a lack of personal identification with the product. The main factors affecting the level of consumer involvement are previous experience, interest, perceived risk of negative consequences (financial, social, and psychological), situation, and social visibility.

4.1 Describe the three categories of consumer decision-making behavior. Name typical products for which each type of consumer behavior is used.

⑤ Identify and understand the cultural factors that affect consumer buying decisions. Cultural influences on consumer buying decisions include culture and values, subculture, and social class. Culture is the essential character of a society that distinguishes it from other cultural groups. The underlying elements of every culture are the values, language, myths, customs, rituals, laws, and the artifacts, or products, that are transmitted from one generation to the next. The most defining element of a culture is its values—the enduring beliefs shared by a society that a specific mode of conduct is personally or socially preferable to another mode of conduct. A culture can be divided into subcultures on the basis of demographic characteristics, geographic regions, national and ethnic background, political beliefs, and religious beliefs. Subcultures share elements of the overall culture as well as cultural elements unique to their own group. A social class is a group of people who are considered nearly equal in status or community esteem, who regularly socialize among themselves both formally and informally, and who share behavioral norms.

5.1 **WRITING** You are a new marketing manager for a firm that produces a line of athletic shoes to be targeted to the college student subculture. In a memo to your boss, list some product attributes that might appeal to this subculture and the steps in your customers' purchase processes, and recommend some marketing strategies that can influence their decision.

⑥ Identify and understand the social factors that affect consumer buying decisions. Social factors include such external influences as reference groups, opinion leaders, and family. Consumers seek out others' opinions for guidance on new products or services and products with image-related attributes or because attribute information is lacking or uninformative. Consumers may use products or brands to identify with or become a member of a reference group. Opinion leaders are members of reference groups who influence others' purchase decisions. Family members also influence purchase decisions; children tend to shop in similar patterns as their parents.

6.1 Family members play many different roles in the buying process: initiator, influencer, decision maker, purchaser, and consumer. In your family, name who might play each of these roles in the purchase of a dinner at Pizza Hut, a summer vacation, Froot Loops breakfast cereal, an Abercrombie & Fitch sweater, golf clubs, an Internet service provider, and a new car.

⑦ Identify and understand the individual factors that affect consumer buying decisions. Individual factors that affect consumer buying decisions include gender; age and family life-cycle stage; and personality, self-concept, and lifestyle. Beyond obvious physiological differences, men and women differ in their social and economic roles that affect consumer buying decisions. How old a consumer is generally indicates what products he or she may be interested in purchasing. Marketers often define their target markets in terms of consumers' life-cycle stage, following changes in consumers' attitudes and behavioral tendencies as they mature. Finally, certain products and brands reflect consumers' personality, self-concept, and lifestyle.

7.1 Assume you are involved in the following consumer decision situations: (a) renting a video to watch with your roommates, (b) choosing a fast-food restaurant to go to with a new friend, (c) buying a popular music compact disc, (d) buying jeans to wear to class. List the individual factors that would influence your decision in each situation and explain your responses.

⑧ Identify and understand the psychological factors that affect consumer buying decisions. Psychological factors include perception, motivation, learning, values, beliefs, and attitudes. These factors allow consumers to interact with the world around them, recognize their feelings, gather and analyze information, formulate thoughts and opinions, and take action. Perception allows consumers to recognize their consumption problems. Motivation is what drives consumers to take action to satisfy specific consumption needs. Almost all consumer behavior results from learning, which is the process that creates changes in behavior through experience. Consumers with similar beliefs and attitudes tend to react alike to marketing-related inducements.

8.1 How do beliefs and attitudes influence consumer behavior? How can negative attitudes toward a product be changed? How can marketers alter beliefs about a product? Give some examples of how marketers have changed negative attitudes about a product or added or altered beliefs about a product.

8.2 *INFOTRAC COLLEGE EDITION* How can nonmarketing periodicals help you understand consumer behavior? Using InfoTrac (**http://www.infotrac-college.com**), research articles from such publications as the *Journal of Psychology, Journal of American Ethnic History, Psychology Today, Race and Class, Working Women, Society,* and others. Select and read three articles that explore different topics (i.e., do not select three articles on psychology). Then, make a list of factors you think could affect consumer purchasing behavior. Include with each factor a way marketers could use this information to their benefit.

■ DEFINE IT

Application for Entrepreneurs

Deli Depot is a new franchise opportunity offering cold and hot sandwiches, soup, chili, yogurt, pies, and cookies. It is positioned to compete with Subway and similar sandwich restaurants. Its unique advantages include special sauces on sandwiches, supplementary menu items like soup and pies, and quick delivery within specified zones.

The franchise package offered to franchisees includes information on the factors that typically influence consumers' selection of casual restaurants. These selection factors, in order from most important to least important, include food taste, food variety, value for the money, restaurant reputation, friendliness of employees, and convenience of location.

Robert Powell and a group of investors purchased the right to all franchise locations in the Atlanta metropolitan area. His group estimates that five units can be opened successfully in the first year and that a total of thirty can be opened in the first five years.

Because this is a new franchise, potential customers must first be made aware of Deli Depot and then be convinced to try it. Over the long run, a loyal customer base must be established to make each Deli Depot a success.

Questions

1. Are Deli Depot's unique advantages strong enough to attract customers from Subway and other sandwich competitors? Why or why not?

2. Are all the important customer selection factors for sandwich restaurants included in the list? Do you agree with the importance rankings? Explain your answers.

3. How can Robert and his group make potential customers aware of the new Deli Depot locations and menu selections?

4. How can Robert and his group convince individuals who try Deli Depot to become regular customers?

THINK ABOUT IT

Ethics Exercise

EyeOnU operates a Web filter service for public schools and libraries to protect students from inappropriate material on the Internet. Like the industry as a whole, the company's market share has been stagnant for the past two years. Looking for new sources of revenue, the company is considering selling the data it has collected about student surfing habits to marketers trying to learn more about students' behavior on the Web. The data are anonymous, but privacy advocates are concerned about the precedent of selling information about children to marketers.

Questions

1. What should EyeOnU do? Should it protect the student's data, or should it take the opportunity to create new revenues? Why?

2. Does the AMA Code of Ethics address this issue? Go to **http://www.marketingpower.com** and review the code. Then, write a brief paragraph on how the AMA Code of Ethics relates to EyeOnU's dilemma.

TRY IT

Entrepreneurship Case

Bucking the Trend: Is "Family" the Next Theme Restaurant?

In 1995, attorney and real estate investor Stephen Waite sparked a revitalization in Albany, New York, when he opened his Big House Brewing Company in a century-old vacant downtown building. The extremely successful restaurant and pub set off a chain reaction of development and improvement projects that have transformed downtown Albany into a very different place, especially after five o'clock. In 2002, Waite hoped to leverage his experience downtown to create an entirely new type of restaurant concept, this time in Clifton Park, an Albany suburb.

Although financiers were not terribly eager to underwrite the Big House in 1995, Waite and his new business partner, Eric Shilling, are having much less trouble garnering support for their idea this time around. The pair wants to create a family-friendly restaurant with miniature golf in the summer and outdoor ice skating in the winter, plus clowns and magicians the whole year round. Providing recreational activities in conjunction with family dining is not a new trend: Places like Chuck E. Cheese and Dave & Buster's have been doing it for years. But what Waite and Shilling know will set their establishment apart is the fact that it is a unique facility. The restaurant menu will incorporate dishes made with locally grown products, like local apples. Having dishes that are indigenous to the area will set the restaurant apart from the bevy of national chain restaurants and attractions that make up the American suburban landscape. In fact, the location of the new complex is not near any strip mall or commercial area. The proposed site is a wooded six-acre site near the community sports complex and local schools.

Waite and Shilling's whole project is bucking the trend of locating chains near other chains to drive traffic, forecasting that people are getting tired of chains. In fact, there is some evidence that Americans are getting tired of the sameness that pervades their culture. And even companies once thought of as innovators, like Hard Rock Café and The Gap, are struggling to some degree as consumers' attentions fade. Some former innovators, like Planet Hollywood, are now defunct. In some cases, consumers have stayed away because they are weary of the theme; in some cases it's because consumers demand higher quality than the theme restaurants provide. Amex conducted a series of seminars that examined consumer dining trends. Panelists included people from the marketing research discipline and chefs and owners of major restaurants. One trend identified by Barbara Caplan of Yankelovitch Partners, a national marketing research firm, was that of authenticity. Bobby Flay, popular chef and owner of the Mesa Grill and Bob in New York City, added to that by stating that consumers want an experience. But do theme restaurants provide that experience consumers seek?

With ten consecutive years of growth, the National Restaurant Association looked to top $408 billion in sales for 2002. And despite the hard times at many theme-based retailers (not just restaurants), Waite and Shilling are not alone in looking for the next successful theme. McDonald's opened its second-largest outlet in Columbus, Ohio's Easton Town Center in 2002. Not just a restaurant, this McDonald's includes an interactive miniature drive-thru for kids, a karaoke booth for customers to record CDs, a separate area where adults can eat, a merchandise area where customers can purchase McDonald's apparel and souvenirs, and a McTreat Center that sells ice cream treats, cookies, pastries, and imported Lavazza specialty coffee.

Although family-oriented dining is not new, it may very well be the new trend in theme restaurants. And even though Waite and Shilling want their family entertainment venue to be distinct from the chains in the nearby area, they are already looking at turning their idea into a regional chain, should it be as successful as they anticipate. Rick Sampson, the president of the New York State Restaurant Association, an Albany-based trade group, thinks that the popularity of themes is here to stay. "When the Hard Rock (Café) started off, they only had a couple," notes Sampson. "Their popularity made them what they are today."

Questions

1. What type of consumer buying decision best describes dining at Waite and Shilling's new family restaurant and entertainment complex? Is it different than the decision made to dine at McDonald's new Edu-Tainment restaurant? At a regular McDonald's restaurant? How?

2. List the factors that would influence a consumer to spend his or her dining budget at a family entertainment-themed restaurant. Include cultural, social, individual, and psychological factors on your list.

3. What influences on consumer decision making do you think are contributing to the declining performance of once-popular theme chains, like Hard Rock Café, Gap, the Disney Store, the Warner Bros. Store, and so forth? Based on the factors you identify, do you think that opening a new theme restaurant is wise? Why or why not?

Short **SUPERBOWL**

On your dedicated PowerPoint CD-ROM, you will find various ads that illustrate consumer decision making. Ads from Budweiser, Monster, and Radio Shack are examples of how marketers dealt with the terrorist attacks of September 11. Ads from McDonald's and Charles Schwab illustrate other issues working in the consumer buying process.

Medium **CNN VIDEO**

How important is perception in driving consumer behavior? In the early 2000s, while the media were reporting economic decline, consumers were still spending as they had in previous years because they felt that personally, things weren't so bad. So is perception or reality the more important factor in assessing consumer behavior? Watch the CNN clip and decide for yourself. The CNN clip for Chapter 15 on the yacht boom also illustrates consumer behavior concepts.

Long **SmallBusinessSchool**
the Series on PBS stations and the Web

To give you insight into Chapter 4, Small Business School will introduce you to Cowgirl Enterprises and its founder, Donna Baase. Baase invented Cowgirl Cream in her kitchen, and now the company sells a full line of skin products to a certain type of woman. What type? Well, a cowgirl. Watch the segment and work the questions on the supplemental video CD-ROM.

FLIP IT

 Flip to Chapter 4 in your *Grademaker Study Guide* for more review opportunities, including the pretest, vocabulary review, Internet activities, study test questions, and consumer behavior scenarios. Do you know the major factors that influence consumer behavior? Can you close your book and diagram the consumer decision-making process? Open your Study Guide to find out how much you know—or don't know.

CLICK IT

The *Essentials of Marketing* Web site links you to all the Internet-based activities in this chapter, like "Use It," "Review It" Questions 2.1 and 8.2, and the On-Line exercises in the chapter margins. As a review, do the Chapter 4 quiz and crossword puzzle. You can also work the Career Exersite that shows you different resources for marketing careers in the area of consumer behavior. Or review the main concepts in the PowerPoint presentation for Chapter 4. Go to **http://lamb.swlearning.com**, read the material, and follow the links right from the site.

Surf to Xtra! and test your understanding of consumer behavior by completing the worksheets for Exhibits 4.1, 4.2, 4.3, 4.4, 4.5, 4.6, 4.8, 4.11, and 4.12. If your instructor has assigned a marketing plan project, worksheets on Xtra! can help you organize your work. In addition to the quiz on the Web site, there's another quiz on Xtra!, plus video of the authors answering frequently asked questions about consumer behavior, such as "Which is more important in the purchasing decision—perception or reality?"

Still Shaky? Here's a Tip.

Imagine you are the professor, and make up your own test for Chapter 4. What are the main topics and key concepts that students should know? If you work with a study group, exchange practice tests. Work them individually then "grade" them collectively. This way you can discuss trouble spots and answer each other's questions.

CHAPTER **FIVE**
BUSINESS MARKETING

Learning Objectives

1 Describe business marketing

2 Describe the role of the Internet in business marketing

3 Discuss the role of relationship marketing and strategic alliances in business marketing

4 Identify the four major categories of business market customers

5 Explain the North American Industry Classification System

6 Explain the major differences between business and consumer markets

7 Describe the seven types of business goods and services

8 Discuss the unique aspects of business buying behavior

General Motors Corporation has spent the past several years weaving together a web of alliances and joint ventures to build its Asian presence. Now, the No. 1 automaker is trying to show it can turn this sprawling network into a real competitive advantage.

With profits in its home market slumping, GM is under pressure to make its Asian strategy deliver. So far, the results haven't been very encouraging. The most they can tout is that, combined with the sales of its alliance partners, GM's share of the Asian market is more than 16 percent, second only to Toyota Motor Corporation. "Cooperation between GM and our alliance partners is still in its infancy," says Asia chief Rudy Schlais. Though some of GM's Asian relationships date back decades, GM didn't devote much attention to them until recently. But after years of trying without much success to crack Asian markets on its own, GM now is counting on its partners to help. For example, in Japan GM has given up trying to sell large numbers of its U.S. or European models after years of trying without success. Instead, GM will begin selling the Chevrolet Cruze mini-SUV, a vehicle designed and built by Suzuki. GM and its allies hope that together they will be able to build a successful distribution network.

GM offers its partners the chance to lower parts costs thanks to volume discounts and big savings on costly research into future technologies. Already, they are winning deeper discounts from suppliers thanks to their larger buying power. But the Japanese companies, which rely more heavily on suppliers for engineering, are reluctant to adopt GM's approach for all their buying. Fuji officials say they don't expect to buy more than 30 percent of their parts through GM's system, for fear of compromising the uniqueness of their vehicles.

GM is finding out that sharing across regions and between independent companies is often complex. Though GM insists that minority-stake alliance deals avoid much of the pain and tension of a full-blown merger, the partners' independence can complicate efforts to cooperate. Take GM's $650 million plant in Thailand. On paper, the factory looks like a model for 21st century globalization. Located in a low-wage country, the factory is flexible enough to build everything from small Zafira minivans for European customers to sports cars for Italy's Fiat SpA, GM's European ally, to Asia-bound pickup trucks for Isuzu.

On the ground, things aren't so neat. Consider a slight rippling in the paint known as "orange peel." Engineers from Fuji wanted it reduced to a minimum on the Zafiras they will sell in Japan, since Japanese consumers expect a near-flawless paint job. But GM's Opel European unit didn't want orange peel eliminated entirely, since minor imperfections in the sheet metal are more obvious to the eye where the paint is smooth.

Though the factory employs the latest in GM's quality-control techniques, Opel insisted on an extra round of inspections to make sure the Zafiras it is getting are up to European standards. After passing that test, along with a test drive over a bumpy track designed to expose latent squeaks and rattles, Fuji submits them to another, even more thorough, once-over by quality checkers looking for defects that might put off picky buyers in Japan.[1]

What motivated General Motors to form strategic alliances and joint ventures with Asian automakers? What does GM bring to these relationships? What do the partners have to contribute?

What Is Business Marketing?

Business marketing is the marketing of goods and services to individuals and organizations for purposes other than personal consumption. The sale of an overhead projector to your college or university is an example of business marketing. Business products include those that are used to manufacture other products, become part of another product, aid the normal operations of an organization, or are acquired for resale without any substantial change in form. The key characteristic distinguishing business products from consumer products is intended use, not physical characteristics. A product that is purchased for personal or family consumption or as a gift is a consumer good. If that same product, such as a microcomputer or a cellular telephone, is bought for use in a business, it is a business product.

Business Marketing on the Internet

It is hard to imagine that commercial use of the Internet began as recently as the mid-1990s.[2] In 1995, those commercial Web sites that did exist were static. Only a few had data-retrieval capabilities. Frames, tables, and styles were not available. Security of any sort was rare, and streaming video did not exist. In early 1995, the entire Internet could have been stored on fewer than fifty compact discs.[3]

What a difference a few years have made! Today, Dell Computer sells over $1 million worth of computer equipment every day on the Internet, and IBM purchases over $6 billion of goods and services annually through Internet transactions. The worldwide purchase of business goods and services runs into the trillions of dollars annually. Cost savings just from purchasing goods and services on-line are estimated to exceed $2 trillion annually.[4]

Business marketing on the Internet offers tremendous opportunities for firms to increase efficiency, reduce costs, improve customer service, create one-to-one relationships, introduce new products, and expand markets. One study, sponsored by Cisco Systems, reported that over 80 percent of all U.S. companies with five thousand or more employees have some form of Internet presence.[5]

COURTESY OF CARRIER CORP.

One company that has successfully deployed its e-business initiative is Carrier, maker of air conditioners. Particularly noteworthy is how the company's Brazilian division used the Internet to increase sales, inventory turns, and customer satisfaction, all while decreasing delivery times.

Two Success Stories

Carrier Corporation and the resins division of General Electric Company illustrate the opportunities for businesses to use the Internet to reduce costs, streamline order processing, and enhance customer service and satisfaction.

At Carrier, the world's largest manufacturer of air conditioners, company officials claim to have reduced costs by $100 million annually by buying and selling on the Internet.[6] Carrier now sells over $1 billion worth of products through the company's Web site. International sales and service results have been particularly remarkable.

The time required for Brazilian customers to place an order with Carrier and get confirmation has gone from six days to six minutes. Inventory turnover has increased from seventeen to twenty-four times per year. And 77 percent of the Brazilian customers report that they are "satisfied" or "highly satisfied" with the service they are receiving.[7] A similar initiative in Korea has resulted in 50 percent of all sales passing through the Web site and orders being delivered in eighteen days compared to thirty-three days in the past.[8]

In 1997, General Electric's resins division launched an e-commerce site that was affectionately named GEPolymerland. Employees thought it sounded like a magical place, like Disneyland or Never-Never Land. It has produced what some might call magical results. Sales made through the Web site increased twelve-fold from 1999 to 2000 and grew from $1.2 billion in 1999 to $3 billion in 2001.[9]

GE's goals for the site are reducing costs and helping customers streamline their buying. Since 95 percent of on-line orders go straight into GEPolymerland's information-management system without human intervention, the site cuts GE's costs and speeds up orders. There are savings on customer service costs, too. Answering a technical question by telephone might cost $80, but if the customer accesses the same information using a search tool, the cost is only 50 cents.[10]

GEPolymerland

Is GEPolymerland just an e-commerce site, or is it also a virtual community? Visit the site and see what it offers beyond on-line ordering of resins.

http://www.gepolymerland.com

On Line

Potential Unrealized

Carrier and GE's resins division were both successful marketers before they created easy-to-use Web sites. Putting the operations on-line didn't require changing fundamental business relationships: The Web sites were just a way to make the firms more efficient.

Most business buying and selling is done off-line. One recent study found that only 18 percent of business marketers with an on-line presence sell on-line at all. Another study found that corporate purchasing agents make a mere 20 percent of purchases on-line. As one person put it, "if you are buying a stapler, you have no problems clicking around on-line. If you're buying fifteen thousand staplers, you want to talk to someone."[11] What are the 82 percent of business marketers that have a presence on the Internet but are not selling goods and services offering? Most provide product information and promotion. Some answer questions. Others provide contact and ordering information. Business Internet marketing represents trillions of dollars of sales potential per year. It has currently reached only a fraction of its potential.

Benefits of Business Marketing on the Internet

As many examples in this book demonstrate, companies that use the Internet effectively gain clear advantages. These include:

1. *Lower prices:* Competition among on-line vendors leads to lower prices for business buyers.

2. *Greater selection of products and vendors:* The Web makes it possible for corporate purchasing agents to find numerous vendors for almost any product.

3. *Access to customer and product sales data:* Companies can develop customer lists and learn their buying characteristics. They can also immediately learn which products are selling best.

4. *Around-the-clock ordering and customer service:* Company Web sites provide extensive product information for prospective customers around the world on a "24/7" basis, thereby expanding markets and facilitating more transactions—without hiring additional personnel. Customers themselves decide how much information they require by clicking on site links. Well-designed sites offer solutions to customer problems and make product suggestions.

5. *Lower costs:* Cost savings are a major benefit of e-commerce. These can take many forms, from distribution savings to staff reductions and lower costs of

purchasing supplies. Carrier used the Web to cut costs by $100 million. GEPolymerland.com contributed substantially to General Electric's $1 billion in cost savings in 2001.

6. *Customized products:* The Internet is revolutionizing product design and manufacturing. No longer do companies have to design and build products well in advance of the sale, basing product decisions on market research. They can use the Internet to take orders for products tailored to customer specifications. Dell Computer was one of the first to allow computer buyers to configure their ideal computer from menus at Dell's Web site. Even though Dell's build-to-order procedures were remarkably efficient when customers phoned in all their orders, the Web has increased its efficiency and profitability. Warehouses receive supply orders via Internet messages every two hours instead of daily faxes. Suppliers know about the company's inventory and production plans and get feedback on their performance in meeting shipping deadlines.

 Many business marketers now realize that the Internet is a valuable tool for expanding markets and better serving customers. Exhibit 5.1 identifies seven Internet sites that contain important information for firms interested in competing in foreign markets. Exhibit 5.2 provides examples of popular Internet sites that cater to small businesses.

Exhibit 5.1

An Internet Guide to Small-Business Exporting

One of the easiest ways to delve into exporting is to utilize the Internet. Visit these sites, which offer valuable resources as well as links to additional information.

http://www.exim.gov   The Export-Import Bank of the United States was established to aid in financing and to facilitate U.S. exports.

http://www.exporthotline.com   Export Hotline contains thousands of market research reports, a trade library, and a variety of other resources focused on all aspects of global trade and investment.

http://www.fita.org   Trade associations are invaluable resources on exporting. Visit the Federation of International Trade Associations Web site to take advantage of all of its resources, including a network of three hundred thousand companies belonging to three hundred international trade associations in North America.

http://www.ita.doc.gov   The International Trade Administration of the U.S. Department of Commerce is "dedicated to helping U.S. businesses compete in the global marketplace." It offers many resources to encourage, assist, and advocate U.S. exports.

http://www.sba.gov   The U.S. Small Business Administration offers a wealth of basic information and resources, including various export support programs. It provides financial, technical, and management assistance to help Americans start, run, and help their businesses grow.

SOURCE: Based on information from Christopher Farrell and Edith Updike, "So You Think the World Is Your Oyster," *Business Week*, June 9, 1997, p. ENT8.

Exhibit 5.2

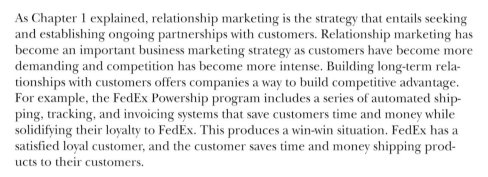

http://www.allbusiness.com   AllBusiness provides entrepreneurs with the knowledge and tools to start, manage, and grow their business. The site links to hundreds of how-to articles and provides expert answers to questions.

http://www.bcentral.com   Microsoft bCentral offers small-business solutions such as assistance in establishing an on-line business presence, enhancing sales or services, or managing business operations. The site also contains practical tips, advice, and links to how-to articles.

http://office.com   Office.com offers practical information on how to start or run a business and how to transform an existing company into an e-business. Users access over five hundred databases for news that affects their companies or industries. Office.com is one of the ten most visited business Web sites on the Internet.

http://www.quicken.com/small_business/   This site offers information on starting, running, and growing a small business. It also provides links to a variety of other Quicken sites that are useful to small-business owners and managers.

Relationship Marketing and Strategic Alliances

Discuss the role of relationship marketing and strategic alliances in business marketing

As Chapter 1 explained, relationship marketing is the strategy that entails seeking and establishing ongoing partnerships with customers. Relationship marketing has become an important business marketing strategy as customers have become more demanding and competition has become more intense. Building long-term relationships with customers offers companies a way to build competitive advantage. For example, the FedEx Powership program includes a series of automated shipping, tracking, and invoicing systems that save customers time and money while solidifying their loyalty to FedEx. This produces a win-win situation. FedEx has a satisfied loyal customer, and the customer saves time and money shipping products to their customers.

Strategic Alliances

A **strategic alliance**, sometimes called a *strategic partnership*, is a cooperative agreement between business firms. Strategic alliances can take the form of licensing or distribution agreements, joint ventures, research and development consortia, and partnerships. They may be between manufacturers, manufacturers and customers, manufacturers and suppliers, and manufacturers and channel intermediaries.

strategic alliance (strategic partnership)
A cooperative agreement between business firms.

Business marketers form strategic alliances to leverage what they have (technology, financial resources, access to markets) by combining these assets with those of other firms. Sometimes the alliance partners' assets are complementary. For example, UPS has developed strategic alliances with Ford, Nike, and DaimlerChrysler to employ its information-technology expertise to track shipments and handle on-line orders. Ford uses UPS to track the more than four million cars and trucks it produces annually. Dealers log onto an Internet site to find out exactly where their orders are in the distribution system, much the way customers already can track UPS packages on the Internet using a tracking number.[12]

Some strategic alliances are formed to achieve economies of scale. General Motors, Ford, DaimlerChrysler, Nissan Motor Company, and Renault SA created an Internet automobile parts exchange, called Covisint, that is expected to account for

Strategic alliances are at the heart of business marketing. Nobody knows this better than UPS. Its alliance with Office Depot makes UPS services available to the multitude of businesspeople that shop the supply superstore.

keiretsu
A network of interlocking corporate affiliates.

$300 billion in sales per year.[13] Covisint officials claim that the exchange will benefit small suppliers because they will have access to advanced technology that will provide them with faster and better access to buyers. Covisint officials also say smaller firms will be able to improve profit margins by reducing inventory and saving time.[14]

Relationships in Other Cultures

Although the terms "relationship marketing" and "strategic alliances" are fairly new, and popularized mostly by American business executives and educators, the concepts have long been familiar in other cultures. Businesses in countries such as Mexico, China, Japan, Korea, and much of Europe rely heavily on personal relationships.

In Japan, for example, the basis of exchange between firms is personal relationships that are developed through what is called *amae*, or indulgent dependency. *Amae* is the feeling of nurturing concern for, and dependence upon, another. Reciprocity and personal relationships contribute to *amae*. Relationships between companies can develop into a **keiretsu**—a network of interlocking corporate affiliates. Within a keiretsu, executives may sit on the boards of their customers or their suppliers. Members of a keiretsu trade with each other whenever possible and often engage in joint product development, finance, and marketing activity. For example, the Toyota Group keiretsu includes fourteen core companies and another 170 that receive preferential treatment. Toyota holds an equity position in many of these 170 member firms and is represented on many of their boards of directors.

Many American firms have found that the best way to compete in Asian countries is to form relationships with Asian firms. For example, Fuji-Xerox markets copiers in Japan and other Asian countries. Whirlpool has spent over $200 million buying controlling interests in competing firms in China and in India. The "Global Perspectives" box in this chapter describes a strategic alliance between General Motors and Shanghai Automotive to create a "Farmer Car" for rural residents of China.

Major Categories of Business Customers

4
Identify the four major categories of business market customers

The business market consists of four major categories of customers: producers, resellers, governments, and institutions.

Producers

The producer segment of the business market includes profit-oriented individuals and organizations that use purchased goods and services to produce other products, to incorporate into other products, or to facilitate the daily operations of the organization. Examples of producers include construction, manufacturing, transportation, finance, real estate, and food service firms. In the United States there are over thirteen million firms in the producer segment of the business market. Some of these firms are small and others are among the world's largest businesses.

Individual producers often buy large quantities of goods and services. Companies like General Motors spend more than $70 billion annually—more than the gross domestic product of Ireland, Portugal, Turkey, or Greece—on such business products as steel, metal components, and tires.

Shanghai Auto and GM to Market Farmer's Car

Under a new agreement, Shanghai Automotive, one of China's biggest auto companies, will license GM technology to build a cheap, bare-bones combination pickup-delivery truck designed specifically for the country's farmers.

With nearly one billion consumers and a fast-growing network of national highways, China boasts an auto market expected to be the biggest in the world someday. The rural focus, however, is a major shift for GM and Shanghai Automotive, which so far have focused on catering to the country's white-collar urban workers. The two already make Buick sedans, which sell for around $40,000, and will soon begin regular production of a new, more affordable compact car, the Sail, priced around $10,000.

But with almost every major auto maker in the world competing to sell cars to the few Chinese urbanites who can afford them, sales of the Buicks haven't lived up to expectations, and some auto analysts say the new compact car could also face a lukewarm reception. In fact, total car sales in Chinese cities grew just 6 percent last year, less than half the rate of rural auto sales, initial figures show.

The new Farmer's Car, as it is currently called, is based on GM's Corsa Combo and will be sold under Shanghai Auto's brand, retailing for about $7,000. Shanghai Auto and GM are betting the car will be a hit among China's 800 million rural inhabitants, a huge group of consumers mostly overlooked by foreign investors because of their skimpy earnings and frugal lifestyle.

For now, that is the biggest stumbling block the new car faces. Though living standards in the countryside have leapt in the past decade, rural dwellers remain the country's lowest earners, making less than $300 a year on average. And with grain and some produce prices falling, that figure is unlikely to rise significantly during the next few years.

Shanghai Auto is so confident in the rural car that it recently bought an unprofitable government auto company in coastal Jiangsu province, where it will produce the new Combo. Already, dozens of executives from Shanghai GM, the joint venture, are being lent to the Combo factory, where they plan to retool the outdated plant using GM's Corsa platform. Plans call for the Combo to use some parts, possibly including the engine made at Shanghai GM's plant, a $1.5 billion facility that now makes Buicks, family wagons, and, soon, the new Sail compact car.

Though China has a handful of auto companies that make simple pickup trucks for farmers, Shanghai Auto and GM are the first two major concerns to step into the vast countryside market. If the Combo proves successful, auto analysts say, that could change quickly. "This is a part of the market that hasn't registered on most companies' radar screens, but given the sheer number of farmers out there, these vehicles could end up dominating the market," says Yale Zhang, a Beijing executive with industry consultant Automotive Resources Asia.[15]

Do you think the first product of the Shanghai Auto/GM alliance, the Farmer's Car, will be successful? What are the benefits to each company in establishing such a partnership? The disadvantages?

Resellers

The reseller market includes retail and wholesale businesses that buy finished goods and resell them for a profit. A retailer sells mainly to final consumers; wholesalers sell mostly to retailers and other organizational customers. There are approximately 1.5 million retailers and five hundred thousand wholesalers operating in the United States. Consumer-product firms like Procter & Gamble, Kraft General Foods, and Coca-Cola sell directly to large retailers and retail chains and through wholesalers to smaller retail units.

Business product distributors are wholesalers that buy business products and resell them to business customers. They often carry thousands

© ANDY SACKS/TONY STONE IMAGES

The producer segment of the business market includes manufacturing, like this globe production line, as well as construction, finance, transportation, real estate, and others.

of items in stock and employ sales forces to call on business customers. Businesses that wish to buy a gross of pencils or a hundred pounds of fertilizer typically purchase these items from local distributors rather than directly from manufacturers such as Empire Pencil or Dow Chemical.

Governments

A third major segment of the business market is government. Government organizations include thousands of federal, state, and local buying units. They make up what may be the largest single market for goods and services in the world.

Contracts for government purchases are often put out for bid. Interested vendors submit bids (usually sealed) to provide specified products during a particular time. Sometimes the lowest bidder is awarded the contract. When the lowest bidder is not awarded the contract, strong evidence must be presented to justify the decision. Grounds for rejecting the lowest bid include lack of experience, inadequate financing, or poor past performance. Bidding allows all potential suppliers a fair chance at winning government contracts and helps ensure that public funds are spent wisely.

Federal Government

Name just about any good or service and chances are that someone in the federal government uses it. The U.S. federal government is the world's largest customer.

Although much of the federal government's buying is centralized, no single federal agency contracts for all the government's requirements, and no single buyer in any agency purchases all that the agency needs. We can view the federal government as a combination of several large companies with overlapping responsibilities and thousands of small independent units.

 One popular source of information about government procurement is *Commerce Business Daily*. Until recently, businesses hoping to sell to the federal government found the document unorganized, and it often arrived too late to be useful. The new on-line version (**http://www.cbd-net.com**) is more timely and lets contractors find leads using keyword searches. *Doing Business with the General Services Administration*, *Selling to the Military*, and *Selling to the U.S. Air Force* are other examples of publications designed to explain how to do business with the federal government.

State, County, and City Government

Selling to states, counties, and cities can be less frustrating for both small and large vendors than selling to the federal government. Paperwork is typically simpler and more manageable than it is at the federal level. On the other hand, vendors must decide which of the over eighty-two thousand government units are likely to buy their wares. State and local buying agencies include school districts, highway departments, government-operated hospitals, and housing agencies.

Institutions

The fourth major segment of the business market is institutions that seek to achieve goals other than the standard busi-

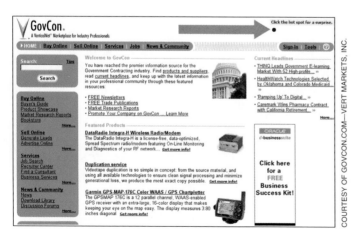

For doing business with the federal government, there is no better on-line resource than http://govcon.com. Users can check industry news, consult government databases, and view active contracts.

ness goals of profit, market share, and return on investment. This segment includes schools, hospitals, colleges and universities, churches, labor unions, fraternal organizations, civic clubs, foundations, and other so-called nonbusiness organizations.

The North American Industry Classification System

The **North American Industry Classification System (NAICS)** is an industry classification system introduced in 1997 to replace the standard industrial classification system (SIC). NAICS (pronounced *nakes*) is an all-new system for classifying North American business establishments. The system, developed jointly by the United States, Canada, and Mexico, provides a common industry classification system for the North American Free Trade Association (NAFTA) partners. Goods- or service-producing firms that use identical or similar production processes are grouped together.

NAICS is an extremely valuable tool for business marketers engaged in analyzing, segmenting, and targeting markets. Each classification group is relatively homogeneous in terms of raw materials required, components used, manufacturing processes employed, and problems faced. The more digits in a code, the more homogenous the group is. Therefore, if a supplier understands the needs and requirements of a few firms within a classification, requirements can be projected for all firms in that category. The number, size, and geographic dispersion of firms can also be identified. This information can be converted to market potential estimates, market share estimates, and sales forecasts. It can also be used for identifying potential new customers. NAICS codes can help identify firms that may be prospective users of a supplier's goods and services.

Exhibit 5.3 (on page 166) provides an overview of NAICS. Exhibit 5.4 (on page 167) illustrates the six-digit classification system for two of the twenty NAICS economic sectors: manufacturing and information. The hierarchical structure of NAICS allows industry data to be summarized at several levels of detail. To illustrate:

- The first two digits designate a major economic sector such as agriculture (11) or manufacturing (31–33).

- The third digit designates an economic subsector such as crop production or apparel manufacturing.

- The fourth digit designates an industry group, such as grain and oil seed farming or fiber, yarn, and thread mills.

- The fifth digit designates the NAICS industry, such as wheat farming or broadwoven fabric mills.

- The sixth digit, when used, identifies subdivisions of NAICS industries that accommodate user needs in individual countries.[16]

For a complete listing of all NAICS codes, see **http://www.census.gov/epcd/www/naics.html**.

5

Explain the North American Industry Classification System

North American Industry Classification System (NAICS)
A detailed numbering system developed by the United States, Canada, and Mexico to classify North American business establishments by their main production processes.

Business versus Consumer Markets

The basic philosophy and practice of marketing are the same whether the customer is a business organization or a consumer. Business markets do, however, have characteristics different from consumer markets. Exhibit 5.5 on page 168 summarizes the main differences between business and consumer markets.

6

Explain the major differences between business and consumer markets

Exhibit 5.3

NAICS Code	Economic Sector
11	Agriculture, forestry, and fishing
21	Mining
22	Utilities
23	Construction
31–33	Manufacturing
43	Wholesale trade
44–45	Retail trade
47–48	Transportation
51	Information
52	Finance and insurance
53	Real estate and rental and leasing
56	Professional and technical services
57	Management and support services
56	Professional and technical services
57	Management and support services
61	Education services
62	Health and social assistance
71	Arts, entertainment, and recreation
72	Food services, drinking places, and accommodations
81	Other services, except public administration
93	Public administration
98	Estates and trusts
99	Nonclassifiable

Exhibit 5.4

NAICS Level	Example 1		Example 2	
	NAICS Code	Description	NAICS Code	Description
Sector	31–33	Manufacturing	51	Information
Subsector	334	Computer and electronic product manufacturing	513	Broadcasting and telecommunications
Industry group	3346	Manufacturing and reproduction of magnetic and optical media	5133	Telecommunications
Industry	33461	Manufacturing and reproduction of magnetic and optical media	51332	Wireless telecommunications carriers, except satellite
U.S. industry	334611	Reproduction of software	513321	Paging

SOURCE: U.S. Census Bureau, "New Code System in NAICS," http://www.census.gov/epcd/www/naics.html.

Demand

Consumer demand for products is quite different from demand in the business market. Unlike consumer demand, business demand is derived, inelastic, joint, and fluctuating. (Chapter 15 explains consumer demand in more detail.)

Derived Demand

The demand for business products is called **derived demand** because organizations buy products to be used in producing their customers' products. For example, the market for CPUs, hard drives, and CD-ROMs is derived from the demand for personal computers. These items are only valuable as components of computers. Demand for these items rises and falls with the demand for PCs.

> **derived demand**
> The demand for business products.

Because demand is derived, business marketers must carefully monitor demand patterns and changing preferences in final consumer markets, even though their customers are not in those markets. Moreover, business marketers must carefully monitor their customers' forecasts, because derived demand is based on expectations of future demand for those customers' products.

Some business marketers not only monitor final consumer demand and customer forecasts but also try to influence final consumer demand. Aluminum producers use television and magazine advertisements to point out the convenience and recycling opportunities that aluminum offers to consumers who can choose to purchase soft drinks in either aluminum or plastic containers.

Inelastic Demand

The demand for many business products is inelastic with regard to price. *Inelastic demand* means that an increase or decrease in the price of the product will not significantly affect demand for the product. This will be discussed further in Chapter 15.

The price of a product used in the production of or as part of a final product is often a minor portion of the final product's total price. Therefore, demand for

Exhibit 5.5

Major Characteristics of Business Markets Compared to Consumer Markets

Characteristic	Business Market	Consumer Market
Demand	Organizational	Individual
Purchase volume	Larger	Smaller
Number of customers	Fewer	Many
Location of buyers	Geographically concentrated	Dispersed
Distribution structure	More direct	More indirect
Nature of buying	More professional	More personal
Nature of buying influence	Multiple	Single
Type of negotiations	More complex	Simpler
Use of reciprocity	Yes	No
Use of leasing	Greater	Lesser
Primary promotional method	Personal selling	Advertising

the final consumer product is not affected. If the price of automobile paint or spark plugs rose significantly, say, 200 percent in one year, do you think the number of new automobiles sold that year would be affected? Probably not.

Joint Demand

joint demand
The demand for two or more items used together in a final product.

Joint demand occurs when two or more items are used together in a final product. For example, a decline in the availability of memory chips will slow production of microcomputers, which will in turn reduce the demand for disk drives. One of the largest markets for Caterpillar diesel engines is over-the-road, heavy-duty truck manufacturers. A recent decline in sales of the behemoth trucks has led to fewer engines being purchased.[17]

Fluctuating Demand

multiplier effect (accelerator principle)
Phenomenon in which a small increase or decrease in consumer demand can produce a much larger change in demand for the facilities and equipment needed to make the consumer product.

The demand for business products—particularly new plants and equipment—tends to be more unstable than the demand for consumer products. A small increase or decrease in consumer demand can produce a much larger change in demand for the facilities and equipment needed to make the consumer product. Economists refer to this phenomenon as the **multiplier effect** (or **accelerator principle**).

Cummins Engine Company, a producer of heavy-duty diesel engines, uses sophisticated surface grinders to make parts. Suppose Cummins is using twenty surface grinders. Each machine lasts about ten years. Purchases have been timed so two machines will wear out and be replaced annually. If the demand for engine parts does not change, two grinders will be bought this year. If the demand for parts declines slightly, only eighteen grinders may be needed and Cummins won't replace the worn ones. However, suppose in the next year demand returns to previous levels plus a little more. To meet the new level of demand, Cummins will need to replace the two machines that wore out in the first year, the two that wore out in the second year, plus one or more additional machines. The multiplier effect works this way in many industries, producing highly fluctuating demand for business products.

Purchase Volume

Business customers buy in much larger quantities than consumers. Just think how large an order Kellogg typically places for the wheat bran and raisins used to manufacture Raisin Bran. Imagine the number of tires that DaimlerChrysler buys at one time.

Number of Customers

Business marketers usually have far fewer customers than consumer marketers. The advantage is that it is a lot easier to identify prospective buyers, monitor current customers' needs and levels of satisfaction, and personally attend to existing customers. The main disadvantage is that each customer becomes crucial—especially for those manufacturers that have only one customer. In many cases, this customer is the U.S. government. The success or failure of one bid can make the difference between prosperity and bankruptcy. In 2001, after five years of development, testing, and politicking, the Pentagon awarded Lockheed Martin a multidecade contract to build three thousand jet fighter airplanes.[18] Boeing Aircraft Company, the only other bidder on the $200 billion contract, immediately announced plans for substantial layoffs.

Winning major contracts, particularly high-volume ones, is definitely a reason to cheer. Lockheed Martin employees celebrate after the announcement that the company won the U.S. Defense Department contract to build the Joint Striker Fighter aircraft.

Location of Buyers

Business customers tend to be much more geographically concentrated than consumers. For instance, more than half the nation's business buyers are located in New York, California, Pennsylvania, Illinois, Ohio, Michigan, and New Jersey. The aircraft and microelectronics industries are concentrated on the West Coast, and many of the firms that supply the automobile manufacturing industry are located in and around Detroit.

Distribution Structure

Many consumer products pass through a distribution system that includes the producer, one or more wholesalers, and a retailer. However, because of many of the characteristics already mentioned, channels of distribution are typically shorter in business marketing. Direct channels, where manufacturers market directly to users, are much more common.

ON LINE

Many businesses that market directly to users are discovering that the Internet offers great potential for reaching new and existing customers domestically and around the world, while reducing costs to both buyers and sellers. Several examples of the expanding potential of the Internet are cited in this chapter.

Nature of Buying

Unlike consumers, business buyers usually approach purchasing rather formally. Businesses use professionally trained purchasing agents or buyers who spend their entire career purchasing a limited number of items. They get to know the items and the sellers well. Some professional purchasers earn the designation of Certified Purchasing Manager (CPM) after participating in a rigorous certification program.

Nature of Buying Influence

Typically, more people are involved in a single business purchase decision than in a consumer purchase. Experts from fields as varied as quality control, marketing, and finance, as well as professional buyers and users, may be grouped in a buying center (discussed later in this chapter).

Type of Negotiations

Consumers are used to negotiating price on automobiles and real estate. In most cases, however, American consumers expect sellers to set the price and other conditions of sale, such as time of delivery and credit terms. In contrast, negotiating is common in business marketing. Buyers and sellers negotiate product specifications, delivery dates, payment terms, and other pricing matters. Sometimes these negotiations occur during many meetings over several months. Final contracts are often very long and detailed.

Use of Reciprocity

reciprocity
A practice where business purchasers choose to buy from their own customers.

Business purchasers often choose to buy from their own customers, a practice known as **reciprocity**. For example, General Motors buys engines for use in its automobiles and trucks from Borg Warner, which in turn buys many of the automobiles and trucks it needs from GM. This practice is neither unethical nor illegal unless one party coerces the other and the result is unfair competition. Reciprocity is generally considered a reasonable business practice. If all possible suppliers sell a similar product for about the same price, doesn't it make sense to buy from those firms that buy from you?

Use of Leasing

Consumers normally buy products rather than lease them. But businesses commonly lease expensive equipment such as computers, construction equipment and vehicles, and automobiles. Leasing allows firms to reduce capital outflow, acquire a seller's latest products, receive better services, and gain tax advantages.

The lessor, the firm providing the product, may be either the manufacturer or an independent firm. The benefits to the lessor include greater total revenue from leasing compared to selling and an opportunity to do business with customers who cannot afford to buy.

Primary Promotional Method

Business marketers tend to emphasize personal selling in their promotion efforts, especially for expensive items, custom-designed products, large-volume purchases, and situations requiring negotiations. The sale of many business products requires a great deal of personal contact. Personal selling is discussed in more detail in Chapter 13.

Types of Business Products

Business products generally fall into one of the following seven categories, depending on their use: major equipment, accessory equipment, raw materials, component parts, processed materials, supplies, and business services.

⑦

Describe the seven types of business goods and services

Major Equipment

Major equipment includes such capital goods as large or expensive machines, mainframe computers, blast furnaces, generators, airplanes, and buildings. (These items are also commonly called **installations**.) Major equipment is depreciated over time rather than charged as an expense in the year it is purchased. In addition, major equipment is often custom-designed for each customer. Personal selling is an important part of the marketing strategy for major equipment because distribution channels are almost always direct from the producer to the business user.

Accessory Equipment

Accessory equipment is generally less expensive and shorter-lived than major equipment. Examples include portable drills, power tools, microcomputers, and fax machines. Accessory equipment is often charged as an expense in the year it is bought rather than depreciated over its useful life. In contrast to major equipment, accessories are more often standardized and are usually bought by more customers. These customers tend to be widely dispersed. For example, all types of businesses buy microcomputers.

Local industrial distributors (wholesalers) play an important role in the marketing of accessory equipment because business buyers often purchase accessories from them. Regardless of where accessories are bought, advertising is a more vital promotional tool for accessory equipment than for major equipment.

Raw Materials

Raw materials are unprocessed extractive or agricultural products—for example, mineral ore, lumber, wheat, corn, fruits, vegetables, and fish. Raw materials become part of finished products. Extensive users, such as steel or lumber mills and food canners, generally buy huge quantities of raw materials. Because there is often a large number of relatively small sellers of raw materials, none can greatly influence price or supply. Thus, the market tends to set the price of raw materials, and individual producers have little pricing flexibility. Promotion is almost always via personal selling, and distribution channels are usually direct from producer to business user.

Component Parts

Component parts are either finished items ready for assembly or products that need very little processing before becoming part of some other product. The Caterpillar diesel engines used in heavy-duty trucks that were mentioned earlier in this chapter are component parts. Other examples include spark plugs, tires, and electric motors for automobiles. A special feature of component

major equipment (installations)
Capital goods such as large or expensive machines, mainframe computers, blast furnaces, generators, airplanes, and buildings.

accessory equipment
Goods, such as portable tools and office equipment, that are less expensive and shorter-lived than major equipment.

raw materials
Unprocessed extractive or agricultural products, such as mineral ore, lumber, wheat, corn, fruits, vegetables, and fish.

component parts
Either finished items ready for assembly or products that need very little processing before becoming part of some other product.

© INDEX STOCK IMAGERY / GARY CONNER

Raw materials constitute a large part of business purchasing. Buyers typically order raw materials, such as lumber and steel, in large quantity.

OEM
The acronym OEM stands for original equipment manufacturer. OEMs buy business goods that they incorporate into the products that they produce for eventual sale to other producers or to consumers.

parts is that they can retain their identity after becoming part of the final product. For example, automobile tires are clearly recognizable as part of a car. Moreover, because component parts often wear out, they may need to be replaced several times during the life of the final product. Thus, there are two important markets for many component parts: the original equipment manufacturer (OEM) market and the replacement market.

Many of the business features listed earlier in Exhibit 5.5 characterize the **OEM** market. The difference between unit costs and selling prices in the OEM market is often small, but profits can be substantial because of volume buying.

The replacement market is composed of organizations and individuals buying component parts to replace worn-out parts. Because components often retain their identity in final products, users may choose to replace a component part with the same brand used by the manufacturer—for example, the same brand of automobile tires or battery. The replacement market operates differently from the OEM market, however. Whether replacement buyers are organizations or individuals, they tend to demonstrate the characteristics of consumer markets that were shown in Exhibit 5.5. Consider, for example, an automobile replacement part. Purchase volume is usually small and there are many customers, geographically dispersed, who typically buy from car dealers or parts stores. Negotiations do not occur, and neither reciprocity nor leasing is usually an issue.

Manufacturers of component parts often direct their advertising toward replacement buyers. Cooper Tire & Rubber, for example, makes and markets component parts—automobile and truck tires—for the replacement market only. General Motors and other car makers compete with independent firms in the market for replacement automobile parts.

Processed Materials

processed materials
Products used directly in manufacturing other products.

Processed materials are products used directly in manufacturing other products. Unlike raw materials, they have had some processing. Examples include sheet metal, chemicals, specialty steel, lumber, corn syrup, and plastics. Unlike component parts, processed materials do not retain their identity in final products.

Most processed materials are marketed to OEMs or to distributors servicing the OEM market. Processed materials are generally bought according to customer specifications or to some industry standard, as is the case with steel and lumber. Price and service are important factors in choosing a vendor.

Supplies

supplies
Consumable items that do not become part of the final product.

Supplies are consumable items that do not become part of the final product—for example, lubricants, detergents, paper towels, pencils, and paper. Supplies are normally standardized items that purchasing agents routinely buy. Supplies typically have relatively short lives and are inexpensive compared to other business goods. Because supplies generally fall into one of three categories—maintenance, repair, or operating supplies—this category is often referred to as MRO items.

Competition in the MRO market is intense. Bic and Paper Mate, for example, battle for business purchases of inexpensive ballpoint pens.

Business Services

business services
Expense items that do not become part of a final product.

Business services are expense items that do not become part of a final product. Businesses often retain outside providers to perform janitorial, advertising, legal, management consulting, marketing research, maintenance, and other services. Hiring an outside provider makes sense when it costs less than hiring or assigning an employee to perform the task and when an outside provider is needed for particular expertise.

Business Buying Behavior

As you probably have already concluded, business buyers behave differently from consumers. Understanding how purchase decisions are made in organizations is a first step in developing a business selling strategy. Business buying behavior has five important aspects: buying centers, evaluative criteria, buying situations, business ethics, and customer service.

Buying Centers

A **buying center** includes all those persons in an organization who become involved in the purchase decision. Membership and influence vary from company to company. For instance, in engineering-dominated firms like Bell Helicopter, the buying center may consist almost entirely of engineers. In marketing-oriented firms like Toyota and IBM, marketing and engineering have almost equal authority. In consumer goods firms like Procter & Gamble, product managers and other marketing decision makers may dominate the buying center. In a small manufacturing company, almost everyone may be a member.

The number of people involved in a buying center varies with the complexity and importance of a purchase decision. The composition of the buying group will usually change from one purchase to another and sometimes even during various stages of the buying process. To make matters more complicated, buying centers do not appear on formal organization charts.

For example, even though a formal committee may have been set up to choose a new plant site, it is only part of the buying center. Other people, like the company president, often play informal yet powerful roles. In a lengthy decision-making process, such as finding a new plant location, some members may drop out of the buying center when they can no longer play a useful role. Others whose talents are needed then become part of the center. No formal announcement of "who is in" and "who is out" is ever made.

Roles in the Buying Center

As in family purchasing decisions, several people may play a role in the business purchase process:

- *Initiator:* the person who first suggests making a purchase.

- *Influencers/evaluators:* people who influence the buying decision. They often help define specifications and provide information for evaluating options. Technical personnel are especially important as influencers.

- *Gatekeepers:* group members who regulate the flow of information. Frequently, the purchasing agent views the gatekeeping role as a source of his or her power. A secretary may also act as a gatekeeper by determining which vendors get an appointment with a buyer.

- *Decider:* the person who has the formal or informal power to choose or approve the selection of the supplier or brand. In complex situations, it is often difficult to determine who makes the final decision.

- *Purchaser:* the person who actually negotiates the purchase. It could be anyone from the president of the company to the purchasing agent, depending on the importance of the decision.

- *Users:* members of the organization who will actually use the product. Users often initiate the buying process and help define product specifications.

An example illustrating these basic roles is shown in Exhibit 5.6.

Discuss the unique aspects of business buying behavior

buying center
All those persons in an organization who become involved in the purchase decision.

Buying-Center Roles for
Computer Purchases

Role	Illustration
Initiator	Division general manager proposes to replace company's computer network.
Influencers/evaluators	Corporate controller's office and vice president of data processing have an important say about which system and vendor the company will deal with.
Gatekeepers	Corporate departments for purchasing and data processing analyze company's needs and recommend likely matches with potential vendors.
Decider	Vice president of administration, with advice from others, selects vendor the company will deal with and system it will buy.
Purchaser	Purchasing agent negotiates terms of sale.
Users	All division employees use the computers.

Implications of Buying Centers for the Marketing Manager

Successful vendors realize the importance of identifying who is in the decision-making unit, each member's relative influence in the buying decision, and each member's evaluative criteria. Successful selling strategies often focus on determining the most important buying influences and tailoring sales presentations to the evaluative criteria most important to these buying-center members.

For example, Loctite Corporation, the manufacturer of Super Glue and industrial adhesives and sealants, found that engineers were the most important influencers and deciders in adhesive and sealant purchase decisions. As a result, Loctite focused its marketing efforts on production and maintenance engineers.

Evaluative Criteria

Business buyers evaluate products and suppliers against three important criteria: quality, service, and price—in that order.

Quality

In this case, quality refers to technical suitability. A superior tool can do a better job in the production process, and superior packaging can increase dealer and consumer acceptance of a brand. Evaluation of quality also applies to the salesperson and the salesperson's firm. Business buyers want to deal with reputable salespeople and companies that are financially responsible. Quality improvement should be part of every organization's marketing strategy.

Service

Almost as much as they want satisfactory products, business buyers want satisfactory service. A purchase offers several opportunities for service.

One way that business buyers evaluate products and suppliers is by looking at the service the prospect provides. Covisint advertises itself as a more efficient way to conduct business with other businesses.

Suppose a vendor is selling heavy equipment. Prepurchase service could include a survey of the buyer's needs. After thorough analysis of the survey findings, the vendor could prepare a report and recommendations in the form of a purchasing proposal. If a purchase results, postpurchase service might consist of installing the equipment and training those who will be using it. Postsale services may also include maintenance and repairs. Another service that business buyers seek is dependability of supply. They must be able to count on delivery of what was ordered when it is scheduled to be delivered. Buyers also welcome services that help them sell their finished products. Services of this sort are especially appropriate when the seller's product is an identifiable part of the buyer's end product.

Price

Business buyers want to buy at low prices—at the lowest prices, under most circumstances. However, a buyer who pressures a supplier to cut prices to a point where the supplier loses money on the sale almost forces shortcuts on quality. The buyer also may, in effect, force the supplier to quit selling to him or her. Then a new source of supply will have to be found.

Buying Situations

Often business firms, especially manufacturers, must decide whether to make something or buy it from an outside supplier. The decision is essentially one of economics. Can an item of similar quality be bought at a lower price elsewhere? If not, is manufacturing it in-house the best use of limited company resources? For example, Briggs & Stratton Corporation, a major manufacturer of four-cycle engines, might be able to save $150,000 annually on outside purchases by spending $500,000 on the equipment needed to produce gas throttles internally. Yet Briggs & Stratton could also use that $500,000 to upgrade its carburetor assembly line, which would save $225,000 annually. If a firm does decide to buy a product instead of making it, the purchase will be a new buy, a modified rebuy, or a straight rebuy.

New Buy

A **new buy** is a situation requiring the purchase of a product for the first time. For example, suppose a manufacturing company needs a better way to page managers while they are working on the shop floor. Currently, each of the several managers has a distinct ring, for example, two short and one long, that sounds over the plant intercom whenever he or she is being paged by anyone in the factory. The company decides to replace its buzzer system of paging with handheld wireless radio technology that will allow managers to communicate immediately with the department initiating the page. This situation represents the greatest opportunity for new vendors. No long-term relationship has been established for this product, specifications may be somewhat fluid, and buyers are generally more open to new vendors.

new buy
A situation requiring the purchase of a product for the first time.

If the new item is a raw material or a critical component part, the buyer cannot afford to run out of supply. The seller must be able to convince the buyer that the seller's firm can consistently deliver a high-quality product on time.

Modified Rebuy

A **modified rebuy** is normally less critical and less time-consuming than a new buy. In a modified-rebuy situation, the purchaser wants some change in the original good or service. It may be a new color, greater tensile strength in a component part, more respondents in a marketing research study, or additional services in a janitorial contract.

Because the two parties are familiar with each other and credibility has been established, buyer and seller can concentrate on the specifics of the modification. But in some cases, modified rebuys are open to outside bidders. The purchaser uses this strategy to ensure that the new terms are competitive. An example would be the manufacturing company buying radios with a vibrating feature for managers who have trouble hearing the ring over the factory noise. The firm may open the bidding to examine the price/quality offerings of several suppliers.

Straight Rebuy

A **straight rebuy** is a situation vendors prefer. The purchaser is not looking for new information or other suppliers. An order is placed and the product is provided as in previous orders. Usually, a straight rebuy is routine because the terms of the purchase have been agreed to in earlier negotiations. An example would be the manufacturing company previously cited purchasing additional radios for new managers from the same supplier on a regular basis.

One common instrument used in straight-rebuy situations is the purchasing contract. Purchasing contracts are used with products that are bought often and in high volume. In essence, the purchasing contract makes the buyer's decision making routine and promises the salesperson a sure sale. The advantage to the buyer is a quick, confident decision and, to the salesperson, reduced or eliminated competition.

Suppliers must remember not to take straight-rebuy relationships for granted. Retaining existing customers is much easier than attracting new ones.

Business Ethics

The ethics of business buyer and seller relationships are often scrutinized and sometimes criticized by superiors, associates, other prospective suppliers, the general public, and the news media. Lockheed Martin Corporation, mindful of the key problems often faced by professional buyers and sellers, developed the ethical principles shown in the "Ethics in Marketing" box.

Customer Service

Business marketers are increasingly recognizing the benefits of developing a formal system to monitor customer opinions and perceptions of the quality of customer service. Companies like McDonald's, L.L. Bean, and Lexus build their strategies not only around products but also around a few highly developed service skills. Many firms are finding new ways to enhance customer service through technology. Business marketers are leading the way in adoption of new media technologies such as on-line services and CD-ROMs. For example, Honeywell has an on-line store that sells measurement and control instruments directly to corporate buyers. Honeywell's Industrial Store carries

The Code of Ethics at Lockheed Martin

The booklet, *Setting the Standard*, has been adopted by the Lockheed Martin Board of Directors as this company's Code of Ethics and Business Conduct, and summarizes the virtues and principles that are to guide actions in the global marketplace. The code deals both with "doing things right" and with "the right thing to do" so as to maintain personal and institutional integrity.

While maintaining sensitivity to the diverse social and cultural settings in which the company conducts business, Lockheed Martin aims to set the standard for ethical conduct at all of its localities throughout the world. The company strives to achieve this through behavior in accordance with six virtues: honesty, integrity, respect, trust, responsibility, and citizenship.

THE CODE

Honesty:
to be truthful in all our endeavors; to be honest and forthright with one another and with our customers, communities, suppliers, and shareholders.

Integrity:
to say what we mean, to deliver what we promise, and to stand for what is right.

Respect:
to treat one another with dignity and fairness, appreciating the diversity of our workforce and the uniqueness of each employee.

Trust:
to build confidence through teamwork and open, candid communication.

Responsibility:
to speak up—without fear of retribution—and report concerns in the workplace, including violations of laws, regulations, and company policies, and seek clarification and guidance whenever there is doubt.

Citizenship:
to obey all the laws of the countries in which we do business and to do our part to make the communities in which we live and work better.[19]

---

instruments used by industries ranging from refineries and chemicals to metal, mining, oil, gas, food, and pharmaceuticals. Prospective customers can get quotes and place orders on-line twenty-four hours per day, seven days per week. Orders are quickly filled by the company's order management system. W. W. Grainger sells about 20 percent of its $9 million per month sales on-line outside of normal business hours. Management believes that its electronic commerce business would grow more if its customer base of plant managers and janitors were more computer literate. Grainger is addressing the problem with workshops for customers.[20]

CONNECT IT

Look back at the story about General Motors at the beginning of the chapter. You now know that a strategic alliance is a cooperative agreement between business firms.

GM was motivated to form strategic alliances and joint ventures with Asian automakers to offset weak profits in the United States and to increase its share of the Asian market. GM has tried for several years to "crack" the Asian market on its own, but has not been very successful.

GM helps the Asian automakers by providing financial resources, technology, and lower parts costs. The Asian partners have access to markets through existing distribution networks. They also have a better understanding of local markets and customer buying behaviors.

USE IT

Explore the Possibilities
Starting a business at home is one of the easiest ways to become self-employed. Using the Home Office Association of America (HOAA) Web site (**http://www.hoaa.com**) for ideas, choose a possible business opportunity that interests you and that has business marketing possibilities. Then explore both the HOAA site and the American Association of Home-Based Businesses Web site (**http://www.aahbb.org**) to learn more about how to set up your business.

Learn from an Entrepreneur
What does it really take to become an entrepreneur? Find out by interviewing a local entrepreneur or researching an entrepreneur you've read about in this chapter or in the business press. Get answers to the following questions, as well as any others you'd like to ask:

- How did you develop your vision for the company?
- What are the most important entrepreneurial characteristics that helped you succeed?
- Where did you learn the business skills you needed to run and grow the company?
- How did you research the feasibility of your idea? Prepare your business idea?
- What were the biggest challenges you had to overcome?
- Where did you obtain financing for the company?
- How do you market your products and services to other businesses?
- What are the most important lessons you learned by starting this company?
- What advice do you have for would-be entrepreneurs?

REVIEW IT

1 **Describe business marketing.** Business marketing provides goods and services that are bought for use in business rather than for personal consumption. Intended use, not physical characteristics, distinguishes a business product from a consumer product.

1.1 **WRITING** As the marketing manager for Huggies diapers made by Kimberly-Clark, you are constantly going head-to-head with Pampers, produced by rival Procter & Gamble. You are considering unlocking the potential of the business market to increase your share of the disposable diaper market, but how? Write an outline of several ways you could transform this quintessentially consumer product into a successful business product as well.

2 **Describe the role of the Internet in business marketing.** The rapid expansion and adoption of the Internet have made business markets more competitive than ever before. The number of business buyers and sellers using the Internet is rapidly increasing. Firms are seeking new and better ways to expand markets and sources of supply, increase sales and decrease costs, and better serve customers. With the Internet, every business in the world is potentially a local competitor.

2.1 **ON LINE** How could you use the Web site **http://www.b2business.net** to help define a target market and develop a marketing plan?

2.2 **ON LINE** Reconsider question 1.1. How could you use the Internet in your business marketing of Huggies diapers?

3 **Discuss the role of relationship marketing and strategic alliances in business marketing.** Relationship marketing entails seeking and establishing long-term alliances or partnerships with customers. A strategic alliance is a cooperative agreement between business firms. Firms form alliances to leverage what they do well by partnering with others who have complementary skills.

3.1 Why is relationship or personal selling the best way to promote in business marketing?

④ Identify the four major categories of business market customers. Producer markets consist of for-profit organizations and individuals that buy products to use in producing other products, as components of other products, or in facilitating business operations. Reseller markets consist of wholesalers and retailers that buy finished products to resell for profit. Government markets include federal, state, county, and city governments that buy goods and services to support their own operations and serve the needs of citizens. Institutional markets consist of very diverse nonbusiness institutions whose main goals do not include profit.

4.1 *WRITING* *INFOTRAC COLLEGE EDITION* Understanding businesses is key to business marketing. Use Info-Trac (**http://www.infotrac-college.com**) to learn more about a variety of industries. Publications like *Manufacturing Automation, Computer Weekly, Power Generation Technology & Markets,* and *Biotech Equipment Update* can give you insights into many business marketing concepts. Research the industrial publications to find an article on a business marketer that interests you. Write a description of the company using as many concepts from the chapter as possible. What major category or categories of business market customers does this firm serve?

⑤ Explain the North American Industry Classification System. The NAICS provides a way to identify, analyze, segment, and target business and government markets. Organizations can be identified and compared by a numeric code indicating business sector, subsector, industry group, industry, and country industry. NAICS is a valuable tool for analyzing, segmenting, and targeting business markets.

5.1 *ON LINE* Explain how a marketer can use the Web site **http://www.census. gov/epcd/www/naics.html** to convert SIC data to the NAICS.

⑥ Explain the major differences between business and consumer markets. In business markets, demand is derived, price-inelastic, joint, and fluctuating. Purchase volume is much larger than in consumer markets, customers are fewer in number and more geographically concentrated, and distribution channels are more direct. Buying is approached more formally using professional purchasing agents, more people are involved in the buying process, negotiation is more complex, and reciprocity and leasing are more common. And, finally, selling strategy in business markets normally focuses on personal contact rather than on advertising.

6.1 How might derived demand affect the manufacturing of an automobile?

6.2 Your boss has just asked you, the company purchasing manager, to buy new computers for an entire department. Since you have just recently purchased a new home computer, you are well-educated about the various products available. How will your buying process for the company differ from your recent purchase for yourself?

⑦ Describe the seven types of business goods and services. Major equipment includes capital goods, such as heavy machinery. Accessory equipment is typically less expensive and shorter-lived than major equipment. Raw materials are extractive or agricultural products that have not been processed. Component parts are finished or near-finished items to be used as parts of other products. Processed materials are used to manufacture other products. Supplies are consumable and not used as part of a final product. Business services are intangible products that many companies use in their operations.

7.1 *WRITING* *TEAM* In small groups, brainstorm examples of companies that feature the products in different business categories. (Avoid examples already listed in the chapter.) Compile a list of ten specific business products including at least one in each category. Then match up with another group. Have each group take turns naming a product and have the other group identify its appropriate category. Try to resolve all discrepancies by discussion. Some identified products might appropriately fit into more than one category.

(8) Discuss the unique aspects of business buying behavior. Business buying behavior is distinguished by five fundamental characteristics. First, buying is normally undertaken by a buying center consisting of many people who range widely in authority level. Second, business buyers typically evaluate alternative products and suppliers based on quality, service, and price—in that order. Third, business buying falls into three general categories: new buys, modified rebuys, and straight rebuys. Fourth, the ethics of business buyers and sellers are often scrutinized. Fifth, customer service before, during, and after the sale plays a big role in business purchase decisions.

8.1 **WRITING** A colleague of yours has sent you an e-mail seeking your advice as he attempts to sell a new voice-mail system to a local business. Send him a return e-mail describing the various people who might influence the customer's buying decision. Be sure to include suggestions for dealing with the needs of each of these individuals.

8.2 Intel Corporation supplies microprocessors to Hewlett-Packard for use in its computers. Describe the buying situation in this relationship, keeping in mind the rapid advance of technology in this industry.

DEFINE IT

accessory equipment 171
business marketing 158
business services 172
buying center 173
component parts 171
derived demand 167
joint demand 168
keiretsu 162
major equipment
   (installations) 171

modified rebuy 176
multiplier effect (accelerator
   principle) 168
new buy 175
North American Industry
   Classification System
   (NAICS) 165
OEM 172
processed materials 172
raw materials 171

reciprocity 170
straight rebuy 176
strategic alliance (strategic
   partnership) 161
supplies 172

APPLY IT

Application for Entrepreneurs

ENTREPRENEUR Dan White is an independent video producer whose biggest client is the State of Illinois Agricultural Department. Although this account is big enough to support the entire business, Dan has developed other lines of business to eliminate the risks involved with having only one customer. Dan has also landed a sizable account through a high school friend who is the vice president of Good Hands Insurance. This also happens to be the company that underwrites Dan's life insurance. Additionally, Dan is hired to work on various projects for large production companies. Dan generated this business through long-term relationships built by working on projects for the state of Illinois.

As Dan prepares his business plan for the upcoming year, he is contemplating several strategic changes. Because of the increasing speed at which the video industry is evolving, Dan has observed two important trends. First, he is finding it increasingly difficult to own the latest video equipment that his customers are demanding. Second, Dan's clients are not able to keep up with the recent developments in the industry and would be willing to pay more for his expertise. Dan is looking into a lease for new equipment, and he is contemplating increasing the price of his services.

Questions

1. What two-digit NAICS code would you assign to Dan's business? For a complete list of all NAICS codes, see **http://www.census.gov/epcd/www/naics.html**.

2. Is Dan's choice to use Good Hands Insurance ethical? Why or why not?

3. How can Dan use the inelasticity of demand to his advantage?

4. Would you advise Dan to lease or buy the new equipment? Why?

THINK ABOUT IT

Ethics Exercise

Cameron Stock, purchasing manager for Goalie Keepaway, a sports equipment manufacturer, is responsible for buying $5 million of component parts and supplies every year. He has a preferred list of certified suppliers, many of which are awarded a large percentage of this business annually. Cameron has been offered an all-expense paid weekend for two in Las Vegas as a Christmas present from a major supplier with whom he has done business for close to a decade. Over this time, Cameron has built a very good relationship with the vendor.

Questions

1. Would it be legal and ethical for Cameron Stock to accept this gift?

2. How is this addressed in the AMA Code of Ethics? Go to the AMA Web site at **http://www.marketingpower.com** and reread the Code of Ethics. Write a brief paragraph summarizing where the AMA stands on the issue of supplier gifts.

TRY IT

Intrapreneurship Case
W. W. Grainger: Moving Maintenance to the Internet Space

 For more than seventy years, W. W. Grainger has kept the manufacturing and other labor-intensive industries on their collective feet by supplying the much-needed parts that help keep the machinery and operations running. From tape to electric motors, from chemicals to industrial-strength mops, and from lubricating fluids to lightbulbs, Grainger lists seventy thousand parts in its legendary seven-pound red catalog. In the $220 billion maintenance, repair, and operating supplies (MRO) market, this Chicago-based company has staked its claim to a $5 billion piece. It has shipped its catalog to purchasing and procurement officers in manufacturing and office-related environments for over seventy years, and has always enjoyed the reputation of being America's premier industrial supplier of replacement and supplemental parts. An Old Economy stalwart, Grainger is the kind of company that many would have predicted would have trouble with the dawning of widespread adoption of the Internet. Using Net storefronts, Grainger's suppliers would be able to sell directly to its customers, and its New Economy competition would be able to move faster, having built completely Internet-focused business models. Grainger, however, has adapted in a way few Old Economy companies have, and its successful entrepreneurship in the Internet space has quieted doubters and reaffirmed its position as the nation's leader in the MRO market.

To battle inefficiencies in its order taking and fulfillment process, Grainger looked to the Internet for a viable solution that would allow it to move quicker and offer more parts and more value-added services to its customer base. Grainger.com sells the complete Grainger catalog of parts. Search functions allow customers to drastically reduce the time needed to leaf through the standard catalog for parts. The site also shows real-time inventory status of those parts and greatly simplifies the process of placing large orders. The success of the initiative is reflected in the fact that the average order placed on-line is twice as large as traditional orders, and customers who buy primarily on-line spend

20 percent more over the course of the year than those ordering through the old red catalog.

Perhaps what has contributed to Grainger's success on the Internet is that its Web site is well laid out, intuitive to navigate, and void of unwanted clutter like annoying and intrusive banner ads. There is a simplicity in browsing Grainger's on-line catalog, placing an order, and searching for parts and service information that is not normally found on business-to-consumer Internet retail sites. Grainger knows its buyers are people who know what they want, who are probably repeat customers, and who will buy based on cost or quality alone. Branding and advertising are not likely to sway the industrial purchasing manager whose job it is to find the most cost-effective and reliable parts, regardless of looks, style, or presentation. That is not to say that there is no place for branding in business-to-business marketing. Quite the opposite. Functionality rules in that market, and purchasers are judged on whether they save money or procure reliable parts (not parts that represent any great style). So instead of differentiating their parts based on style or self-image, business-to-business marketers brand their products to convey images of performance, endurance, or low cost.

Grainger has taken a fresh approach to the art of business-to-business messaging. Instead of taking the traditional approach of showing a picture of a product in the center of the page and filling the surrounding space with text heralding the product's superiority, Grainger borrowed a technique generally reserved for business-to-consumer marketers.

Grainger is not worried about its Web business cannibalizing its existing paper catalog business. In fact, it has made the on-line ordering and fulfillment process so efficient and accurate that it is much more cost-effective than filling orders the old way. Don Bielinsky, the Grainger group president, envisions and hopes for a time when over 50 percent of all Grainger orders are placed and filled through the digital medium. Only those who are too slow or too small to conduct business on the Internet would place orders through the paper catalog, and in a world of cheap PCs and available free Internet access, those types of customers are rapidly dwindling.

Questions

1. List the benefits Grainger has enjoyed by moving its business on-line.

2. How would you classify the types of business products Grainger sells? To what business market does it sell?

3. How has Grainger adopted consumer-style promotions to improve its business marketing?

WATCH IT

Short

The FedEx ad on your dedicated PowerPoint CD-ROM shows how important business services are to companies in defraying costs and improving efficiencies. The ad uses humor to convey its message.

Medium

Companies dictating business practices to suppliers is all too common in today's business environment. Although often this arrangement is to the detriment of the supplier, sometimes it is to the supplier's benefit. Such is the case with the Conservation Company, which works to create sustainable farming practices in the coffee industry and raise the standard of living of coffee producers and coffee producing countries. Compare what you see in the CNN clip for

Chapter 5 with what you discover at the Wal-Mart supplier Web page from the "On-Line" activity on page 333. Decide how involved you think companies should be in their suppliers' affairs.

Long    SmallBusinessSchool ▣
the Series on PBS stations and the Web

To give you insight into Chapter 5, Small Business School will introduce you to the Souto family, owners of Rowland Roasters and its trademark brand of coffee, Café Pilon. When the Souto family immigrated to the United States from Cuba, it had to start over with nothing. Watch how this dynamic family rebuilt its business and grew it into a multimillion dollar enterprise that sells almost exclusively to other businesses.

 FLIP IT

Flip to Chapter 5 in your *Grademaker Study Guide* for more review opportunities, including the pretest, vocabulary review, Internet activities, study test questions, and business marketing scenarios. Do you know what distinguishes consumer products from business products? And can you list the four major categories of business market customers? Close your book and describe the seven types of business goods and services. Can't? Then flip open your Study Guide to brush up.

 CLICK IT

The *Essentials of Marketing* Web site links you to all the Internet-based activities in this chapter, like "Use It," "Review It" questions 2.1, 2.2, 4.1, and 5.1, "Apply It," and the On-Line exercises in the chapter margins. As a review, do the Chapter 5 quiz and crossword puzzle. You can also work the Career Exersite that shows you different resources for careers in the area of business marketing. Or review the main concepts in the PowerPoint presentation for Chapter 5. Go to **http://lamb.swlearning.com**, read the material, and follow the links right from the site.

Surf to Xtra! to test your understanding of business marketing by completing the worksheets for Exhibits 5.1, 5.2, and 5.6. If your instructor has assigned a marketing plan project, worksheets on Xtra! can help you organize your work. In addition to the quiz on the Web site, there's another quiz on Xtra!, plus video of the authors answering frequently asked questions about business marketing, such as "How can demand for business products be both derived and widely fluctuating?" and "What is an extranet?"

Still Shaky? Here's a Tip.

Find a study partner and have him or her quiz you using the end-of-chapter materials and the quizzes on Xtra!. Try to give the rationale for each of your answers.

CHAPTER **SIX**

SEGMENTING AND TARGETING MARKETS

Learning Objectives

1 Describe the characteristics of markets and market segments

2 Explain the importance of market segmentation

3 Discuss criteria for successful market segmentation

4 Describe the bases commonly used to segment consumer markets

5 Describe the bases for segmenting business markets

6 List the steps involved in segmenting markets

7 Discuss alternative strategies for selecting target markets

8 Explain how and why firms implement positioning strategies and how product differentiation plays a role

9 Discuss global market segmentation and targeting issues

Hair care in the United States is a $45 billion industry. Hair care for kids under age twelve makes up approximately $5 billion of that market. Therefore, servicing only kids excludes nearly 90 percent of the market, and thus does not appear to represent a viable market segment. Furthermore, stylists have traditionally avoided this market because the customers tend to wiggle and wail and may even bite the hand that shears them.

However, the kids' haircutting industry is growing. Since 1995, at least four new children's haircutting chains have opened around the country. They join established kids' salons such as Cartoon Cuts, a $4.5 billion, sixteen-unit outfit whose first facility opened in Fairfax, Virginia, in 1991, and $2 million-plus Kids' Hair, Inc., which launched the first of ten stores in 1992 in Edina, Minnesota. The growth spurt is similar to that of children's specialty retail stores like GapKids and Gymboree, which emerged in the mid-1980s to take advantage of baby boomers' lavish spending on their kids.

Most of the new kids' haircutting chains began as regional enterprises, but many have plans to expand. One exception is Cool Cuts, whose founder from the start envisioned a national chain with hundreds of outlets. The company uses computer systems to capture point-of-sale customer data to learn each potential location's socioeconomic makeup. These data, combined with sophisticated mapping that superimposes spending habits on demographic and economic data such as median home values, household income, and number and ages of children, allow the company to pinpoint the most lucrative spots for new sites.

While the chains have similarities—all claim to have superior customer service and consistent offerings—each one has its own variation on the kids theme. Cool Cuts, for example, divides its waiting area into two sides. For kids age six and under, a gated-in play space is stocked with Legos and videos such as *Barney* and *Sesame Street*. For older children there is an area stocked with Nintendo 64 stations. Kid Snips sells toys and splashes whimsical jungle creatures on its walls. Stylists at Cartoon Cuts wash as well as cut their customers' hair, dousing the suds with hoses that project from the trunks of green fiberglass elephants. For the most part, though, kids' salons make use of universal elements. Crayons, toys, and videos entertain waiting customers. Televisions (with or without VCRs) and video game systems are placed at cutting stations.

Specialty chairs—a rocket ship, a jeep, a racecar—or standard salon chairs outfitted with booster seats are the furniture of choice. Stylists blow bubbles and offer balloons and lollipops or small prizes.

The child is not the only customer in this niche, however. Parents are customers too. For example, at Snip-its, there are no crayons or toys. Nor are there the specialty chairs that are typically found at kids' salons. Instead, each station has either a child-sized salon chair or a standard salon chair (for older kids and lap sitters), as well a big cushy "parents" chair, which allows moms and dads to instruct the stylist without feeling they are in the way. Treehouse bills itself as a family destination, cutting the hair of little ones, their teenage siblings, and adults, and offering family packages.[1]

Based on this story, how would you define market segmentation and targeting? What type of targeting strategy are kids' hair salons using? Do you think the kids' market is a viable segment for salons to target? Explain your answer. This chapter will help you answer these questions and more.

Market Segmentation

1

Describe the characteristics of markets and market segments

market
People or organizations with needs or wants and the ability and willingness to buy.

market segment
A subgroup of people or organizations sharing one or more characteristics that cause them to have similar product needs.

market segmentation
The process of dividing a market into meaningful, relatively similar, and identifiable segments or groups.

The term *market* means different things to different people. We are all familiar with the supermarket, stock market, labor market, fish market, and flea market. All these types of markets share several characteristics. First, they are composed of people (consumer markets) or organizations (business markets). Second, these people or organizations have wants and needs that can be satisfied by particular product categories. Third, they have the ability to buy the products they seek. Fourth, they are willing to exchange their resources, usually money or credit, for desired products. In sum, a **market** is (1) people or organizations with (2) needs or wants and with (3) the ability and (4) the willingness to buy. A group of people or an organization that lacks any one of these characteristics is not a market.

Within a market, a **market segment** is a subgroup of people or organizations sharing one or more characteristics that cause them to have similar product needs. At one extreme, we can define every person and every organization in the world as a market segment because each is unique. At the other extreme, we can define the entire consumer market as one large market segment and the business market as another large segment. All people have some similar characteristics and needs, as do all organizations.

From a marketing perspective, market segments can be described as somewhere between the two extremes. The process of dividing a market into meaningful, relatively similar, and identifiable segments or groups is called **market segmentation**. The purpose of market segmentation is to enable the marketer to tailor marketing mixes to meet the needs of one or more specific segments.

Exhibit 6.1 illustrates the concept of market segmentation. Each box represents a market consisting of seven persons. This market might vary as follows: one homogeneous market of seven people, a market consisting of seven individual segments, a market composed of two segments based on gender, a market composed of three age segments, or a market composed of five age and gender market segments. Age and gender and many other bases for segmenting markets are examined later in this chapter.

The Importance of Market Segmentation

2

Explain the importance of market segmentation

Until the 1960s, few firms practiced market segmentation. When they did, it was more likely a haphazard effort than a formal marketing strategy. Before 1960, for example, the Coca-Cola Company produced only one beverage and aimed it at the entire soft drink market. Today, Coca-Cola offers over a dozen different products to market segments based on diverse consumer preferences for flavors and calorie and caffeine content. Coca-Cola offers traditional soft drinks, energy drinks (such as Power Ade), flavored teas, fruit drinks (Fruitopia), and water (Dasani).

Market segmentation plays a key role in the marketing strategy of almost all successful organizations and is a powerful marketing tool for several reasons. Most importantly, nearly all markets include groups of people or organizations with different product needs and preferences. Market segmentation helps marketers define customer needs and wants more precisely. Because market segments differ in size and potential, segmentation helps decision makers more accurately define marketing objectives and better allocate resources. In turn, performance can be better evaluated when objectives are more precise.

Chico's, a successful women's fashion retailer, thrives by marketing to women aged thirty-five to fifty-five who like to wear comfortable, yet stylish clothing. It sells private-label clothing that comes in just a few nonjudgmental sizes: zero (regular sizes 4–6), one (8–10), two (10–12), and three (14–16). The Chico's look, built mainly around wash-and-wear fabrics, is loose and colorful. Prices are mod-

Exhibit 6.1

Concept of Market Segmentation

No market segmentation

Fully segmented market

Market segmentation
by gender: M, F

Market segmentation
by age group: 1, 2, 3

Market segmentation
by gender and age group

erate, ranging from $20 to $150. Chico's has developed a loyal base of customers and is a fast-growing retailer.[2]

Criteria for Successful Segmentation

Marketers segment markets for three important reasons. First, segmentation enables marketers to identify groups of customers with similar needs and to analyze the characteristics and buying behavior of these groups. Second, segmentation provides marketers with information to help them design marketing mixes specifically matched with the characteristics and desires of one or more segments. Third, segmentation is consistent with the marketing concept of satisfying customer wants and needs while meeting the organization's objectives.

To be useful, a segmentation scheme must produce segments that meet four basic criteria:

*   *Substantiality:* A segment must be large enough to warrant developing and maintaining a special marketing mix. This criterion does not necessarily mean that a segment must have many potential customers. Marketers of custom-designed homes and business buildings, commercial airplanes, and large computer systems typically develop marketing programs tailored to each potential customer's needs. In most cases, however, a market segment needs many potential customers to make commercial sense. In the 1980s, home banking failed because not enough people owned personal computers. Today, a larger number of people own computers, and home banking is a growing industry.

*   *Identifiability and measurability:* Segments must be identifiable and their size measurable. Data about the population within geographic boundaries, the

Discuss criteria for successful market segmentation

number of people in various age categories, and other social and demographic characteristics are often easy to get, and they provide fairly concrete measures of segment size. Suppose that a social service agency wants to identify segments by their readiness to participate in a drug and alcohol program or in prenatal care. Unless the agency can measure how many people are willing, indifferent, or unwilling to participate, it will have trouble gauging whether there are enough people to justify setting up the service.

- *Accessibility:* The firm must be able to reach members of targeted segments with customized marketing mixes. Some market segments are hard to reach—for example, senior citizens (especially those with reading or hearing disabilities), individuals who don't speak English, and the illiterate.

- *Responsiveness:* As Exhibit 6.1 illustrates, markets can be segmented using any criteria that seem logical. Unless one market segment responds to a marketing mix differently from other segments, however, that segment need not be treated separately. For instance, if all customers are equally price-conscious about a product, there is no need to offer high-, medium-, and low-priced versions to different segments.

Bases for Segmenting Consumer Markets

Describe the bases commonly used to segment consumer markets

segmentation bases (variables)
Characteristics of individuals, groups, or organizations.

Marketers use **segmentation bases,** or **variables,** which are characteristics of individuals, groups, or organizations, to divide a total market into segments. The choice of segmentation bases is crucial because an inappropriate segmentation strategy may lead to lost sales and missed profit opportunities. The key is to identify bases that will produce substantial, measurable, and accessible segments that exhibit different response patterns to marketing mixes.

Markets can be segmented using a single variable, such as age group, or several variables, such as age group, gender, and education. Although it is less precise, single-variable segmentation has the advantage of being simpler and easier to use than multiple-variable segmentation. The disadvantages of multiple-variable segmentation are that it is often harder to use than single-variable segmentation; usable secondary data are less likely to be available; and as the number of segmentation bases increases, the size of individual segments decreases. Nevertheless, the current trend is toward using more rather than fewer variables to segment most markets. Multiple-variable segmentation is clearly more precise than single-variable segmentation.

Consumer goods marketers commonly use one or more of the following characteristics to segment markets: geography, demographics, psychographics, benefits sought, and usage rate.

Geographic Segmentation

geographic segmentation
Segmenting markets by region of a country or the world, market size, market density, or climate.

Geographic segmentation refers to segmenting markets by region of a country or the world, market size, market density, or climate. Market density means the number of people within a unit of land, such as a census tract. Climate is commonly used for geographic segmentation because of its dramatic impact on residents' needs and purchasing behavior. Snowblowers, water and snow skis, clothing, and air-conditioning and heating systems are products with varying appeal, depending on climate.

Consumer goods companies take a regional approach to marketing for four reasons. First, many firms need to find new ways to generate sales because of sluggish and intensely competitive markets. Second, computerized checkout stations with scanners enable retailers to assess accurately which brands sell best in their region. Third, many packaged-goods manufacturers are introducing new regional brands intended to appeal to local preferences. Fourth, a more regional approach

Bringing Science to Weight Loss in China

On a recent afternoon, five chubby teenagers, two women of normal build, and a man with a potbelly came to the Sino-Japanese Friendship Hospital. They are asked about their eating habits, then step on a high-tech scale connected to a computer, which calculates body mass and prints out an elaborate diet and exercise regimen. Each person also leaves the hospital with a bottle of a weight-loss drug called Xenical.

"I feel more secure seeing a doctor. At least there's less of a chance of getting cheated," says Cai Shuang, an eighteen-year old in baggy denim shorts and high tops who says she has tried several weight-loss pills advertised on television.

This is the kind of customer Roche Holding AG, the Swiss maker of Xenical, is hoping will help it conquer China's booming market in weight-loss products. China has hundreds of weight-loss treatments ranging from "slimming soups" to a traditional herb laxative, *dahuang*, derived from the rhubarb plant. As with the rest of China's pharmaceutical industry, shams and scams abound, piracy is rampant, claims are overblown, and regulation is minimal—a situation that has led many foreign drugmakers to target the country.

Roche is hoping to bring science to the business of weight loss in China. Its patented Xenical, which works by blocking fat absorption and was introduced in China in January 2001, is the first prescription weight-loss drug approved by the Chinese government: All other weight-loss products are labeled "health products" and cannot be sold in hospitals or prescribed by doctors. Roche has set up high-end hospital clinics in major cities and trained doctors at each one. It is counting on the doctors to help sell patients on the benefits of Xenical.

As China's economy is growing, obesity is becoming a serious national health problem. Western pharmaceutical companies are trying to bring science to China's weight-loss market, but they are having difficulty penetrating a market that is comfortable self-prescribing traditional medicines, like those pictured here, without consulting a physician.

Roche, as well as other drug companies, face cultural hurdles in China. Many Chinese have some knowledge of traditional medicine and feel comfortable prescribing for themselves instead of seeing a doctor. Also, most Chinese people see weight as more of a cosmetic than a health issue, as do many doctors. Furthermore, it is not clear that Chinese consumers want to go to hospitals for their dieting advice. Many state-run hospitals have outdated facilities and require hours-long waits.

China ranks second after the United States in terms of the number of obese people, which numbers about seventy million. Over the past ten years, consumption of meat, fast food, and soft drinks in the country has increased with incomes. A generation that can still remember malnutrition and famine now worries about diseases like diabetes, hypertension, and the obesity that facilitates both. However, unlike in the United States, where many people understand basic nutrition and exercise, China is awash in ignorance. And the rapid pace of change in people's lives means that they are still eating as they used to even though they are no longer engaged in the physical labor they once were.

While Roche will not reveal actual numbers, it says sales of Xenical in China are growing between 30 percent and 50 percent a month.[3]

What cultural differences do manufacturers of obesity drugs like Roche have to contend with in China? Do you think China will continue to be a lucrative market segment for makers of obesity drugs to target? Explain your answer.

---

allows consumer goods companies to react more quickly to competition. For example, Cracker Barrel, a restaurant known in the South for home-style cooking, is altering its menu outside its core southern market to reflect local tastes. Customers in upstate New York can order Reuben sandwiches, and those in Texas can get eggs with salsa. Miller Lite developed the "Miller Lite True to Texas" marketing program, a statewide campaign targeting Texas beer drinkers. The "Global Perspectives" box provides another example of geographic market segmentation.

Demographic Segmentation

Marketers often segment markets on the basis of demographic information because it is widely available and often related to consumers' buying and consuming behavior. Some common bases of **demographic segmentation** are age, gender, income, ethnic background, and family life cycle. The discussion here provides some important information about the main demographic segments.

Age Segmentation

Attracting children is a popular strategy for many companies because they hope to instill brand loyalty early. Furthermore, children influence a great deal of family consumption. There are three subsegments in the children's market: young children (under age nine), tweens (ages nine to twelve), and teens (ages twelve to nineteen).

The U.S. Census projects there will be more than thirty-eight million children under age nine in the United States in 2005. High-end playthings like luxurious playhouses and BMW skateboards are gaining in popularity with children.[4] Nickelodeon, once simply a television network for kids, now publishes three magazines for this target market: *Nickelodeon*, an entertainment and humor book; *Rugrats Comic Adventures*, a comic book spun off from the popular TV show; and *Crayola Kids*, aimed at kids and their parents.[5] Older children, dubbed "tweens," number about twenty million and have an estimated spending power of $20 billion.[6] Tweens desire to be kids, but also want some of the fun and glamour of being a teenager.[7] Many retailers, such as Limited Too and abercrombie, are targeting tweens by selling clothing that is similar in style to the more teen- and young adult–oriented stores Limited and Abercrombie & Fitch. Teens, sometimes referred to as Generation Y, number thirty-two million, and represent approximately $153 billion in spending power. Teens spend most of their money on clothing, entertainment, and food. Teens can be loyal to companies that reach them, and they seem to prefer smaller, niche brands, such as Burton Snowboards, Femme Arsenal (a cosmetics firm), and Razor USA (markets push scooters and apparel).[8] The dairy industry is trying to make drinking milk cool among teenagers by selling sixteen-ounce bottles of milk in vending machines decorated with large pictures of the famous "Got Milk?" ads featuring skateboarder Tony Hawk or members of the Backstreet Boys band wearing milk mustaches.[9]

Age segmentation can clearly define your target, but it can also be restrictive. Volvo has broken out of its older, family image by launching a new ad campaign with ads like the one pictured. The goal is to attract youthful Gen X-ers to a brand most typically associated with family life.

COURTESY OF VOLVO CARS OF NORTH AMERICA

Other age segments are also appealing targets for marketers. The approximately fifty-eight million people classified as young adults, between twenty and thirty-four years of age, are being targeted by many beer, wine, and spirits companies. For example, Bacardi Ltd. hired a young marketing team to develop ads for Dewars Scotch. The team dropped the "mixability" angle stressed in previous ads and revived the famous Dewars profiles campaign, showing adventure-seeking twenty-five- to thirty-four-year olds. The campaign appeals to Generation X by focusing on people following their dreams and not just evoking money and success.[10] The computer-literate Gen X-ers also are a large and viable market for the Internet.

The baby boom generation, born between 1946 and 1964, comprises the largest age segment—about 30 percent of the entire U.S. population. Many in this group are approaching (or past) fifty years of age and are continuing to lead active, fully involved lifestyles. Now that many in this group are in or headed toward their fifties, they are changing the way people look at aging, which presents an opportunity for brands to reposition themselves and to be more lifestyle oriented. Starwood Hotels, for instance, designed its W chain to appeal to a young, hip crowd. But the company has been surprised at how much the hotels are attracting baby boomers.[11] Walgreens is opening many new drugstores in Sun Belt states, such as Florida, Texas, California, and Arizona, because that is where the baby boomers will retire and prescription sales will soar.[12]

Seniors (aged sixty-five and over) are especially attracted to companies that build relationships by taking the time to get to know them and their preferences. As an example, older customers say they prefer catalog shopping to retail outlets because of dissatisfaction with customer service at retail stores. People of this age group are more likely than most to have the combination of free time, money, and health that lets them pursue leisure-time activities, especially education and travel. Boston-based Elderhostel, a large education organization for older adults, enrolled 250,000 students last year in about ten thousand courses worldwide. And travelers fifty-five and older took nearly a third of the trips made within the United States in 1999.[13] In addition, though the senior audience may be coming on-line later than their younger counterparts, it is a large audience— one that is driven by a desire to stay in touch and stay connected.[14]

Gender Segmentation

Marketers of products such as clothing, cosmetics, personal-care items, magazines, jewelry, and footwear commonly segment markets by gender. Men aged eighteen to forty-nine are the segment most likely to purchase goods on-line. Many Internet companies have advertised to this group to build their brands and get exposure for their sites. For example, Blue Nile, one of the most successful on-line jewelry retailers, targets men who dislike jewelry stores, even though most of the jewelry it sells is for women.[15] However, brands that have traditionally been marketed to men, such as Gillette razors and Rogaine baldness remedy, are increasing their efforts to attract women. Computer and video game companies have traditionally targeted young men, but Interactive Digital Software Association, a trade group, found that women are buying just as much game software as men. As a result, more game companies and Web sites are focusing their marketing efforts on girls and women.[16] Conversely, "women's" products such as cosmetics, household products, and furniture are also being marketed to men. About 35 percent of the buyers of Tommy Hilfiger's beauty-care products are young men, who buy items such as Tommy's Remote Control Hair gel and Juiced Up orange-scented soap.[17] Rodale, Inc., is bringing out a new magazine for teenage boys called MH-18, which focuses on teen boys' lifestyles.[18]

© L. CLARKE/CORBIS

Gender segmentation can be a tricky, yet profitable, form of segmentation, particularly for companies that launch unique product offerings for each gender. One such example is video games. Once marketers discovered that girls and women buy as much game software as boys and men, more companies began to focus marketing efforts on both genders— and with great success.

Income Segmentation

Income is a popular demographic variable for segmenting markets because income level influences consumers' wants and determines their buying power. Many markets are segmented by income, including the markets for housing, clothing, automobiles, and food. For example, wholesale clubs Costco and Sam's Club appeal to different income segments. Costco attracts more upscale customers with warehouse prices for gourmet foods and upscale brands like Waterford crystal, Raymond Weil watches, and Ralph Lauren clothing. Sam's Club, on the other hand, originally focused more on members' business needs, offering bulk packages of the kinds of items sold in Wal-Mart's discount stores and supercenters. Sam's Club is now trying to win more upscale customers by adding items like jewelry and gourmet food.[19]

Ethnic Segmentation

Many companies are segmenting their markets by ethnicity. The three largest ethnic markets are the African American, Hispanic American, and Asian American. These three groups collectively are projected to make up one-third of the country's population by 2010, and have a combined buying power of more than $1 trillion. Ethnic communities also make up significant portions of many major metropolitan areas, including New York, Chicago, Los Angeles, and Miami.[20]

African Americans African Americans are the largest minority group in the United States, and their population is expected to grow to more than forty-five million by 2020. They spend more than whites on luxury items such as cars, clothing, and home furnishings. Consequently, a number of companies market specifically to African Americans. Coca-Cola runs television ads featuring as-yet-undiscovered black music artists like Tyrese and Ja Rule before they hit the big time.[21] As part of its sponsorship of the National Association of Black Journalists convention, DaimlerChrysler AG offers a "Ride & Drive" program that provides cars to attendees so that they can visit local attractions.[22] The Internet is of growing importance as a medium to reach the African American consumer. While Net use among this group lags behind that of the white population (28 percent of blacks versus 37 percent of whites), African Americans who are on-line are younger, more affluent, and better educated than African Americans who do not use the Internet. In addition, nearly 30 percent intend to place orders on-line, compared with 21 percent of the general population.[23] Web sites such as **http://www.netnoir.com** and **http://www.afronet.com** attract thousands of African Americans with news, information, entertainment, and products of interest to their audiences.

Hispanic Americans The U.S. Hispanic population numbers more than thirty million, accounting for more than 11 percent of the total population. By 2050, Hispanic Americans will comprise almost a quarter of the population. This group also has substantial buying power, estimated to be between $273 billion and $445 billion.[24]

Companies are increasingly directing marketing efforts at Hispanic Americans. Gateway, the computer manufacturer, launched a marketing program that included TV and radio ads in Spanish, a toll-free number for Spanish-speaking clients, and representatives in sales, customer service, and tech support who are fluent in the language.[25] Hormel has developed a family of Mexican brands, including salsas, peppers, juices, and chiles, called Herdez, and its advertising highlights the line's authentic heritage.[26] Hallmark Cards has designed a line of greeting cards to commemorate the Mexican holiday, Cinco de Mayo.[27] Liz Claiborne launched Mambo, advertising it as the first-ever "Latino" scent for young Americans.[28]

Asian Americans Like Hispanic Americans, Asian Americans are a diverse group with thirteen submarkets. The five largest are Chinese, Filipino, Japanese, Asian Indian, and Korean. This fast-growing market of 10.2 million is younger and better educated than the general market and has the highest average household income in the United States.

Some entrepreneurs are building large enclosed malls that cater to Asian consumers. At the Aberdeen Centre near Vancouver, British Columbia, nearly 80 percent of the merchants are Chinese Canadians, as are 80 percent of the customers. The mall offers fashions made in Hong Kong, a shop for traditional Chinese medicines, and a theater showing Chinese movies. Kung fu martial arts demonstrations and Chinese folk dances are held in the mall on weekends.

Family Life-Cycle Segmentation

The demographic factors of gender, age, and income often do not sufficiently explain why consumer buying behavior varies. Frequently, consumption patterns among people of the same age and gender differ because they are in different stages of the family life cycle. The **family life cycle (FLC)** is a series of stages determined by a combination of age, marital status, and the presence or absence of children.

Traditional families—married couples with children younger than eighteen years—constituted just 23.5 percent of all U.S. households according to the 2000 census data. Such families represented 30.2 percent of households in 1980 and 45 percent in 1960.[29] Exhibit 6.2 on page 194 illustrates both traditional and contemporary FLC patterns and shows how families' needs, incomes, resources, and expenditures differ at each stage. The horizontal flow shows the traditional family life cycle. The lower part of the exhibit gives some of the characteristics and purchase patterns of families in each stage of the traditional life cycle. The exhibit also acknowledges that about half of all first marriages end in divorce. When young marrieds move into the young divorced stage, their consumption patterns often revert back to those of the young single stage of the cycle. About four out of five divorced persons remarry by middle age and reenter the traditional life cycle, as indicated by the "recycled flow" in the exhibit. Charles Schwab Corporation, the San Francisco financial-services firm, ran a television ad featuring Sarah Ferguson, the Duchess of York and a divorced mom. The ad shows Ferguson telling a bedtime story to a little girl, and the story ends with the importance of girls understanding their financial choices. Schwab is eager to reach single women because they have a heightened interest in financial strategies.[30]

Psychographic Segmentation

Age, gender, income, ethnicity, family life-cycle stage, and other demographic variables are usually helpful in developing segmentation strategies, but often they don't paint the entire picture. Demographics provides the skeleton, but psychographics adds meat to the bones. **Psychographic segmentation** is market segmentation on the basis of the following variables:

- *Personality:* Personality reflects a person's traits, attitudes, and habits. Porsche Cars North America understood well the demographics of the Porsche owner: a forty-something male college graduate earning over $200,000 per year. However, research discovered that this general demographic category included five personality types that more effectively segmented Porsche buyers. Exhibit 6.3 on page 195 describes the five segments. Porsche refined its marketing as a result of the study, and, after a previous seven-year slump, the company's U.S. sales rose 48 percent.[31]

- *Motives:* Marketers of baby products and life insurance appeal to consumers' emotional motives—namely, to care for their loved ones. Using appeals to economy, reliability, and dependability, carmakers like Subaru and Suzuki target customers with rational motives. Carmakers like Mercedes-Benz, Jaguar, and Cadillac appeal to customers with status-related motives.

- *Lifestyles:* Lifestyle segmentation divides people into groups according to the way they spend their time, the importance of the things around them, their beliefs, and socioeconomic characteristics such as income and education. For example, Harley-

family life cycle (FLC)
A series of stages determined by a combination of age, marital status, and the presence or absence of children.

psychographic segmentation
Market segmentation on the basis of personality, motives, lifestyles, and geodemographics.

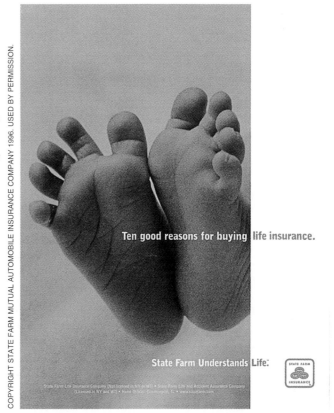

COPYRIGHT STATE FARM MUTUAL AUTOMOBILE INSURANCE COMPANY 1996. USED BY PERMISSION.

Ten good reasons for buying life insurance.

State Farm Understands Life.

This ad for State Farm clearly appeals to consumers' emotional motives by associating the purchase of life insurance with the caring and responsibility of parenting.

| **Exhibit 6.2** | Family Life Cycle |

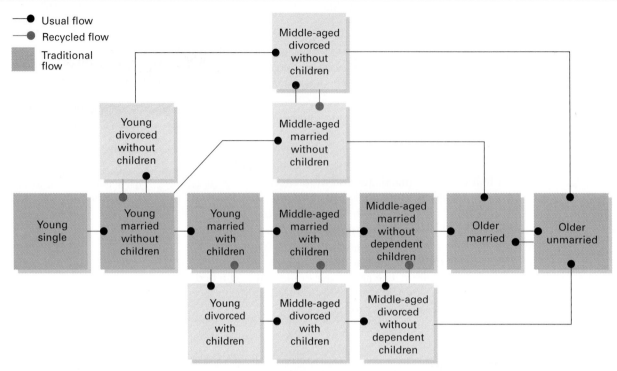

- Usual flow
- Recycled flow
- Traditional flow

Young single
Few financial burdens
Fashion opinion leaders
Recreation-oriented
Buy: basic kitchen equipment, basic furniture, cars, equipment for mating game, vacations

Young married without children
Better off financially than they will be in near future
Highest purchase rate and highest average purchase of durables
Buy: cars, refrigerators, stoves, sensible and durable furniture, vacations

Young married with children
Home purchasing at peak
Liquid assets low
Dissatisfied with financial position and amount of money saved
Interested in new products
Like advertised products
Buy: washers, dryers, televisions, baby food, chest rubs, cough medicine, vitamins, dolls, wagons, sleds, skates

Middle-aged married with children
Financial position still better
More wives work
Some children get jobs
Hard to influence with advertising
High average purchase of durables
Buy: new and more tasteful furniture, auto travel, unnecessary appliances, boats, dental services, magazines

Middle-aged married without children
Home ownership at peak
Most satisfied with financial position and money saved
Interested in travel, recreation, self-education
Make gifts and contributions
Not interested in new products
Buy: vacations, luxuries, home improvements

Older married
Drastic cut in income
Keep home
Buy: medical appliances, medical care, products that aid health, sleep, and digestion

Older unmarried
Drastic cut in income
Special need for attention, affection, and security
Buy: same medical and product needs as other retired group

Davidson divides its customers into seven lifestyle segments, from "cocky misfits" who are most likely to be arrogant troublemakers, to "laid-back camper types" committed to cycling and nature, to "classy capitalists" who have wealth and privilege.[32]

geodemographic segmentation
Segmenting potential customers into neighborhood lifestyle categories.

- *Geodemographics:* **Geodemographic segmentation** clusters potential customers into neighborhood lifestyle categories. It combines geographic, demographic, and lifestyle segmentations. Geodemographic segmentation helps marketers develop marketing programs tailored to prospective buyers who live in small geographic regions, such as neighborhoods, or who have very specific lifestyle and demographic characteristics. Central Market, an upscale H-E-B Company food store that sells groceries and prepared foods, has several locations in

Exhibit 6.3

Taxonomy of Porsche Buyers

Type	% of All	Owners Description
Top Guns	27%	Driven, ambitious types. Power and control matter. They expect to be noticed.
Elitists	24%	Old-money blue bloods. A car is just a car, no matter how expensive. It is not an extension of personality.
Proud Patrons	23%	Ownership is an end in itself. Their car is a trophy earned for hard work, and who cares if anyone sees them in it?
Bon Vivants	17%	Worldly jet setters and thrill seekers. Their car heightens the excitement in their already passionate lives.
Fantasists	9%	Walter Mitty types. Their car is an escape. Not only are they uninterested in impressing others with it, they also feel a little guilty about owning one.

Texas, and the merchandise mix varies according to the location. In Fort Worth there is a strong Western influence, so the company installed a smoker at that store to smoke beef and poultry—something its other stores do not have. The Hispanic market is strong in San Antonio and Fort Worth, so those stores stock a wide selection of fresh and dried peppers, avocados, and tomatoes.[33]

Psychographic variables can be used individually to segment markets or be combined with other variables to provide more detailed descriptions of market segments. One combination approach is the Claritas PRIZM Lifestyle software program that divides Americans into sixty-two "clusters," or consumer types, all with catchy names. The clusters combine basic demographic data such as age, ethnicity, and income with lifestyle information, such as magazine and sports preferences, taken from consumer surveys. For example, the "Kids and Cul-de-Sacs" group are upscale, suburban families with a median household income of $68,900 who tend to shop on-line and visit Disney theme parks. The "Bohemian Mix" cluster are professionals aged twenty-five to forty-four with a median income of $38,500 who are likely to shop at Gap, and read *Elle* magazine. The program also predicts to which neighborhoods across the country the clusters are likely to gravitate. Using PRIZM, Hyundai chose zip codes with a high percentage of promising clusters and sent test-drive offers only to those areas (instead of blanketing entire cities with the offer). In those markets, Hyundai not only increased the number of people showing up for a test-drive but also increased its sales and cut its costs per vehicle sold in half.[34]

Benefit Segmentation

Benefit segmentation is the process of grouping customers into market segments according to the benefits they seek from the product. Most types of market segmentation are based on the assumption that this variable and customers' needs are related. Benefit segmentation is different because it groups potential customers on

benefit segmentation
The process of grouping customers into market segments according to the benefits they seek from the product.

the basis of their needs or wants rather than some other characteristic, such as age or gender. The snack-food market, for example, can be divided into six benefit segments, as shown in Exhibit 6.4.

Customer profiles can be developed by examining demographic information associated with people seeking certain benefits. This information can be used to match marketing strategies with selected target markets. Procter & Gamble introduced Pampers Rash Guard, a diaper designed to combat diaper rash. To attract time-pressed consumers, Tops Friendly Markets supermarket chain is building stores half the size of some existing ones and emphasizing efficient shopping by locating carry-out foods near the front of the store and similar features.[35]

Usage-Rate Segmentation

usage-rate segmentation
Dividing a market by the amount of product bought or consumed.

Usage-rate segmentation divides a market by the amount of product bought or consumed. Categories vary with the product, but they are likely to include some combination of the following: former users, potential users, first-time users, light or irregular users, medium users, and heavy users. Segmenting by usage rate enables marketers to focus their efforts on heavy users or to develop multiple marketing mixes aimed at different segments. Because heavy users often account for a sizable portion of all product sales, some marketers focus on the heavy-user segment.

80/20 principle
A principle holding that 20 percent of all customers generate 80 percent of the demand.

The **80/20 principle** holds that 20 percent of all customers generate 80 percent of the demand. Although the percentages usually are not exact, the general idea often holds true. For example, in the fast-food industry, the heavy user accounts for only one of five fast-food patrons, but makes about 60 percent of all visits to fast-food restaurants. Using this definition, the heavy user (who is most

Exhibit 6.4   Lifestyle Segmentation of the Snack-Food Market

	Nutritional Snackers	Weight Watchers	Guilty Snackers	Party Snackers	Indiscriminate Snackers	Economical Snackers
% of Snackers	22%	14%	9%	15%	15%	18%
Lifestyle Characteristics	Self-assured, controlled	Outdoorsy, influential, venturesome	Highly anxious, isolated	Sociable	Hedonistic	Self-assured, price-oriented
Benefits Sought	Nutritious, without artificial ingredients, natural	Low in calories, quick energy	Low in calories, good tasting	Good to serve guests, served with pride, go well with beverages	Good tasting, satisfies hunger	Low in price, best value
Consumption Level of Snacks	Light	Light	Heavy	Average	Heavy	Average
Type of Snacks Usually Eaten	Fruits, vegetables, cheese	Yogurt, vegetables	Yogurt, cookies, crackers, candy	Nuts, potato chips, crackers, pretzels	Candy, ice cream, cookies, potato chips, pretzels, popcorn	No specific products
Demographics	Better educated, have younger children	Younger, single	Younger or older, female, lower socio-economic status	Middle-aged, nonurban	Teenager	Have large family, better educated

Are Brewers Using the Internet to Target Underage Drinkers?

Reluctantly nudged into the on-line world, major brewers are finding the Web offers a new way to win brand loyalty—especially among the young adult males who drank more than half of the 2.7 billion cases of beer sold in the United States in 2000. "We want to get that one-on-one time," says Tony Ponturo, vice president of marketing for Anheuser-Busch Companies, the brewer of Budweiser. "If [consumers] are on the Budweiser.com site and interacting with your site, that is something special and different. They will feel some loyalty to you."

Brewers are also adding features to their sites that have less to do with beer and more to do with the lifestyle of beer drinkers. For example, Miller and Budweiser offer on-line fantasy race-car leagues. Miller created a "beer pager" on its site that allows a user to send a message to a group of friends and track their responses. There are also concert promotions, interactive chats with sports stars, and on-line sweepstakes.

As the sites try to be more hip and youth-oriented, some public-health advocates worry that the on-line campaigns will increasingly attract underage drinkers. Beer companies, like other manufacturers of consumer products, strive to make a connection with consumers as early as possible. That requires a delicate balancing act of trying not to appeal to underage drinkers while still targeting the twenty-one-and-over crowd.

"We take great care to ensure people visiting our site are twenty-one and older," says Francine Katz, vice president of consumer affairs for Anheuser-Busch. "Our site is intended for adults." She notes that all visitors to the Budweiser site must enter a date of birth before being granted access to the site—a standard feature on beer Web pages.

But skeptics say the warning screen requiring a date of birth may actually attract underage drinkers because it suggests the site is taboo. In addition, the age screen is based on the honor system—there is no way to verify whether the user is entering his or her real date of birth.

The addition of games, concert promotions, and other pop culture to beer Web sites will inevitably lead to an increase in visits from teenagers, believes Kathryn Montgomery, the president of the Center for Media Education, a nonprofit organization that promotes television and Internet safeguards for children. She notes, "The whole nature of the Web creates new opportunities to make the products more fun and exciting and the site more about play than traditional advertising. I think there is an ulterior motive, one that is hard for us to prove, but it appears targeted at young people. [Youths who see the beer sites] connect consuming alcohol with having a lot of fun. It is very playful. There is no discussion of consequences."

George Hacker, director of the Alcohol Policies Project of the Center for Science in the Public Interest, says Coors Brewing Company is the only major brewer to operate a Web site devoid of the glitzy promotions that might attract underage users. "The Internet represents another means for beer to be in young kids' faces," says Hacker. "There are so many young people in the [on-line] audience that any standards brewers hold relating to targeting young people are worthless."[37]

Discuss the ethical implications of the beer industry's design and use of Web sites to promote alcoholic products. Do you think the beer industry is targeting children with its sites? Explain your answer.

---

often a single male) accounted for roughly $66 billion of the $110 billion the National Restaurant Association said was spent on fast food in 1999.[36]

Developing customers into heavy users is the goal behind many frequency/loyalty programs like the airlines' frequent flyer programs. Many supermarkets have also designed loyalty programs that reward the heavy-user segment with deals available only to them, such as in-store coupon dispensing systems, loyalty card programs, and special price deals on selected merchandise.

The "Ethics in Marketing" box describes how the brewing industry's use of the Internet to market beer to heavy users may also attract those who are too young to drink.

Bases for Segmenting Business Markets

The business market consists of four broad segments: producers, resellers, institutions, and government (for a detailed discussion of the characteristics of these segments, see Chapter 5). Whether marketers focus on only one or on all four of these segments, they are likely to find diversity among potential customers. Thus,

5

Describe the bases for segmenting business markets

further market segmentation offers just as many benefits to business marketers as it does to consumer-product marketers.

Company Characteristics

Company characteristics, such as geographic location, type of company, company size, and product use, can be important segmentation variables. Some markets tend to be regional because buyers prefer to purchase from local suppliers, and distant suppliers may have difficulty competing in terms of price and service. Therefore, firms that sell to geographically concentrated industries benefit by locating close to their markets.

Segmenting by customer type allows business marketers to tailor their marketing mixes to the unique needs of particular types of organizations or industries. Many companies are finding this form of segmentation to be quite effective. For example, Home Depot, one of the largest do-it-yourself retail businesses in the United States, has targeted professional repair and remodeling contractors in addition to consumers.

Volume of purchase (heavy, moderate, light) is a commonly used basis for business segmentation. Another is the buying organization's size, which may affect its purchasing procedures, the types and quantities of products it needs, and its responses to different marketing mixes. Banks frequently offer different services, lines of credit, and overall attention to commercial customers based on their size.

Many products, especially raw materials like steel, wood, and petroleum, have diverse applications. How customers use a product may influence the amount they buy, their buying criteria, and their selection of vendors. For example, a producer of springs may have customers that use the product in applications as diverse as making machine tools, bicycles, surgical devices, office equipment, telephones, and missile systems.

Buying Processes

Many business marketers find it helpful to segment customers and prospective customers on the basis of how they buy. For example, companies can segment some business markets by ranking key purchasing criteria, such as price, quality, technical support, and service. Atlas Corporation developed a commanding position in the industrial door market by providing customized products in just four weeks, which was much faster than the industry average of twelve to fifteen weeks. Atlas's primary market is companies with an immediate need for customized doors.

The purchasing strategies of buyers may provide useful segments. Two purchasing profiles that have been identified are satisficers and optimizers. **Satisficers** contact familiar suppliers and place the order with the first one to satisfy product and delivery requirements. **Optimizers** consider numerous suppliers (both familiar and unfamiliar), solicit bids, and study all proposals carefully before selecting one.

The personal characteristics of the buyers themselves (their demographic characteristics, decision style, tolerance for risk, confidence level, job responsibilities, etc.) influence their buying behavior and thus offer a viable basis for segmenting some business markets. IBM computer buyers, for example, are sometimes characterized as being more risk averse than buyers of less expensive computers that perform essentially the same functions. In advertising, therefore, IBM stressed its reputation for high quality and reliability.

Customer Relationship

More and more, companies are beginning to go beyond the traditional segmentation variables by focusing on the type of relationship they have with their customers. For example, Cable & Wireless, a British telephone company, had tradi-

satisficers

Business customers who place an order with the first familiar supplier to satisfy product and delivery requirements.

optimizers

Business customers who consider numerous suppliers, both familiar and unfamiliar, solicit bids, and study all proposals carefully before selecting one.

tionally segmented customers based on size. This meant that a *Fortune* 500 organization would have priority over a midsize customer, even if the midsize client accounted for more business. Recently, the company reevaluated this method and began using other factors, such as revenue generated by each customer, and how cost-effective and efficient it is for Cable & Wireless to serve particular customers.[38]

The Chapman Group, a Columbia, Maryland, company that specializes in sales and marketing process improvement, has designed a segmentation strategy based on types of relationships companies have with their customers. They developed three segments of relationships: client accounts, customer accounts, and buyer accounts. Clients collaborate with the organization on attaining mutual goals of profitability. They appreciate support, consistently offer profitable revenue, and have reasonable expectations of services for the prices they pay. They are willing to work on teams and expand relationships between both organizations. Customers are less interested in building a relationship network, are indifferent about mutual profitability, want most goods and services for lower-than-market prices, and are more costly to service. Buyers focus on price only. Value, relationships, and services typically do not offset pricing differences in this segment. Companies using this segmentation strategy can then offer different service approaches for each segment.[39]

Steps in Segmenting a Market

The purpose of market segmentation, in both consumer and business markets, is to identify marketing opportunities. Exhibit 6.5 traces the steps below in segmenting a market. Note that steps 5 and 6 are actually marketing activities that follow market segmentation (steps 1 through 4).

6

List the steps involved in segmenting markets

1. *Select a market or product category for study:* Define the overall market or product category to be studied. It may be a market in which the firm already competes, a new but related market or product category, or a totally new one. For instance, Anheuser-Busch closely examined the beer market before introducing Michelob Light and Bud Light. Anheuser-Busch also carefully studied the market for salty snacks before introducing the Eagle brand.

2. *Choose a basis or bases for segmenting the market:* This step requires managerial insight, creativity, and market knowledge. There are no scientific procedures for selecting segmentation variables. However, a successful segmentation scheme must produce segments that meet the four basic criteria discussed earlier in this chapter.

3. *Select segmentation descriptors:* After choosing one or more bases, the marketer must select the segmentation descriptors. Descriptors identify the specific segmentation variables to use. For example, if a company selects demographics as

Steps in Segmenting a Market and Subsequent Activities   **Exhibit 6.5**

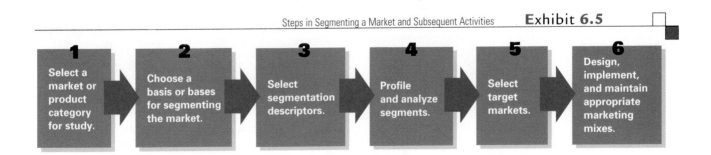

a basis of segmentation, it may use age, occupation, and income as descriptors. A company that selects usage segmentation needs to decide whether to go after heavy users, nonusers, or light users.

4. *Profile and analyze segments:* The profile should include the segments' size, expected growth, purchase frequency, current brand usage, brand loyalty, and long-term sales and profit potential. This information can then be used to rank potential market segments by profit opportunity, risk, consistency with organizational mission and objectives, and other factors important to the firm.

5. *Select target markets:* Selecting target markets is not a part of but a natural outcome of the segmentation process. It is a major decision that influences and often directly determines the firm's marketing mix. This topic is examined in greater detail later in this chapter.

6. *Design, implement, and maintain appropriate marketing mixes:* The marketing mix has been described as product, distribution, promotion, and pricing strategies intended to bring about mutually satisfying exchange relationships with target markets. Chapters 8 through 15 explore these topics in detail.

Strategies for Selecting Target Markets

7

Discuss alternative strategies for selecting target markets

target market
A group of people or organizations for which an organization designs, implements, and maintains a marketing mix intended to meet the needs of that group, resulting in mutually satisfying exchanges.

So far this chapter has focused on the market segmentation process, which is only the first step in deciding whom to approach about buying a product. The next task is to choose one or more target markets. A **target market** is a group of people or organizations for which an organization designs, implements, and maintains a marketing mix intended to meet the needs of that group, resulting in mutually satisfying exchanges. The three general strategies for selecting target markets—undifferentiated, concentrated, and multisegment targeting—are illustrated in Exhibit 6.6. Exhibit 6.7 illustrates the advantages and disadvantages of each targeting strategy.

Exhibit 6.6

Three Strategies for Selecting Target Markets

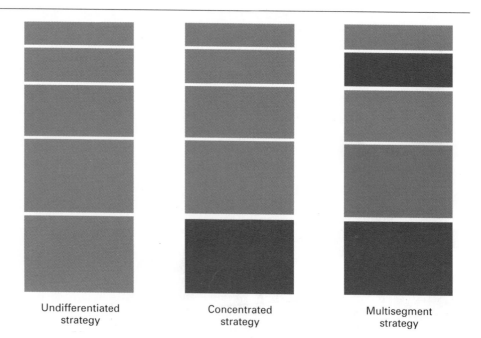

Undifferentiated strategy   Concentrated strategy   Multisegment strategy

Exhibit 6.7

Targeting Strategy	Advantages	Disadvantages
Undifferentiated Targeting	• Potential savings on production/marketing costs • Company more susceptible to competition	• Unimaginative product offerings
Concentrated Targeting	• Concentration of resources • Can better meet the needs of a narrowly defined segment • Allows some small firms to better compete with larger firms • Strong positioning	• Segments too small, or changing • Large competitors may more effectively market to niche segment
Multisegment Targeting	• Greater financial success • Economies of scale in production/marketing	• High costs • Cannibalization

Undifferentiated Targeting

A firm using an **undifferentiated targeting strategy** essentially adopts a mass-market philosophy, viewing the market as one big market with no individual segments. The firm uses one marketing mix for the entire market. A firm that adopts an undifferentiated targeting strategy assumes that individual customers have similar needs that can be met with a common marketing mix.

The first firm in an industry sometimes uses an undifferentiated targeting strategy. With no competition, the firm may not need to tailor marketing mixes to the preferences of market segments. Henry Ford's famous comment about the Model T is a classic example of an undifferentiated targeting strategy: "They can have their car in any color they want, as long as it's black." At one time, Coca-Cola used this strategy with a single product and a single size of its familiar green bottle. Marketers of commodity products, such as flour and sugar, are also likely to use an undifferentiated targeting strategy.

One advantage of undifferentiated marketing is the potential for saving on production and marketing. Because only one item is produced, the firm should be able to achieve economies of mass production. Also, marketing costs may be lower when there is only one product to promote and a single channel of distribution. Too often, however, an undifferentiated strategy emerges by default rather than by design, reflecting a failure to consider the advantages of a segmented approach. The result is often sterile, unimaginative product offerings that have little appeal to anyone.

Another problem associated with undifferentiated targeting is that it makes the company more susceptible to competitive inroads. Hershey lost a big share of the candy market to Mars and other candy companies before it changed to a multisegment targeting strategy. Coca-Cola forfeited its position as the leading seller of cola drinks in supermarkets to Pepsi-Cola in the late 1950s, when Pepsi began offering several sizes of containers.

You might think a firm producing a standard product like toilet tissue would adopt an undifferentiated strategy. However, this market has industrial segments and consumer segments. Industrial buyers want an economical, single-ply product sold in boxes of a hundred rolls. The consumer market demands a more versatile product in smaller quantities. Within the consumer market, the product is differentiated with designer print or no print, cushioned or noncushioned, and

undifferentiated targeting strategy
Marketing approach that views the market as one big market with no individual segments and thus requires a single marketing mix.

Charleston Gardens

What segmentation strategy does Charleston Gardens employ on its Web site? Why do you think as you do?

http://www.charlestongardens.com

On Line

concentrated targeting strategy
A strategy used to select one segment of a market for targeting marketing efforts.

niche
One segment of a market.

economy priced or luxury priced. Fort Howard Corporation, the market share leader in industrial toilet paper, does not even sell to the consumer market.

Concentrated Targeting

With a **concentrated targeting strategy**, a firm selects a market **niche** (one segment of a market) for targeting its marketing efforts. Because the firm is appealing to a single segment, it can concentrate on understanding the needs, motives, and satisfactions of that segment's members and on developing and maintaining a highly specialized marketing mix. Some firms find that concentrating resources and meeting the needs of a narrowly defined market segment is more profitable than spreading resources over several different segments.

  For example, Starbucks became successful by focusing on a group of consumers that wanted gourmet coffee products. America Online (AOL) became one of the worlds' leading Internet providers by targeting Internet newcomers. By making the Internet interface easy to use, AOL was able to attract millions of people who otherwise might not have subscribed to an on-line service.[40] The City University of Hong Kong is restructuring its entire focus and transforming its programs into an e-business curriculum.[41]

 Small firms often adopt a concentrated targeting strategy to compete effectively with much larger firms. For example, Enterprise Rent-A-Car rose to number one in the car rental industry by catering to people with cars in the shop. It has now expanded into the airport rental market.

Some firms, on the other hand, use a concentrated strategy to establish a strong position in a desirable market segment. Porsche, for instance, targets an upscale automobile market through "class appeal, not mass appeal."

Concentrated targeting violates the old adage "Don't put all your eggs in one basket." If the chosen segment is too small or if it shrinks because of environmental changes, the firm may suffer negative consequences. For instance, OshKosh B'Gosh, Inc., was highly successful selling children's wear in the 1980s. It was so successful, however, that the children's line came to define OshKosh's image to the extent that the company could not sell clothes to anyone else. Attempts at marketing older children's clothing, women's casual clothes, and maternity wear were all abandoned. Recognizing it was in the children's-wear business, the company expanded into products such as kids' shoes, children's eyewear, and plush toys.

A concentrated strategy can also be disastrous for a firm that is not successful in its narrowly defined target market. Before Procter & Gamble introduced Head and Shoulders shampoo, several small firms were already selling antidandruff shampoos. Head and Shoulders was introduced with a large promotional campaign, and the new brand captured over half the market immediately. Within a year, several of the firms that had been concentrating on this market segment went out of business.

AP/WIDE WORLD PHOTOS

Starbucks deploys a very concentrated marketing strategy by focusing on gourmet coffee drinkers. How serious is the company about its strategy? Senior Vice President Mary Williams, pictured here, slurps more than three hundred cups of coffee a day. She is in charge of coffee tasting, buying, and education for the company.

Multisegment Targeting

A firm that chooses to serve two or more well-defined market segments and develops a distinct marketing mix for each has a **multisegment targeting strategy**. Stouffer's, for example, offers gourmet entrées for one segment of the frozen dinner market and Lean Cuisine for another. Hershey offers premium candies like Golden Almond chocolate bars, packaged in gold foil, that are marketed to an adult audience. Another chocolate bar, called RSVP, is targeted toward consumers who crave the taste of Godiva chocolates at the price of a Hershey bar.

Cosmetics companies seek to increase sales and market share by targeting multiple age and ethnic groups. Maybelline and Cover Girl, for example, market different lines to teenage women, young adult women, older women, and African American women. Mattel targets multiple markets with its Barbie doll. To make Barbie relevant to older girls, the brand has a new logo, new packaging, and an expanded product line of books and trendy apparel. Other new items include an electronic Barbie scrapbook to keep voice-recorded secrets and activity sets for fingernails and make-your-own lip-gloss. To target preteen girls, the company is introducing Barbie dolls with strands of hair studded with rhinestones, street-fashion clothing, and a first ever Barbie belly button.[42]

AP/WIDE WORLD PHOTOS

Sometimes organizations use different promotional appeals, rather than completely different marketing mixes, as the basis for a multisegment strategy. Beer marketers such as Adolph Coors and Anheuser-Busch advertise and promote special events targeted toward African American, Hispanic American, and Asian American market segments. The beverages and containers, however, do not differ by ethnic market segment.

Multisegment targeting offers many potential benefits to firms, including greater sales volume, higher profits, larger market share, and economies of scale in manufacturing and marketing. Yet it may also involve greater product design, production, promotion, inventory, marketing research, and management costs. Before deciding to use this strategy, firms should compare the benefits and costs of multisegment targeting to those of undifferentiated and concentrated targeting.

Another potential cost of multisegment targeting is **cannibalization**, which occurs when sales of a new product cut into sales of a firm's existing products. In many cases, however, companies prefer to steal sales from their own brands rather than lose sales to a competitor. Also, in today's fast-paced world of Internet business, some companies are willing to cannibalize existing business to build new business. Bank One launched WingspanBank.com as a freestanding all-Internet bank that would be free to poach Bank One's customers. Likewise, the pet-supply chain Petsmart spun off its on-line venture, Petsmart.com, as a separate company.

Positioning

The development of any marketing mix depends on **positioning**, a process that influences potential customers' overall perception of a brand, product line, or organization in general. **Position** is the place a product, brand, or group of products occupies in consumers' minds relative to competing offerings. Consumer goods marketers are particularly concerned with positioning. Procter & Gamble, for example, markets eleven different laundry detergents, each with a unique position, as illustrated in Exhibit 6.8 on page 204.

multisegment targeting strategy
A strategy that chooses two or more well-defined market segments and develops a distinct marketing mix for each.

Mattel targets multiple markets with its Barbie doll. In an attempt to appeal to today's generation of young girls, the company rolled out "Generation" dolls. Traditional Barbies now share shelf space with the new line, which includes a doll with a nose ring and one with a butterfly tattoo on her stomach.

cannibalization
A situation that occurs when sales of a new product cut into sales of a firm's existing products.

8
Explain how and why firms implement positioning strategies and how product differentiation plays a role

positioning
Developing a specific marketing mix to influence potential customers' overall perception of a brand, product line, or organization in general.

position
The place a product, brand, or group of products occupies in consumers' minds relative to competing offerings.

Use the Internet to see how the positionings of the detergents listed in Exhibit 6.8 are reflected on their Web sites.

On Line

Exhibit 6.8

Positioning of Procter & Gamble Detergents

Brand	Positioning	Market Share
Tide	Tough, powerful cleaning	31.1%
Cheer	Tough cleaning and color protection	8.2%
Bold	Detergent plus fabric softener	2.9%
Gain	Sunshine scent and odor-removing formula	2.6%
Era	Stain treatment and stain removal	2.2%
Dash	Value brand	1.8%
Oxydol	Bleach-boosted formula, whitening	1.4%
Solo	Detergent and fabric softener in liquid form	1.2%
Dreft	Outstanding cleaning for baby clothes, safe for tender skin	1.0%
Ivory Snow	Fabric and skin safety on baby clothes and fine washables	0.7%
Ariel	Tough cleaner, aimed at Hispanics	0.1%

Positioning assumes that consumers compare products on the basis of important features. Marketing efforts that emphasize irrelevant features are therefore likely to misfire. For example, Crystal Pepsi and a clear version of Coca-Cola's Tab failed because consumers perceived the "clear" positioning as more of a marketing gimmick than a benefit.

Effective positioning requires assessing the positions occupied by competing products, determining the important dimensions underlying these positions, and choosing a position in the market where the organization's marketing efforts will have the greatest impact. For example, Ford Motor Company styled the new Taurus models with conventional lines and installed new high-tech protection features. It positioned the Taurus as a safe, family sedan, based on marketing research that revealed consumers view safety as a top priority in automobiles.

product differentiation
A positioning strategy that some firms use to distinguish their products from those of competitors.

As the previous example illustrates, **product differentiation** is a positioning strategy that many firms use to distinguish their products from those of competitors. The distinctions can be either real or perceived. Tandem Computer designed machines with two central processing units and two memories for computer systems that can never afford to be down or lose their databases (for example, an airline reservation system). In this case, Tandem used product differentiation to create a product with very real advantages for the target market. However, many everyday products, such as bleaches, aspirin, unleaded regular gasoline, and some soaps, are differentiated by such trivial means as brand names, packaging, color, smell, or "secret" additives. The marketer attempts to convince consumers that a particular brand is distinctive and that they should demand it over competing brands.

Some firms, instead of using product differentiation, position their products as being similar to competing products or brands. Artificial sweeteners advertised as tasting like sugar or margarine tasting like butter are two examples.

Perceptual Mapping

Perceptual mapping is a means of displaying or graphing, in two or more dimensions, the location of products, brands, or groups of products in customers' minds. For example, after several years of decreasing market share and the perception of teenagers that Levi's were not "cool," Levi Strauss has developed a number of youth-oriented fashions, ranging from oddly cut jeans to nylon pants that unzip into shorts. It has also introduced apparel appealing to adults by extending the Dockers and Slates casual-pants brands.[43] The perceptual map in Exhibit 6.9 shows Levi's dozens of brands and subbrands, from cheap basics to high-priced fashion.

perceptual mapping
A means of displaying or graphing, in two or more dimensions, the location of products, brands, or groups of products in customers' minds.

Positioning Bases

Firms use a variety of bases for positioning, including the following:

- *Attribute:* A product is associated with an attribute, product feature, or customer benefit. Rockport shoes are positioned as an always comfortable brand that is

Exhibit 6.9

Perceptual Map and Positioning Strategy for Levi Strauss Products

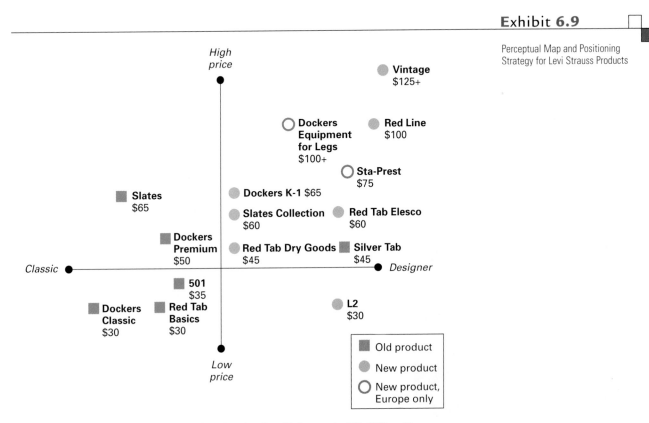

SOURCE: Nina Munk, "How Levi's Trashed a Great American Brand," *Fortune,* April 12, 1999, p. 84.

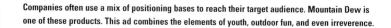
Companies often use a mix of positioning bases to reach their target audience. Mountain Dew is one of these products. This ad combines the elements of youth, outdoor fun, and even irreverence.

MOUNTAIN DEW, DEW, AND DO THE DEW ARE REGISTERED TRADEMARKS OF PEPSICO, INC. USED WITH PERMISSION.

available in a range of styles from working shoes to dress shoes.

- *Price and quality:* This positioning base may stress high price as a signal of quality or emphasize low price as an indication of value. Neiman Marcus uses the high-priced strategy; Wal-Mart has successfully followed the low-price and value strategy. The mass merchandiser Target has developed an interesting position based on price and quality. It is an "upscale discounter," sticking to low prices but offering higher quality and design than most discount chains.

- *Use or application:* AT&T telephone service advertising emphasized communicating with loved ones using the "Reach Out and Touch Someone" campaign. Stressing uses or applications can be an effective means of positioning a product with buyers. Kahlúa liqueur used advertising to point out 228 ways to consume the product.

- *Product user:* This positioning base focuses on a personality or type of user. Zale Corporation has several jewelry store concepts, each positioned to a different user. The Zale stores cater to middle-of-the-road consumers with traditional styles. Its Gordon's stores appeal to a slightly older clientele with a contemporary look. Guild is positioned for the more affluent fifty-plus consumer.

- *Product class:* The objective here is to position the product as being associated with a particular category of products; for example, positioning a margarine brand with butter.

- *Competitor:* Positioning against competitors is part of any positioning strategy. The Avis rental car positioning as number two exemplifies positioning against specific competitors.

It is not unusual for a marketer to use more than one of these bases. The AT&T "Reach Out and Touch Someone" campaign that stressed use also emphasized the relatively low cost of long-distance calling. Mountain Dew positioned its soft drink to the youth market as a thirst-quenching drink that is associated with teens having fun outdoors.

repositioning
Changing consumers' perceptions of a brand in relation to competing brands.

Repositioning

Sometimes products or companies are repositioned in order to sustain growth in slow markets or to correct positioning mistakes. **Repositioning** is changing consumers' perceptions of a brand in relation to competing brands. One of the most successful product repositioning campaigns ever was the National Pork Board's repositioning of pork as "the other white meat." In the late 1980s, when consumers became more health-conscious, pork producers were making changes in response to the demand for a leaner, higher quality product, but few people knew about it. While poultry sales were increasing, sales of pork products declined by more than 20 percent. The Pork Board launched the "Pork: The Other White Meat" campaign, which highlighted pork's conve-

AP/WIDE WORLD PHOTOS

When the Pork Board launched the "Pork: The Other White Meat" campaign, it saw pork consumption rise to the point where pork is now the most eaten meat in the world. Building on this success, a new campaign has been developed in which ads repeat old adages, then unexpectedly drop in the word "Pork." Pictured here: "One potato, two potato, three potato, pork."

nience and nutritional benefits. By 1996, almost 90 percent of consumers surveyed recognized the slogan—up from 64 percent four years earlier. In 2000, new print, television, and Internet campaigns were introduced, and the slogan was named the fifth most memorable tag line in contemporary advertising by Northwestern University. Since the start of the campaign, pork production has increased nearly 40 percent, and pork is now the most eaten meat in the world.[44] Another company that has capitalized on the trend of health-consciousness in an effort to target baby boomers is Johnson & Johnson. The company repositioned St. Joseph baby aspirin as a low-dose aspirin for adults who want to reduce the risk of heart attack and stroke.[45]

United States Department of Agriculture

Review Exhibit 6.4 on the snack-food market. Then, visit the USDA Web site for an article on the snack-food market in Shanghai. Do the segments seem all that different? If you were a manufacturer of cheese popcorn, how would you penetrate the Shanghai snack market? A manufacturer of caramels?

http://www.fas.usda.gov/info/agexporter/1997/shangsnk.html

On Line

Global Issues in Market Segmentation and Targeting

Chapter 3 discussed the trend toward global market standardization, which enables firms like Coca-Cola, Colgate-Palmolive, McDonald's, and Nike to market similar products using similar marketing strategies in many different countries. This chapter has also discussed the trend toward targeting smaller, more precisely defined markets.

The tasks involved in segmenting markets, selecting target markets, and designing, implementing, and maintaining appropriate marketing mixes (described in Exhibit 6.5) are the same whether the marketer has a local perspective or a global vision. The main difference is the segmentation variables commonly used. Countries are commonly grouped using such variables as per capita gross domestic product, geography, religion, culture, or political system.

Some firms have tried to group countries or customer segments around the world using lifestyle or psychographic variables. So-called Asian yuppies in places like Singapore, Hong Kong, Japan, and South Korea have substantial spending power and exhibit purchase and consumption behavior similar to that of their better-known counterparts in the United States. In this case, firms may be able to use a global market standardization approach.

 Recall from Chapter 3 that Metabolife International has introduced a line of Chinese herb formulas designed to treat five common ailments, such as the common cold and upset stomach. The line, called Chinac, is being marketed to both American and Chinese consumers. For Americans, Chinac offers an easy way to access what is for most consumers an unfamiliar field of medicine. For Chinese, Chinac may offer a welcome change to the numerous and confusing choices they face in a traditional Chinese pharmacy.[46]

Discuss global market segmentation and targeting issues

CONNECT IT

As you read at the beginning of this chapter, market segmentation refers to the process of dividing a market into meaningful, relatively similar, and identifiable segments or groups. Targeting is selecting one or more market segments for which an organization designs, implements, and maintains distinctive marketing mixes. Most of the hair salons discussed in

(continued)

the opening story are using a niche tartgeting strategy. They are attempting to appeal to one segment of the market: children. (One salon in the story, Treehouse, also targets parents, so it is using a multisegmentation strategy.) The kids' market would appear to violate one of the criteria for successful segmentation—substantiality—because it represents only 10 percent of the total hair care market. For individual salons in specific geographic locations, however, this niche is proving to be profitable, probably because few salons in those locations target kids.

USE IT

The principles of positioning discussed in this chapter do not apply solely to products that you buy. Many people position themselves in different "marketplaces" based on how they present themselves through the clothing they choose, the hairstyles they wear, and the activities they engage in. For example, a young woman may position herself in the dating market by wearing short skirts, sporting a trendy hairstyle, and spending time at night clubs. Another woman may dress modestly, wear a conservative hairstyle, and attend singles events at her church. These two women are positioning themselves to attract different kinds of men.

Apply what you have learned in this chapter about positioning by developing a written strategy for a female friend who is interviewing for a job in two different industries: banking and advertising. How would you suggest this friend dress and wear her hair for each of the two interviews? What activities should she stress on her résumé for the bank interview and the advertising agency interview? How would you advise a male friend?

REVIEW IT

1 **Describe the characteristics of markets and market segments.** A market is composed of individuals or organizations with the ability and willingness to make purchases to fulfill their needs or wants. A market segment is a group of individuals or organizations with similar product needs as a result of one or more common characteristics.

1.1 Mercedes-Benz is thinking about advertising its cars to college students. Do you think that college students are a viable potential market for Mercedes? Why or why not?

1.2 ON LINE How are visitors to the following Web site segmented when seeking relevant job openings? Try this search engine and report your results: **http://www.careermag.com**.

2 **Explain the importance of market segmentation.** Before the 1960s, few businesses targeted specific market segments. Today, segmentation is a crucial marketing strategy for nearly all successful organizations. Market segmentation enables marketers to tailor marketing mixes to meet the needs of particular population segments. Segmentation helps marketers identify consumer needs and preferences, areas of declining demand, and new marketing opportunities.

2.1 Describe market segmentation in terms of the historical evolution of marketing.

3 **Discuss criteria for successful market segmentation.** Successful market segmentation depends on four basic criteria: (1) a market segment must be substantial and have enough potential customers to be viable; (2) a market segment must be identifiable and measurable; (3) members of a market segment must be accessible to marketing efforts; and (4) a market segment must respond to particular marketing efforts in a way that distinguishes it from other segments.

3.1   **WRITING**   Refer to the story about kids' hair salons at the beginning of the chapter. As a marketing consultant for a chain of hair salons, you have been asked to evaluate the kids' market as a potential segment for the chain to target. Write a memo to your client discussing your evaluation of the kids' segment in terms of the four criteria for successful market segmentation.

(4) Describe the bases commonly used to segment consumer markets. Five bases are commonly used for segmenting consumer markets. Geographic segmentation is based on region, size, density, and climate characteristics. Demographic segmentation is based on age, gender, income level, ethnicity, and family life-cycle characteristics. Psychographic segmentation includes personality, motives, and lifestyle characteristics. Benefits sought is a type of segmentation that identifies customers according to the benefits they seek in a product. Finally, usage segmentation divides a market by the amount of product purchased or consumed.

4.1   **WRITING**   Choose magazine ads for five different consumer products. For each ad, write a description of what you think the demographic characteristics of the targeted market are.

4.2   **ON LINE**   Investigate how Delta Airlines (**http://www.delta.com**) uses its Web site to cater to its market segments.

(5) Describe the bases for segmenting business markets. Business markets can be segmented on three general bases. First, businesses segment markets based on company characteristics, such as customers' geographic location, type of company, company size, and product use. Second, companies may segment customers based on the buying processes those customers use. Third, companies are increasingly basing market segmentation on the type of relationship they have with their customers.

5.1   **WRITING**   Choose five ads from business publications such as the *Wall Street Journal, Fortune,* and *Business Week.* For each ad, write a description of how you think the company has segmented its business market.

(6) List the steps involved in segmenting markets. Six steps are involved when segmenting markets: (1) selecting a market or product category for study; (2) choosing a basis or bases for segmenting the market; (3) selecting segmentation descriptors; (4) profiling and evaluating segments; (5) selecting target markets; and (6) designing, implementing, and maintaining appropriate marketing mixes.

6.1   **WRITING**   Write a letter to the president of your bank suggesting ideas for increasing profits and enhancing customer service by improving segmentation and targeting strategies.

(7) Discuss alternative strategies for selecting target markets. Marketers select target markets using three different strategies: undifferentiated targeting, concentrated targeting, and multisegment targeting. An undifferentiated targeting strategy assumes that all members of a market have similar needs that can be met with a single marketing mix. A concentrated targeting strategy focuses all marketing efforts on a single market segment. Multisegment targeting is a strategy that uses two or more marketing mixes to target two or more market segments.

7.1   Form a team with two or three other students. Create an idea for a new product. Describe the segment (or segments) you are going to target with the product, and explain why you chose the targeting strategy you did.

8 **Explain how and why firms implement positioning strategies and how product differentiation plays a role.** Positioning is used to influence consumer perceptions of a particular brand, product line, or organization in relation to competitors. The term *position* refers to the place that the offering occupies in consumers' minds. To establish a unique position, many firms use product differentiation, emphasizing the real or perceived differences between competing offerings. Products may be differentiated on the basis of attribute, price and quality, use or application, product user, product class, or competitor.

8.1 Choose a product category (e.g., cars), and identify at least three different brands and their respective positioning strategies. How is each position communicated to the target audience?

9 **Discuss global market segmentation and targeting issues.** The key tasks in market segmentation, targeting, and positioning are the same regardless of whether the target market is local, regional, national, or multinational. The main differences are the variables used by marketers in analyzing markets and assessing opportunities and the resources needed to implement strategies.

9.1 Find an article in a business newspaper or magazine that describes how a U.S. company is marketing its products in another country. Create a chart that compares the U.S. marketing mix elements with the same elements for the other country. You may also wish to consult foreign periodicals to see how multinational companies advertise their products in other countries.

DEFINE IT

benefit segmentation 195
cannibalization 203
concentrated targeting
   strategy 202
demographic segmentation
   190
80/20 principle 196
family life cycle (FLC) 193
geodemographic segmenta-
   tion 194
geographic segmentation
   188
market 186

market segment 186
market segmentation 186
multisegment targeting
   strategy 203
niche 202
optimizers 198
perceptual mapping 205
position 203
positioning 203
product differentiation 204
psychographic segmenta-
   tion 193
repositioning 206

satisficers 198
segmentation bases (vari-
   ables) 188
target market 200
undifferentiated targeting
   strategy 201
usage-rate segmentation
   196

APPLY IT

Application for Entrepreneurs

Judy Brown has always loved working with animals. She has experience in pet grooming, boarding, and in-home pet sitting. Judy wants to open a full-service business utilizing her skills that is uniquely positioned in relation to the traditional pet grooming/boarding businesses that operate in the town where she lives. Customers that use these current pet services deliver their pets to the firms and later pick them up. Most are open between 9 A.M. and 6 P.M. from Monday through Friday.

Judy lives in a midsize city that is close to a major airport. Many high-tech companies are located in or near her city, so there are a large number of men and women in managerial and information-technology positions who must travel frequently as part of their jobs. A lot of families have pets, so Judy thinks there is a market for pet-related services, despite the current competition.

Questions

1. How should Judy segment the market for pet services?

2. What targeting strategy should Judy use to start her business? Should this strategy change as her business prospers and grows?

3. How should Judy position her pet services business against her competition?

THINK ABOUT IT

Ethics Exercise

Tobacco companies are frequently criticized for targeting potential customers below the legal age to purchase and use their products. Critics cite Joe Camel and the Marlboro man as images meant to make smoking appealing to young people. If tobacco companies are actually following this particular demographic targeting strategy, most would agree that it is unethical if not illegal.

Questions

1. Is marketing tobacco products to younger consumers unethical?

2. Many are beginning to argue that fast-food companies, such as McDonald's and Burger King, are knowingly marketing unhealthy food to consumers. Is it unethical for fast-food companies to market kids' meals to children?

3. What does the AMA Code of Ethics have to say about marketing unhealthy or harmful products to consumers, particularly children and young adults? Go to the AMA Web site at **http://www.marketingpower.com** to review the code. Write a brief paragraph summarizing where the AMA stands on this important issue.

TRY IT

Entrepreneurship Case

Segmenting the On-line Market: The Case of eBay

When Pam Omidyar dreamed of a place where she could meet, talk, and trade with other collectors of Pez candy dispensers, her computer-programming and soon-to-be husband, Pierre Omidyar, immediately set to work on developing the software that would enable such interaction on-line. Together, in September 1995, they launched eBay.com, and within five short years it was one of the most recognizable brand names on the Internet. From its humble beginnings as a niche Web site, it has become the premier Internet auction showcase. eBay's 4,300 categories include everything from tie-dyed Grateful Dead Beanie Babies to bubblegum cards to nearly new Ferraris and even fine jewelry. Once you find what you're looking for, you can haggle for it in one of the four million daily auctions.

eBay positions itself as a folksy and friendly facilitator of an on-line community that caters to traders with varying tastes and preferences, but the original idea was to service one type of collector in a single geographic area—Pam and Pierre's neighborhood in San Francisco. The Omidyars' customer-focused strategy led to such a high degree of customer satisfaction that awareness of the site quickly spread through the entire Bay area. High customer loyalty, repeat usage, and very strong word-of-mouth advertising (*viral marketing*) fueled eBay's growth. eBay is unique in that it has equal appeal to the occasional Internet surfer, the nostalgic trader, the fanatic trader, the small business in search of used or inexpensive equipment, and those who simply love the thrill of the deal.

In trying to nurture its growing enterprise, eBay's entrepreneurial management team was faced with many marketing challenges that it still grapples with today:

- Attracting users who are accustomed to trading in traditional venues such as auction houses, estate sales, and flea markets
- Convincing Internet users to execute transactions on-line
- Organizing many specific product categories into a much smaller number of broad categories and corresponding market segments
- Developing a marketing mix to reach multiple targets

The first step for eBay was to build a killer product. eBay focuses on delivering a first-class user experience by providing frequent content and auction updates. The site's help areas are customized for either experienced or new users, and detailed collector news and information are available. The second step was developing a pricing schedule to satisfy its broad spectrum of users. Transactions can be executed for as little as twenty-five cents for the seller of a Pez dispenser, but eBay can claim as much as a 5 percent commission on the selling price of an expensive item like a diamond necklace. Under the direction of Senior Vice President of Marketing Brian Swette, the company rethought its past strategy of restricting on-line promotions to its own Web site and has accomplished prolific distribution on the World Wide Web. eBay has struck deals to gain presence on major entry portals like AOL, shopping verticals like MySimon.com, and destination sites like AutoTrader.com.

The final component of the marketing mix, promotion, was the most complex to address. At first glance, eBay has only one product—the on-line auction forum—that it sells to traders and consumers. To that end, eBay has remained faithful to its grass-roots marketing effort in the off-line world. It has also maintained its presence at trade and collector shows of all kinds in order to evangelize the benefits of auctioning on-line. A closer look at what transpires at the site, however, reveals that eBay is the auction utility of choice for a range of collectors so stratified that on any one day a browser at eBay can encounter auctions for coins, clothes, model airplanes, or more controversial and hence discouraged items like hate-group materials, used underwear, or a human kidney. The challenge for eBay, therefore, is not so much that it has so many different consumers, but that each one of its consumers has very different needs. With that in mind, eBay has chosen to divide markets using a variety of segmentation strategies. It has employed demographic, psychographic, geodemographic, benefit, and usage-rate segmentation techniques to better understand and serve customer needs across a broad range in each.

In order to effectively promote the site to its eclectic audience, eBay developed a complex and comprehensive print advertising campaign aimed at several targets. Working with the advertising agency of Ogilvy & Mather, eBay decided to avoid mass print media and use niche publications. This way, the company could reach an audience that would be more captive at the point of exposure to the advertisement. Unique messaging and advertising copy was developed for campaigns deployed in twelve different vertical markets. Across those twelve markets, eBay selected seventy-five specialty magazines for their highly tailored advertisements. eBay still supports this strategy today. Although segmenting its market into multiple niches was a demanding and complex initiative, it has clearly been a successful tactic.

Currently, over ten million registered users buy and sell one of 450,000 new items posted to the auction site every day. Customers range from infrequent traders to traders who use eBay regularly to generate personal profit streams. eBay has special services such as My eBay and Mister Lister for frequent users and has gone so far as to build a Business Exchange area where it caters to needs of small businesses. Customers can participate in local auctions specific to their geographic region, bid on items whose proceeds go directly to one of many charities, or sign up for eBay magazine. Chat rooms, an on-line library of articles organized by collection category, and eBay's own newsletter all provide information to enhance and empower the customer's trading experience. eBay's success has inspired a proliferation of copycat auction sites, but none enjoys the customer base or widespread brand recognition of the original.

Questions

1. What types of segmentation does eBay use?

2. Does eBay use an undifferentiated, a niche, or a multiple targeting strategy? Discuss the range of tactics eBay uses to reach its target market.

3. Explain the tools eBay has developed for usage-rate segmentation and consider how eBay might use those tools to enhance its profitability.

4. How did eBay tackle the marketing challenges it faced as it grew from an entrepreneurial venture to a multimillion-dollar operation?

5. Describe eBay's target market.

WATCH IT

Short 

The Kellogg's ad on your dedicated PowerPoint CD-ROM illustrates the concepts of usage-rate segmentation. The series of six Mlife ads taken together are a wonderful example of demographic segmentation. After watching the full series, identify which market segments the company is targeting with each ad.

Medium   **VIDEO**

As the multiracial population grows, identifying distinct market segments based on race will become increasingly difficult. CNN reported on the growth of the self-identified multiracial population after the 2000 census. Watch the clip and consider the implications of multiracial market segments on marketing practices.

Long 
the Series on PBS stations and the Web

To give you insight into Chapter 6, Small Business School will take you to Le Travel Store in San Diego. This specialty retail shop has been serving a unique and specific group of customers for over twenty years. Bill and Joan Keller, owners of the store, will show you how identifying your market segment—and targeting it well—can lead to success.

FLIP IT

 Flip to Chapter 6 in your *Grademaker Study Guide* for more review opportunities, including the pretest, vocabulary review, Internet activities, study test questions, and segmentation scenarios. Can you explain why market segmentation is important? What are the most common bases that marketers use to segment markets? Don't know? Then you need to review with your Grademaker.

CLICK IT

The *Essentials of Marketing* Web site links you to all the Internet-based activities in this chapter, like "Review It" questions 1.2 and 4.2, and the On-Line exercises in the chapter margins. As a review, do the Chapter 6 quiz and crossword puzzle. And don't forget the Career Exersite that shows you different resources if you'd like to incorporate segmenting and targeting markets into your marketing career. Review the main concepts in the PowerPoint presentation for Chapter 6, too. Go to **http://lamb. swlearning.com**, read the material, and follow the links right from the site.

Surf to Xtra! and test your understanding of market segmentation by completing the worksheets for Exhibits 6.2, 6.5, 6.6, and 6.7. If your instructor has assigned a marketing plan project, worksheets on Xtra! can help you organize your work. In addition to the quiz on the Web site, there's another quiz on Xtra!, plus video of the authors answering frequently asked questions about target marketing, such as "How do firms choose NOT to target certain markets?" and "Could you explain perceptual mapping in more detail?"

CHAPTER **SEVEN**
DECISION SUPPORT SYSTEMS AND MARKETING RESEARCH

Learning Objectives

1 Explain the concept and purpose of a marketing decision support system

2 Define marketing research and explain its importance to marketing decision making

3 Describe the steps involved in conducting a marketing research project

4 Discuss the profound impact of the Internet on marketing research

5 Discuss the growing importance of scanner-based research

6 Explain the concept of competitive intelligence

In many ways, it's a common marketing situation: A manufacturer faces dwindling sales of a venerable product due to a shrinking core market; an ancillary market holds some promise, but its growth potential is hindered by pricing issues. In other ways, it's almost unique: Most of the people who buy the product do so because they have to, not because they want to; and most of them have no idea what the product is used for.

Then there's the product itself: duck stamps. Known in official parlance as Migratory Bird Hunting and Conservation Stamps, duck stamps are a required annual purchase for duck hunters. (Most hunters say they have little idea of what duck stamp fees are used for. They just know that you have to buy a stamp if you want to hunt ducks.) But the number of hunters is decreasing, and though the stamps are sought after by collectors, their hefty price (last year's stamp was $15) makes accumulating them an expensive proposition for the garden-variety philatelist. "We needed to find a way to reach a new audience, to broaden our market, as with any product," says Margaret Wendy, manager of sales and marketing, Federal Duck Stamp Office, Department of the Interior, U.S. Fish and Wildlife Service, Washington, D.C.

Initially, the idea was to focus the marketing campaign on the stamps themselves, their beauty, and the value of collecting them. But in focus groups conducted during the development of the campaign by The Ball Group, a Lancaster, Pennsylvania–based research and advertising firm, the stamps themselves weren't enough to make the sale. "The collecting aspect was of minimal interest," says Wes Ball, the firm's president.

Focus groups were held in cities around the country, two groups per city, one with environmentally active people and the other with people who were not environmentally active but who were not predisposed against environmental issues. (In addition, a telephone survey with a random national sample was conducted to determine awareness of the Duck Stamp program and to gauge interest and participation in environmental issues.)

Thanks to new strategies based upon the marketing research, hunters and stamp collectors won't be the only ones making an annual duck stamp purchase.

"We discovered a huge contingent who are concerned about the environment, especially air and water quality, and they believed that wetlands are a primary water filter for us, and felt that [up to] a $30 contribution was not only attractive but one that they would actively support again and again. We had people say, 'Now that I know about this I'll contribute money every year,'" Ball says.[1]

What are the various techniques for conducting marketing research? Should managers always do marketing research before they make a decision? How does marketing research relate to decision support systems? We will explore all these topics and others in Chapter 7.

On Line ◄ ►

U.S. Fish and Wildlife Service
How well is the government marketing duck stamps over the Internet? Does the U.S. Fish and Wildlife Service Web site reflect the desire to market the stamps to environmental groups?
http://www.fws.gov
http://www.duckstamp.com

Marketing Decision Support Systems

Explain the concept and purpose of a marketing decision support system

marketing information
Everyday information about developments in the marketing environment that managers use to prepare and adjust marketing plans.

decision support system (DSS)
An interactive, flexible computerized information system that enables managers to obtain and manipulate information as they are making decisions.

Accurate and timely information is the lifeblood of marketing decision making. Good information can help maximize an organization's sales and efficiently use scarce company resources. To prepare and adjust marketing plans, managers need a system for gathering everyday information about developments in the marketing environment—that is, for gathering **marketing information**. The system most commonly used these days for gathering marketing information is called a *marketing decision support system.*

A marketing **decision support system (DSS)** is an interactive, flexible computerized information system that enables managers to obtain and manipulate information as they are making decisions. A DSS bypasses the information-processing specialist and gives managers access to useful data from their own desks.

These are the characteristics of a true DSS:

- *Interactive:* Managers give simple instructions and see immediate results. The process is under their direct control; no computer programmer is needed. Managers don't have to wait for scheduled reports.

- *Flexible:* A DSS can sort, regroup, total, average, and manipulate the data in various ways. It will shift gears as the user changes topics, matching information to the problem at hand. For example, the CEO can see highly aggregated figures, and the marketing analyst can view very detailed breakouts.

- *Discovery-oriented:* Managers can probe for trends, isolate problems, and ask "what if" questions.

- *Accessible:* Managers who aren't skilled with computers can easily learn how to use a DSS. Novice users should be able to choose a standard, or default, method of using the system. They can bypass optional features so they can work with the basic system right away while gradually learning to apply its advanced features.

As a hypothetical example of how a DSS can be used, consider Renee Smith, vice president and manager of new products for Central Corporation. To evaluate sales of a recently introduced product, Renee can "call up" sales by the week, then by the month, breaking them out at her option by, say, customer segments. As she works at her desktop computer, her inquiries can go in several directions, depending on the decision at hand. If her train of thought raises questions about monthly sales last quarter compared to forecasts, she can use her DSS to analyze problems immediately. Renee might see that her new product's sales were significantly below forecasts. Were her forecasts too optimistic? She compares other products' sales to her forecasts and finds that the targets were very accurate. Was something wrong with the product? Is her sales department getting insufficient leads, or is it not putting leads to good use? Thinking a minute about how to examine that question, she checks ratios of leads converted to sales, product by product. The results disturb her. Only 5 percent of the new product's leads generated orders, compared to the company's 12 percent all-product average. Why? Renee guesses that the sales force is not supporting the new product vigorously enough. Quantitative information from the DSS could perhaps provide more evidence to back that suspicion. But already having enough quantitative knowledge to satisfy herself, the VP acts on her intuition and experience and decides to have a chat with her sales manager.

database marketing
The creation of a large computerized file of customers' and potential customers' profiles and purchase patterns.

 Perhaps the fastest-growing use of DSSs is for **database marketing**, which is the creation of a large computerized file of customers' and potential customers' profiles and purchase patterns. It is usually the key tool for successful micromarketing, which relies on very specific information about a market.

The Role of Marketing Research

Marketing research is the process of planning, collecting, and analyzing data relevant to a marketing decision. The results of this analysis are then communicated to management. Marketing research plays a key role in the marketing system. It provides decision makers with data on the effectiveness of the current marketing mix and also with insights for necessary changes. Furthermore, marketing research is a main data source for both management information systems and DSS.

Marketing research has three roles: descriptive, diagnostic, and predictive. Its *descriptive* role includes gathering and presenting factual statements. For example, what is the historic sales trend in the industry? What are consumers' attitudes toward a product and its advertising? Its *diagnostic* role includes explaining data. For instance, what was the impact on sales of a change in the design of the package? Its *predictive* function is to address "what if" questions. For example, how can the researcher use the descriptive and diagnostic research to predict the results of a planned marketing decision?

Define marketing research and explain its importance to marketing decision making

marketing research
The process of planning, collecting, and analyzing data relevant to a marketing decision.

Management Uses of Marketing Research

Marketing research can help managers in several ways. It improves the quality of decision making and helps managers trace problems. Most important, sound marketing research helps managers focus on the paramount importance of keeping existing customers, aids them in better understanding the marketplace, and alerts them to marketplace trends. Marketing research helps managers gauge the perceived value of their goods and services as well as the level of customer satisfaction.

AP/WIDE WORLD PHOTOS

Marketing research can help managers in several ways. For example, research revealed which brands of plumbing fixtures were traditional to New York City. This helped the Brooklyn Home Depot's store manager Rich Kantor to arrange his small pilot store designed to meet the needs of urban communities.

Improving the Quality of Decision Making

Managers can sharpen their decision making by using marketing research to explore the desirability of various marketing alternatives. For example, despite the growing popularity of cruise ships—nearly six million North American passengers boarded U.S.-based ships in 2001—cruises still get only a tiny slice of Americans' vacation time. Just 5 percent of people who take vacations longer than five days and are willing to spend $1,000 per person take cruises.[2] Royal Caribbean Cruise Lines liked the tremendous potential in the cruising market. Its job was to find a way to woo those people who wouldn't be caught dead on a cruise ship. The classic objections that people raise to vacationing on a cruise ship have not changed in nearly twenty years. Marketing research found that people worry about feeling trapped; they'd rather participate in activities than sit in a pool lounge all day long; they don't like having to eat in an elegant dining room, seven nights in a row, and share a table with strangers; and they don't like having to eat at a set time. In other words, they want options.

Royal Caribbean tackled those objections. That's how *Voyager of the Sea* ended up with an in-line skating track, a kids-only pool, a rock-climbing wall, an English pub, a Johnny Rockets restaurant, and a roulette wheel so big that gamblers can ride around its rim as if it were a carousel. To date, the ship has been very successful at attracting first-time cruisers.

Tracing Problems

Another way managers use marketing research is to find out why a plan backfires. Was the initial decision incorrect? Did an unforeseen change in the external environment cause the plan to fail? How can the same mistake be avoided in the future?

Keebler introduced Sweet Spots, a shortbread cookie with a huge chocolate drop on it. It has had acceptable sales and is still on the market, but only after the company used marketing research to overcome several problems. Soon after the cookie's introduction, Keebler increased the box size from 10 ounces at $2.29 to 15 ounces at $3.19. Demand immediately fell. Market research showed that Sweet Spots were now considered more of a luxury than an everyday item. Keebler lowered the price and went back to the 10-ounce box. Even though Sweet Spots originally was aimed at upscale adult females, the company also tried to appeal to kids. In subsequent research, Keebler found that the package graphics appealed to mothers but not to children.[3]

Focusing on the Paramount Importance of Keeping Existing Customers

An inextricable link exists between customer satisfaction and customer loyalty. Long-term relationships don't just happen but are grounded in the delivery of service and value by the firm. Customer retention pays big dividends for organizations. Powered by repeat sales and referrals, revenues and market share grow. Costs fall because firms spend less money and energy attempting to replace defectors. Steady customers are easy to serve because they understand the modus operandi and make fewer demands on employees' time. Increased customer retention also drives job satisfaction and pride, which lead to higher employee retention. In turn, the knowledge employees acquire as they stay longer increases productivity. A Bain & Company study estimates that a 5 percent decrease in the customer defection rate can boost profits by 25 to 95 percent.[4]

The ability to retain customers is based on an intimate understanding of their needs. This knowledge comes primarily from marketing research. For example, British Airways recast its first-class transatlantic service based on detailed marketing research. Most airlines stress top-of-the-line service in their transatlantic first-class cabins, but British Air's research found that most first-class passengers simply want to sleep. British Air now gives premium flyers the option of dinner on the ground, before takeoff, in the first-class lounge. Then, once on board, they can slip into British Air pajamas, put their heads on real pillows, slip under blankets, and enjoy an interruption-free flight. On arrival at their destination, first-class passengers can have breakfast, use comfortable dressing rooms and showers, and even have their clothes pressed before they set off. These changes in British Air's first-class service were driven strictly by marketing research.

Fly to London in the world's first fully flat bed in business class, and you will not only get hours of peaceful sleep, but for a short time you will also get two free economy tickets to wherever you like. Simply become a new member of British Airways Executive Club when you book your roundtrip Club World ticket and travel before June 30th, 2002.

To register for this promotion visit britishairways.com/tny. Then, just lie back and dream of where you'll fly next.

Fly flat. Fly free.

oneworld

BRITISH AIRWAYS

COURTESY OF BRITISH AIRWAYS.

British Airways refined its first class service based on marketing research that revealed that travelers often want to sleep during long-haul flights. The company further applied this information to create the world's first fully flat bed in business class (Club World) as shown above.

Understanding the Ever-Changing Marketplace

Marketing research also helps managers understand what is going on in the marketplace and take advantage of opportunities. Historically, marketing research has been practiced for as long as marketing has existed. The early Phoenicians carried out market demand studies as they traded in the various ports of the Mediterranean Sea. Marco Polo's diary indicates he was performing a marketing research function as he traveled to China. There is even evidence that the Spanish systematically conducted "market surveys" as they explored the New World, and there are examples of marketing research conducted during the Renaissance.

 Today, Internet marketing research can help companies quickly and efficiently understand what is happening in the marketplace. For example, Women.com, an on-line community site that offers editorial content and e-commerce services, has surveyed visitors for several years but recently boosted its research efforts. The surveys are designed to discover visitors' demographic and psychographic profiles for the network's internal use, as well as to share with advertisers.

Along with collecting basic demographic data, the site also asks visitors about their e-commerce habits (whether they've shopped for or purchased anything on-line recently, for instance), their feelings about privacy on the Internet, and value and attitudinal questions, such as whether they agree or disagree with statements like "I'm usually the first in my peer group to try something new." Such information provides a picture of the person on the other side of the computer that goes beyond her average age and income, says Regina Lewis, director of research for Women.com Networks, Inc. Understanding whether visitors are more risk oriented, family focused, or career minded helps Women.com set the right tone when talking to visitors, Lewis says, and has resulted in page redesigns.[5]

Steps in a Marketing Research Project

Virtually all firms that have adopted the marketing concept engage in some marketing research because it offers decision makers many benefits. Some companies spend millions on marketing research; others, particularly smaller firms, conduct informal, limited-scale research studies. For example, when Eurasia restaurant, serving Eurasian cuisine, first opened along Chicago's ritzy Michigan Avenue, it drew novelty seekers. But it turned off the important business lunch crowd, and sales began to decline. The owner surveyed several hundred businesspeople working within a mile of the restaurant. He found that they were confused by Eurasia's concept and wanted more traditional Asian fare at lower prices. In response, the restaurant altered its concept; it hired a Thai chef, revamped the menu, and cut prices. The dining room was soon full again.

Whether a research project costs $200 or $2 million, the same general process should be followed. The marketing research process is a scientific approach to decision making that maximizes the chance of getting accurate and meaningful results. Exhibit 7.1 on page 222 traces the steps: (1) identifying and formulating the problem/opportunity, (2) planning the research design and gathering primary data, (3) specifying the sampling procedures, (4) collecting the data, (5) analyzing the data, (6) preparing and presenting the report, and (7) following up.

The research process begins with the recognition of a marketing problem or opportunity. As changes occur in the firm's external environment, marketing managers are faced with the questions, "Should we change the existing marketing mix?" and, if so, "How?" Marketing research may be used to evaluate product, promotion, distribution, or pricing alternatives. In addition, it is used to find and evaluate new market opportunities.

For example, more than twenty million babies have been born in the United States since 1995, forming the largest generation since the baby boomers. More impressive than their numbers, though, is their wealth. The increase in single-parent and dual-earner households means kids are making shopping decisions

3

Describe the steps involved in conducting a marketing research project

Exhibit 7.1

The Marketing Research Process

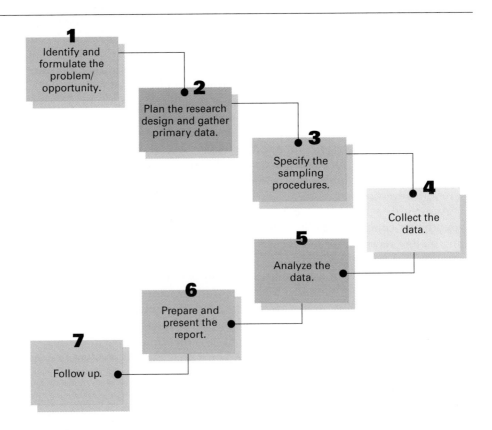

once left to mom. Combining allowance, earnings, and gifts, kids fourteen and under will directly spend an estimated $23 billion this year, and they will influence the spending of another $200 billion.

For savvy marketers, these statistics represent opportunity. Marketing research can identify and clarify where the best opportunities lie. Walt Disney, for example, is launching a twenty-four-hour kids' radio network based on its marketing research. Sometimes research can lead to unexpected results requiring creative uses of the marketing mix. General Motors recently completed an analysis of "backseat consumers," that is, children between five and fifteen years of age. Marketing research discovered that parents often let their children play a tie-breaking role in deciding what car to purchase. Marketing managers, armed with this information, launched several programs. GM purchased the inside cover of *Sports Illustrated for Kids*, a magazine targeted to boys from eight to fourteen years old. The ad featured a brightly colored two-page spread for the Chevy Venture minivan, a vehicle targeted toward young families. GM also sent the minivan into malls and showed Disney movies on a VCR inside the van.

The GM story illustrates an important point about problem/opportunity definition. The **marketing research problem** is information oriented. It involves determining what information is needed and how that information can be obtained efficiently and effectively. The **marketing research objective**, then, is to provide insightful decision-making information. This requires specific pieces of information needed to answer the marketing research problem. Managers must combine this information with their own experience and other information to make a proper decision. In the GM scenario, the marketing research objective was to determine what role, if any, backseat consumers play in a family's decision to purchase an automobile. In contrast, the **management decision problem** is action oriented. Management problems tend to be much broader in scope and far more general, whereas marketing research problems must be more narrowly defined and specific if the research effort is to be successful. Sometimes several research studies must be conducted to solve a broad management problem. Once GM determined that children

marketing research problem
Determining what information is needed and how that information can be obtained efficiently and effectively.

marketing research objective
The specific information needed to solve a marketing research problem; the objective should be to provide insightful decision-making information.

management decision problem
A broad-based problem that requires marketing research in order for managers to take proper actions.

GM continues to reap the benefits of its marketing research revealing how important kids are in the family decision-making process. The company's Warner Bros. Edition Chevy Venture minivan includes a built-in child's restraining seat, a video player, and an ongoing package called VentureTainment!

AP/WIDE WORLD PHOTOS

within this target market played a tiebreaker role, the question became one of what should be done to influence the tiebreakers. GM used marketing research to determine that direct advertising to children in the target market and mall promotions would be the best form of promotion.

Secondary Data

A valuable tool throughout the research process but particularly in the problem/opportunity identification stage is **secondary data**—data previously collected for any purpose other than the one at hand. Secondary information originating within the company includes documents such as annual reports, reports to stockholders, product testing results perhaps made available to the news media, and house periodicals composed by the company's personnel for communication to employees, customers, or others. Often this information is incorporated into a company's internal database.

secondary data
Data previously collected for any purpose other than the one at hand.

Innumerable outside sources of secondary information also exist, principally in the forms of government (federal, state, and local) departments and agencies that compile and publish summaries of business data. Trade and industry associations also publish secondary data. Still more data are available in business periodicals and other news media that regularly publish studies and articles on the economy, specific industries, and even individual companies. The unpublished summarized secondary information from these sources corresponds to internal reports, memos, or special-purpose analyses with limited circulation. Economic considerations or priorities in the organization may preclude publication of these summaries. Most of the sources listed above can be found on the Internet.

Secondary data save time and money if they help solve the researcher's problem. Even if the problem is not solved, secondary data have other advantages. They can aid in formulating the problem statement and suggest research methods and other types of data needed for solving the problem. In addition, secondary data can pinpoint the kinds of people to approach and their locations and serve as a basis of comparison for other data. The disadvantages of secondary data stem mainly from a mismatch between the researcher's unique problem and the purpose for which the secondary data were originally gathered, which are typically different. For example, a major consumer-products manufacturer wanted to determine the market potential for a fireplace log made of coal rather than compressed wood by-products. The researcher found plenty of secondary data about total wood consumed as fuel, quantities consumed in each state, and types of wood burned. Secondary data were also available about consumer attitudes and purchase patterns of wood by-product fireplace logs. The wealth of secondary data provided the researcher with many insights into the artificial log market. Yet nowhere was there any information that would tell the firm whether consumers would buy artificial logs made of coal.

The quality of secondary data may also pose a problem. Often secondary data sources do not give detailed information that would enable a researcher to assess their quality or relevance. Whenever possible, a researcher needs to address these important questions: Who gathered the data? Why were the data obtained? What methodology was used? How were classifications (such as heavy users versus light users) developed and defined? When was the information gathered?

The New Age of Secondary Information: The Internet

Gathering secondary data, while necessary in almost any research project, has traditionally been a tedious and boring job. The researcher often had to write to government agencies, trade associations, or other secondary data providers and then wait days or weeks for a reply that might never come. Often, one or more trips to the library were required and the researcher might find that needed reports were checked out or missing. With the rapid development of the Internet and World Wide Web in the last few years, however, much of the drudgery associated with the collection of secondary data has been eliminated.

Finding Secondary Data on the Internet

If you know the address of a particular Web site that contains the secondary data that you are searching for, you can type a description of what you are looking for directly into your Web browser (Netscape Navigator and Microsoft Internet Explorer are the dominant browsers).

Search Engines Sites such as AltaVista, Excite, and Google have become popular with researchers looking for information on the Web. These organizations offer what are called *search engines* that scan the Web looking for sites on a designated topic. Each search engine uses its own indexing system to locate relevant information. All of them allow users to enter one or more keywords that will initiate a search of the databases of Web sites for all occurrences of those words. They then return listings that allow users to go immediately to the sites described.

Remember that the Internet is a self-publishing medium. Your visits to search engines will yield files with a wide range of quality from a variety of sources. Try out multiple sites when you are investigating a topic.

Directories In addition to search engines, you can use subject directories on the Web to explore a subject. There are two basic types of directories: (1) academic and professional directories, often created and maintained by subject experts to support the needs of researchers, and (2) commercial portals, which cater to the general public and are competing for traffic. Directories depend upon people to compile their listings.

- *Academic and professional directories* are created by librarians or subject experts and tend to be associated with libraries and academic institutions. These collections are created to enhance the research process and help users find high-quality sites of interest. A careful selection process is applied, and links to the selected resources are usually annotated. These collections are often created to serve an institution's constituency but may be useful to any researcher. As a rule, these sites do not generate income or carry advertising. INFOMINE, from the University of California, is an example of an academic directory.

- *Commercial portals* are created to generate income and serve the general public. These services link to a wide range of topics and often emphasize entertainment, commerce, hobbies, sports, travel, and other interests not necessarily covered by academic directories. These sites seek to draw traffic in order to support advertising. As a part of this goal, the directory is offered in conjunction with a number of additional customer services. Yahoo! is an example of a commercial portal.

The lines between directories and search engines are blurring. Directories are present at some search engine sites, and sometimes their contents are searched along with content from the general Web. For example, AltaVista offers the LookSmart directory; Infoseek shares the screen with the directory at the Go Network; Excite has its own directory; and Lycos offers the directory contents from the Netscape Open Directory. Directory results are sometimes placed before search results to steer users to the directory's content. This can be a useful way of getting at substantive content relating to your query. Most subject directories offer a search engine mechanism to query the database.

Sites of Interest to Marketing Researchers A number of Web sites are accessed daily by marketing researchers in search of information. These sites offer an incredible variety of information. A list of those used most often is shown in Exhibit 7.2 on pages 226–227.

Periodical, Newspaper, and Book Databases

Several excellent periodical, newspaper, and book databases are available to researchers. Some can be directly accessed via the Internet and others through your local library's Web site. A list of these databases is shown in Exhibit 7.3 on page 228.

Internet Discussion Groups and Special Interest Groups as Sources of Secondary Data

A primary means of communicating with other professionals and special interest groups on the Internet is through newsgroups. With an Internet connection and newsreader software, you can visit any newsgroup supported by your service provider. If your service provider does not offer newsgroups or does not carry the group in which you are interested, you can find one of the publicly available newsgroup servers that does carry the group you would like to read.

Newsgroups function much like bulletin boards for a particular topic or interest. A newsgroup is established to focus on a particular topic. Readers stop by that newsgroup to read messages left by other people, post responses to others' questions, and send rebuttals to comments with which they disagree. Generally, there is some management of the messages to keep discussions within the topic area and to remove offensive material. However, readers of a newsgroup are free to discuss any issue and communicate with anyone in the world that visits that newsgroup. Images and data files can be exchanged in newsgroups, just as they can be exchanged via e-mail.

With over 250,000 newsgroups currently in existence and more being added every day, there is a newsgroup for nearly every hobby, profession, and lifestyle. Newsgroup messages look like e-mail messages. They contain a subject title, author, and a message body. Unlike normal e-mail messages, though, newsgroup messages are threaded discussions. This means that any reply to a previous message will appear linked to that message. Therefore, you can follow a discussion between two or more people by starting at the original message and following the links (or threads) to each successive reply. You can send images, sound files, and video clips attached to your message for anyone to download and examine.

newsgroups
Function like bulletin boards on the Internet. They are established to focus on a particular topic.

Planning the Research Design and Gathering Primary Data

Good secondary data can help researchers conduct a thorough situation analysis. With that information, researchers can list their unanswered questions and rank them. Researchers must then decide the exact information required to answer the questions. The **research design** specifies which research questions must be answered, how and when the data will be gathered, and how the data will be analyzed. Typically, the project budget is finalized after the research design has been approved.

research design
Specifies which research questions must be answered, how and when the data will be gathered, and how the data will be analyzed.

Organization	URL	Description
American Demographics/ Marketing Tools	http://www.marketingtools.com	Searches the full text of all of *American Demographics* and *Marketing Tools.*
American Marketing Association	http://www.ama.org	Searches all of the AMA's publications by using keywords.
BLS Consumer Expenditure Surveys	http://www.bls.gov/cex	Provides information on the buying habits of consumers, including data on their expenditures, income, and consumer credit.
Bureau of Economic Analysis	http://.bea.gov	Provides a wide range of economic statistics.
Bureau of Transportation Statistics	http://www.bts.gov	Comprehensive source for a wide range of statistics on transportation.
Centers for Disease Control and Prevention	http://www.cdc.gov/nchs	As the federal government's principal vital and health statistical agency, the National Center for Health Statistics has a lot to offer. The NCHS, a subdivision of the Centers for Disease Control and Prevention, maintains data on vital events, health status, lifestyle and exposure to unhealthy influences, the onset and diagnosis of illness and disability, and the use of health care.
Cyberatlas	http://www.cyberatlas.com	Viewers can browse the latest research compiled from several reputable firms, including Media Metrix, Greenfield Online, Intelliquest, and Inteco. The geography page fills you in on surveys about on-line populations around the world. There's also a generous section on e-commerce that breaks out research in different markets, like advertising, finance, and retail. Peek into the stats toolbox for a mother lode of lists on everything from weekly usage data to the top-ten banner ads.
The Dismal Scientist	http://www.dismal.com	An authoritative site offering timely economic information, with comprehensive data and analysis at the metro, state, and national levels. There's also data and analyses of global issues, including situations facing Asia, South America, and Europe. Visitors can rank states and metro areas on more than 100 economic, socioeconomic, and demographic categories.
Easy Analytic Software	http://www.easidemo graphics.com	Easy Analytic Software, a New York City-based developer and marketer of demographic data, offers demographic site reports, or three-ring studies, including current estimates for population and households. Each three-ring study offers census estimates for race, ethnicity, age distribution, income distribution, and weather data. The site also offers one million pages of demographic reports for all zip codes, counties, metropolitan areas, cities, sectional centers, television markets, states, and other geographies.
EconData	http://www.econdata.net	A premier site for researchers interested in economics and demographics. There is a tremendous number of links to government, private, and academic data sources. Check out the top-ten data sources list.
Economic Research Service, Department of Agriculture	http://www.ers.usda.gov	Provides a wide range of agricultural statistics.
Encyclopedia Britannica	http://www.britannica.com	Entire 32-volume encyclopedia is available free on-line.

Organization	URL	Description
Equifax National Decision Systems	http://www.equifax.com/biz/index.shtml	Provides access to a wide range of secondary data on many topics. Most must be purchased.
ESRI	http://www.esribis.com	On ESRI Business Information Solutions' site, users can type in their zip codes to get a snapshot of the dominant profile type in their town. Population figures are available for the zips, as are percentages for race and gender. Median house hold income, average home values, and average rent are also presented.
Find/SVP	http://www.findsvp.com	Offers consulting and research services. Claims to offer access to the largest private information center in the United States.
Harris Info Service	http://www.harrisinfo.com	Offers business-to-business data on American manufacturers and key decision makers.
Marketing Research Association	http://www.MRA-net.org	Analyzes causes and solutions of "declining respondent cooperation"; links to research suppliers.
Mediamark Research	http://www.mediamark.com/mri/docs/toplinereports.html	Marketers and researchers looking for demographic data on magazines, cable TV, or 53 different product or service categories can find it at Top-Line Reports site. Top-Line Reports breaks down cable TV networks according to viewers' age, gender, median age, and income. Magazines are listed by total audience, circulation, readers per copy, median age, and income.
Nielsen Media Research	http://www.nielsen-netratings.com	Course on Internet audience information. Researchers can find data and Internet growth and user patterns.
Office of Research & Statistics, SSA	http://www.ssa.gov/	Provides a range of government statistics.
Pcensus for Windows	http://www.tetrad.com	Provides detailed information about the population of metropolitan areas.
Population Reference Bureau	http://www.prb.org/	Source of demographic information on population issues.
Service Intelligence	http://www.serviceintelligence.com	The site has an area devoted to customer stories of unpleasant experiences with airlines, banks, restaurants, and other service businesses. It's not all bad news, though—"hero" stories are also included.
Strategic Mapping	http://www.stratmap.org	Offers an extensive selection of geographic files, includes detailed geography for the entire United States.
U.S. Census Bureau	http://www.census.gov	Very useful source of virtually all census data.
U.S. Demography	http://www.ciesin.org	Excellent source of U.S. demographic information.
USA Data	http://www.usadata.com	Provides access to consumer lifestyle data on a local, regional, or national basis.
World Opinion	http://www.worldopinion.com	Perhaps the premier site for the marketing research industry; thousands of marketing research reports available.

Exhibit 7.3

Full-Text Periodical, Newspaper, and Book Databases Used by Marketing Researchers

Source	Description
ABI/Inform Global	Updated monthly; provides bibliographic information and abstracts for approximately 1,000 journals in business and management. Includes full-text entries for approximately 520 journals. Among the major marketing journals now included in full-text format are *Journal of Marketing; JMR: Journal of Marketing Research;* and *Journal of the Academy of Marketing Science.*
Dow Jones Interactive	Includes full-text news and articles from over 3,400 sources including newspapers from around the world, as well as information on companies, industries, stocks, bonds, mutual funds, and foreign exchange rates; updated daily.
Electric Library	Contains over 5 million full-text documents in all subject areas. Content is updated daily and includes an archive of up to twelve years. Covers six separate media types: newspapers and news wires, periodicals, TV and radio program transcripts, literature and reference books, photos, and maps.
Lexis-Nexis	The Lexis-Nexis database contains 2.5 billion searchable documents. Each week, 14.7 million new documents are added. It includes 18,871 news and business sources. Lexis-Nexis is the largest business information service. It offers access to thousands of worldwide newspapers, magazines, trade journals, industry newsletters, tax and accounting information, financial data, public records, legislative data, and company information.
Periodical Abstracts Research II (PAR)	Covers current affairs, business, industry news, cultural events, editorial material, and general interest topics from more than 1,800 general and academic periodicals. Includes full-text articles from more than 600 journals. Full-text coverage began in 1992; updated monthly. Marketing journals are not heavily indexed in this database, but those that are available full-text include *Direct Marketing; Journal of Consumer Affairs;* and *Sales & Marketing Management.*

primary data
Information collected for the first time. Can be used for solving the particular problem under investigation.

Sometimes research questions can be answered by gathering more secondary data; otherwise, primary data may be needed. **Primary data**, or information collected for the first time, can be used for solving the particular problem under investigation. The main advantage of primary data is that they will answer a specific research question that secondary data cannot answer. For example, suppose Pillsbury has two new recipes for refrigerated dough for sugar cookies. Which one will consumers like better? Secondary data will not help answer this question. Instead, targeted consumers must try each recipe and evaluate the tastes, textures, and appearances of each cookie. Moreover, primary data are current and researchers know the source. Sometimes researchers gather the data themselves rather than assign projects to outside companies. Researchers also specify the methodology of the research. Secrecy can be maintained because the information is proprietary. In contrast, secondary data are available to all interested parties for relatively small fees.

Gathering primary data is expensive; costs can range from a few thousand dollars for a limited survey to several million for a nationwide study. For instance, a nationwide, fifteen-minute telephone interview with one thousand adult males can cost $50,000 for everything, including a data analysis and report. Because primary data gathering is so expensive, firms commonly cut back on the number of interviews to save money. Larger companies that conduct many research projects use another cost-saving technique. They piggyback studies, or gather data on two different projects using one questionnaire. The drawback is that answering questions about, say, dog food and gourmet coffee may be confusing to respondents. Piggybacking also requires a longer interview (sometimes a half hour or longer), which

Do convenience polls qualify as bona fide survey research? The woman pictured here is casting a poll vote in a survey asking Australians whether they should cut constitutional ties with Britain (Country) or retain Queen Elizabeth as Australia's constitutional monarch (Queen).

© REUTERS NEWMEDIA INC./CORBIS

tires respondents. The quality of the answers typically declines, with people giving curt replies and thinking, "When will this end!" A lengthy interview also makes people less likely to participate in other research surveys.[6]

Nevertheless, the disadvantages of primary data gathering are usually offset by the advantages. It is often the only way of solving a research problem. And with a variety of techniques available for research—including surveys, observations, and experiments—primary research can address almost any marketing question.

Survey Research

The most popular technique for gathering primary data is **survey research**, in which a researcher interacts with people to obtain facts, opinions, and attitudes. Exhibit 7.4 summarizes the characteristics of traditional forms of research.

In-Home Personal Interviews Although in-home personal interviews often provide high-quality information, they tend to be very expensive because of the interviewers' travel time and mileage costs. Therefore, they are rapidly disappearing from the marketing researcher's survey toolbox.

survey research
The most popular technique for gathering primary data in which a researcher interacts with people to obtain facts, opinions, and attitudes.

Characteristics of Traditional Forms of Survey Research **Exhibit 7.4**

Characteristic	In-Home Personal Interviews	Mall Intercept Interviews	Central-Location Telephone Interviews	Self-Administered and One-Time Mail Surveys	Mail Panel Surveys	Executive Interviews	Focus Groups
Cost	High	Moderate	Moderate	Low	Moderate	High	Low
Time span	Moderate	Moderate	Fast	Slow	Relatively slow	Moderate	Fast
Use of interviewer probes	Yes	Yes	Yes	No	Yes	Yes	Yes
Ability to show concepts to respondent	Yes (also taste tests)	Yes (also taste tests)	No	Yes	Yes	Yes	Yes
Management control over interviewer	Low	Moderate	High	n/a	n/a	Moderate	High
General data quality	High	Moderate	High to moderate	Moderate to low	Moderate	High	Moderate
Ability to collect large amounts of data	High	Moderate	Moderate to low	Low to moderate	Moderate	Moderate	Moderate
Ability to handle complex questionnaires	High	Moderate	High if computer-aided	Low	Low	High	Low

mall intercept interview

A survey research method that involves interviewing people in the common areas of shopping malls.

Mall Intercept Interviews The **mall intercept interview** is conducted in the common areas of shopping malls or in a market research office within the mall. It is the economy version of the door-to-door interview with personal contact between interviewer and respondent, minus the interviewer's travel time and mileage costs. To conduct this type of interview, the research firm rents office space in the mall or pays a significant daily fee. One drawback is that it is hard to get a representative sample of the population.

However, an interviewer can also probe when necessary—a technique used to clarify a person's response. For example, an interviewer might ask, "What did you like best about the salad dressing you just tried?" The respondent might reply, "Taste." This answer doesn't provide a lot of information, so the interviewer could probe by saying, "Can you tell me a little bit more about taste?" The respondent then elaborates: "Yes, it's not too sweet, it has the right amount of pepper, and I love that hint of garlic."

Mall intercept interviews must be brief. Only the shortest ones are conducted while respondents are standing. Usually, researchers invite respondents to their office for interviews, which are still rarely over fifteen minutes long. The researchers often show respondents concepts for new products or a test commercial or have them taste a new food product. The overall quality of mall intercept interviews is about the same as telephone interviews.

Marketing researchers are applying computer technology in mall interviewing. The first technique is **computer-assisted personal interviewing**. The researcher conducts in-person interviews, reads questions to the respondent off a computer screen, and directly keys the respondent's answers into the computer. A second approach is **computer-assisted self-interviewing**. A mall interviewer intercepts and directs willing respondents to nearby computers. Each respondent reads questions off a computer screen and directly keys his or her answers into a computer. The third use of technology is fully automated self-interviewing. Respondents are guided by interviewers or independently approach a centrally located computer station or kiosk, read questions off a screen, and directly key their answers into the station's computer.

computer-assisted personal interviewing

An interviewing method in which the interviewer reads the questions from a computer screen and enters the respondent's data directly into the computer.

computer-assisted self-interviewing

An interviewing method in which a mall interviewer intercepts and directs willing respondents to nearby computers where the respondent reads questions off a computer screen and directly keys his or her answers into a computer.

central-location telephone (CLT) facility

A specially designed phone room used to conduct telephone interviewing.

Telephone Interviews Compared to the personal interview, the telephone interview costs less and may provide the best sample of any traditional survey procedure. Most telephone interviewing is conducted from a specially designed phone room called a **central-location telephone (CLT) facility**. A phone room has many phone lines, individual interviewing stations, sometimes monitoring equipment, and headsets. The research firm typically will interview people nationwide from a single location.

Many CLT facilities offer computer-assisted interviewing. The interviewer reads the questions from a computer screen and enters the respondent's data directly into the computer. The researcher can stop the survey at any point and immediately print out the survey results. Thus, a researcher can get a sense of the project as it unfolds and fine-tune the research design as necessary. An on-line interviewing system can also save time and money because data entry occurs as the response is recorded rather than as a separate process after the interview. Hallmark Cards found that an interviewer administered a printed questionnaire for its Shoebox Greeting cards in twenty-eight minutes. The same questionnaire administered with computer assistance took only eighteen minutes.

Mail Surveys Mail surveys have several benefits: relatively low cost, elimination of interviewers and field supervisors, centralized control, and actual or promised anonymity for respondents (which may draw more candid responses). Some researchers feel that mail questionnaires give the respondent a chance to reply more thoughtfully and to check records, talk to family members, and so forth. A disadvantage is that mail questionnaires usually produce low response rates.

Low response rates pose a problem because certain elements of the population tend to respond more than others. The resulting sample may therefore not represent the surveyed population. For example, the sample may have too many retired people and too few working people. In this instance, answers to a question about attitudes toward Social Security might indicate a much more favorable overall view of the system than is actually the case. Another serious problem with mail surveys is that no one probes respondents to clarify or elaborate on their answers.

Mail panels like those operated by Market Facts, National Family Opinion Research, and NPD Research offer an alternative to the one-shot mail survey. A mail panel consists of a sample of households recruited to participate by mail for a given period. Panel members often receive gifts in return for their participation. Essentially, the panel is a sample used several times. In contrast to one-time mail surveys, the response rates from mail panels are high. Rates of 70 percent (of those who agree to participate) are not uncommon.

Executive Interviews Marketing researchers use **executive interviews** to conduct the industrial equivalent of door-to-door interviewing. This type of survey involves interviewing businesspeople, at their offices, concerning industrial products or services. For example, if Dell wanted information regarding user preferences for different features that might be offered in a new line of computer printers, it would need to interview prospective user-purchasers of the printers. It is appropriate to locate and interview these people at their offices.

This type of interviewing is very expensive. First, individuals involved in the purchase decision for the product in question must be identified and located. Sometimes lists can be obtained from various sources, but more frequently screening must be conducted over the telephone. A particular company is likely to have individuals of the type being sought, but locating those people within a large organization can be expensive and time-consuming. Once a qualified person is located, the next step is to get that person to agree to be interviewed and to set a time for the interview. This is not as hard as it might seem because most professionals seem to enjoy talking about topics related to their work.

Finally, an interviewer must go to the particular place at the appointed time. Long waits are frequently encountered; cancellations are not uncommon. This type of survey requires the very best interviewers because they are frequently interviewing on topics that they know very little about. Executive interviewing has essentially the same advantages and disadvantages as in-home interviewing.

Focus Groups A **focus group** is a type of personal interviewing. Often recruited by random telephone screening, seven to ten people with certain desired characteristics form a focus group. These qualified consumers are usually offered an incentive (typically $30 to $50) to participate in a group discussion. The meeting place (sometimes resembling a living room, sometimes featuring a conference table) has audiotaping and perhaps videotaping equipment. It also likely has a viewing room with a one-way mirror so that clients (manufacturers or retailers) may watch the session. During the session, a moderator, hired by the research company, leads the group discussion.

Focus groups are much more than question-and-answer interviews. Market researchers draw a distinction between "group dynamics" and "group interviewing." The interaction provided in **group dynamics** is essential to the success of focus-group research; this interaction is the reason for conducting group rather than individual research. One of the essential postulates of group-session usage is the idea that a response from one person may become a stimulus for another, thereby generating an interplay of responses that may yield more information than if the same number of people had contributed independently.

executive interviews
A type of survey that involves interviewing businesspeople at their offices concerning industrial products or services.

focus group
Seven to ten people who participate in a group discussion led by a moderator.

group dynamics
Group interaction essential to the success of focus-group research.

Because of the group dynamics of focus groups, researchers can uncover more information than in a single interview. Here people are tasting cookies while a food scientist takes notes. Later they will conduct a focus group regarding the cookies.

© DANA WHITE/PHOTOEDIT

Focus groups are occasionally used to brainstorm new product ideas or to screen concepts for new products. Ford Motor Company, for example, asked consumers to drive several automobile prototypes. These "test drivers" were then brought together in focus groups. During the discussions, consumers complained that they were scuffing their shoes because the rear seats lacked foot room. In response, Ford sloped the floor underneath the front seats, widened the space between the seat adjustment tracks, and made the tracks in the Taurus and Sable models out of smooth plastic instead of metal.

A new system by Focus Vision Network allows client companies and advertising agencies to view live focus groups in Chicago, Dallas, Boston, and fifteen other major cities. For example, the private satellite network lets a General Motors researcher observing a San Diego focus group control two cameras in the viewing room. The researcher can get a full-group view or a close-up, zoom, or pan the participants. The researcher can also communicate directly with the moderator using an ear receiver. Ogilvy & Mather (a large New York advertising agency whose clients include StarKist Sea Foods, Seagram's, MasterCard, and Burger King) has installed the system.

 The newest development in qualitative research is the on-line or cyber focus group. A number of organizations are currently offering this new means of conducting focus groups. The process is fairly simple.

- The research firm builds a database of respondents via a screening questionnaire on its Web site.

- When a client comes to a firm with a need for a particular focus group, the firm goes to its database and identifies individuals who appear to qualify. It sends an e-mail message to these individuals, asking them to log on to a particular site at a particular time scheduled for the group. The firm pays them an incentive for their participation.

- The firm develops a discussion guide similar to the one used for a conventional focus group.

- A moderator runs the group by typing in questions on-line for all to see. The group operates in an environment similar to that of a chat room so that all participants see all questions and all responses.

- The firm captures the complete text of the focus group and makes it available for review after the group has finished.

Many advantages are claimed for cyber groups. Cyber Dialogue, a marketing research company specializing in cyber groups, lists the following benefits of on-line focus groups on its Web site:

- *Speed:* Typically, focus groups can be recruited and conducted, with delivery of results, within five days of client approval.

- *Cost effectiveness:* Off-line focus groups incur costs for facility rental, air fare, hotel, and food. None of these costs is incurred with on-line focus groups.

- *Broad geographic scope:* In a given focus group, you can speak to people in Boise, Idaho, and Miami, Florida, at the same time.

- *Accessibility:* On-line focus groups give you access to individuals who otherwise might be difficult to recruit (e.g., business travelers, doctors, mothers with infants).

- *Honesty:* From behind their screen names, respondents are anonymous to other respondents and tend to talk more freely about issues that might create inhibitions in a face-to-face group.

Cyber Dialogue charges $3,000 for its focus groups. This compares very favorably to a cost in the range of $7,000 without travel costs for conventional focus groups. Unfortunately, no systematic evaluation comparing on-line focus groups and conventional focus groups has been done at this time.

Open-Ended Questions	Closed-Ended Questions	Scaled-Response Question
1. What advantages, if any, do you think ordering from a mail-order catalog offers compared to shopping at a local retail outlet? (*Probe:* What else?)	**Dichotomous** 1. Did you heat the Danish product before serving it? Yes . . . . .1 No 2	Now that you have used the rug cleaner, would you say that you . . . *(Circle one.)* Would definitely buy it . . . . .1 Would probably buy it 2
2. Why do you have one or more of your rugs or carpets professionally cleaned rather than having you or someone else in the household clean them?	2. The federal government doesn't care what people like me think. Agree . . . . .1 Disagree 2	Might or might not buy it . . . . .3 Probably would not buy it . . . . .4 Definitely would not buy it 5
3. What is there about the color of the eye shadow that makes you like it the best?	**Multiple choice** 1. I'd like you to think back to the last footwear of any kind that you bought. I'll read you a list of descriptions and would like for you to tell me which category they fall into. *(Read list and circle proper category.)* Dress and/or formal . . . . .1 Casual . . . . .2 Canvas/trainer/gym shoes . . . . .3 Specialized athletic shoes . . . . .4 Boots 5	
	2. In the last three months, have you used Noxzema skin cream . . . (Circle all that apply.) As a facial wash .1 For moisturizing the skin . . . . .2 For treating blemishes . . . . .3 For cleansing the skin . . . . .4 For treating dry skin . . . . .5 For softening skin . . . . .6 For sunburn . . . . .7 For making the facial skin smooth 8	

Questionnaire Design

All forms of survey research require a questionnaire. Questionnaires ensure that all respondents will be asked the same series of questions. Questionnaires include three basic types of questions: open-ended, closed-ended, and scaled-response (see Exhibit 7.5). An **open-ended question** encourages an answer phrased in the respondent's own words. Researchers get a rich array of information based on the respondent's frame of reference. In contrast, a **closed-ended question** asks the respondent to make a selection from a limited list of responses. Traditionally, marketing researchers separate the two-choice question (called *dichotomous*) from the many-item type (often called *multiple choice*). A **scaled-response question** is a closed-ended question designed to measure the intensity of a respondent's answer.

Closed-ended and scaled-response questions are easier to tabulate than open-ended questions because response choices are fixed. On the other hand, unless the researcher designs the closed-ended question very carefully, an important choice may be omitted.

For example, suppose a food study asked this question: "Besides meat, which of the following items do you normally add to a taco that you prepare at home?"

open-ended question
An interview question that encourages an answer phrased in the respondent's own words.

closed-ended question
An interview question that asks the respondent to make a selection from a limited list of responses.

scaled-response question
A closed-ended question designed to measure the intensity of a respondent's answer.

Avocado	1	Olives (black/green)	6
Cheese (Monterey Jack/cheddar)	2	Onions (red/white)	7
Guacamole	3	Peppers (red/green)	8
Lettuce	4	Pimento	9
Mexican hot sauce	5	Sour cream	0

The list seems complete, doesn't it? However, consider the following responses: "I usually add a green, avocado-tasting hot sauce"; "I cut up a mixture of lettuce and spinach"; "I'm a vegetarian; I don't use meat at all. My taco is filled only with guacamole." How would you code these replies? As you can see, the question needs an "other" category.

A good question must also be clear and concise, and ambiguous language must be avoided. Take, for example, the question "Do you live within ten minutes of here?" The answer depends on the mode of transportation (maybe the person walks), driving speed, perceived time, and other factors. Instead, respondents should see a map with certain areas highlighted and be asked whether they live in one of those areas.

Designing and interpreting scaled-response questions can be particularly difficult in global marketing research. A researcher must fully understand cultural differences, as the "Global Perspectives" box explains.

Clarity also implies using reasonable terminology. A questionnaire is not a vocabulary test. Jargon should be avoided, and language should be geared to the target audience. A question such as "What is the level of efficacy of your preponderant dishwasher powder?" would probably be greeted by a lot of blank stares. It would be much simpler to say "Are you (1) very satisfied, (2) somewhat satisfied, or (3) not satisfied with your current brand of dishwasher powder?"

Stating the survey's purpose at the beginning of the interview also improves clarity. The respondents should understand the study's intentions and the inter-

GLOBAL PERSPECTIVES

Culture Complicates Global Marketing Research

Except in very unusual circumstances, customer interviews should always be conducted in the local language by local interviewers. That would include even those interviews conducted with respondents who speak English well. Few people are as at ease or articulate in a second or third language as they are in their own mother tongue. By forcing respondents to speak a foreign language, you are, from the outset, limiting their ability to express their opinions and needs clearly and articulately.

Even something as straightforward as a scaled-response question should be given careful thought. It is best to utilize rating scales that make the most sense to the given population. For example, Americans may be very comfortable giving performance ratings using an A–F "school grade" system. That scale, however, is meaningless to Germans, who are more familiar with a 1–6 rating scale, with 1 indicating the best performance and 6 indicating the worst performance. And of course the Japanese wouldn't understand our letter grades at all—they generally use a 100-point scale for these purposes. You may even find that different populations use the same rating scales differently. For example, Germans may consistently give lower grades than Italians, while Italians may consistently rate every attribute as more important than Spaniards. These differences need to be factored in during the analysis phase.

Cultural differences can also surface with an issue like participation incentives. The first question is, "Are cash incentives appropriate in this market?" In Japan, for example, incentives for businesspeople often take the form of a gift, rather than cash. Sometimes it is better to offer gift certificates to major department stores as incentives. Charitable donations might also be an option.[7]

Americans, Australians, and the English all speak a common language. Therefore, cultural considerations are not important when designing and interpreting a marketing research study. Do you agree or disagree? Why? Door-to-door interviewing is almost nonexistent anymore in the United States. Do you think this is a worldwide trend? Why or why not? If a person in the United States and another person in Beijing, responding to the same questionnaire (the only difference being that one is in English and one is in Mandarin), both give something a "6" rating, do their responses really mean the same thing? Isn't a "6" always a "6" on a scale of 1–7?

viewer's expectations. Sometimes, of course, to get an unbiased response, the interviewer must disguise the true purpose of the study. If an interviewer says, "We're conducting an image study for American National Bank" and then proceeds to ask a series of questions about the bank, chances are the responses will be biased. Many times respondents will try to provide answers that they believe are "correct" or that the interviewer wants to hear.

Finally, to ensure clarity, the interviewer should avoid asking two questions in one; for example, "How did you like the taste and texture of the Pepperidge Farm coffee cake?" This should be divided into two questions, one concerning taste and the other texture.

A question should also be unbiased. A question such as "Have you purchased any quality Black & Decker tools in the past six months?" biases respondents to think of the topic in a certain way (in this case, to link quality and Black & Decker tools). Questions can also be leading: "Weren't you pleased with the good service you received last night at the Holiday Inn?" (The respondent is all but instructed to say yes.) These examples are quite obvious; unfortunately, bias is usually more subtle. Even an interviewer's clothing or gestures can create bias.

Often getting people to answer a questionnaire is not easy. One innovative approach that ties research to gaming is thriving on the Internet. The "Ethics in Marketing" box discusses this new approach to data gathering.

Observation Research

In contrast to survey research, **observation research** depends on watching what people do. Specifically, it can be defined as the systematic process of recording the behavioral patterns of people, objects, and occurrences without questioning or communicating with them. A market researcher using the observation technique witnesses and records information as events occur or compiles evidence from records of past events. Carried a step further, observation may involve watching people or phenomena and may be conducted by human observers or machines. Examples of these various observational situations are shown in Exhibit 7.6 on page 236.

Two common forms of people-watching-people research are mystery shoppers and one-way mirror observations. **Mystery shoppers** are researchers posing as customers who gather observational data about a store (i.e., are the shelves neatly stocked?) and collect data about customer/employee interactions. In the latter case, of course, there is communication between the mystery shopper and the employee. The mystery shopper may ask, "How much is this item?" "Do you have this in blue?" or "Can you deliver this by Friday?" The interaction is not an interview, and communication occurs only so that the mystery shopper can observe the actions and comments of the employee. Mystery shopping is, therefore, classified as an observational marketing research method even though communication is often involved. Conducted on a continuous basis, mystery shopping can motivate and recognize service performance. Used as a benchmark, mystery shopping can pinpoint strengths and weaknesses for training operations and policy refinements.

observation research
A research method that relies on three types of observation: people watching people, people watching an activity, and machines watching people.

mystery shoppers
Researchers posing as customers who gather observational data about a store.

Find the Monkey and You Get to Fill Out a Questionnaire

Not all Internet sites have fallen on hard times. Sites like FreeLotto.com, Flipside.com, and TreeLoot.com are continuing to grow at a rapid pace. By offering free gifts, prizes, coupons, or big cash winnings, gaming and sweepstakes sites are able to sign up game players and get them to divulge their names, addresses, and, in some cases, hobbies, interests, and buying patterns. The sites then use the information to sell advertisers targeted e-mail lists or space in a daily e-mail message to players.

That is gold to advertisers who want to get better results by targeting their ads to specific users. Ford Motor Company, for example, could put ads in e-mails sent to users who indicated they might buy a car in the next twelve months. Or a credit card company could offer a new card with a bigger limit to someone who plans to buy a computer.

"It's market research disguised as a game," says analyst Jim Magahad of PC Data Corporation, a research firm in Reston, Virginia. "And the information they are getting is very valuable."

To lure players to those games, sites have come up with some pretty catchy campaigns. One of the most memorable approaches is TreeLoot's "Punch the Monkey" banner ad that has run for almost the past two years. The ad invites Web surfers to try to knock out a monkey zooming across a banner at the top of their screen. If you can click on the elusive monkey, you win $20 in credits that can be exchanged for discounts at Web retailers or other prizes—and you get linked to TreeLoot's Web site, where you can play the site's money-tree game to win more credits.

FreeLotto runs a daily lotto drawing that has $11 million in cash prizes available to be won each day. Players must provide a valid e-mail and postal address and the name that will be on the check if they win. While choosing lottery numbers, users answer questions about interests in travel or any plans to buy a computer, car, or house. Plus, to submit their lotto numbers for the daily drawing, the players must click on one of several featured ads.

"It's direct mail without the postage, and the consumer does your daily entry—what could be better?" asks FreeLotto's chief executive Kevin Aronin.

Further, Jim Magahad of PC Data says the proliferation of Internet use among a broader population has helped boost the use of these sites. Gaming sites were the fastest-growing segment of the Internet last year, according to PC Data, and that is largely due to the willingness of people to give out information about themselves for the chance to win big.

"Now you have Middle America on-line—it's not just the affluent—and Middle America loves lotto," says Magahad.

Privacy concerns have largely been a moot point for the companies. Most promise not to disclose information without the players' consent, but the players, who volunteer the information, generally agree to let it be used.[8]

Are FreeLotto and TreeLoot really conducting marketing research? Is it ethical to require game participants to answer questions about purchase plans as a requirement to continue in the game? Is it ethical for a marketing research company to sell names, addresses, and question responses to companies? What if the respondent consents? Do you see any privacy issues here?

Exhibit 7.6

Observational Situations

Situation	Example
People watching people	Observers stationed in supermarkets watch consumers select frozen Mexican dinners; the purpose is to see how much comparison shopping people do at the point of purchase.
People watching phenomena	Observer stationed at an intersection counts traffic moving in various directions.
Machines watching people	Movie or videotape cameras record behavior as in the people-watching-people example above.
Machines watching phenomena	Traffic-counting machines monitor traffic flow.

One interesting observation situation is toy-testing day camp. Pictured here, Fama Ana tries on a pair of "spy glasses" at Durcell Toy Testing Camp. In one week, over one thousand children in fifteen U.S. cities test twenty-five different toys while marketers look on.

© MICHAEL GREENLAR/THE IMAGE WORKS

At the Fisher-Price Play Laboratory, children are invited to spend twelve sessions playing with toys. Toy designers watch through one-way mirrors to see how children react to Fisher-Price's and other makers' toys. Fisher-Price, for example, had difficulty designing a toy lawn mower that children would play with. A designer, observing behind the mirror, noticed the children's fascination with soap bubbles. He then created a lawn mower that spewed soap bubbles. It sold over a million units in the first year.

Experiments

An **experiment** is a method a researcher can use to gather primary data. The researcher alters one or more variables—price, package design, shelf space, advertising theme, advertising expenditures—while observing the effects of those alterations on another variable (usually sales). The best experiments are those in which all factors are held constant except the ones being manipulated. The researcher can then observe that changes in sales, for example, result from changes in the amount of money spent on advertising.

Holding all other factors constant in the external environment is a monumental and costly, if not impossible, task. Such factors as competitors' actions, weather, and economic conditions are beyond the researcher's control. Yet market researchers have ways to account for the ever-changing external environment. Mars, the candy company, was losing sales to other candy companies. Traditional surveys showed that the shrinking candy bar was not perceived as a good value. Mars wondered whether a bigger bar sold at the same price would increase sales enough to offset the higher ingredient costs. The company designed an experiment in which the marketing mix stayed the same in different markets but the size of the candy bar varied. The substantial increase in sales of the bigger bar quickly proved that the additional costs would be more than covered by the additional revenue. Mars increased the bar size—and its market share and profits.

experiment
A method a researcher uses to gather primary data.

Specifying the Sampling Procedures

Once the researchers decide how they will collect primary data, their next step is to select the sampling procedures they will use. A firm can seldom take a census of all possible users of a new product, nor can they all be interviewed. Therefore, a firm must select a sample of the group to be interviewed. A **sample** is a subset from a larger population.

Several questions must be answered before a sampling plan is chosen. First, the population, or **universe**, of interest must be defined. This is the group from which the sample will be drawn. It should include all the people whose opinions, behavior, preferences, attitudes, and so on are of interest to the marketer. For example, in a study whose purpose is to determine the market for a new canned dog food, the universe might be defined to include all current buyers of canned dog food.

After the universe has been defined, the next question is whether the sample must be representative of the population. If the answer is yes, a probability sample is needed. Otherwise, a nonprobability sample might be considered.

sample
A subset from a large population.

universe
The population from which a sample will be drawn.

Probability Samples

A **probability sample** is a sample in which every element in the population has a known statistical likelihood of being selected. Its most desirable feature is that scientific rules can be used to ensure that the sample represents the population.

probability sample
A sample in which every element in the population has a known statistical likelihood of being selected.

random sample

A sample arranged in such a way that every element of the population has an equal chance of being selected as part of the sample.

nonprobability sample

Any sample in which little or no attempt is made to get a representative cross section of the population.

convenience sample

A form of nonprobability sample using respondents who are convenient or readily accessible to the researcher—for example, employees, friends, or relatives.

One type of probability sample is a **random sample**—a sample arranged in such a way that every element of the population has an equal chance of being selected as part of the sample. For example, suppose a university is interested in getting a cross section of student opinions on a proposed sports complex to be built using student activity fees. If the university can acquire an up-to-date list of all the enrolled students, it can draw a random sample by using random numbers from a table (found in most statistics books) to select students from the list. Common forms of probability and nonprobability samples are shown in Exhibit 7.7.

Nonprobability Samples

Any sample in which little or no attempt is made to get a representative cross section of the population can be considered a **nonprobability sample**. A common form of a nonprobability sample is the **convenience sample**, which uses respondents who are convenient or readily accessible to the researcher—for instance, employees, friends, or relatives.

Exhibit 7.7

Types of Samples

Probability Samples	
Simple Random Sample	Every member of the population has a known and equal chance of selection.
Stratified Sample	Population is divided into mutually exclusive groups (such as gender or age); then random samples are drawn from each group.
Cluster Sample	Population is divided into mutually exclusive groups (such as geographic areas); then a random sample of clusters is selected. The researcher then collects data from all the elements in the selected clusters or from a probability sample of elements within each selected cluster.
Systematic Sample	A list of the population is obtained—i.e., all persons with a checking account at XYZ Bank—and a *skip interval* is obtained by dividing the sample size by the population size. If the sample size is 100 and the bank has 1,000 customers, then the skip interval is 10. The beginning number is randomly chosen within the skip interval. If the beginning number is 8, then the skip pattern would be 8, 18, 28, ...
Nonprobability Samples	
Convenience Sample	The researcher selects the easiest population members from which to obtain information.
Judgment Sample	The researcher's selection criteria are based on personal judgment that the elements (persons) chosen will likely give accurate information.
Quota Sample	The researcher finds a prescribed number of people in several categories—i.e., owners of large dogs versus owners of small dogs. Respondents are not selected on probability sampling criteria.
Snowball Sample	Additional respondents are selected on the basis of referrals from the initial respondents. This method is used when a desired type of respondent is hard to find—i.e., persons who have taken round-the-world cruises in the last three years. This technique employs the old adage "Birds of a feather flock together."

Nonprobability samples are acceptable as long as the researcher understands their nonrepresentative nature. Because of their lower cost, nonprobability samples are the basis of much marketing research.

Types of Errors

Whenever a sample is used in marketing research, two major types of error may occur: measurement error and sampling error. **Measurement error** occurs when there is a difference between the information desired by the researcher and the information provided by the measurement process. For example, people may tell an interviewer that they purchase Coors beer when they do not. Measurement error generally tends to be larger than sampling error.

Sampling error occurs when a sample somehow does not represent the target population. Sampling error can be one of several types. *Nonresponse error* occurs when the sample actually interviewed differs from the sample drawn. This error happens because the original people selected to be interviewed either refused to cooperate or were inaccessible. For example, people who feel embarrassed about their drinking habits may refuse to talk about them.

Frame error, another type of sampling error, arises if the sample drawn from a population differs from the target population. For instance, suppose a telephone survey is conducted to find out Chicago beer drinkers' attitudes toward Coors. If a Chicago telephone directory is used as the *frame* (the device or list from which the respondents are selected), the survey will contain a frame error. Not all Chicago beer drinkers have a phone, and many phone numbers are unlisted. An ideal sample (for example, a sample with no frame error) matches all important characteristics of the target population to be surveyed. Could you find a perfect frame for Chicago beer drinkers?

Random error occurs when the selected sample is an imperfect representation of the overall population. Random error represents how accurately the chosen sample's true average (mean) value reflects the population's true average (mean) value. For example, we might take a random sample of beer drinkers in Chicago and find that 16 percent regularly drink Coors beer. The next day we might repeat the same sampling procedure and discover that 14 percent regularly drink Coors beer. The difference is due to random error.

measurement error
An error that occurs when there is a difference between the information desired by the researcher and the information provided by the measurement process.

sampling error
An error that occurs when a sample somehow does not represent the target population.

frame error
An error that occurs when a sample drawn from a population differs from the target population.

random error
An error that occurs when the selected sample is an imperfect representation of the overall population.

Collecting the Data

Marketing research field service firms collect most primary data. A **field service firm** specializes in interviewing respondents on a subcontracted basis. Many have offices throughout the country. A typical marketing research study involves data collection in several cities, requiring the marketer to work with a comparable number of field service firms. To ensure uniformity among all subcontractors, detailed field instructions should be developed for every job. Nothing should be open to chance; no interpretations of procedures should be left to subcontractors.

Besides conducting interviews, field service firms provide focus-group facilities, mall intercept locations, test product storage, and kitchen facilities to prepare test food products. They also conduct retail audits (counting the amount of a product sold off retail shelves).

field service firm
A firm that specializes in interviewing respondents on a subcontracted basis.

Analyzing the Data

After collecting the data, the marketing researcher proceeds to the next step in the research process: data analysis. The purpose of this analysis is to interpret and draw conclusions from the mass of collected data. The marketing researcher tries to organize and analyze those data by using one or more techniques common to marketing research: one-way frequency counts, cross-tabulations, and more sophisticated statistical analysis. Of these three techniques, *one-way*

Exhibit 7.8

Brand	Purchase by Gender	
	Male	Female
Orville Reddenbacher	31%	48%
T.V. Time	12	6
Pop Rite	38	4
Act Two	7	23
Weight Watchers	4	18
Other	8	0

cross-tabulation
A method of analyzing data that
lets the analyst look at the responses to one question in relation to the responses to one or
more other questions.

frequency counts are the simplest. One-way frequency tables record the responses
to a question. For example, the answers to the question "What brand of microwave popcorn do you buy most often?" would provide a one-way frequency
distribution. One-way frequency tables are always done in data analysis, at least
as a first step, because they provide the researcher with a general picture of the
study's results.

A **cross-tabulation**, or "cross-tab," lets the analyst look at the responses to one
question in relation to the responses to one or more other questions. For example,
what is the association between gender and the brand of microwave popcorn
bought most frequently? Hypothetical answers to this question are shown in Exhibit 7.8. Although the Orville Reddenbacher brand was popular with both males
and females, it was more popular with females. Compared with women, men
strongly preferred Pop Rite, whereas women were more likely than men to buy
Weight Watchers popcorn.

Researchers can use many other more powerful and sophisticated statistical
techniques, such as hypothesis testing, measures of association, and regression
analysis. A description of these techniques goes beyond the scope of this book but
can be found in any good marketing research textbook. The use of sophisticated
statistical techniques depends on the researchers' objectives and the nature of the
data gathered.

Preparing and Presenting the Report

After data analysis has been completed, the researcher must prepare the report
and communicate the conclusions and recommendations to management. This is
a key step in the process. If the marketing researcher wants managers to carry out
the recommendations, he or she must convince them that the results are credible
and justified by the data collected.

Researchers are usually required to present both written and oral reports on
the project. Today, the written report is no more than a copy of the PowerPoint
slides used in the oral presentation. Both reports should be tailored to the audience. They should begin with a clear, concise statement of the research objectives,
followed by a complete, but brief and simple, explanation of the research design
or methodology employed. A summary of major findings should come next. The
conclusion of the report should also present recommendations to management.

Most people who enter marketing will become research users rather than research suppliers. Thus, they must know what to notice in a report. As with many other items we purchase, quality is not always readily apparent. Nor does a high price guarantee superior quality. The basis for measuring the quality of a marketing research report is the research proposal. Did the report meet the objectives established in the proposal? Was the methodology outlined in the proposal followed? Are the conclusions based on logical deductions from the data analysis? Do the recommendations seem prudent, given the conclusions?

Following Up

The final step in the marketing research process is to follow up. The researcher should determine why management did or did not carry out the recommendations in the report. Was sufficient decision-making information included? What could have been done to make the report more useful to management? A good rapport between the product manager, or whoever authorized the project, and the market researcher is essential. Often they must work together on many studies throughout the year.

The Profound Impact of the Internet on Marketing Research

 In many ways, the Internet has turned the world of marketing research upside-down. Old ways of conducting some types of research may soon seem as quaint as a steam-engine train. New techniques and new ways of conducting traditional marketing research are coming on-line in increasing numbers every day. By 2005, Internet marketing research will account for about 50 percent of all marketing research revenue in the United States.[9]

There are several reasons for the success of Internet marketing research:

- It allows for better and faster decision making through much more rapid access to business intelligence.
- It improves the ability to respond quickly to customer needs and market shifts.
- It makes follow-up studies and longitudinal research much easier to conduct and more fruitful.
- It slashes labor- and time-intensive research activities (and associated costs), including mailing, telephone solicitation, data entry, data tabulation, and reporting.[10]

Advantages of Internet Surveys

 The huge growth in the popularity of Internet surveys is the result of the many advantages offered by the Internet. The specific advantages of Internet surveys are related to many factors:

4

Discuss the profound impact of the Internet on marketing research

The Internet is becoming a powerful tool in marketing research as more and more Americans get on-line. *Inc. Magazine* is one of a growing number of companies turning to the Internet to gather data about customers and their opinions.

- *Rapid development, real-time reporting:* Internet surveys can be broadcast to thousands of potential respondents simultaneously. Respondents complete surveys simultaneously; then results are tabulated and posted for corporate clients to view as the returns arrive. The result: survey results can be in a client's hands in significantly less time than would be required for traditional surveys.

- *Dramatically reduced costs:* The Internet can cut costs by 25 to 40 percent and provide results in half the time it takes to do traditional telephone surveys. Data-collection costs account for a large proportion of any traditional market research budget. Telephone surveys are labor-intensive efforts incurring training, telecommunications, and management costs. Electronic methods eliminate these completely. While costs for traditional survey techniques rise proportionally with the number of interviews desired, electronic solicitations can grow in volume with little increase in project costs.

- *Personalized questions and data:* Internet surveys can be highly personalized for greater relevance to each respondent's own situation, thus speeding the response process. Respondents enjoy a personalized survey because they are asked to answer only pertinent questions, can pause and resume the survey as needed, and can see previous responses and correct inconsistencies.

- *Improved respondent participation:* Busy respondents may be growing increasingly intolerant of "snail mail" or telephone-based surveys. Internet surveys take half as much time to complete as phone interviews, can be accomplished at the respondent's convenience (after work hours), and are much more stimulating and engaging. Graphics, interactivity, links to incentive sites and real-time summary reports make the interview enjoyable. The result? Much higher response rates.

- *Contact with the hard-to-reach:* Certain groups—doctors, high-income professionals, top management in Global 2000 firms—are among the most surveyed on the planet and the most difficult to reach. Many of these groups are well represented on-line. Internet surveys provide convenient anytime/anywhere access that makes it easy for busy professionals to participate.[11]

The rapid growth of Internet survey research is a result of the mushrooming number of Americans on-line—the current estimate being more than 50 percent. This in turn has meant that researchers are finding that on-line and off-line research results are the same. For example, America Online's (AOL) Digital Marketing Services (DMS), an on-line research organization, has done a number of surveys with both on-line and off-line samples. DMS's clients include IBM, Eastman Kodak, and Procter & Gamble. In well over a hundred side-by-side comparisons of on-line and off-line studies, both techniques led clients to the same business decisions.[12] The guidance from both sets of data was the same.

Internet Samples

unrestricted Internet sample
A survey in which anyone with a computer and modem can fill out the questionnaire.

Internet samples may be classified as unrestricted, screened, or recruited.[13] In an **unrestricted Internet sample**, anyone who desires can complete the questionnaire. It is fully self-selecting and probably representative of nothing except Web surfers. The problem is exacerbated if the same Internet user can access the questionnaire repeatedly. For example, *InfoWorld*, a computer user magazine, decided to conduct its Readers Choice survey for the first time on the Internet. The results were so skewed by repeat voting for one product that the entire survey was publicly abandoned and the editor asked for readers' help to avoid the problem again. A simple solution to repeat respondents is to lock respondents out of the site after they have filled out the questionnaire.

screened Internet sample
An Internet sample with quotas based on desired sample characteristics.

Screened Internet samples adjust for the unrepresentativeness of the self-selected respondents by imposing quotas based on some desired sample characteristics. These are often demographic characteristics such as gender, income, and geographic region, or product-related criteria such as past purchase behavior, job responsibilities, or current product use. The applications for screened samples are generally similar to those for unrestricted samples.

Screened sample questionnaires typically use a branching or skip pattern for asking screening questions to determine whether the full questionnaire should be presented to a respondent. Some Web survey systems can make immediate market segment calculations that first assign a respondent to a particular segment based on screening questions and then select the appropriate questionnaire to match the respondent's segment.

Alternatively, some Internet research providers maintain a "panel house" that recruits respondents who fill out a preliminary classification questionnaire. This information is used to classify respondents into demographic segments. Clients specify the desired segments, and the respondents who match the desired demographics are permitted to fill out the questionnaires of all clients who specify that segment.

Recruited Internet samples are used for targeted populations in surveys that require more control over the makeup of the sample. Respondents are recruited by telephone, mail, e-mail, or in person. After qualification, they are sent the questionnaire by e-mail or are directed to a Web site that contains a link to the questionnaire. At Web sites, passwords are normally used to restrict access to the questionnaire to the recruited sample members. Since the makeup of the sample is known, completions can be monitored, and the participation rate can be improved by sending follow-up messages to those who do not complete the questionnaire.

Recruited samples are ideal in applications that already have a database from which to recruit the sample. For example, a good application would be a survey that used a customer database to recruit respondents for a purchaser satisfaction study.

recruited Internet sample
A sample in which respondents are prerecruited and must qualify to participate. They are then e-mailed a questionnaire or directed to a secure Web site.

Other Uses of the Internet by Marketing Researchers

The Internet revolution in marketing research has had an impact on more than just the way surveys are conducted. The management of the research process and the dissemination of information have also been greatly enhanced by the Internet. Several key areas have been affected by the Internet:

- *The distribution of requests for proposals (RFPs) and proposals:* Companies can now quickly and efficiently send RFPs to a select e-mail list of research suppliers. In turn, research suppliers can develop proposals and e-mail them back to clients. A process that used to take days using snail mail now occurs in a matter of hours.

- *Collaboration between the client and the research supplier in the management of a research project:* Now a researcher and client may both be looking at a proposal, RFP, report, or some type of statistical analysis at the same time on their respective computer screens while discussing it over the telephone. This is very powerful and efficient. Changes in the sample size, quotas, and other aspects of the research plan can be discussed and made immediately.

- *Data management and on-line analysis:* Clients can access their survey via the research supplier's secure Web site and monitor the data gathering in real time. The client can use sophisticated tools to actually do data analysis as the survey develops. This real-time analysis may result in changes in the questionnaire, sample size, or the types of respondents being interviewed. The research supplier and the client become partners in "just-in-time" marketing research.

- *Publication and distribution of reports:* Reports can be published to the Web directly from programs such as PowerPoint and all the latest versions of leading word-processing, spreadsheet, and presentation software packages. This means that results are available to appropriate managers worldwide on an almost instantaneous basis. Reports can be searched for the content of interest using the same Web browser used to view the report.

- *Viewing of oral presentations of marketing research surveys by widely scattered audiences:* By placing oral presentations on password-protected Web sites, managers throughout the world can see and hear the actual client presentation. This saves time and money by avoiding the need for the managers to travel to a central meeting site.[14]

Discuss the growing importance of scanner-based research

IRI's BehaviorScan product allows IRI to track individual household purchases over time. Participants in the household panel present an ID card at the checkout of a scanner-equipped grocery store.

scanner-based research
A system for gathering information from a single group of respondents by continuously monitoring the advertising, promotion, and pricing they are exposed to and the things they buy.

BehaviorScan
A scanner-based research program that tracks the purchases of three thousand households through store scanners.

InfoScan
A scanner-based sales-tracking service for the consumer packaged-goods industry.

Scanner-Based Research

Scanner-based research is a system for gathering information from a single group of respondents by continuously monitoring the advertising, promotion, and pricing they are exposed to and the things they buy. The variables measured are advertising campaigns, coupons, displays, and product prices. The result is a huge database of marketing efforts and consumer behavior. Scanner-based research is bringing ever closer the Holy Grail of marketing research: an accurate, objective picture of the direct causal relationship between different kinds of marketing efforts and actual sales.

The two major scanner-based suppliers are Information Resources. Inc. (IRI) and the A. C. Nielsen Company. Each has about half the market. However, IRI is the founder of scanner-based research.

IRI's first product is called **BehaviorScan**. A household panel (a group of three thousand long-term participants in the research project) has been recruited and maintained in each BehaviorScan town. Panel members shop with an ID card, which is presented at the checkout in scanner-equipped grocery stores and drugstores, allowing IRI to track electronically each household's purchases, item by item, over time. It uses microcomputers to measure TV viewing in each panel household and can send special commercials to panel member television sets. With such a measure of household purchasing, it is possible to manipulate marketing variables, such as TV advertising or consumer promotions, or to introduce a new product and analyze real changes in consumer buying behavior.

IRI's most successful product is **InfoScan**—a scanner-based sales-tracking service for the consumer packaged-goods industry. Retail sales, detailed consumer purchasing information (including measurement of store loyalty and total grocery basket expenditures), and promotional activity by manufacturers and retailers are monitored and evaluated for all bar-coded products. Data are collected weekly from more than thirty-one thousand supermarkets, drugstores, and mass merchandisers.[15]

When Should Marketing Research Be Conducted?

When managers have several possible solutions to a problem, they should not instinctively call for marketing research. In fact, the first decision to make is whether to conduct marketing research at all.

Some companies have been conducting research in certain markets for many years. Such firms understand the characteristics of target customers and their likes and dislikes about existing products. Under these circumstances, further research would be repetitive and waste money. Procter & Gamble, for example, has extensive knowledge of the coffee market. After it conducted initial taste tests with Folgers Instant Coffee, P&G went into national distribution without further research. Consolidated Foods Kitchen of Sara Lee followed the same strategy with its frozen croissants, as did Quaker Oats with Chewy Granola Bars. This tactic, however, does not always work. P&G marketers thought they understood the pain reliever market thoroughly, so they bypassed market research for Encaprin aspirin in capsules. Because it lacked a distinct competitive advantage over existing products, however, the product failed and was withdrawn from the market.

Managers rarely have such great trust in their judgment that they would refuse more information if it were available and free. But they might have enough confidence that they would be unwilling to pay very much for the information or to wait a long time to receive it. The willingness to acquire additional decision-making information depends on managers' perceptions of its quality, price, and timing. Of course, if perfect information were available—that is, the data conclusively showed which alternative to choose—decision makers would be willing to pay more for it than for information that still left uncertainty. In summary, research should be undertaken only when the expected value of the information is greater than the cost of obtaining it.

Society for Competitive Intelligence Professionals

Find out more about competitive intelligence at the Society for Competitive Intelligence (SCIP) Web site. Research a career in CI by checking out the job marketplace at SCIP.

http://www.scip.org

On Line

Competitive Intelligence

Derived from military intelligence, competitive intelligence is an important tool for helping a firm overcome a competitor's advantage. Specifically, competitive intelligence can help identify the advantage, play a major role in determining how the advantage was achieved, and then provide insights on how it was achieved.

Competitive intelligence (CI) is the creation of a system that helps managers assess their competitors and their vendors in order to become a more efficient and effective competitor. Intelligence is analyzed information. It becomes decision-making intelligence when it has implications for the organization. For example, a primary competitor may have plans to introduce a product with performance standards equal to ours but with a 15 percent cost advantage. The new product will reach the market in eight months. This intelligence has important decision-making and policy consequences for management. Competitive intelligence and environmental scanning (where management gathers data about the external environment—see Chapter 1) combine to create marketing intelligence. Marketing intelligence is then used as input into a marketing decision support system.

Explain the concept of competitive intelligence

competitive intelligence (CI)
An intelligence system that helps managers assess their competition and vendors in order to become more efficient and effective competitors.

Advantages of Competitive Intelligence

Competitive intelligence is one of the hottest areas in marketing today. Firms like General Motors, Ford, GTW, AT&T, Motorola, and many others have large, well-established CI units. The Ford Taurus came about after Ford engineers, aided by CI, examined competitors' cars and incorporated the best features into one auto.

Competitive intelligence helps managers assess their competition and their vendors, which, in turn, means fewer surprises. Competitive intelligence allows managers to predict changes in business relationships, identify marketplace opportunities, guard against threats, forecast a competitor's strategy, discover new or potential competitors, learn from the success or failure of others, learn about new technologies that can affect the company, and learn about the impact of government regulations on the competition. In summary, CI promotes effective and efficient decision making, which should lead to greater profitability. Sheena Sharp, principal, Sharp Information Research, says: "CI gives the company the competitive advantage of foresight and allows it to learn today what will be discovered by others tomorrow."[16]

Several years ago NutraSweet's patent on the artificial sweetener *aspartame* was expiring, and the company faced potential disaster. Management was afraid that chemical and food companies would move into the market. NutraSweet analyzed competitors' prices, customer relations, expansion plans, and advertising campaigns. The company used the information to cut costs, improve service, and preserve most of its market. "We maintained over 80 percent of our market," said NutraSweet's Robert E. Flynn. He said that CI practices are worth $50 million a year to his company.

Sources of Competitive Intelligence

The Internet and its databases are a great source of CI. A CI researcher can use Internet databases to answer these and other questions:

- What articles were written about this market?

- What companies are associated with this product group?

- What patents have been filed for this technology?

- What are the major magazines or texts in this industry?

- What are the chances that I will find something in print on the target company?

- How many companies are in the same industry as the target company?

- Who are the reporters studying this industry?

- How can I be updated on industry and company events without having to constantly request the information?

- How can I compile a list of the leading experts in the industry and the key institutions they are associated with?

Non-computer-based sources of CI can be found in a variety of areas:

- A company's salespeople, who can directly observe and ask questions about the competition.

- Experts with in-depth knowledge of a subject or activity.

- CI consultants, who can use their knowledge and experience to gather needed information quickly and efficiently.

- Government agencies, a valuable source of all types of data.

- Uniform Commercial Code (UCC) filings, a system that identifies goods that are leased or pledged as collateral. This is an excellent source for learning about a company's latest additions to plant assets.

- Suppliers, a group that may offer information on products shipped to a competitor.

- Periodicals, a good source for timely articles on successes, failures, opportunities, and threats.

- The Yellow Pages, which often provide data on number of competitors, trading areas, and special offerings.

- Trade shows, official gatherings where competitors display their latest offerings.

This list is not exhaustive but it does provide an idea of how CI can be gathered.

Read more about competitive intelligence in the supplemental module on Xtra!

CONNECT IT

Look back at the story about duck stamps at the beginning of this chapter. A company can use survey research, observations, or experiments to conduct marketing research.

Unless a company has extensive knowledge, based on research, of the problem at hand, it should probably conduct marketing research. Yet managers should also be reasonably sure that the cost of gathering the information will be less than the value of the data gathered.

Key marketing data often come from a company's own decision support system, which continually gathers data from a variety of sources and funnels the information to decision makers. They then manipulate the data to make better decisions. DSS data are often supplemented by marketing research information.

As a consumer, you participate in shaping consumer products by the choices you make and the products and services you buy. You can become a better consumer by actively participating in marketing surveys and learning more about the products you buy.

Participate in Marketing Research Surveys

All of us get tired of telephone solicitations where people try to sell us everything from new carpet to chimney cleaning. Recognize that marketing research surveys are different. A true marketing research survey will *never* involve a sales pitch nor will the research firm sell your name to a database marketer. The purpose of marketing research is to build better goods and services for you and me. If you help out such researchers, you ultimately help yourself. The Council for Marketing and Opinion Research (CMOR) is an organization of hundreds of marketing research professionals that is dedicated to preserving the integrity of the research industry. If you receive a call from someone who tries to sell you something under the guise of marketing research, get the name and address of the organization. Call CMOR at 1 (800) 887-CMOR and report the abuse.

REVIEW IT

(1) **Explain the concept and purpose of a marketing decision support system.** A decision support system (DSS) makes data instantly available to marketing managers and allows them to manipulate the data themselves to make marketing decisions. Four characteristics make DSSs especially useful to marketing managers: They are interactive, flexible, discovery oriented, and accessible. Decision support systems give managers access to information immediately and without outside assistance. They allow users to manipulate data in a variety of ways and to answer "what if" questions. And, finally, they are accessible to novice computer users.

1.1 In the absence of company problems, is there any reason to develop a marketing DSS?

1.2 Explain the difference between marketing research and a DSS.

(2) **Define marketing research and explain its importance to marketing decision making.** Marketing research is a process of collecting and analyzing data for the purpose of solving specific marketing problems. Marketers use marketing research to explore the profitability of marketing strategies. They can examine why particular strategies failed and analyze characteristics of specific market segments. Managers can use research findings to help keep current customers. Moreover, marketing research allows management to behave proactively, rather than reactively, by identifying newly emerging patterns in society and the economy.

2.1 The task of marketing is to create exchanges. What role might marketing research play in the facilitation of the exchange process?

2.2 Marketing research has traditionally been associated with manufacturers of consumer goods. Today, however, an increasing number of organizations, both profit and nonprofit, are using marketing research. Why do you think this trend exists? Give some examples of specific reasons why organizations might use marketing research.

2.3 **WRITING** Write a reply to the following statement: "I own a restaurant in the downtown area. I see customers every day whom I know on a first-name basis. I understand their likes and dislikes. If I put something on the menu and it doesn't sell, I know that they didn't like it. I also read the magazine *Modern Restaurants*, so I know what the trends are in the industry. This is all of the marketing research I need to do."

2.4 Give an example of (a) the descriptive role of marketing research, (b) the diagnostic role, and (c) the predictive function of marketing research.

(3) **Describe the steps involved in conducting a marketing research project.** The marketing research process involves several basic steps. First, the researcher and the decision maker must agree on a problem statement or set of research objectives. The researcher then creates an overall research design to specify how primary data will be gathered and analyzed. Before collecting data, the researcher decides whether the group to be interviewed will be a probability or nonprobability sample. Field service firms are often hired to carry out data collection. Once data have been collected, the researcher analyzes them using statistical analysis. The researcher then prepares and presents oral and written reports, with conclusions and recommendations, to management. As a final step, the researcher determines whether the recommendations were implemented and what could have been done to make the project more successful.

3.1 Critique the following methodologies and suggest more appropriate alternatives:

a. A supermarket was interested in determining its image. It dropped a short questionnaire into the grocery bag of each customer before putting in the groceries.

b. To assess the extent of its trade area, a shopping mall stationed interviewers in the parking lot every Monday and Friday evening. Interviewers walked up to people after they had parked their cars and asked them for their zip codes.

c. To assess the popularity of a new movie, a major studio invited people to call a 900 number and vote yes, they would see it again, or no, they would not. Each caller was billed a $2 charge.

3.2 *WRITING* You have been charged with determining how to attract more business majors to your school. Write an outline of the steps you would take, including the sampling procedures, to accomplish the task.

3.3 Why are secondary data sometimes preferable to primary data?

3.4 Discuss when focus groups should and should not be used.

3.5 *TEAM* Divide the class into teams of eight persons. Each group will conduct a focus group on the quality and number of services that your college is providing to its students. One person from each group should be chosen to act as moderator. Remember, it is the moderator's job to facilitate discussion, not to lead the discussion. These groups should last approximately forty-five minutes. If possible, the groups should be videotaped or recorded. Upon completion, each group should write a brief report of its results. Consider offering to meet with the dean of students to share the results of your research.

(4) **Discuss the profound impact of the Internet on marketing research.** The Internet has vastly simplified the secondary data search process, placing more sources of information in front of researchers than ever before. Internet survey research is surging in popularity. Internet surveys can be created rapidly and reported in real time. They are also relatively inexpensive and can easily be personalized. Often researchers can use the Internet to contact respondents who are difficult to reach by other means. The Internet can also be used to distribute research proposals and reports and to facilitate collaboration between the client and the research supplier. Clients can access real-time data and analyze the information as the collection process continues.

4.1 *ON LINE* Use the Internet and a Web browser, such as Lycos or Yahoo!, and type "marketing research." You will then have thousands of options. Pick a Web site that you find interesting and report on its content to the class.

4.2 Why has the Internet been of such great value to researchers seeking secondary data?

⑤ Discuss the growing importance of scanner-based research. A scanner-based research system enables marketers to monitor a market panel's exposure and reaction to such variables as advertising, coupons, store displays, packaging, and price. By analyzing these variables in relation to the panel's subsequent buying behavior, marketers gain useful insight into sales and marketing strategies.

5.1 Why has scanner-based research been seen as "the ultimate answer" for marketing researchers? Do you see any disadvantages of this methodology?

5.2 Detractors claim that scanner-based research is like "driving a car down the road looking only in the rearview mirror." What does this mean? Do you agree?

⑥ Explain the concept of competitive intelligence. Competitive intelligence (CI) is the creation of an intelligence system that helps managers assess their competition and their vendors in order to become more efficient and effective competitors. Intelligence is analyzed information, and it becomes decision-making intelligence when it has implications for the organization.

By helping managers assess their competition and vendors, CI leads to fewer surprises. CI allows managers to predict changes in business relationships, guard against threats, forecast a competitor's strategy, and develop a successful marketing plan.

The Internet and databases accessed via the Internet offer excellent sources of CI. Company personnel, particularly sales and service representatives, are usually good sources of CI. Many companies require their salespersons to routinely fill out CI reports. Other external sources of CI include experts, CI consultants, government agencies, UCC filings, suppliers, newspapers and other publications, Yellow Pages, and trade shows.

6.1 Why do you think that CI is so hot in today's environment?

6.2 Prepare a memo to your boss at United Airlines and outline why the organization needs a CI unit.

6.3 Form a team with three other students. Each team must choose a firm in the PC manufacturing industry and then go to the Web site of the firm and acquire as much CI as possible. Each team will then prepare a five-minute oral presentation on its findings.

DEFINE IT

BehaviorScan 244
central-location telephone (CLT) facility 230
closed-ended question 233
competitive intelligence (CI) 245
computer-assisted personal interviewing 230
computer-assisted self-interviewing 230
convenience sample 238
cross-tabulation 240
database marketing 218
decision support system (DSS) 218

executive interviews 231
experiment 237
field service firm 239
focus group 231
frame error 239
group dynamics 231
InfoScan 244
mall intercept interview 230
management decision problem 222
marketing information 218
marketing research 219
marketing research objective 222

marketing research problem 222
measurement error 239
mystery shoppers 235
newsgroups 225
nonprobability sample 238
observation research 235
open-ended question 233
primary data 228
probability sample 237
random error 239
random sample 238
recruited Internet sample 243
research design 225

APPLY IT

Application for Entrepreneurs

Bill and Mary Osborn hit it lucky with dot-com stocks. At the age of thirty-nine, they have amassed $5.2 million from astutely playing the stock market. They cashed out before the dot-com crash, and now they are ready to pursue their dream.

The Osborns have always wanted to live in Colorado and have dreamed of owning a small hotel. Mary hit upon the idea of doing both—that is, building a hotel in Colorado that they could manage. Initial research uncovered the following information.

When asked which two or three things are most important in choosing a hotel for a vacation, Americans put nonsmoking rooms first (40 percent). Twenty-four-hour access to food (36 percent), quality in-room amenities such as coffeemakers and hair dryers (34 percent), athletic facilities (31 percent), and "good evening facilities" (26 percent) are next. Vacationers rank supervised activities for children much higher than business travelers (10 percent versus 3 percent).

Overnight business travelers, who traveled in the past year, in contrast, focus on things that will make their trip more productive. Like vacationers, they rate nonsmoking rooms tops (46 percent). But they put quality in-room amenities (39 percent) and transportation to the airport (32 percent) next. And, while they cite many of the same things as vacationers as being important, they put a much higher priority on some things, particularly in-room connections for computer, fax, and on-line access (21 percent, seventeen points higher than vacationers), being able to earn airline miles (15 percent, eight points higher), and frequent guest programs (14 percent, five points higher).

Questions

Use the Internet to help determine the following:

1. What price range should be offered?

2. Where in Colorado should the hotel be built?

3. Should the hotel cater primarily to business or vacation travelers?

4. What amenities and features should the hotel offer?

5. Should Mary and Bill consider becoming a franchisee?

THINK ABOUT IT

Ethics Exercise

John Michael Smythe owns a small marketing research firm in Cleveland, Ohio, which employs seventy-five people. Most employees are sole breadwinners in their families. John's firm has not fared well for the past two years and is on the verge of bankruptcy. The company recently surveyed over 2,500 people in Ohio about new car purchase plans for the Ohio Department of Economic Development. Because the study identified many hot prospects for new cars, a new car dealer has offered John $8,000 for the names and phone numbers of people saying they are "likely" or "very likely" to buy a new car within the next twelve months. John needs the money to avoid laying off a number of employees.

Questions

1. Should John Smythe sell the names?

2. Does the AMA Code of Ethics address this issue? Go to **http://www.marketingpower.com** and review the code. Then, write a brief paragraph on what the AMA Code of Ethics contains that relates to John Smythe's dilemma.

Entrepreneursip Case

Cool and How to Find It: Look-Look

COURTESY LOOK-LOOK, INC.

You can't always believe what you hear, particularly in the fast-moving world of youth trends. That is, unless you listen to Sharon Lee and DeeDee Gordon, founders of Look-Look, the most accurate information resource on the global youth culture. The pair founded the company in 1999, determined to find whatever makes the cultural spider-sense tingle—music, shoes, clothes, games, makeup, food, and technology. Lee and Gordon took Look-Look on-line in 2000, and the company has quickly risen to be the paragon of trend forecasting in the youth market. How?

When Sharon Lee needs to know what's cool, she taps into a network of experts the CIA would envy. It's a Web-linked weave of nearly ten-thousand volunteers and part-timers, aged fourteen to thirty, recruited over several years at clubs and hangouts around the country, from New York to Los Angeles and points in between, to report on their world.

Look-Look's multilevel database is populated with thousands of prescreened recruits who log on to answer surveys and polls, register opinions, and communicate for points that can lead to cash, digital cameras, and other techie toys. Some of the recruits, armed with digital cameras, can photograph their world, then upload the pictures, send e-mail reports, and use Look-Look's Intranet message boards. The young field agents might snap anything from a rave to their bedroom walls. Look-Look relies on "early adopters" and "influencers" to provide the layers of information that traditional research only skims.

Look-Look is a cool seeker, paid by major marketers to get the first bead on what's next on the horizon. With a cool seeker's expertise, even the most staid company can be on the razor's edge: Look-Look ferreted out the then-uncharted popularity of under-a-dollar stores, fold-up scooters, and over-the-shoulder bags.

Cornerstone Promotion, a Look-Look rival, was behind Microsoft's successful launch of the Xbox video-gaming system. "Seventy kids got units," said Cornerstone's president. "They were plugged into the local clubs and set up gaming parties with music giveaways from our record label clients. They'd do it in campus rec centers or at night clubs or on radio shows." By the time Xbox made its debut, "we created a huge frenzy." Microsoft was no longer stodgy compared to Sega or PlayStation.

In addition to youth market environmental scanning, a client might ask Look-Look to check the coolness quotient of a product. After the small army is canvassed with on-line polls and surveys, the results are arranged into categories. "The turnaround," says Lee, "can be as little as forty-eight hours." Look-Look categorizes information into ten channels: fashion, entertainment, technology, activities, eating and drinking, health and beauty, mood of culture (how kids feel about life), spirituality, city guide, and Look Out (a "best of" findings in a snapshot). The information is put through rigorous paces. "Methodology is crucial, especially with the quantity and quality of the sample," says Lee. "We can take a sample of 300 or thousands. That's up to Gallup standards."

To ensure the most accurate information, Look-Look steers away from focus groups because peer pressure is a factor at this age; teens are more likely to bend to pressure and follow the leader of a peer group. One-on-one interviews are, therefore, preferred. They keep the responses truer and uninfluenced by external pressures. To get to cool, Look-Look has to keep its sources cool.

And what is cool, anyway? Says Lee, "For young people now it's pure raw emotion—it's anything that inspires you to think 'I want that because it fits me so well.' It can be a person, a product, a place, anything." according to Que Gaskins, the chief marketing officer of Ad*itive, a multicultural marketing firm, cool really starts with the "what if" factor: "'What if I wore that hat or that jersey?' Then you give it your own twist, the way African American males sport Asian tattoos or middle-class white kids wear dreadlocks or corn-rows. But there's just no formula for cool."

"Cool burns out so fast that by the time companies know it's cool, it's not cool anymore," says Lee. "The old-time corporate methodology was to treat it like the annual report for shareholders—going out and testing a sample size of a few hundred people, then retesting it again the next year. But a year in youth culture is like a year in dog years."

Still, cool is as hard to pin down as a weather forecast for next week. But the real arbiters of cool are those who can afford to lead. "Ultimately," says Gaskins, "the future of cool belongs to whoever has the most buying power."

Questions

1. What is Look-Look offering businesses that traditional market research firms cannot offer?

2. Describe the role of the Internet in youth trend spotting. Do you think a research firm can accurately forecast youth trends without an on-line component to its research plan?

3. Go to Look-Look's Web site at **http://www.look-look.com** and check out some of the free information in each category. How accurate do you find the information? Have you seen any of these trends in your city or region, or among your friends and classmates?

4. Make a list of products or companies that you think could benefit from Look-Look's form of predictive market research. Next to each item, write a brief reason why and how you think cool seeking would benefit the company or product.

 ## WATCH IT

Short

It's not often that marketing research topics are depicted in advertisements. The two ads for Quiznos in the Chapter 7 PowerPoint presentation on the *Essentials of Marketing* PowerPoint CD-ROM spoof research validity.

Medium **VIDEO**

Staying abreast of current trends is difficult enough without trying to forecast what will be popular in the future. One researcher takes candid shots of people throughout Tokyo and then uploads them to the Web so that clients can view the pictures. Watch this cool hunter in action in the CNN clip for Chapter 7.

Long Small**BusinessSchool** ▫
the Series on PBS stations and the Web

To give you insights into Chapter 7, Small Business School will take you the Specialty Cheese Company in Lowell, Wisconsin. Vickie and Paul Scharfman develop new products, avoid product bombs, and transform an old business into a thriving company, all through marketing research.

 ## FLIP IT

 Flip to Chapter 7 in your *Grademaker Study Guide* for more review opportunities, including the pretest, vocabulary review, Internet activities, study test questions, and marketing research scenarios. Can you explain why market research is so important? Can you close your book and outline the marketing research process? Can't? Then you need to review with your *Grademaker*.

CLICK IT

The *Essentials of Marketing* Web site links you to all the Internet-based activities in this chapter, like "Review It" questions 4.1, 4.2, and 6.3, "Apply It," and the On-Line exercises in the chapter margins. As a review, do the Chapter 7 quiz and crossword puzzle. And don't forget the Career Exersite that shows you different resources if you're interested in a career in marketing research. Review the main concepts in the PowerPoint presentation for Chapter 7, too. Go to **http://lamb.swlearning.com**, read the material, and follow the links right from the site.

Surf to Xtra! to find out more about competitive intelligence in the supplemental content module. Then test your understanding of marketing research by completing the worksheets for Exhibits 7.1, 7.4, 7.6, and 7.7. If your instructor has assigned a marketing plan project, worksheets on Xtra! can help you organize your work. In addition to the quiz on the Web site, there's another quiz on Xtra!, plus video of the authors answering frequently asked quesitons about marketing research, such as "Are there ever conflicts between marketing researchers and product managers?" and "What is the difference between qualitative and quantitative research?"

Still Shaky? Here's a Tip.

Review your class notes. Do they give you enough information? If they are lacking, visit your campus study center to learn how to take good notes.

MARKETING MISCUES

Metricom's Ricochet Fails to Rebound

In 1995, Metricom, Inc., introduced a wireless data service that it promised would replicate a desktop in the field. Ten years after its 1985 start as a company focused on developing technology to enable utilities to check meters remotely, Metricom was the first company to offer reliable wireless access and expected to be way ahead of the wireless pack. Six years, and millions of dollars later, the company went bankrupt. What was to blame? Flawed marketing.

The Product

Metricom, Inc., based in Los Gatos, California, offered both a product (Ricochet modem) and a service (Microcellular Data Network). The Ricochet wireless modem, which sold for about $350, was a small black box that plugged into the serial port of a computer. The modem was equipped with a rechargeable battery and came with a power adapter/charger. The Ricochet technology provided wireless data speeds up to 128 kilobits per second.

Metricom's Microcellular Data Network consisted of Ricochet transmitter repeater radios installed on existing poles (e.g., light poles) less than half a mile apart in market areas where Metricom had decided to do business. Because the transmitters were placed on existing infrastructure, Metricom had to obtain permission from landlords or city offices to install them. Once the transmitters were installed in a given city, a Ricochet modem could be used.

By 2001, the company offered high-speed wireless service in fifteen market areas in the United States. These included fifteen major cities: Atlanta, Baltimore, Dallas, Denver, Detroit, Houston, Los Angeles, Minneapolis, New York, Philadelphia, Phoenix, San Diego, San Francisco, Seattle, and Washington, D.C. Reseller partners included WorldCom, Inc., Juno Online, GoAmerica, Aether Systems, Wireless WebConnect!, and IP communications.

The Promotion

Why didn't customers buy the Ricochet system? Analysts and industry observers claim that a weak marketing program was to blame for Metricom's demise. While the market did not fault Metricom's products, the rest of the company's marketing mix received considerable criticism. The lack of overall market coverage (only a few cities) and the length of time it took to roll out to new cities were problems. Furthermore, at $80 a month, Metricom's mobile access cost three times as much as dial-up services and was not price-competitive with local cable providers and phone-company DSLs.

The company's advertising campaign was considered confusing, especially for a product that could, itself, be confusing to potential users. Metricom advertised its Ricochet wireless system in markets as they opened. The advertising used two characters, Rico and Chet, a spy duo who obtained top set information off the Internet while in their car.

Possibly the most important problem, however, was that Metricom may have targeted the wrong market segment. With a small change in its pricing model, the company could have offered wireless technology to homes and offices within its access cities. Why didn't the company realize that business users would need Internet access from more than fifteen cities, but that there were millions of home and office users in the markets within the company's network?

Questions

1. Where did Metricom go wrong?

2. How important was the target market to Metricom's success?

CRITICAL THINKING CASE

Square Two: On Par with Female Golfers' Needs

As a supplier of low-priced yet high-quality golf clubs for men and women since 1974, Square Two golf has always targeted the budget-minded segment of new golf equipment buyers. The golf equipment industry has changed markedly, and the game's surge in popularity has pushed the market for golf equipment and supplies to almost $2.5 billion per year. Fighting for survival among traditional golf giants such as Taylor-Made, Titleist, Ping, and Callaway, Square Two Golf has used a crafty positioning and segmentation strategy to fortify its business.

Having long ago identified differentiation as the key to its survival, Square Two determined that the best way to grow its business would be to turn its attention to a very specific segment of the golf equipment market. During the past several years, the number of female golfers in the United States surged past five million, or almost 20 percent of the country's total participants. The average female player has a household income of $70,000. In light of these environmental factors, the company undertook a gradual repositioning initiative that aligned it almost exclusively with the women's game.

The company's first major step was its launch of a national television ad campaign in 1999. Set in a golf shop, the ads featured a woman who informed viewers that buying the latest in women's golf technology does not have to be prohibitively expensive. Doug Buffington, the company's chief operating officer, affirms that the ad's message reinforces Square Two's unique selling proposition: supplying women with more choices of affordable golf equipment using patented technology than better-known brands. Buffington also notes that the ads communicate the products' value and inspire viewers to ask store representatives what the differences are between Square Two's clubs and those made by the competition. The advertising spots led Square Two to its first year of profitability.

Not resting on his laurels, Buffington initiated a deal in June 2001 to acquire a leading women's golf shoe manufacturer, Lady Fairway, in order to extend Square Two's product lines. That deal inspired the chairman of Nancy Lopez Golf, a maker of high-end women's clubs named after the eponymous Hall of Fame golfer, to approach Square Two with a similar acquisition deal. Since the Nancy Lopez line would complement Square Two's existing line of affordable clubs, thus enabling it to serve the entire women's market at multiple price levels, Square Two agreed.

The Lopez line caters to the more affluent golfer, so there is little chance that one line will cannibalize the other. Moreover, both companies have a strong history of targeting women, and their deal opens new and improved distribution channels. Though costs of marketing the new lines initially hurt Square Two's bottom line, the acquisitions have led to increased revenues, and stronger positioning promises to increase profitability in the future.

Buffington's repositioning strategy culminated with the public announcement that Square Two changed its corporate name to Women's Golf Unlimited (WGU). The new company oversees the development and marketing of its two club brands, Square Two Golf and Nancy Lopez Golf, and its shoe, apparel, and accessories brand, Lady Fairway. The synergies, however, are not limited to product development. Retail outlets carrying the new company's three product lines can offer their customers a one-stop source for all of their equipment needs.

Square Two's repositioning effort proved to be extremely insightful. Critics may point out that although women represent 20 percent of the golfing population, they only account for 15 percent of the market's $2.5 billion in spending. Critics may also cite the statistic that shows the number of female golfers has slightly decreased from 5.8 million to 5.1 million in the last couple of years. Both facts are true, but one of the reasons many female golfers may have left the game is that equipment manufacturers have not sufficiently met their unique needs. WGU, however, manufactures golf clubs and supporting equipment designed to meet the needs of women's smaller bodies and swing speeds, while providing pleasing aesthetics.

That is where WGU sees a huge opportunity. It has the potential to use its knowledge of and sensitivity towards the women's market to motivate female players to spend proportionately to their share of the total market's population. It is an untapped market value of well over $100 million.

Questions

1. Does the group of consumers to which WGU targets its products satisfy the definition of a market, a market segment, or both? Explain.

2. Discuss the importance of market segmentation strategy to WGU.

3. Describe the positioning strategy for WGU as an organization.

4. Describe the positioning for each of the two golf club brands that WGU markets.

MARKETING PLANNING ACTIVITIES

To complete all seven activities, use the Part 2 Marketing Planning Worksheets on *Xtra!* If you need a company for the basis of your work, follow the "Marketing Plan Project" link on the *Essentials of Marketing* Web site (**http://lamb.swcollege.com**).

Analyzing Marketing Opportunities

For continued general assistance on business plans and marketing plans, visit **http://www.bplans.com** or **http://www.businessplans.org**. For electronic sources of information, search the Electric Library at **http://www.elibrary.com** or the Internet Public Library at **http://www.ipl.org**. Another excellent source of information is the Sales and Marketing Executives Marketing Library at **http://www.smei.org**.

The next step in preparing a marketing plan for the company you have chosen is to get a thorough understanding of the marketing opportunities in terms of marketing to customers. Investigate Internet opportunities, with a special focus on potential customers. Try to understand both consumer and business decision making because Internet business can be built to serve either market. In fact, most experts predict that the business-to-business sector of the Internet will be several times larger than the business-to-consumer sector. Knowing how to perform marketing research to find out more about both customers and competitors is key for any strategic marketing plan.

Use the following exercises to guide you through the second part of your strategic marketing plan:

1. Identify the NAICS code for your chosen company's industry. Perform a brief industry analysis (from U.S. *Industrial Outlook*, for example) of your firm's industry, based on the NAICS code. You can find SIC codes at **http://www.wave.net/upg/immigration/sic_index.html**. These codes will help you perform further research. For example, register with the free site **http://www.zapdata.com** and get market analyses and profiles for your firm and industry. The Statistical Data Locators site (**http://www.ntu.edu.sg/library/stat/statdata.htm**) is a good collection of statistical and economic sources from countries and regions outside the United States.

2. To whom does your company market (consumer, industrial, government, not-for-profit, or a combination of targets)? Within each market, are there specific segments or niches that your company can concentrate on? If so, which one(s) would you focus on and why? What are the factors used to create these segments? What are the Internet capabilities in those markets? If you try to encourage those segments to access your product or service via the Internet, will that change which segments are most important to your business? How? What are the factors used to create these segments? Which segments should your company focus on and why? A resource indicating segment-specific resources is available at **http://www.awool.com/**. Additionally, the U.S. Census Bureau has a number of databases you can access with statistics for different marketing segments at **http://www.census.gov**. You can also look at the unique challenges of business-to-business e-marketing at **www.clickz.com**.

3. Describe your company's target market segment(s). Use demographics, psychographics, geographics, economic factors, size, growth rates, trends, NAICS codes, and any other appropriate descriptors. What role does the Internet play in your target market's life? How is the target market for your Internet business different from that of a traditional business in your market?

4. Describe the decision-making process that customers go through when purchasing your company's product or service. What are the critical factors that influence this purchase-behavior process? How will this decision making affect your e-marketing focus and your market offering? If you have a brick-and-mortar presence, will you encourage any existing customers to shop online? Why?

5. Using the list of key differential advantages described in the first part of your marketing plan, create a series of positioning grids, using two factors as dimensions (see Exhibit 6.9 for example). Then plot the list of key competitors identified earlier onto these positioning grids. Is your company too close to a key competitor? Are there spaces where the consumer's needs and wants are unsatisfied? Check out the concepts and models used by Positioning Strategies at **http://www.positioning.com** to increase your understanding of positioning strategies. Consider how the Internet changes what factors are important to success in your market space. Is technology the most important factor for your firm, or are there other ways for you to differentiate from and beat your competition?

6. Are there any critical issues you must explore with primary marketing research before you can implement your marketing plan? These might include items such as customer demand, purchase intentions, customer perceptions of product quality, price perceptions, and reaction to critical promotion. List some critical research questions and decide which form of research you would use. Design a brief Internet customer satisfaction survey that you could place on your Web site. Use the "Survey Wiz" at **http://psych.fullerton.edu/ mbirnbaum/programs/surveyWiz.HTM** to help you with your questionnaire. Also check out Insight Express at **http://www.insightexpress.com**.

7. What type of competitive intelligence will you need to gather in order to monitor your market space? How can analyzing the job offerings, mission or "about us" statements, products and services descriptions, or other general information on your competitors' Web sites help you figure out their strategic direction? What areas of a Web site could you scan to gather competitive information? Perhaps you will need to select a clipping service. Go to **http://www.looksmart.com** and search for "News Clipping Services." For an excellent compilation of competitive intelligence tools, go to **http://www.fuld.com/i3/index.html**.

CROSS-FUNCTIONAL CONNECTIONS SOLUTIONS

Information Intergration to Satisfy Customer Wants and Needs

Questions

1. Why has information historically been perceived as "owned" by the marketing department?

   There are probably several general answers to this question. One is that because the information is referred to as "marketing research" rather than "market" or "marketplace," it automatically denotes that it is part of the marketing department. Also, the research has traditionally been conducted by the marketing department—reinforcing the notion that the marketing department owns it. Additionally, prior to the 1990s, the marketing department was the only formal link between the company and the customer. Because a primary focus of marketing research is the customer, it was always owned by the marketing department.

2. What data differences exist across functions?

   The historical data debate between marketing and other business functions centers on the qualitative versus quantitative format of the data. The data collected by marketers are perceived to be "touchy-feely" data in contrast to the "hard" data utilized by other functional areas. In addition to unit sales and competitive offerings, marketing data look at customers' perceptions—something very "soft" when compared to other functional data. For example, manufacturing can cite exact production output, cost, and cycle data, and R&D has precise specifications for tensile strength, electrical usage, and battery power. Add accounting data with their general accounting standards to the "hard" data side of the picture, and it's not surprising that data differences cause cross-functional conflict within a firm.

3. What is the job of a chief knowledge officer?

   The chief knowledge officer (CKO) is a company executive who manages institutional learning. CKOs are responsible for integrating internal and external knowledge into their companies. In addition to monitoring this information, the CKO creates and propagates new knowledge based on industry observations, best practices, and benchmarking studies. The CKO shares the collected knowledge with all members of the firm, thereby providing them with consistently important and relevant information.

Suggested Readings

James A. Cook, "Web Browser Brings Product Demand into Focus," *Logistics Management and Distribution*, May 1999, 67–70.

Alex Taylor III, "Kellogg Cranks Up Its Idea Machine," *Fortune*, July 5, 1999, 181–182.

Product and Distribution Decisions

PART 3

CROSS-FUNCTIONAL CONNECTIONS

CROSS-FUNCTIONAL COLLABORATION IN SPEEDING PRODUCTS TO MARKET

Achieving customer satisfaction means that the company must have the right product at the right place at the right time (and at the right price). The need for cross-functional coordination in developing, producing, and delivering a high-quality product is clear. The giant retailer Wal-Mart has based much of its competitive success on its ability to get the right product in the right stores at the right time—products that are then sold to customers via the company's helpful, friendly sales people.

Efficient processes developed on the technical side of business have been meshed with customers' demands for high-quality, highly customized products that can be delivered immediately. For example, research and development and manufacturing functional groups have become efficient at working together—using processes referred to as "design-factory fit," "concurrent engineering," "design for manufacturability and assembly," and "early manufacturing involvement." All of these concepts refer to advance linkage between a product's design and its manufacturing needs such that it can be made and shipped soon after it is designed. Companies have been quite successful at implementing these concepts. Ryobi Group, a Japanese manufacturer of power tools and power equipment, used design for manufacturability and assembly in the development of a new engine for hand-held power equipment. The company's marketing group got involved in the new product development process by collecting input with respect to customers' desired product features.

Such attention to customers' expectations is in direct contrast to traditional thinking. Traditionally, companies made standardized products available immediately, with customers understanding that customization would mean delays in delivery. Today's marketplace increasingly demands that companies compete on both time and customization.

The key to providing customized products quickly is a multidisciplinary approach to business. Traditionally, products were conceptualized by one function, given to another function to produce, and then handed over to yet another to sell. New models, however, are replacing linear product development. Now, companies are expected to move products through all functional processes in at least half the time previously considered acceptable.

Harley-Davidson uses cross-functional teams from concept to market. Implementing the cross-functional team approach helped pull the company from the brink of disaster in the late twentieth century. The company began to design and deliver a product that satisfied customers' demands, while at the same time designing a product that was quicker and easier to assemble. This type of design and assembly requires a high level of coordination among marketing, R & D, and manufacturing.

Boeing refers to this type of coordination as "paperless design." Teams of R & D, manufacturing, marketing, customers, and finance designed the Boeing 777 by assembling an airplane on a computer system that allowed them to model the airplane and iron out bugs long before the major expense of building a prototype.

Manufacturers also have focused on meeting customization and speed to market demands with "modularization." With modular components, some of a product's component parts fit in all, or most, of the company's products. Many of the power tools made by Black & Decker are made with modular components. Modularity standardizes a large part of the product and allows the firm to quickly customize the product beyond its core architecture. However, modularization increases the time and cost of (re)designing products, so it is critical to demonstrate the long-term payoff.

As expected, considerable costs are associated with getting a high-quality product out the door, and manufacturing has been a key marketing partner in making the delivery process successful. Advanced manufacturing systems (AMS) have been developed that not only reduce costs (and therefore price), but also allow faster product delivery. Just-in-time (JIT) and electronic data interchange (EDI) are two of the more popular advanced manufacturing systems.

A JIT manufacturing system produces the product as needed, instead of producing for stock. JIT ultimately changes the channel structure. Customers may be able to receive products directly from the manufacturer rather than through a distribution channel. The lack of channel intermediaries not only makes products available quickly, but it also results in fewer channel members and, in turn, decreased costs—the ultimate in efficiency of operations. Before eliminating intermediaries, marketing must determine if the channel intermediary provides a service that would otherwise be unavailable if the product were shipped directly to the customer from the manufacturer.

Electronic data interchange can also significantly increase the efficiency of operations between the shop floor and distribution network. With EDI, data are collected at the point-of-sale and transmitted automatically to the manufacturing department. Manufacturing then knows the exact number of available units at any point in time and can schedule its production and delivery to meet the customer's specific needs. Eli Lilly Canada is a health-care company that must be able to trace its product movements from the time of manufacture to the point of customer delivery. The company uses wireless data communication to track this movement. Its radio-frequency-based warehouse management system was implemented by a cross-functional team comprised of manufacturing, technology, and marketing experts.

As you can see, successful cross-functional plans result in operational efficiencies by linking marketing's product development and distribution processes to manufacturing's production processes.

Both marketing and manufacturing should have a hand in developing these plans. Why? To give consumers both dollar savings and improved customer service.

Increased focus on customer service has added another function to this marketing-production coupling—human resources. Employees are at the heart of customer service. The front-line employee is key to delivering high-quality service and a high-quality product. A company's profitability and growth objectives are driven by customer loyalty, which is in turn driven by customer satisfaction, which is the direct result of human interaction with the distributor of the final product.

Coordination between marketing and other business functions is necessary to get a high-quality, competitively priced product to the end-user in a timely manner. Whether it is developing a new product/service or managing the existing product line or service offerings, cross-functional teamwork is necessary for company-wide success and for maintaining competitive advantage in today's rapidly changing marketplace.

Questions

1. What are some of the popular business terms used to describe cross-functional integration?

2. What are some of the popular advanced manufacturing systems, and how do they interact with marketing?

3. How do production and delivery happen simultaneously in the service sector? What other functional areas are important partners in the service arena?

Check It Out

For articles and exercises on the material in this part, and for other great study aids, visit the *Essentials of Marketing* Web site at

http://lamb.swlearning.com

CHAPTER **EIGHT**
PRODUCT AND SERVICES CONCEPTS

Learning Objectives

1 Define the term product

2 Classify consumer products

3 Discuss the importance of services to the economy

4 Discuss the differences between services and goods

5 Define the terms product item, product line, *and* product mix

6 Describe marketing uses of branding

7 Describe marketing uses of packaging and labeling

8 Describe how and why product warranties are important marketing tools

In the summer of 1999, Design Continuum's parking lot could have doubled as a Texas barbecue cook-off. However, the consultants at the Boston product design company were researching a new product for Coleman, the company known for its lanterns and camping stoves. Coleman was about to introduce the first gas grill in its hundred-year history. While grills do not pose a difficult engineering problem, the marketing of a Coleman backyard grill was a challenge. Coleman has a successful brand name, but it had never produced anything besides camping products. "If you know the Coleman brand, it's radical to propose having a backyard grill," noted Mark Prince, Continuum's director of marketing. "They were taking the brand into new territory." Moreover, Coleman had no branding guide to help designers.

The Continuum team examined years of Coleman catalogs to try and define what made the Coleman brand unique. It found several things that Coleman products had in common, including their weight and their signature green enamel finish. The design team tried a few radical ideas, including a design for a grill that resembled a Coleman lantern. But customer surveys found that customers preferred the sturdy, traditional designs that Coleman was known for. People expected the new grills to carry on the Coleman heritage, which meant reliable and durable products.

The challenge was to translate this heritage into a new product category. The Continuum/Coleman team decided to create not the most advanced grill in the industry, but one that had the unique aspects of the Coleman brand: weight and the green enamel color. "When you see this grill in Home Depot, you don't say,

'Wow, that's better than anything I've seen,'" Prince says. "You look at it and say it's a Coleman."

To introduce the product, Coleman used its connections with stores like Home Depot and Sears to persuade them to carry the new grills, priced in the $300 to $500 range. A print ad campaign ran in outdoor-enthusiast magazines. The company also sponsored cook-offs at Nascar events. The grill got a public relations boost from *Consumer Reports*, which gave it one of its highest ratings.

The new line of grills captured 4 percent of the market and was one of the most successful launches in Sunbeam's (Coleman's parent company) history. In fact, the new grills have helped attract people to the entire Coleman brand.[1]

Explain how Coleman's new grill fits into the company's product mix. Why do you think that Coleman was so successful with its new grill? What other new products might Coleman be successful with? We will answer these questions and more in Chapter 8.

What Is a Product?

1

Define the term *product*

product
Everything, both favorable and unfavorable, that a person receives in an exchange.

The product offering, the heart of an organization's marketing program, is usually the starting point in creating a marketing mix. A marketing manager cannot determine a price, design a promotion strategy, or create a distribution channel until the firm has a product to sell. Moreover, an excellent distribution channel, a persuasive promotion campaign, and a fair price have no value with a poor or inadequate product offering.

A **product** may be defined as everything, both favorable and unfavorable, that a person receives in an exchange. A product may be a tangible good like a pair of shoes, a service like a haircut, an idea like "don't litter," or any combination of these three. Packaging, style, color, options, and size are some typical product features. Just as important are intangibles such as service, the seller's image, the manufacturer's reputation, and the way consumers believe others will view the product.

To most people, the term *product* means a tangible good. However, services and ideas are also products. The marketing process identified in Chapter 1 is the same whether the product marketed is a good, a service, an idea, or some combination of these.

Types of Consumer Products

2

Classify consumer products

business product (industrial product)
A product used to manufacture other goods or services, to facilitate an organization's operations, or to resell to other customers.

consumer product
A product bought to satisfy an individual's personal wants.

Products can be classified as either business (industrial) or consumer products, depending on the buyer's intentions. The key distinction between the two types of products is their intended use. If the intended use is a business purpose, the product is classified as a business or industrial product. As explained in Chapter 5, a **business product** is used to manufacture other goods or services, to facilitate an organization's operations, or to resell to other customers. A **consumer product** is bought to satisfy an individual's personal wants. Sometimes the same item can be classified as either a business or a consumer product, depending on its intended use. Examples include lightbulbs, pencils and paper, and computers.

We need to know about product classifications because business and consumer products are marketed differently. They are marketed to different target markets and tend to use different distribution, promotion, and pricing strategies.

Chapter 5 examined seven categories of business products: major equipment, accessory equipment, component parts, processed materials, raw materials, supplies, and services. The current chapter examines an effective way of categorizing consumer products. Although there are several ways to classify them, the most popular approach includes these four types: convenience products, shopping products, specialty products, and unsought products (see Exhibit 8.1). This approach classifies products according to how much effort is normally used to shop for them.

Convenience Products

convenience product
A relatively inexpensive item that merits little shopping effort.

A **convenience product** is a relatively inexpensive item that merits little shopping effort—that is, a consumer is unwilling to shop extensively for such an item. Candy, soft drinks, combs, aspirin, small hardware items, dry cleaning, and car washes fall into the convenience product category.

Consumers buy convenience products regularly, usually without much planning. Nevertheless, consumers do know the brand names of popular convenience products, such as Coca-Cola, Bayer aspirin, and Right Guard deodorant. Convenience products normally require wide distribution in order to sell sufficient quantities to meet profit goals.

Exhibit 8.1

Classification of Consumer Products

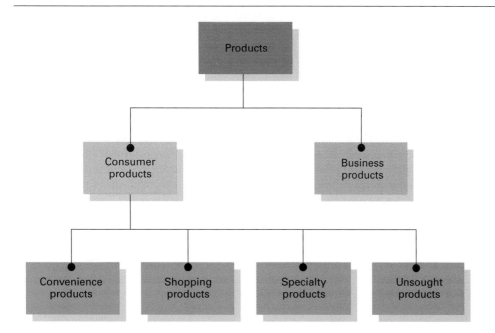

Shopping Products

A **shopping product** is usually more expensive than a convenience product and is found in fewer stores. Consumers usually buy a shopping product only after comparing several brands or stores on style, practicality, price, and lifestyle compatibility. They are willing to invest some effort into this process to get the desired benefits.

There are two types of shopping products: homogeneous and heterogeneous. Consumers perceive *homogeneous* shopping products as basically similar—for example, washers, dryers, refrigerators, and televisions. With homogeneous shopping products, consumers typically look for the lowest-priced brand that has the desired features.

In contrast, consumers perceive *heterogeneous* shopping products as essentially different—for example, furniture, clothing, housing, and universities. Consumers often have trouble comparing heterogeneous shopping products because the prices, quality, and features vary so much. The benefit of comparing heterogeneous shopping products is "finding the best product or brand for me"; this decision is often highly individual.

shopping product
A product that requires comparison shopping because it is usually more expensive than a convenience product and is found in fewer stores.

specialty product
A particular item that consumers search extensively for and are very reluctant to accept substitutes.

Specialty Products

When consumers search extensively for a particular item and are very reluctant to accept substitutes, that item is a **specialty product**. Fine watches, Rolls Royce automobiles, expensive stereo equipment, gourmet restaurants, and highly specialized forms of medical care are generally considered specialty products.

Marketers of specialty products often use selective, status-conscious

With homogeneous products such as stoves, consumers typically buy the lowest-priced brand that has the desired features.

© GETTY IMAGES/PHOTODISC

advertising to maintain their product's exclusive image. Distribution is often limited to one or a very few outlets in a geographic area. Brand names and quality of service are often very important.

Unsought Products

unsought product
A product unknown to the potential buyer or a known product that the buyer does not actively seek.

A product unknown to the potential buyer or a known product that the buyer does not actively seek is referred to as an **unsought product**. New products fall into this category until advertising and distribution increase consumer awareness of them.

Some goods are always marketed as unsought items, especially needed products we do not like to think about or care to spend money on. Insurance, burial plots, encyclopedias, and similar items require aggressive personal selling and highly persuasive advertising. Salespeople actively seek leads to potential buyers. Because consumers usually do not seek out this type of product, the company must go directly to them through a salesperson, direct mail, or direct-response advertising.

The Importance of Services

Discuss the importance of services to the economy

service
The result of applying human or mechanical efforts to people or objects.

A **service** is the result of applying human or mechanical efforts to people or objects. Services involve a deed, a performance, or an effort that cannot be physically possessed. Today, the service sector substantially influences the U.S. economy. The service sector accounts for 76 percent of the U.S. gross domestic product and 79 percent of employment.[2] The demand for services is expected to continue. According to the Bureau of Labor Statistics, service occupations will be responsible for all net job growth through the year 2005, as can be seen in Exhibit 8.2. Much of this demand results from demographics. An aging population will need nurses, home health care, physical therapists, and social workers. Two-earner families need child-care, housecleaning, and lawn-care services. Also increasing will be the demand for information managers, such as computer engineers and systems analysts. There is also a growing market for service companies worldwide. U.S. service exports are expected to reach $650 billion by 2010—about the same value as current U.S. exports of farm and manufactured goods.[3]

Many ideas and strategies discussed throughout this book have been illustrated with service examples. In many ways, marketing is marketing, regardless of the product's characteristics. In addition, although a comparison of goods and ser-

Exhibit 8.2 Service-Producing Industries and Job Growth

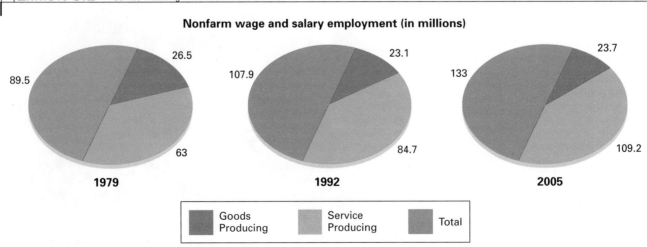

Nonfarm wage and salary employment (in millions)

1979	1992	2005
89.5, 26.5, 63	107.9, 23.1, 84.7	133, 23.7, 109.2

Goods Producing · Service Producing · Total

SOURCE: *Arlington Star Telegram*, September 2, 1996, B9.

vices marketing can be beneficial, in reality it is hard to distinguish clearly between manufacturing and service firms. Indeed, many manufacturing firms can point to service as a major factor in their success. For example, maintenance and repair services offered by the manufacturer are important to buyers of copy machines. Nevertheless, services have some unique characteristics that distinguish them from goods, and marketing strategies need to be adjusted for these characteristics.

How Services Differ from Goods

Services have four unique characteristics that distinguish them from goods. Services are intangible performances, they are produced and consumed simultaneously, they have greater variability in inputs and outputs than goods, and they are perishable.

Discuss the differences between services and goods

Services Are Intangible Performances

The basic difference between services and goods is that services are intangible performances. Because of their **intangibility**, they cannot be touched, seen, tasted, heard, or felt in the same manner that goods can be sensed. Services cannot be stored and are often easy to duplicate.

Evaluating the quality of services before or even after making a purchase is harder than evaluating the quality of goods because, compared to goods, services tend to exhibit fewer search qualities. A **search quality** is a characteristic that can be easily assessed before purchase—for instance, the color of an appliance or automobile. At the same time, services tend to exhibit more experience and credence qualities. An **experience quality** is a characteristic that can be assessed only after use, such as the quality of a meal in a restaurant or the actual experience of a vacation. A **credence quality** is a characteristic that consumers may have difficulty assessing even after purchase because they do not have the necessary knowledge or experience. Medical and consulting services are examples of services that exhibit credence qualities.

These characteristics also make it harder for marketers to communicate the benefits of an intangible service than to communicate the benefits of tangible goods. Thus, marketers often rely on tangible cues to communicate a service's nature and quality. For example, Travelers Insurance Company's use of the umbrella symbol helps make tangible the benefit of protection that insurance provides.

The facilities that customers visit, or from which services are delivered, are a critical tangible part of the total service offering. Messages about the organization are communicated to customers through such elements as the decor, the clutter or neatness of service areas, and the staff's manners and dress. The Sheraton hotel chain is replacing its outdated shag carpeting and flowered bedspreads with pin stripes and sleigh beds. Its goal is to restore a reputation for reliability and comfort and to avoid scaring off travelers with tacky accommodations. The new design will feature clubby library-like furnishings and practical amenities like ergonomic desk chairs and two-line phones. The remodeling is also a part of the strategy followed by Sheraton's parent company, Starwood Hotels & Resorts Worldwide, to differentiate the company's hotel brands aesthetically. For example, it wants its Sheratons to attract conservative business travelers, while its Westin Hotels are targeting younger, hipper, and somewhat richer overnighters.[4]

intangibility
The inability of services to be touched, seen, tasted, heard, or felt in the same manner that goods can be sensed.

search quality
A characteristic that can be easily assessed before purchase.

experience quality
A characteristic that can be assessed only after use.

credence quality
A characteristic that consumers may have difficulty assessing even after purchase because they do not have the necessary knowledge or experience.

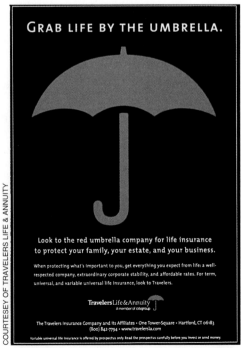

COURTESY OF TRAVELERS LIFE & ANNUITY

To communicate the benefits of intangible services, marketers often rely on concrete symbols. The umbrella symbol used by Travelers Insurance signifies protection. This helps give the company's service substance.

Services Are Produced and Consumed Simultaneously

Goods are produced, sold, and then consumed. In contrast, services are often sold, produced, and consumed at the same time. In other words, their production and consumption are inseparable activities. This means that, because consumers must be present during the production of services like haircuts or surgery, they are actually involved in the production of the services they buy. That type of consumer involvement is rare in goods manufacturing.

Simultaneous production and consumption also means that services normally cannot be produced in a centralized location and consumed in decentralized locations, as goods typically are. Services are also inseparable from the perspective of the service provider. Thus, the quality of service that firms are able to deliver depends on the quality of their employees.

Services Have Greater Variability

One great strength of McDonald's is consistency. Whether customers order a Big Mac and french fries in Fort Worth, Tokyo, or Moscow, they know exactly what they are going to get. This is not the case with many service providers. Because services have greater variability of inputs and outputs, they tend to be less standardized and uniform than goods. For example, physicians in a group practice or barbers in a barber shop differ within each group in their technical and interpersonal skills. A given physician's or barber's performance may even vary depending on time of day, physical health, or some other factor. Because services tend to be labor-intensive and production and consumption are inseparable, consistency and quality control can be hard to achieve.

Standardization and training help increase consistency and reliability. Limited-menu restaurants like Pizza Hut and KFC offer customers high consistency from one visit to the next because of standardized preparation procedures. Another way to increase consistency is to mechanize the process. Banks have reduced the inconsistency of teller services by providing automated teller machines (ATMs). Automatic coin receptacles on toll roads have replaced human collectors.

Services Are Perishable

Services are perishable, which means that they cannot be stored, warehoused, or inventoried. An empty hotel room or airplane seat produces no revenue that day. The revenue is lost. Yet service organizations are often forced to turn away full-price customers during peak periods.

One of the most important challenges in many service industries is finding ways to synchronize supply and demand. The philosophy that some revenue is better than none has prompted many hotels to offer deep discounts on weekends and during the off-season and has prompted airlines to adopt similar pricing strategies during off-peak hours. Car rental agencies, movie theaters, and restaurants also use discounts to encourage demand during nonpeak periods.

Product Items, Lines, and Mixes

Define the terms *product item*, *product line*, and *product mix*

product item
A specific version of a product that can be designated as a distinct offering among an organization's products.

Rarely does a company sell a single product. More often, it sells a variety of things. A **product item** is a specific version of a product that can be designated as a distinct offering among an organization's products. Gillette's MACH 3 razor is an example of a product item (see Exhibit 8.3).

A group of closely related product items is a **product line**. For example, the column in Exhibit 8.3 titled "Blades and Razors" represents one of Gillette's product lines. Different container sizes and shapes also distinguish items in a

Exhibit 8.3

Gillette's Product Lines
and Product Mix

	Width of the Product Mix			
	Blades and Razors	Toiletries	Writing Instruments	Lighters
Depth of the Product Lines	MACH 3	Series	Paper Mate	Cricket
	Sensor	Adorn	Flair	S.T. Dupont
	Trac II	Toni		
	Atra	Right Guard		
	Swivel	Silkience		
	Double-Edge	Soft and Dri		
	Lady Gillette	Foamy		
	Super Speed	Dry Look		
	Twin Injector	Dry Idea		
	Techmatic	Brush Plus		

product line. Diet Coke, for example, is available in cans and various plastic containers. Each size and each container are separate product items.

An organization's **product mix** includes all the products it sells. All Gillette's products—blades and razors, toiletries, writing instruments, and lighters—constitute its product mix. Each product item in the product mix may require a separate marketing strategy. In some cases, however, product lines and even entire product mixes share some marketing strategy components. Nike promoted all of its product items and lines with the theme "Just Do It."

Organizations derive several benefits from organizing related items into product lines, including the following:

- *Advertising economies:* Product lines provide economies of scale in advertising. Several products can be advertised under the umbrella of the line. Campbell's can talk about its soup being "m-m-good" and promote the entire line.

- *Package uniformity:* A product line can benefit from package uniformity. All packages in the line may have a common look and still keep their individual identities. Again, Campbell's soup is a good example.

- *Standardized components:* Product lines allow firms to standardize components, thus reducing manufacturing and inventory costs. For example, many of the components Samsonite uses in its folding tables and chairs are also used in its patio furniture. General Motors uses the same parts on many automobile makes and models.

- *Efficient sales and distribution:* A product line enables sales personnel for companies like Procter & Gamble to provide a full range of choices to customers. Distributors and retailers are often more inclined to stock the company's products if it offers a full line. Transportation and warehousing costs are likely to be lower for a product line than for a collection of individual items.

- *Equivalent quality:* Purchasers usually expect and believe that all products in a line are about equal in quality. Consumers expect that all Campbell's soups and all Mary Kay cosmetics will be of similar quality.

Product mix width (or breadth) refers to the number of product lines an organization offers. In Exhibit 8.3, for example, the width of Gillette's product mix is four product lines. **Product line depth** is the number of product items in a product line. As shown in Exhibit 8.3, the blades and razors product line consists of ten product items; the toiletries product line also includes ten product items.

Firms increase the *width* of their product mix to diversify risk. To generate sales and boost profits, firms spread risk across many product lines rather than depend on only one or two. Firms also widen their product mix to capitalize on established

product line
A group of closely related product items.

product mix
All products that an organization sells.

product mix width
The number of product lines an organization offers.

product line depth
The number of product items in a product line.

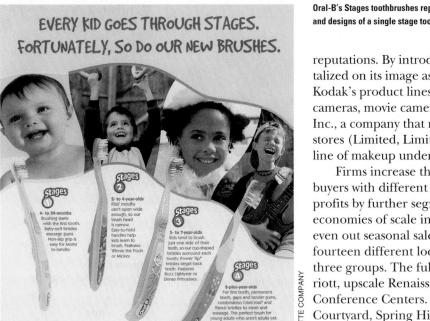

Oral-B's Stages toothbrushes represent a functional modification to adult toothbrushes. Numerous colors and designs of a single stage toothbrush would be a style modification.

reputations. By introducing new product lines, Kodak capitalized on its image as a leader in photographic products. Kodak's product lines now include film, processing, still cameras, movie cameras, paper, and chemicals. Limited, Inc., a company that mostly comprises women's apparel stores (Limited, Limited Too, Victoria's Secret) developed a line of makeup under the Victoria's Secret brand.

Firms increase the *depth* of product lines to attract buyers with different preferences, to increase sales and profits by further segmenting the market, to capitalize on economies of scale in production and marketing, and to even out seasonal sales patterns. Marriott International has fourteen different lodging brands that are divided into three groups. The full-service group includes flagship Marriott, upscale Renaissance Hotels and Resorts, and Marriott Conference Centers. The select service group includes Courtyard, Spring Hill Suites, and Fairfield Inn. The extended stay group includes Residence Inn and ExecuStay.

Adjustments to Product Items, Lines, and Mixes

Over time, firms change product items, lines, and mixes to take advantage of new technical or product developments or to respond to changes in the environment. They may adjust by modifying products, repositioning products, or extending or contracting product lines.

Product Modification

product modification
Changing one or more of a product's characteristics.

Marketing managers must decide if and when to modify existing products. **Product modification** changes one or more of a product's characteristics:

- *Quality modification:* change in a product's dependability or durability. Reducing a product's quality may let the manufacturer lower the price and appeal to target markets unable to afford the original product. On the other hand, increasing quality can help the firm compete with rival firms. Increasing quality can also result in increased brand loyalty, greater ability to raise prices, or new opportunities for market segmentation. Inexpensive ink-jet printers have improved in quality to the point that they produce photo-quality images. These printers are now competing with camera film. To appeal to a more upscale market, Robert Mondavi Winery introduced a high-end wine called Twin Oaks to prestige restaurants and hotels. This wine is positioned as a higher quality wine than the one Mondavi sells in supermarkets.

- *Functional modification:* change in a product's versatility, effectiveness, convenience, or safety. Oral-B introduced Stages toothbrushes, a line of toothbrushes for children. For example, Stage 2, designed for toddlers, has an easy-to-grip handle and a narrow brush that makes it easier to reach all teeth.[5] Lea & Perrins offers its steak sauce in a value-priced squeeze bottle with a "no mess, stay clean" cap.

- *Style modification:* aesthetic product change, rather than a quality or functional change. Pontiac modified the style of its Aztec car based on focus-group results after initial sales were weak. The original two-tone color scheme that featured gray trim was replaced by a monochromatic color scheme, and the small wheels were replaced with sixteen-inch cast aluminum wheels. A spoiler was also added to soften some of the car's sharp lines.[6] Clothing and auto manufacturers also commonly use style modifications to motivate customers to replace products before they are worn out. **Planned obsolescence** is a term commonly used to describe the practice of modifying products so that those that have already been sold become obsolete before they actually need replacement. Some argue that planned obsolescence is wasteful; some claim it is unethical. Marketers respond that consumers favor style modifications because they like changes in the appearance of goods like clothing and cars. Marketers also contend that consumers, not manufacturers and marketers, decide when styles are obsolete.

Unilever

Can Unilever delete anything from its product lines? Visit the company's product category pages on its "Brands" Web page to see the number of existing products and new products planned. Write a proposal for contracting one of Unilever's product lines.

http://www.unilever.com

On Line

Repositioning

Repositioning, as Chapter 6 explained, involves changing consumers' perceptions of a brand. For example, Tommy Hilfiger started out as a company offering classic, preppy clothing. During the 1990s, Hilfiger was repositioned as a hipper, more urban brand to appeal to a younger audience. During 2001, to combat decreasing sales and to regain its core market, Hilfiger once again repositioned itself and returned to its clean-cut image.[7]

planned obsolescence
The practice of modifying products so those that have already been sold become obsolete before they actually need replacement.

GLOBAL Changing demographics, declining sales, or changes in the social environment often motivate firms to reposition established brands. The Japanese cosmetics company Shiseido changed the positioning of its cosmetics from masking products to products to enhance women's inner beauty. Based on this repositioning, the company introduced a new skin-care line that has helped to attract a younger audience (twenty-five- to thirty-year olds) than its traditional market of women aged thirty to forty-five.[8]

©TERRI MILLER/E-VISUAL COMMUNICATIONS, INC.

Product Line Extensions

A **product line extension** occurs when a company's management decides to add products to an existing product line in order to compete more broadly in the industry. Minute Maid has added two calcium-fortified juices—Premium Home-Squeezed Style orange juice and Ruby Red Grapefruit Blend—to attract health-conscious baby boomers.[9] Jolly Rancher launched Fruit Chews to compete in the chewy candy product category.[10] Procter & Gamble has developed numerous extensions of its Tide laundry detergent, including Tide with Bleach, Tide Free (which has no fragrance), Tide WearCare (which claims to keep fabrics brighter longer), and Tide Kick (whose package has a nozzle to rub detergent directly into fabrics).[11]

The story in the "Global Perspectives" box illustrates how Coca-Cola and Procter & Gamble expanded their beverage lines to respond to consumer needs in developing countries.

Product extensions enable a company to compete more broadly in an industry. Coca-Cola's Minute Maid was successful building upon its original Premium orange juice brand with a variety of juices. Other product extensions include Minute Maid Coolers, Minute Maid Smoothies, and Minute Maid Frozen Fruit Bars.

product line extension
Adding additional products to an existing product line in order to compete more broadly in the industry.

Product Line Contraction

Does the world really need thirty-one varieties of Head and Shoulders shampoo? Or fifty-two versions of Crest? Black & Decker has decided the answer is no. The company has deleted a number of household products—Dustbusters, SnakeLight flashlights, and toaster ovens—and is concentrating on power tools. Symptoms of product line overextension include the following:

• Some products in the line do not contribute to profits because of low sales or cannibalize sales of other items in the line.

Drinks for Developing Countries

In the spring of 2001, Coca-Cola Company conducted a clinical test of a special drink on children in Gabarone, Botswana. The beverage looked and tasted like the company's Hi-C orange-flavored drink, but this drink contained twelve vitamins and minerals chronically lacking in the diets of people in developing countries. The test was part of "Project Mission," a continuing research and development effort aimed at creating a drink to help fight diseases like anemia, blindness, and other afflictions that are common in poorer parts of the world. At the end of eight weeks, results of the test showed that levels of iron and zinc in the children's blood had grown. Some parents said their children, whose diets consist mostly of cornmeal and rice, had more energy and had become more attentive at school. The new drink, to be called Vitango, could help Coke increase sales at a time when growth of carbonated beverages is slowing.

After its launch, Vitango will put Coca-Cola in direct competition with Procter & Gamble Company, which has a similar drink that is already being sold. P&G launched its product, Nutristar, in late 2001 in Venezuela after years of research and development and clinical tests. A powdered drink that contains eight vitamins and five minerals, Nutristar is sold at most food stores in flavors like mango and passion fruit. So far, the drink is doing well. Available also at McDonald's, Nutristar is the chosen beverage with about half the Happy Meals the restaurants sell. Nutristar is also being sampled in schools.

While the market for such drinks is limited, they are meant to offer Coke and P&G a chance to attempt the role of good corporate citizen at a time when being perceived as such is increasingly important for U.S. multinational firms. Coke has high hopes for Vitango in Africa and Latin America, where its products already reach some of the most remote areas. A second clinical test, to determine how well Vitango's nutrients are absorbed into the bloodstream, was just finished in Peru.

"Micronutrient" deficiencies, or a lack of vitamins and minerals such as vitamin A, iron, and zinc, are believed to afflict about two billion children around the world. With vitamin pills costly to distribute and pill-taking regimes hard to enforce, fortification of foods offers the most promising prospects for combating some deficiencies.

Coke's Project Mission began in April 2000, when a group of marketing and innovation executives visited the company's operations in Ecuador. Local managers there were looking for a less obtru-sive way to advance the Coca-Cola name in secondary schools than through bottle-cap contests that promoted sales of cola. With economic conditions in the country deteriorating, children were poorly nourished and inattentive in class. In developing the beverage, Coke found out that a powdered version of Hi-C sold to restaurants appealed to consumer groups tested in South Africa. With that information, the company put together a "worldwide nutrition advisory board" to create a combination of vitamins and minerals that would be absorbed well and whose taste would not be too strong. Powder, liquid, and even carbonated forms of the beverage were developed. Concerned with water quality in Africa, Coke wants to sell the beverage there in a ready-to-drink form. The beverage is not intended to replace drinking milk or juice, but as a supplement that augments a healthy diet.[12]

Would you consider Vitango to be a product modification for Coca-Cola? If so, what type of modification does it represent? What type of branding strategy does Coca-Cola appear to be using with Vitango? Do you think that this brand name would be successful in other countries? Support your answer.

- Manufacturing or marketing resources are disproportionately allocated to slow-moving products.
- Some items in the line are obsolete because of new product entries in the line or new products offered by competitors.

Three major benefits are likely when a firm contracts overextended product lines. First, resources become concentrated on the most important products. Second, managers no longer waste resources trying to improve the sales and profits of poorly performing products. Third, new product items have a greater chance of being successful because more financial and human resources are available to manage them.

▌ Branding

6

Describe marketing uses of branding

The success of any business or consumer product depends in part on the target market's ability to distinguish one product from another. Branding is the main tool marketers use to distinguish their products from the competition's.

Lesson Plans

It's hard to resist a large group of consumers that is always looking for the Next Big Thing and is a guaranteed captive audience seven to eight hours a day, five days a week, nine months of the year. While advertising to kids under eighteen is tricky enough, reaching them at school takes marketers even further into an ethical gray area.

Teenage Research Unlimited, a marketing research firm based in Northbrook, Illinois, estimates that U.S. teens, ages twelve to nineteen, spent a total of about $155 billion in 2000. While no statistic exists for the total amount spent by corporations each year on in-school marketing programs, Milwaukee-based Center for the Analysis of Commercialism in Education (CACE), a nonprofit academic group dedicated to tracking marketing in U.S. schools, reports that the last decade has seen a 395 percent increase in the number of stories on the subject published or broadcast in the U.S. media.

Despite the increased media attention, in-school marketing programs are nearly irresistible—for the administration as well as the marketers—because of the money that goes to the school above and beyond what local communities and state and federal governments provide. For example, programs to help students with special needs often lack sufficient funds, and the money from marketing agreements can be a boost to districts seeking to fill this void.

Soft drink vending machines in schools are among the most common, and the most controversial, types of in-school marketing agreements. The machines may generate hundreds of thousands of dollars a year in extra revenue for the schools that have them, but they have in the past increased concerns of parents and others about the mix of marketing and education. For example, in 1998, a Georgia high school senior wore a Pepsi-branded t-shirt on the school-designated "Coke Day." The result was a day's suspension—and nationwide publicity, including a number of editorials decrying corporate America's involvement in the classroom. (The principal ultimately withdrew the suspension and cleared his [the student's] record.)

More recently, the machines have been targeted because of the lack of nutritional value in carbonated drinks. One thing that soft drink marketers have done to address these concerns has been to make sure a variety of beverages, such as fruit juice and water, are available in school vending machines. However, the move does not make many nutritionists happy. They note that many juice drinks found in vending machines are high in calories, low on nutrition, and not much healthier for kids than soft drinks.

Another education-based program is Pizza Hut's Book It. This program is positioned as a teacher's aid, and awards certificates to students in elementary schools who complete reading assignments. "We are not marketing to kids, but providing a literacy curriculum to teachers," says Patty Sullivan, director of public relations for Pizza Hut. Since the Book It program's creation in 1985, Pizza Hut has given away $178 million in pizza to schoolchildren. The program has also probably generated additional revenue for the company, assuming that family and friends accompanying the awardee make additional purchases. Meanwhile, the program has escaped much of the criticism that has been leveled at other in-school marketing programs. Indeed, the U.S. Department of Education has granted Book It several Certificates of Recognition, citing it as a model educational partnership between a corporation and schools.[13]

Is in-school marketing ethical? Do you think that there is a difference between types of in-school marketing (for example, vending machines versus the Book It program)? Explain your answers.

A **brand** is a name, term, symbol, design, or combination thereof that identifies a seller's products and differentiates them from competitors' products. A **brand name** is that part of a brand that can be spoken, including letters (GM, YMCA), words (Chevrolet), and numbers (WD-40, 7-Eleven). The elements of a brand that cannot be spoken are called the **brand mark**—for example, the well-known Mercedes-Benz and Delta Airlines symbols.

Benefits of Branding

Branding has three main purposes: product identification, repeat sales, and new-product sales. The most important purpose is *product identification*. Branding allows marketers to distinguish their products from all others. Many brand names are familiar to consumers and indicate quality.

The term **brand equity** refers to the value of company and brand names. A brand that has high awareness, perceived quality, and brand loyalty among customers has high brand equity. A brand with strong brand equity is a valuable asset. As the "Ethics in Marketing" box shows, however, concerns have been raised about the way some companies attempt to build brand equity.

brand
A name, term, symbol, design, or combination thereof that identifies a seller's products and differentiates them from competitors' products.

brand name
That part of a brand that can be spoken, including letters, words, and numbers.

brand mark
The elements of a brand that cannot be spoken.

brand equity
The value of company and brand names.

Exhibit 8.4

The World's Ten Most Valuable Brands

Rank	Brand	2003 Brand Value ($ billions)	Country of Ownership
1	Coca-Cola	70.5	U.S.
2	Microsoft	65.1	U.S.
3	IBM	51.8	U.S.
4	GE	42.4	U.S.
5	Intel	31.1	U.S.
6	Nokia	29.4	Finland
7	Disney	28.0	U.S.
8	McDonald's	25.3	U.S.
9	Marlboro	22.2	U.S.
10	Mercedes	21.4	Germany

SOURCE: "The Best Global Brands," *Business Week*, August 4, 2003.

global brand
A brand where at least 20 percent of the product is sold outside its home country or region.

The term **global brand** has been used to refer to brands where at least 20 percent of the product is sold outside their home country or region. "A strong global brand acts as an ambassador when companies enter new markets or offer new products." It also helps guide corporate strategy decisions by indicating which new ideas fit within the brand concept and which do not.[14] Yum Brands (formerly Tricon Global Restaurants), which owns Pizza Hut, KFC, and Taco Bell, is a good example of a company that has developed strong global brands. Yum believes that it has to adapt its restaurants to local tastes and different cultural and political climates. In Japan, for instance, KFC sells tempura crispy strips. In northern England, KFC focuses on gravy and potatoes, while in Thailand it offers rice with soy or sweet chili sauce. In China, the company recruits employees who balance an understanding of the Chinese mind-set with Western business training.[15] Exhibit 8.4 lists the world's ten most valuable brands.

What constitutes a good brand name? Most effective brand names have several of the following features:

- Is easy to pronounce (by both domestic and foreign buyers)
- Is easy to recognize

- Is easy to remember
- Is short
- Is distinctive, unique
- Describes the product
- Describes product use
- Describes product benefits
- Has a positive connotation
- Reinforces the desired product image
- Is legally protectable in home and foreign markets of interest

Obviously, no brand exhibits all of these characteristics. The most important issue is that the brand can be protected for exclusive use by its owner.

The best generator of *repeat sales* is satisfied customers. Branding helps consumers identify products they wish to buy again and avoid those they do not. **Brand loyalty**, a consistent preference for one brand over all others, is quite high in some product categories. Over half the users in product categories such as cigarettes, mayonnaise, toothpaste, coffee, headache remedies, photographic film, bath soap, and ketchup are loyal to one brand. Brand identity is essential to developing brand loyalty.

brand loyalty
A consistent preference for one brand over all others.

The third main purpose of branding is to *facilitate new-product sales*. Company and brand names like those listed in Exhibit 8.4 are extremely useful when introducing new products.

The Internet provides firms a new alternative for generating brand awareness, promoting a desired brand image, stimulating new and repeat brand sales, and enhancing brand loyalty and building brand equity. A number of packaged-goods firms, such as Procter & Gamble, Campbell's soup, and Gerber, have a presence on-line. Tide.com offers a useful feature called Stain Detective, a digital tip sheet on how to remove almost any substance from almost any fabric. Reflect.com lets women mix and match various options to create their own "brands" of makeup, perfume, and other beauty-care products.[16]

Branding Strategies

Firms face complex branding decisions. As Exhibit 8.5 illustrates, the first decision is whether to brand at all. Some firms actually use the lack of a brand name as a selling point. These unbranded products are called generic products. Firms that decide to brand their products may choose to follow a policy of using manufacturers' brands, private (distributor) brands, or both. In either case, they must then decide among a policy of individual branding (different brands for different products), family branding (common names for different products), or a combination of individual branding and family branding.

Generic Products versus Branded Products

A **generic product** is typically a no-frills, no-brand-name, low-cost product that is simply identified by its product category. (Note that a generic product and a brand name that becomes generic, such as cellophane, are not the same thing.) Generic products have captured significant market shares in some product categories, such as canned fruits, canned vegetables, and paper products. These unbranded products are frequently identified only by black stenciled lettering on white packages.

generic product
A no-frills, no-brand-name, low-cost product that is simply identified by its product category.

The main appeal of generics is their low price. Generic grocery products are usually 30 to 40 percent less expensive than manufacturers' brands in the same product category and 20 to 25 percent less expensive than retailer-owned brands.

Pharmaceuticals are another product category where generics have made inroads. When patents on successful pharmaceutical products expire, low-cost generics rapidly appear on the market. For example, when the patent on Merck's

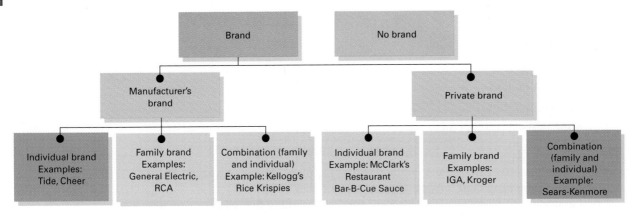

popular antiarthritis drug Clinoril expired, sales declined by 50 percent almost immediately.

Manufacturers' Brands versus Private Brands

manufacturer's brand
The brand name of a manufacturer.

The brand name of a manufacturer—such as Kodak, Lazy Boy, and Fruit of the Loom—is called a **manufacturer's brand**. Sometimes "national brand" is used as a synonym for "manufacturer's brand." This term is not always accurate, however, because many manufacturers serve only regional markets. Using "manufacturer's brand" more precisely defines the brand's owner.

private brand
A brand name owned by a wholesaler or a retailer.

A **private brand**, also known as a private label or store brand, is a brand name owned by a wholesaler or a retailer. Hunt Club (a JCPenney brand), Sam's American Choice (Wal-Mart), and IGA (Independent Grocers' Association) are all private brands. Private brands now account for over 20 percent of sales at all U.S. mass merchandisers, drugstores, and supermarkets. At some stores, the penetration is much higher: At Target, for example, more than 50 percent of the merchandise is exclusive to the store. And across the board, store brands are growing faster than national brands.[17] Marketing experts predict that private labels will make up as much as 30 percent of grocery sales within five years—particularly as big supermarkets continue to consolidate.[18]

Exhibit 8.6 illustrates key issues that wholesalers and retailers should consider in deciding whether to sell manufacturers' brands or private brands. Many firms, such as JCPenney, Kmart, and Safeway, offer a combination of both. In fact, JCPenney and Sears have turned their low-priced, private-label jeans into some of the most popular brands around, thanks to hip marketing campaigns that feature rock bands, Web sites, and imagery targeted at teens.

Individual Brands versus Family Brands

individual branding
Using different brand names for different products.

Many companies use different brand names for different products, a practice referred to as **individual branding**. Companies use individual brands when their products vary greatly in use or performance. For instance, it would not make sense to use the same brand name for a pair of dress socks and a baseball bat. Procter & Gamble targets different segments of the laundry-detergent market with Bold, Cheer, Dash, Dreft, Era, Gain, Ivory Snow, Oxydol, Solo, and Tide. Marriott International also targets different market segments with Courtyard by Marriott, Residence Inn, and Fairfield Inn.

family brand
Marketing several different products under the same brand name.

In contrast, a company that markets several different products under the same brand name is using a **family brand**. Sony's family brand includes radios, television sets, stereos, and other electronic products. A brand name can only be stretched so far, however. Do you know the differences among Holiday Inn, Holiday Inn Express, Holiday Inn Select, Holiday Inn Sunspree Resort, Holiday Inn Garden Court, and Holiday Inn Hotel & Suites? Neither do most travelers.

Procter & Gamble has an extensive Web presence to support its complete slate of brands. In 2000, the company launched the pg.com network, touting it as "the one place where all our brands hang out together."

Cobranding

Cobranding entails placing two or more brand names on a product or its package. There are three types of cobranding. *Ingredient branding* identifies the brand of a part that makes up the product. Examples of ingredient branding are Intel (a microprocessor) in a personal computer, such as Dell, or a premium leather interior (Coach) in an automobile (Lincoln). *Cooperative branding* occurs when two brands receiving equal treatment (in the context of an advertisement) borrow on each other's brand equity. A promotional contest jointly sponsored by Ramada Inns, American Express, and Continental Airlines is an example of cooperative branding. Guests at Ramada who paid with an American Express card were automatically entered in the contest and were eligible to win more than a hundred getaways for two at any Ramada in the continental United States and round-trip airfare from Continental.[19] Finally, there is *complementary branding*, where products are advertised or marketed together to suggest usage, such as a spirits brand (Seagram's) and a compatible mixer (7-Up).

Cobranding is a useful strategy when a combination of brand names enhances the prestige or perceived value of a product or when it benefits brand owners and users. Toyota Motor's luxury division introduced a Platinum version of its Lexus brand. For a premium of as much as 10 percent above the base sticker prices, buyers get upgraded paint, leathers and accessories, and a free two-year subscription to the $300-a-year American Express Platinum Card. Both companies say that the Platinum Series models will reinforce their brands while delivering added value.[20]

where's the one place all our brands hang out together?

introducing the **PG.com** network

The new pg.com lets you **do more, learn more** and **get more** from P&G and our brands than ever before...

Discover the surprising number of online resources our brands have to offer.	Try and buy products before they're available in stores.	Share your ideas for improving our products and creating new ones.	and coming soon... Take advantage of new tools to help manage your P&G shareholders account.

w w w . p g . c o m

cobranding
Placing two or more brand names on a product or its package.

Exhibit 8.6

Comparing Manufacturers' and Private Brands from the Reseller's Perspective

Key Advantages of Carrying Manufacturers' Brands	Key Advantages of Carrying Private Brands
• Heavy advertising to the consumer by manufacturers like Procter & Gamble helps develop strong consumer loyalties.	• A wholesaler or retailer can usually earn higher profits on its own brand. In addition, because the private brand is exclusive, there is less pressure to mark the price down to meet competition.
• Well-known manufacturers' brands, such as Kodak and Fisher-Price, can attract new customers and enhance the dealer's (wholesaler's or retailer's) prestige.	• A manufacturer can decide to drop a brand or a reseller at any time or even to become a direct competitor to its dealers.
• Many manufacturers offer rapid delivery, enabling the dealer to carry less inventory.	• A private brand ties the customer to the wholesaler or retailer. A person who wants a Die-Hard battery must go to Sears.
• If a dealer happens to sell a manufacturer's brand of poor quality, the customer may simply switch brands and remain loyal to the dealer.	• Wholesalers and retailers have no control over the intensity of distribution of manufacturers' brands. Wal-Mart store managers don't have to worry about competing with other sellers of Sam's American Choice products or Ol' Roy dog food. They know that these brands are sold only in Wal-Mart and Sam's Wholesale Club stores.

trademark
The exclusive right to use a brand or part of a brand.

service mark
A trademark for a service.

generic product name
Identifies a product by class or type and cannot be trademarked.

Cobranding may be used to increase a company's presence in markets in which it has little or no market share. For example, Disney is attempting to increase its share of the food and beverage market by developing cobranding deals with Minute Maid for an eighteen-variety line of Disney Xtreme! Coolers based on Mickey and Friends and with Kellogg for cobranded cereals.[21]

European firms have been slower to adopt cobranding than U.S. firms have. One reason is that European customers seem to be more skeptical than U.S. customers about trying new brands. European retailers also typically have less shelf space than their U.S. counterparts and are less willing to give new brands a try.

Trademarks

A **trademark** is the exclusive right to use a brand or part of a brand. Others are prohibited from using the brand without permission. A **service mark** performs the same function for services, such as H&R Block and Weight Watchers. Parts of a brand or other product identification may qualify for trademark protection. Some examples are

- Shapes, such as the Jeep front grille and the Coca-Cola bottle
- Ornamental color or design, such as the decoration on Nike tennis shoes, the black-and-copper color combination of a Duracell battery, Levi's small tag on the left side of the rear pocket of its jeans, or the cutoff black cone on the top of Cross pens
- Catchy phrases, such as Prudential's "Own a piece of the rock," Merrill Lynch's "We're bullish on America," and Budweiser's "This Bud's for you"
- Abbreviations, such as Bud, Coke, or The Met
- Sounds, such as General Electric Broadcasting Company's ship's bell clock sound and the MGM lion's roar.

The Trademark Revision Act of 1988 allows organizations to register trademarks based on a bona fide intention to use them (normally, within six months following the issuance of the trademark) for ten years. To renew the trademark, the company must prove it is using it. Rights to a trademark last as long as the mark is used. Normally, if the firm does not use it for two years, the trademark is considered abandoned, and a new user can claim exclusive ownership of the mark.

In November 1999, legislation went into effect that explicitly applies trademark law to the on-line world. This law includes financial penalties for those who violate trademarked products or who register an otherwise trademarked term as a domain name.[22]

Companies that fail to protect their trademarks face the possibility that their product names will become generic. A **generic product name** identifies a product by class or type and cannot be trademarked. Former brand names that were not sufficiently protected by their owners and were subsequently declared to be generic product names by U.S. courts include aspirin, cellophane, linoleum, thermos, kerosene, monopoly, cola, and shredded wheat.

Companies like Rolls Royce, Cross, Xerox, Levi Strauss, Frigidaire, and McDonald's aggressively enforce their trademarks. Rolls Royce, Coca-Cola, and Xerox even run newspaper and magazine ads stating that their names are trademarks and should not be used as descriptive or generic terms. Some ads threaten lawsuits against competitors that violate trademarks.

Despite severe penalties for trademark violations, trademark infringement lawsuits are not uncommon. One of the major battles is over brand names that closely resemble another brand name. Donna Karan filed a lawsuit against Donnkenny Inc., whose Nasdaq trading symbol—DNKY—was too close to Karan's DKNY trademark.

Companies must also contend with fake or unauthorized brands, such as fake Levi's jeans, Microsoft software, Rolex watches, Reebok and Nike footwear, and Louis Vuitton handbags. Sales of copycat golf clubs, such as Big Bursa, a knockoff of Callaway's popular Big Bertha, are growing.

 In Europe, you can sue counterfeiters only if your brand, logo, or trademark is formally registered. Until recently, formal registration was required in each country in which a company sought protection. A company can now register its trademark in all European Union (EU) member countries with one application.

Packaging

Packages have always served a practical function—that is, they hold contents together and protect goods as they move through the distribution channel. Today, however, packaging is also a container for promoting the product and making it easier and safer to use.

Describe marketing uses of packaging and labeling

Packaging Functions

The three most important functions of packaging are to contain and protect products, promote products, and facilitate the storage, use, and convenience of products. A fourth function of packaging that is becoming increasingly important is to facilitate recycling and reduce environmental damage.

Containing and Protecting Products

The most obvious function of packaging is to contain products that are liquid, granular, or otherwise divisible. Packaging also enables manufacturers, wholesalers, and retailers to market products in specific quantities, such as ounces.

Physical protection is another obvious function of packaging. Most products are handled several times between the time they are manufactured, harvested, or otherwise produced and the time they are consumed or used. Many products are shipped, stored, and inspected several times between production and consumption. Some, like milk, need to be refrigerated. Others, like beer, are sensitive to light. Still others, like medicines and bandages, need to be kept sterile. Packages protect products from breakage, evaporation, spillage, spoilage, light, heat, cold, infestation, and many other conditions.

Promoting Products

Packaging does more than identify the brand, list the ingredients, specify features, and give directions. A package differentiates a product from competing products and may associate a new product with a family of other products from the same manufacturer. Welch's repackaged its line of grape juice–based jams, jellies, and juices to unify the line and get more impact on the shelf.

Packages use designs, colors, shapes, and materials to try to influence consumers' perceptions and buying behavior. For example, marketing research shows that health-conscious consumers are likely to think that any food is probably good for them as long as it comes in green packaging. Two top brands of low-fat foods—SnackWell's and Healthy Choice—use green packaging. Sunsweet Growers, appealing to baby boomers' interest in health foods, used the theme "Be good to yourself" on new packages for its line of prune products.[23]

Packaging has a measurable effect on sales. Quaker Oats revised the package for Rice-a-Roni without making any other changes in marketing strategy and experienced a 44 percent increase in sales in one year.

Pringles invented the innovative tube package that has become as much a part of the product as the chip itself. New packaging ideas, however, are crucial to Pringles in the twenty-first century. Why? The patent on the package just expired, and rivals are quickly entering the market with their own version of the chip tube.

© THE PROCTER & GAMBLE COMPANY. USED BY PERMISSION.

Facilitating Storage, Use, and Convenience

Wholesalers and retailers prefer packages that are easy to ship, store, and stock on shelves. They also like packages that protect products, prevent spoilage or breakage, and extend the product's shelf life.

Consumers' requirements for storage, use, and convenience cover many dimensions. Consumers are constantly seeking items that are easy to handle, open, and reclose, although some consumers want packages that are tamperproof or childproof. Consumers also want reusable and disposable packages. Surveys conducted by *Sales & Marketing Management* magazine revealed that consumers dislike—and avoid buying—leaky ice cream boxes, overly heavy or fat vinegar bottles, immovable pry-up lids on glass bottles, key-opener sardine cans, and hard-to-pour cereal boxes. Such packaging innovations as zipper tear strips, hinged lids, tab slots, screw-on tops, and pour spouts were introduced to solve these and other problems. H.J. Heinz Company developed a new container for ketchup designed to fit the hands of children and encourage extra squeezing, which facilitates use for this target market.[24] Miracle-Gro's new packages have pictures on the front of the plants for which the products are formulated, so gardeners can more easily identify which product best fits their needs.[25]

Some firms use packaging to segment markets. For example, a C&H sugar carton with an easy-to-pour, reclosable top is targeted to consumers who don't do a lot of baking and are willing to pay at least twenty cents more for the package. Different-size packages appeal to heavy, moderate, and light users. Salt is sold in package sizes ranging from single serving to picnic size to giant economy size. Campbell's soup is packaged in single-serving cans aimed at the elderly and singles market segments. Beer and soft drinks are similarly marketed in various package sizes and types. Packaging convenience can increase a product's utility and, therefore, its market share and profits. Guinness Bass Import is testing a packaged-draft system that allows consumers to drink nitrogenated Guinness Stout right out of the bottle. This package could win converts among consumers who prefer to drink beer straight from the bottle and in nightclubs that offer beer only in bottles rather than in a glass or on draft.[26]

ON LINE The Internet will soon give consumers more packaging options. Indeed, the Internet may significantly change the purpose and appearance of packaging. Packaging for products sold on the Internet will be more under the customer's control and will be customized by consumers to fit their needs. Some designers are already offering to personalize, for a fee, packages such as wine bottle labels.[27]

Facilitating Recycling and Reducing Environmental Damage

One of the most important packaging issues today is compatibility with the environment.

Some firms use their packaging to target environmentally concerned market segments. Brocato International markets shampoo and hair conditioner in bottles that are biodegradable in landfills. Procter & Gamble markets Sure Pro and Old Spice in "eco-friendly" pump-spray packages that do not rely on aerosol propellants. Other firms that have introduced pump sprays include S. C. Johnson (Pledge furniture polish) and Reckitt & Coleman Household Products (Woolite rug cleaner).

Labeling

An integral part of any package is its label. Labeling generally takes one of two forms: persuasive or informational. **Persuasive labeling** focuses on a promotional theme or logo, and consumer information is secondary. Price Pfister developed a new, persuasive label—featuring a picture of a faucet, the brand name, and the logo—with the goal of strengthening brand identity and becoming known as a brand instead of as a manufacturer. Note that the standard promotional claims—such as "new," "improved," and "super"—are no longer very persuasive. Consumers have been saturated with "newness" and thus discount these claims.

Informational labeling, in contrast, is designed to help consumers make proper product selections and lower their cognitive dissonance after the purchase. Sears attaches a "label of confidence" to all its floor coverings. This label gives such product information as durability, color, features, cleanability, care instructions, and construction standards. Most major furniture manufacturers affix labels to their wares that explain the products' construction features, such as type of frame, number of coils, and fabric characteristics. The Nutritional Labeling and Education Act of 1990 mandated detailed nutritional information on most food packages and standards for health claims on food packaging. An important outcome of this legislation has been guidelines from the Food and Drug Administration for using terms like *low fat, light, reduced cholesterol, low sodium, low calorie,* and *fresh.*

Universal Product Codes

The **universal product codes (UPCs)** that appear on most items in supermarkets and other high-volume outlets were first introduced in 1974. Because the numerical codes appear as a series of thick and thin vertical lines, they are often called *bar codes.* The lines are read by computerized optical scanners that match codes with brand names, package sizes, and prices. They also print information on cash register tapes and help retailers rapidly and accurately prepare records of customer purchases, control inventories, and track sales. The UPC system and scanners are also used in single-source research (see Chapter 7).

Product Warranties

Just as a package is designed to protect the product, a **warranty** protects the buyer and gives essential information about the product. A warranty confirms the quality or performance of a good or service. An **express warranty** is a written guarantee. Express warranties range from simple statements—such as "100 percent cotton" (a guarantee of quality) and "complete satisfaction guaranteed" (a statement of performance)—to extensive documents written in technical language. In contrast, an **implied warranty** is an unwritten guarantee that the good or service is fit for the purpose for which it was sold. All sales have an implied warranty under the Uniform Commercial Code.

Congress passed the Magnuson-Moss Warranty–Federal Trade Commission Improvement Act in 1975 to help consumers understand warranties and get action from manufacturers and dealers. A manufacturer that promises a full warranty must meet certain minimum standards, including repair "within a reasonable time and without charge" of any defects and replacement of the merchandise or a full refund if the product does not work "after a reasonable number of attempts" at repair. Any warranty that does not live up to this tough prescription must be "conspicuously" promoted as a limited warranty.

persuasive labeling
A type of package labeling that focuses on a promotional theme or logo and consumer information is secondary.

informational labeling
A type of package labeling designed to help consumers make proper product selections and lower their cognitive dissonance after the purchase.

universal product codes (UPCs)
A series of thick and thin vertical lines (bar codes), readable by computerized optical scanners, that represent numbers used to track products.

Describe how and why product warranties are important marketing tools

warranty
A confirmation of the quality or performance of a good or service.

express warranty
A written guarantee.

implied warranty
An unwritten guarantee that the good or service is fit for the purpose for which it was sold.

CONNECT IT

Look back at the chapter-opening story about Coleman's new outdoor gas grill. The grill represents both a new product item and a new product line for Coleman. Coleman's success with the grill is likely due to consumers' familiarity with the Coleman brand and the perception that the company offers good-quality products. High brand equity helps companies introduce new products because consumers trust the brand. Also, although the grill was the first home-use product Coleman developed, consumers may have perceived that if Coleman makes good camping stoves, it would probably also make a good outdoor gas grill. Based on that logic, Coleman might be successful with charcoal grills, grill accessories, or backyard lanterns.

USE IT

As a student, you are required to hand in written assignments, such as papers and group projects. Have you ever thought about these class projects as a product that you exchange for a grade? Maybe not, but some of the product concepts discussed in this chapter are as applicable to class projects as they are to products. One of the most applicable product concepts in this context is that of packaging. Think about the four functions of packaging, and how they might apply to class projects. How could you more effectively package your class projects to contain and protect the project? As a tool for promotion, packaging is not only important for identification purposes, but also serves the critical function of differentiating your project from the competition (other students' projects). It is also important to facilitate storage, use, and convenience of the project for your customer—the instructor! What are some things you could do to make your project more convenient for the instructor to read and to grade? Finally, packaging facilitates recycling. How might you facilitate the environmental recycling of your project?

REVIEW IT

(1) **Define the term _product_.** A product is anything, desired or not, that a person or organization receives in an exchange. The basic goal of purchasing decisions is to receive the tangible and intangible benefits associated with a product. Tangible aspects include packaging, style, color, size, and features. Intangible qualities include service, the retailer's image, the manufacturer's reputation, and the social status associated with a product. An organization's product offering is the crucial element in any marketing mix.

1.1 Form a team of four or five. Have the team determine what the tangible and intangible benefits are for a computer, a tube of toothpaste, a beauty salon, and a dentist.

(2) **Classify consumer products.** Consumer products are classified into four categories: convenience products, shopping products, specialty products, and unsought products. Convenience products are relatively inexpensive and require limited shopping effort. Shopping products are of two types: homogeneous and heterogeneous. Because of the similarity of homogeneous products, they are differentiated mainly by price and features. In contrast, heterogeneous products appeal to consumers because of their distinct characteristics. Specialty products possess unique benefits that are highly desirable to certain customers. Finally, unsought products are either new products or products that require aggressive selling because they are generally avoided or overlooked by consumers.

2.1 **TEAM** Break into groups of four or five. Have the members of the group classify each of the following products into the category (convenience, shopping, specialty, unsought) that they think fits best from their perspective as consumers (i.e., if they were buying the product): Coca-Cola (brand), car stereo, winter coat, pair of shoes, life insurance, blue jeans, fast-food hamburgers, shampoo, canned vegetables, frozen pizza.

3 **Discuss the importance of services to the economy.** The service sector plays a crucial role in the U.S. economy, employing about three-quarters of the workforce and accounting for more than 70 percent of the gross domestic product.

3.1 **ON LINE** What services does the Web site **http://www.travelweb.com** offer? How do visitors use the Special Offer List?

4 **Discuss the differences between services and goods.** Services are distinguished by four characteristics. Services are intangible performances in that they lack clearly identifiable physical characteristics, making it difficult for marketers to communicate their specific benefits to potential customers. The production and consumption of services occur simultaneously. Services are variable because their quality depends on such elements as the service provider, individual consumer, location, and so on. Finally, services are perishable in the sense that they cannot be stored or saved. As a result, synchronizing supply with demand is particularly challenging in the service industry.

4.1 **WRITING** Assume that you are a manager of a bank branch. Write a list of the implications of intangibility for your firm.

5 **Define the terms** *product item, product line,* **and** *product mix.* A product item is a specific version of a product that can be designated as a distinct offering among an organization's products. A product line is a group of closely related products offered by an organization. An organization's product mix includes all the products it sells. Product mix width refers to the number of product lines an organization offers. Product line depth is the number of product items in a product line. Firms modify existing products by changing their quality, functional characteristics, or style. Product line extension occurs when a firm adds new products to existing product lines.

5.1 **WRITING** A local civic organization has asked you to give a luncheon presentation about planned obsolescence. Rather than pursuing a negative approach by talking about how businesses exploit customers through planned obsolescence, you have decided to talk about the benefits of producing products that do not last forever. Prepare a one-page outline of your presentation.

5.2 **ON LINE** What is the product mix offered at Web site **http://www.rubbermaid.com**?

6 **Describe marketing uses of branding.** A brand is a name, term, or symbol that identifies and differentiates a firm's products. Established brands encourage customer loyalty and help new products succeed. Branding strategies require decisions about individual, family, manufacturers', and private brands.

6.1 **WRITING** A local supermarket would like to introduce its own brand of paper goods (i.e., paper towels, facial tissue, etc.) to sell alongside its current inventory. The company has hired you to generate a report outlining the advantages and disadvantages of doing so. Write the report.

7 **Describe marketing uses of packaging and labeling.** Packaging has four functions: containing and protecting products; promoting products; facilitating product storage, use, and convenience; and facilitating recycling and reducing environmental damage. As a tool for promotion, packaging identifies the brand and its features. It also serves the critical function of differentiating a product from competing products and linking it with related products from the same manufacturer. The label is an integral part of the package, with persuasive and informational functions. In essence, the package is the marketer's last chance to influence buyers before they make a purchase decision.

7.1 **WRITING** Find a product at home that has a distinctive package. Write a paragraph evaluating that package based on the four functions of packaging discussed in the chapter.

8 **Describe how and why product warranties are important marketing tools.** Product warranties are important tools because they offer consumers protection and help them gauge product quality.

8.1 **INFOTRAC COLLEGE EDITION** Learn more about how product warranties are handled worldwide. Using InfoTrac (**http://infotrac-college.com**), run a keyword search for "warranty" or "guarantee" and a country of interest. For example, search for "warranty" and "Germany" or "guarantee" and "Mexico." Write a paragraph about what you discover.

DEFINE IT

brand 273
brand equity 273
brand loyalty 275
brand mark 273
brand name 273
business product (industrial
    product) 264
cobranding 277
consumer product 264
convenience product 264
credence quality 267
experience quality 267
express warranty 281
family brand 276
generic product 275

generic product name 278
global brand 274
implied warranty 281
individual branding 276
informational labeling 281
intangibility 267
manufacturer's brand 276
persuasive labeling 281
planned obsolescence 271
private brand 276
product 264
product item 268
product line 269
product line depth 269
product line extension 271

product mix 269
product mix width 269
product modification 270
search quality 267
service 266
service mark 278
shopping product 265
specialty product 265
trademark 278
universal product code
    (UPC; bar code) 281
unsought product 266
warranty 281

APPLY IT

Application for Entrepreneurs

ENTREPRENEUR The Baker family owns one of the largest catfish farms in central Texas and is known for raising the sweetest catfish in the area. After graduating from college with a degree in marketing, Frank Baker returned to the farm with lots of ideas for new ways to cash in on the farm's reputation. At the time, the family allowed the butcher at the local supermarket to use the Baker name on their catfish. In central Texas, eating Baker Farms catfish was a sign of status. Frank, eager to put his degree to work, convinced his family that they could make money off their name by selling their catfish products already packaged to supermarkets. After hearing the idea, the family quickly met to formulate a plan to begin selling Baker Farms catfish.

Questions

1. What type of product is the Baker family selling? List your reasons.

2. What type of branding is the Baker family using? List your reasons.

3. How should Baker Farms catfish be packaged?

4. Assuming that the Baker family wishes to reposition their catfish products, what would be an optimal strategy?

Ethics Exercise

Web sites such as Oncology.com, cancerpage.com, and CancerSource.com offer cancer patients sophisticated medical data and advice in exchange for personal data that are then sold to advertisers and business partners and used by the Web sites to create products to sell back to patients. Some argue that cancer patients visiting these sites are willingly exchanging their personal information for the sites' medical information. Others would contend that this kind of exchange is unethical.

Questions

1. Is this practice ethical?

2. Does the AMA Code of Ethics have anything to say about this issue? Go to **http://www.marketingpower.com** and review the code. Then, write a brief paragraph on what the AMA Code of Ethics contains that relates to this scenario.

⟩ **TRY IT**

Entrepreneurship Case

Maps à la Carte

A love of maps combined with some computer savvy may have translated into a viable business for two Massachusetts entrepreneurs. Ed McNierney and Bill Everett, both former executives at Kodak Company's software subsidiary in Billerica, Massachusetts, launched Maps à la Carte's Topozone.com Web site in November 1999. Founded in 1999, Maps à la Carte is a Digital Cartographic Business Partner with the U.S. Geological Survey.

Topographic maps are used extensively by hikers, hunters, surveyors, and geologists. The maps contain information such as elevation, positioning, and landmarks and are produced by the U.S. Geological Survey. Unfortunately, these sixty thousand different maps do not fit together when users try to move from map to map. For example, some maps are curved at the edges, while others are rectangles, and they may even come in different scales. McNierney and Everett were able to solve such problems with Topozone.com.

Targeting the more than fifty million outdoor recreation enthusiasts (both McNierney and Everett are avid outdoorsmen), the Topozone.com site is the first interactive, seamless U.S. topographic map site on the Web. Prior to this on-line capability, outdoor recreation enthusiasts had to use paper and CD-ROM topographic maps to plan their outdoor adventures. Map giant DeLorme Publishing Company offers topographic maps on CD-ROMs, and Maptech, Inc., includes topographic maps on its site. DeLorme's CD-ROMs sell for around $100, however, and Maptech, with its emphasis on nautical areas, has tended to target boaters rather than hikers. Therefore, U.S. Geological Survey and industry experts suggest that Topozone.com, with its high quality and extensive site search tools, is the map industry leader.

Within six months of launch, the Topozone.com site was averaging around 150,000 visitors a month. In addition to outdoor enthusiasts, the site was reaching beyond the intended target market. Visitors included genealogists, hobbyists, and cemetery associations. Additionally, the site won About.com's "1999 Best of the Net" award and was designated as the number one on-line geography site, replacing MapQuest.

While Maps à la Carte's new product offering appeared to be a huge success, company executives were not experiencing overnight wealth. With a good product service idea that was lauded by many, the company was not charging consumers to print out screen maps. By June 2000, the company had made only $50,000 in revenue from advertising and licensing fees. Maps à la Carte licensed its Topozone.com topographic map content to leading Web sites such as MapQuest.com, Trails.com, and GreatLodge.com, and the company was offering banner advertising opportunities.

To make money on this new product venture, McNierney and Everett developed a business model wherein they would give away the topographic map data and sell consumers the software that allowed users to make full use of the better quality maps available at Topozone.com. To work within this new product development business model, Maps à la Carte sold almost 20 percent of the company to Navitrak, a Canadian mapping company, in June 2000 for approximately $1 million. Navitrak is a wireless navigation technology company specializing in the development and manufacture of personal navigation devices. Along with this 20 percent acquisition, the companies will work together to further develop topographic mapping systems for the outdoor recreation market.

As entrepreneurs, McNierney and Everett developed and introduced a product that satisfied a need of outdoor enthusiasts and others. With a major investment by Navitrak, the two must focus upon extending the product concept into new markets and/or product extensions. With the fast pace of change and development in Internet-related offerings and a slew of potential competitors, McNierney and Everett have to move quickly.

Questions

1. What type of product does Topozone.com offer?
2. Should Maps à la Carte consider a branding strategy?
3. Should Maps à la Carte combine with Navitrak in a cobranding strategy? What would be the benefits of cobranding?

  WATCH IT

Short  SUPERBOWL

The *Essentials of Marketing* PowerPoint CD-ROM has four ad videos in the Chapter 8 slide presentation. The concepts of homogeneous shopping products, product line, cobranding, private brands, and warranty are illustrated in ads for AOL/WebMD, Kenmore, Chrysler, and Radio Shack. While watching the ads, write about the concepts you see in each ad.

Medium **VIDEO**

What makes a product organic, and what does hypoallergenic actually mean? The first CNN clip for Chapter 8 addresses products and issues relating to standardizing the organic claim. A second CNN clip shows how Marvel Comics and others have extended their comic book brands (like Superman, Spiderman, and the Hulk) to the big screen, effectively transforming their products into services.

Long  SmallBusinessSchool ▣
the Series on PBS stations and the Web

To give you insight into Chapter 8, Small Business School will take you to Fluker Cricket Farms in Baton Rouge, Louisiana. Richard Fluker started the business when he couldn't find bait before going fishing. Now his product line includes gourmet snacks! Watch the segment and see how real businesspeople are working with the concepts of product item, line, and mix.

 FLIP IT

Flip to Chapter 8 in your *Grademaker Study Guide* for more review opportunities, including the pretest, vocabulary review, Internet activities, study test questions, and a marketing application based on product concepts. Can you describe branding? Do you know the difference between product lines, items, and mixes? If you're not quite sure, then you need to review with your *Grademaker*.

Still Shaky? Here's a Tip.

Pick up a recent copy of the *Wall Street Journal* at a newsstand or library and read several articles in the Marketplace section (section B). What product issues are facing the companies you read about? Make two lists: one of marketing concepts you read about and one of product topics.

The *Essentials of Marketing* Web site links you to all the Internet-based activities in this chapter, like "Review It" questions 3.1, 5.2, and 8.1 and the On-Line exercises in the chapter margins. As a review, do the Chapter 8 quiz and crossword puzzle. And don't forget the Career Exersite that shows you different resources if you're interested in a brand management or other product-related career. Review the main concepts in the Power-Point presentation for Chapter 8, too. Go to **http://lamb.swlearning.com**, read the material, and follow the links right from the site.

Surf to Xtra! to test your understanding of the product concepts in the chapter by completing the worksheets for exhibits 8.1, 8.5, and 8.6. If your instructor has assigned a marketing plan project, worksheets on Xtra! can help you organize your work. In addition to the quiz on the Web site, there's another quiz on Xtra!, plus video of the authors answering frequently asked questions about product and services concepts, like "If a product falls into one of the four types discussed in the text, does it stay in that category as long as it is on the market?" and "Is it really meaningful to distinguish between goods and services firms?" Surf to Xtra! and find out.

CHAPTER **NINE**

DEVELOPING AND MANAGING PRODUCTS

Learning Objectives

1 Explain the importance of developing new products and describe the six categories of new products

2 Explain the steps in the new-product development process

3 Explain the diffusion process through which new products are adopted

4 Explain the concept of product life cycles

Every carmaker in the world is trying to figure out how to use the Internet to streamline the new-product development process, which traditionally can take four to six years and cost billions of dollars for a major launch. The Chrysler Group has reason to be trying harder than the rest. The company is losing money, and the Germans have arrived from the parent company to supervise a turnaround.

Part of Chrysler's answer to the pressure it faces is FastCar. The project is still in the early stages, but two hundred workstations at Chrysler's Auburn Hills, Michigan, headquarters have been tied into the Web-based system.

FastCar allows the company to link the flow of information from at least six major information systems that until now have not been able to communicate seamlessly—finance has had its system, engineering had a different one, purchasing relied on a third, and so on. There were even smaller, largely secret "shadow" systems. Because each arm of Chrysler had spent huge sums of money building information systems that suited its individual needs, headquarters could never force all of the departments onto one centrally controlled system. So far, the various arms of Chrysler are communicating over the Internet only in designing a large car for the 2004 model year.

The sheer scale and complexity of the auto industry are daunting for even the most intrepid Net maven. The rule of thumb is that any given car has roughly 12,000 moving parts. Chrysler has 50,000 different components that it draws upon internally. Every screw, bolt, and button has detailed specifications. When other variations are introduced (Do you want 16-inch or 17-inch tires? What color paint do you want?), there are billions of permutations for Chrysler vehicles. So, even though Net-based collaboration is old hat for some newer, smaller companies, it's an enormous undertaking for the auto industry.

The whole point of FastCar is to keep everyone working on the same design at the same time. As designers go through hundreds of variations, colleagues at other arms of Chrysler can understand what is changing in real time. In the past, if the designers changed something, engineers would have to catch up later to see what effect that would have on manufacturing; finance would have to reassess the costs; and quality control would have to reexamine its own issues. By then, the designers could be on to the next iteration.

Now FastCar offers everyone what Chrysler calls a "unified data model" or a "single point of truth" that they can see in three dimensions. The goal of FastCar is to move from theme selection to design completion to mass manufacturing within two years, roughly half the current industry standard.

FastCar is not aimed only at Chrysler's internal processes. Chrysler says FastCar will eventually work seamlessly with Covisint, an industry consortium set up with General Motors, Ford Motor, Renault, and Nissan. FastCar and Covisint fit together "like Lego blocks," the company says.

Using Covisint's standards, FastCar hopes to send e-mail messages to suppliers with hyperlinks to 3-D renderings of the parts or systems that are changing. Suppliers can use a personal computer or a laptop and don't need expensive workstations.

No one knows how fast the auto industry can migrate to Net-based systems. It is the most wrenching period of change since Henry Ford introduced the assembly line nearly ninety years ago. Aside from cutting the cost of each auto by as much as $1,500, moving to newer Internet-based systems should make the industry much more responsive to fashion trends. Chris Cedergren, managing director of Nextrend, a consultancy in Thousand Oaks, California, argues that to survive, an automaker will have to become more like a Calvin Klein or Ralph Lauren design house. "They have to be able to get a concept from the design studio to the dealer's showroom in eighteen months and do it for 30 to 35 percent less than it costs today," says Cedergren. If the FastCar project succeeds, that type of speed, savings, and flexibility could become standard operating procedure for an industry mired today in lags, costs, and rigidity.[1]

How has the Internet helped Chrysler to reduce the time it takes to design and develop a new car and at the same time dramatically reduce costs and increase flexibility? Could these processes be helpful to firms in other industries?

On Line ◀ ▶

DaimlerChrysler

How does Chrysler's Web site advertise its new products? Review the design concepts for this year. Which ones do you think are the most likely to succeed?

http://www.chrysler.com

The Importance of New Products

Explain the importance of developing new products and describe the six categories of new products

New products are important to sustain growth and profits and to replace obsolete items. 3M Company introduces about five hundred new products each year. Of the products Corning, Inc., sold in 2000, 84 percent had been introduced within the past four years. [2] As Exhibit 9.1 illustrates, the number of new-product introductions rose rapidly throughout the 1970s, 1980s, and early- to mid-1990s. In the late 1990s, fewer new products were introduced annually. The decline in new-food-item introductions is particularly dramatic. What accounts for this reversal after twenty-five years of annual increases? The cost of new-product failures is a contributing factor. Others include the intense competitive pressure and rigorous financial scrutiny that marketers face from Wall Street analysts. [3] The decline in the U.S. economy in 2000 and 2001 also left many firms risk averse.

Categories of New Products

new product
A product new to the world, the market, the producer, the seller, or some combination of these.

The term **new product** is somewhat confusing because its meaning varies widely. Actually, the term has several "correct" definitions. A product can be new to the world, to the market, to the producer or seller, or to some combination of these. There are six categories of new products:

• *New-to-the-world products* (also called *discontinuous innovations*): These products create an entirely new market. The telephone, television, computer, and facsim-

Exhibit 9.1

New-Product Introductions, 1964–2000

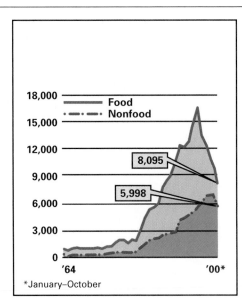

*January–October

SOURCE: Gary Strauss, "Squeezing New from Old," *USA Today*, January 4, 2000, B1.

ile machine are commonly cited examples of new-to-the-world products. New-to-the-world products represent the smallest category of new products.

- *New product lines:* These products, which the firm has not previously offered, allow it to enter an established market. Heinz Frozen Foods introduced a new product line called Boston Market Home Style following a ten-year licensing deal with Boston Chicken, Inc. The new line anchors the premium end of three Heinz lines that include Budget Gourmet (a value product line) and Smart Ones (a nutritionally oriented product line).

- *Additions to existing product lines:* This category includes new products that supplement a firm's established line. Examples of product line additions include Tide detergent in tablet form, Downey Wrinkle Releaser fabric softener, and Yoplait's Go-Gurt, packaged in kid-friendly Popsicle-style tubes.[4] Kimberly-Clark has added a moistened version of toilet paper to its Cottonelle line.[5]

- *Improvements or revisions of existing products:* The "new and improved" product may be significantly or slightly changed. For example, Breyers Soft 'n Creamy! ice cream "scoops right out without bending the spoon." Anyone who has ever sat around for fifteen minutes waiting for a half-gallon of ice cream to thaw would certainly agree that this is a product improvement. Another type of revision is package improvement. The Heinz EZ Squirt Ketchup bottle is short, is made from easy-to-squeeze plastic, and has a needle-shaped nozzle that lets small hands use it to decorate food.[6] Most new products fit into the revision or improvement category.

- *Repositioned products:* These are existing products targeted at new markets or market segments. The bottle for Beefeater gin was totally redesigned in an effort to appeal to a younger, more upscale market.[7] Dippity-Do, the "green colored goo" that has been marketed to adult women since 1965, is being repositioned to target teen buyers, according to managers at White Rain, the corporate parent.[8]

- *Lower-priced products:* This category refers to products that provide performance similar to competing brands at a lower price. Hewlett-Packard Laser Jet 3100 is a scanner, copier, printer, and fax machine combined. This new product is priced lower than many conventional color copiers and much lower than the combined price of the four items purchased separately. The so-called e-machines that have been introduced for under $500 also fit into this category of new product!

Sometimes a product's claim to be safer than an existing product raises ethical issues, as the "Ethics in Marketing" box discusses.

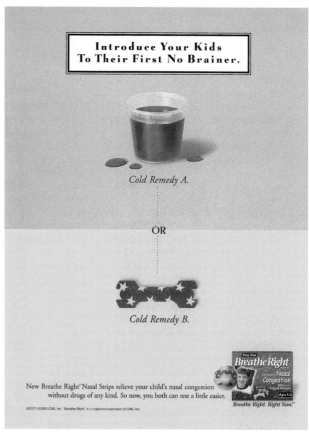

COURTESY OF CNS INC.

Into what category of new products do you think the Breathe Right Nasal Strip falls? It could possibly fall into more than one: additions to existing product lines and repositioned products. How?

The New-Product Development Process

The management and technology consulting firm Booz, Allen, & Hamilton has studied the new-product development process for over thirty years. Analyzing five major studies undertaken during this period, the firm has concluded that the companies most likely to succeed in developing and introducing new products are those that take the following actions:

Explain the steps in the new-product development process

Less Toxins, Great Taste

Vector Tobacco Ltd. recently introduced a new cigarette called Omni, with the slogan, "Reduced carcinogens, premium taste." The ad says that Omni was created to "significantly" cut levels of chemicals that are the "major causes of lung cancer" in smokers. "Now there's actually a reason to change brands," it says.

The tobacco in the Omni cigarette is treated with a combination of chemicals, including palladium, a metal most commonly found in the catalytic converters of cars. Vector says that the treatment, combined with a new, carbon-filled filter, has resulted in a cigarette that tastes as good as competitors' brands but has lower levels of a number of toxic and cancer-causing compounds.

Vector says that its palladium catalyst reduces various cancer-causing compounds known as polycyclic aromatic hydrocarbons, or PAHs, by 15 to 60 percent. It also cuts down on a tobacco-specific nitrosamine, known as NNK, that is considered an especially potent lung carcinogen. Levels of another nitrosamine, however, aren't reduced. The filter removes nearly all the benzene from the cigarette's smoke and also makes significant cuts in other chemicals, Vector scientist Robert Bereman says.

Vector acknowledges there is no scientific proof that these reductions will make its cigarettes any less dangerous than the average Marlboro or Camel. It has yet to complete any human or animal tests of the effects of smoking the new cigarettes. In an open letter to be published in magazines and newspapers, Vector's chief executive, Bennett S. LeBow, writes that "there is no such thing as a safe cigarette, and we do not encourage anyone to smoke." But, he adds: "We strongly believe that if you do smoke, Omni is the best alternative."

"We're doing what we have to do to do the right thing," Mr. LeBow says. "If we have this technology, we have to come out with it. I wouldn't be able to sleep at night if I were sitting on this."

Vector's strategy already is drawing fire from antismoking activists, public-health experts and some of its larger rivals in the cigarette business, who say the ads are misleading. "Everything is designed to imply that this cigarette is safer, with Vector having no proof whatsoever that this is the case," says Matthew L. Myers, president of the Campaign for Tobacco-Free Kids, a Washington advocacy group. "That has the potential to cause serious harm to consumers."

The whole notion of a less hazardous cigarette is controversial. Proponents say it would be wrong not to try to reduce the harm caused by smoking, which contributes to more than 400,000 deaths a year in the United States. But some anti-tobacco activists worry that the newfangled cigarettes will discourage smokers from quitting and possibly entice nonsmokers to light up.[9]

Is Omni a new product? If so, what category of new product does it fit into? Are Vector's claims for Omni legal and ethical?

- Make the long-term commitment needed to support innovation and new-product development
- Use a company-specific approach, driven by corporate objectives and strategies, with a well-defined new-product strategy at its core
- Capitalize on experience to achieve and maintain competitive advantage
- Establish an environment—a management style, organizational structure, and degree of top-management support—conducive to achieving company-specific new-product and corporate objectives

Most companies follow a formal new-product development process, usually starting with a new-product strategy. Exhibit 9.2 traces the seven-step process, which is discussed in detail in this section. The exhibit is funnel-shaped to highlight the fact that each stage acts as a screen. The purpose is to filter out unworkable ideas.

New-Product Strategy

new-product strategy
A plan that links the new-product development process with the objectives of the marketing department, the business unit, and the corporation.

A **new-product strategy** links the new-product development process with the objectives of the marketing department, the business unit, and the corporation. A new-product strategy must be compatible with these objectives, and in turn, all three objectives must be consistent with one another.

A new-product strategy is part of the organization's overall marketing strategy. It sharpens the focus and provides general guidelines for generating, screening, and evaluating new-product ideas. The new-product strategy specifies the roles

Exhibit 9.2

New-Product Development Process

1 New-product strategy
2 Idea generation
3 Idea screening
4 Business analysis
5 Development
6 Test marketing
7 Commercialization

New product

that new products must play in the organization's overall plan and describes the characteristics of products the organization wants to offer and the markets it wants to serve.

Idea Generation

New-product ideas come from many sources, including customers, employees, distributors, competitors, research and development (R&D), and consultants.

- *Customers:* The marketing concept suggests that customers' wants and needs should be the springboard for developing new products. Thermos, the vacuum bottle manufacturer, provides an interesting example of how companies tap customers for ideas. The company's first step in developing an innovative home barbecue grill was to send ten members of its interdisciplinary new-product team into the field for about a month. Their assignment was to learn all about people's cookout needs and to invent a product to meet them. In various cities including Boston, Los Angeles, and Columbus, Ohio, the team conducted focus groups, visited people's homes, and even videotaped barbecues.

- *Employees:* Marketing personnel—advertising and marketing research employees, as well as salespeople—often create new-product ideas because they analyze and are involved in the marketplace. The very successful introduction of Post-it

Notes started with an employee's idea. In 1974, the R&D department of 3M's commercial tape division developed and patented the adhesive component of Post-it Notes. However, it was a year before an employee of the commercial tape division, who sang in a church choir, identified a use for the adhesive. He had been using paper clips and slips of paper to mark places in hymn books. But the paper clips damaged his books, and the slips of paper fell out. The solution, as we now all know, was to apply the adhesive to small pieces of paper and sell them in packages.

- *Distributors:* A well-trained sales force routinely asks distributors about needs that are not being met. Because they are closer to end users, distributors are often more aware of customer needs than are manufacturers. The inspiration for Rubbermaid's litter-free lunch box, named Sidekick, came from a distributor. The distributor suggested that Rubbermaid place some of its plastic containers inside a lunch box and sell the box as an alternative to plastic wrap and paper bags.

- *Competitors:* No firms rely solely on internally generated ideas for new products. A big part of any organization's marketing intelligence system should be monitoring the performance of competitors' products. One purpose of competitive monitoring is to determine which, if any, of the competitors' products should be copied.

There is plenty of information about competitors on the World Wide Web. For example, AltaVista (**http://www.altavista.com**) is a powerful index tool that can be used to locate information about products and companies. Fuld & Company's competitive intelligence guide provides links to a variety of market intelligence sites.

- *Research and development:* R&D is carried out in four distinct ways. Basic research is scientific research aimed at discovering new technologies. Applied research takes these new technologies and tries to find useful applications for them. **Product development** goes one step further by converting applications into marketable products. *Product modification* makes cosmetic or functional changes in existing products. Many new-product breakthroughs come from R&D activities. Pert Plus, Procter & Gamble's combination shampoo and conditioner, was invented in the laboratory. So was Take Heart, a new product line from Quaker Oats, that includes an ingredient called Reducol, which has been found to lower the level of low-density lipoprotein or LDL, cholesterol.[10]

- *Consultants:* Outside consultants are always available to examine a business and recommend product ideas. Examples include the Weston Group; Booz, Allen, & Hamilton; and Management Decisions. Traditionally, consultants determine whether a company has a balanced portfolio of products and, if not, what new-product ideas are needed to offset the imbalance. For instance, an outside consultant conceived Airwick's highly successful Carpet Fresh carpet cleaner.

Creativity is the wellspring of new-product ideas, regardless of who comes up with them. A variety of approaches and techniques have been developed to stimulate creative thinking. The two considered most useful for generating new-product ideas are brainstorming and focus-group exercises. The goal of **brainstorming** is to get a group to think of unlimited ways to vary a product or solve a problem. Group members avoid criticism of an idea, no matter how ridiculous it may seem. Objective evaluation is postponed. The sheer quantity of ideas is what matters. As noted in Chapter 7, an objective of focus-group interviews is to stimulate insightful comments through group interaction. Focus groups usually consist of seven to ten people. Sometimes consumer focus groups generate excellent new-product ideas—for example, Cycle dog food, Stick-Up room deodorizers, Dustbuster vacuum cleaners, and Wendy's salad bar. In the industrial market, machine tools, keyboard designs, aircraft interiors, and backhoe accessories have evolved from focus groups.

product development
A marketing strategy that entails the creation of marketable new products; the process of converting applications for new technologies into marketable products.

brainstorming
The process of getting a group to think of unlimited ways to vary a product or solve a problem.

Idea Screening

After new ideas have been generated, they pass through the first filter in the product development process. This stage, called **screening**, eliminates ideas that are inconsistent with the organization's new-product strategy or are obviously inappropriate for some other reason. The new-product committee, the new-product department, or some other formally appointed group performs the screening review. General Motors' Advanced Portfolio Exploration Group (APEx) knows that only one out of every twenty new car concepts developed by the group will ever become a reality. That's not a bad percentage. In the pharmaceutical business, one new product out of five thousand ideas is not uncommon.[11] Most new-product ideas are rejected at the screening stage.

Concept tests are often used at the screening stage to rate concept (or product) alternatives. A **concept test** evaluates a new-product idea, usually before any prototype has been created. Typically, researchers get consumer reactions to descriptions and visual representations of a proposed product.

Concept tests are considered fairly good predictors of success for line extensions. They have also been relatively precise predictors of success for new products that are not copycat items, are not easily classified into existing product categories, and do not require major changes in consumer behavior—such as Betty Crocker Tuna Helper, Cycle dog food, and Libby Fruit Float. However, concept tests are usually inaccurate in predicting the success of new products that create new consumption patterns and require major changes in consumer behavior—such as microwave ovens, videocassette recorders, computers, and word processors.

screening
The first filter in the product development process, which eliminates ideas that are inconsistent with the organization's new-product strategy or are obviously inappropriate for some other reason.

concept test
A test to evaluate a new-product idea, usually before any prototype has been created.

Business Analysis

New-product ideas that survive the initial screening process move to the **business analysis** stage, where preliminary figures for demand, cost, sales, and profitability are calculated. For the first time, costs and revenues are estimated and compared. Depending on the nature of the product and the company, this process may be simple or complex.

The newness of the product, the size of the market, and the nature of the competition all affect the accuracy of revenue projections. In an established market like soft drinks, industry estimates of total market size are available. Forecasting market share for a new entry is a bigger challenge.

Analyzing overall economic trends and their impact on estimated sales is especially important in product categories that are sensitive to fluctuations in the business cycle. If consumers view the economy as uncertain and risky, they will put off buying durable goods like major home appliances, automobiles, and homes. Likewise, business buyers postpone major equipment purchases if they expect a recession.

These questions are commonly asked during the business analysis stage:

- What is the likely demand for the product?

- What impact would the new product probably have on total sales, profits, market share, and return on investment?

- How would the introduction of the product affect existing products? Would the new product cannibalize existing products?

business analysis
The second stage of the screening process where preliminary figures for demand, cost, sales, and profitability are calculated.

New-product development is the lifeblood of many companies. IBM is working on a flexible panel/e-newspaper device that will allow users to download news services through wireless access.

- Would current customers benefit from the product?

- Would the product enhance the image of the company's overall product mix?

- Would the new product affect current employees in any way? Would it lead to hiring more people or reducing the size of the workforce?

- What new facilities, if any, would be needed?

- How might competitors respond?

- What is the risk of failure? Is the company willing to take the risk?

Answering these and related questions may require studies of markets, competition, costs, and technical capabilities. But at the end of this stage, management should have a good understanding of the product's market potential. This full understanding is important because costs increase dramatically once a product idea enters the development stage.

Development

development
The stage in the product development process in which a prototype is developed and a marketing strategy is outlined.

In the early stage of **development**, the R&D department or engineering department may develop a prototype of the product. During this stage, the firm should start sketching a marketing strategy. The marketing department should decide on the product's packaging, branding, labeling, and so forth. In addition, it should map out preliminary promotion, price, and distribution strategies. The technical feasibility of manufacturing the product at an acceptable cost should also be thoroughly examined.

The development stage can last a long time and thus be very expensive. Crest toothpaste was in the development stage for ten years. It took eighteen years to develop Minute Rice, fifteen years to develop the Polaroid Colorpack camera, fifteen years to develop the Xerox copy machine, and fifty-five years to develop television. Gillette spent six years developing the MACH 3 razor.

simultaneous product development
A team-oriented approach to new-product development.

The development process works best when all the involved areas (R&D, marketing, engineering, production, and even suppliers) work together rather than sequentially, a process called **simultaneous product development.** This approach allows firms to shorten the development process and reduce costs. With simultaneous product development, all relevant functional areas and outside suppliers participate in all stages of the development process. Rather than proceeding through highly structured stages, the cross-functional team operates in unison. Involving key suppliers early in the process capitalizes on their specialized knowledge and enables them to design and develop critical component parts.

ON LINE The Internet is a useful tool for implementing simultaneous product development. On the Net, multiple partners from a variety of locations can meet regularly to assess new-product ideas, analyze markets and demographics, and review cost information. Ideas judged to be feasible can quickly be converted into new products. For example, Procter & Gamble has created an autonomous idea laboratory called Corporate New Ventures. Its mission is to encourage ideas for products and put the best ideas into speedy production. Corporate New Ventures has $250 million in seed money and reports directly to top management. The story at the beginning of this chapter about the Chrysler Group of DaimlerChrysler using the Internet to connect various groups both inside and outside the company illustrates the value of the Internet in simultaneous product development efforts.

Dannon chose to test market its successful European product Actimel in Colorado before rolling out the bacteria-loaded dairy product nationwide. Test marketing for two years allowed the company to refine its marketing strategy and determine customer reaction.

Laboratory tests are often conducted on prototype models during the development stage. User safety is an important aspect of laboratory testing, which actually subjects products to much more severe treatment than is expected by end users. The Consumer Product Safety Act of 1972 requires manufacturers to conduct a "reasonable testing program" to ensure that their products conform to established safety standards.

Many products that test well in the laboratory are also tried out in homes or businesses. Examples of product categories well suited for such use tests include human and pet food products, household cleaning products, and industrial chemicals and supplies. These products are all relatively inexpensive, and their performance characteristics are apparent to users. For example, at the W. K. Kellogg Institute for Food and Nutrition Research, cross-functional teams of employees spend their days cooking, eating, and comparing notes. Management believes that creativity comes from diversity, so researchers with unusual backgrounds are recruited. The Institute employs people from twenty-two different countries. The company is quite pleased with the results produced by the Institute. In one month, researchers generated sixty-five new product ideas and ninety-four new packaging ideas.[12]

Most products require some refinement based on the results of laboratory and use tests. General Mills tested various package prototypes of Go-Gurt with mothers and their children. "If you could squeeze it, push it, pump it, peel it, or sip it, we tried it."[13] A second stage of development often takes place before test marketing.

Test Marketing

After products and marketing programs have been developed, they are usually tested in the marketplace. **Test marketing** is the limited introduction of a product and a marketing program to determine the reactions of potential customers in a market situation. Test marketing allows management to evaluate alternative strategies and to assess how well the various aspects of the marketing mix fit together. Quaker Oats test marketed the Take Heart line of food products including ready-to-eat cereals, snack bars, and fruit juice beverages in selected markets in the New York State area before introducing the line nationwide.[14] Even established products are test marketed to assess new marketing strategies. One-dollar bottles of chocolate, strawberry, and coffee-flavored milk, distributed through vending machines, were offered in schools in Texas, California, Massachusetts, Nebraska, and Florida to assess this alternative distribution strategy. Initial weekly sales ran about two hundred bottles per machine.[15]

The cities chosen as test sites should reflect market conditions in the new product's projected market area. Yet no "magic city" exists that can universally represent market conditions, and a product's success in one city doesn't guarantee that it will be a nationwide hit. When selecting test market cities, researchers should therefore find locations where the demographics and purchasing habits mirror the overall market. The company should also have good distribution in test cities. Moreover, test locations should be isolated from the media. If the TV stations in a particular market reach a very large area outside that market, the advertising used for the test product may pull in many consumers from outside the market. The product may then appear more successful than it really is. Exhibit 9.3 on page 298 provides a useful checklist of criteria for selecting test markets.

The High Costs of Test Marketing

Test marketing frequently takes one year or longer, and costs can exceed $1 million. Some products remain in test markets even longer. McDonald's spent twelve years developing and testing salads before introducing them. Despite the cost, many firms believe it is a lot better to fail in a test market than in a national introduction.

Because test marketing is so expensive, some companies do not test line extensions of well-known brands. For example, because the Folgers brand is well

What can you find out on the Internet about current test marketing? Use the AlltheWeb search engine and type in "Test Marketing."
http://www.alltheweb.com
On Line

test marketing
The limited introduction of a product and a marketing program to determine the reactions of potential customers in a market situation.

Exhibit 9.3

Checklist for Selecting Test Markets

In choosing a test market, many criteria need to be considered, especially the following:
Similarity to planned distribution outlets
Relative isolation from other cities
Availability of advertising media that will cooperate
Diversified cross section of ages, religions, cultural-societal preferences, etc.
No atypical purchasing habits
Representative population size
Typical per capita income
Good record as a test city, but not overly used
Not easily "jammed" by competitors
Stability of year-round sales
No dominant television station; multiple newspapers, magazines, and radio stations
Availability of research and audit services
Availability of retailers that will cooperate
Freedom from unusual influences, such as one industry's dominance or heavy tourism

known, Procter & Gamble faced little risk in distributing its instant decaffeinated version nationally. Consolidated Foods Kitchen of Sara Lee followed the same approach with its frozen croissants. Other products introduced without being test marketed include General Foods' International Coffees, Quaker Oats' Chewy Granola Bars and Granola Dipps, and Pillsbury's Milk Break Bars.

The high cost of test marketing is not just financial. One unavoidable problem is that test marketing exposes the new product and its marketing mix to competitors before its introduction. Thus, the element of surprise is lost. Several years ago, for example, Procter & Gamble began testing a ready-to-spread Duncan Hines frosting. General Mills took note and rushed to market with its own Betty Crocker brand, which now is the best-selling brand of ready-to-spread frosting. Competitors can also sabotage or "jam" a testing program by introducing their own sales promotion, pricing, or advertising campaign. The purpose is to hide or distort the normal conditions that the testing firm might expect in the market.

Alternatives to Test Marketing

Many firms are looking for cheaper, faster, safer alternatives to traditional test marketing. In the early 1980s, Information Resources, Inc., pioneered one alternative: single-source research using supermarket scanner data (discussed in Chapter 7). A typical supermarket scanner test costs about $300,000. Another alternative to traditional test marketing is **simulated (laboratory) market testing**. Advertising and other promotional materials for several products, including the test product, are shown to members of the product's target market. These people are then taken to shop at a mock or real store, where their purchases are recorded. Shopper behavior, including repeat purchasing, is monitored to assess the product's likely performance under true market conditions. Research firms offer simulated market tests for $25,000 to $100,000, compared to $1 million or more for full-scale test marketing.

On-Line Test Marketing

Despite these alternatives, most firms still consider test marketing essential for most new products. The high price of failure simply prohibits the widespread introduction of most new products without testing. Many firms are finding that the Internet offers a fast, cost-effective way to conduct test marketing.

Procter & Gamble is an avid proponent of using the Internet as a means for gauging customer demand for potential new products. The company reportedly conducts 40 percent of its product tests and other studies on-line and hopes to cut its $140 million annual research budget in half by shifting efforts to the Internet.[16]

Many products that are not available in grocery stores or drugstores can be sampled or purchased from P&G's corporate Web site **http://PG.com**. Crest Whitestrips provides an illustration.

In August 2000, when P&G brand manager Val Bogdan-Powers was ready to launch Crest Whitestrips, a new home tooth-bleaching kit, management wasn't sure that consumers would be willing to pay the proposed $44 retail price. She then began an eight-month campaign offering the strips exclusively on P&G's **http://whitestrips.com**. TV spots and magazine ads were run to promote the on-line sale. In eight months, 144,000 whitening kits were sold on-line. The product was introduced in retail outlets in 2001, and $50 million worth of kits were sold in the first three months at the $44 per kit price.[17]

Other consumer goods firms that have recently begun on-line test marketing include General Mills and Quaker Oats. Other sites have appeared that offer consumers prototype products developed by all sizes of firms.

Commercialization

The final stage in the new-product development process is **commercialization**, the decision to market a product. The decision to commercialize the product sets several tasks in motion: ordering production materials and equipment, starting production, building inventories, shipping the product to field distribution points, training the sales force, announcing the new product to the trade, and advertising to potential customers. "Our goal," says Bruce Thompson, senior vice president of product development and engineering at Sea Ray Boats, "is to deliver to the customer what they want even before they need it."[18]

The time from the initial commercialization decision to the product's actual introduction varies. It can range from a few weeks for simple products that use existing equipment to several years for technical products that require custom manufacturing equipment.

The total cost of development and initial introduction can be staggering. Gillette spent $750 million developing MACH 3, and the first-year marketing budget for the new three-bladed razor was $300 million.

simulated (laboratory) market testing
The presentation of advertising and other promotion materials for several products, including a test product, to members of the product's target market.

commercialization
The decision to market a product.

The Spread of New Products

Managers have a better chance of successfully marketing products if they understand how consumers learn about and adopt products. A person who buys a new product never before tried may ultimately become an **adopter**, a consumer who was happy enough with his or her trial experience with a product to use it again.

Explain the diffusion process through which new products are adopted

adopter
A consumer who was happy enough with his or her trial experience with a product to use it again.

innovation
A product perceived as new by a potential adopter.

diffusion
The process by which the adoption of an innovation spreads.

Diffusion of Innovation

An **innovation** is a product perceived as new by a potential adopter. It really doesn't matter whether the product is "new to the world" or some other category of new product. If it is new to a potential adopter, it is an innovation in this context. **Diffusion** is the process by which the adoption of an innovation spreads.

Five categories of adopters participate in the diffusion process:

- *Innovators:* the first 2.5 percent of all those who adopt the product. Innovators are eager to try new ideas and products, almost as an obsession. In addition to having higher incomes, they are more worldly and more active outside their community than noninnovators. They rely less on group norms and are more self-confident. Because they are well educated, they are more likely to get their information from scientific sources and experts. Innovators are characterized as being venturesome.

- *Early adopters:* the next 13.5 percent to adopt the product. Although early adopters are not the very first, they do adopt early in the product's life cycle. Compared to innovators, they rely much more on group norms and values. They are also more oriented to the local community, in contrast to the innovators' worldly outlook. Early adopters are more likely than innovators to be opinion leaders because of their closer affiliation with groups. The respect of others is a dominant characteristic of early adopters.

- *Early majority:* the next 34 percent to adopt. The early majority weighs the pros and cons before adopting a new product. They are likely to collect more information and evaluate more brands than early adopters, therefore extending the adoption process. They rely on the group for information but are unlikely to be opinion leaders themselves. Instead, they tend to be opinion leaders' friends and neighbors. The early majority is an important link in the process of diffusing new ideas because they are positioned between earlier and later adopters. A dominant characteristic of the early majority is deliberateness.

- *Late majority:* the next 34 percent to adopt. The late majority adopts a new product because most of their friends have already adopted it. Because they also rely on group norms, their adoption stems from pressure to conform. This group tends to be older and below average in income and education. They depend mainly on word-of-mouth communication rather than on the mass media. The dominant characteristic of the late majority is skepticism.

- *Laggards:* the final 16 percent to adopt. Like innovators, laggards do not rely on group norms. Their independence is rooted in their ties to tradition. Thus, the past heavily influences their decisions. By the time laggards adopt an innovation, it has probably been outmoded and replaced by something else. For example, they may have bought their first black-and-white TV set after color television was already widely diffused. Laggards have the longest adoption time and the lowest socioeconomic status. They tend to be suspicious of new products and alienated from a rapidly advancing society. The dominant value of laggards is tradition. Marketers typically ignore laggards, who do not seem to be motivated by advertising or personal selling.

Exhibit 9.4 illustrates the diffusion of three familiar products throughout the United States. Virtually every household is equipped with one or more color televisions. Note that some product categories, such as monochrome televisions, may never be adopted by 100 percent of the population. The adopter categories refer to all of those who will eventually adopt a product, not the entire population.

Product Characteristics and the Rate of Adoption

Five product characteristics can be used to predict and explain the rate of acceptance and diffusion of a new product:

- *Complexity:* the degree of difficulty involved in understanding and using a new product. The more complex the product, the slower is its diffusion. For instance, before many of their functions were automated, 35mm cameras were used primarily by hobbyists and professionals. The cameras were just too complex for most people to learn to operate.

- *Compatibility:* the degree to which the new product is consistent with existing values and product knowledge, past experiences, and current needs. Incompatible products diffuse more slowly than compatible products. For example, the introduction of contraceptives is incompatible in countries where religious beliefs discourage the use of birth control techniques.

- *Relative advantage:* the degree to which a product is perceived as superior to existing substitutes. For example, because it reduces cooking time, the microwave oven has a clear relative advantage over a conventional oven.

- *Observability:* the degree to which the benefits or other results of using the product can be observed by others and communicated to target customers. For instance, fashion items and automobiles are highly visible and more observable than personal-care items.

- *"Trialability":* the degree to which a product can be tried on a limited basis. It is much easier to try a new toothpaste or breakfast cereal than a new automobile

Diffusion of Three Familiar Products among U.S. Households **Exhibit 9.4**

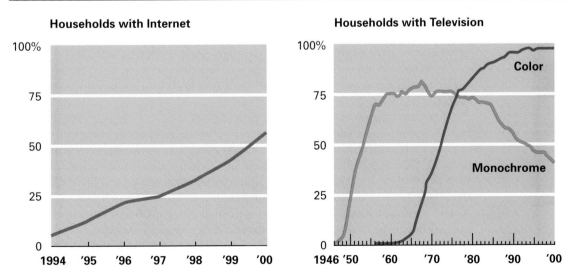

SOURCE: Julia Angwin, "Consumer Adoption Rate Slows in Replay of TV's History; Bad News for Online Firms," *Wall Street Journal*, July 16, 2001, B1. Reprinted by permission of the *Wall Street Journal*. © 2001 Dow Jones & Company, Inc. All rights reserved worldwide. 2001. Dow Jones & Company, Inc. Data supplied by Forrester Research; Consumer Electronics Association.

or microcomputer. Demonstrations in showrooms and test-drives are different from in-home trial use. To stimulate trials, marketers use free-sampling programs, tasting displays, and small package sizes.

Marketing Implications of the Adoption Process

Two types of communication aid the diffusion process: *word-of-mouth communication* among consumers and communication from marketers to consumers. Word-of-mouth communication within and across groups speeds diffusion. Opinion leaders discuss new products with their followers and with other opinion leaders. Marketers must therefore ensure that opinion leaders have the types of information desired in the media that they use. Suppliers of some products, such as professional and health-care services, rely almost solely on word-of-mouth communication for new business.

The second type of communication aiding the diffusion process is *communication directly from the marketer to potential adopters*. Messages directed toward early adopters should normally use different appeals than messages directed toward the early majority, the late majority, or the laggards. Early adopters are more important than innovators because they make up a larger group, are more socially active, and are usually opinion leaders.

As the focus of a promotional campaign shifts from early adopters to the early majority and the late majority, marketers should study the dominant characteristics, buying behavior, and media characteristics of these target markets. Then they should revise messages and media strategy to fit. The diffusion model helps guide marketers in developing and implementing promotion strategy.

Product Life Cycles

Explain the concept of product life cycles

product life cycle (PLC)
A concept that provides a way to trace the stages of a product's acceptance, from its introduction (birth) to its decline (death).

product category
All brands that satisfy a particular type of need.

The **product life cycle (PLC)** is one of the most familiar concepts in marketing. Few other general concepts have been so widely discussed. Although some researchers have challenged the theoretical basis and managerial value of the PLC, most believe it has great potential as a marketing management tool.

The product life cycle is a concept that provides a way to trace the stages of a product's acceptance, from its introduction (birth) to its decline (death). As Exhibit 9.5 shows, a product progresses through four major stages: introduction, growth, maturity, and decline. Note that the product life cycle illustrated does not refer to any one brand; rather, it refers to the life cycle for a product category or product class. A **product category** includes all brands that satisfy a particular type of need. Product categories include passenger cars, cigarettes, soft drinks, and coffee. When we trace the product life cycle of a product such as DVD players, we are including the aggregate sales of all brands of DVD players, not just a single brand.

The time a product spends in any one stage of the life cycle may vary dramatically. Some products, such as fad items, move through the entire cycle in weeks. Others, such as electric clothes washers and dryers, stay in the maturity stage for decades. Exhibit 9.5 illustrates the typical life cycle for a consumer durable good, such as a washer or dryer. In contrast, Exhibit 9.6 illustrates typical life cycles for styles (such as formal, business, or casual clothing), fashions (such as miniskirts or stirrup pants), and fads (such as leopard-print clothing). Changes in a product, its uses, its image, or its positioning can extend that product's life cycle.

The product life cycle concept does not tell managers the length of a product's life cycle or its duration in any stage. It does not dictate marketing strategy. It is simply a tool to help marketers forecast future events and suggest appropriate strategies. Look at Exhibit 9.7 on page 304. What conclusions can you draw about the product life cycle of DVD players based on four and a half years of sales data?

Exhibit 9.5

Four Stages of the Product Life Cycle

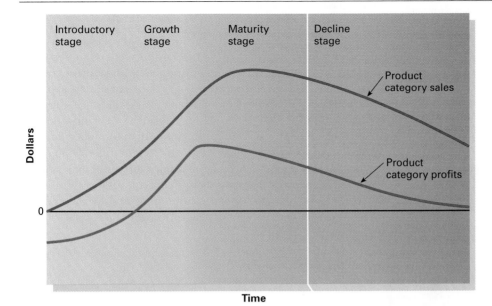

Introductory Stage

The **introductory stage** of the product life cycle represents the full-scale launch of a new product into the marketplace. Computer databases for personal use, room-deodorizing air-conditioning filters, and wind-powered home electric generators are all product categories that have recently entered the product life cycle. A high failure rate, little competition, frequent product modification, and limited distribution typify the introduction stage of the PLC.

Marketing costs in the introductory stage are normally high for several reasons. High dealer margins are often needed to obtain adequate distribution, and incentives are needed to get consumers to try the new product. Advertising expenses are high because of the need to educate consumers about the new product's benefits. Production costs are also often high in this stage, as product and manufacturing flaws are identified and corrected and efforts are undertaken to develop mass-production economies.

As Exhibit 9.5 illustrates, sales normally increase slowly during the introductory stage. Moreover, profits are usually negative because of R&D costs, factory tooling, and high introduction costs. The length of the introductory phase is largely determined by product characteristics, such as the product's advantages over substitute products, the educational effort required to make the product known, and management's commitment of resources to the new item. A short introductory period is usually preferred to help reduce the impact of negative earnings and cash flows. As soon as the product gets off the ground, the financial burden should begin to

introductory stage
The full-scale launch of a new product into the marketplace.

Exhibit 9.6

Product Life Cycles for Styles, Fashions, and Fads

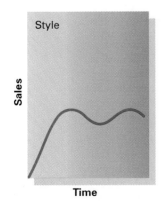

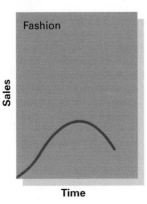

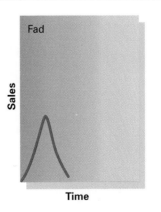

Introducing **Vitaball**, the vitamin gumball

A whole new way to take your vitamins℠

You may never have to remind your kids to take their vitamins again. With new Vitaball, there's no begging, no pleading, no fuss.

The first 5 minutes or so your kids chew Vitaball, they get 100% RDA of 11 essential vitamins kids need every day. And it comes in all their favorite gumball colors and flavors.

At last there's a multi-vitamin kids won't outgrow. You'll love Vitaball as a kid, a teen and beyond. Get Vitaball for the whole family.

When was the last time your kids reminded you to give them their vitamins?

Get a FREE SAMPLE and coupon

visit www.vitaball.com or call 888-565-6699

While supplies last

COURTESY AMERIFIT NUTRITION, INC.

growth stage
The second stage of the product life cycle when sales typically grow at an increasing rate, many competitors enter the market, large companies may start acquiring small pioneering firms, and profits are healthy.

maturity stage
A period during which sales increase at a decreasing rate.

Styles, fashions, and fads tend to follow different product life cycles. Based on what you see in Exhibits 9.5 and 9.6, what is the life cycle for Vitaballs, a new vitamin-infused bubblegum? Do you think it will be adopted by the mainstream? If so, how quickly?

diminish. Also, a short introduction helps dispel some of the uncertainty as to whether the new product will be successful.

Promotion strategy in the introductory stage focuses on developing product awareness and informing consumers about the product category's potential benefits. At this stage, the communication challenge is to stimulate primary demand—demand for the product in general rather than for a specific brand. Intensive personal selling is often required to gain acceptance for the product among wholesalers and retailers. Promotion of convenience products often requires heavy consumer sampling and couponing. Shopping and specialty products demand educational advertising and personal selling to the final consumer.

Growth Stage

If a product category survives the introductory stage, it advances to the **growth stage** of the life cycle. In this stage, sales typically grow at an increasing rate, many competitors enter the market, and large companies may start to acquire small pioneering firms. Profits rise rapidly in the growth stage, reach their peak, and begin declining as competition intensifies. Emphasis switches from primary demand promotion (for example, promoting personal digital assistants [PDAs]) to aggressive brand advertising and communication of the differences between brands (for example, promoting Casio versus Palm and Visor).

Distribution becomes a major key to success during the growth stage, as well as in later stages. Manufacturers scramble to sign up dealers and distributors and to build long-term relationships. Without adequate distribution, it is impossible to establish a strong market position.

Maturity Stage

A period during which sales increase at a decreasing rate signals the beginning of the **maturity stage** of the life cycle. New users cannot be added indefinitely, and sooner or later the market approaches saturation. Normally, this is the longest stage

☐ **Exhibit 9.7**

Sales of DVD Players in the United States

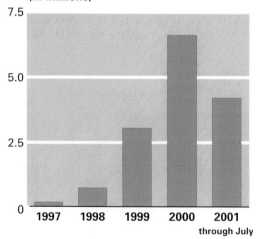

Annual Sales of DVD Players (in Millions)*

SOURCE: Marten Peers, "For Now, At Least, DVD Sales Are Soaring As Prices Drop," *Wall Street Journal,* September 11, 2001, B4. Reprinted by permission of the *Wall Street Journal.* ©2001. Dow Jones & Company, Inc. All rights reserved worldwide. 2001. Dow Jones & Company, Inc. Data supplied by NPD Intellect Market Tracking.

of the product life cycle. Many major household appliances are in the maturity stage of their life cycles.

For shopping products and many specialty products, annual models begin to appear during the maturity stage. Product lines are lengthened to appeal to additional market segments. Service and repair assume more important roles as manufacturers strive to distinguish their products from others. Product design changes tend to become stylistic (How can the product be made different?) rather than functional (How can the product be made better?).

As prices and profits continue to fall, marginal competitors start dropping out of the market. Dealer margins also shrink, resulting in less shelf space for mature items, lower dealer inventories, and a general reluctance to promote the product. Thus, promotion to dealers often intensifies during this stage in order to retain loyalty.

Heavy consumer promotion by the manufacturer is also required to maintain market share. Consider these well-known examples of competition in the maturity stage: the "cola war" featuring Coke and Pepsi, the "beer war" featuring Anheuser-Busch's Budweiser brands and Philip Morris's Miller brands, and the "burger wars" pitting leader McDonald's against challengers Burger King and Wendy's.

Another characteristic of the maturity stage is the emergence of "niche marketers" that target narrow, well-defined, underserved segments of a market. Starbucks Coffee targets its gourmet line at the only segment of the coffee market that is growing: new, younger, more affluent coffee drinkers.

AP/WIDE WORLD PHOTOS

Coffee is an example of a product in the maturity stage where niche marketers have emerged. Starbucks, for example, targets its gourmet products at newer, younger, more affluent coffee drinkers.

Decline Stage

A long-run drop in sales signals the beginning of the **decline stage**. The rate of decline is governed by how rapidly consumer tastes change or substitute products are adopted. Many convenience products and fad items lose their market overnight, leaving large inventories of unsold items, such as designer jeans. Others die more slowly, like citizen band (CB) radios, black-and-white console television sets, and nonelectronic wristwatches.

Some firms have developed successful strategies for marketing products in the decline stage of the product life cycle. They eliminate all nonessential marketing expenses and let sales decline as more and more customers discontinue purchasing the products. Eventually, the product is withdrawn from the market.

Management sage Peter Drucker says that all companies should practice "organized abandonment," which entails reviewing every product, service, and policy every two or three years and asking the critical question, "If we didn't do this already, would we launch it now?" Would we introduce the product, service, or policy now? If the answer is no, it's time to begin the abandonment process.[19]

decline stage
A long-run drop in sales.

Implications for Marketing Management

The product life cycle concept encourages marketing managers to plan so that they can take the initiative instead of reacting to past events. The product life cycle

Exhibit **9.8** Typical Marketing Strategies during the Product Life Cycle

Marketing Mix Strategy	Product Life Cycle Stage			
	Introduction	Growth	Maturity	Decline
Product Strategy	Limited number of models; frequent product modifications	Expanded number of models; frequent product modifications	Large number of models	Elimination of unprofitable models and brands
Distribution Strategy	Distribution usually limited, depending on product; intensive efforts and high margins often needed to attract wholesalers and retailers	Expanded number of dealers; intensive efforts to establish long-term relationships with wholesalers and retailers	Extensive number of dealers; margins declining; intensive efforts to retain distributors and shelf space	Unprofitable outlets phased out
Promotion Strategy	Develop product awareness; stimulate primary demand; use intensive personal selling to distributors; use sampling and couponing for consumers	Stimulate selective demand; advertise brand aggressively	Stimulate selective demand; advertise brand aggressively; promote heavily to retain dealers and customers	Phase out all promotion
Pricing Strategy	Prices are usually high to recover development costs (see Chapter 15)	Prices begin to fall toward end of growth stage as result of competitive pressure	Prices continue to fall	Prices stabilize at relatively low level; small price rises are possible if competition is negligible

is especially useful as a predicting or forecasting tool. Because products pass through distinctive stages, it is often possible to estimate a product's location on the curve using historical data. Profits, like sales, tend to follow a predictable path over a product's life cycle.

Exhibit 9.8 briefly summarizes some typical marketing strategies during each stage of the product life cycle. Exhibit 9.9 shows the relationship between the adopter categories and stages of the product life cycle. Note that the various categories of adopters first buy products in different stages of the product life cycle. Almost all sales in the maturity and decline stages represent repeat purchasing.

Exhibit **9.9**

Relationship between the Diffusion Process and the Product Life Cycle

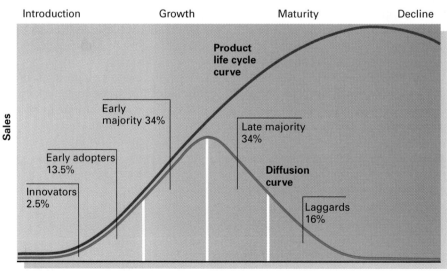

Diffusion curve: Percentage of total adoptions by category
Product life cycle curve: Time

Look back at the story at the beginning of this chapter about how the Chrysler Group is using the Internet to streamline the new-product development process. You now know that involving design, production, finance, and other areas including outside suppliers in the new-product development process is called simultaneous product development. The process reduces product development time by keeping everyone up-to-date on design and development changes and allows a stamping engineer, for example, to watch what is happening so that he or she can make sure the company's stamping plants (where multistory-high presses stamp sheets of metal) can actually make the body that designers select.[20]

The Internet has been particularly helpful to Chrysler because the industry is very complex. Web technology has linked areas within the company that must communicate with one another and that previously had been using different information systems. In addition, the Covisint system will help coordinate activities with suppliers. Other firms such as Procter & Gamble are also using the Internet to implement simultaneous product development processes.

Stay Informed
To keep current with the changing trends and new products in the financial-services industry, arm yourself with information. A banking Web site that will help you make informed decisions is **http://www.bankrate.com**. It has a How-to section that teaches the basics of banking and helps you calculate your payment on loans. The site's collection of interest rate information covers everything from car loans to money market accounts and enables you to compare rates from financial institutions in all fifty states. You can also check the fees different banks charge for their services and compare them to on-line banking service charges.

Locate Lenders
More and more financial institutions are expanding their lending to entrepreneurs and small-business owners. The following Web sites help start-ups and small businesses find financing:

- **http://quicken.com and http://intuit.com** Both of these sites offer numerous tools for small business and personal finance. Lending Tree offers access to several financial institutions through its site. You can fill out a single loan application at its Web site, **http://lendingtree.com**, and you will receive quotes from various lenders.

- **http://www.icba.org** The Web site of the Independent Community Bankers of America provides leads to all U.S. community banks.

- **http://www.Yahoo.com** This site links to various sources of financial information, news, and advice.

(1) Explain the importance of developing new products and describe the six categories of new products. New products are important to sustain growth and profits and to replace obsolete items. New products can be classified as new-to-the-world products (discontinuous innovations), new product lines, additions to existing product lines, improvements or revisions of existing products, repositioned products, or lower cost products. To sustain or increase profits, a firm must introduce at least one new successful product before a previous product advances to the maturity stage and profit levels begin to drop. Several factors make it more important than ever for firms to consistently introduce new products: shortened product life cycles, rapidly changing technology and consumer priorities, the high rate of new-product failures, and the length of time needed to implement new-product ideas.

1.1 How many new products can you identify? Visit the supermarket and make a list of at least fifteen items with the word "New" on the label. Include on your list anything that looks like a new product. Next to each item on your list, write the category of new product that best describes the item. Share your results with the class.

(2) **Explain the steps in the new-product development process.** First, a firm forms a new-product strategy by outlining the characteristics and roles of future products. Then new-product ideas are generated by customers, employees, distributors, competitors, and internal R&D personnel. Once a product idea has survived initial screening by an appointed screening group, it undergoes business analysis to determine its potential profitability. If a product concept seems viable, it progresses into the development phase, in which the technical and economic feasibility of the manufacturing process is evaluated. The development phase also includes laboratory and use testing of a product for performance and safety. Following initial testing and refinement, most products are introduced in a test market to evaluate consumer response and marketing strategies. Finally, test market successes are propelled into full commercialization. The commercialization process involves starting up production, building inventories, shipping to distributors, training a sales force, announcing the product to the trade, and advertising to consumers.

2.1 List the advantages of simultaneous product development.

2.2 **WRITING** You are a marketing manager for Nike. Your department has come up with the idea of manufacturing a baseball bat for use in colleges around the nation. Assuming you are in the business analysis stage, write a brief analysis based on the questions in the "Business Analysis" section of the chapter.

2.3 What are the major disadvantages to test marketing, and how might they be avoided?

2.4 **ON LINE** How could information from customer orders at **http://www.pizzahut.com** help the company's marketers plan new-product developments?

2.5 **ON LINE** How is customer input affecting the development of Baked Lay's potato chips? Go to **http://www.fritolay.com** to find out.

(3) **Explain the diffusion process through which new products are adopted.** The diffusion process is the spread of a new product from its producer to ultimate adopters. Adopters in the diffusion process belong to five categories: innovators, early adopters, the early majority, the late majority, and laggards. Product characteristics that affect the rate of adoption include product complexity, compatibility with existing social values, relative advantage over existing substitutes, visibility, and "trialability." The diffusion process is facilitated by word-of-mouth communication and communication from marketers to consumers.

3.1 Describe some products whose adoption rates have been affected by complexity, compatibility, relative advantage, observability, and/or "trialability."

3.2 What type of adopter behavior do you typically follow? Explain.

(4) **Explain the concept of product life cycles.** All product categories undergo a life cycle with four stages: introduction, growth, maturity, and decline. The rate at which products move through these stages varies dramatically. Marketing managers use the product life cycle concept as an analytical tool to forecast a product's future and devise effective marketing strategies.

4.1 INFOTRAC COLLEGE EDITION Place the personal computer on the product life cycle curve, and give reasons for placing it where you did. Use InfoTrac (**http://www.infotrac-college.com**) to consult publications like *Technology Review, Computer World,* and *Computer Weekly* to help support your position.

DEFINE IT

adopter 300
brainstorming 294
business analysis 295
commercialization 299
concept test 295
decline stage 305
development 296
diffusion 300

growth stage 304
innovation 300
introductory stage 303
maturity stage 304
new product 290
new-product strategy 292
product category 302
product development 294

product life cycle (PLC) 302
screening 295
simulated (laboratory) market testing 299
simultaneous product development 296
test marketing 297

APPLY IT

Application for Entrepreneurs

Joyce Strand went to the oven to remove the newest batch of beef jerky that she would later sell to the Frontenac Central Store. To her surprise, she had turned the oven up too high, and the beef jerky had dried to a crisp. Although the texture was much different, the jerky still had its unmistakable taste. Joyce decided to take it to the Central Store anyway and let the customers decide. The new snack became a huge success in the snack-food section of the store. Because of her recent success, Joyce began experimenting with different tastes and textures of snack foods that she sells at the Central Store. Realizing that innovation can be very profitable, Joyce now actively looks for new ways to please her customers.

Questions

1. How might Joyce ensure that proper attention is paid to developing new products?

2. What factors should she be aware of that might lead to product failure?

THINK ABOUT IT

Ethics Exercise

One source of new-product ideas is competitors. Steven Fischer recently joined Frankie and Alex Specialty Products as a brand manager. His new boss told him, "We don't have a budget for new-product development. We just monitor our competitors' new-product introductions and offer 'knock-offs' or copies of any that look like they will be successful."

Questions

1. Is this practice ethical?

2. Does the AMA Code of Ethics address this issue? Go to **http://www.marketingpower. com** and review the code. Then, write a brief paragraph on what the AMA Code of Ethics contains that relates to knock-off products.

Entrepreneurship Case

Valvoline: Coming to a Pep Rally Near You

Be prepared for surprises at Valvoline's research and development lab in Lexington, Kentucky. You might picture lab director Fran Lockwood poring over bottles of colored fluids or frowning over mathematical equations. But recently, she was touching up a picture she'd drawn on the wall by her desk with a can of black Spirit Foam.

The foam, a decorative spray that will not drip, was developed by Lockwood's crew of scientists. Lockwood had drawn a pumpkin, a lopsided one with two bats—not birds, she insisted—flying overhead. She wasn't happy with the way the eyes on the pumpkin had turned out.

This is not what you'd expect from the top scientist at Valvoline, a chemist who runs a $4.9 million lab. But then, Spirit Foam isn't the kind of product you'd expect from a company like Valvoline, the world's oldest premium motor-oil brand.

During three years of research, testing, and tweaking, Lockwood's scientists revved up their creative engines to create Spirit Foam. Valvoline is taking the product, its first non-automotive invention brought to market in its 108-year history, for a test-drive at Wal-Mart stores across the nation.

Analysts are applauding Valvoline's move, one the company's competitors have also made in recent years. Pennzoil–Quaker State introduced Glass Chalk, a chalk that can be used to write on glass, about two years ago, and its Medo division makes air fresheners for the home. Industry observers think it is time Valvoline stepped out, too.

"They're pretty well-known, so it makes sense for them to spin into other products to take advantage of that," says Mike Beall of Davenport & Company LLC in Richmond, Virginia. "It's clever of them to try it. They have the maturity to carry it out."

Spirit Foam has sold beyond the company's expectations. The product contributed about $500,000 in profits to the company in September 2001, its first month on the shelf. Wal-Mart quickly asked Valvoline to move the product out of testing mode and into full production.

According to Jim O'Brien, the company's president, Valvoline wanted its first steps out of its motor oil box to be made with a product that would easily capture the public's attention: "We wanted to prove that we can call on customers we don't normally call on and be welcomed in, and have an audience."

O'Brien says that while the motor oil market will be a profitable market for Valvoline for many years, it is growing at only 1 to 2 percent per year. Valvoline's 2001 fiscal year wasn't great for the company. For the year, operating income climbed only slightly, from $78 million to $81 million, while sales and revenues improved from $1.07 billion to $1.09 billion.

Plans for other products are already in the works. Lockwood has formed a strategic group dedicated to exploring new project areas, and she plans to have a new product idea every year.

"We're not going to leave our core business to chase a few whiffs," O'Brien says. "We were feeling around outside the box, but we're not jumping out. This is more of an evolution than a revolution."

Questions

1. How you think Spirit Foam's characteristics will affect its rate of adoption?

2. What advantages does Valvoline have when introducing a new product into a new marketplace?

3. Why is a new product like Spirit Foam so important to Valvoline's future? What kind of marketing strategy is Valvoline following?

4. To what category of new products does Spirit Foam belong? Why is this an advantage for Valvoline? Explain.

WATCH IT

Short **SUPERBOWL**

The *Essentials of Marketing* PowerPoint CD-ROM has four ad videos in the Chapter 9 slide presentation. The concepts of new products are illustrated by ads for Pizza Hut's new Pizzone and Cool Relief Tums. Watch how companies advertise a product in the mature stage of the PLC in the Tylenol ad.

Medium **CNN VIDEO**

New products are often in the news, but do you know how companies launch new products using trade shows? Visit a technology trade show in the CNN news clip for Chapter 9.

Long  **SmallBusinessSchool** ◼
the Series on PBS stations and the Web

To give you insights into Chapter 9, Small Business School will take you to Karsten Manufacturing, creators and makers of Ping golf clubs. What started out to be a club banned by the Professional Golf Association has become the industry standard. When Karsten Solheim invented the now-famous putter, the innovation did not take off quite as well as he had hoped. Step into the SBS Master Class to learn more about product development and diffusion of innovation.

FLIP IT

 Flip to Chapter 9 in your *Grademaker Study Guide* for more review opportunities, including the pretest, vocabulary review, study test questions, and a marketing application based on product concepts. Can you describe the product life cycle? Do you know which marketing mix strategies work best at each point in the product life cycle? What about the diffusion of innovation? If you're unsure, then pick up your *Grademaker* and review.

CLICK IT

 The *Essentials of Marketing* Web site links you to all the Internet-based activities in this chapter, like the "Use It," "Review It" questions 2.4, 2.5, and 4.1, and the On-Line exercises in the chapter margins. As a review, do the Chapter 9 quiz and crossword puzzle. And don't forget the Career Exersite that gives you resources for exploring product-development career opportunities. Review the main concepts in the PowerPoint presentation for Chapter 9, too. Go to **http://lamb.swlearning.com**, read the material, and follow the links right from the site.

Surf to Xtra! to test your understanding of the new-product development concepts in the chapter by completing the worksheets for Exhibits 9.2, 9.3, 9.5, 9.6, 9.8, and 9.9. If your instructor has assigned a marketing plan project, worksheets on Xtra! can help you organize your work. In addition to the quiz on the Web site, there's another quiz on Xtra!, plus video of the authors answering frequently asked questions about new products and product diffusion, such as "Why is such a small proportion of the new products introduced each year 'new-to-the-world' products?"

Still Shaky? Here's a Tip.

The main diagrams in this chapter are Exhibits 9.2, 9.5, 9.6, and 9.9. On a separate sheet, write the titles of these exhibits. Then, with your book closed, try to reproduce the diagrams exactly as they are in the book. Write a short description of what each diagram depicts, and then open your book to check your work.

CHAPTER **TEN**

MARKETING CHANNELS AND SUPPLY CHAIN MANAGEMENT

Learning Objectives

1 Explain what a marketing channel is and why intermediaries are needed

2 Define the types of channel intermediaries and describe their functions and activities

3 Describe the channel structures for consumer and business-to-business products and discuss alternative channel arrangements

4 Define supply chain management and discuss its benefits

5 Discuss the issues that influence channel strategy

6 Explain channel leadership, conflict, and partnering

7 Describe the logistical components of the supply chain

8 Discuss new technology and emerging trends in supply chain management

9 Discuss channels and distribution decisions in global markets

10 Identify the special problems and opportunities associated with distribution in service organizations

How does a traditional grocery store profitably compete head-to-head with Wal-Mart Supercenters? Leadership at the H-E-B Grocery Company believes excellence in supply chain management is one key.

In the early 1990s when Wal-Mart began opening its combination grocery and general merchandise stores, grocery companies were forced to look at their own strengths and weaknesses to determine the best strategy to compete. Some companies decided to concede price to Wal-Mart and to compete instead with customer service. Others decided to cut services to the bare bones and compete on price. H-E-B Grocery Company decided that with excellence in supply chain management it could compete successfully with Wal-Mart without sacrificing low prices or customer service.

To meet this goal, leadership groups from every aspect of the supply chain work as a team to reduce supply chain costs and to increase customer service. For starters, in addition to negotiating lower prices, managers in H-E-B's procurement office communicate directly with suppliers to ensure reliable just-in-time delivery to the company's stores and warehouses. The procurement department also works closely with suppliers to develop more efficient product packaging. For example, produce is shipped in green plastic containers that can be used to display products in the stores. The new packaging improves product quality by reducing damage during shipping and handling and saves time in the stores by dramatically reducing the need for product handling. Finally, the new packaging reduces waste because the packages can be returned to the vendor and used again.

Order processing is handled using advanced computer technology. Store management sends daily orders to the warehouse electronically using a handheld computer system. The system saves time and paper at both the store and warehouse levels. In addition, order information is simultaneously shared with suppliers including H-E-B's own manufacturing units, which then begin production to replenish the company's inventory. The combination of supplier relations and advanced technology enables H-E-B to operate effectively with lean inventories without sacrificing the company's ability to have the right products on store shelves at the right time.

Another critical part of H-E-B's supply chain is the company's state-of-the-art warehouse and distribution centers, which are designed to increase accuracy and reduce time by minimizing product handling and delivery times. Every product in the warehouse system is tracked with radio frequency technology, making it easy for an order selector to find a specific product at any time. Warehouses are organized according to the layout of the company's retail stores. Therefore, when order selectors build a pallet to ship to a store, items are unpacked in the order they are displayed. Finally, each pallet is scanned to confirm that the order is correct before it is loaded onto a truck.

When an order is ready to ship to the store, H-E-B's distribution team uses computer technology to plan deliveries based on mileage, order size, and traffic patterns. In fact, the company has a strategic alliance with Houston's Metro system that gives dispatchers real-time traffic information so that drivers can avoid being caught in traffic delays.

Distribution centers are also strategically placed throughout H-E-B's market area to allow for same-day deliveries.

Finally, the company is investing in a new fleet of alternative fuel trucks. By using cleaner burning fuel, the company is able to save money through lower fuel costs and a reduction in maintenance requirements.

The result of all this attention to detail is the largest privately owned grocery company in the United States. Today, H-E-B operates more than 275 stores, twelve manufacturing plants, and four warehouse and distribution centers throughout Texas and Mexico. How has technology enabled H-E-B to become the largest privately owned grocery company in the United States? What other factors have helped H-E-B become a leader in its field? As you read the following chapter, you will learn more about how supply chain management adds competitive advantage to companies of all kinds.

On Line

H-E-B Grocery

What elements of H-E-B's supply chain are evident on the company's Web site?

http://www.heb.com

Marketing Channels

Explain what a marketing channel is and why intermediaries are needed

marketing channel (channel of distribution)
A set of interdependent organizations that ease the transfer of ownership as products move from producer to business user or consumer.

channel members
All parties in the marketing channel that negotiate with one another, buy and sell products, and facilitate the change of ownership between buyer and seller in the course of moving the product from the manufacturer into the hands of the final consumer.

supply chain
The connected chain of all of the business entities, both internal and external to the company, that perform or support the logistics function.

The term *channel* is derived from the Latin word *canalis*, which means canal. A marketing channel can be viewed as a large canal or pipeline through which products, their ownership, communication, financing and payment, and accompanying risk flow to the consumer. Formally, a **marketing channel** (also called a **channel of distribution**) is a business structure of interdependent organizations that reach from the point of product origin to the consumer with the purpose of moving products to their final consumption destination. Marketing channels facilitate the physical movement of goods through the supply chain, representing "place" in the marketing mix (product, price, promotion, and place) and encompassing the processes involved in getting the right product to the right place at the right time.

Many different types of organizations participate in marketing channels. **Channel members** (also called *intermediaries*, *resellers*, and *middlemen*) negotiate with one another, buy and sell products, and facilitate the change of ownership between buyer and seller in the course of moving the product from the manufacturer into the hands of the final consumer. An important aspect of marketing channels is the joint effort of all channel members to create a continuous and seamless supply chain. The **supply chain** is the connected chain of all of the business entities, both internal and external to the company, that perform or support the marketing channel functions. As products move through the supply chain, channel members facilitate the distribution process by providing specialization and division of labor, overcoming discrepancies, and providing contact efficiency.

Providing Specialization and Division of Labor

According to the concept of specialization and division of labor, breaking down a complex task into smaller, simpler ones and allocating them to specialists will create greater efficiency and lower average production costs. Manufacturers achieve economies of scale through the use of efficient equipment capable of producing large quantities of a single product.

Marketing channels can also attain economies of scale through specialization and division of labor by aiding producers who lack the motivation, financing, or expertise to market directly to end users or consumers. In some cases, as with most consumer convenience goods, such as soft drinks, the cost of marketing directly to millions of consumers—taking and shipping individual orders—is prohibitive. For this reason, producers hire channel members, such as wholesalers and retailers, to do what the producers are not equipped to do or what channel members are better prepared to do. Channel members can do some things more efficiently than producers because they have built good relationships with their customers. Therefore, their specialized expertise enhances the overall performance of the channel.

Overcoming Discrepancies

Marketing channels also aid in overcoming discrepancies of quantity, assortment, time, and space created by economies of scale in production. For example, assume that Pillsbury can efficiently produce its Hungry Jack instant pancake mix only at a rate of 5,000 units in a typical day. Not even the most ardent pancake fan could consume that amount in a year, much less in a day. The quantity produced to achieve low unit costs has created a **discrepancy of quantity**, which is the difference between the amount of product produced and the amount an end user wants to buy. By storing the product and distributing it in the appropriate amounts, marketing channels overcome quantity discrepancies by making products available in the quantities that consumers desire.

Mass production creates not only discrepancies of quantity but also discrepancies of assortment. A **discrepancy of assortment** occurs when a consumer does not have all of the items needed to receive full satisfaction from a product. For pancakes

discrepancy of quantity
The difference between the amount of product produced and the amount an end user wants to buy.

discrepancy of assortment
The lack of all the items a customer needs to receive full satisfaction from a product or products.

to provide maximum satisfaction, several other products are required to complete the assortment. At the very least, most people want a knife, fork, plate, butter, and syrup. Others might add orange juice, coffee, cream, sugar, eggs, and bacon or sausage. Even though Pillsbury is a large consumer-products company, it does not come close to providing the optimal assortment to go with its Hungry Jack pancakes. To overcome discrepancies of assortment, marketing channels assemble in one place many of the products necessary to complete a consumer's needed assortment.

A **temporal discrepancy** is created when a product is produced but a consumer is not ready to buy it. Marketing channels overcome temporal discrepancies by maintaining inventories in anticipation of demand. For example, manufacturers of seasonal merchandise, such as Christmas decorations, are in operation all year even though consumer demand is concentrated during certain months of the year.

Furthermore, because mass production requires many potential buyers, markets are usually scattered over large geographic regions, creating a **spatial discrepancy**. Often global, or at least nationwide, markets are needed to absorb the outputs of mass producers. Marketing channels overcome spatial discrepancies by making products available in locations convenient to consumers. For example, automobile manufacturers overcome spatial discrepancies by franchising dealerships close to consumers.

temporal discrepancy
A situation that occurs when a product is produced but a customer is not ready to buy it.

spatial discrepancy
The difference between the location of a producer and the location of widely scattered markets.

Providing Contact Efficiency

The third need fulfilled by marketing channels is a way to provide contact efficiency. Consider your extra costs if supermarkets, department stores, and shopping centers or malls did not exist. Suppose you had to buy your milk at a dairy and your meat at a stockyard. Imagine buying your eggs and chicken at a hatchery and your fruits and vegetables at various farms. You would spend a great deal of time, money, and energy just shopping for a few groceries. Supply chains simplify distribution by cutting the number of transactions required to get products from manufacturers to consumers and making an assortment of goods available in one location.

Consider the example illustrated in Exhibit 10.1 on page 316. Four consumers each want to buy a television set. Without a retail intermediary like Circuit City, television manufacturers JVC, Zenith, Sony, Toshiba, and RCA would each have to make four contacts to reach the four buyers who are in the target market, totaling twenty transactions. However, when Circuit City acts as an intermediary between the producer and consumers, each producer only has to make one contact, reducing the number of transactions to nine. Each producer sells to one retailer rather than to four consumers. In turn, consumers buy from one retailer instead of from five producers.

Channel Intermediaries and Their Functions

Intermediaries in a channel negotiate with one another, facilitate the change of ownership between buyers and sellers, and physically move products from the manufacturer to the final consumer. The most prominent difference separating intermediaries is whether or not they take title to the product. *Taking title* means they own the merchandise and control the terms of the sale—for example, price and delivery date. Retailers and merchant wholesalers are examples of intermediaries who take title to products in the marketing channel and resell them. **Retailers** are firms that sell mainly to consumers. Retailers will be discussed in more detail in Chapter 11.

Merchant wholesalers are those organizations that facilitate the movement of products and services from the manufacturer to producers, resellers, governments, institutions, and retailers. All merchant wholesalers take title to the goods they sell, and most of them operate one or more warehouses where they receive goods, store them, and later reship them. Customers are mostly small- or moderate-sized retailers, but merchant wholesalers also market to manufacturers and institutional clients.

Define the types of channel intermediaries and describe their functions and activities

retailer
A channel intermediary that sells mainly to consumers.

merchant wholesaler
An institution that buys goods from manufacturers and resells them to businesses, government agencies, and other wholesalers or retailers and that receives and takes title to goods, stores them in its own warehouses, and later ships them.

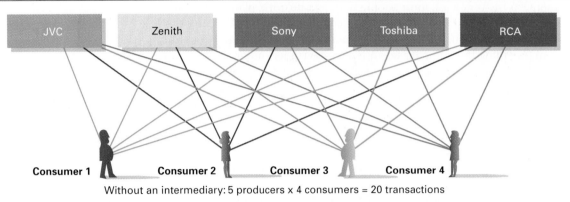

Without an intermediary: 5 producers x 4 consumers = 20 transactions

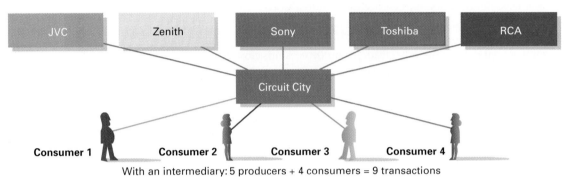

With an intermediary: 5 producers + 4 consumers = 9 transactions

agents and brokers
Wholesaling intermediaries who do not take title to a product but facilitate its sale from producer to end user by representing retailers, wholesalers, or manufacturers.

Other intermediaries do not take title to goods and services they market but do facilitate the exchange of ownership between sellers and buyers. **Agents and brokers** simply facilitate the sale of a product from producer to end user by representing retailers, wholesalers, or manufacturers. Title reflects ownership, and ownership usually implies control. Unlike wholesalers, agents or brokers only facilitate sales and generally have little input into the terms of the sale. They do, however, get a fee or commission based on sales volume.

Variations in channel structures are due in large part to variations in the numbers and types of wholesaling intermediaries. Generally, product characteristics, buyer considerations, and market conditions determine the type of intermediary the manufacturer should use. Product characteristics that may dictate a certain type of wholesaling intermediary include whether the product is standardized or customized, the complexity of the product, and the gross margin of the product. Buyer considerations affecting wholesaler choice include how often the product is purchased and how long the buyer is willing to wait to receive the product. Market characteristics determining the wholesaler type include how many buyers are in the market and whether they are concentrated in a general location or are widely dispersed. Exhibit 10.2 shows these determining factors. For example, a manufacturer that produces only a few engines a year for space rockets will probably use an agent or broker to sell its product. In addition, the handful of customers that need the product are most likely concentrated near rocket launching sites, again making an agent or broker more practical. On the other hand, a book publisher that prints thousands of books and has many widely dispersed customers with year-round demand for its product will probably use a merchant wholesaler.

Channel Functions Performed by Intermediaries

Retailing and wholesaling intermediaries in marketing channels perform several essential functions that make the flow of goods between producer and buyer possible. The three basic functions that intermediaries perform are summarized in Exhibit 10.3.

Exhibit 10.2

Factor	Merchant Wholesalers	Agents or Brokers
Nature of Product	Standard	Nonstandard, custom
Technicality of Product	Complex	Simple
Product's Gross Margin	High	Low
Frequency of Ordering	Frequent	Infrequent
Time between Order and Receipt of Shipment	Buyer desires shorter lead time	Buyer satisfied with long lead time
Number of Customers	Many	Few
Concentration of Customers	Dispersed	Concentrated

SOURCE: Reprinted by permission of the publisher. From Donald M. Jackson and Michael F. D'Amico, "Products and Markets Served by Distributors and Agents," 27–33 in *Industrial Marketing Management*. Copyright 1989 by Elsevier Science Inc.

Transactional functions involve contacting and communicating with prospective buyers to make them aware of existing products and explain their features, advantages, and benefits. Intermediaries in the supply chain also provide *logistical* functions. **Logistics** is a term borrowed from the military that describes the process of strategically managing the efficient flow and storage of raw materials,

logistics
The process of strategically managing the efficient flow and storage of raw materials, in-process inventory, and finished goods from point of origin to point of consumption.

Exhibit 10.3

Type of Function	Description
Transactional Functions	**Contacting and promoting:** Contacting potential customers, promoting products, and soliciting orders **Negotiating:** Determining how many goods or services to buy and sell, type of transportation to use, when to deliver, and method and timing of payment **Risk taking:** Assuming the risk of owning inventory

Logistical Functions	**Physically distributing:** Transporting and sorting goods to overcome temporal and spatial discrepancies
	Storing: Maintaining inventories and protecting goods
	Sorting: Overcoming discrepancies of quantity and assortment by
	  Sorting out: Breaking down a heterogeneous supply into separate homogeneous stocks
	  Accumulation: Combining similar stocks into a larger homogeneous supply
	  Allocation: Breaking a homogeneous supply into smaller and smaller lots ("breaking bulk")
	  Assortment: Combining products into collections or assortments that buyers want available at one place

Facilitating Function	**Researching:** Gathering information about other channel members and consumers **Financing:** Extending credit and other financial services to facilitate the flow of goods through the channel to the final consumer

in-process inventory, and finished goods from point of origin to point of consumption. Logistical functions include transporting, storing, sorting out, accumulating, allocating, and assorting products into either homogeneous or heterogeneous collections. For example, grading agricultural products typifies the sorting-out process while consolidation of many lots of grade A eggs from different sources into one lot illustrates the accumulation process. Supermarkets or other retailers perform the assorting function by assembling thousands of different items that match their customers' desires. Similarly, while large companies typically have direct channels, many small companies depend on wholesalers to champion and distribute their products. For example, small beverage manufacturers like Jones Soda, Honest Tea, and Energy Brands depend on wholesalers to distribute their products in a marketplace dominated by large competitors like Coca-Cola and Pepsi.[1]

The third basic channel function, *facilitating*, includes research and financing. Research provides information about channel members and consumers by getting answers to key questions: Who are the buyers? Where are they located? Why do they buy? Financing ensures that channel members have the money to keep products moving through the channel to the ultimate consumer.

A single company may provide one, two, or all three functions. Consider Kramer Beverage Company, a Coors beer distributor. As a beer distributor, Kramer provides transactional, logistical, and facilitating channel functions. Sales representatives contact local bars and restaurants to negotiate the terms of the sale, possibly giving the customer a discount for large purchases, and arrange for delivery of the beer. At the same time, Kramer also provides a facilitating function by extending credit to the customer. Kramer merchandising representatives, meanwhile, assist in promoting the beer on a local level by hanging Coors beer signs and posters. Kramer also provides logistical functions by accumulating the many types of Coors beer from the Coors manufacturing plant in Golden, Colorado, and storing them in its refrigerated warehouse. When an order needs to be filled, Kramer then sorts the beer into heterogeneous collections for each particular customer. For example, the local Chili's Grill & Bar may need two kegs of Coors, three kegs of Coors Light, and two cases of Killian's Red in bottles. The beer will then be loaded onto a refrigerated truck and transported to the restaurant. Upon arrival, the Kramer delivery person will transport the kegs and cases of beer into the restaurant's refrigerator and may also restock the coolers behind the bar.

Although individual members can be added to or deleted from a channel, someone must still perform these essential functions. They can be performed by producers, end users, or consumers, channel intermediaries such as wholesalers and retailers, and sometimes nonmember channel participants. For example, if a manufacturer decides to eliminate its private fleet of trucks, it must still have a way to move the goods to the wholesaler. This task may be accomplished by the wholesaler, which may have its own fleet of trucks, or by a nonmember channel participant, such as an independent trucking firm. Nonmembers also provide many other essential functions that may at one time have been provided by a channel member. For example, research firms may perform the research function; advertising agencies, the promotion function; transportation and storage firms, the physical distribution function; and banks, the financing function.

Channel Structures

Describe the channel structures for consumer and business-to-business products and discuss alternative channel arrangements

A product can take many routes to reach its final consumer. Marketers search for the most efficient channel from the many alternatives available. Marketing a consumer convenience good like gum or candy differs from marketing a specialty good like a Mercedes-Benz. The two products require very different distribution channels. Likewise, the appropriate channel for a major equipment supplier like Boeing Aircraft would be unsuitable for an accessory equipment producer like

Black & Decker. To illustrate the differences in typical marketing channels for consumer and business-to-business products like these, the next sections discuss the structures of marketing channels for each product type. Alternative channel structures are also discussed.

What kind of marketing channel functions can be performed over the Internet? Why do you think so?

On Line

Channels for Consumer Products

Exhibit 10.4 illustrates the four ways manufacturers can route products to consumers. Producers use the **direct channel** to sell directly to consumers. Direct marketing activities—including telemarketing, mail-order and catalog shopping, and forms of electronic retailing like on-line shopping and shop-at-home television networks—are a good example of this type of channel structure. For example, home computer users can purchase Dell computers directly over the telephone or directly from Dell's Internet Web site. There are no intermediaries. Producer-owned stores and factory outlet stores—like Sherwin-Williams, Polo Ralph Lauren, Oneida, and West Point Pepperel—are other examples of direct channels. Farmers' markets are also direct channels. Direct marketing and factory outlets are discussed in more detail in Chapter 11.

At the other end of the spectrum, an *agent/broker channel* involves a fairly complicated process. Agent/broker channels are typically used in markets with many small manufacturers and many retailers that lack the resources to find each other. Agents or brokers bring manufacturers and wholesalers together for negotiations, but they do not take title to merchandise. Ownership passes directly to one or more wholesalers and then to retailers. Finally, retailers sell to the ultimate consumer of the product. For example, a food broker represents buyers and sellers of grocery products. The broker acts on behalf of many different producers and negotiates the sale of their products to wholesalers that specialize in foodstuffs. These wholesalers in turn sell to grocers and convenience stores.

Most consumer products are sold through distribution channels similar to the other two alternatives: the retailer channel and the wholesaler channel. A *retailer channel* is most common when the retailer is large and can buy in large quantities

direct channel
A distribution channel in which producers sell directly to consumers.

Marketing Channels for Consumer Products   **Exhibit 10.4**

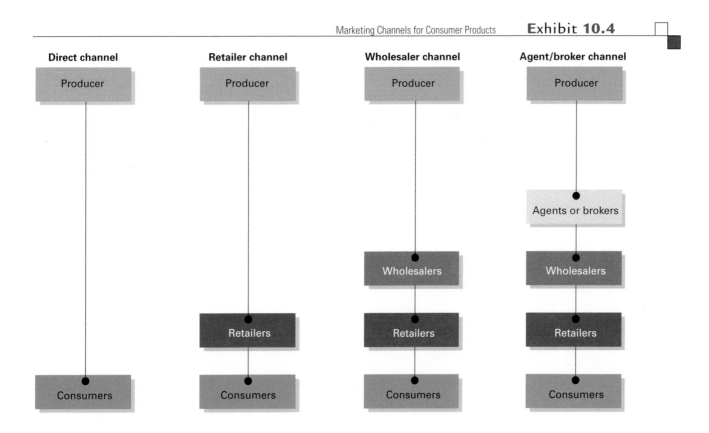

Direct channel	Retailer channel	Wholesaler channel	Agent/broker channel
Producer	Producer	Producer	Producer
			Agents or brokers
		Wholesalers	Wholesalers
	Retailers	Retailers	Retailers
Consumers	Consumers	Consumers	Consumers

directly from the manufacturer. Wal-Mart, Sears, and car dealers are examples of retailers that often bypass a wholesaler. A *wholesaler channel* is frequently used for low-cost items that are frequently purchased, such as candy, cigarettes, and magazines. For example, M&M/Mars sells candies and chocolates to wholesalers in large quantities. The wholesalers then break these quantities into smaller quantities to satisfy individual retailer orders.

Channels for Business-to-Business and Industrial Products

As Exhibit 10.5 illustrates, five channel structures are common in business-to-business and industrial markets. First, direct channels are typical in business-to-business and industrial markets. For example, manufacturers buy large quantities of raw materials, major equipment, processed materials, and supplies directly from other manufacturers. Manufacturers that require suppliers to meet detailed technical specifications often prefer direct channels. The direct communication required between DaimlerChrysler and its suppliers, for example, along with the tremendous size of the orders, makes anything but a direct channel impractical. The channel from producer to government buyers is also a direct channel. Since much of government buying is done through bidding, a direct channel is attractive. Dell Computer Corporation, for example, the top seller of desktop computers to federal, state, and local government agencies in the United States, sells the computers through direct channels.[2]

Companies selling standardized items of moderate or low value often rely on *industrial distributors*. In many ways, an industrial distributor is like a supermarket for organizations. Industrial distributors are wholesalers and channel members that buy and take title to products. Moreover, they usually keep inventories of their products and sell and service them. Often small manufacturers cannot afford to employ their own sales force. Instead, they rely on manufacturers' representatives or selling agents to sell to either industrial distributors or users.

Increasingly, companies are using the Internet to create more direct and efficient business-to-business channels. Industry analysts predict that more than $5.7 trillion in business-to-business commerce will be conducted on-line by 2004. Currently, three major forms of business-to-business ex-

Exhibit 10.5   Channels for Business-to-Business and Industrial Products

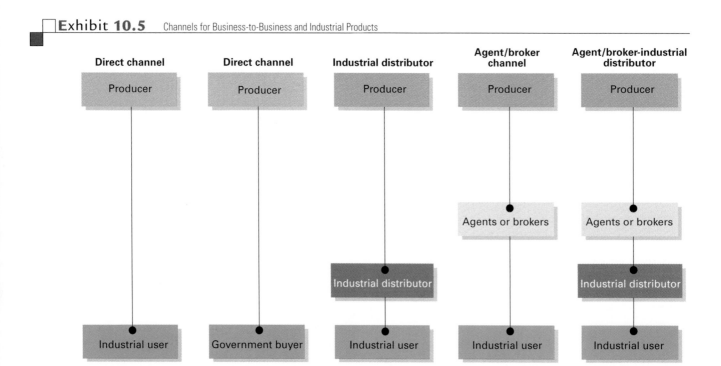

changes are taking place on the Internet. The first and smallest sector is made up of new Internet companies that have been developed to link buyers and sellers. These companies act as agents and charge a service fee. A second form of marketplace has been developed by existing companies looking for a way to drop the intermediary from the supply chain. For example, the Worldwide Retail Exchange is a marketplace created by more than fifty major retailers including Target, JCPenney, and Safeway. Retailers use the exchange to make purchases that in the past would have required telephone, fax, or face-to-face sales calls. Retailers using the exchange estimate they have saved approximately 15 percent in their purchasing costs. Finally, the third type of Internet marketplace is a "private exchange." Private exchanges allow companies to automate their supply chains while sharing information only with select suppliers. Ace Hardware and Hewlett-Packard, for example, use private exchanges to manage their inventory supplies.[3]

Alternative Channel Arrangements

Rarely does a producer use just one type of channel to move its product. It usually employs several different or alternative channels, which include multiple channels, nontraditional channels, and strategic channel alliances.

Multiple Channels

When a producer selects two or more channels to distribute the same product to target markets, this arrangement is called **dual distribution** (or **multiple distribution**). For example, Whirlpool sells its washers, dryers, and refrigerators directly to home and apartment builders and contractors, but it also sells these same appliances to retail stores that sell to consumers. Avon, which has traditionally sold its products only through a company sales force, launched a new cosmetic line with JCPenney. The venture into retail, called "Avon Centers," was part of an overall strategy to update Avon's image. However, the new cosmetic line did not sell, and it was taken out of the stores.[4] Similarly, Dell Computer recently made a radical departure from its direct channel sales model by testing retail kiosks in shopping malls as a way to increase its market share of personal home computers. The company has also tried selling computers directly to home users through cable shopping channels.[5] Multiple channels may also be employed by producers with unique second brands. For example, the Walt Disney Company routinely releases first-run animated films to movie theaters and then releases a sequel directly to the home-video market. Such sequels as *Aladdin and the King of Thieves* and *Beauty and the Beast: The Enchanted Christmas* follow up its theater blockbusters.

dual distribution (multiple distribution)
The use of two or more channels to distribute the same product to target markets.

COURTESY OF BECOMING

TAYLOR FOSTER IS BECOMING

CHILDISH

beComing
redefine
airbrush foundation
SPF 10
AVON

Adding a new supply chain can renew a company's image. Such is the case with Avon, the leading company in direct selling, which broke its own mold with the launch of beComing, the company's first brand distributed exclusively in retail outlets. beComing floundered and was eventually pulled from JCPenney. The brand is still available through Avon's direct channel.

Nontraditional Channels

GLOBAL

Often nontraditional channel arrangements help differentiate a firm's product from the competition. For example, manufacturers may decide to use nontraditional channels such as the Internet, mail-order channels, or infomercials, to sell products instead of going through traditional retailer channels. Although nontraditional channels may limit a brand's coverage, they can give a producer serving a niche market a way to gain market access and customer attention

Why Just Collapse The Supply Chain When You Can Flatten The Competition?

strategic channel alliance
A cooperative agreement between business firms to use the other's already established distribution channel.

Supply chain management is the key to competitiveness, and numerous companies market tools to help other businesses manage their supply chains effectively. Rockwell Automation is one such solutions provider, helping companies share critical production information across the business enterprise.

without having to establish channel intermediaries. Nontraditional channels can also provide another avenue of sales for larger firms. For example, a London publisher has begun selling short stories through a vending machine in the London Underground. Instead of the traditional book format, the stories are printed like folded maps making them an easy-to-read alternative for commuters.[6]

Strategic Channel Alliances

Producers often form **strategic channel alliances**, which enable the producers to use another manufacturer's already-established channel. Alliances are used most often when the creation of marketing channel relationships may be too expensive and time-consuming. Amazon and Circuit City have a multiyear agreement to expand the selection of electronics available on Amazon.com. Under the agreement, Amazon.com customers have the option of purchasing items from Amazon's inventory of electronic items or from the broader selection offered by Circuit City. The arrangement benefits both companies: It allows Amazon.com to deepen its selection without increasing its own inventory expense, and it increases sales for Circuit City. Similarly, Amazon.com and Target formed an alliance involving the customer service and distribution operations for Target.com. The deal increases Target's on-line selection of books, music, and entertainment while adding clothing, jewelry, and other products to Amazon's selection.[7]

Strategic channel alliances are proving to be more successful for growing businesses than mergers and acquisitions. This is especially true in global markets where cultural differences, distance, and other barriers can prove challenging. For example, Heinz has a strategic alliance with Kagome, one of Japan's largest food companies. The companies are working together to find ways to reduce operating costs while expanding both brands' market presence globally.[8]

Supply Chain Management

(4)

Define supply chain management and discuss its benefits

supply chain management
A management system that coordinates and integrates all of the activities performed by supply chain members into a seamless process, from the source to the point of consumption, resulting in enhanced customer and economic value.

In today's sophisticated marketplace, many companies are turning to supply chain management for competitive advantage. The goal of **supply chain management** is to coordinate and integrate all of the activities performed by supply chain members into a seamless process from the source to the point of consumption, ultimately giving supply chain managers "total visibility" of the supply chain both inside and outside the firm. The philosophy behind supply chain management is that by visualizing the entire supply chain, supply chain managers can maximize strengths and efficiencies at each level of the process to create a highly competitive, customer-driven supply system that is able to respond immediately to changes in supply and demand.

An important element of supply chain management is that it is completely customer driven. In the mass-production era, manufacturers produced standardized products that were "pushed" down through the supply channel to the consumer. In contrast, in today's marketplace, products are being driven by customers, who expect to receive product configurations and services matched to their unique needs. For example, Dell only builds computers according to its customers' precise specifications, such as the amount of RAM memory; type of monitor, modem, or CD drive; and amount of hard disk space. Similarly, car companies offer customers the option to customize even economy-priced cars. For less than $20,000, customers can order a Mitsubishi Lancer with spoilers and flashy colors or a Mazda Protégé with a faster engine, special transmission, and 280-watt MP3 sound system. The focus is on pulling products into the marketplace and partnering with members of the supply chain to enhance customer value. Customizing an automobile is now possible because of new supply chain relationships between the automobile manufacturers and the after-market auto-parts industry.[9]

This reversal of the flow of demand from a "push" to a "pull" has resulted in a radical reformulation of both market expectations and traditional marketing, production, and distribution functions. Through the channel partnership of suppliers, manufacturers, wholesalers, and retailers along the entire supply chain who work together toward the common goal of creating customer value, supply chain management allows companies to respond with the unique product configuration and mix of services demanded by the customer. Today, supply chain management plays a dual role: first, as a *communicator* of customer demand that extends from the point of sale all the way back to the supplier, and second, as a *physical flow process* that engineers the timely and cost-effective movement of goods through the entire supply pipeline.[10]

Accordingly, supply chain managers are responsible for making channel strategy decisions, coordinating the sourcing and procurement of raw materials, scheduling production, processing orders, managing inventory, transporting and storing supplies and finished goods, and coordinating customer service activities. Supply chain managers are also responsible for the management of information that flows through the supply chain. Coordinating the relationships between the company and its external partners, such as vendors, carriers, and third-party companies, is also a critical function of supply chain management. Because supply chain managers play such a major role in both cost control and customer satisfaction, they are more valuable than ever. In fact, average salaries for supply chain graduates have increased more than 25 percent in spite of the recent recession.[11]

In summary, supply chain managers are responsible for directing raw materials and parts to the production department and the finished or semifinished product through warehouses and eventually to the intermediary or end user. Above all, supply chain management begins and ends with the customer. Instead of forcing into the market a product that may or may not sell quickly, supply chain managers react to actual customer demand. By doing so, they minimize the flow of raw materials, finished product, and packaging materials at every point in the supply chain, resulting in lower costs and increased customer value. Exhibit 10.6 on page 324 depicts the supply chain process.

Benefits of Supply Chain Management

Supply chain management is a key means of differentiation for a firm and a critical component in marketing and corporate strategy. Companies that focus on supply chain management commonly report lower inventory, transportation, warehousing, and packaging costs; greater supply chain flexibility; improved customer service; and higher revenues. Research has shown a clear relationship between supply chain performance and profitability. Leaders in supply chain management report a 5 percent increase in revenue due to reducing supply chain costs, a 65 percent increase in supply chain flexibility, and an 18 percent improvement in cash flow.[12]

Dreyer's ice cream has built its success on its logistics system. The company recently invested $150 million in a new fleet of trucks, manufacturing centers, additional employees, and a computerized delivery system that enables dispatchers to design delivery routes around sales volume, mileage, traffic patterns, road tolls, and a store's hours of operation. As a return on its investment, the company has experienced a 33 percent increase in sales accounts, eliminated more than 42,000 unnecessary stops, saved $11 million

AP/WIDE WORLD PHOTOS

Dreyer's Ice Cream's successful logistics systems starts with its state-of-the-art manufacturing facility. The return on investment the company experienced subsequent to its supply chain upgrades was extremely impressive.

Exhibit 10.6   The Supply Chain Process

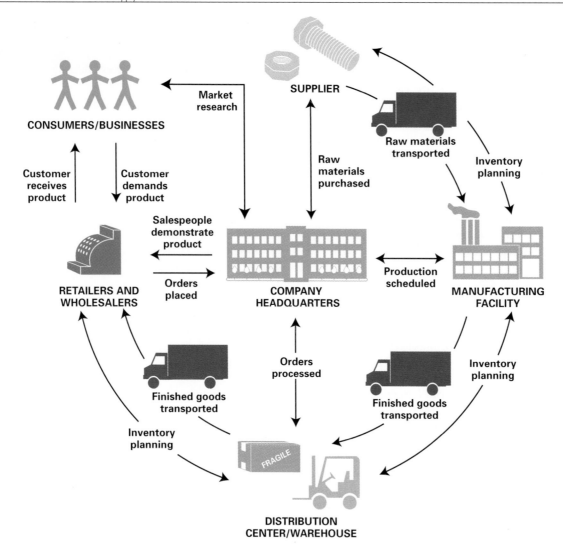

The Supply Chain Process

in gas and labor hours, and increased its net income by 150 percent between 1999 and 2000. In fact, the system provides such strong customer service capability and cost savings that nearly one-third of Dreyer's revenue comes from deals to distribute its competitors' brands such as Häagen-Dazs and Ben & Jerry's.[13] On a more individual level, one materials analyst for a company that produces seat belts reported that when her company began focusing on supply chain management, it shortened her workweek by fifteen to twenty hours and reduced her inventory costs by 75 percent.[14]

Making Channel Strategy Decisions

Discuss the issues that influence channel strategy

Devising a marketing channel strategy requires several critical decisions. Supply chain managers must decide what role distribution will play in the overall marketing strategy. In addition, they must be sure that the channel strategy chosen is consistent with product, promotion, and pricing strategies. In making these decisions, marketing managers must analyze what factors will influence the choice of channel and what level of distribution intensity will be appropriate.

Factors Affecting Channel Choice

Supply chain managers must answer many questions before choosing a marketing channel. The final choice depends on the analysis of several factors, which often interact. These factors can be grouped as market factors, product factors, and producer factors.

Market Factors

Among the most important market factors affecting the choice of distribution channel are target customer considerations. Specifically, supply chain managers should answer the following questions: Who are the potential customers? What do they buy? Where do they buy? When do they buy? How do they buy? Additionally, the choice of channel depends on whether the producer is selling to consumers or to industrial customers. Industrial customers' buying habits are very different from those of consumers. Industrial customers tend to buy in larger quantities and require more customer service. Consumers usually buy in very small quantities and sometimes do not mind if they get no service at all, as in a discount store.

The geographic location and size of the market are also important to channel selection. As a rule, if the target market is concentrated in one or more specific areas, then direct selling through a sales force is appropriate. When markets are more widely dispersed, intermediaries would be less expensive. The size of the market also influences channel choice. Generally, a very large market requires more intermediaries. For instance, Procter & Gamble has to reach millions of consumers with its many brands of household goods. It needs many intermediaries, including wholesalers and retailers.

Product Factors

Products that are more complex, customized, and expensive tend to benefit from shorter and more direct marketing channels. These types of products sell better through a direct sales force. Examples include pharmaceuticals, scientific instruments, airplanes, and mainframe computer systems. On the other hand, the more standardized a product is, the longer its distribution channel can be and the greater the number of intermediaries that can be involved. For example, the formula for chewing gum is about the same from producer to producer, with the exception of flavor and shape. Chewing gum is also very inexpensive. As a result, the distribution channel for gum tends to involve many wholesalers and retailers.

The product's life cycle is also an important factor in choosing a marketing channel. In fact, the choice of channel may change over the life of the product. For example, when photocopiers were first available, they were typically sold by a direct sales force. Now, however, photocopiers can be found in several places, including warehouse clubs, electronics superstores, and mail-order catalogs. As products become more common and less intimidating to potential users, producers tend to look for alternative channels. Gatorade was originally sold to sports teams, gyms, and fitness clubs. As the drink became more popular, mainstream supermarket channels were added, followed by convenience stores and drugstores. Now Gatorade can be found in vending machines and even in some fast-food restaurants.

Another factor is the delicacy of the product. Perishable products like vegetables and milk have a relatively short life span. Fragile

Vending machines are becoming a popular way to sell everything from boxer shorts to cameras. Kodak teamed up with Maytag to roll out thousands of camera-and-film vending machines within a couple of years. Kodak wants to satisfy instant cravings for a must-have snapshot in places like amusement parks, ski resorts, and the beach.

AP/WIDEWORLD PHOTOS

products like china and crystal require a minimum amount of handling. Therefore, both require fairly short marketing channels.

Producer Factors

Several factors pertaining to the producer itself are important to the selection of a marketing channel. In general, producers with large financial, managerial, and marketing resources are better able to use more direct channels. These producers have the ability to hire and train their own sales force, warehouse their own goods, and extend credit to their customers. Smaller or weaker firms, on the other hand, must rely on intermediaries to provide these services for them. Compared to producers with only one or two product lines, producers that sell several products in a related area are able to choose channels that are more direct. Sales expenses then can be spread over more products.

A producer's desire to control pricing, positioning, brand image, and customer support also tends to influence channel selection. For instance, firms that sell products with exclusive brand images, such as designer perfumes and clothing, usually avoid channels in which discount retailers are present. Manufacturers of upscale products, such as Gucci (handbags) and Godiva (chocolates), may sell their wares only in expensive stores in order to maintain an image of exclusivity. Many producers have opted to risk their image, however, and test sales in discount channels. Levi Strauss expanded its distribution to include JCPenney and Sears. JCPenney is now Levi Strauss's biggest customer.

Levels of Distribution Intensity

Organizations have three options for intensity of distribution: intensive distribution, selective distribution, or exclusive distribution (see Exhibit 10.7).

Intensive Distribution

intensive distribution
A form of distribution aimed at having a product available in every outlet where target customers might want to buy it.

Intensive distribution is a form of distribution aimed at maximum market coverage. The manufacturer tries to have the product available in every outlet where potential customers might want to buy it. If buyers are unwilling to search for a product (as is true of convenience goods and operating supplies), the product

---

▢ Exhibit 10.7

Intensity of Distribution Levels

Intensity Level	Distribution Intensity Objective	Number of Intermediaries in Each Market	Examples
Intensive	Achieve mass-market selling; popular with health and beauty aids and convenience goods that must be available everywhere	Many	Pepsi-Cola, Frito-Lay potato chips, Huggies diapers, Alpo dog food, Crayola crayons
Selective	Work closely with selected intermediaries who meet certain criteria; typically used for shopping goods and some specialty goods	Several	Donna Karan clothing, Hewlett-Packard printers, Burton snowboards, Aveda aromatherapy products
Exclusive	Work with a single intermediary for products that require special resources or positioning; typically used for specialty goods and major industrial equipment	One	BMW cars, Rolex watches, Subway franchise

must be very accessible to buyers. A low-value product that is purchased frequently may require a lengthy channel. For example, candy is found in almost every type of retail store imaginable. It is typically sold to retailers in small quantities by a food or candy wholesaler. The Wrigley Company could not afford to sell its gum directly to every service station, drugstore, supermarket, and discount store. The cost would be too high.

Most manufacturers pursuing an intensive distribution strategy sell to a large percentage of the wholesalers willing to stock their products. Retailers' willingness (or unwillingness) to handle items tends to control the manufacturer's ability to achieve intensive distribution. For example, a retailer already carrying ten brands of gum may show little enthusiasm for one more brand.

Selective Distribution

Selective distribution is achieved by screening dealers and retailers to eliminate all but a few in any single area. Because only a few are chosen, the consumer must seek out the product. For example, when Heeling Sports Ltd. launched Heelys, thick-soled sneakers with a wheel embedded in each heel, the company hired a group of forty teens to perform Heelys exhibitions in targeted malls, skate parks, and college campuses across the country to create demand. Then the company made the decision to avoid large stores like Target and FAO Schwarz and to distribute the shoes only through selected mall retailers and skate and surf shops in order to position the product as "cool and kind of irreverent."[15]

Selective distribution strategies often hinge on a manufacturer's desire to maintain a superior product image so as to be able to charge a premium price. DKNY clothing, for instance, is sold only in select retail outlets, mainly full-price department stores. Likewise, premium pet food brands such as Hill's Pet Nutrition and Ralston-Purina's ProPlan are distributed chiefly through specialty pet food stores and veterinarians, rather than mass retailers like Wal-Mart, so that a premium price can be charged. Procter & Gamble, which purchased rival premium pet food brand Iams, recently expanded Iams's selective distribution strategy to include mass retailer Target. The strategy could jeopardize Iams's high-price strategy and disenfranchise the breeders and veterinarians who have been the brand's primary source of strength over the years.[16]

Exclusive Distribution

The most restrictive form of market coverage is **exclusive distribution**, which entails only one or a few dealers within a given area. Because buyers may have to search or travel extensively to buy the product, exclusive distribution is usually confined to consumer specialty goods, a few shopping goods, and major industrial equipment. Products such as Rolls Royce automobiles, Chris-Craft power boats, and Pettibone tower cranes are distributed under exclusive arrangements. Sometimes exclusive territories are granted by new companies (such as franchisers) to obtain market coverage in a particular area. Limited distribution may also serve to project an exclusive image for the product.

Retailers and wholesalers may be unwilling to commit the time and money necessary to promote and service a product unless the manufacturer guarantees them an exclusive territory. This arrangement shields the dealer from direct competition and enables it to be the main beneficiary of the manufacturer's promotion efforts in that geographic area. With exclusive distribution, channels of communication are usually well established because the manufacturer works with a limited number of dealers rather than many accounts.

Exclusive distribution has been part of retailing for years. Toys are often made exclusively for certain retailers and cannot be found elsewhere. Exclusive distribution may also take place within a retailer's store rather than a geographic area—for example, when a retailer agrees not to sell a manufacturer's competing

selective distribution
A form of distribution achieved by screening dealers to eliminate all but a few in any single area.

exclusive distribution
A form of distribution that establishes one or a few dealers within a given area.

brands. Radio Shack, for instance, has prospered in recent years by offering electronics manufacturers exclusivity within its stores. When Sprint Corporation was looking for a retail base from which to sell its new wireless phone network, Radio Shack offered to make Sprint its exclusive national wireless provider. The agreement helped Sprint become the leader in digital personal communications services, selling more wireless phones than rivals Best Buy, Circuit City, and Sears. Radio Shack cut similar exclusive distribution deals with HP-Compaq Computers, satellite television provider DirecTV, and RCA for audio and video equipment.[17]

Managing Channel Relationships

6

Explain channel leadership, conflict, and partnering.

A marketing channel is more than a set of institutions linked by economic ties. Social relationships play an important role in building unity among channel members. A critical aspect of supply chain management, therefore, is managing the social relationships among channel members to achieve synergy. The basic social dimensions of channels are power, control, leadership, conflict, and partnering.

Channel Power, Control, and Leadership

channel power

The capacity of a particular marketing channel member to control or influence the behavior of other channel members.

channel control

A situation that occurs when one marketing channel member intentionally affects another member's behavior.

channel leader (channel captain)

A member of a marketing channel that exercises authority and power over the activities of other channel members.

Channel power is a channel member's capacity to control or influence the behavior of other channel members. **Channel control** occurs when one channel member affects another member's behavior. To achieve control, a channel member assumes channel leadership and exercises authority and power. This member is termed the **channel leader**, or **channel captain**. In one marketing channel, a manufacturer may be the leader because it controls new-product designs and product availability. In another, a retailer may be the channel leader because it wields power and control over the retail price, inventory levels, and postsale service.

The exercise of channel power is a routine element of many business activities in which the outcome is often more efficient operations and cost savings. For instance, grain has traditionally been stored and transported by an inefficient system controlled by unrelated small-town grain elevators. In a new trend, more than 150 large, high-speed elevators have been opened, making the system faster and more cost-efficient. The new elevators are capable of loading twice as many cars in half the time of the traditional elevators. As a result, the new system has lowered transportation costs, making U.S. grain more competitive globally and enabling farmers to make higher profits.[18]

Channel Conflict

channel conflict

A clash of goals and methods between distribution channel members.

Inequitable channel relationships often lead to **channel conflict**, which is a clash of goals and methods among the members of a distribution channel. In a broad context, conflict may not be bad. Often it arises because staid, traditional channel members refuse to keep pace with the times. Removing an outdated intermediary may result in reduced costs for the entire supply chain.

Conflicts among channel members can be due to many different situations and factors. Oftentimes, conflict arises because channel members have conflicting goals. For instance, athletic footwear retailers want to sell as many shoes as possible in order to maximize profits, regardless of whether the shoe is manufactured by Nike, adidas, or Saucony. But the Nike manufacturer wants a certain sales volume and market share in each market.

Conflict can also arise when channel members fail to fulfill expectations of other channel members—for example, when a franchisee does not follow the rules set down by the franchiser, or when communications channels break down between channel members. As another example, if a manufacturer reduces the length of warranty coverage and fails to communicate this change to dealers, then conflict may occur when dealers make repairs with the expectation that they will be reimbursed by the manufacturer. Further, ideological differences and different perceptions of reality can also cause conflict among channel members. For instance, retailers may believe "the customer is always right" and offer a very liberal return policy. Wholesalers and manufacturers may feel that people "try to get something for nothing" or don't follow product instructions carefully. Their differing views of allowable returns will undoubtably conflict with those of retailers.

Conflict within a channel can be either horizontal or vertical. **Horizontal conflict** occurs among channel members on the same level, such as two or more different wholesalers or two or more different retailers, that handle the same manufacturer's brands. This type of channel conflict is found most often when manufacturers practice dual or multiple distribution strategies. For instance, there was considerable channel conflict after computer manufacturers began distributing their computers beyond the traditional computer resellers and to discount stores, department stores, warehouse clubs, and giant electronic superstores, such as Circuit City and Comp-USA. Horizontal conflict can also occur when channel members on the same level feel they are being treated unfairly by the manufacturer. For example, the American Booksellers Association, a group representing small independent booksellers, filed a lawsuit against bookstore giants Barnes & Noble and Borders, claiming they had violated antitrust laws by using their buying power to demand "illegal and secret" discounts from publishers. These deals, the association contended, put independent booksellers at a serious competitive disadvantage.[19]

Many regard horizontal conflict as healthy competition. Much more serious is **vertical conflict**, which occurs between different levels in a marketing channel, most typically between the manufacturer and wholesaler or the manufacturer and retailer. Producer-versus-wholesaler conflict occurs when the producer chooses to bypass the wholesaler and deal directly with the consumer or retailer. For example, conflict arose when several producers agreed to Wal-Mart's request to deal with it directly, bypassing intermediaries altogether.

Dual distribution strategies can also cause vertical conflict in the channel. For example, high-end fashion designers have traditionally sold their products through luxury retailers such as Neiman Marcus and Saks Fifth Avenue. Interested in increasing sales and gaining additional presentation control, many designers such as Giorgio Armani, Donna Karan, and Louis Vuitton have begun opening their own boutiques in the same shopping centers that are anchored by Neiman Marcus and Saks Fifth Avenue stores. As a result, the department stores are seeing a huge decline in revenue.[20] Similarly, manufacturers that are experimenting with selling to customers directly over the Internet are also creating conflict with their traditional retailing intermediaries. For example, Baby Jogger worked closely with retailers to build a business with $15 million in sales. But when numerous look-alike products began appearing on the market, the company decided to try to increase sales by selling directly to consumers on the Internet. Angry retailers responded by promoting other brands. Recognizing how important the retailers were to its success, Baby Jogger halted Internet sales.[21]

Producers and retailers may also disagree over the terms of the sale or other aspects of the business relationship. When Procter & Gamble introduced "everyday low pricing" to its retail channel members, a strategy designed to standardize wholesale prices and eliminate most trade promotions, many retailers retaliated. Some cut the variety of P&G sizes they carried or eliminated marginal brands. Others moved P&G brands from prime shelf space to less visible shelves.

Channel Partnering

Regardless of the locus of power, channel members rely heavily on one another. Even the most powerful manufacturers depend on dealers to sell their products; even the most powerful retailers require the products provided by suppliers. In sharp contrast to the adversarial relationships of the past between buyers and sellers,

horizontal conflict
A channel conflict that occurs among channel members on the same level.

vertical conflict
A channel conflict that occurs between different levels in a marketing channel, most typically between the manufacturer and wholesaler or between the manufacturer and retailer.

channel partnering (channel cooperation)
The joint effort of all channel members to create a supply chain that serves customers and creates a competitive advantage.

contemporary management thought emphasizes the development of close working partnerships among channel members. **Channel partnering**, or **channel cooperation**, is the joint effort of all channel members to create a supply chain that serves customers and creates a competitive advantage. Channel partnering is vital if each member is to gain something from other members. By cooperating, retailers, wholesalers, manufacturers, and suppliers can speed up inventory replenishment, improve customer service, and reduce the total costs of the marketing channel.

Channel alliances and partnerships help supply chain managers create the parallel flow of materials and information required to leverage the supply chains' intellectual, material, and marketing resources. The rapid growth in channel partnering is due to new enabling technology and the need to lower costs. A comparison between companies that approach the marketplace unilaterally and those that engage in channel cooperation and form partnerships is detailed in Exhibit 10.8.

Collaborating channel partners meet the needs of consumers more effectively by ensuring that the right products are available at the right time and for a lower cost, thus boosting sales and profits. Forced to become more efficient, many companies are turning formerly adversarial relationships into partnerships. For example, when all three branches of the U.S. and British militaries went shopping for more than three thousand new stealth fighter jets, long-time rivals in the defense industry had to work together to win the $200 billion contract. If the project is successful, the Joint Strike Fighter jet will be the first plane adapted to meet the needs of all three branches of the U.S. and British militaries. To meet that goal, Lockheed Martin, BAE Systems, and Northrop Grumman will have to work as partners. According to the partnership, Lockheed Martin will design and oversee the project, BAE Systems will be responsible for major subassembly, and Northrop Grumman will build the central fuselage and design its radar and stealth systems.[22]

Managing the Logistical Components of the Supply Chain

Describe the logistical components of the supply chain

Now that you are familiar with the structure and strategy of marketing channels and the role of supply chain management, it is important to also understand the physical means through which products move through the supply chain. As men-

Exhibit 10.8

Transaction- versus Partnership-Based Firms

	Transaction-Based	Partnership-Based
Relationships between Manufacturer and Supplier	• Short-term • Adversarial • Independent • Price more important	• Long-term • Cooperative • Dependent • Value-added services more important
Number of Suppliers	Many	Few
Level of Information Sharing	Minimal	High
Investment Required	Minimal	High

SOURCE: David Frederick Ross, *Competing Through Supply Chain Management: Creating Market-Winning Strategies Through Supply Chain Partnerships* (New York: Chapman & Hall, 1998), 61.

tioned earlier, supply chain management coordinates and integrates all of the activities performed by supply chain members into a seamless process. The supply chain consists of several interrelated and integrated logistical components: (1) sourcing and procurement of raw materials and supplies, (2) production scheduling, (3) order processing, (4) inventory control, (5) warehousing and materials-handling, and (6) transportation. These components are shown in Exhibit 10.9.

Integrating and linking all of the logistics components of the supply chain is the **logistics information system**. Today's supply chain logisticians are at the forefront of information technology, which is not just a functional affiliate of supply chain management. Rather it is the enabler, the facilitator, the linkage that connects the various components and partners of the supply chain into an integrated whole. Electronic data interchange, on-board computers, satellite and cellular communications systems, materials-handling and warehouse-management software, enterprise-wide systems solutions, and the Internet are among the information enablers of successful supply chain management.

The **supply chain team**, in concert with the logistics information system, orchestrates the movement of goods, services, and information from the source to the consumer. Supply chain teams typically cut across organizational boundaries, embracing all parties who participate in moving the product to market. The best supply chain teams also move beyond the organization to include the external participants in the chain, such as suppliers, transportation carriers, and third-party logistics suppliers. Members of the supply chain communicate, coordinate, and cooperate extensively.

Today's corporate supply chain logisticians have become so efficient that the U.S. Marine Corps is now consulting with companies like Wal-Mart, United Parcel Service, and Unilever to improve its own supply chain efficiency. The Marine Corps's goal is to reduce the time it takes to deliver supplies to the front lines from one week to twenty-four hours and lower costs by cutting inventories in half.[23]

Sourcing and Procurement

One of the most important links in the supply chain is that between the manufacturer and the supplier. Purchasing professionals are on the front lines of supply

logistics information system
Information technology that integrates and links all of the logistics functions of the supply chain.

supply chain team
An entire group of individuals who orchestrate the movement of goods, services, and information from the source to the consumer.

Exhibit 10.9

Integrated Logistical Components of the Supply Chain

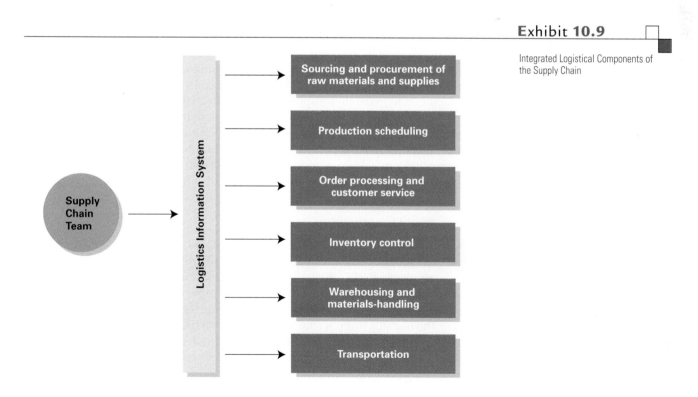

chain management. Purchasing departments plan purchasing strategies, develop specifications, select suppliers, and negotiate price and service levels.

The goal of most sourcing and procurement activities is to reduce the costs of raw materials and supplies. Purchasing professionals have traditionally relied on tough negotiations to get the lowest price possible from suppliers of raw materials, supplies, and components. Perhaps the biggest contribution purchasing can make to supply chain management, however, is in the area of vendor relations. Companies can use the purchasing function to strategically manage suppliers in order to reduce the total cost of materials and services. Through enhanced vendor relations, buyers and sellers can develop cooperative relationships that reduce costs and improve efficiency with the aim of lowering prices and enhancing profits. By integrating suppliers into their companies' businesses, purchasing managers have become better able to streamline purchasing processes, manage inventory levels, and reduce overall costs of the sourcing and procurement operations.

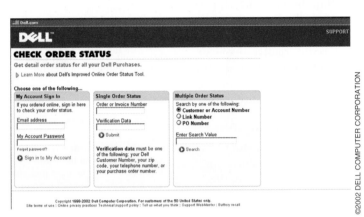

©2002 DELL COMPUTER CORPORATION

Build-to-order computers are more than commonplace today, thanks to the direct selling model of Dell Computer. The company allows customers to track their orders throughout manufacturing and shipping.

Production Scheduling

In traditional mass-market manufacturing, production begins when forecasts call for additional products to be made or inventory control systems signal low inventory levels. The firm then makes a product and transports the finished goods to its own warehouses or those of intermediaries, where the goods wait to be ordered by retailers or customers. Production scheduling based on pushing a product down to the consumer obviously has its disadvantages, the most notable being that companies risk making products that may become obsolete or that consumers don't want in the first place.

In a customer "pull" manufacturing environment, which is growing in popularity, production of goods or services is not scheduled until an order is placed by the customer specifying the desired configuration. This process, known as **mass customization**, or **build-to-order**, uniquely tailors mass-market goods and services to the needs of the individuals who buy them. Companies as diverse as BMW, Dell Computer, Levi Strauss, Mattel, and a slew of Web-based businesses are adopting mass customization to maintain or obtain a competitive edge.

As more companies move toward mass customization—and away from mass marketing—of goods, the need to stay on top of consumer demand is forcing manufacturers to make their supply chains more flexible. Flexibility is critical to a manufacturer's success when dramatic swings in demand occur. For example, automobile manufacturers such as Honda and Toyota have been modifying their assembly plants to make it easier to shift production based on demand. As a result, the companies can move new models into production in only a few months to keep up with the frequently changing tastes of consumers.[24]

mass customization (build-to-order)
A production method whereby products are not made until an order is placed by the customer; products are made according to customer specifications.

Just-in-Time Manufacturing

An important manufacturing process common today among manufacturers is just-in-time manufacturing. Borrowed from the Japanese, **just-in-time production (JIT)**, sometimes called *lean production*, requires manufacturers to work closely with suppliers and transportation providers to get necessary items to the assembly line or factory floor at the precise time they are needed for production. For the manufacturer, JIT means that raw materials arrive at the assembly line in guaranteed working order "just in time" to be installed, and finished products are generally shipped to the customer immediately after completion. For the supplier,

just-in-time production (JIT)
A process that redefines and simplifies manufacturing by reducing inventory levels and delivering raw materials just when they are needed on the production line.

Exhibit 10.10

Inventory Replenishment Example

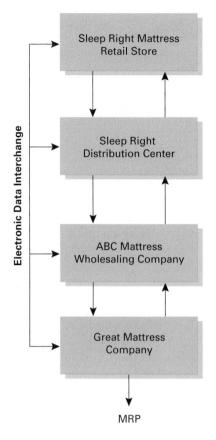

Sleep Right is planning a promotion on the Great Mattress Company's Gentle Rest mattress. Sales forecast is for fifty units to be sold. Sleep Right has ten open Gentle Rest orders with its distribution center. New mattresses must be delivered in two weeks in time for the promotion.

Sleep Right's Distribution Center is electronically notified of the order of fifty new Gentle Rest mattresses. It currently has twenty Gentle Rest mattresses in inventory and begins putting together the transportation plans to deliver these to the Sleep Right Store. Delivery takes one day. It orders forty new mattresses from its mattress wholesaler to make up the difference.

ABC Mattress Wholesaling Company is electronically notified of Sleep Right DC's order of forty new Gentle Rest mattresses. It currently does not have any of these in stock but electronically orders forty from the Great Mattress Company's factory. Once it receives the new mattresses, it can have them delivered to the Sleep Right DC in two days.

The Great Mattress Company electronically receives ABC's order and forwards it to the factory floor. Production of a new mattress takes twenty minutes. The total order of forty mattresses can be ready to be shipped to ABC in two days. Delivery takes one day. Raw material supplies for this order are electronically requested from Great Mattress's supply partners, who deliver the needed materials just-in-time to its stitching machines.

Although JIT manufacturing processes may eliminate the need to warehouse many raw materials, manufacturers may often keep some safety stock on hand in the event of an emergency, such as a strike at a supplier's plant or a catastrophic event that temporarily stops the flow of raw materials to the production line. Likewise, the final user may not need or want the goods at the same time the manufacturer produces and wants to sell them. Products like grain and corn are produced seasonally, but consumers demand them year-round. Other products, such as Christmas ornaments and turkeys, are produced year-round, but consumers do not want them until autumn or winter. Therefore, management must have a storage system to hold these products until they are shipped.

Storage is what helps manufacturers manage supply and demand, or production and consumption. It provides time utility to buyers and sellers, which means that the seller stores the product until the buyer wants or needs it. Even when products are used regularly, not seasonally, many manufacturers store excess products in case the demand surpasses the amount produced at a given time. Storing additional product does have disadvantages, however, including the costs of insurance on the stored product, taxes, obsolescence or spoilage, theft, and warehouse operating costs. Another drawback is opportunity costs—that is, the opportunities lost because money is tied up in stored product instead of being used for something else.

Because businesses are focusing on cutting supply chain costs, the warehousing industry is also changing to better serve its customers. For example, many warehouses are putting greater emphasis on more efficient unloading and reloading layouts and customized services that move merchandise through the warehouse faster, often in the same day. They also are investing in services using sophisticated tracking technology such as materials-handling systems.[30]

A **materials-handling system** moves inventory into, within, and out of the warehouse. Materials-handling includes these functions:

materials-handling system
A method of moving inventory into, within, and out of the warehouse.

- Receiving goods into the warehouse or distribution center
- Identifying, sorting, and labeling the goods
- Dispatching the goods to a temporary storage area
- Recalling, selecting, or picking the goods for shipment (may include packaging the product in a protective container for shipping)

The goal of the materials-handling system is to move items quickly with minimal handling. With a manual, nonautomated materials-handling system, a product may be handled more than a dozen times. Each time it is handled, the cost and risk of damage increase; each lifting of a product stresses its package. Consequently, most manufacturers today have moved to automated systems. Scanners quickly identify goods entering and leaving a warehouse through bar-coded labels affixed to the packaging. Automatic storage and retrieval systems automatically store and pick goods in the warehouse or distribution center. Automated materials-handling systems decrease product handling, ensure accurate placement of product, and improve the accuracy of order picking and the rates of on-time shipment.

Transportation

Transportation typically accounts for 5 to 10 percent of the price of goods.[31] Supply chain logisticians must decide which mode of transportation to use to move products from supplier to producer and from producer to buyer. These decision are, of course, related to all other logistics decisions. The five major modes of transportation are railroads, motor carriers, pipelines, water transportation, and airways. Supply chain managers generally choose a mode of transportation on the basis of several criteria:

- *Cost:* The total amount a specific carrier charges to move the product from the point of origin to the destination
- *Transit time:* The total time a carrier has possession of goods, including the time required for pickup and delivery, handling, and movement between the point of origin and the destination
- *Reliability:* The consistency with which the carrier delivers goods on time and in acceptable condition
- *Capability:* The ability of the carrier to provide the appropriate equipment and conditions for moving specific kinds of goods, such as those that must be transported in a controlled environment (for example, under refrigeration)
- *Accessibility:* A carrier's ability to move goods over a specific route or network
- *Traceability:* The relative ease with which a shipment can be located and transferred

The mode of transportation used depends on the needs of the shipper, as they relate to these six criteria. Exhibit 10.11 compares the basic modes of transportation on these criteria.

In many cases, especially in a JIT manufacturing environment, the transportation network replaces the warehouse or eliminates the expense of storing inventories as goods are timed to arrive the moment they're needed on the assembly line or for shipment to customers. In fact, Toyota is so committed to JIT that it has no parts warehouses in the United States. Instead, it works closely with its suppliers to make sure that parts will be delivered on time even during a crisis. For example, Continental Teves, Inc., supplies Toyota with German-made steering sensors for its Sequoia SUV. Traditionally, the parts were flown from Germany and delivered to Toyota when they were needed for installation. Following the September 11 terrorist attacks, however, Continental decided to begin shipping the parts via ship to ensure that Toyota will receive shipments on time even if U.S. airspace is shut down. Although the change will increase Continental's costs, the company decided it was necessary to meet Toyota's needs.[32]

Exhibit 10.11

Criteria for Ranking Modes
of Transportation

	Highest				Lowest
Relative Cost	Air	Truck	Rail	Pipe	Water
Transit Time	Water	Rail	Pipe	Truck	Air
Reliability	Pipe	Truck	Rail	Air	Water
Capability	Water	Rail	Truck	Air	Pipe
Accessibility	Truck	Rail	Air	Water	Pipe
Traceability	Air	Truck	Rail	Water	Pipe

Trends in Supply Chain Management

Several technological advances and business trends are affecting the job of the supply chain manager today. Three of the most outstanding trends are advanced computer technology, outsourcing of logistics functions, and electronic distribution.

8
Discuss new technology and emerging trends in supply chain management

Advanced Computer Technology

Advanced computer technology has boosted the efficiency of logistics dramatically with tools such as automatic identification systems (auto ID) using bar coding and radio frequency technology, communications technology, and supply chain software systems that help synchronize the flow of goods and information with customer demand. Amazon.com's state-of-the-art distribution centers, for instance, use sophisticated order picking systems that utilize computer terminals to guide workers through the picking and packing process. Radio frequency technology, which uses radio signals that work with scanned bar codes identifying products, directs Amazon's workers to the exact locations in the warehouse where the product is stored. Warehouse management software examines pick rates, location, and picking and storage patterns, and builds combinations of customer orders for shipping. After installing these supply chain technology tools, Amazon saw a 70 percent improvement in operational efficiency.[33]

One of the major goals of technology is to bring up-to-date information to the supply chain manager's

Matt Spangler and others are pictured here picking orders from the media cage at Amazon.com's Seattle distribution center. Amazon's command of the supply chain has translated into increased sales and customer satisfaction, but the company is still struggling to turn a profit.

© DAVID SAMUEL ROBBI/CORBIS SYGMA

desk. The transportation system has long been referred to as a "black hole," where products and materials fall out of sight until they reappear some time later in a plant, store, or warehouse. Now carriers have systems that track freight, monitor the speed and location of carriers, and make routing decisions on the spur of the moment. For instance, Roadway Express handles more than sixty thousand shipments a day, many for large retailers like Wal-Mart and Home Depot. New computer technology allows each package to be tracked from the minute it is received at one of Roadway's terminals until it is delivered. Anxious customers can check on the progress of their shipment anytime by checking with the Roadway Express call center or by using the company's password-protected Web site.[34] And, Swedish-based communications giant Ericsson, whose operations span the globe, uses specialized supply chain software to gain visibility over the fifty thousand outbound shipments it makes a year. As products leave its manufacturing facilities, transportation providers transmit status information at specified intervals to Ericsson's information system, which is accessible to management using a standard Web browser. The company has benefited greatly from the increased visibility of shipments the system has provided. Ericsson's management is now in a position to identify bottlenecks and respond before a crisis occurs, as well as measure the performance of its supply chain at different checkpoints.[35]

Outsourcing Logistics Functions

outsourcing (contract logistics)
A manufacturer's or supplier's use of an independent third party to manage an entire function of the logistics system, such as transportation, warehousing, or order processing.

External partners are becoming increasingly important in the efficient deployment of supply chain management. **Outsourcing**, or **contract logistics**, is a rapidly growing segment of the distribution industry in which a manufacturer or supplier turns over the entire function of buying and managing transportation or another function of the supply chain, such as warehousing, to an independent third party. Many manufacturers are turning to outside partners for their logistics expertise in an effort to focus on the core competencies that they do best. Partners create and manage entire solutions for getting products where they need to be, when they need to be there. Logistics partners offer staff, an infrastructure, and services that reach consumers virtually anywhere in the world. Because a logistics provider is focused, clients receive service in a timely, efficient manner, thereby increasing customers' level of satisfaction and boosting their perception of added value to a company's offerings. The trend is so strong that the supply chain outsourcing industry is expected to generate almost $1.8 billion in revenue by the year 2005.[36]

 Third-party contract logistics allow companies to cut inventories, locate stock at fewer plants and distribution centers, and still provide the same service level or even better. The companies then can refocus investment on their core business. Recall from Chapter 5 that Ford Motor Company decided to use third-party logistics provider UPS Worldwide Logistics Group to manage the delivery of Ford, Lincoln, and Mercury cars and trucks in the United States, Canada, and Mexico. The companies say they expect the alliance will reduce the time it takes to move vehicles from Ford's plants to dealers and customers by up to 40 percent. The alliance will also provide Web-based information systems that allow Ford and its dealers to track individual vehicle status from production through final delivery.[37]

Many firms are taking outsourcing one step further by allowing business partners to take over the final assembly of their product or its packaging in an effort to reduce inventory costs, speed up delivery, or meet customer requirements better. Ryder Truck Lines assembles and packages twenty-two different combinations of shrink-wrapped boxes that contain the ice trays, drawers, shelves, doors, and other accessories for the various refrigerator models Whirlpool sells. Similarly, outsourcing firm, StarTek, Inc., packages and ships products for Microsoft, provides technical support to customers of AOL Time Warner, and maintains AT&T communication systems.[38]

Electronic Distribution

Electronic distribution is the most recent development in the logistics arena. Broadly defined, **electronic distribution** includes any kind of product or service that can be distributed electronically, whether over traditional forms such as fiber-optic cable or through satellite transmission of electronic signals. For instance, instead of buying and installing software from stores, computer users increasingly can purchase software over the Internet and download it electronically to their personal computers or rent the same software from Internet services that have the program available for use on their servers. For example, Intuit, Inc., allows people to fill out their tax returns on its Web site rather than buying its TurboTax software.[39] Postage stamps can now be purchased on-line through E-Stamp, which uses a silver-dollar size "vault" attached to the purchaser's computer to keep track of postage purchases.[40] Similarly, on-line ticket companies and movie theaters have recently developed the technology to sell tickets to sporting events, concerts, and movies via the Internet; consumers can print the tickets at home on a standard computer printer.[41]

Hollywood movie studios are getting ready to deliver their products directly to consumers through digital pipelines.[42] Consumers can already download digital files of their favorite music, movies, and television shows to be played on their computers, portable players, and televisions, often without paying for the file. This controversial form of electronic distribution is discussed in the "Ethics in Marketing" box.

© IRS PUBLIC SERVICE ANNOUNCEMENT

electronic distribution
A distribution technique that includes any kind of product or servive that can be distributed electronically, whether over traditional forms such as fiber optic cable or through satellite transmission of electronic signals.

Channels and Distribution Decisions for Global Markets

With the surging popularity of free-trade agreements and treaties, such as the European Union and the North American Free Trade Agreement (NAFTA) over the past decade, global marketing channels and management of the supply chain have become increasingly important to U.S. corporations that export their products or manufacture abroad.

9

Discuss channels and distribution decisions in global markets

Developing Global Marketing Channels

Executives should recognize the unique cultural, economic, institutional, and legal aspects of each market before trying to design marketing channels in foreign countries. Manufacturers introducing products in global markets face a tough decision: what type of channel structure to use. Specifically, should the product be marketed directly, mostly by company salespeople, or through independent foreign intermediaries, such as agents and distributors? Using company salespeople generally provides more control and is less risky than using foreign intermediaries. However, setting up a sales force in a foreign country also entails a greater commitment, both financially and organizationally.

Video Piracy

As discussed in the chapter, new Internet and computer technology has been largely responsible for advances in supply chain management. However, the new technology and the Internet are also creating serious supply chain problems for the entertainment industry. For example, the invention of MP3 music files, which can be swapped on the Internet and burned onto compact discs, had a dramatic effect on traditional music sales. The music industry was forced to sue Napster, the leading music file swapping Web site, which eventually filed for bankruptcy, for copyright infringement and to develop both new distribution channels and new technologies to prevent music swapping.

Similarly, new technology now allows consumers to make and swap digital copies of television shows and movies. For instance, digital video recorders (DVRs) allow consumers to record their favorite television shows and movies via traditional cable, broadcast, satellite, and Internet connections. With DVRs, consumers can watch their favorite programs when it is convenient and even pause live programming. As adoption of the technology increases, DVRs could have an impact on television advertising sales and program scheduling. The industry is more concerned, however, about SonicBlue's introduction of ReplayTV 4000, which not only enables consumers to automatically skip commercials but also allows them to send copies over the Internet to other Replay users.

Consumers can also obtain copies of their favorite movies and television shows by going on-line with one of two popular software programs that make it easy to swap video files on the Internet—Morpheus and Kazaa. With more than forty million users between the two, experts say that more than one million users are downloading copies of their favorite television shows and movies at any given time. Available downloads include every *Simpsons* episode ever recorded, film classics such as *Breakfast at Tiffany's*, and episodes of HBO's *The Sopranos* and *Sex in the City*. Finally, digital video cameras with FireWire are even making it easy to share copies of movies currently being shown in theaters.

All of these new technologies are leading to a dramatic increase in video piracy. Movie theaters around the globe are reporting heavy losses as a result. In fact, the Motion Picture Association of America claims that consumers illegally copy 350,000 films a day on the Internet. Other piracy experts put the number closer to a million a day. What's more, experts predict the trend will grow as technology improves and Internet speed increases.

To protect its product, the television industry has sued SonicBlue, claiming that ReplayTV 4000 illegally jeopardizes the industry's two main revenue sources: advertising and subscription fees. SonicBlue claims that copyright laws give consumers a "fair use" right to share—an argument the courts rejected in the Napster trial. Further, the company contends that it is creating innovative products that give consumers more control over how they use entertainment. The film industry has also sued StreamCast Networks, the distributor of Morpheus, for copyright infringement. StreamCast argues that the software enables people to share home movies and films that are in the public domain.

Regardless of the outcome of these lawsuits, the entertainment industry is examining the future of its distribution channels. Television studios are looking for a way to use electronic tags within a broadcast to prevent copying and are asking the federal government to require that all television sets, receivers, and computers be capable of reading the tags. For the tags to be effective, the studios would have to cease all nondigital broadcasts—a move that could eliminate free television, forcing consumers to use a cable or satellite company for program access.

In contrast, in an effort to satisfy consumers, MGM, Sony, Paramount, Universal, and Warner Brothers studios have started a joint venture called Moviefly to provide consumers with a secure, reliable way to "rent" movies on the Internet. Of course, if successful, the joint venture would eliminate cable and satellite companies from the pay-per-view distribution channel.[43]

What other distribution options does the entertainment industry have? Will new technology give the industry a way to protect its products, or will the industry be forced to reinvent the way it operates? How do you think television programs and movies will be distributed in the future?

Marketers should be aware that channel structures and types abroad may differ from those of channels in the United States. For instance, the more highly developed a nation is economically, the more specialized its channel types. Therefore, a marketer wishing to sell in Germany or Japan will have several channel types to choose from. Conversely, developing countries like India, Ethiopia, and Venezuela have limited channel types available; there are typically few mail-order channels, vending machines, or specialized retailers and wholesalers.

 Marketers must also be aware that many foreign countries have "gray" marketing channels, in which products are distributed through unauthorized channel intermediaries. It is estimated that sales of coun-

Challenges and Opportunities in China

Thanks to the Internet, new technology, and international trade agreements, global supply chains are bringing the world's businesses closer together. Today, large multinational corporations and small businesses alike look to markets around the world for their sourcing and procurement needs. Critics argue that this trend is widening the gap between the nations that have and those that do not. Proponents counter that globalization has brought education and economic development to developing nations and lower prices to the world's markets. Either way, both sides agree that globalization is here to stay. One development that global supply chain managers are watching closely is China's admission into the World Trade Organization (WTO).

For the many companies hoping to market their products to the world's largest market, opportunities abound. So do challenges for supply chain managers since China does not function as a single market but as hundreds, each with its own unique trade barriers. For example, each province and municipality has its own tariffs and trade restrictions. Transportation is particularly difficult. Not only is infra-

structure questionable outside urban areas but many provinces also have their own government-controlled transportation companies and outside transportation companies are not welcome. As a result, cargo must be unloaded and reloaded at each border crossing within the country. In fact, current supply chain costs in China are typically 30 to 40 percent of wholesale prices, compared to 5 to 20 percent in the United States.

On the other hand, China's participation in the WTO will secure the opening of additional markets to Chinese exports. With the greater availability of cheap Chinese goods, companies everywhere, including those already doing business with Chinese companies, may see lower sourcing and procurement costs. This should be good for consumers, but for emerging economies like India and Thailand, the competition could be deadly. Therefore, many companies are tightening up operations and focusing on quality to improve their ability to compete against the cheaper Chinese products. One such company is Bajaj Auto, a motorcycle manufacturer in New Delhi. Bajaj has expanded operations to take advantage of

economies of scale, invested heavily in R&D to stay on the cutting edge, and put its finances in order so that it can take advantage of future growth opportunities.

Supply chain managers will have to manage relationships with their Chinese supply chain partners closely to protect company interests from design piracy. For example, one of Black & Decker's Chinese sources turned around and competed head-to-head with Black & Decker in Germany using the American company's own design. The Japanese motorcycle manufacturers Yamaha, Honda, and Suzuki have also had problems with Chinese companies stealing their designs.

In the end, experts agree that China's participation in world markets will make the global economy more competitive, ultimately benefiting consumers. In the meantime, global supply chain managers will have to monitor developments around the world, particularly in Asia.[45]

What other global supply chain challenges and opportunities do you see in working with China? Will China's participation in world markets strengthen globalization, or will it have a negative impact?

---

terfeit luxury items like Prada handbags and Big Bertha golf clubs have reached almost $2 billion a year. The new fakes are harder to detect and hit the market almost instantly. For instance, a fake Christian Dior saddlebag was available just weeks after the original arrived on retailers' shelves. Similarly, Chinese companies

 are producing so many knockoffs of Yamaha, Honda, and Suzuki motorcycles that the Japanese companies are seeing a drop in sales. What's more, many companies are getting so good at design piracy that they are beginning to launch their own new products.[44] The "Global Perspectives" box provides more details on the impact of supply chain globalization.

 The Internet has also proved to be a way for pirates to circumvent authorized distribution channels, especially in the case of popular prescription drugs. In recent years, the U.S. Customs Service has seized millions of dollars worth of prescription drugs, most of which were purchased from foreign Internet sites. Some were seized because they had not been approved for use in the United States, others because they did not comply with U.S. labeling laws. Most sites offer just a handful of the most popular drugs, such as Viagra and the diet drug Xenical; consumers can get the drugs after obtaining the approval of a doctor who is affiliated with the site and who never sees the patient.

Global Logistics and Supply Chain Management

As global trade becomes a more decisive factor in success or failure for firms of all sizes, a well-thought-out global logistics strategy becomes more important.

One of the most critical global logistical issues for importers of any size is coping with the legalities of trade in other countries. Shippers and distributors must be aware of the permits, licenses, and registrations they may need to acquire and, depending on the type of product they are importing, the tariffs, quotas, and other regulations that apply in each country. This multitude of different rules is why multinational companies like Eastman Kodak are so committed to working through the World Trade Organization to develop a global set of rules and to encourage countries to participate. Other goals for these companies include reducing trade barriers such as tariffs. As these barriers fall, the flow of merchandise across borders is increasing as more companies are sourcing from multiple countries. For instance, a Kodak camera sold in France may have been assembled there, but the camera mechanism probably came from China and the film from the United States.[46]

The presence of different rules hasn't slowed the spread of supply chain globalization, however. In spite of the added costs associated with importing and exporting goods, many companies are looking to other countries for their sourcing and procurement needs. For example, Applica, Inc., a U.S. maker of small appliances, is committed to using technology to improve its relationships with suppliers in Mexico. The company has linked its suppliers directly to sales data from Wal-Mart stores to help manage production and inventory costs.[47]

Transportation can also be a major issue for companies dealing with global supply chains. Uncertainty regarding shipping usually tops the list of reasons why companies, especially smaller ones, resist international markets. Even companies that have scored overseas successes often are vulnerable to logistical problems. Large companies have the capital to create global logistics systems, but smaller companies often must rely on the services of carriers and freight forwarders to get their products to overseas markets.

In some instances, poor infrastructure makes transportation dangerous and unreliable. And the process of moving goods across the borders of even the most industrialized nations can still be complicated by government regulations. For example, NAFTA was supposed to improve the flow of goods across the continent, but moving goods across the border still requires approvals from dozens of government agencies, broker intervention, and hours spent at border checks. Shipping companies like Ryder are working to make the process easier. Currently, Ryder operates a cross-border facility in San Antonio to help clients like General Motors and Xerox with customs and logistics costs. The company also is part of a pilot project to automate border crossings with technology similar to that of an E-Z pass. The new system sends and receives short-range radio signals containing information on the load to toll booths, weigh stations, and border crossings. If the cargo meets requirements, the truck or train receives a green light to go ahead. Questionable cargo is set aside for further inspection. Transportation industry experts believe the system could reduce delivery times by more than three hours.[48]

10

Identify the special problems and opportunities associated with distribution in service organizations

Channels and Distribution Decisions for Services

The fastest-growing part of our economy is the service sector. Although distribution in the service sector is difficult to visualize, the same skills, techniques, and strategies used to manage inventory can also be used to manage service inventory—for instance, hospital beds, bank accounts, or airline seats. The quality of the planning and execution of distribution can have a major impact on costs and customer satisfaction.

Does your bank deliver any of its services on-line? Visit its Web site to find out. Which on-line services would you be inclined to use? Are there any that you would definitely *not* use? Why not?

On Line

One thing that sets service distribution apart from traditional manufacturing distribution is that, in a service environment, production and consumption are simultaneous. In manufacturing, a production setback can often be remedied by using safety stock or a faster mode of transportation. Such substitution is not possible with a service. The benefits of a service are also relatively intangible—that is, you can't normally see the benefits of a service, such as a doctor's physical exam. But a consumer can normally see the benefits provided by a product—for example, a vacuum cleaner removing dirt from the carpet.

Because service industries are so customer oriented, customer service is a priority. Service distribution focuses on three main areas:

Modeled after successful programs like ExxonMobil's Speedpass, McDonald's is testing a program to minimize the time customers spend at the register. Customers run a small wand over the electronic reader to pay for food they order. People can load the wand electronically with dollars by using a credit or debit card. Reduced time paying for food means that McDonald's can sell hamburgers almost as fast as customers can order them.

- *Minimizing wait times:* Minimizing the amount of time customers wait in line to deposit a check, wait for their food at a restaurant, or wait in a doctor's office for an appointment is a key factor in maintaining the quality of service. People tend to overestimate the amount of time they spend waiting in line, researchers report, and unexplained waiting seems longer than explained waits. To reduce anxiety among waiting customers, some restaurants give patrons pagers that allow them to roam around or go to the bar. Banks sometimes install electronic boards displaying stock quotes or sports scores. Car rental companies reward repeat customers by eliminating their waits altogether.[49] Airports have designed comfortable sitting areas with televisions and children's play areas for those waiting to board planes. Some service companies are using sophisticated technology to further ease their customers' waiting time. Similarly, many hotels are experimenting with electronic check-in kiosks. Travelers can insert their credit cards to check in upon arrival to receive their room key, get directions and print maps to area restaurants and attractions, and print out their hotel bills.[50]

- *Managing service capacity:* For product manufacturers, inventory acts as a buffer, enabling them to provide the product during periods of peak demand without extraordinary efforts. Service firms don't have this luxury. If they don't have the capacity to meet demand, they must either turn down some prospective customers, let service levels slip, or expand capacity. For instance, at tax time a tax preparation firm may have so many customers desiring its services that it has to either turn business away or add temporary offices or preparers. Popular restaurants risk losing business when seating is unavailable or the wait is too long.

- *Improving service delivery:* Like manufacturers, service firms are now experimenting with different distribution channels for their services. Choosing the right distribution channel can increase the times that services are available (such as using the Internet to disseminate information and services 24/7) or add to customer convenience (like pizza delivery, walk-in medical clinics, or a dry cleaner located in a supermarket). The airline industry has found that using the Internet for ticket sales both reduces distribution costs and raises the level of customer service by making it easier for customers to plan their own travel. Cruise lines, on the other hand, have found that travel agents add value by helping customers sort through the abundance of information and complicated options available when booking a cruise.[51]

The Internet is fast becoming an alternative channel for delivering services. Consumers can now purchase plane tickets, plan a vacation cruise, reserve a hotel room, pay bills, purchase mutual funds, and receive electronic newspapers in cyberspace. Insurance giant Allstate, for instance, now sells auto and home insurance directly to consumers in some states through the Internet in addition to its traditional network of agents. The effort reduces costs so that Allstate can stay competitive with rival insurance companies Progressive and Geico that already target customers directly.[52] Similarly, several new residential real estate Web sites are making it easier for customers to shop for a new home on the Web. Traditionally, the only way for customers to gain access to realtors' listings was to work through a real estate agent who would search the listings and then show customers homes that met their requirements. The new companies offer direct access to the listings, enabling customers to review properties for sale on their own, and choose which ones they would like to visit.[53]

CONNECT IT

As you complete this chapter, you should be able to see how marketing channels operate and how supply chain management is necessary to move goods from the manufacturer to the final consumer. Companies can choose from several different marketing channels to sell their products. For example, as the opening story discussed, H-E-B is using supply chain concepts and technology to compete successfully with giants like Wal-Mart. This strategy has made H-E-B the largest privately owned grocery distribution company in the United States.

USE IT

Buy Your Textbooks through a Direct Marketing Channel

Save money and valuable loafing or study time by buying your textbooks from on-line textbook sellers, such as Big Words (**bigwords.com**), **ecampus.com**, or **VarsityBooks. com**. These sites provide students with the right textbooks, at the right price, right in time for classes to begin. And, instead of having to wait in line at the bookstore with your course curriculum, you can zap your book list to any of the cyber-bookstores that work with your school and then have them delivered directly to your dorm room. Since approximately nine out of ten of the fifteen million students enrolled in higher-education institutions use the Internet, buying textbooks on-line is a natural fit.

Have a Product You Want to Sell on the Web?

Specialized Web sites can help you set up an e-commerce site with minimal effort and cost. Sites such as **BizLand.com**, **Bigstep.com**, and **Go2Net** help small-business owners create e-commerce Web sites where purchases can be accepted on-line with a credit card. BizLand's site, for instance, provides free on-line storefronts and shopping carts, custom domain names, e-mail, business promotional tools, site monitoring, plus lots more. Easy-to-use software helps merchants build and maintain catalogs of products and services to sell over the Internet. The sites are becoming very popular; Bizland's membership swelled to over 500,000 small-business owners from all 50 states plus 150 countries in just one year.

① Explain what a marketing channel is and why intermediaries are needed. A marketing channel is a business structure of interdependent organizations that reach from the point of product origin to the consumer with the purpose of physically moving products to their final consumption destination, representing "place" in the marketing mix and encompassing the processes involved in getting the right product to the right place at the right time. Members of a marketing channel create a continuous and seamless supply chain that performs or supports the marketing channel functions. Channel members provide economies to the distribution process in the form of specialization and division of labor; overcoming discrepancies in quantity, assortment, time, and space; and providing contact efficiency.

1.1 Your family runs a specialty ice cream parlor, Graeter's, that manufactures its own ice cream in small batches and sells it only in pint-sized containers. Recently, someone not affiliated with the company sent six pints of its ice cream to Oprah Winfrey, who proclaimed on her national TV show that it was the best ice cream she had ever eaten. Immediately after the broadcast, orders came flooding in, overwhelming your small-batch production schedule and your rudimentary distribution system. The company's shipping manager thinks she can handle it, but you disagree. List the reasons why you need to restructure your supply chain.[54]

② Define the types of channel intermediaries and describe their functions and activities. The most prominent difference separating intermediaries is whether or not they take title to the product. Retailers and merchant wholesalers take title, but agents and brokers do not. Retailers are firms that sell mainly to consumers. Merchant wholesalers are those organizations that facilitate the movement of products and services from the manufacturer to producers, resellers, governments, institutions, and retailers. Agents and brokers do not take title to the goods and services they market, but do they facilitate the exchange of ownership between sellers and buyers. Channel intermediaries perform three basic types of functions. Transactional functions include contacting and promoting, negotiating, and risk taking. Logistical functions performed by channel members include physical distribution, storing, and sorting functions. Finally, channel members may perform facilitating functions, such as researching and financing.

2.1 Discuss the reasons intermediaries are important to the distribution of most goods. What important functions do they provide?

③ Describe the channel structures for consumer and business-to-business products and discuss alternative channel arrangements. Marketing channels for consumer and business-to-business products vary in degree of complexity. The simplest consumer-product channel involves direct selling from producers to consumers. Businesses may sell directly to business or government buyers. Marketing channels grow more complex as intermediaries become involved. Consumer-product channel intermediaries include agents, brokers, wholesalers, and retailers. Business-product channel intermediaries include agents, brokers, and industrial distributors. Marketers often use alternative channel arrangements to move their products to the consumer. With dual distribution or multiple distribution, they choose two or more different channels to distribute the same product. Nontraditional channels help differentiate a firm's product from the competitor's or provide a manufacturer with another avenue for sales. Finally, strategic channel alliances are arrangements that use another manufacturer's already established channel.

3.1 Describe the most likely marketing channel structure for each of these consumer products: candy bars, Tupperware products, nonfiction books, new automobiles, farmers' market produce, and stereo equipment. Now, construct alternative channels for these same products.

3.2 *∫ INFOTRAC* COLLEGE EDITION Dell Computer successfully uses a direct channel to sell computers and equipment it manufactures to consumers over the telephone and Internet. How has Dell affected traditional computer retailers with brick-and-mortar buildings? How have other computer manufacturers, such as Compaq and IBM, countered Dell's competitive advantage in its direct channel? Use Info-Trac (**http://www.infotrac-college.com**) to search for articles on this topic. You may also need to consult your campus library's databases on companies and articles to search for this information.

3.3 **WRITING** You have been hired to design an alternative marketing channel for a firm specializing in the manufacturing and marketing of novelties for college student organizations. In a memo to the president of the firm, describe how the channel operates.

3.4 **WRITING** Building on question 1.1, determine a new channel structure for Graeter's. Write a proposal to present to your key managers.

4 **Define supply chain management and discuss its benefits.** Supply chain management coordinates and integrates all of the activities performed by supply chain members into a seamless process from the source to the point of consumption. The responsibilities of a supply chain manager include developing channel design strategies, managing the relationships of supply chain members, sourcing and procurement of raw materials, scheduling production, processing orders, managing inventory and storing product, and selecting transportation modes. The supply chain manager is also responsible for managing customer service and the information that flows through the supply chain. The benefits of supply chain management include reduced costs in inventory management, transportation, warehousing, and packaging; improved service through techniques like time-based delivery and make-to-order; and enhanced revenues, which result from such supply chain–related achievements as higher product availability and more customized products

4.1 Discuss the benefits of supply chain management. How does the implementation of supply chain management result in enhanced customer value?

5 **Discuss the issues that influence channel strategy.** When determining marketing channel strategy, the supply chain manager must determine what market, product, and producer factors will influence the choice of channel. The manager must also determine the appropriate level of distribution intensity. Intensive distribution is distribution aimed at maximum market coverage. Selective distribution is achieved by screening dealers to eliminate all but a few in any single area. The most restrictive form of market coverage is exclusive distribution, which entails only one or a few dealers within a given area.

5.1 Decide which distribution intensity level—intensive, selective, or exclusive—is used for each of the following products, and explain why: Rolex watches, Land Rover sport utility vehicles, M&Ms, special edition Barbie dolls, Crest toothpaste.

5.2 **TEAM** Now that you have a basic channel structure for Graeter's (from question 3.4), form a team of three to four students and list the market, product, and producer factors that will affect your final channel structure.

6 **Explain channel leadership, conflict, and partnering.** Power, control, leadership, conflict, and partnering are the main social dimensions of marketing channel relationships. Channel power refers to the capacity of one channel member to control or influence other channel members. Channel control occurs when one channel member intentionally affects another member's behavior. Channel leadership is the exercise of authority and power. Channel conflict occurs when there is a clash of goals and methods among the members of a distribution channel. Channel conflict can be either horizontal, among channel members at the same level, or vertical, among channel members at different levels of the channel. Channel partnering is the joint effort of all channel members to create a supply chain that serves customers and creates a competitive advantage. Collaborating channel partners meet the needs of consumers more effectively by ensuring that the right products reach shelves at the right time and at a lower cost, boosting sales and profits.

6.1 Procter & Gamble and Wal-Mart are key partners in a shared supply chain. P&G is one of Wal-Mart's biggest suppliers, and Wal-Mart provides extremely detailed scanner data about customer purchases of P&G products. Wal-Mart recently began selling its own brand of Sam's Choice laundry detergent in bright orange bottles alongside P&G's Tide but for a greatly reduced price. What do you think will be the impact of this new product on what has been a stable channel relationship?

7 **Describe the logistical components of the supply chain.** The logistics supply chain consists of several interrelated and integrated logistical components: (1) sourcing and procurement of raw materials and supplies, (2) production scheduling, (3) order processing, (4) inventory control, (5) warehousing and materials-handling, and (6) transportation. Integrating and linking all of the logistics functions of the supply chain is the logistics information system. Information technology connects the various components and partners of the supply chain into an integrated whole. The supply chain team, in concert with the logistics information system, orchestrates the movement of goods, services, and information from the source to the consumer. Supply chain teams typically cut across organizational boundaries, embracing all parties who participate in moving product to market. Procurement deals with the purchase of raw materials, supplies, and components according to production scheduling. Order processing monitors the flow of goods and information (order entry and order handling). Inventory control systems regulate when and how much to buy (order timing and order quantity) Warehousing provides storage of goods until needed by the customer while the materials-handling system moves inventory into, within, and out of the warehouse. Finally, the major modes of transportation include railroads, motor carriers, pipelines, waterways, and airways.

7.1 Discuss the impact of just-in-time production on the entire supply chain. Specifically, how does JIT affect suppliers, procurement planning, inventory levels, mode of transportation selected, and warehousing? What are the benefits of JIT to the end consumer?

7.2 Assume that you are the supply chain manager for a producer of expensive, high-tech computer components. Identify the most suitable method(s) of transporting your product in terms of cost, transit time, reliability, capability, accessibility, and traceability. Now, assume you are the supply chain manager for a producer of milk. How does this change your choice of transportation?

8 **Discuss new technology and emerging trends in supply chain management.** Several trends are emerging that affect the job of today's supply chain manager. Technology and automation are bringing up-to-date distribution information to the decision maker's desk. Technology is also linking suppliers, buyers, and carriers for joint decision making, and it has created a new electronic distribution channel. Many companies are saving money and time by outsourcing third-party carriers to handle some or all aspects of the distribution process.

8.1 Visit the Web site of Menlo Logistics at **http://www.menlolog.com**. What logistics functions can this third-party logistics supplier provide? How does its mission fit in with the supply chain management philosophy?

8.2 Use InfoTrac (**http://www.infotrac-college.com**) to locate the following article in *Computerworld* magazine: "Filling Orders a Hot E-Business: Companies Race to Offer Logistics Services" by Julia King. Read the article and write a summary of the implications of Internet commerce for the U.S. transportation and logistics industries.

9 **Discuss channels and distribution decisions in global markets.** Global marketing channels are becoming more important to U.S. companies seeking growth abroad. Manufacturers introducing products in foreign countries must decide what type of channel structure to use—in particular, whether the product should be marketed through direct channels or through foreign intermediaries. Marketers should be aware that channel structures in foreign markets may be very different from those they are accustomed to in the United States. Global distribution expertise is also emerging as an important skill for supply chain managers as many countries are removing trade barriers.

9.1 ꞁINFOTRAC° COLLEGE EDITION How are transportation and logistics issues handled around the world? To find out, consult the *Transportation Journal* using Info-Trac (**http://www.infotrac-college.com**). Create a grid comparing at least two countries according to standard procedures, particular challenges faced, and creative solutions to problems they have encountered.

(10) Identify the special problems and opportunities associated with distribution in service organizations. Managers in service industries use the same skills, techniques, and strategies to manage logistics functions as managers in goods-producing industries. The distribution of services focuses on three main areas: minimizing wait times, managing service capacity, and improving service delivery.

10.1 WRITING Assume that you are the marketing manager of a hospital. Write a report indicating the distribution functions that concern you. Discuss the similarities and dissimilarities of distribution for services and for goods.

DEFINE IT

agents and brokers 316
channel conflict 328
channel control 328
channel leader (channel captain) 328
channel members 314
channel partnering (channel cooperation) 330
channel power 328
direct channel 319
discrepancy of assortment 314
discrepancy of quantity 314
distribution resource planning (DRP) 334
dual distribution (multiple distribution) 321
electronic data interchange (EDI) 333
electronic distribution 339

exclusive distribution 327
horizontal conflict 329
intensive distribution 326
inventory control system 334
just-in-time production (JIT) 332
logistics 317
logistics information system 331
marketing channel (channel of distribution) 314
mass customization (build-to-order) 332
materials-handling system 335
materials requirement planning (MRP) (materials management) 334
merchant wholesaler 315

order processing system 333
outsourcing (contract logistics) 338
retailer 315
selective distribution 327
spatial discrepancy 315
strategic channel alliance 322
supply chain 314
supply chain management 322
supply chain team 331
temporal discrepancy 315
vertical conflict 329

APPLY IT

Application for Entrepreneurs

 Boudreaux has owned and operated a small spice-manufacturing business in south Louisiana for about ten years. Boudreaux has also experimented with preparing and selling several sauces, mostly for meats and salads. For the most part, the firm has sold its products locally, but on occasion, distributors have signed contracts to sell Boudreaux's products regionally. Boudreaux's most recent product—a spicy Cajun mayonnaise—has been a huge success locally, and several inquiries have come from large distributors about the possibilities of selling the mayonnaise regionally and perhaps nationally. No research has been conducted to determine the level or scope of demand for the mayonnaise. Also, it has been packaged and sold in only a twelve-ounce bottle. The red-and-white label just says "Boudreaux's Cajun Mayonnaise" and lists the major ingredients.

Questions

1. What should Boudreaux do to help the firm decide how best to market the new Cajun mayonnaise?

2. Should Boudreaux sign a contract with one of the distributors to sell the Cajun mayonnaise, or should his firm try to sell the product directly to one or more of the major supermarket chains?

THINK ABOUT IT

Ethics Exercise

Wholesome Snacks Inc., the maker of a variety of cookies and crackers, has just created a new vitamin-packed cookie. The new cookie has the potential to combat many of the health issues caused by malnutrition in children throughout poverty-stricken parts of the world. To date, however, many of the larger developing markets have resisted opening distribution channels to Wholesome's products. Wholesome realizes that its new cookie could also help open the door for the company to sell its less nutritious products in these markets. Therefore, the company is offering the new cookie at a low cost to government relief programs in exchange for long sought after distribution channels. The company feels the deal is good for business, but the countries feel it is corporate bullying.

Questions

1. What do you think about Wholesome's idea for opening a new distribution channel?

2. Does the AMA Code of Ethics address this issue? Go to **http://www.marketingpower. com** and review the code. Then, write a brief paragraph stating what the AMA Code of Ethics contains that relates to distribution channels in developing nations.

TRY IT

Entrepreneurship Case

CarsDirect.com: Driving Car Buyers to the Internet

CarsDirect.com is heating up the new car industry. The country's first direct broker of cars on the Internet has sent automakers, on-line-buying services, and dealer groups scrambling to control the growing number of customers going on-line to shortcut the traditional process of shopping for new and used vehicles. The Internet start-up sparked a flurry of copycat Web sites dedicated to the direct-to-consumer purchase of cars, like CarOrder.com, DriveOff.com, Carpoint.com, and Greenlight.com. But several have now gone out of business.

Backed by Michael Dell's personal investment firm, CarsDirect.com was conceived by Bill Gross, chairman of Idealab, a venture incubator that has also launched other Internet businesses, such as eToys, Tickets.com, and Cooking.com. After becoming frustrated with his own efforts at buying an auto on-line, Gross realized that current Internet options for car buying were not only inadequate but did nothing to leverage available technology on behalf of the consumer. At the time of his search, on-line car sites functioned only as lead generators for local dealers, requiring him to close the sale of his car the old-fashioned way: haggling at the dealership with the untrustworthiest of people—a car salesperson.

His vision, CarsDirect.com, sells cars entirely through the Internet, allowing consumers to bypass traditional car dealers in their negotiations. As a car broker, CarsDirect.com offers Web buyers a car at a fixed price based on recent average selling prices. Then,

CarsDirect.com works through its network of existing dealers to get the car at that price. Since CarsDirect.com doesn't hold franchise agreements with any car manufacturers, consumers enjoy an impartial and unbiased shopping experience as well as an unrivaled selection. In contrast, buying cars the old-fashioned way makes consumers travel from car dealer to car dealer looking for the models they are interested in or the best price.

Car buyers visiting CarsDirect.com can research a car by searching the site's extensive database, which provides objective information on price, performance, and options for more than 2,500 different makes and models—virtually every production vehicle available in the United States. CarsDirect.com's research tools let buyers compare the features of vehicles and see in seconds the manufacturer's suggested retail price, the invoice, and, most importantly, the price CarsDirect.com can get for them. If a consumer wants to buy, payment is arranged completely on-line to close the deal. Financing options are provided through CarsDirect.com's financial partner Bank One, one of the nation's largest banks and a major automotive lender. Then, the buyer can arrange for delivery of the vehicle at home or the office or pick it up from a local automotive retailer.

With on-line auto sales expected to exceed 5 percent of total sales soon, there are still big hurdles ahead for car brokers like CarsDirect.com. General Motors, for instance, recently warned its 7,700 dealers to cease and desist from using on-line car-buying sites like CarsDirect.com. The largest obstacle, however, is the myriad of state franchise laws that protect car dealers and restrict direct sales of automobiles. Car brokers have found that no two states' franchise laws are the same, and many include rules that are arcane or impractical. Texas, the nation's second biggest automotive market, has the most restrictive dealer-protection laws in the country. There, only state-licensed dealers can sell cars. Brokering of cars to consumers by anyone other than a dealer is strictly prohibited. As a result, car brokers have had to redesign their direct-sales model around Texas laws. CarsDirect.com, for instance, currently does not offer cars to residents of Texas. Often, instead of trying to bypass dealers, Internet car brokers are forming alliances with dealers or reworking their strategies to become more dealer-friendly to comply with state law.

Questions

1. Explain how CarsDirect.com fits into the channel structure for car retailing to consumers.

2. How has CarsDirect.com's selling model caused channel conflict?

3. Visit CarsDirect.com's Web site at **http://www.carsdirect.com**. Give examples of how its Web site simplifies the car-buying process for consumers.

WATCH IT

Short  SUPERBOWL

The *Essentials of Marketing* PowerPoint CD-ROM has two ad videos in the Chapter 10 slide presentation. An eTrade ad shows how companies advertise products with electronic distribution. What do you think is the issue illustrated by the Columbia TriStar ad?

Medium **CNN VIDEO**

Distribution is a key issue for a Palestinian brewery. Watch the CNN clip on Taybeh Beer and identify ways that Taybeh can overcome the serious obstacles that it faces. Issues related to the concepts in Chapters 2 and 3 are also presented in the Taybeh segment.

To give you insight into Chapter 10, Small Business School will take you back to Karsten Manufacturing in Phoenix, Arizona, to see how this company manages its supply chain. Although you will see the same segment you viewed for Chapter 9, this time concentrate on issues like channel structure, channel relationships, and the logistical components of Karsten's supply chain.

FLIP IT

Flip to Chapter 10 in your *Grademaker Study Guide* for more review opportunities, including the pretest, vocabulary review, Internet activities, study test questions, and an application exercise based on marketing channel concepts. Can you close your book and diagram the various channel structures discussed in the book? Do you know the issues that marketers must consider when determining a channel strategy? If not, then pick up your *Grademaker* and review.

CLICK IT

The *Essentials of Marketing* Web site links you to all the Internet-based activities in this chapter, like the "Use It," "Review It" questions 3.2, 8.1, 8.2, and 9.1, and the On-Line exercises in the chapter margins. As a review, do the Chapter 10 quiz and crossword puzzle. And don't forget the Career Exersite that gives you resources for exploring marketing career opportunities in supply chain management. Review the main concepts in the PowerPoint presentation for Chapter 10, too. Go to **http://lamb.swlearning.com**, read the material, and follow the links right from the site.

Surf to Xtra! to test your understanding of the service marketing concepts in the chapter by completing the worksheets for Exhibits 10.1 through 10.7, 10.9, and 10.11. If your instructor has assigned a marketing plan project, worksheets on Xtra! can help you organize your work. In addition to the quiz on the Web site, there's another quiz on Xtra!, plus video of the authors answering frequently asked questions about supply chain management topics, such as "What factors should be considered when deciding the best channels of distribution?" and "Why should management be concerned about supply chain management?"

Still Shaky? Here's a Tip.

In the margin next to each paragraph or section in the chapter, write the question that the section answers. For example, "What discrepancies do marketing channels aid in overcoming?" could go on page 315. Once you have questions throughout the chapter, you can quiz yourself by using a blank piece of paper to cover the content. To check yourself, reveal each paragraph after you have answered the corresponding question.

CHAPTER **ELEVEN**

RETAILING

Learning Objectives

1 Discuss the importance of retailing in the U.S. economy

2 Explain the dimensions by which retailers can be classified

3 Describe the major types of retail operations

4 Discuss nonstore retailing techniques

5 Define franchising and describe its two basic forms

6 List the major tasks involved in developing a retail marketing strategy

7 Discuss the challenges of expanding retailing operations into global markets

8 Describe future trends in retailing

Target, it seems, is right on target. With sales of $29 billion annually and approximately a thousand stores in forty-six states, Target strives to be the best place to buy high-quality merchandise at low prices in surroundings that make shopping fun. With that goal in mind, Target has successfully branded itself as the fashionable place to buy discount.

Unlike its discount competitors, Target seeks an affluent, educated clientele. Therefore, the chain doesn't sell the cheapest products possible or use advertising gimmicks. Instead Target draws on its department store roots to offer customers quality, stylish merchandise at low prices. Eighty percent of the chain's apparel merchandise is private-label knockoffs of the more expensive brands found in traditional department stores like Marshall Field's or Nordstrom. In addition, the stores also carry exclusive branded products such as household accessories by Michael Graves and Todd Oldham and apparel for juniors by Mossimo. Target's merchandising strategy of offering upscale items is carried over in its new Super Target combination general merchandise and grocery stores, where customers can buy gourmet food items such as fresh sushi, Starbucks coffee, and Dean & Deluca cooking oils. Being so narrowly focused on the type of products its customers want has helped the chain to consistently meet customer expectations.

Another important part of Target's success has been the company's advertising and promotions campaign. The current campaign, which presents a "bull's eye world" on television and in fashion magazines, is more about fun and fashion than price. It also has made Target's logo a cultural icon. For instance, when Target was a sponsor of CBS's *Survivor* series, customers everywhere recognized the logo on the parachute that appeared in almost every episode. But most importantly the campaign's print and television ads make consumers want to shop at Target.

Target's management also applies consistency and discipline to store presentation. Target customers often cite cleanliness, attractive displays, and availability of merchandise as reasons they like to shop there. As one customer commented, "I'm just drawn to Target. Something about that place makes me want to spend money."

Finally, in spite of the discount nature of the stores, Target operates under the mentality that customers are guests. The staff treats customers courteously and will even drop what they are doing to help a customer locate an item. The same focus on customer service led Target to create both its popular Club Wedd bridal registry and The Lullaby Club baby registry.[1]

So what's next? How will Target continue to grow sales and open new stores in an increasingly tight market? What has made the chain stand out from its competitors? How does a retailer's target market determine its merchandise selection? What factors are involved in developing a store's atmosphere? This chapter seeks to answer these questions and many more by discussing retailers' important role in moving products and services to the ultimate consumer. We begin with a discussion of the role of retailing and the ways in which retail operations can be classified, followed by a description of the decisions involved in developing a retail marketing strategy.

On Line

Target Stores

How does Target use its Web site to reach the niche it seeks to occupy? Compare Target's site to those of Wal-Mart and Sears. Are the sites as differentiated as the stores?

http://www.target.com

http://www.walmart.com

http://www.sears.com

The Role of Retailing

1

Discuss the importance of retailing in the U.S. economy

retailing
All the activities directly related to the sale of goods and services to the ultimate consumer for personal, nonbusiness use.

Retailing—all the activities directly related to the sale of goods and services to the ultimate consumer for personal, nonbusiness use—has enhanced the quality of our daily lives. When we shop for groceries, hair styling, clothes, books, and many other products and services, we are involved in retailing. The millions of goods and services provided by retailers mirror the needs and styles of U.S. society.

Retailing affects all of us directly or indirectly. The retailing industry is one of the largest employers; over 1.6 million U.S. retailers employ more than twenty million people, or nearly one out of every five workers. At the store level, retailing is still considered a mom-and-pop business. Almost nine out of ten retail companies employ fewer than twenty employees and, according to the National Retail Federation, 95 percent of all retailers operate just one store.[2]

The U.S. economy is heavily dependent on retailing. Retailers ring up over $3.18 trillion in sales annually, almost a third of the gross domestic product (GDP).[3] Although most retailers are quite small, a few giant organizations dominate the industry, most notably Wal-Mart, whose annual U.S. sales alone account for about 5 percent of all retail sales. Who are these giants? Exhibit 11.1 lists the ten largest U.S. retailers.

Classification of Retail Operations

2

Explain the dimensions by which retailers can be classified

A retail establishment can be classified according to its ownership, level of service, product assortment, and price. Specifically, retailers use the latter three variables to position themselves in the competitive marketplace. (As noted in Chapter 6, positioning is the strategy used to influence how consumers perceive one product in relation to all competing products.) These three variables can be combined in several ways to create distinctly different retail operations. Exhibit 11.2 lists the major types of retail stores discussed in this chapter and classifies them by level of service, product assortment, price, and gross margin.

Ownership

independent retailers
Retailers owned by a single person or partnership and not operated as part of a larger retail institution.

chain stores
Stores owned and operated as a group by a single organization.

franchise
The right to operate a business or to sell a product.

Retailers can be broadly classified by form of ownership: independent, part of a chain, or franchise outlet. Retailers owned by a single person or partnership and not operated as part of a larger retail institution are **independent retailers**. Around the world, most retailers are independent, operating one or a few stores in their community. Local florists, shoe stores, and ethnic food markets typically fit this classification.

Chain stores are owned and operated as a group by a single organization. Under this form of ownership, many administrative tasks are handled by the home office for the entire chain. The home office also buys most of the merchandise sold in the stores.

Franchises are owned and operated by individuals but are licensed by a larger supporting organization. Franchising combines the advantages of independent ownership with those of the chain store organization. Franchising is discussed in more detail later in the chapter.

Level of Service

The level of service that retailers provide can be classified along a continuum, from full service to self-service. Some retailers, such as exclusive clothing stores, offer high levels of service. They provide alterations, credit, delivery, consulting, liberal return policies, layaway, gift wrapping, and personal shopping. Discount stores

Exhibit 11.1

Ten Largest U.S. Retailers

2002 Rank	Company	Retailing Formats	2002 Revenues (in billions)	2002 Number of Stores
1	**Wal-Mart** Bentonville, Arkansas	Discount stores, super-centers, and warehouse clubs	$246.5	4,694
2	**The Home Depot** Atlanta, Georgia	Home centers	$58.2	1,532
3	**Kroger** Cincinnati, Ohio	Supermarkets and convenience stores	$51.7	4,089
4	**Target Corporation*** Minneapolis, Minnesota	Discount stores and department stores	$42.7	1,475
5	**Sears, Roebuck** Hoffman Estates, Illinois	Department stores, catalogs, home centers, and specialty	$41.4	2,192
6	**Costco** Issaquah, Washington	Warehouse clubs	$38.0	401
7	**Albertson's** Boise, Idaho	Supermarkets	$35.6	2,287
8	**Safeway** Pleasanton, California	Supermarkets	$32.4	1,695
9	**JCPenney** Plano, Texas	Department stores, catalogs, and drugstores	$32.3	3,789
10	**Kmart[†]** Troy, Michigan	Discount stores and supercenters	$30.8	1,831

* Renamed Target Corporation in January 2000; formerly was Dayton Hudson Corporation.
[†] Kmart declared bankruptcy in 2002 and emerged from bankruptcy in 2003.
SOURCE: STORES, July 2003, http://www.stores.org. Sales figures include international sales. © 2003 NRF Enterprises, Inc. Used with permission.

usually offer fewer services. Retailers like factory outlets and warehouse clubs offer virtually no services.

Product Assortment

The third basis for positioning or classifying stores is by the breadth and depth of their product line. Specialty stores—for example, Hallmark card stores, Lady Foot Locker, and TCBY yogurt shops—have the most concentrated product assortments, usually carrying single or narrow product lines but in considerable depth. On the other end of the spectrum, full-line discounters typically carry broad assortments of merchandise with limited depth. For example, Target carries automotive supplies, household cleaning products, and pet food. However, Target may carry only four or five brands of canned dog food; a supermarket may carry as many as twenty.

Exhibit 11.2

Types of Stores and Their
Characteristics

Type of Retailer	Level of Service	Product Assortment	Price	Gross Margin
Department store	Moderately high to high	Broad	Moderate to high	Moderately high
Specialty store	High	Narrow	Moderate to high	High
Supermarket	Low	Broad	Moderate	Low
Convenience store	Low	Medium to narrow	Moderately high	Moderately high
Drugstore	Low to moderate	Medium	Moderate	Low
Full-line discount store	Moderate to low	Medium to broad	Moderately low	Moderately low
Discount specialty store	Moderate to low	Medium to broad	Moderately low to low	Moderately low
Warehouse clubs	Low	Broad	Low to very low	Low
Off-price retailer	Low	Medium to narrow	Low	Low
Restaurant	Low to high	Narrow	Low to high	Low to high

Other retailers, such as factory outlet stores, may carry only part of a single line. Liz Claiborne, a major manufacturer of women's clothing, sells only certain items of its own brand in its many outlet stores. Discount specialty stores like Home Depot or Toys "R" Us carry a broad assortment in concentrated product lines, such as building and home supplies or toys.

Price

Price is a fourth way to position retail stores. Traditional department stores and specialty stores typically charge the full "suggested retail price." In contrast, discounters, factory outlets, and off-price retailers use low prices as a major lure for shoppers.

The last column in Exhibit 11.2 shows the typical **gross margin**—how much the retailer makes as a percentage of sales after the cost of goods sold is subtracted. The level of gross margin and the price level generally match. For example, a traditional jewelry store has high prices and high gross margins. A factory outlet has low prices and low gross margins. Markdowns on merchandise during sale periods and price wars among competitors, in which stores lower prices on certain items in an effort to win customers, cause gross margins to decline. When Wal-Mart entered the grocery business in a small Arkansas community, a fierce price war ensued. By the time the price war was in full swing, the price of a quart

gross margin
The amount of money the retailer makes as a percentage of sales after the cost of goods sold is subtracted.

of milk had plummeted by more than 50 percent (below the price of a pint) and a loaf of bread sold for only 9¢, prices at which no retailer could make a profit.

Major Types of Retail Operations

Traditionally, there have been several distinct types of retail stores, with each offering a different product assortment, type of service, and price level, according to its customers' shopping preferences.

In a recent trend, however, retailers are experimenting with alternative formats that make it harder to classify them. For instance, supermarkets are expanding their nonfood items and services, discounters are adding groceries, drugstores are becoming more like convenience stores, and department stores are experimenting with smaller stores.[4] Nevertheless, many stores still fall into the basic types.

Department Stores

Housing several departments under one roof, a **department store** carries a wide variety of shopping and specialty goods, including apparel, cosmetics, housewares, electronics, and sometimes furniture. Purchases are generally made within each department rather than at one central checkout area. Each department is treated as a separate buying center to achieve economies in promotion, buying, service, and control. Each department is usually headed by a **buyer**, a department head who not only selects the merchandise for his or her department but may also be responsible for promotion and for personnel. For a consistent, uniform store image, central management sets broad policies about the types of merchandise carried and price ranges. Central management is also responsible for the overall advertising program, credit policies, store expansion, customer service, and so on.

Large independent department stores are rare today. Most are owned by national chains. Among the largest U.S. department store chains are Sears, Target Corporation, JCPenney, Federated Department Stores, and May Department Stores. All operate more than one chain of retail stores, from discount chains to upscale clothiers. Two newer department store chains are Dillard's, based in Little Rock, Arkansas, and Nordstrom, with corporate headquarters in Seattle. Dillard's is known for its distribution expertise; Nordstrom offers innovative customer service. Both of these growing chains have a very promising future.

In recent years, consumers have become more cost conscious and value oriented. Specialty retailers like Gap, discounters, catalog outlets, and even on-line Internet shopping alternatives are offering superior merchandise selection and presentation, sharper pricing, and greater convenience to take sales away from department stores. They have also been quicker to adopt new technology and invest in labor-saving strategies. In addition, their leaner cost structure translates into lower prices for the customer. Meanwhile, manufacturers like Liz Claiborne, Bass, Calvin Klein, and Polo/Ralph Lauren have opened outlet stores of their own and more discount stores such as Wal-Mart and Target have upgraded their apparel assortments, taking more sales away from department stores.

Recent trends in retailing are making it increasingly difficult to classify retailers, as stores are crossing into each other's domains. This woman is purchasing computer software in her grocery store.

3
Describe the major types of retail operations

department store
A store housing several departments under one roof.

buyer
A department head who selects the merchandise for his or her department and may also be responsible for promotion and personnel.

Department store managers are using several strategies to preserve their market share. One is to reposition department stores as specialty outlets. They are dividing departments into miniboutiques, each featuring a distinct fashion taste, as specialty stores do. For example, many upscale department stores feature Donna Karan and Liz Claiborne boutiques within their stores. Department stores are also enhancing customer service to shift the focus away from price. Services include complimentary alterations, longer store hours, personalized attention, after-sale follow-up, and personal wardrobe planning. And a few department store chains like Bloomingdale's and Macy's are also experimenting with smaller, alternative formats.[5] Finally, department stores are expanding, remodeling, and revitalizing to show off new merchandising directions and to reflect the growth in their marketing areas.

Specialty Stores

Specialty store formats allow retailers to refine their segmentation strategies and tailor their merchandise to specific target markets. A **specialty store** is not only a type of store but also a method of retail operations—namely, specializing in a given type of merchandise. Examples include children's clothing, men's clothing, candy, baked goods, gourmet coffee, sporting goods, and pet supplies. A typical specialty store carries a deeper but narrower assortment of specialty merchandise than does a department store. Generally, specialty stores' knowledgeable sales clerks offer more attentive customer service. The format has become very powerful in the apparel market and other areas. In fact, according to recent studies, consumers buy more clothing from specialty stores than from any other type of retailer.[6] The Disney Store, Gadzooks, Williams-Sonoma, Foot Locker, and Tower Records are examples of successful chain specialty retailers.

Consumers usually consider price to be secondary in specialty outlets. Instead, the distinctive merchandise, the store's physical appearance, and the caliber of the staff determine its popularity. For example, Chico's, a national retail chain, has grown quickly by offering quality, private-label clothing for baby boomer women. The moderately priced clothing is styled to be loose, colorful, and low maintenance. Salesclerks focus on salesmanship, helping customers put together outfits and offering advice on which styles look best.[7] Because of their attention to the customer and limited product line, manufacturers often favor introducing new products in small specialty stores before moving on to larger retail and department stores.

Small specialty stores also provide a low-risk testing ground for many new products. Nike, for instance, often uses athletic footwear retailer Foot Locker as its venue for new shoe introductions. As an example, Nike introduced its $130 Tuned Air running shoe exclusively at Foot Locker shoe outlets. While the arrangement protected Foot Locker from price competition from other retailers, allowing it to charge full retail price, it also created an image of exclusivity for Nike.[8]

Sephora is a specialty cosmetics store that supplements its boutique format with in-store kiosks where customers can consult the company's Web site for items not in the store.

MARK RICHARDS/PHOTOEDIT

Supermarkets

U.S. consumers spend about a tenth of their disposable income in **supermarkets**—large, departmentalized, self-service retailers that specialize in food and some nonfood items.

A decade ago, industry experts predicted the decline of the supermarket industry, whose slim profit margins of just 1 to 2 percent of sales left it vulnerable. These experts originally felt that supermarkets would merely need an ever-growing customer base to sustain volume and compensate for low margins. Although the population continued to grow, albeit at less than 1 percent a year on average, supermarkets still experienced declining sales. As a result, experts were forced to examine not only population trends but also demographic and lifestyle changes of consumers. They discovered several trends affecting the supermarket industry.

For example, as dual-income and single-parent families increase, consumers are eating out more or are too busy to prepare meals at home. According to the U.S. Department of Agriculture, Americans spent only about two-thirds of their food money in retail grocery stores, compared with a third spent for food away from home. In comparison, Americans spent over three-fourths of their food money in grocery stores in 1950.[9] The growth in the away-from-home food market has been driven by the entry of more women into the workforce and their need for convenience and time-saving products. Working couples need one-stop shopping, and the increasing number of affluent customers are willing to pay for specialty and prepared foods.

As stores seek to meet consumer demand for one-stop shopping, conventional supermarkets are being replaced by bigger *superstores*, which are usually twice the size of supermarkets. Superstores meet the needs of today's customers for convenience, variety, and service. Superstores offer one-stop shopping for many food and nonfood needs, as well as many services—including pharmacies, flower shops, salad bars, in-store bakeries, takeout food sections, sit-down restaurants, health food sections, video rentals, dry-cleaning services, shoe repair, photo processing, and banking. Some even offer family dentistry or optical shops. This tendency to offer a wide variety of nontraditional goods and services under one roof is called **scrambled merchandising**. Canada's largest supermarket chain Loblaw exemplifies this trend: Along with dry cleaning, a liquor store, a coffee shop, a pharmacy, and a banking center, it also offers video-game and cellphone sales outlets and leases space to a clothing chain and a fitness club complete with a sauna, tanning beds, and day-care center. Loblaw's ancillary services aim to attract today's time-strapped customers by providing one-stop shopping.[10]

A recent trend in supermarket diversification is the addition of store-owned gas stations. The gas stations are not only a new revenue source for the supermarkets and a convenience for customers, but they also attract customers to the location by offering lower prices than can usually be found at a traditional gas station. Experts expect the trend will continue and that by the year 2005 supermarkets will account for 15 percent of overall gasoline sales.[11]

Another demographic trend affecting supermarkets is expanding ethnicity. Over the next fifty years, nonwhite ethnic groups will constitute the fastest-growing segments of the American population. According to the U.S. Census Bureau, the most pronounced population growth will be seen among Hispanics, Asian Americans, and African Americans. If current trends in shopping patterns among ethnic groups continue, these demographic changes promise to have a vast impact on supermarket retailers. For example, both African American and Hispanic households now outspend white American households on weekly grocery shopping. In terms of shopping habits, African Americans and Hispanics tend to be conservative, looking for products and brands they know and trust and patronizing stores that reliably meet their needs. It will also be increasingly important for supermarkets to tailor their stores' product mix to reflect the demographics of the population they serve.[12]

Many supermarket chains are tailoring marketing strategies to appeal to specific consumer segments to help them stand out in an increasingly competitive marketplace. Most notable is the shift toward *loyalty marketing programs* that reward loyal customers carrying frequent shopper cards with discounts or gifts. Once scanned at the checkout, frequent shopper cards help supermarket retailers electronically track shopper's buying habits. Sixty percent of customers who shop at the 110 stores operated by South Carolina–based Piggly Wiggly, for instance, carry the Pig's Favorite loyalty card. Customers use their card each time they shop to get special discounts on items. Piggly Wiggly also uses consumer purchase data stored in its database to determine customer preferences. If management sees that a customer buys flowers regularly, then it sends that customer a coupon redeemable in its floral department.[13]

scrambled merchandising
The tendency to offer a wide variety of nontraditional goods and services under one roof.

On Line

drugstore
A retail store that stocks pharmacy-related products and services as its main draw.

convenience store
A miniature supermarket, carrying only a limited line of high-turnover convenience goods.

discount store
A retailer that competes on the basis of low prices, high turnover, and high volume.

full-line discount stores
A retailer that offers consumers very limited service and carries a broad assortment of well-known, nationally branded "hard goods."

Drugstores

Drugstores stock pharmacy-related products and services as their main draw. Consumers are most often attracted to a drugstore by its pharmacy or pharmacist, its convenience, or because it honors their third-party prescription drug plan. Drugstores also carry an extensive selection of over-the-counter (OTC) medications, cosmetics, health and beauty aids, seasonal merchandise, specialty items such as greeting cards and a limited selection of toys, and some nonrefrigerated convenience foods. As competition has increased from mass merchandisers and supermarkets with their own pharmacies, as well as from direct-mail prescription services, drugstores have been adding value-added services such as twenty-four-hour operations and drive-through pharmacies.

Demographic trends in the United States look favorable for the drugstore industry. As the baby boom population continues to age, they will spend an increasing percentage of their disposable income on health care and wellness. This is good news for the drugstore industry, as the average sixty-year-old purchases fifteen prescriptions per year, nearly twice as many as the average thirty-year-old. Because baby boomers are attentive to their health and keenly sensitive about their looks, the increased traffic at the pharmacy counter in the future should also spur sales in other traditionally strong drugstore merchandise categories, most notably over-the-counter drugs, vitamins, and health and beauty aids.[14]

Convenience Stores

A **convenience store** can be defined as a miniature supermarket, carrying only a limited line of high-turnover convenience goods. These self-service stores are typically located near residential areas and are open twenty-four hours, seven days a week. Convenience stores offer exactly what their name implies: convenient location, long hours, fast service. However, prices are almost always higher at a convenience store than at a supermarket. Thus, the customer pays for the convenience.

From the mid-1970s to the mid-1980s, hundreds of new convenience stores opened, many with self-service gas pumps. Full-service gas stations fought back by closing service bays and opening miniature stores of their own, selling convenience items like cigarettes, sodas, and snacks. Supermarkets and discount stores also wooed customers with one-stop shopping and quick checkout. To combat the gas stations' and supermarkets' competition, convenience store operators have changed their strategy. They have expanded their offerings of nonfood items with video rentals, health and beauty aids, upscale sandwich and salad lines, and more fresh produce. Some convenience stores are even selling Pizza Hut and Taco Bell products prepared in the store.

Discount Stores

A **discount store** is a retailer that competes on the basis of low prices, high turnover, and high volume. Discounters can be classified into four major categories: full-line discount stores, discount specialty stores, warehouse clubs, and off-price discount retailers.

Full-Line Discount Stores

Compared to traditional department stores, **full-line discount stores** offer consumers very limited service and carry a much broader assortment of well-known, nationally branded "hard goods," including housewares, toys, automotive parts, hardware, sporting goods, and garden items, as well as clothing, bedding, and linens. Some even carry limited nonperishable food items, such as soft drinks, canned goods, and potato chips. As with department stores, national chains dominate the discounters. Full-line discounters are often called mass merchandisers. **Mass merchandising** is the retailing strategy whereby retailers use moderate to low prices on large quantities of merchandise and lower service to stimulate high turnover of products.

Wal-Mart is the largest full-line discount organization in terms of sales. With over four thousand stores, Wal-Mart has expanded rapidly by locating on the outskirts of small towns and absorbing business for miles around. Much of Wal-Mart's success has been attributed to its merchandising foresight, cost consciousness, efficient communication and distribution systems, and involved, motivated employees. Wal-Mart is credited with pioneering the retail strategy of "everyday low pricing," a strategy now widely copied by retailers the world over. Besides expanding throughout all fifty states and Puerto Rico, Wal-Mart has expanded globally into Mexico, Canada, Brazil, Argentina, China, Germany, Korea, and the United Kingdom.[15] Wal-Mart has also become a formidable retailing giant in on-line shopping, concentrating on toys and electronics. With tie-ins to its stores across the country, Wal-Mart is expected to introduce millions of customers to on-line shopping with in-store kiosks linking to the site and the ability to handle returns and exchanges from Internet sales at its physical stores.[16]

A hybrid of the full-line discounter is the hypermarket, a concept adapted from the Europeans. The flashy **hypermarket** format combines a supermarket and full-line discount store in a space ranging from 200,000 to 300,000 square feet. Although they have enjoyed widespread success in Europe, where consumers have fewer retailing choices, hypermarkets have been much less successful in the United States. Most Europeans still need to visit several small stores just for their food needs, which makes hypermarkets a good alternative. Americans, on the other hand, can easily pick among a host of stores that offer large selections of merchandise. According to retailing executives and analysts, American customers have found hypermarkets to be too big. Both Wal-Mart's Hypermart USA and Kmart's American Fare hypermarket formats never got beyond the experimental stage.

Similar to a hypermarket, but only half the size, is the **supercenter**, which combines groceries and general merchandise goods with a wide range of services including pharmacy, dry cleaning, portrait studios, photo finishing, hair salons, optical shops, and restaurants—all in one location. For supercenter operators like Wal-Mart, food is a customer magnet that sharply increases the store's overall volume, while taking customers away from traditional supermarkets. Wal-Mart now operates over 900 supercenters and plans to keep opening them at a rate of more than 150 a year for the near future. Although Target has been the last major discounter to embrace the supercenter concept, it recently doubled the number of Super Target stores and is investing in the development of private-label grocery products.[17]

 Supercenters are also threatening to push Europe's traditional small and medium-sized food stores into extinction. Old-fashioned corner stores and family businesses are giving way to larger chains that offer food, drugs, services, and general merchandise all in one place. Many European countries are passing legislation to make it more difficult for supercenters to open. In France, for example, laws were passed that banned authorizations for new supercenters over 1,000 square meters (10,800 square feet). Belgium and Portugal have passed similar bans. In Britain and the Netherlands, areas outside towns and cities are off limits to superstores. By imposing planning and building restrictions for large stores, these countries are trying to accommodate environmental concerns, movements to revive city centers, and the worries of small shopkeepers.

An increasingly popular variation of off-price retailing at full-line discount stores is *extreme-value retailing*, the most notable examples being Dollar General and Family Dollar. Extreme-value retailers have grown in popularity as major discounters continue to shift toward the supercenter format, broadening their customer base and increasing their offerings of higher priced goods aimed at higher income consumers. This has created an opening for extreme-value retailers to entice shoppers from the low-income segment. Low- and fixed-income customers are drawn to

mass merchandising
A retailing strategy using moderate to low prices on large quantities of merchandise and lower service to stimulate high turnover of products.

hypermarket
A retail store that combines a supermarket and full-line discount store in a space ranging from 200,000 to 300,000 square feet.

supercenter
A retail store that combines groceries and general merchandise goods with a wide range of services.

extreme-value retailers, whose stores are located within their communities. Extreme-value retailers also build smaller stores (a typical store is about the size of one department in a Wal-Mart superstore) with a narrower selection of merchandise emphasizing day-to-day necessities. Rock-bottom prices are also key to their success. With the average transaction under $10, extreme-value retailers have found low price to be far more critical to building traffic and loyalty than any other retailing format.[18]

Specialty Discount Stores

Another discount niche includes the single-line **specialty discount stores**—for example, stores selling sporting goods, electronics, auto parts, office supplies, and toys. These stores offer a nearly complete selection of single-line merchandise and use self-service, discount prices, high volume, and high turnover to their advantage. Specialty discount stores are often termed **category killers** because they so heavily dominate their narrow merchandise segment. Examples include Toys "R" Us in toys, Circuit City and Best Buy in electronics, Staples and Office Depot in office supplies, Home Depot in home improvement supplies, IKEA in home furnishings, and Bed, Bath & Beyond in kitchen and bath accessories.

 Toys "R" Us was the first category killer, offering a giant selection of toys, usually over fifteen thousand different items per store, at prices usually 10 to 15 percent less than competitors'. When Toys "R" Us came on the retail scene, department stores were generally limiting their toy assortments to the Christmas season. Toys "R" Us offered a broad assortment of inventory all year long. Additionally, the playing field was scattered with many small toy chains or mom-and-pop stores. With its bright warehouse-style stores, Toys "R" Us gobbled up market share, and many small toy stores failed and department stores eliminated their toy departments. The Toys "R" Us chain—currently an $11.3 billion company with more than 1,500 stores worldwide—now commands about a quarter of the U.S. retail toy business. Toys "R" Us first went international in 1984 with stores in Canada and Singapore. Since then, the company has opened over 492 stores in more than two dozen foreign countries, the most recent being Japan. Toys "R" Us has also expanded its category-killer retailing concept to include over 200 Kids "R" Us children's clothing stores and 148 Babies "R" Us product stores. In addition, the company's Web site garnered more than $180 million in sales last year thanks in part to an alliance with Amazon.com. The company plans to build on its momentum by also enhancing its Web sites for Babies "R" Us and Imaginarium.com.[19]

Other specialty segments have followed the lead of Toys "R" Us, hoping to build similar retailing empires in highly fragmented mom-and-pop markets. For instance, the home improvement industry was once dominated by professional builders and small hardware stores that offered basic staple products. Similarly, prior to the creation of Petsmart and Petco pet supplies chains, the pet industry was dominated by thousands of independent neighborhood pet stores. Another industry that was very fragmented was the office products industry. As more people began to work from home, replacing their typewriters with personal computers and purchasing fax machines, the local stationery store, with its limited selection of paper and writing materials, quickly became obsolete. The industry is now dominated by Office Depot, Staples, and OfficeMax, each stocking some five to seven thousand different types of products. Category-dominant retailers like these serve their customers by offering a large selection of merchandise, stores that make shopping easy, and low prices every day, which eliminates the need for time-consuming comparison shopping.

Warehouse Membership Clubs

Warehouse membership clubs sell a limited selection of brand-name appliances, household items, and groceries. These are usually sold in bulk from warehouse outlets on a cash-and-carry basis to members only. Individual members of warehouse clubs are charged low or no membership fees. Currently, the leading stores in this category are Wal-Mart's Sam's Club, Costco, and BJ's Wholesale Club.

Warehouse clubs have had a major impact on supermarkets. With 90,000 square feet or more, warehouse clubs offer 60 to 70 percent general merchandise and health- and beauty-care products, with grocery-related items making up the difference. Warehouse club members tend to be more educated and more affluent and have a larger household than regular supermarket shoppers. These core customers use warehouse clubs to stock up on staples; then they go to specialty outlets or food stores for perishables.

Fierce competition is commonplace in the warehouse club industry. Common practices include price slashing, selling below cost, locating outlets to compete directly with each other, and sometimes hiring away rivals' employees to get an edge in local markets. In one recent battle, Sam's Club has been targeting Costco's more affluent clientele. Costco, with annual revenues more than twice those of Sam's Club, dedicates approximately 25 percent of its inventory to high-end products like TaylorMade golf clubs and Coach handbags to attract wealthier customers who tend to spend more per visit. In an effort to beat Costco at its own game, Sam's Club has not only expanded its selection of fresh food, wine, and branded products, but has also begun holding promotional diamond and fine jewelry sales to draw customers.[20]

Off-Price Retailers

An **off-price retailer** sells at prices 25 percent or more below traditional department store prices because it pays cash for its stock and usually doesn't ask for return privileges. Off-price retailers buy manufacturers' overruns at cost or even less. They also absorb goods from bankrupt stores, irregular merchandise, and unsold end-of-season output. Nevertheless, much off-price retailer merchandise is first-quality, current goods. Because buyers for off-price retailers purchase only what is available or what they can get a good deal on, merchandise styles and brands often change monthly. Today there are hundreds of off-price retailers, the best known being T. J. Maxx, Ross Stores, Marshall's, HomeGoods, and Tuesday Morning.

Factory outlets are an interesting variation on the off-price concept. A **factory outlet** is an off-price retailer that is owned and operated by a manufacturer. Thus, it carries one line of merchandise—its own. Each season, from 5 to 10 percent of a manufacturer's output does not sell through regular distribution channels because it consists of closeouts (merchandise being discontinued), factory seconds, and canceled orders. With factory outlets, manufacturers can regulate where their surplus is sold, and they can realize higher profit margins than they would by disposing of the goods through independent wholesalers and retailers. Factory outlet malls typically locate in out-of-the-way rural areas or near vacation destinations. Most are situated at least thirty miles from urban or suburban shopping areas so that manufacturers don't alienate their department store accounts by selling the same goods virtually next door at a discount.

Several manufacturers reaping the benefits of outlet mall popularity include Liz Claiborne, J. Crew, and Calvin Klein clothiers; West Point Pepperel textiles; Oneida silversmiths; and Dansk kitchenwares. Top-drawer department stores—including Saks Fifth Avenue and Neiman Marcus—have also opened outlet stores to sell hard-to-move merchandise. Dillard Department Stores has opened a series of clearance centers to make final attempts to move merchandise that failed to sell in the department store. To move their clearance items, Nordstrom's operates Nordstrom Rack and Boston's Filene's has Filene's Basement.

As outlet malls have gained in popularity, however, they are beginning to act less and less like traditional outlets in which manufacturers sold surplus or damaged goods. For instance, some manufacturers such as Gap, Brooks Brothers, Ann Taylor, and Donna Karan now make lower-quality lines specifically for their outlet stores. Outlet store centers are also becoming less sensitive toward department stores that carry their brands at full retail price and are choosing to compete with

off-price retailer
A retailer that sells at prices 25 percent or more below traditional department store prices because it pays cash for its stock and usually doesn't ask for return privileges.

factory outlet
An off-price retailer that is owned and operated by a manufacturer.

regional malls by adding high-end amenities and entertainment to draw customers. For instance, Silver Sands Factory Stores in Destin, Florida, offers shoppers a two-level, 30,000-square-foot family entertainment center with activities for both children and adults. Similarly, Carlsbad Company Stores' outlet center in Carlsbad, California, features a sculpture garden, state-of-the-art fountain, and bright airy rest rooms designed for easy use by shoppers with bags and families with small children.[21]

Restaurants

Restaurants straddle the line between retailing establishments and service establishments. Restaurants do sell tangible products, food and drink, but they also provide a valuable service for consumers in the form of food preparation and food service. Most restaurants could even fall into the definition of a specialty retailer given that most concentrate their menu offerings on a distinctive type of cuisine—for example, Olive Garden Italian restaurants, Starbucks coffeehouses, Popeye's Fried Chicken, and Pizza Hut pizza restaurants.

As a retailing institution, restaurants must deal with many of the same issues as a more traditional retailer, such as personnel, distribution, inventory management, promotion, pricing, and location. Restaurants and food-service retailers run the spectrum from those offering limited service and inexpensive food, such as fast-food chains or the local snack bar or coffeehouse, to those that offer sit-down service and moderate to high prices, such as the likes of the Outback Steakhouse & Saloon chain or a local trendy Italian bistro.

Eating out is an important part of Americans' daily activities and is growing in strength. According to the National Restaurant Association, more than 54 billion meals are eaten in restaurants or cafeterias annually. This means that Americans consume an average of 4.2 commercially prepared meals per week. Food away from home accounts for about 25 percent of the household food budget for lower income families and as much as 50 percent for those with higher incomes. The trend toward eating out has been fueled by the increase in working mothers and dual-income families who have more money to eat out and less time to prepare meals at home. Money spent on food away from home is expected to grow from 46 percent of household food budgets in 2002 to 53 percent by 2010.[22]

The restaurant industry is one of the most entrepreneurial of businesses and one of the most competitive. Because barriers to entering the restaurant industry are low, the opportunity appeals to many people. The risks, however, are great. About 50 percent of all new restaurants fail within the first year of operation. Restaurants face competition not only from other restaurants but also from the consumer who can easily choose to cook at home. Competition has fostered innovation in the restaurant industry, such as Pizza Hut's introduction of The Edge pizza, to the ever-changing menus at fast-food restaurants. Seeking out and targeting underserved distribution niches is another way restaurants are competing with one another to reach consumers. Fast-food operators are increasingly looking to provide service at locations such as hospitals, airports, schools, and highway rest stops. Companies like Subway, Dunkin' Donuts, and Church's Fried Chicken also are partnering with branded service stations to offer customers one-stop shopping. These partnerships save money on leases, lure more customers, and foster innovation.

More restaurants are now competing directly with supermarkets by offering takeout and delivery in an effort to capture more of the home meal replacement market. Eatzi's Market & Bakery, for instance, is a cross between a gourmet grocery store and an upscale delicatessen where chefs behind counters cook, bake, and prepare meals. Eatzi's now has markets in Dallas, Houston, Atlanta, and Rockville, Maryland, where its chefs create over 100 ready-to-go entrees, 75 cheeses, 50 breads, and 125 desserts, and even fresh sushi. Consumers can even purchase wine, flowers, and cigars to complement their prepared meal.[23]

Nonstore Retailing

The retailing methods discussed so far have been at the origin in-store methods, in which customers must physically shop at stores. In contrast, **nonstore retailing** is shopping without visiting a store. Because consumers demand convenience, nonstore retailing is currently growing faster than in-store retailing. The major forms of nonstore retailing are automatic vending, direct retailing, direct marketing, and electronic retailing.

Discuss nonstore retailing techniques

nonstore retailing
Shopping without visiting a store.

Automatic Vending

A low-profile yet important form of retailing is **automatic vending**, the use of machines to offer goods for sale—for example, the cola, candy, or snack vending machines found in college cafeterias and office buildings. Vending is the most pervasive retail business in the United States, with about six million vending machines selling $30 billion annually. Food and beverages account for about 85 percent of all sales from vending machines. Due to the convenience, consumers are willing to pay higher prices for products from a vending machine than for the same products in traditional retail settings.[24]

automatic vending
The use of machines to offer goods for sale.

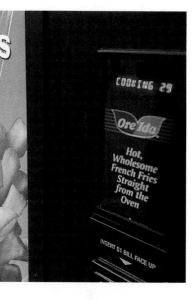

Retailers are constantly seeking new opportunities to sell via vending. For example, United Artists Theaters offer moviegoers the option of purchasing hot popcorn, Tombstone pizza, Kraft macaroni-and-cheese, and chicken fingers from a vending machine instead of waiting in line at the concession stand.[25] Many vending machines today also sell nontraditional kinds of merchandise, such as videos, toys, stickers, and sports cards. Vending machines in college libraries sell computer diskettes, pens and highlighters, and other office-type supplies. Tourists can purchase film and disposable cameras from vending machines in many popular destinations. And Joe Boxer underwear can be purchased with a credit card from vending machines in selected department stores.

Of course, vending machines are also an important tool in the ongoing cola wars between Coca-Cola and Pepsi. Both companies are constantly looking for new ways to improve vending machine sales. For example, Pepsi recently introduced new vending machines that allow customers to pay with a credit card for a soft drink. Coca-Cola is working on a new vending machine for workplaces. By using radio frequency identification to bill customers directly for their purchases, the machines would eventually allow Coca-Cola to offer loyalty awards to its vending machine customers.[26]

Automatic vending is being used to sell everything from hot french fries to prescription medication. In Australia, you can even order a Coke from a vending machine using your mobile phone.

Direct Retailing

In **direct retailing**, representatives sell products door-to-door, office-to-office, or at home sales parties. Companies like Avon, Mary Kay Cosmetics, The Pampered Chef, Usbourne Books, and World Book Encyclopedia depend on these techniques. Even personal computers are now being sold through direct retailing methods. Hand Technologies, based in Austin, Texas, sells computers using a team of consultants to sell computer products via demonstrations in the home and local

direct retailing
The selling of products by representatives who work door-to-door, office-to-office, or at home parties.

seminars for schools and families. The company targets new users of technology who need more support when they purchase, set up, and learn about computers and the Internet. The company now has over one thousand part-time consultants to sell personal computers directly to the customer.[27]

Most direct retailers seem to favor party plans these days in lieu of door-to-door canvassing. Party plans call for one person, the host, to gather as many prospective buyers as possible. The parties are generally part social gathering, part shopping, and part entertainment. For instance, at a Pampered Chef kitchen show, the party starts with a cooking demonstration that is designed to showcase many of the products offered for sale. Following the demonstration, the guests are treated to food and refreshments while they visit with one another and make their purchases.[28] Similarly, when young mothers shop for their children at house parties held by Orient Express, the chance to meet and talk with other young mothers is as much a part of the agenda as the purchases.

The sales of direct retailers have suffered as women have entered the workforce. Working women are not home during the day and have little time to attend selling parties. Although most direct sellers like Avon and Tupperware still advocate the party plan method, the realities of the marketplace have forced them to be more creative in reaching their target customer. Direct sales representatives now hold parties in offices, parks, and even parking lots. Others hold informal gatherings where shoppers can drop in at their convenience or offer self-improvement classes. Many direct retailers are also turning to direct mail, telephone, or more traditional retailing venues to find new avenues to their customers and increase sales. Avon, for instance, has begun opening cosmetic kiosk counters, called Avon Beauty Centers, in malls and strip centers. Direct retailers are also experimenting with the Internet to reach more buyers and increase sales. Amway recently launched an entirely new on-line spin-off, called Quixtar.com. Customers access the site using referral numbers unique to each of the Amway reps, which ensures that the reps earn commissions. Avon, Tupperware, and Mary Kay have followed Amway's lead by setting up Internet retail sites. At Avon's site, individual reps have created home pages that link from Avon's home page so that the sale will still go through them.[29]

In response to the decline in U.S. sales, many direct retailers are exploring opportunities in other countries. For example, Mary Kay, Avon, and Amway have started successful operations in China by adapting their business models to China's laws. Mary Kay agents in China do not purchase and resell the products but are paid a sales commission instead. The company also changed its slogan from "God First, Family Second, Career Third," to "Faith First, Family Second, Career Third."[30]

Direct Marketing

Direct marketing, sometimes called **direct-response marketing**, refers to the techniques used to get consumers to make a purchase from their home, office, or other nonretail setting. Those techniques include direct mail, catalogs and mail order, telemarketing, and electronic retailing. Shoppers using these methods are less bound by traditional shopping situations. Time-strapped consumers and those who live in rural or suburban areas are most likely to be direct-response shoppers because they value the convenience and flexibility that direct marketing provides.

Direct Mail

Direct mail can be the most efficient or the least efficient retailing method, depending on the quality of the mailing list and the effectiveness of the mailing piece. According to the Direct Marketing Association, direct mail generated $580 billion in revenue in 2001. With direct mail, marketers can precisely target their customers according to demographics, geographics, and even psychographics. Good mailing lists come from an internal database or are available from list brokers for about $35 to $150 per thousand names. For example, a Los Angeles computer software manufacturer selling programs for managing medical records may buy a list of all the physicians in the area. The software manufacturer may then design a direct-mail piece explaining the benefits of its system and send the piece to each physician. Today, direct mailers are even using videocassettes in place of letters and brochures to deliver their sales message to consumers.

Direct mailers are becoming more sophisticated in targeting the "right" customers. Using statistical methods to analyze census data, lifestyle and financial information, and past-purchase and credit history, direct mailers can pick out those most likely to buy their products. For example, a direct marketer like Dell Computer might use this technique to target 500,000 people with the right spending patterns, demographics, and preferences. Without it, Dell could easily mail millions of solicitations annually. Some solicitations may be targeted to only ten thousand of the best prospects, saving the company millions in postage while still preserving sales.

Most catalog companies also offer on-line shopping. Visit the Web site of one of your favorite catalogs to see if you can buy on-line. If so, surf the on-line catalog for a few minutes. Then compare the two retailing methods (paper and Internet) for prices, products, and so forth. Do you prefer the paper catalog or on-line shopping? Why?

On Line

Catalogs and Mail Order

Consumers can now buy just about anything through the mail, from the mundane like books, music, and polo shirts to the outlandish, such as the $5 million diamond-and-ruby-studded bra available through the Victoria's Secret catalog. Although women make up the bulk of catalog shoppers, the percentage of male catalog shoppers has recently soared. As changing demographics have shifted more of the shopping responsibility to men, they are viewing shopping via catalog, mail order, and the Internet as more sensible than a trip to the mall.

Successful catalogs are usually created and designed for highly segmented markets. Sears, whose catalog sales had dropped off, replaced its "big book" with a collection of more successful specialty catalogs targeted to specific market segments. Certain types of retailers are also using mail order to good effect. For example, computer manufacturers have discovered that mail order is a lucrative way to sell computers to home and small-business users, evidenced by the huge successes of Dell Computer and Gateway. Dell has used its direct business model to become a $31.8 billion company that is ranked number one in global market share.[31] Dell began shifting its sales to the Internet in the late 1990s and now sells over $50 million worth of computers and computer equipment on-line every day.

Improved customer service and quick delivery policies have boosted consumer confidence in mail order. L.L. Bean and Lands' End are two catalog companies known for their excellent customer service. Shoppers may order twenty-four hours a day and return any merchandise for any reason for a full refund. Other successful mail-order catalogs—including Spiegel, Talbots, Frontgate, and Lillian Vernon—target hardworking, home-oriented baby boomers who don't have time to visit or would rather not visit a retail store. To remain competitive and save time for customers, catalog companies are building computer databases containing customer information so they do not have to repeatedly give their addresses, credit card information, and so on. They also are working with overnight shippers such as UPS and FedEx to speed up deliveries. Indeed, some products can be ordered as late at 12:30 A.M. and still arrive the same day by 10:30 A.M.

Telemarketing

Telemarketing is the use of the telephone to sell directly to consumers. It consists of outbound sales calls, usually unsolicited, and inbound calls—that is, orders through toll-free 800 numbers or fee-based 900 numbers.

Outbound telemarketing is an attractive direct-marketing technique because of rising postage rates and decreasing long-distance phone rates. Skyrocketing field

telemarketing
The use of the telephone to sell directly to consumers.

sales costs have also put pressure on marketing managers to use outbound telemarketing. Searching for ways to keep costs under control, marketing managers are discovering how to pinpoint prospects quickly, zero in on serious buyers, and keep in close touch with regular customers. Meanwhile, they are reserving expensive, time-consuming, in-person calls for closing sales. The large number of outbound telemarketing calls, however, has led many states to pass laws establishing "do not call" lists of consumers who do not want to receive unsolicited phone calls. Although those in the industry insist that these lists help them by eliminating nonbuyers, this trend could have a long-term effect on telemarketing sales.

Inbound telemarketing programs, which use 800 and 900 numbers, are mainly used to take orders, generate leads, and provide customer service. Inbound 800 telemarketing has successfully supplemented direct-response TV, radio, and print advertising for more than twenty-five years. The more recently introduced 900 numbers, which customers pay to call, are gaining popularity as a cost-effective way for companies to target customers. One of the major benefits of 900 numbers is that they allow marketers to generate qualified responses. Although the charge may reduce the total volume of calls, the calls that do come are from customers who have a true interest in the product.

Electronic Retailing

Electronic retailing includes the twenty-four-hour, shop-at-home television networks and on-line retailing.

Shop-at-Home Networks

The shop-at-home television networks are specialized forms of direct-response marketing. These shows display merchandise, with the retail price, to home viewers. Viewers can phone in their orders directly on a toll-free line and shop with a credit card. The shop-at-home industry has quickly grown into a billion-dollar business with a loyal customer following. Shop-at-home networks have the capability of reaching nearly every home that has a television set.

The best-known shop-at-home networks are the Home Shopping Network and the QVC (Quality, Value, Convenience) Network. Home shopping networks attract a broad audience through diverse programming and product offerings and are now adding new products to appeal to more affluent audiences. For instance, on QVC, cooking programs attract both men and women, fashion programs attract mostly women, and the NFL Team Shop attracts primarily men. Since it began broadcasting, the channel has sold everything from Sony electronics to Bugs Bunny to Gucci. In 2000, the company shipped more than 79 million packages worldwide and had a customer file of approximately 20 million people in four countries accounting for its $3.5 billion in sales.[32]

On-line Retailing

For years, shopping at home meant looking through catalogs and then placing an order over the telephone. For many people today, however, it now means turning on a computer, surfing retail Web sites, and selecting and ordering products on-line with the click of a mouse. **On-line retailing**, or *e-tailing*, is a type of shopping available to consumers with personal computers and access to the Internet. According to Nielsen Reports, 60 percent of Americans had Internet access either at home or in the workplace in 2001.[33]

On-line retailing has exploded in the last several years as consumers have found this type of shopping convenient and, in many instances, less costly. Consumers can shop without leaving home, choose from a wide selection of merchants, use shopping comparison services to search the Web for the best price, and then have the items delivered to their doorsteps. As a result, on-line shopping continues to grow at a rapid pace. In fact, according to the National Retail Federation, e-retailers' sales increased by more than 45 percent in 2001 to $65 billion.[34] On-line

on-line retailing
A type of shopping available to consumers with personal computers and access to the Internet.

retailing is also increasing in popularity outside the United States. Read more about e-tailing worldwide in the "Global Perspectives" box.

Original Web-based retailers, like Amazon.com and CDNow, pioneered on-line retailing, selling merchandise more cheaply and conveniently than their brick-and-mortar competition. Both companies have continued to grow and prosper by offering outstanding customer service. Today, CDNow offers customers more than 500,000 CDs, videos, DVDs, and digital music downloads with forty-eight-hour delivery.[35] Similarly, Amazon.com, which opened for business in 1995 with a mission to transform book buying into the fastest, easiest, and most enjoyable shopping experience possible, has grown into a $3.12 billion company selling a combination of both new and used items, ranging from books and electronics to toys and hardware. Amazon has customers in more than 220 countries around the world.[36]

Most traditional retailers have now jumped on the Internet bandwagon, allowing shoppers to purchase the same merchandise found in their stores from their Web site. On-line retailing also fits well with traditional catalog companies, such as Lands' End and Eddie Bauer that already have established distribution networks. In a drastic turnabout in its retail strategy, computer software retailer Egghead recently closed all of its brick-and-mortar stores, moved its entire business onto the Web, and added ".com" to the end of its name. Software purchased at the company's site, **http://www.egghead.com**, can be downloaded directly to the purchaser's computer.

As the popularity of on-line retailing grows, it is becoming critical that retailers be on-line and that their stores, Web sites, and catalogs be integrated. Customers expect to find the same brands, products, and prices whether they purchase on-line, on the phone, or in a store. Therefore, retailers are increasingly using in-store kiosks to help tie the channels together for greater customer service. Retailer

---

GLOBAL PERSPECTIVES

On-Line Retailing Growing Worldwide

Consumers around the world are embracing on-line retailing. In fact, in 2001 about 54 percent of Internet users worldwide used the Internet to gather information about products and services, and 27 percent purchased on-line. What's more, analysts predict that the number of on-line shoppers will double in the next few years.

According to a recent survey, the items most commonly purchased on-line are books, CDs, videos, and computer games. Books are the number one best seller everywhere except Brazil and Canada where music tops the list. British and French shoppers like to purchase food and beverages online, and flowers are popular purchases in Switzerland. Swiss and Spanish shoppers purchase more financial services on-line than customers in other foreign countries.

Almost 60 percent of on-line shoppers have purchased from an on-line retailer in another country.

The main reason they do so is that the product is not available in their country, but finding a product at a lower price in another country also persuades some shoppers to go international.

So what should a retailer know about global on-line retailing? First, having a multichannel approach to retailing is important. Customers worldwide want the option of shopping on-line. Second, contrary to the belief that on-line shoppers are a unique audience, given Internet access, the same customers who shop in stores are buying on-line. Third, consumers expect the same product selection and customer service on-line that they receive in stores. And finally, customers will push retailers to make their Web site work the way they want it to work.

In addition, retailers interested in global on-line retailing can learn by studying the success of global on-line retailers like Amazon.com.

Amazon.com is the most popular place to shop on-line in the United States, United Kingdom, Canada, Italy, and Australia. In 2001, company sales in the United Kingdom, Germany, France, and Japan grew 81 percent, and more than 29 percent of total company sales were to international customers. The top reasons given for shopping at Amazon.com by customers everywhere are product selection, competitive prices, ease-of-use, product availability, and delivery speed.[37]

As Internet usage around the world increases, so will the number of on-line shoppers. How do you think that will affect traditional retailers? Will they learn to operate in the cyberworld, or will they try to compete against their on-line counterparts? Do you think the Internet will create a truly global retail marketplace?

Sylvan Learning

What do you need to do to become a Sylvan Learning franchiser? Visit the Web page to find out. Does anything surprise you?

http://www.sylvanlearning.com

On Line

and cataloger Williams-Sonoma, for example, recently linked its store gift registry to its Web site, allowing brides to see who has bought what in real time. Banana Republic stores in New York and Santa Monica, California, have kiosks where customers can order items that aren't on the shelves. Kiosks are even more popular among retailers that target younger, more computer-oriented customers. For example, Van's operates eight skate parks, which are a combination retail store, entertainment venue, and alternative sports arena. In addition to the skating rink, each park has a lounge area where customers can hang out, watch customized videos, and surf Van's Web site at a bank of kiosks. Each kiosk not only offers a complete selection of Van's footwear, apparel, and accessories, but also includes a full-service pro shop that sells over five hundred skateboards, bicycles, helmets, and other equipment and an information center with the latest tour, special event, and contest information.[38]

A relatively new phenomenon in on-line retailing is the success of auctions run by Internet companies like eBay and Amazon.com. With close to two million items for sale each day, ranging from antique clocks to car stereos, eBay leads the trend in cyberspace auctions. Internet auction services, like eBay, run the Web service and collect a token listing fee, plus a commission of 1 to 5 percent when a sale is completed. Recently, eBay announced a new joint venture with Sotheby's to offer fine art, rare coins, sports collectibles, jewelry, and antiques on-line. Each item carries a stamp of authenticity from Sotheby's or one of the 2,800 art and antiques dealers worldwide who have signed exclusive agreements with Sotheby's. The deal is a boost to eBay's fine arts and antiques division and will allow Sotheby's to continue on-line sales without the overhead expense of managing its own site.[39]

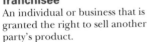

Franchising

⑤

Define franchising and describe its two basic forms

franchiser
The originator of a trade name, product, methods of operation, and so on, that grants operating rights to another party to sell its product.

franchisee
An individual or business that is granted the right to sell another party's product.

A *franchise* is a continuing relationship in which a franchiser grants to a franchisee the business rights to operate or to sell a product. The **franchiser** originates the trade name, product, methods of operation, and so on. The **franchisee**, in return, pays the franchiser for the right to use its name, product, or business methods. A franchise agreement between the two parties usually lasts for ten to twenty years, at which time the agreement can be renewed if both parties are agreeable.

To be granted the rights to a franchise, a franchisee usually pays an initial, one-time franchise fee. The amount of this fee depends solely on the individual franchiser, but it generally ranges from $5,000 to $150,000. In addition to this initial franchise fee, the franchisee is expected to pay weekly, biweekly, or monthly royalty fees, usually in the range of 3 to 7 percent of gross revenues. The franchisee may also be expected to pay advertising fees, which usually cover the cost of promotional materials and, if the franchise organization is large enough, regional or national advertising. A McDonald's franchise, for example, costs an initial $45,000 per store plus a monthly fee based upon the restaurant's sales performance and base rent. In addition, a new McDonald's franchisee can expect start-up costs for equipment and pre-opening expenses to range from $444,800 to $742,150. The size of the restaurant facility, area of the country, inventory, selection of kitchen equipment, signage, and style of decor and landscaping affect new restaurant costs.[40] While the dollar amount will vary depending on the type of franchise, fees such as these are typical for all major franchisers, including Burger King, Jani-King, Athlete's Foot, and Subway.

AP/WIDE WORLD PHOTOS

Franchising is most often associated with restaurants, but some of the most successful franchises of late are not even food related. Sylvan Learning Systems is an example. To learn more about Sylvan, do the On-Line activity at the top of this page.

Franchising is not new. General Motors has used this approach since 1898, and Rexall drugstores, since 1901. Today, there are over half a million franchised establishments in the United States, with combined sales approaching $1 trillion, or about 40 percent of all retail trade. Although franchised restaurants attract most of those dollars, hundreds of retail and service franchises, such as Alphagraphics Printshops, Mail Boxes, Etc., and Sylvan Learning Systems, also are thriving. Indeed, there are over 320,000 franchises in seventy-five industries. Industries expected to see real growth in franchising include home repair, business support services, automotive repairs, hair salons, children's services, and telecommunications.[41] Exhibit 11.3 lists some facts about some of the largest and best-known U.S. franchisers.

Two basic forms of franchises are used today: product and trade name franchising and business format franchising. In *product and trade name franchising*, a dealer agrees to sell certain products provided by a manufacturer or a wholesaler. This approach has been used most widely in the auto and truck, soft drink bottling, tire, and gasoline service industries. For example, a local tire retailer may hold a franchise to sell Michelin tires. Likewise, the Coca-Cola bottler in a particular area is a product and trade name franchisee licensed to bottle and sell Coca-Cola's soft drinks.

Largest U.S. Franchisers **Exhibit 11.3**

Franchiser	Type of Business	Total Units	Initial Investment
McDonald's Corporation Oak Brook, Illinois	Fast food	Franchised units: 18,361 Company-owned units: 5,262	$444,800–$742,150
Southland Corporation (7-Eleven) Dallas, Texas	Convenience stores	Franchised units: 15,572 Company-owned units: 2,666	Not available
Subway Sandwiches & Salads Milford, Connecticut	Fast food	Franchised units: 13,537 Company-owned units: 2	$66,200–$175,000
Burger King Corporation Miami, Florida	Fast food	Franchised units: 7,495 Company-owned units: 758	$73,000–$511,000
KFC Corporation Louisville, Kentucky	Fast food	Franchised units: 3,255 Company-owned units: 1,759	Not available
Pizza Hut, Inc. Dallas, Texas	Pizza	Franchised units: 4,200 Company-owned units: 2,800	Not available
Tandy Corporation Fort Worth, Texas	Consumer electronics	Franchised units: 6,779 Company-owned units: 1,890	$60,000+
Jani-King International Dallas, Texas	Janitorial, cleaning services	Franchised units: 7,700 Company-owned units: 35	$5,500–$80,000
Taco Bell Corporation Dallas, Texas	Fast food	Franchised units: 4,600 Company-owned units: 3,044	$200,000+
International Dairy Queen Minneapolis, Minnesota	Ice cream, fast food	Franchised units: 5,347 Company-owned units: NA	Not available

SOURCE: Franchise Opportunities Guide Online, International Franchise Association, Washington, D.C., http://www.franchise.org.

Business format franchising is an ongoing business relationship between a franchiser and a franchisee. Typically, a franchiser "sells" a franchisee the rights to use the franchiser's format or approach to doing business. This form of franchising has rapidly expanded since the 1950s through retailing, restaurant, food-service, hotel and motel, printing, and real estate franchises. Fast-food restaurants like McDonald's, Wendy's, and Burger King use this kind of franchising, as do other companies such as Hyatt Corporation, Unocal Corporation, and ExxonMobil Corporation. To be eligible to be a Domino's Pizza franchisee, you must have worked in a Domino's pizza store for at least one year. The company believes that after working in an existing location, you will have a better understanding of the company and its values and standards. Then potential franchisees must participate in a series of career development, franchise orientation, presentation skills, and franchise development programs.[42]

 Like other retailers, franchisers are seeking new growth abroad. Hundreds of U.S. franchisers have begun international expansion and are actively looking for foreign franchisees to open new locations. KFC operates approximately five thousand restaurants in the United States and 6,000 abroad in more than eighty countries around the world including Japan, Australia, China, Indonesia, and Saudi Arabia. An additional one thousand overseas locations are planned for the near future. KFC's parent company attributes the franchise's success to its ability to adapt to local cultures and tastes without losing control of quality and brand image.[43] The International Franchise Association now lists over fifty national franchise organizations in countries from Argentina to Zimbabwe.

Franchisers usually allow franchisees to alter their business format slightly in foreign markets. For example, some McDonald's franchisees in Germany sell beer, and in Japan they offer food items that appeal to Japanese tastes, such as steamed dumplings, curry with rice, and roast pork cutlet burgers with melted cheese. McDonald's franchisees in India serve mutton instead of beef because most Indians are Hindu, a religion whose followers believe cows are a sacred symbol of the source of life. The menu also features rice-based Vegetable Burgers made with peas, carrots, red pepper, beans, and Indian spices as well as Vegetable McNuggets. But, in spite of menu differences, McDonald's foreign franchisees still maintain the company's standards of service and cleanliness.

Retail Marketing Strategy

6

List the major tasks involved in developing a retail marketing strategy

Retailers must develop marketing strategies based on overall goals and strategic plans. Retailing goals might include more traffic, higher sales of a specific item, a more upscale image, or heightened public awareness of the retail operation. The strategies that retailers use to obtain their goals might include a sale, an updated decor, or a new advertisement. The key tasks in strategic retailing are defining and selecting a target market and developing the retailing mix to successfully meet the needs of the chosen target market.

Defining a Target Market

The first and foremost task in developing a retail strategy is to define the target market. This process begins with market segmentation, the topic of Chapter 6. Successful retailing has always been based on knowing the customer. Sometimes retailing chains flounder when management loses sight of the customers the stores should be serving. For example, during the 1990s Gap built a retail empire by offering updated, casual classics like white shirts and khaki pants that appealed to everyone from high school through middle age. But the company began losing customers in 1999 when it shifted toward trendier fashions with a limited appeal.

Analysts blame the chain's problems on losing focus and touch with its customers.[44]

Target markets in retailing are often defined by demographics, geographics, and psychographics. For instance, Bluefly.com, a discount fashion e-tailer, targets women who are in their thirties, have a higher-than-average income, read fashion magazines, and favor high-end designers. By understanding who its customer are, the company has been able to tailor its Web site to appeal specifically to its audience. The result is a higher sales rate than most e-tailers.[45]

Determining a target market is a prerequisite to creating the retailing mix. For example, Target's merchandising approach for sporting goods is to match its product assortment to the demographics of the local store and region. The amount of space devoted to sporting goods, as well as in-store promotions, also varies according to each store's target market. Similarly, Ann Taylor caters to working women in their thirties and forties—a group of customers notoriously pressed for time. Consequently, its stores offer a one-stop wardrobe solution with color-coordinated blouses, sweaters, skirts, and trousers that make it easy to create a wardrobe with just a few purchases.[46]

Choosing the Retailing Mix

Retailers combine the elements of the retailing mix to come up with a single retailing method to attract the target market. The **retailing mix** consists of six Ps: the four Ps of the marketing mix (product, place, promotion, and price) plus presentation and personnel (see Exhibit 11.4).

The combination of the six Ps projects a store's image, which influences consumers' perceptions. Using these impressions of stores, shoppers position one store against another. A retail marketing manager must make sure that the store's positioning is compatible with the target customers' expectations. As discussed at the beginning of the chapter, retail stores can be positioned on three broad dimensions: service provided by store personnel, product assortment, and price. Management should use everything else—place, presentation, and promotion—to fine-tune the basic positioning of the store.

retailing mix
A combination of the six Ps—product, place, promotion, price, presentation, and personnel—to sell goods and services to the ultimate consumer.

Exhibit 11.4

The Retailing Mix

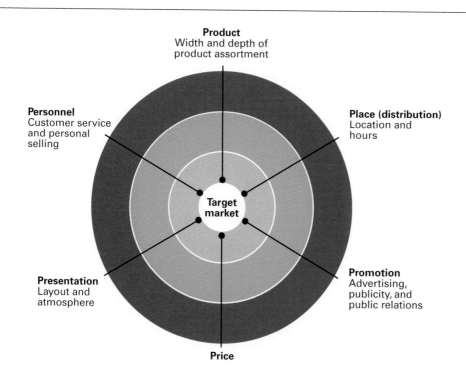

Product
Width and depth of product assortment

Place (distribution)
Location and hours

Personnel
Customer service and personal selling

Target market

Presentation
Layout and atmosphere

Promotion
Advertising, publicity, and public relations

Price

The Product Offering

product offering
The mix of products offered to the consumer by the retailer; also called the *product assortment* or *merchandise mix*.

The first element in the retailing mix is the **product offering**, also called the *product assortment* or *merchandise mix*. Retailers decide what to sell on the basis of what their target market wants to buy. They can base their decision on market research, past sales, fashion trends, customer requests, and other sources. A new technology, called *analytics*, uses complex mathematical models to help retailers make better product mix decisions. Early adopters of the technology, such as Dillard's, are using analytics to determine which products to stock at what price, how to manage markdowns, and how to advertise to draw target customers.[47]

Developing a product offering is essentially a question of the width and depth of the product assortment. *Width* refers to the assortment of products offered; *depth* refers to the number of different brands offered within each assortment. Price, store design, displays, and service are important to consumers in determining where to shop, but the most critical factor is merchandise selection. This reasoning also holds true for on-line retailers. Amazon.com, for instance, has ambitious plans to build the world's biggest on-line department store so that shoppers can get whatever they want with one click on their Web browsers. As with a traditional department store or mass merchandiser, Amazon offers considerable width in its product assortment with millions of different items, including books, music, toys, videos, tools and hardware, health and beauty aids, electronics, and software. Conversely, on-line specialty retailers, such as Garden.com, CDNow, and Blockbuster's Reel.com, focus on a single category of merchandise, hoping to attract loyal customers with a larger depth of products at lower prices and better customer service. Many on-line retailers purposely focus on single product line niches that could never garner enough foot traffic to support a traditional brick-and-mortar store. Mustardstore.com, for instance, offers 660 different gourmet mustards, while Fridgedoor.com sells 1,500 different types of refrigerator magnets to collectors.[48]

After determining what products will satisfy target customers' desires, retailers must find sources of supply and evaluate the products. When the right products are found, the retail buyer negotiates a purchase contract. The buying function can either be performed in-house or be delegated to an outside firm. The goods must then be moved from the seller to the retailer, which means shipping, storing, and stocking the inventory. The trick is to manage the inventory by cutting prices to move slow goods and by keeping adequate supplies of hot-selling items in stock. As in all good systems, the final step is to evaluate the entire process to seek more efficient methods and eliminate problems and bottlenecks.

One of the more efficient new methods of managing inventory and streamlining the way products are moved from supplier to distributor to retailer is called *efficient consumer response* (*ECR*). At the heart of ECR is *electronic data interchange* (*EDI*), the computer-to-computer exchange of information, at every stage of the supply chain. In a full implementation of ECR, products are scanned at the retail store when purchased, which updates the store's inventory lists. Headquarters then polls the stores to retrieve the data needed to produce an order. The vendor confirms the order, shipping date, and delivery time, then ships the order and transmits the invoice electronically. The item is received at the warehouse, scanned into inventory, and then sent to the store. The invoice and receiving data are reconciled, and payment via an electronic transfer of funds completes the process.

Many retailers are experimenting with or have successfully implemented ECR and EDI. Calendar Club, a mall-based kiosk retailer of calendars, uses ECR and EDI to get the right products at its kiosks, some of which sell more than one thousand calendars a day for the 120 days a year they are open. Calendar Club developed an ECR replenishment solution that allows the company to pick, pack, and ship unique replenishment orders for each kiosk every night.[49]

private brands
Brands that are designed and developed using the retailer's name.

As margins drop and competition intensifies, retailers are becoming ever more aware of the advantages of **private brands**, or those brands that are designed and developed using the retailer's name. Because the cost of goods typically makes up between 70 and 85 percent of a retailer's expenses, eliminating intermediaries can shave costs. As a result, prices of private-label goods are typically lower than for national brands, giving customers greater value. Private-label branding is not new. For decades, Sears has fashioned its Kenmore, Craftsman, and DieHard brands into household names. Lately, Wal-Mart has begun rolling out its own private-label brands, such as White Cloud paper products, Spring Valley nutritional supplements, Sam's American Choice laundry detergent, EverActive alkaline batteries, and EverStart auto batteries, with much success. Its Ol' Roy dog food and Sam's American Choice garden fertilizer are now the best-selling brands in their categories. As the nation's largest retailer, Wal-Mart's foray into private labels worries many brand marketers, such as Procter & Gamble, which manufactures Tide laundry detergent. Whereas Wal-Mart was once its biggest customer, the giant retailer is transforming itself into P&G's biggest competitor with the introduction of Sam's American Choice laundry soap that sells for 25 to 30 percent lower. And while Wal-Mart's private labels may not steal significant sales away from popular brands like Tide, in the long run smaller second- and third-tier brands that don't bring consumers to the shelves may have a difficult time surviving.[50]

Kroger Company
How extensive are Kroger's private-label brands? Visit its Web site to find out.
http://www.kroger.com/operations_manufacturing_about.htm

On Line

Promotion Strategy

Retail promotion strategy includes advertising, public relations and publicity, and sales promotion. The goal is to help position the store in consumers' minds. Retailers design intriguing ads, stage special events, and develop promotions aimed at their target markets. For example, today's grand openings are a carefully orchestrated blend of advertising, merchandising, goodwill, and glitter. All the elements of an opening—press coverage, special events, media advertising, and store displays—are carefully planned.

Retailers' advertising is carried out mostly at the local level, although retail giants like Sears and JCPenney can advertise nationally. Local advertising by retailers usually provides specific information about their stores, such as location, merchandise, hours, prices, and special sales. In contrast, national retail advertising generally focuses on image. For example, Target has used its "sign of the times" advertising campaign to effectively position itself as the "chic place to buy cheap."

Target's advertising campaign also takes advantage of cooperative advertising, another popular retail advertising practice. Traditionally, marketers would pay retailers to feature their products in store mailers, or a marketer would develop a TV campaign for the product and simply tack on several retailers' names at the end. But Target's advertising makes use of a more collaborative trend in cooperative advertising by integrating products such as Tide laundry detergent, Tums antacids, or Coca-Cola into the actual campaign.[51] Another common form of cooperative advertising involves promotion of exclusive products. For instance, Kmart's advertising campaign for its Martha Stewart product line has the dual role of promoting the products and attracting customers to the store.

Many retailers are forgoing media advertising these days in favor of direct-mail or frequent shopper programs. Direct-mail and catalog programs are luring many retailers, which hope they will prove to be a cost-effective means of increasing brand loyalty and spending by core customers. Nordstrom, for example, mails catalogs featuring brand-name and private-brand clothing, shoes, and accessories to target the shop-at-home crowd. Home repair outlets such as Lowe's and Home Depot have also used direct mail, often around holidays when people have time off to complete needed repairs. Restaurants and small retailers have successfully used frequent diner or frequent shopper programs for years. Now many retail chains, like Gap, Victoria's Secret, and Eddie Bauer, are offering frequent shopper programs with perks ranging from gift certificates to special "members only" sale prices. For example, customers with a Victoria's Secret Angel credit card are offered monthly specials on store merchandise, including items that generally are not put on sale to the public.

The Proper Location

The retailing axiom "location, location, location" has long emphasized the importance of place to the retail mix. The location decision is important first because the retailer is making a large, semipermanent commitment of resources that can reduce its future flexibility. Second, the location will affect the store's future growth and profitability.

Site location begins by choosing a community. Important factors to consider are the area's economic growth potential, the amount of competition, and geography. For instance, retailers like T. J. Maxx, Wal-Mart, and Toys "R" Us build stores in areas where the population is growing. Often these large retailers will build stores in new communities that are still under development. On the other hand, while population growth is an important consideration for fast-food restaurants, most also look for an area with other fast-food restaurants because being located in clusters helps to draw customers for each restaurant. Finally, for many retailers geography remains the most important factor in choosing a community. For example, Starbucks coffee looks for densely populated urban communities for its stores, Talbots looks for locations near upper-class neighborhoods, and Buckle stores look for locations in small, underserved cities.

After settling on a geographic region or community, retailers must choose a specific site. In addition to growth potential, the important factors are neighborhood socioeconomic characteristics, traffic flows, land costs, zoning regulations, and public transportation. A particular site's visibility, parking, entrance and exit locations, accessibility, and safety and security issues are other variables contributing to site selection success. Additionally, a retailer should consider how its store would fit into the surrounding environment. Retail decision makers probably would not locate a Dollar General store next door to a Neiman Marcus department store.

One final decision about location faces retailers: whether to have a freestanding unit or to become a tenant in a shopping center or mall.

Freestanding Stores An isolated, freestanding location can be used by large retailers like Wal-Mart, Kmart, or Target and sellers of shopping goods like furniture and cars because they are "destination" stores, or those stores consumers will purposely plan to visit. In other words, customers will seek them out. An isolated store location may have the advantages of low site cost or rent and no nearby competitors. On the other hand, it may be hard to attract customers to a freestanding location, and no other retailers are around to share costs.

Freestanding units are increasing in popularity as retailers strive to make their stores more convenient to access, more enticing to shop, and more profitable. Freestanding sites now account for more than half of the millions of square feet of retail construction starts in the United States as more and more retailers are deciding not to locate in pedestrian malls. Perhaps the greatest reason for developing a freestanding site is greater visibility. Retailers often feel they get lost in huge centers and malls, but freestanding units can help stores develop an identity with shoppers. The ability to grow at faster rates through freestanding buildings has also propelled the surge toward stand-alone units. Retailers like The Sports Authority, Linens & Things, and Bed, Bath & Beyond often choose to be freestanding in order to achieve their expansion objectives. An aggressive expansion plan may not allow time to wait for shopping centers to be built. Similarly, drugstore chains like Walgreens and Rite-Aid have been aggressively relocating their existing mall and shopping center stores to freestanding sites, especially street corner sites for drive-through accessibility.

Shopping Centers The tremendous boom in shopping centers began after World War II, as the U.S. population started migrating to the suburbs. The first shopping centers were *strip centers*, typically located along a busy street. They usually included a supermarket, a variety store, and perhaps a few specialty stores. Essentially unplanned business districts, these strip centers remain popular.

Next, the small *community shopping centers* emerged, with one or two small department store branches, more specialty shops, one or two restaurants, and several apparel stores. These centers offer a broader variety of shopping, specialty, and convenience goods, provide large off-street parking lots, and usually include 75,000 to 300,000 square feet of retail space.

Finally, along came the huge *regional malls*, generally offering 400,000 to 800,000 square feet of shopping space. Regional malls are either entirely enclosed or roofed to allow shopping in any weather. Many are landscaped with trees, fountains, sculptures, and the like to enhance the shopping environment. They have acres of free parking. The *anchor stores* or *generator stores* (JCPenney, Sears, or major department stores) are usually located at opposite ends of the mall to create heavy foot traffic. Las Vegas's Fashion Show Mall takes the concept to the extreme. When renovations are completed, the mall will span two million square feet with eight anchor stores including Neiman Marcus, Lord & Taylor, and Nordstrom.[52]

According to shopping center developers, *lifestyle centers* are now emerging as the newest generation of shopping centers offering time-pressed consumers a more convenient alternative to malls. These new open-air shopping centers are targeted to upper-income shoppers with an aversion for "the mall" and seek to create an atmosphere that is part neighborhood park and part urban shopping center. Lifestyle centers generally feature approximately 300,000 square feet of upscale retail space occupied by trendy restaurants and specialty retailers like Pottery Barn and Williams-Sonoma. Other attractions include expensive landscaping and convenient parking. Developers expect that there will be more than fifty lifestyle centers around the country by 2004.[53]

Locating in a community shopping center or regional mall offers several advantages. First, the facilities are designed to attract shoppers. Second, the shopping environment, anchor stores, and "village square" activities draw customers. Third, ample parking is available. Fourth, the center or mall projects a unified image. Fifth, tenants also share the expenses of the mall's common area and promotions for the whole mall. Finally, malls can target different demographic groups. Some malls are considered upscale; others are aimed at people shopping for bargains.

Locating in a shopping center or mall does have disadvantages. These include expensive leases, the chance that common promotion efforts will not attract customers to a particular store, lease restrictions on merchandise carried and hours of operation, the anchor stores' domination of the tenants' association, and the possibility of having direct competitors within the same facility. Consumers have also become more pressed for time in recent years and have decreased the number of visits and the time they spend in malls in favor of more convenient stand-alone stores and neighborhood centers. Faced with this trend, mall developers have improved the layout of many malls to make it more convenient for customers to shop. For instance, the RiverTown Crossings center in Grandville, Michigan, clusters competing stores, like Abercrombie Kids, GapKids, Gymboree, and other kids' clothing stores in one section of the mall to accommodate time-strapped parents.[54]

Retail Prices

Another important element in the retailing mix is price. It is important to understand that retailing's ultimate goal is to sell products to consumers and that the right price is critical in ensuring sales. Because retail prices are usually based on the cost of the merchandise, an essential part of pricing is efficient and timely buying.

Price is also a key element in a retail store's positioning strategy and classification. Higher prices often indicate a level of quality and help reinforce the prestigious image of retailers, as they do for Lord & Taylor, Saks Fifth Avenue, Gucci, Cartier, and Neiman Marcus. On the other hand, discounters and off-price retailers, such as Target and T. J. Maxx, offer a good value for the money. There are even stores, such as Dollar Tree, where everything costs shoppers one dollar. Dollar

How can a company create an atmosphere on its Web site? Visit the pages of some of your favorite retailers to see if they have been able to re-create the store atmosphere on the Internet.

◄ ►   **On Line**

Tree's single-price-point strategy is aimed at getting higher-income customers to make impulse purchases through what analysts call the "wow factor"—the excitement of discovering that an item costs only a dollar.[55]

A pricing trend among American retailers that seems to be here to stay is *everyday low pricing*, or EDLP. Introduced to the retail industry by Wal-Mart, EDLP offers consumers a low price all the time rather than holding periodic sales on merchandise. Even large retail giants, like Federated Department Stores, parent of Macy's and Bloomingdale's, have phased out deep discounts and sales in favor of lower prices every day. Similarly, Gap reduced prices on denim jeans, denim shirts, socks, and other items to protect and broaden the company's share of the casual clothes market. Supermarkets such as Albertson's and Winn Dixie have also found success in EDLP.

Presentation of the Retail Store

The presentation of a retail store helps determine the store's image and positions the retail store in consumers' minds. For instance, a retailer that wants to position itself as an upscale store would use a lavish or sophisticated presentation.

The main element of a store's presentation is its **atmosphere**, the overall impression conveyed by a store's physical layout, decor, and surroundings. The atmosphere might create a relaxed or busy feeling, a sense of luxury or of efficiency, a friendly or cold attitude, a sense of organization or of clutter, or a fun or serious mood. For example, the look at Express stores is designed to make suburban shoppers feel as though they have just strolled into a Parisian boutique. Signage is often in French, and the background music has a European flair. Likewise, REI sporting-goods stores feature indoor rock-climbing walls, bike test trails, and rain rooms for testing outdoor gear.

More often these days retailers are adding an element of entertainment to their store atmosphere. The Nike Town store in Chicago looks more like a museum than a traditional retail store. The three-story space displays products amid life-size Michael Jordan statues and glassed-in relics like baseball legend Nolan Ryan's shoes. A History of Air exhibit explains the pockets of air on the bottom of some Nike shoes. A video theater plays Nike commercials and short films featuring Nike gear.

The layout of retail stores is a key factor in their success. Layout is planned so that all space in the store is used effectively, including aisles, fixtures, merchandise displays, and nonselling areas. Effective store layout ensures the customer's shopping ease and convenience, but it also has a powerful influence on customer traffic patterns and purchasing behavior. For instance, Kohl's is known for its unique circular store layout, which encourages customers to pass all of a store's departments to reach the checkout lanes. The stores are smaller than most department stores but have a wide aisle designed to allow plenty of room for customers and shopping carts. Each department is limited to five display racks on the main aisle. Displays are spaced widely apart and are set at varying heights so that a customer can see everything in the department, including wall displays, from the main aisle. To further enhance the store's clean crisp presentation, merchandise is displayed from light to dark, which research suggests is most pleasing to the eye. Finally, to encourage last-minute, impulse purchases, Kohl's displays low-cost items at the checkout register. The result

atmosphere
The overall impression conveyed by a store's physical layout, decor, and surroundings.

© DAVID SAMUEL ROBBINS/CORBIS

Retailers use the physical space of the store to entice customers to buy merchandise. REI encourages customers to try out the rock-climbing wall at its flagship Seattle, Washington, store.

of the store layout is a $279 sales per square foot average (sales per square foot is a standard industry measurement).[56]

Layout also includes where products are placed in the store. Many technologically advanced retailers are using a technique called *market-basket analysis* to analyze the huge amounts of data collected through their point-of-purchase scanning equipment. The analysis looks for products that are commonly purchased together to help retailers remerchandise their stores to place products in the right places. Wal-Mart uses market-basket analysis to determine where in the store to stock products for customer convenience. Bananas are placed not only in the produce section but also in the cereal aisle. Kleenex tissues are in the paper-goods aisle and also mixed in with the cold medicines. Measuring spoons are in the housewares and also hanging next to Crisco shortening. During October, flashlights are not only in the hardware aisle but also with the Halloween costumes.[57]

These are the most influential factors in creating a store's atmosphere:

- *Employee type and density:* Employee type refers to an employee's general characteristics—for instance, neat, friendly, knowledgeable, or service oriented. Density is the number of employees per thousand square feet of selling space. A discounter like Kmart has a low employee density that creates a "do-it-yourself," casual atmosphere. In contrast, Neiman Marcus's density is much higher, denoting readiness to serve the customer's every whim. Too many employees and not enough customers, however, can convey an air of desperation and intimidate customers.

- *Merchandise type and density:* The type of merchandise carried and how it is displayed add to the atmosphere the retailer is trying to create. A prestigious retailer like Saks or Marshall Field's carries the best brand names and displays them in a neat, uncluttered arrangement. Discounters and off-price retailers may sell some well-known brands, but many carry seconds or out-of-season goods. Their merchandise may be stacked so high that it falls into the aisles, helping create the impression that "We've got so much stuff, we're practically giving it away."

- *Fixture type and density:* Fixtures can be elegant (rich woods), trendy (chrome and smoked glass), or consist of old, beat-up tables, as in an antiques store. The fixtures should be consistent with the general atmosphere the store is trying to create. Gap creates a relaxed and uncluttered atmosphere by displaying its merchandise on tables and shelves, rather than on traditional pipe racks, allowing customers to see and touch the merchandise more easily. Adding technology as a fixture is a recent successful trend in coffee shops and lounges. The most popular examples include adding PCs to provide Internet access to customers and ultimately get them to remain in the store longer. E-Trade's flagship bank branch is technologically hip with computer workstations and flat-panel televisions tuned to financial networks instead of the traditional teller windows and doctor's-office-style waiting areas.[58]

- *Sound:* Sound can be pleasant or unpleasant for a customer. Classical music at a nice Italian restaurant helps create ambience, just as country-and-western music does at a truck stop. Music can also entice customers to stay in the store longer and buy more or eat quickly and leave a table for others. For instance, rapid music tends to make people eat more, chew less, and take bigger bites whereas slow music prompts people to dine more leisurely and eat less. Retailers can tailor their musical atmosphere to their shoppers' demographics and the merchandise they're selling. Music can control the pace of the store traffic, create an image, and attract or direct the shopper's attention. For example, Harrods in London features music by live harpists, pianists, and marching bagpipers to create different atmospheres in different departments. Coffee shops are also getting into the music business as are theme restaurants like Hard Rock Cafe, Planet Hollywood, Harley Davidson Cafe, and Rainforest Cafe, which turn

This enormous frog sculpture crowns the entrance to the Rainforest Cafe in Chicago, Illinois. Coupled with the giant toadstools that flank the doors, the sculptures that decorate the outside of the restaurant create an impression of fun and whimsy.

© RICHARD CUMMINS/CORBIS

eating a hamburger and fries into an experience. Au Bon Pain, Starbucks, and Victoria's Secret have all sold copies of their background music, hoping that the music will remind consumers of the feeling of being in their stores.

- *Odors:* Smell can either stimulate or detract from sales. The wonderful smell of pastries and breads entices bakery customers. Conversely, customers can be repulsed by bad odors such as cigarette smoke, musty smells, antiseptic odors, and overly powerful room deodorizers. If a grocery store pumps in the smell of baked goods, sales in that department increase threefold. Department stores have pumped in fragrances that are pleasing to their target market, and the response has been favorable. Not surprisingly, retailers are increasingly using fragrance as a key design element, as important as layout, lighting, and background music. Research suggests that people evaluate merchandise more positively, spend more time shopping, and are generally in a better mood when an agreeable odor is present. Retailers use fragrances as an extension of their retail strategy. The Rainforest Cafe, for instance, pumps fresh-flower extracts into its retail sections. Similarly, the Christmas Store at Disney World, which is open year-round, is infused with the scents of evergreen and spiced apple cider. Jordan's Furniture in Massachusetts and New Hampshire uses the scent of pine in its country-style sections to make the environment more interesting and encourage customers to linger longer.[59]

- *Visual factors:* Colors can create a mood or focus attention and therefore are an important factor in atmosphere. Red, yellow, and orange are considered warm colors and are used when a feeling of warmth and closeness is desired. Cool colors like blue, green, and violet are used to open up closed-in places and create an air of elegance and cleanliness. Some colors are better for display. For instance, diamonds appear most striking against black or dark blue velvet. The lighting can also have an important effect on store atmosphere. Jewelry is best displayed under high-intensity spotlights and cosmetics under more natural lighting. Many retailers have found that natural lighting, either from windows or skylights, can lead to increased sales. Outdoor lighting can also affect consumer patronage. Consumers often are afraid to shop after dark in many areas and prefer strong lighting for safety. The outdoor facade of the store also adds to its ambience and helps create favorable first impressions by shoppers. For example, on the top of the roof over the door at Cup o' Joe specialty coffee shop in Lennox Town Square, Columbus, Ohio, sits a twelve-foot-wide by six-foot-tall coffee mug. The coffee shop's designers used the exaggerated storefront to call attention to its site, which would have otherwise gotten lost amid its big-box neighbors Old Navy, Target, and an AMC Theater.[60]

Personnel and Customer Service

People are a unique aspect of retailing. Most retail sales involve a customer–salesperson relationship, if only briefly. When customers shop at a grocery store, the cashiers check and bag their groceries. When customers shop at a prestigious clothier, the salesclerks may help select the styles, sizes, and colors. They may also assist in the fitting process, offer alteration services, wrap purchases, and even offer a glass of champagne. Sales personnel provide their customers with the amount of service prescribed in the retail strategy of the store.

Retail salespeople serve another important selling function: They persuade shoppers to buy. They must therefore be able to persuade customers that what they are selling is what the customer needs. Salespeople are trained in two common selling techniques: trading up and suggestion selling. Trading up means persuading customers to buy a higher-priced item than they originally intended to buy. To avoid selling customers something they do not need or want, however, salespeople should take care when practicing trading-up techniques. Suggestion selling, a common practice among most retailers, seeks to broaden customers' original purchases with related items. For example, McDonald's cashiers may ask customers whether they would like a hot apple pie with their hamburger and fries. Suggestion selling and trading up should always help shoppers recognize true needs rather than sell them unwanted merchandise. To learn about problems retailers sometimes have with overzealous employees, read about racial profiling by retailers in the "Ethics in Marketing" box.

Providing great customer service is one of the most challenging elements in the retail mix because customer expectations for service are so varied. What customers expect in a department store is very different from their expectations for a discount store. Customer expectations also change. Ten years ago, shoppers wanted personal one-on-one attention. Today, most customers are happy to help themselves as long as they can easily find what they need. For example, Home Depot has always had a reputation for great customer service. Shoppers enjoy talking to the store's knowledgeable staff in the busy, do-it-yourself, warehouse atmosphere. But as store sales increased, the company began receiving customer feedback that the salespeople seemed too busy to help and the stores were too cluttered. To meet customers' new

ETHICS IN MARKETING

Racial Profiling in Retail

As discussed in the chapter, in most cases retailers rely on their salespeople to represent the company to the customer. Therefore, to make customers feel welcome and appreciated, retailers look for salespeople who are courteous and outgoing. But what if some customers don't feel welcome?

As racial profiling has become an important issue in the United States, many African Americans say they often feel unwelcome in retail stores and restaurants. According to a recent Gallup poll, 46 percent of African Americans feel they have been mistreated in stores or malls, and 39 percent feel they have been treated unfairly in restaurants. Whether or not the perception is reality, rumors of discrimination are harmful to a retailer, and if the perception is widespread, it can have a negative effect on business.

Why do so many African Americans feel unwelcome, and what can retailers do about it? One reason may be that many retail and restaurant owners hire off-duty police officers to provide security. Police officers are trained to be police officers, not salespeople.

They are not trained to believe the customer is always right, and they are not hired to help customers. Instead, they may be there to make customers feel safe or to prevent shoplifting. In other words, they are in the store to discourage wrongdoing. And if the officers believe that African Americans are more likely to cause trouble, they may watch African American customers more closely, thereby creating the customers' perception of being mistreated.

Several high-profile incidents of racial profiling involving off-duty police officers have been in the news. In one of the most blatant examples, an off-duty police officer who was working as a security guard at an Eddie Bauer warehouse sale confronted an African American teenager and accused him of stealing the shirt he was wearing. When the customer explained that he had purchased the shirt at the sale the previous day, the officer insisted that he remove the shirt and come back with the receipt to prove he had purchased it. The incident led to community outrage, a lawsuit, and an out-of-court settlement. Similarly, Dil-

lard's currently faces multiple lawsuits involving charges of racial profiling by off-duty police officers.

As a result of these incidents, Eddie Bauer and many other retailers have decided not to use off-duty police officers for store security. But to be fair, not all racial profiling accusations are the result of off-duty police officers. For instance, community activists in the Detroit area claim that civilian security guards at both Lord & Taylor and Kroger engage in racial profiling. In fact, all it takes for customers to feel mistreated is one salesperson who shadows or asks for additional identification from minority customers. Many large chains are following Eddie Bauer's lead and have started including diversity training in their employee orientation programs.[61]

What do you think? Can retailers prevent racial profiling in their stores? How important is it for retailers to be proactive about racial profiling? Is the risk of racial profiling by security justified by the fact that retailers lose almost $8.5 billion annually to shoplifters?

expectations, the company recently changed its store policy to free up staff time to help customers and has eliminated merchandise displays from the aisles.[62]

 Customer service is also critical for on-line retailers. On-line shoppers expect a retailer's Web site to be easy to use, products to be available, and returns to be simple. Therefore, customer-friendly retailers like Bluefly.com design their sites to give their customers the information they need such as what's new and what's on sale. Other companies like Amazon.com and LandsEnd.com offer product recommendations and personal shoppers. Many on-line retailers have also begun including a return envelope with all orders to make returns easier for the customer.[63]

Global Retailing

7

Discuss the challenges of expanding retailing operations into global markets

It is no accident that U.S. retailers are now testing their store concepts on a global basis. With the battle for market share among domestic retailers showing no sign of abating and growth prospects dismal, mature retailers are looking for growth opportunities in the growing consumer economies of other countries. American retailers have made quite an impact on the global market, as Exhibit 11.5 displays. Seven of the top ten global retailers are from the

Exhibit 11.5

Ranking of Global Retailers

Rank	Retailer	Country of Origin	Format	2001 Retail Sales ($ millions)
1	Wal-Mart	U.S.	Discount/Warehouse	217,799
2	Carrefour	France	Cash & Carry/Convenience/Discount/Hypermarket/Supermarket	61,565
3	Ahold	Netherlands	Cash & Carry/Convenience/Discount/Drug/Hypermarket	57,976
4	Home Depot	U.S.	DIY/Specialty	53,553
5	Kroger	U.S.	Convenience/Department/Discount/Drug/Supermarket	50,098
6	Metro	Germany	Department/DIY/Hypermakret/Specialty/Supermarket/Warehouse/Mail Order	43,357
7	Target	U.S.	Department/Discount	39,455
8	Albertson's	U.S.	Drug/Supermarket	37,931
9	Kmart	U.S.	Discount	36,151
10	Sears, Roebuck	U.S.	Department/Mail Order/Specialty	35,843

SOURCE: Nation Retail Federation, "Top 200 Global Retailers 2003," http://www.stores.org. © 2003 NRF Enterprises, Inc. Used with permission.

United States, with Wal-Mart holding the top spot with sales about three times that of its nearest competitors.

Several events have made expansion across national borders more feasible. First, the spread of communication networks and mass media has homogenized tastes and product preferences to some extent around the world. As a result, the casual American lifestyle and the products that symbolize it, such as Levi's jeans and Nike sportswear, have become more appealing. Second, the lowering of trade barriers and tariffs has facilitated the expansion of American retailers to Mexico, Canada, and Europe. Last, high growth potential in underserved markets is also luring U.S. retailers abroad into Latin America, South America, and Asia. China contains a quarter of the world's population and only recently opened its markets to outside concerns. Although the majority of China's population still lacks adequate consumer spending power, projections call for the country's economy to eclipse all others in the next twenty-five years.

Before taking the plunge into the international retailing arena, the soundest advice retailers can heed is to do their homework (see Exhibit 11.6). Analysts from consulting firm Ernst & Young count among the prerequisites for going global a secure and profitable position domestically, a long-term perspective

Factors Used to Analyze Global Retail Markets **Exhibit 11.6**

- **Market size and economics:** Analyzing factors such as population and demographic trends, economics (including gross domestic product and consumer spending), and political trends that could make or break the success of a retailer in a foreign country. For instance, in China the central government has been urging middle-income Chinese to buy their own housing. For retailers, this means plenty of new apartments and homes to fill with more electronics, bigger refrigerators and kitchens for edibles, and roomier closets.

- **Infrastructure and distribution:** Building global supply chains and securing qualified labor can be particularly challenging in emerging markets. Expansion to Canada and Mexico is simpler logistically for U.S. retailers than transporting their stores across oceans. In many developing countries such as China, underdeveloped transportation infrastructures as well as few logistics providers pose daunting distribution challenges to retailers trying to stock products in stores.

- **Competition:** Assessing the current competitive landscape and how the retailer could bring innovations to the market. Compared to the United States, Mexico, for instance, is considered grossly understored; the country has less than 550 square feet of food and apparel stores per thousand people, compared to 20,000 square feet per thousand people in the United States. Similarly, Europe has a higher percentage of independent, mom-and-pop operations. The highly fragmented European market appears ripe for well-capitalized U.S. big-box retailers.

- **Operations:** Assessing how operational concerns, such as real estate, labor, and inventory, will affect the success of an overseas unit. For instance, labor laws vary drastically from country to country. Cultural differences also affect holidays, number of vacation days for employees, and hours of operation. U.S. retail stores are open an average of seventy hours a week whereas retail stores in Greece are open only about forty-six hours a week.

- **Financial and tax reporting:** Addressing issues such as currency fluctuations, the hedging of risks, and how a region's tax regime and incentives would fit in to a retailer's overall tax strategy. A lot of retailers are entering Brazil and Chile because their markets are open and their business economies and financial systems are more "Western-like."

- **Merchandise acceptability:** Conducting research to understand local consumer needs, preferences, and buying habits, and then reinventing the assortment to match the culture of the region. For instance, back-to-school sales occur in April in Japan, and August in Europe is a traditionally slow retailing month because most Europeans are on vacation. When IKEA came to the United States, it learned that it needed to offer larger beds, furniture with larger drawers, and different assortments of kitchen utensils.

- **Partnering capability:** Considering the availability of suitable partners in a desired country or region. Starbucks coffee typically picks distribution and supply partners before it decides on a country or region because poor strategic alliances or logistics partnering can make or break a retail operation.

SOURCE: From "Global Retailing '97," Ernst & Young special report for *Chain Store Age*, December 1997. Reprinted by permission from Chain Store Age. Copyright Lebhar-Friedman, Inc., 425 Park Avenue, NY, NY 10022.

because many foreign operations take a long time to set up and even longer to turn a profit, and a global strategy that meshes with the retailer's overall corporate strategy. Retailers should first determine what their core competency is, whether it be low prices, a distinctive fashion look, or excellent customer service, and determine whether this differentiation is what the local market wants. For instance, Gap's international success is attributable to its allegiance to the "American casual" formula that made it so successful in its home market, including the Gap name. Similarly, wherever shoppers travel, they can reasonably expect to experience Wal-Mart's friendliness, the quality, service, and cleanliness of McDonald's.

In addition to keeping their core strengths when going global, retailers need to understand the cultural differences of new markets because the differences can affect almost every area of the retail mix. Differences in color, style, or taste preferences can affect a company's product choices. For example, lime green is a popular color on the sunny beaches of St. Tropez, but customers in northern Europe feel it leaves them looking sickly. Tight skirts are popular in France but not in countries like Holland where women often bicycle to work. Cultural differences also should be taken into consideration on all location, presentation, and promotion decisions. For instance, Canadian retailer Pop Shoppes failed in the United States because most U.S. consumers don't call soft drinks pop and therefore failed to understand what the store sold. Differences in supply chain, real estate, and employment costs can undermine a retailer's price strategy. And, as always, great customer service depends on a retailer's understanding of customer expectations.[64]

Trends in Retailing

8

Describe future trends in retailing

Predicting the future is always risky, but the use of entertainment to lure customers, a shift toward providing greater convenience to receive the patronage of today's precision shoppers, and the emergence of customer management programs to foster loyalty and enhance communications with a retailer's best customers are three of the more important trends for retailing's future.

Entertainment

Adding entertainment to the retail environment is one of the most popular strategies in retailing in recent years. Small retailers as well as national chains are using entertainment to set themselves apart from the competition.

Entertainment is not limited to music, videos, fashion shows, or guest appearances by soap opera stars or book authors. Entertainment includes anything that makes shoppers have a good time, stimulates their senses or emotions, and gets them into a store, keeps them there, and encourages them to buy and to keep coming back. The quiet, comfortable couches and cafes of bookstores and combination book and music retailers such as Barnes & Noble, Books-a-Million, Borders, and Media Play are entertaining as are the Gershwin tunes coming from the piano in a Nordstrom's atrium. Video screens and loud, energetic music capture the attention of many younger consumers. To attract affluent, young professionals, Brooks Brothers stores host in-store cocktail parties with margaritas, food, and store discounts. Similarly, many high-end retailers like Bergdorf Goodman are using exclusive trunk shows to attract affluent women in their thirties and forties to shop. Trunk shows also allow retailers to increase sales of full-price items.[65]

Convenience and Efficiency

Today's consumer is increasingly looking for ways to shop more quickly and efficiently. The trend not only reflects the increase in women working full- or part-time but also can be attributed to all consumers being more stretched for time. Consumers are visiting malls only about half as often as they used to, and the number of stores they visit when they get there is down substantially, too. According to a recent survey, 61 percent of shoppers said that convenience was the most important factor in deciding where to shop. Shoppers in the same study also indicated that they are shopping in only 1.9 stores per week, compared to 2.9 the year before.[66] Therefore, retailers must make sure that customers have a positive experience every time they shop.

Retailers must also learn to better manage the patronage experience. Consumers are no longer satisfied when a store merely meets their expectations. They desire delightful experiences brought about by retailers who anticipate consumers' expectations and go the extra mile to exceed them on a regular basis. Dimensions in which retailers can far exceed expectations include shopping assistance, the buying process, delivery and installation of the product, service after the sale, and disposal and renewal of the product.

Examples of ways this can be done include offering amenities such as pick-up service for shoppers who do not want to fight traffic, baby-sitting services, free drinks and refreshments during shopping, and preferred shopper parking spaces. For example, IGA supermarkets offer parents a child-care center where they can leave their kids while buying groceries. The play area includes computers, puzzles and crayons, television, and other entertainment activities. Drugstores are offering flu shots, cholesterol screenings, and in-store health clinics. In addition, retailers that maintain records of consumers' preferences in product features are able to offer individualized attention to consumers during product selection. Sales associates can preselect items that are most likely to be preferred by the customer. For example, the store's records may indicate that a consumer prefers a particular style of suit, leading the sales associate to show the consumer the new suits for the season in that style.

To improve customer service, many retailers are also implementing multichannel strategies. Retailers like Eddie Bauer and Talbots are using their catalogs and Web sites to familiarize customers with their merchandise selection and then offering special in-store incentives designed to entice customers to the store. Once inside the store, customers have access to catalogs and Web sites for purchasing items out-of-stock at the time of their visit.[67] Retailers that successfully integrate multiple channels are finding that doing so increases sales in each channel.

Experts predict that in the future retailers, especially supermarkets, will become true marketers rather than marketers that act as distribution centers. For instance, packaged goods and staples won't be sold in supermarkets. Instead, they will be delivered directly to consumers at home, within fifteen minutes of an order's placement, freeing shoppers to visit stores for things they enjoy buying—fresh produce, meats, and the fixings for a dinner party. Consumers who need staples would use hand scanners to record products' bar codes and update electronic shopping lists. Magazine ads would also carry bar codes so that consumers could scan pages to put new products on their lists. Already, Frigidaire has produced a concept model refrigerator that comes complete with a video screen and bar-code scanner, which consumers can use to reorder products by scanning their used-up container across the door. The scanner picks up the UPC and automatically reorders a fresh supply. The video screen also connects to the Internet, allowing consumers to check e-mail, pay bills, check their bank account, and shop on-line.[68]

Customer Management

Today, prime locations and unique merchandise are not the primary indicators of success they once were in the retail environment. Instead, retailers are recognizing that customer equity is one of the only ways to sustain true competitive advantage. Through customer management strategies, leading retailers are intensifying their

Entertainment in the retail environment is at its pinnacle in the Donna Karan New York boutique. Customers sit at a coffee bar while a grid of televisions provides the single screen for a fashion show broadcast.

efforts to identify, satisfy, retain, and maximize the value of their best customers. Enabled by database technology, these forward-focused retailers are employing strategies designed to capture customers' share of mind, wallet, and time.

Emerging customer management strategies that retailers are embracing include customer relationship marketing, loyalty programs, and clienteling. Regardless of the strategy used, the intent is the same—to foster loyalty and develop an ongoing dialogue with a retailer's best customers. *Customer relationship marketing (CRM)* originated out of the need to more accurately target a fragmented customer base that was becoming increasingly more difficult to reach with mass advertising vehicles like television and newspapers.

Armed with richer customer databases and the technology to gather and analyze customer and sales data, retailers are now taking active measures to develop loyalty programs that identify and reward their best customers. Sears' KidVantage program, for example, provides savings to members with young children. Similarly, specialty retailer Loehmann's, which offers women's designer apparel at discounted prices, uses data from its Insider Club to understand what customers are purchasing, when they are purchasing, and the type of events they prefer. In addition to periodic coupon and members-only savings, Insider Club members, currently 1.6 million strong, are notified of items and sales events. Loehmann's also launched a cobranded Insider Club Platinum Visa Card that provides a rebate on purchases.

Another approach to managing and building long-term relationships with best customers is *clienteling*. Saks Fifth Avenue, for example, strongly emphasizes personal contact with customers on the part of managers and sales associates. Associates collect and maintain detailed electronic client profiles that can be used to provide enhanced service. Sales associates are also encouraged to service clients across all departments so that the associates, already familiar with size and style preferences, can address clients' complete wardrobe needs as opposed to merely selling merchandise from their assigned department.

CONNECT IT

Think back now to the opening story about Target's phenomenal success as an upscale discounter. With sales growing exponentially, the chain's retailing strategy of providing quality, fashionable products at a low price in a fun atmosphere has proved to be a big hit with its core target market. Every element in Target's retailing mix, from merchandise assortment to price levels, service levels, atmosphere, and location, must be carefully considered to provide its customers with the products and shopping experience they are looking for. This is no easy feat for retailers, but finding the right combination can mean the difference between success and failure. And Target has indeed found success.

USE IT

Study Franchise Opportunities

Franchising offers an alternative to starting a business on your own. But which franchise is a good match for your interests and skills? Narrow the field of the thousands of different franchise opportunities by visiting the Franchise Handbook Online at **http://www.franchise1.com**. There you will find articles with checklists to help you thoroughly research a franchise and its industry, as well as a directory of franchise opportunities. Armed with this information, you can develop a questionnaire to evaluate a prospective franchise. Also visit the

International Franchise Association, a Washington, D.C., trade group, at **http://www.franchise.org** to find more information about franchising and learn if it's right for you.

Stop Junk Mail
If you are upset about junk mail, contact the Direct Marketing Association and have

your name removed from mailing lists. The e-mail address is **http://www.the-dma.org.** You can also join an umbrella organization dedicated to stopping the flood of junk e-mail, intrusive telemarketing calls, and junk mail. One such organization is Stop Junk Mail, found at **http://www.stopjunkmail.com**.

REVIEW IT

1 **Discuss the importance of retailing in the U.S. economy.** Retailing plays a vital role in the U.S. economy for two main reasons. First, retail businesses contribute to our high standard of living by providing a vast number and diversity of goods and services. Second, retailing employs a large part of the U.S. working population—over twenty million people.

1.1 INFOTRAC COLLEGE EDITION In order to fully appreciate the role retailing plays in the U.S. economy, it may be helpful to review a selection of press articles related to the retailing industry. Using InfoTrac (**http://www.infotrac-college.com**), run a keyword search for articles pertaining to retailing. Read a selection of articles, and report your findings to the class.

2 **Explain the dimensions by which retailers can be classified.** Many different kinds of retailers exist. A retail establishment can be classified according to its ownership, level of service, product assortment, and price. On the basis of ownership, retailers can be broadly differentiated as independent retailers, chain stores, or franchise outlets. The level of service retailers provide can be classified along a continuum of high to low. Retailers also classify themselves by the breadth and depth of their product assortments; some retailers have concentrated product assortments, whereas others have extensive product assortments. Last, general price levels also classify a store, from discounters offering low prices to exclusive specialty stores where high prices are the norm. Retailers use these latter three variables to position themselves in the marketplace.

2.1 TEAM WRITING Form a team of three classmates to identify different retail stores in your city where pet supplies are sold. Include nonstore forms of retailing as well, such as catalogs, the Internet, or the local veterinarian. Team members should divide up and visit all the different retailing outlets for pet supplies. Prepare a report describing the differences in brands and products sold at each of the retailing formats and the differences in store characteristics and service levels. For example, which brands are sold via mass merchandiser, independent specialty store, or other venue. Suggest why different products and brands are distributed through different types of stores.

3 **Describe the major types of retail operations.** The major types of retail stores are department stores, specialty retailers, supermarkets, drugstores, convenience stores, discount stores, and restaurants. Department stores carry a wide assortment of shopping and specialty goods, are organized into relatively independent departments, and offset higher prices by emphasizing customer service and decor. Specialty retailers typically carry a narrower but deeper assortment of merchandise, emphasizing distinctive products and a high level of customer service. Supermarkets are large self-service retailers that offer a wide variety of food products and some nonfood items. Drugstores are retail formats that sell mostly prescription and over-the-counter medications, health and beauty aids, cosmetics, and specialty items. Convenience stores carry a limited line of high-turnover convenience goods. Discount stores offer low-priced general merchandise and consist of four types: full-line discounters, discount specialty retailers, warehouse clubs, and off-price retailers. Finally, restaurants straddle the line between the retailing and services industries; whereas restaurants sell a product, food and drink, to final consumers, they can also be considered service marketers because they provide consumers with the service of preparing food and providing table service.

3.1 Discuss the possible marketing implications of the recent trend toward supercenters, which combine a supermarket and a full-line discount store.

3.2 Explain the function of warehouse clubs. Why are they classified as both wholesalers and retailers?

4 **Discuss nonstore retailing techniques.** Nonstore retailing, which is shopping outside a store setting, has three major categories. Automatic vending uses machines to offer products for sale. In direct retailing, the sales transaction occurs in a home setting, typically through door-to-door sales or party plan selling. Direct marketing refers to the techniques used to get consumers to buy from their homes or place of business. Those techniques include direct mail, catalogs and mail order, telemarketing, and electronic retailing, such as home shopping channels and on-line retailing using the Internet.

4.1 Go to the Gift Shop at on-line wine retailer Wine.com's Web site at **http://www.wine.com/**. How does this site help shoppers select gifts?

4.2 How much does the most powerful computer with the fastest modem, most memory, largest monitor, biggest hard drive, and all the available peripherals cost at **http://www.dell.com**? Then visit a store like Best Buy or Circuit City and price a comparable computer. How can you explain any price differences between the two retail operations? Explain any differences in features that you encountered. What conclusions can you draw from your research?

4.3 Why should retailers market their printed catalogs on-line? Look at Web site **http://www.catalogsite.com**.

5 **Define franchising and describe its two basic forms.** Franchising is a continuing relationship in which a franchiser grants to a franchisee the business rights to operate or to sell a product. Modern franchising takes two basic forms. In product and trade name franchising, a dealer agrees to buy or sell certain products or product lines from a particular manufacturer or wholesaler. Business format franchising is an ongoing business relationship in which a franchisee uses a franchiser's name, format, or method of business in return for several types of fees.

5.1 What advantages does franchising provide to franchisers as well as franchisees?

6 **List the major tasks involved in developing a retail marketing strategy.** Retail management begins with defining the target market, typically on the basis of demographic, geographic, or psychographic characteristics. After determining the target market, retail managers must develop the six variables of the retailing mix: product, promotion, place, price, presentation, and personnel.

6.1 Identify a successful retail business in your community. What marketing strategies have led to its success?

6.2 WRITING You want to convince your boss, the owner of a retail store, of the importance of store atmosphere. Write a memo citing specific examples of how store atmosphere affects your own shopping behavior.

7 **Discuss the challenges of expanding retailing operations into global markets.** With increased competition and slow domestic growth, mature retailers are looking for growth opportunities in the developing consumer economies of other countries. The homogenization of tastes and product preferences around the world, the lowering of trade barriers, and the emergence of underserved markets have made the prospects of expanding across national borders more feasible for many retailers. Retailers wanting to expand globally should first determine what their core competency is and determine whether this differentiation is what the local market wants. Retailers also need to skillfully make adjustments in product mix to meet local demands.

7.1 Your retail clothing company is considering expanding into Mexico. What information about the country and its customs should you collect before opening a store in Mexico?

8 **Describe future trends in retailing.** Three major trends are evident in retailing today. First, adding entertainment to the retail environment is one of the most popular strategies in retailing in recent years. Small retailers as well as national chains are using entertainment to set themselves apart from the competition. Second, retailers of the future will offer more convenience and efficiency to consumers as consumers become more precise on their shopping trips. Staples won't be sold in stores but instead will be delivered directly to the consumer, freeing shoppers to visit stores for products they enjoy buying. Advances in technology will make it easier for consumers to obtain the products they want. Last, more and more retailers are using the information they collect about their customers at the point of sale to develop customer management programs, including customer relationship marketing, loyalty programs, and clienteling.

8.1 *WRITING* *INFOTRAC COLLEGE EDITION* You have been asked to write a brief article about the way consumer demand for convenience and efficiency is influencing the future of retailing. Write the outline for your article. Once you have written your outline, use InfoTrac (**http://www.infrotrac-college.com**) to locate the article in *Business Credit* magazine titled, "Electronic Retailing: A Threat to Brick and Mortar Retailers?" by Keith Ackerman. How does your article differ? Is Ackerman's article still relevant?

DEFINE IT

atmosphere 378	franchise 354	retailing 354
automatic vending 365	franchisee 370	retailing mix 373
buyer 357	franchiser 370	scrambled merchandising
category killers 362	full-line discount store 360	359
chain stores 354	gross margin 356	specialty discount store
convenience store 360	hypermarket 361	362
department store 357	independent retailers 354	specialty store 358
direct marketing (direct-	mass merchandising 361	supercenter 361
response marketing) 366	nonstore retailing 365	supermarket 358
direct retailing 365	off-price retailer 363	telemarketing 367
discount store 360	on-line retailing 368	warehouse membership
drugstore 360	private brands 374	clubs 362
factory outlet 363	product offering 374	

APPLY IT

Application for Entrepreneurs

ENTREPRENEUR Ron Johnson is developing a retail strategy to open up his new athletic shoe and sports equipment store. He has decided to carry Nike and Converse as his two lines of athletic shoes. This will give him top-of-the-line merchandise (Nike) and a lower priced, high-quality alternative (Converse). He obtained permission from one of his former professors to hold brainstorming sessions in a couple of his classes. From these sessions, he identified the following evaluative criteria customers might use in selecting a particular athletic shoe to purchase: (1) attractiveness/style/color, (2) brand name, (3) comfort, (4) price, (5) endorsement, and (6) quality. He also determined that location, a friend's recommendation, brands carried, and store atmosphere are important in selecting a place to purchase athletic shoes.

Questions

1. What type of retailing strategy should Ron use?

2. Which elements of the retailing mix are relatively more important?

3. Should Ron incorporate a Web site into his retail strategy? Why or why not?

THINK ABOUT IT

Ethics Exercise

A–Z Grocery Company is well known for offering quality grocery products at the lowest prices in the market. When the company applied for a zoning change to build a new store in a middle-class neighborhood, several city council members objected because the company has no stores in low-income neighborhoods, where they argue the low prices are needed most. The company contends it cannot operate profitably in these neighborhoods because of higher security and operating costs.

Questions

1. Should low-cost retailers be required to locate near low-income customers? Why or why not?

2. Does the AMA Code of Ethics address this issue? Go to **http://www.marketingpower.com** and review the code. Then, write a brief paragraph on how the AMA Code of Ethics relates to retailing locations.

TRY IT.

COURTESY OF DELIA'S CORP.

Entrepreneurship Case
Delia's Retails to Teens

Stephen Kahn knew he had a good idea for a new direct retailing business: sell funky clothes and accessories targeted to Sabrina-wannabe girls between the ages of ten and twenty-four. The problem was convincing financial backers that his idea was more than good—it was very lucrative. When he first presented his idea to venture capitalists, they scoffed at his business plan and refused to lend him money. Teens, they said, are an elusive group with limited financial resources and no access to credit cards. Moreover, teens are fickle, and the pace in teen fashion trends is often too fast for retailers to keep up.

Convinced that this overlooked niche had potential, Kahn, a former leveraged-buyout specialist and recent Yale grad, put up $100,000 of his own money and turned to family and friends for the other $1 million start-up capital he needed to print and mass mail his first catalog, called Delia's. Launched from a Brooklyn garage in 1993, Delia's startled Wall Street with its success, quickly becoming the nation's leading direct retailer of teen fashion.

Kahn's hunch about preteen and teenage girls, it turns out, was right on target. According to Teenage Research Unlimited, a consulting firm specializing in the teen market, young adults between the ages of twelve and nineteen spend an estimated $153 billion a year, or roughly $90 a week. Parents provide over half of their teens' incomes on an as-needed basis, with the rest coming from odd jobs, gifts, and allowances. Further, teens increasingly have access to their parents' credit cards and, in a growing number of cases, are acquiring their own credit cards with an adult sponsor. Parents are also setting up "digital on-line credit accounts" for their teens' on-line spending funded by their own credit cards. Not obligated to pay rent or other household expenses, most teens are free to spend their money on whatever they choose—accessories, CDs, and, most importantly, apparel. Additionally, buying decisions in teen apparel are being made at increasingly younger ages.

One of the most significant reasons for Delia's phenomenal success is the fact that it makes funky fashion accessible and affordable to preteen and teenage girls all across the nation. For young girls in rural and remote areas that lack options to buy cool clothes, Delia's serves as an equalizer of teen fashion. Now, teens in small midwestern or southern towns have the same fashion choices as their counterparts living in Los Angeles or New York. In schools all across the country, critiquing the latest Delia's catalog has become a lunchtime ritual.

After some fairly harrowing experiences with several suppliers early on, Kahn and partner Christopher Edgar, his ex-Yale University roommate, developed more of their own private-label merchandise in order to offer Delia's target market more unique clothing and accessories. More recent catalogs also attempt to target a slightly older demographic, aiming to be aspirational to preteens while not turning off older girls. The duo also weeded out suppliers that couldn't make consistent product and on-time shipments and opened their own warehousing facility to better control the fulfillment process and improve quality. These measures paid off for Delia's: Revenue hit $215 million in 2000, and its mailing list numbers more than 11 million. Not bad for a company that had sales of $150,000 just five years earlier.

Delia's has taken a multichannel approach to retailing. In addition to its successful direct-mail catalog, the company has opened some two dozen retail stores, operates several e-commerce sites. With virtually no advertising, the on-line store has attracted over 100,000 on-line buyers and more than five thousand catalog requests each day.

Questions

1. What type of retailer is Delia's?

2. Describe Delia's retailing strategy as best as you can in terms of product, price, place, promotion, people, and presentation.

3. Visit Delia's Web site at **http://www.delias.com**. How does it entertain and involve young girls in its brand? What is the focal point of the Web site?

WATCH IT

Short

The *Essentials of Marketing* PowerPoint CD-ROM has four video ad clips in the Chapter 11 slide presentation. The concepts of franchising, specialty retailing, discount stores, and direct retailing are illustrated in ads for Blockbuster, Office Depot, the NFL Store, and RadioShack.

Medium **CNN VIDEO**

How can retailers leverage the Internet when selling products that people are more comfortable buying in person, like bathing suits? CNN takes you to Lands' End so that you can see the creation of the company's virtual fitting room.

Long
the Series on PBS stations and the Web

To give you insight into Chapter 11, Small Business School goes to The Art Store in San Diego, California. Started by George Granoff, The Art Store has locations in several California cities and in New York City. Granoff, who lives in Boston, will take you inside the world of retail—and also inside a very targeted retail store. His market is so specific that you may be reminded of concepts from Chapter 6 regarding segmenting and targeting markets.

Still Shaky? Here's a Tip.

Make up a crossword puzzle using the key terms in this chapter. Writing the clues will help you remember the definition and the context of each concept. Make photocopies for exam time and for your study group.

FLIP IT

Flip to Chapter 11 in your *Grademaker Study Guide* for more review opportunities, including the pretest, vocabulary review, Internet activities, study test questions, and an application exercise based on retailing concepts. Can you close your book and describe the major types of retail operations? Can you clearly explain to a friend who's not in the class how to classify retailers? Do you know the tasks involved in developing a retailing strategy? If not, then pick up your *Grademaker* and review.

CLICK IT

The *Essential of Marketing* Web site links you to all the Internet-based activities in this chapter, like the "Use It," "Review It" questions 1.1, 4.1, 4.2, 4.3, and 8.1, and the On-Line exercises in the chapter margins. As a review, do the Chapter 11 quiz and crossword puzzle. And don't forget the Career Exersite that gives you resources for exploring marketing career opportunities in retailing. Review the main concepts in the PowerPoint presentation for Chapter 11, too. Go to **http://lamb.swlearning.com**, read the material, and follow the links right from the site.

Surf to Xtra! to test your understanding of the retailing concepts in the chapter by completing the worksheets for Exhibits 11.2, 11.4, and 11.6. If your instructor has assigned a marketing plan project, worksheets on Xtra! can help you organize your work. In addition to the quiz on the Web site, there's another quiz on Xtra!, plus video of the authors answering frequently asked questions about retailing topics, such as "How can small retailers compete with companies like Wal-Mart?"

MARKETING MISCUES

Jeremy's MicroBatch Ice Creams Gets Licked in Distribution

After only three years, Jeremy's MicroBatch Ice Creams, Inc. discontinued operations. Founded by Jeremy Kraus, a junior at the Wharton School of the University of Pennsylvania, the company and its guerrilla marketing techniques had drawn considerable attention. Kraus received two "entrepreneur of the year" awards, one from the Pennsylvania governor's office and the other from Mail Boxes, Etc. In the second annual Mail Boxes, Etc.'s "See Your Small Business on the Super Bowl Search," Kraus won $5,000 and the opportunity to feature his company's product in a $1.6 million television spot during the second quarter of Super Bowl XXXIII.

Kraus seemed to have everything going for him. In the company's initial public offering in February 2000, Kraus raised approximately $6 million. But, in October 2000, the company ran out of money after its marketing and distribution strategies failed. The collapse occurred despite attempts, in July 2000, to salvage the firm by replacing Kraus as CEO and revising its marketing efforts.

Jeremy's MicroBatch Ice Creams was inspired by successes in the microbrewery business. The company actually grew out of a business plan that Kraus had prepared for a class at Wharton. The idea was to make high-quality ice cream in limited quantities. The major points of Kraus's marketing plan included the following:

- *Target market:* Generation Y, teens, and twenty-somethings. The target market was comprised of consumers similar to the company's founder.
- *Product:* high-quality ice cream. Ice cream flavors included Vanilla Cream Stout (vanilla, cream stout swirl, chocolate-covered pretzels), Wired (vanilla with caffeine), Purple Passion Pills (purple mint, fudge swirl, chocolate-covered blue mint candies), Welcome to Tiramisu (tiramisu with espresso swirl, chocolate chunks, vanilla wafer cookies), Eve's Sinful Cider (apple cider, chunks of apple, apple swirl), Triple Espresso (coffee, espresso swirl, chocolate truffle chunks, chocolate-covered espresso beans), and Revenge of Chocolate Overload (chocolate, fudge swirl, chocolate truffle chunks, chocolate-covered almonds). Old flavors would be removed when new flavors were introduced, making each product available for a limited time only. Production of the ice cream was outsourced.
- *Promotion:* an aggressive guerrilla marketing campaign. The company budgeted (and spent) $2.4 million for magazine ads, radio spots, posters, Internet ads, and its "Secret Service." The "Secret Service" was made up of a hundred part-time student employees who distributed free samples of the product in fifteen northeastern cities via the company's MicroBatch Mobiles.
- *Distribution:* supermarket chains. Jeremy's MicroBatch ice cream was available in over five thousand grocery stores, such as Roche Brothers, Stop & Shop, A&P Food Mart, Donelan's, Tedeschi, and Victory Markets, in New England, Colorado, Minnesota, Florida, Texas, and Arizona.
- *Price:* $3.29 to $3.59 per pint. The high price was intended to reinforce the company's positioning as a high-quality, limited edition ice cream product.

Unfortunately, Jeremy's MicroBatch Ice Creams made a couple of obvious distribution errors. First, the company failed to match its distribution strategy to where its target market would likely shop for specialty-flavored, pint-sized ice cream. The company was promoting its product on college campuses via its team of Secret Service salespeople, but it failed to secure distribution in outlets where these college students were likely to shop. Second, the company spent almost half of its annual revenues on slotting fees to grocery stores. It was battling for a limited quantity of freezer space, and larger competitors had deeper pockets to pay the supermarket chains for this space.

In its third year, the company, under new leadership, decided to alter its distribution strategy and focus on placing MicroBatch freezers in coffeehouses, movie theaters, bookstores, and convenience stores, as well as opening Jeremy's MicroBatch Ice Creams retail shops. The strategy was never implemented, however, as the company went out of business the month after new leaders took the helm.

Questions

1. What was wrong with the initial distribution strategy at Jeremy's MicroBatch Ice Creams?

2. Were any other components of the marketing plan out of sync with the company's aspirations?

CRITICAL THINKING CASE

The Segway Human Transporter

A product code-named after Ginger Rogers and a media frenzy about an invention bigger than the Internet set the stage for DEKA Research and Development Corporation's Segway human transporter (Segway HT; http://www.segway.com). But was the buzz about the product too much? Did it create expectations beyond the product's capabilities? Was it too early? Was the buzz leak really an accident? Will the Segway HT change the transportation marketplace? Just as important, what is the market for this new product?

DEKA Research and Development Corporation

Founded in 1982 by Dean Kamen, DEKA focuses on the product market of radical technologies, with a mission to foster innovations that enhance quality of life. Though technically a research and development group, DEKA has the capabilities to take a product from concept to low-volume manufacturing runs. Based in Manchester, New Hampshire, the company remains relatively small and employs about two hundred engineers, technicians, and machinists.

Kamen is a well-known inventor and entrepreneur, holding more than 150 U.S. and foreign patents. His innovative, scientific achievements have resulted in numerous awards and public recognition. *Smithsonian* magazine labeled him "the Pied Piper of technology" and the *New York Times* called him "a new kind of hero for American youth." He is the recipient of the Kilby Award (for extraordinary contributions to society), the Heinz Award in Technology, and the National Medal of Technology.

Innovative health-care products resulting from Kamen's inventions are numerous. His infusion devices gained immediate and international recognition. The market for these devices was huge, prompting Kamen to found AutoSyringe, Inc., to manufacture and market the products. The company's wearable infusion pump gained rapid acceptance in chemotherapy, neonatology, and endocrinology. AutoSyringe also produced and marketed the first insulin pump for diabetics. Eventually, Kamen sold AutoSyringe, Inc., to Baxter International Corporation and then went on to start DEKA.

Since its inception, DEKA has worked closely with several large companies in the health-care industry. Major corporate partners include Baxter Healthcare Corporation, Davol, Inc., and Johnson & Johnson. DEKA designs and develops products for its corporate partners. For Baxter Healthcare Corporation, DEKA developed a relatively small, lightweight peritoneal dialysis machine that allows greater mobility for the user. In conjunction with Davol, Inc., DEKA developed a one-system irrigation pump for common medical procedures such as laparoscopy, arthroscopy, and hysteroscopy. Various companies within Johnson & Johnson (Cordis Corporation, THERAKOS, and Independence Technology) have used DEKA's medical innovations. DEKA and Cordis introduced the first intravascular stent to reduce artery blockage, and DEKA and THERAKOS developed the most advanced and innovative technology used to treat cutaneous T-cell lymphoma. DEKA and Independence Technology are working together to develop and market a product similar to a wheelchair that can climb stairs, raise the user to eye level, and traverse uneven terrain.

Introducing the Segway Human Transporter

The Segway HT, referred to as a disruptive technology, could soon hit the sidewalks, streets, and hallways of a few cities and businesses. This new-age people mover has been described as a cross between a rotary lawn mower and a scooter or a large weed whacker that a person can stand on. This description is somewhat deceptive, however, in that the Segway HT is not as straightforward as a rotary lawn mower, scooter, or weed whacker. It has three personal computers' worth of computer technology, dual-motored wheels, five solid-state gyroscopes, tubeless and flat-resistant lightweight tires, and handlebars for balance. The product does not have a brake, engine, throttle, gearshift, or steering wheel. It works with human equilibrium by responding to movements. Leaning forward on the Segway HT causes it to accelerate, and leaning backward causes it to stop. Basically, the gyroscopes act like the inner ear, the computer acts like a brain, the motors act like muscles, and the wheels act like feet.

Product specifications include a maximum speed of 5 to 17 miles per hour depending upon settings and terrain, a battery charge of 17 miles on flat surfaces, one hour of charge for two hours of operation, a passenger load of 250 pounds, a weight of 65 to 80 pounds, and a cost of $3,000 for the consumer model and $8,000 for the industrial model.

Bringing the Segway HT to market has not been without obstacles. One of the earliest problems was raised by the Church of Christ, Scientist, which owns the rights to anything referring to Ginger Rogers. Another obstacle is that the federal government must determine whether the product should be classified as a motor vehicle. If it is not a motor vehicle, the Segway HT will likely fall under the auspices of the Consumer Product Safety Commission.

Empowering Pedestrians

DEKA has no mass-market experience, yet it has developed a product that could change the way pedestrians get from point A to point B. Early product-related buzz prompted mixed opinions. While people who had seen or tried the Segway HT were enthusiastic about its potential for success, others were skeptical of its ability to make it to market. The bottom line—would the practicalities of manufacturing and marketing the invention keep it out of consumer hands?

Questions

1. Why is the Segway HT considered a disruptive technology? Is it really just a high-end toy?
2. Can DEKA make the transition from inventing to selling?
3. How can DEKA garner a portion of the $300 billion transportation industry? Who are likely the purchasers of this latest product?
4. Is the Segway HT a consumer product or a business-to-business product?

MARKETING PLANNING ACTIVITIES

To complete all nine product activities and all six distribution activities, use the Part 3 Marketing Planning Worksheets on Xtra!. If you need a company for the basis of your work, follow the "Marketing Plan Project" link on the *Essentials of Marketing* Web site (**http://lamb.swlearning.com**).

Product Decisions

For continued general assistance on business plans and marketing plans, visit **http://www.bplans.com** or **http://www.businessplans.org**. For electronic sources of information, search on the Electric Library at **http://wwws.elibrary.com/** or the Internet Public Library at **http://www.ipl.org/**. Another excellent source of information is the Sales and Marketing Executives Marketing Library at **http://www.smei.org/**.

In the first part of your strategic marketing plan, you stated your business mission and objectives and performed a detailed SWOT analysis. In the second part of the plan, you identified and described target market segments and described their buying behaviors and decision-making processes. In addition, you identified sources of competitive intelligence and determined whether any further marketing research would be needed before the marketing plan could be implemented.

The next stage of the strategic planning process involves defining the elements of the marketing mix: product, place, promotion, and pricing strategies. This third part of the planning process will focus on product and service components. Be sure that the strategies recommended here match the needs and wants of the target audience(s) you identified earlier.

Use the following exercises to guide you through the third part of your strategic marketing plan:

1. How would you classify the offering to your customers? Is it a consumer product? A business-to-business product? A good or a service? Both? How does this classification change the focus of your marketing plan? Is your product unique enough to be patented? Check with the U.S. Patent and Trademark Office at **http://www.uspto.gov**.

2. Place your company's offerings into a product portfolio. Consider the broader impact of marketing a product item within a line or mix. Factors to consider include price, image, complementary products, distribution relationship, and the like. Are there any special product features that selling on the Internet would allow you to add or force you to take away?

3. Does your chosen company have a brand name and brand mark? If not, design both. If so, evaluate the ability of the brand name and mark to communicate effectively to the target market. Is strong branding more or less important in an Internet environment? Why? What makes branding so important? If your firm needs to hire a professional branding company, look for "Naming and Branding Marketing Firms" on **http://www.looksmart.com**. Of particular importance are firms that can translate your brand name into other languages and check for negative implications. Try translations yourself at **http://www.iTools.com**. You can also try to generate brand names made up of random syllables or test a brand name's meaning at **http://www.nomina.net/**.

What will your company's Internet address be? To see what URLs are available, go to **http://www.companyname.com** and try some out. Should your URL be the same as your company's name? Why or why not? What happens if a customer mistypes your name? Should you register under alternative spellings?

4. Is the product packaged and labeled? How should it be packaged and why? Do the package and the label design match other communications tools? How is this an opportunity to communicate with your customers?

5. Evaluate warranties or guarantees offered by your firm, including product return policies. How will customers return products they purchased from the Web site? Design the parameters for warranties and return policies. Should your return policy be stricter on-line than off-line? Why or why not?

6. Place your company's product in the appropriate stage of the product life cycle. What are the implications of being in this stage? Would the product life cycle be lengthened, shortened, or not affected by selling your product or service on-line? Would selling your offering on the Internet make it seem earlier on the product life cycle to your customers? Why?

7. What categories of adopters are likely to buy your company's product? Is the product diffusing slowly or quickly through the marketplace? Why? What elements of the diffusion process can you control to make sure your offering diffuses more quickly throughout the adopter categories and marketplace in general? Will positive word-of-mouth communication be easier or harder to generate on-line?

8. What service aspects are provided with the product? List specific examples of how you can incorporate all five elements of service quality into your offering. What tactics can you define that would minimize any potential service quality gaps? How is customer service handled? What elements of service quality can your firm focus on? What impact would selling on the Internet have on your customer service operation?

9. With whom should your chosen company practice relationship marketing? Marketing on the Internet is particularly vulnerable to breakdowns in client relationships. Which sorts of bonds should be stressed in the relationship marketing strategy? How can your company "touch" its customers differently on-line than off-line? Are there advantages to on-line customer service? Disadvantages?

Distribution Decisions

Let's continue the plan by focusing on place, or distribution. Distribution is a key component of any business. For the e-business, distribution seems "invisible" to the consumer who may not care where your firm is located but wants the product delivered quickly and inexpensively. Creating a worldwide distribution system is an additional challenge to the marketer.

Use the following exercises to guide you through the distribution part of your strategic marketing plan:

1. Discuss the implications of dual/multiple distribution. If your firm sells through a major department store and its own catalog and then decides to have an on-line World Wide Web site or open its own store in a factory outlet, what will happen to channel relationships? To the final price offered to consumers? To promotional vehicles? Most e-marketers assume that a direct distribution channel, with no intermediaries, is the most efficient and least costly method for getting product offerings to customers. However, if you decide on a different distribution channel, you will also have to identify warehouses, fulfillment services, transportation firms, packing companies, and many other facilitating agencies. Does your firm have the capabilities to handle this, or should your firm invest in channel members to take over these tasks and functions?

2. Decide what channel(s) your chosen company should be using. Describe the intermediaries involved and their likely behavior. What are the implications of these channels? Describe the conflict that might arise from having both an e-marketing offering and a brick-and-mortar offering. If distribution costs are different, will your firm set the same or different prices for end customers?

3. Which distribution intensity level would be best for your company's product? Justify your decision.

4. What physical distribution facilities will be needed to complete delivery of products and services to the buyer? Where should these facilities be located? Check out the Warehouse Location Simulation at **http://www.orie.cornell.edu/~jackson.whsloc.html**. How should the product be distributed? Justify your selection of transportation mode(s). What other types of channel facilitators will you require to get your product offering to your customers? Search under **http://www.looksmart.com** for either "Full Service Direct Marketing Firms" or "E-commerce Transaction Management Products."

5. What types of retail establishments might be used for your firm's product? Are they in locations convenient to the target customers? What is the atmosphere of each type of facility? How can you get the atmosphere of the brick-and-mortar offering to match the offering of your Web site?

6. If you have developed an Internet-based service, to what other Web sites might you "distribute" your service? How will working with these other Web sites help you reach your target audience? Are there other Web sites from which you might accept distribution deals that would make your product or service offering stronger? Explain how strategic distribution with other Web sites or services can give you a competitive advantage.

CROSS-FUNCTIONAL CONNECTIONS SOLUTIONS

Cross-Functional Collaboration in Speeding Products to Market

1. What are some of the popular business terms used to describe cross-functional integration?

   - Design-factory fit
   - Concurrent engineering
   - Design for manufacturability and assembly
   - Early manufacturing involvement
   - Paperless design
   - Modularization

2. What are some of the popular advanced manufacturing systems, and how do they interact with marketing?

   Advanced manufacturing systems include just-in-time (JIT) and electronic data interchange (EDI). These systems allow a firm to compete on both time and quality. They allow for a quicker response to customers' demands as well as shorten the new-product production cycle. The systems allow firms to produce a large variety of high-quality products in a reduced cycle time, resulting in more timely deliveries.

3. How do production and delivery happen simultaneously in the service sector? What other functional areas are important partners in the service arena?

A unique characteristic of a service is its inseparability; that is, services are generally sold, produced, and consumed at the same time. Consumers must be present during the production and delivery of a service. For example, a consumer receives a haircut at the same time as the haircut is being produced. This inseparability means that the service cannot be produced in one location and delivered at another location. Thus, the quality of the service depends upon the quality of the employee—making human resources a very important cross-functional partner.

Suggested Readings

Alexander E. Ellinger, "Improving Marketing/Logistics Cross-Functional Collaborations in the Supply Chain," *Industrial Marketing Management,* January 2000, 85–96.

Donald Gerwin, "Team Empowerment in New Product Development," *Business Horizons,* July/August 1999, 29–36.

Avan R. Jassawalla and Hemant C. Sashittal, "Cross-Functional Dynamics in New Product Development," *Research Technology Management,* January/February 2000, 46–49.

PART 4

Promotion and Pricing Decisions

CROSS-FUNCTIONAL CONNECTIONS

UNDERSTANDING MARKETING COMMUNICATIONS' CONTRIBUTION TO FIRM VALUE

When purchasing a product or service, a customer does not think in terms of advertising, sales promotion, public relations, and personal selling, nor does he or she think in terms of marketing, manufacturing, accounting, finance, research and development, and human resources. Rather, the product or service received by the customer is the sum of all of the internal processes, just as the communications message is the sum of all of the communications vehicles available to the firm. It is the company's responsibility to make certain that the product/service received by the customer is consistent with the message that the customer has received via the firm's integrated marketing communications. For example, advertising for Priceline.com touts its ease of use. Therefore, when a potential customer attempts to buy something using Priceline.com, there should not be complicating features that make it difficult for the customer to buy products on-line.

Product quality is an issue that touches at the heart of a firm's operational processes. Marketers love to tout a product's superior quality when communicating with potential customers. When a company's communications strategy focuses upon promoting quality features, pressure is placed on research and development, manufacturing, and human resources to deliver on quality. Unfortunately, issues that mean quality to a scientist or an engineer in a manufacturing or research and development department may not readily translate to perceptions of quality by the customer.

If a firm's communications program entices the consumer to try a product or service, the product or service must then be consistent with the consumer's expectations of the quality. Too frequently, marketers have developed award-winning communications campaigns for a new product, only to see the product fail in the market due to inconsistency between what the communications program is conveying and what is delivered in the product.

The need for interaction between marketing and manufacturing does not stop with the product introduction campaign, however. At any point in a product's life cycle, marketing may decide to promote the product. For example, Colgate-Palmolive may decide to offer a price discount over a two- or three-week period, to advertise heavily, and/or to offer coupons in a freestanding insert for one of its bar soaps. From marketing's perspective, the hope is that a consumer will try the soap due to the heavy marketing communications effort (and keep using the product even after the communications effort has stopped).

Marketing at Colgate-Palmolive would need to work closely with manufacturing when planning such an extensive product promotion. Otherwise manufacturing will be producing the product at its traditional level, which will be inconsistent with marketing's promotional sales plan. An integrated marketing communications program that generates high demand for a product is only as good as the product's availability. That is, a well-orchestrated marketing campaign can create a powerful purchasing stimulus. But when manufacturing cannot meet demand, consumers consider competitive brands in order to satisfy the product want or need stimulated by the marketing communications program.

Advertising and promotional efforts tend to be a source of friction between marketing and financial managers. Oddly, advertising and promotional expenditures are generally viewed as cost elements rather than investments in the product or brand. Marketers view these expenditures as investments in building the business, much like companies invest in personnel in order to have a well-managed organization. Customer satisfaction and repeat business depend upon constant maintenance by the marketing department. In contrast, accountants often view advertising and promotional expenses as variable costs. Unfortunately, viewed as variable costs, advertising expenses are tied directly to sales increases and decreases, and marketing budgets are often cut when they are needed most.

Personal selling is a component of integrated marketing communications where considerable interaction among functions has been occurring and where expenses tend to be viewed as investments since human capital is involved. It is no longer sufficient for a salesperson to have good personal interaction skills to be successful. Now, salespeople have to possess intimate knowledge of the products they present to potential consumers. For example, a sales representative for South-Western College Publishing has to understand the topics covered in a particular textbook in order to talk knowledgeably to professors in the area. At Kele & Associates, a business-to-business supplier of building automation peripherals, sales and accounting collaborate to better understand national account profitability. The company understands that nurturing a current account is less expensive than identifying and developing new accounts.

At the same time, it is no longer sufficient for research and development engineers or manufacturing specialists to work only within their limited domains. Many firms are now insisting that research and development and manufacturing talk directly with customers. Not surprisingly, such an external emphasis is in direct contrast with the technical orientation of research and development and manufacturing employees. Additionally, it is often assumed that salespeople are more extroverted than research and development and manufacturing employees, who are considered to be inherently introverted. Firms such as Motorola and Intuit expect that their engineers will go on sales calls. These engineers may visit customers with a marketing person as part of a sales call or separately in order to watch the customer use the product. There seems to be no better way of developing and manufacturing innovative, cutting-edge products than to have the people who work directly with the product also working closely with the end user.

On the flip side of this, companies could consider including salespeople on cross-functional new-product development teams. Salespeople are the ones out in the field who see how customers use the company's products on a daily basis and hear what customers are saying as far as preferences. They can bring the voice of the customer into the firm. Additionally, salespeople are great sources of competitive intelligence as they are often the first to hear (from a customer) about a competitor's new product.

The sales area is also beginning to work closely with the finance, accounting, and human resource groups with regard to compensation systems. Firms are beginning to move from sales objectives (volume and/or revenue) to financial objectives (profit). By linking sales commissions to profit-related objectives, firms stress the importance of understanding the firm's margin versus focusing solely upon product revenue. Computer giants such as IBM and Hewlett-Packard follow a variable commission strategy that links a salesperson's commission to a product's profit margin.

While finance and accounting will generally be focused upon the profit aspect of the salesperson's objectives, human resources will have to work closely with the salesperson in order to develop the most appropriate compensation system for the types of accounts in the salesperson's territory. Additionally, the human resources staff is trained in methods to help the salesperson clarify individual goals, regarding responsibilities and desired accomplishments, that will be consistent with company-wide strategic goals. In today's business environment of teamwork and cross selling, the human resources department may also be called upon to help interview and train potential sales personnel.

The clear linkage among finance, accounting, human resources, and marketing with regard to a firm's selling strategy is exemplified in IBM's focus on profits and customer satisfaction. As mentioned earlier, IBM follows a variable commission strategy that ties a salesperson's commission to margins on the company's products. Sixty percent of the commission is tied to profit margin. Interestingly, the other 40 percent of the commission is linked to customer satisfaction. Customer satisfaction is measured according to the customer's perception of how well its IBM sales team has helped it achieve its own company objectives.

A successful integrated marketing communications program is dependent upon marketing working closely with research and development and manufacturing with regard to quality and availability. Simultaneously, marketing has to interact closely with finance, accounting, and human resources in order to establish appropriate goals and objectives for its marketing communications programs. It is the sum of the external messages and internal operations that produces a satisfied customer.

Questions for Discussion

1. Why is the company's marketing communications of particular concern to research and development and manufacturing?
2. Why do financial managers view advertising and promotional expenditures as costs?
3. How has personal selling become functionally integrated?

Check It Out

For articles and exercises on the material in this part, and for other great study aids, visit the *Marketing* Web site at

http://lamb.swlearning.com

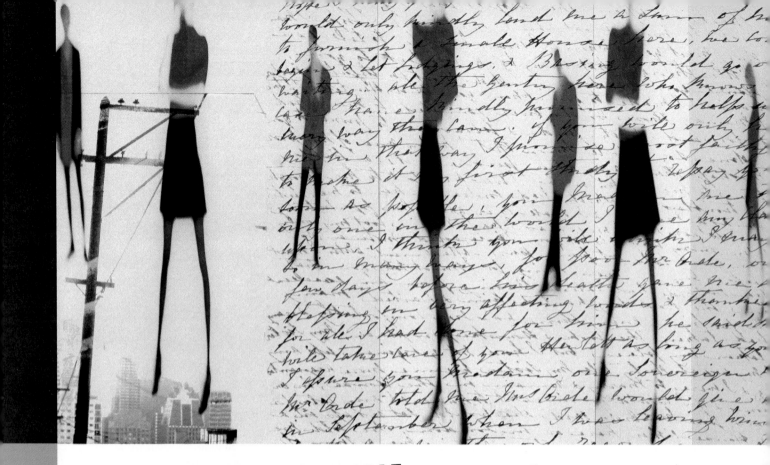

CHAPTER **TWELVE**
MARKETING COMMUNICATIONS AND PERSONAL SELLING

Learning Objectives

1 Discuss the role of promotion in the marketing mix

2 Discuss the elements of the promotional mix

3 Discuss the concept of integrated marketing communications

4 Describe the communication process

5 Explain the goals and tasks of promotion

6 Discuss the AIDA concept and its relationship to the promotional mix

7 Describe the factors that affect the promotional mix

8 Describe personal selling

9 Discuss the key differences between relationship selling and traditional selling

10 List the steps in the selling process

11 Describe the functions of sales management

In the five years since *Maxim* was first introduced to the United States, the publication with its formula of "sex, sports, beer, gadgets, clothes, and fitness" has upset the leaders in the men's magazine industry such as *Gentlemen's Quarterly* and *Esquire*. A newcomer in an industry that has recently seen ad revenues decline sharply, *Maxim* now sells 2.5 million copies each month—two and a half times as many as either *GQ* or *Esquire*. Its recent $115 million worth of advertising was more than *GQ* has and twice as much as *Esquire*; with statistics like these, *Maxim* joins the elite ranks of *Cosmo*, *Glamour*, and a handful of other established magazines.

How has *Maxim* realized such success while more seasoned marketers are experiencing sluggish ad sales and a declining subscriber base? *Maxim* uses an approach that emphasizes low entry costs, a proven editorial formula, and a guerrilla-style approach to marketing that is redefining the magazine industry. *Maxim* started by asking potential readers what they wanted. But instead of hosting traditional focus groups, the publishers felt they could get more information by going where men congregate. Using unofficial focus groups held at bars or sporting events in select U.S. cities, the publishers of *Maxim* gained invaluable knowledge about the needs of its target audience—males twenty-six to thirty-two years old. By giving its readers what they want, the magazine has seen unprecedented growth in its subscriber base. With an initial run of 250,000 copies, *Maxim* has had impressive gains in newsstand appeal, recently reaching one million in single-copy sales. The magazine regularly receives 35,000 to 50,000 blow-in subscription cards from each issue.

Maxim's strategy to becoming a success in the United States included keeping initial expenses low and incorporating a unique marketing mix. Instead of relying on traditional advertising, *Maxim* plans elaborate parties and other marketing events, then reaps the rewards of the free publicity and media coverage. Its first party, "Circus Maximus," was held on a closed-off Sunset Boulevard complete with a parade led by actress Jamie Presley riding on an elephant. Another promotional party took place at the Farmer's Daughter Motor Inn and included a performance by The Cult and motel rooms decorated in twenty-one exotic themes. The magazine also generated a great deal of public relations mileage from its annual "Hot 100 Women" special edition.

Maxim also knows the importance of on-line marketing. Statistics show that 76 percent of *Maxim*'s readers finish reading the magazine the first day they get it. So *Maxim* updates its Web site (**http://www.maximonline.com**) daily, offering interactive programs that include its *Maxim Challenge* football pool, games, and live chats with *Maxim* cover girls like actress Tara Reid. *Maxim* has also teamed up with other companies for cross-promotions that include joint parties with Smirnoff Ice in cities throughout the country and weekend getaways at the trendy W Hotel in ten cities.[1]

As you can see, *Maxim* places considerable emphasis on promotion in its marketing mix. What types of promotional tools are available to companies, and what factors influence the choice of tool? Why is consistent integrated marketing important to the promotional plan? These questions, and others, will be answered as you read this chapter.

The Role of Promotion in the Marketing Mix

Discuss the role of promotion in the marketing mix

promotion
Communication by marketers that informs, persuades, and reminds potential buyers of a product in order to influence an opinion or elicit a response.

promotional strategy
A plan for the optimal use of the elements of promotion: advertising, public relations, personal selling, and sales promotion.

competitive (differential) advantage
One or more unique aspects of an organization that cause target consumers to patronize that firm rather than competitors.

Few goods or services, no matter how well developed, priced, or distributed, can survive in the marketplace without effective **promotion**—communication by marketers that informs, persuades, and reminds potential buyers of a product in order to influence their opinion or elicit a response.

Promotional strategy is a plan for the optimal use of the elements of promotion: advertising, public relations, personal selling, and sales promotion. As Exhibit 12.1 shows, the marketing manager determines the goals of the company's promotional strategy in light of the firm's overall goals for the marketing mix—product, place (distribution), promotion, and price. Using these overall goals, marketers combine the elements of the promotional strategy (the promotional mix) into a coordinated plan. The promotion plan then becomes an integral part of the marketing strategy for reaching the target market.

The main function of a marketer's promotional strategy is to convince target customers that the goods and services offered provide a differential advantage over the competition. A **competitive advantage,** sometimes called a differential advantage, is the set of unique features of a company and its products that are perceived by the target market as significant and superior to the competition. Such features can include high product quality, rapid delivery, low prices, excellent service, or a feature not offered by the competition. For example, Gatorade promises superior refreshment for active consumers when they are "hot and thirsty." By effectively communicating this differential advantage through advertising highlighting the

Exhibit 12.1

Role of Promotion in the Marketing Mix

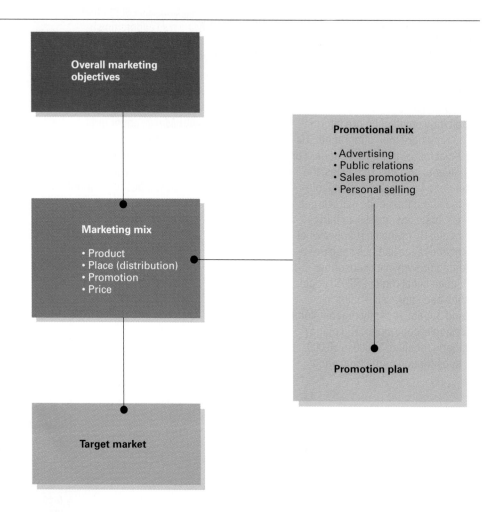

sports drink's origin as a drink developed by scientists for the University of Florida's football team, Gatorade maintains an 85 percent share of the sports-drink market.[2] Promotion is therefore a vital part of the marketing mix, informing consumers of a product's benefits and thereby positioning the product in the marketplace.

The Promotional Mix

Discuss the elements of the promotional mix

Most promotional strategies use several ingredients—which may include personal selling, advertising, public relations, and sales promotion—to reach a target market. That combination is called the **promotional mix**. The proper promotional mix is the one that management believes will meet the needs of the target market and fulfill the organization's overall goals. The more funds allocated to each promotional ingredient and the more managerial emphasis placed on each technique, the more important that element is thought to be in the overall mix.

promotional mix
The combination of promotional tools—including personal selling, advertising, public relations, and sales promotion—used to reach the target market and fulfill the organization's overall goals.

Personal Selling

Personal selling is a purchase situation in which two people communicate in an attempt to influence each other. In this dyad, both the buyer and the seller have specific objectives they wish to accomplish. The buyer may need to minimize cost or assure a quality product, for instance, while the salesperson may need to maximize revenue and profits.[3]

Traditional methods of personal selling include a planned presentation to one or more prospective buyers for the purpose of making a sale. Whether it takes place face-to-face or over the phone, personal selling attempts to persuade the buyer to accept a point of view or convince the buyer to take some action. For example, a car salesperson may try to persuade a car buyer that a particular model is superior to a competing model in certain features, such as gas mileage, roominess, and interior styling. Once the buyer is somewhat convinced, then the salesperson may attempt to elicit some action from the buyer, such as a test-drive or a purchase. Frequently, in this traditional view of personal selling, the objectives of the salesperson are at the expense of the buyer, creating a win-lose outcome.

More current notions on the subject of personal selling emphasize the relationship that develops between a salesperson and a buyer. This concept is more typical with business- and industrial-type goods, such as heavy machinery or computer systems, than with consumer goods. Relationship selling emphasizes a win-win outcome and the accomplishment of mutual objectives that benefits both buyer and salesperson in the long term. Rather than focusing on a quick sale, relationship selling attempts to create a long-term, committed relationship based on trust, increased customer loyalty, and a continuation of the relationship between the salesperson and the customer.[4] Personal selling and relationship selling are discussed further in this chapter.

personal selling
A purchase situation in which two people communicate in an attempt to influence each other.

Advertising

Almost all companies selling a good or a service use some form of advertising, whether it be in the form of a multimillion-dollar campaign or a simple classified ad in a newspaper. **Advertising** is any form of paid communication in which the sponsor or company is identified. Traditional media—such as television, radio, newspapers, magazines, books, direct mail, billboards, and transit cards (advertisements on buses and taxis and at bus stops)—are most commonly used to transmit advertisements to consumers. With the increasing fragmentation of traditional media choices, marketers are sending their advertisements to consumers in many new and innovative ways, such as with interactive video technology located in department stores and supermarkets and through Internet Web sites and electronic mail.

advertising
Impersonal, one-way mass communication about a product or organization that is paid for by a marketer.

You've Got Mail

Turn the computer on, check your e-mail, and more than likely you're bombarded with messages like "You can lose twenty pounds by the summer!" "Cut your mortgage payments in half!" and "Click here to find out how you can take the dream vacation of a lifetime!" Welcome to the Internet! You've got mail—now how do you get rid of it?

Some marketers have been making money by sending unwanted e-mail for years. It seems like the perfect way to reach hundreds, even thousands, with your marketing message. Research shows that e-mail users recently received an average of 1,465 messages during the year, and 571 of them were spam. These figures are expected to more than double to 3,846 messages, 1,479 of them junk, within four years. Spamming—sending out unsolicited advertise-

ments over a computer network to many addresses—annoys most consumers and is now coming under scrutiny from the government.

Just how do marketers get your e-mail address in the first place? Chat rooms, message boards, Internet directories, Web pages, and on-line shopping are prime "harvesting" sites for spammers. Other companies may sell their customer data lists. When Toysmart.com filed for bankruptcy, the company tried to sell its customer database—after promising customers it wouldn't share the information gathered on-line.

Some corporations are now making privacy a competitive advantage. Atlanta-based Internet provider EarthLink is proud of its Spaminator, which the company describes as a "state-of-the-art solution for removing unsolicited

e-mail from your mailbox before it gets to you." America Online, the nation's largest Internet provider, has been blocking mail from known spammers for years. Several states have passed laws limiting unsolicited mass commercial e-mail in an attempt to protect computer users from unwanted intrusions. Under many of the laws, unsolicited e-mail is prohibited or must contain opt-out instructions.

Unsolicited e-mail is a huge inconvenience to consumers. Companies that employ this practice should worry about consumer backlash. Marketers have an ethical and, in some states, legal obligation to keep consumers and their privacy concerns in mind.[5]

Is e-mail an effective marketing tool to use with college students? When does e-mail as a marketing tool become spamming?

One of the primary benefits of advertising is its ability to communicate to a large number of people at one time. Cost per contact, therefore, is typically very low. Advertising has the advantage of being able to reach the masses (for instance, through national television networks), but it can also be microtargeted to small groups of potential customers, such as television ads on a targeted cable network or through print advertising in a trade magazine.

Although the cost per contact in advertising is very low, the total cost to advertise is typically very high. This hurdle tends to restrict advertising on a national basis to only those companies that are financially able to do so. For instance, when Degree antiperspirant introduced its new line of clear gel products aimed at men, the company spent $25 to $30 million in media advertising alone.[6] Few small companies can match this level of spending for a national campaign. Chapter 13 examines advertising in greater detail.

Many companies are including Internet advertising as a vital component in their marketing mix. Banner ads, viral marketing, and interactive promotions are all ways that marketers utilize the Internet to try and reach their target audience. But some consumers and lawmakers feel that privacy issues are being violated. Read about this issue in the "Ethics in Marketing" box.

Public Relations

public relations
The marketing function that evaluates public attitudes, identifies areas within the organization the public may be interested in, and executes a program of action to earn public understanding and acceptance.

Concerned about how they are perceived by their target markets, organizations often spend large sums to build a positive public image. **Public relations** is the marketing function that evaluates public attitudes, identifies areas within the organization the public may be interested in, and executes a program of action to earn public understanding and acceptance. Public relations helps an organization communicate with its customers, suppliers, stockholders, government officials, employees, and the community in which it operates. Marketers use public relations not only to maintain a positive image but also to educate the public about the company's goals and objectives, introduce new products, and help support the sales effort.

HBO, as part of its effort to add 20 percent to its subscriber base over a five-year period, created a ten-hour miniseries based on Stephen Ambrose's best-selling novel *Band of Brothers*. The story follows Easy Company's real-life journey from basic training to V-E Day. The made-for-television miniseries had all the elements of a Hollywood blockbuster: brand-name producers (Steven Spielberg and Tom Hanks), $120 million budget, stellar cast, and a marketing blitz that was one of HBO's most extensive to date. The marketing campaign included billboards, traditional advertising to promote the series, and a savvy public relations and publicity plan. A behind-the-scenes feature and tie-ins with AOL Time Warner, Inc., helped gain public exposure for the series. For example, *Band of Brothers* appeared prominently on the welcome screen, which is the first thing AOL's thirty million subscribers see when they log on. A separate Web site allowed visitors to "experience the war" through the latest Internet technology. TBS, Time Warner's cable TV network, featured a war movie every Monday night for eleven weeks, and the Turner Classic Movies cable TV channel ran a thirty-six-hour marathon of war films prior to the *Band of Brothers* debut. HBO also distributed student magazines, posters, and study guides to as many as three million tenth and eleventh graders—some of whom were also treated to school visits from Easy Company veterans. The miniseries was a critical and commercial success with 9.9 million viewers tuning in during its two-hour premiere.[7]

A solid public relations program can generate favorable **publicity**—public information about a company, good, or service appearing in the mass media as a news item. The organization generally is not identified as the source of the information. The soy industry received favorable publicity and an increase in sales after the Food and Drug Administration (FDA) approved a health claim for food labeling suggesting a link between soy protein and the reduced risk of coronary heart disease.[8] This incident underscores a peculiar reality of marketing: No matter how many millions are spent on advertising, nothing sells a product better than free publicity.

Although an organization does not pay for this kind of mass-media exposure, publicity should not be viewed as free. Preparing news releases, staging special events, and persuading media personnel to print or broadcast them costs money. During the year-and-a-half it took the FDA to approve the soy claim, meatless burger marketer Gardenburger was busy capitalizing on the pre-approval buzz on soy and readying a public relations plan to put its brand at the forefront should the FDA approve the claim. While the FDA was mulling its final decision, Gardenburger used interim packaging touting its soy burgers as "great-tasting and packed with soy protein" to spark interest among those who were hearing about soy's health attributes in the press. Gardenburger also provided footage of its factory lines to major media outlets. These tactics proved quite beneficial for the soy marketer: Seventy-five newspapers and one hundred television stations used Gardenburger's packaging and production line footage in their coverage of the soy story, reaching some thirty-five million consumers. Two months after the FDA's approval, Gardenburger's sales had risen 25 percent.[9] Public relations and publicity are examined further in Chapter 13.

Sales Promotion

Sales promotion consists of all marketing activities—other than personal selling, advertising, and public relations—that stimulate consumer purchasing and dealer effectiveness. Sales promotion is generally a short-run tool used to stimulate immediate increases in demand. Sales promotion can be aimed at end consumers, trade customers, or a company's employees. Sales promotions include free samples, contests, premiums, trade shows, vacation giveaways, and coupons. A major promotional campaign might use several of these sales promotion tools. For example, Motorola, a sponsor of a mountain bike event called "24 Hours of Adrenaline," teamed up recently with Canadian Future Shop to debut the Motorola Gear Grab. This promotion gave ten people twenty-four seconds to grab as much Motorola

Nabisco

Nabisco lists its promotions on its Web site. What do you think the advantages and disadvantages of this are? Visit the site to get more information.

http://www.nabiscoworld.com

On Line

publicity
Public information about a company, good, or service appearing in the mass media as a news item.

sales promotion
Marketing activities—other than personal selling, advertising, and public relations—that stimulate consumer buying and dealer effectiveness.

gear as they could in a Future Shop store. Contestants worked in pairs and used Motorola two-way radios so that one partner could provide the other with the name, description, and location of a Motorola product—including cellphones and messaging devices—within the store. Contestants were also eligible for a grand prize of various Motorola and mountain biking gear. Besides the Gear Grab, Motorola sponsored several mini–Gear Grabs during mountain bike event weekends in different cities.[10]

Often marketers use sales promotion to improve the effectiveness of other ingredients in the promotional mix, especially advertising and personal selling. Research shows that sales promotion complements advertising by yielding faster sales responses. In a new trend, many marketers have been employing teams of young people to create excitement on the street for a new product or advertising campaign in a practice sometimes referred to as "guerrilla marketing." For instance, Hyatt Hotels recently sent a team of "brand ambassadors" dressed as bellhops onto the streets of Manhattan to spend the day doing random favors such as opening doors, carrying packages, and distributing mints to thousands of people. The bellhops also distributed collateral materials about travel deals to complement the company's national print and direct-mail campaign.[11] Sales promotion is discussed in more detail in Chapter 13.

Integrated Marketing Communications

3

Discuss the concept of integrated marketing communications

Ideally, marketing communications from each promotional mix element (personal selling, advertising, sales promotion, and public relations) should be integrated—that is, the message reaching the consumer should be the same regardless of whether it is from an advertisement, a salesperson in the field, a magazine article, or a coupon in a newspaper insert.

From the consumer's standpoint, a company's communications are already integrated. Consumers do not think in terms of the four elements of promotion: personal selling, advertising, public relations, and sales promotion. Instead, everything is an "ad." The only people who recognize the distinctions among these communications elements are the marketers themselves. Unfortunately, many marketers neglect this fact when planning promotional messages and fail to integrate their communication efforts from one element to the next. The most common rift typically occurs between personal selling and the other elements of the promotional mix.

integrated marketing communications (IMC)
The careful coordination of all promotional messages for a product or a service to assure the consistency of messages at every contact point where a company meets the consumer.

This unintegrated, disjointed approach to promotion has propelled many companies to adopt the concept of **integrated marketing communications (IMC)**. IMC is the careful coordination of all promotional messages—traditional advertising, direct marketing, interactive, public relations, sales promotion, personal selling, event marketing, and other communications—for a product or service to assure the consistency of messages at every contact point where a company meets the consumer.[12] Following the concept of IMC, marketing managers carefully work out the roles that various promotional elements will play in the marketing mix. Timing of promotional activities is coordinated, and the results of each campaign are carefully monitored to improve future use of the promotional mix tools. Typically, a marketing communications director is appointed who has overall responsibility for integrating the company's marketing communications.

Movie marketing campaigns benefit greatly from an IMC approach. Those campaigns that are most integrated generally have more impact and make a deeper impression on potential moviegoers, leading to higher box-office sales. Columbia Pictures, a unit of Sony Corporation, launched an aggressive integrated campaign for the release of *Spider-Man* in the summer of 2002. Months before the movie was released, Columbia began running trailers and advertisements on the Internet. Toy stores were full of Spider-Man action figures, night goggles, walkie-talkies, and video games. Promotional support for the movie included specially marked Dr. Pepper products with a chance for customers to register to win a trip to New York for the movie premiere. Kellogg's created Spider-Man cereal, and Cingular Wireless launched its own integrated marketing plan around the movie including special Spider-Man mobile phone face plates. As the release date approached, the film's stars, who were carefully chosen to broaden the movie's appeal, were sent on an extensive media tour. As a result, *Spider-Man* enjoyed a record weekend opening with $114 million in ticket sales.[13]

The IMC concept of has been growing in popularity for several reasons. First, the proliferation of thousands of media choices beyond traditional television has made promotion a more complicated task. Instead of promoting a product just through mass-media options, like television and magazines, promotional messages today can appear in many varied sources. Further, the mass market has also fragmented—more selectively segmented markets and an increase in niche marketing have replaced the traditional broad market groups that marketers promoted to in years past. Finally, marketers have slashed their advertising spending in favor of promotional techniques that generate immediate sales responses and those that are more easily measured, such as direct marketing. Thus, the interest in IMC is largely a reaction to the scrutiny that marketing communications has come under and, particularly, to suggestions that uncoordinated promotional activity leads to a strategy that is wasteful and inefficient.[14]

Marketing Communication

4

Describe the communication process

Promotional strategy is closely related to the process of communication. As humans, we assign meaning to feelings, ideas, facts, attitudes, and emotions. **Communication** is the process by which we exchange or share meanings through a common set of symbols. When a company develops a new product, changes an old one, or simply tries to increase sales of an existing good or service, it must communicate its selling message to potential customers. Marketers communicate information about the firm and its products to the target market and various publics through its promotion programs. Nestlé Crunch, for example, set out to reverse a decline in sales by establishing a consistent brand message that emphasized the candy's "crunchy" personality and key attributes. The company then signed Los Angeles basketball star Shaquille O'Neal as its spokesperson because it felt his personality—confident, witty, and entertaining—matched the attributes of the candy bar. Nestlé promoted the relationship through special events and television commercials. In the first three months of the campaign, dollar volume of Nestlé Crunch was up 5.2 percent over the previous year.[15] Read Shaq's own words about the power of marketing and advertising in Exhibit 12.2.

Communication can be divided into two major categories: interpersonal communication and mass communication. **Interpersonal communication** is direct, face-to-face communication between two or more people. When communicating face-to-face, people see the other person's reaction and can respond almost immediately. A salesperson speaking directly with a client is an example of marketing communication that is interpersonal.

Mass communication refers to communicating a concept or message to large audiences. A great deal of marketing communication is directed to consumers as a whole, usually through a mass medium such as television or newspapers. When a company advertises, it generally does not personally know the people with whom it is trying to communicate. Furthermore, the company is unable to respond immediately to consumers' reactions to its message. Instead, the marketing manager must wait to see whether people are reacting positively or negatively to the mass-communicated promotion. Any clutter from competitors' messages or other distractions in the environment can reduce the effectiveness of the mass communication effort.

communication
The process by which we exchange or share meanings through a common set of symbols.

interpersonal communication
Direct, fact-to-face communication between two or more people.

mass communication
The communication of a concept or message to large audiences.

Exhibit 12.2

Dreamful Attraction: Shaquille O'Neal's Thoughts on Marketing and Advertising

While on the outside looking in, I did not realize that marketing was so complicated. I never knew that a person, such as an athlete, could have such a powerful effect on peoples' thought processes and purchasing behavior. The use of a well-known athlete in marketing a product or service can have a great impact on the sales of that product or service. Look at Michael Jordan. Almost overnight most every kid either was wearing or wanted to wear Air Jordan shoes.

Why does this happen? Is it the appeal of a great athlete or is it great marketing? The answer is "none of the above." It's both. In my years as a professional basketball player, I have seen firsthand the dramatic appeal that athletes have for the fans and public in general. Top-name athletes are like E. F. Hutton—when they talk, people listen. But why do they listen? I believe they listen to us, the athletes, because we have credibility. The effectiveness of celebrity endorsements depends largely on how credible and attractive the spokesperson is and how familiar people are with him or her. Companies sometimes use sports figures and other celebrities to promote products hoping they are appropriate opinion leaders.

Because of an athlete's fame and fortune, or attraction, the athlete can often have the right credibility to be a successful spokesperson. The best definition of credibility that I could find was by James Gordon in his book, *Rhetoric of Western Thought.* He said that attraction "can come from a person's observable talents, achievements, occupational position or status, personality and appearance, and style."* That may be why a famous athlete's personality and position can help him or her communicate more effectively than a not-so-famous athlete.

Credibility is a positive force in the persuasive promotion used predominantly by cola marketers like Pepsi because of what I like to call "dreamful attraction." For example, when I was young, I dreamed that I was like Dr. J., the famous basketball player for the Philadelphia 76ers. I would take his head off a poster and put my head on it. I wanted to be Dr. J. That is dreamful attraction. The youth of today are no different. Just the other day a kid stopped me and told me that he wanted to be like me. He had a dreamful attraction. This dreamful attraction can help sell products. In my case, Pepsi, Spalding, Kenner, and Reebok are hoping that they are able to package properly and market whatever dreamful attraction I might have for their target audience—kids.

There are many ways to communicate to my target audience. I find that the most effective way for me is through television commercials. This avenue gives me a chance to express myself and show my real feelings about a message we are trying to communicate—either visually or vocally. I feel that I have what Clint Eastwood has—"Sudden Impaq." My impact is revealed through my sense of humor and my nonverbal communication.

Why does Shaq sell? Communication. Although the verbal communication in many of my commercials is slim, the impact is still there. This makes me believe even more in the quote that who you are can almost be as important as what you say. But if you can blend the two together—who you are and what you have to say—then imagine how much more successful the communication message can be in the marketing process. Andre Agassi's favorite quote from his Canon commercial is "Image is everything." If it is not everything, it is almost everything. If you have the right image, match it with the right product, and market it properly, then success should follow.

I have been involved in commercials and the marketing of products for only a short time, but I have learned a great deal. If there is one formula for success in selling products, it would be this: Marketing plus credibility and image plus effective communications equals increase in sales—hopefully.

Now, you can call me Dr. Shaq, M.E. (Marketing Expert).

*James Gordon, *Rhetoric of Western Thought,* (Dubuque, Iowa: Kendall-Hunt Publishing Co., 1976), 207.

The Communication Process

Marketers are both senders and receivers of messages. As *senders,* marketers attempt to inform, persuade, and remind the target market to adopt courses of action compatible with the need to promote the purchase of goods and services. As *receivers,* marketers attune themselves to the target market in order to develop the appropriate messages, adapt existing messages, and spot new communication opportunities. In this way, marketing communication is a two-way, rather than one-way, process.[16] The two-way nature of the communication process is shown in Exhibit 12.3.

The Sender and Encoding

sender
The originator of the message in the communication process.

The **sender** is the originator of the message in the communication process. In an interpersonal conversation, the sender may be a parent, a friend, or a salesperson. For an advertisement or press release, the sender is the company or organization itself. For example, the International Olympics Committee and its television partner NBC were the senders of messages promoting the 2002 Winter Games in Salt Lake City to a younger target audience. To appeal to eighteen-to thirty-four-year-olds, the Winter Games promoted more of the extreme sports—the fast, gravity-defying, and often dangerous activities that have surged in popularity among American youth.[17]

Encoding is the conversion of the sender's ideas and thoughts into a message, usually in the form of words or signs. Thus, to promote the Winter Games, NBC might encode its Olympics messages into advertisements. In addition, an NBC sports announcer, covering other extreme sports events, might encode the promotional message into a sports update to the prospective audience watching the event.

A basic principle of encoding is that what matters is not what the source says but what the receiver hears. One way of conveying a message that the receiver will hear properly is to use concrete words and pictures. For example, one television commercial for the Winter Games featured skater Tara Lipinski gliding across the ice to classical music. "To some people," said the smooth voice-over, "the Winter Olympics looks like this. Others see it like this." On the word "this," Lipinski disappeared from the screen; with a crash of noise and techno music, she was replaced by images of crashing skiers, somersaulting freestylers, careening hockey players, soaring ski jumpers, and speeding lugers. The voice-over then read the tagline, "Something for everyone."[18]

Message Transmission

Transmission of a message requires a **channel**—a voice, radio, newspaper, or other communication medium. A facial expression or gesture can also serve as a channel.

Reception occurs when the message is detected by the receiver and enters his or her frame of reference. In a two-way conversation such as a sales pitch given by a sales representative to a potential client, reception is normally high. In contrast,

AP/WIDE WORLD PHOTOS

For the 2002 Winter Games in Salt Lake City, Utah, Olympic organizers (and broadcasters) chose to highlight the extreme sports. Czech athlete Ales Valenta is pictured here upside-down and mid-air during his gold-medal winning jump.

encoding
The conversion of a sender's ideas and thoughts into a message, usually in the form of words or signs.

channel
A medium of communication—such as a voice, radio, or newspaper—for transmitting a message.

Communication Process · **Exhibit 12.3**

Noise
- Other advertisements
- News articles
- Other store displays

Sender	**Encoding the message**	**Message channel**	**Decoding the message**	**Receiver**
• Marketing manager • Advertising manager • Advertising agency	• Advertisement • Sales presentation • Store display • Coupon • Press release	• Media • Salesperson • Retail store • Local news show	• Receiver interpretation of message	• Customers • Viewers/listeners • News media • Clients

Feedback channel
- Market research
- Sales results
- Change in market share

noise
Anything that interferes with, distorts, or slows down the transmission of information.

the desired receivers may or may not detect the message when it is mass communicated because most media are cluttered by **noise**—anything that interferes with, distorts, or slows down the transmission of information. In some media overcrowded with advertisers, such as newspapers and television, the noise level is high and the reception level is low. For example, competing network advertisements, other entertainment option advertisements, or other programming on the network itself might hamper reception of the Winter Games' television ads. Transmission can also be hindered by situational factors such as physical surroundings like light, sound, location, and weather; the presence of other people; or the temporary moods consumers might bring to the situation. Mass communication may not even reach all the right consumers. Some members of the target audience may have been watching television when advertisements for the Winter Games were shown, but others may not have been.

The Receiver and Decoding

receiver
The person who decodes a message.

decoding
Interpretation of the language and symbols sent by the source through a channel.

Marketers communicate their message through a channel to customers, or **receivers**, who will decode the message. **Decoding** is the interpretation of the language and symbols sent by the source through a channel. Common understanding between two communicators, or a common frame of reference, is required for effective communication. Therefore, marketing managers must ensure a proper match between the message to be conveyed and the target market's attitudes and ideas.

Even though a message has been received, it will not necessarily be properly decoded—or even seen, viewed, or heard—because of selective exposure, distortion, and retention (refer to Chapter 4).[19] Even when people receive a message, they tend to manipulate, alter, and modify it to reflect their own biases, needs, knowledge, and culture. Factors that can lead to miscommunication include differences in age, social class, education, culture, and ethnicity. Further, because people don't always listen or read carefully, they can easily misinterpret what is said or written. In fact, researchers have found that a large proportion of both printed and televised communications are misunderstood by consumers. Bright colors and bold graphics have been shown to increase consumers' comprehension of marketing communication. Even these techniques are not foolproof, however. A classic example of miscommunication occurred when Lever Brothers mailed out samples of its then new dishwashing liquid, Sunlight, which contains real lemon juice. The package clearly stated that Sunlight was a household cleaning product. However, many people saw the word *sunlight,* the large picture of lemons, and the phrase "with real lemon juice" and thought the product was lemon juice.

Marketers targeting consumers in foreign countries must also worry about the translation and possible miscommunication of their promotional messages by other cultures. An important issue for global marketers is whether to standardize or customize the message for each global market in which they sell. Read about how some global marketers create messages to appeal to consumers in different cultures in the "Global Perspectives" box.

Feedback

feedback
The receiver's response to a message.

In interpersonal communication, the receiver's response to a message is direct **feedback** to the source. Feedback may be verbal, as in saying "I agree," or nonverbal, as in nodding, smiling, frowning, or gesturing.

Because mass communicators like NBC are often cut off from direct feedback, they must rely on market research or analysis of television ratings for indirect feedback. NBC might use such measurements as the percentage of television viewers who recognized, recalled, or stated that they were exposed to the Winter Games messages. Indirect feedback enables mass communicators to decide whether to continue, modify, or drop a message.

Conquering the World—Who's Buying?

Global marketing—being able to sell your products or services worldwide—is a huge undertaking. Marketing products or services overseas requires both cultural sensitivity and an understanding of the consumers in the market. Recall from Chapter 3 that words in English may have a totally different connotation in other countries. When a U.S. company wanted to market a cosmetic product called "Mist Stick" in Europe, it found that the name would have been a bad idea in German-language countries. The name looks and sounds like the German equivalent of "piece of manure." Even the emotional and psychological properties associated with color used in logos, packaging, and other collateral marketing materials vary from culture to culture.

One of the hottest debates among global marketing professionals is whether to customize or standardize promotional messages. Some believe the message should be tailored to each country or region to be most effective since different cultures perceive and react to promotional messages differently. Kodak, for example, favors a customized approach to advertising in China because consumer tastes and values vary between mainland China and the more progressive Taiwan and Hong Kong areas. Others believe marketers should develop one message, translate it into the language of each country, and deliver it to all target markets. They say consumers everywhere

Global marketers must pay attention to cultural differences, linguistic differences, and the attitudes of consumers in the given market. Heinz, however, was able to use a generally standardized approach because it discovered that teens around the world were more alike in their use of ketchup than they were different.

have the same basic needs and desires and can therefore be persuaded by universal appeals. For example, Heinz concluded from its research that teens around the world are really more alike in their use of ketchup than they are different. As a result, it rolled out a $50 million global advertising campaign to seventy-five countries with only minor creative tweaks in the food the teens were pouring the ketchup over. Probably the best answer to this dilemma is to use a mixture of standardization and customization—standardize the message but pay attention to local differences when executing it. For example,

Coca-Cola uses a standardized appeal when promoting cola, but it tailors the message to regional and international markets. All ads include the tagline "Coca-Cola. Enjoy," but the campaign's "Enjoy" melody has nineteen different versions in genres as varied as reggae, techno, hip-hop, and country depending on demographic and regional preferences.[20]

So what can marketers do to ensure their message is received in other cultures as it is intended? What other barriers to communication exist for global marketers?

The Communication Process and the Promotional Mix

The four elements of the promotional mix differ in their ability to affect the target audience. For instance, promotional mix elements may communicate with the consumer directly or indirectly. The message may flow one way or two ways. Feedback may be fast or slow, a little or a lot. Likewise, the communicator may have varying degrees of control over message delivery, content, and flexibility. Exhibit 12.4 outlines differences among the promotional mix elements with respect to mode of communication, marketer's control over the communication process, amount and speed of feedback, direction of message flow, marketer's control over the message, identification of the sender, speed in reaching large audiences, and message flexibility.

From Exhibit 12.4, you can see that most elements of the promotional mix are indirect and impersonal when used to communicate with a target market, providing

Exhibit 12.4   Characteristics of the Elements in the Promotional Mix

	Advertising	Public Relations	Sales Promotion	Personal Selling
Mode of Communication	Indirect and nonpersonal	Usually indirect and nonpersonal	Usually indirect and nonpersonal	Direct and face-to-face
Communicator Control over Situation	Low	Moderate to low	Moderate to low	High
Amount of Feedback	Little	Little	Little to moderate	Much
Speed of Feedback	Delayed	Delayed	Varies	Immediate
Direction of Message Flow	One-way	One-way	Mostly one-way	Two-way
Control over Message Content	Yes	No	Yes	Yes
Identification of Sponsor	Yes	No	Yes	Yes
Speed in Reaching Large Audience	Fast	Usually fast	Fast	Slow
Message Flexibility	Same message to all audiences	Usually no direct control over message	Same message to varied target audiences	Tailored to prospective buyer

only one direction of message flow. For example, advertising, public relations, and sales promotion are generally impersonal, one-way means of mass communication. Because they provide no opportunity for direct feedback, they cannot easily adapt to consumers' changing preferences, individual differences, and personal goals.

Personal selling, on the other hand, is personal, two-way communication. The salesperson is able to receive immediate feedback from the consumer and adjust the message in response. Personal selling, however, is very slow in dispersing the marketer's message to large audiences. Because a salesperson can only communicate to one person or a small group of persons at one time, it is a poor choice if the marketer wants to send a message to many potential buyers.

The Goals and Tasks of Promotion

Explain the goals and tasks of promotion

People communicate with one another for many reasons. They seek amusement, ask for help, give assistance or instructions, provide information, and express ideas and thoughts. Promotion, on the other hand, seeks to modify behavior and thoughts in some way. For example, promoters may try to persuade consumers to eat at Burger King rather than at McDonald's. Promotion also strives to reinforce existing behavior—for instance, getting consumers to continue to dine at Burger King once they have switched. The source (the seller) hopes to project a favorable image or to motivate purchase of the company's goods and services.

Promotion can perform one or more of three tasks: *inform* the target audience, *persuade* the target audience, or *remind* the target audience. Often a marketer will try to accomplish two or more of these tasks at the same time. Exhibit 12.5 lists the three tasks of promotion and some examples of each.

Informing

Informative promotion may seek to convert an existing need into a want or to stimulate interest in a new product. It is generally more prevalent during the early stages of the product life cycle. People typically will not buy a product service or support a nonprofit organization until they know its purpose and its benefits to them. Informative messages are important for promoting complex and technical products such as automobiles, computers, and investment services. Informative promotion is also important for a "new" brand being introduced into an "old" product class—for example, a new brand of frozen pizza entering the frozen pizza industry, which is dominated by well-known brands like Kraft's DiGiorno and Schwan's Grocery Products' Red Baron. The new product cannot establish itself against more mature products unless potential buyers are aware of it, understand its benefits, and understand its positioning in the marketplace.

Persuading

Persuasive promotion is designed to stimulate a purchase or an action—for example, to drink more Coca-Cola or to use H&R Block tax services. Persuasion normally becomes the main promotion goal when the product enters the growth stage of its life cycle. By this time, the target market should have general product awareness and some knowledge of how the product can fulfill their wants. Therefore, the promotional task switches from informing consumers about the product category to persuading them to buy the company's brand rather than the competitor's. At this time, the promotional message emphasizes the product's real and perceived differential advantages, often appealing to emotional needs such as love, belonging, self-esteem, and ego satisfaction.

AP/WIDE WORLD PHOTOS

A "new" brand being introduced into an "old" category, like Disney brand children's clothing, for example, can benefit from informative promotion. Explain the product's benefits and advantages in a way that will draw attention to it and help it compete against mature brands like HealthTex, Garanimals, and McKids.

Exhibit 12.5

Promotion Tasks and Examples

- **Informative promotion**
  Increasing the awareness of a new brand, product class, or product attribute
  Explaining how the product works
  Suggesting new uses for a product
  Building a company image

- **Persuasive promotion**
  Encouraging brand switching
  Changing customers' perceptions of product attributes
  Influencing customers to buy now
  Persuading customers to call

- **Reminder promotion**
  Reminding consumers that the product may be needed in the near future
  Reminding consumers where to buy the product
  Maintaining consumer awareness

Persuasion can also be an important goal for very competitive mature product categories such as many household items, soft drinks, beer, and banking services. In a marketplace characterized by many competitors, the promotional message often encourages brand switching and aims to convert some buyers into loyal users. For example, to persuade new customers to switch their checking accounts, a bank's marketing manager may offer a year's worth of free checks with no fees.

Critics believe that some promotional messages and techniques can be too persuasive, causing consumers to buy products and services they really don't need.

Reminding

Reminder promotion is used to keep the product and brand name in the public's mind. This type of promotion prevails during the maturity stage of the life cycle. It assumes that the target market has already been persuaded of the good's or service's merits. Its purpose is simply to trigger a memory. Crest toothpaste, Tide laundry detergent, Miller beer, and many other consumer products often use reminder promotion.

Discuss the AIDA concept and its relationship to the promotional mix

AIDA concept
A model that outlines the process for achieving promotional goals in terms of stages of consumer involvement with the message; the acronym stands for *attention, interest, desire,* and *action.*

Promotional Goals and the AIDA Concept

The ultimate goal of any promotion is to get someone to buy a good or service or, in the case of nonprofit organizations, to take some action (for instance, donate blood). A classic model for reaching promotional goals is called the **AIDA concept**.[21] The acronym stands for *attention, interest, desire,* and *action*—the stages of consumer involvement with a promotional message.

This model proposes that consumers respond to marketing messages in a cognitive (thinking), affective (feeling), and conative (doing) sequence. First, the promotion manager attracts a person's *attention* by (in personal selling) a greeting and approach or (in advertising and sales promotion) loud volume, unusual contrasts, bold headlines, movement, bright colors, and so on. Next, a good sales presentation, demonstration, or advertisement creates *interest* in the product and then, by illustrating how the product's features will satisfy the consumer's needs, arouses *desire.* Finally, a special offer or a strong closing sales pitch may be used to obtain purchase *action.*

The AIDA concept assumes that promotion propels consumers along the following four steps in the purchase-decision process:

1. *Attention:* The advertiser must first gain the attention of the target market. A firm cannot sell something if the market does not know that the good or service exists. Imagine that Acme Company, a pet food manufacturer, is introducing a new brand of cat food called Stripes, specially formulated for finicky cats. To increase the general awareness of its new brand, Acme heavily publicizes the introduction and places several ads on TV and in consumer magazines.

2. *Interest:* Simple awareness of a brand seldom leads to a sale. The next step is to create interest in the product. A print ad or TV commercial can't actually tell pet owners whether their cats will like Stripes. Thus, Acme might send samples of the new cat food to cat owners to create interest in the new brand.

3. *Desire:* Even though owners (and their cats) may like Stripes, they may not see any advantage over competing brands, especially if owners are brand loyal. Therefore, Acme must create brand preference by explaining the product's differential advantage over the competition. Specifically, Acme has to show that cats want to eat nothing else. Advertising at this stage claims that Stripes will satisfy "even the pickiest of the litter." Although pet owners may come to prefer Stripes to other brands, they still may not have developed the desire to buy the new brand. At this stage Acme might offer the consumer additional reasons to buy

Stripes, such as easy-to-open, zip-lock packaging that keeps the product fresh; additional vitamins and minerals that healthy cats need; or feline taste-test results.

4. *Action:* Some members of the target market may now be convinced to buy Stripes but have yet to make the purchase. Displays in grocery stores, coupons, premiums, and trial-size packages can often push the complacent shopper into purchase.

Most buyers involved in high-involvement purchase situations pass through the four stages of the AIDA model on the way to making a purchase. The promoter's task is to determine where on the purchase ladder most of the target consumers are located and design a promotion plan to meet their needs. For instance, if Acme has determined that about half its buyers are in the preference or conviction stage but have not bought Stripes cat food for some reason, the company may mail cents-off coupons to cat owners to prompt them to buy.

The AIDA concept does not explain how all promotions influence purchase decisions. The model suggests that promotional effectiveness can be measured in terms of consumers progressing from one stage to the next. However, the order of stages in the model, as well as whether consumers go through all steps, has been much debated. For example, a purchase can occur without interest or desire, perhaps when a low-involvement product is bought on impulse. Regardless of the order of the stages or consumers' progression through these stages, the AIDA concept helps marketers by suggesting which promotional strategy will be most effective.[22]

AIDA and the Promotional Mix

Exhibit 12.6 depicts the relationship between the promotional mix and the AIDA model. It shows that, although advertising does have an impact in the later stages, it is most useful in gaining attention for goods or services. In contrast, personal selling reaches fewer people at first. Salespeople are more effective at creating customer interest for merchandise or a service and at creating desire. For example, advertising may help a potential computer purchaser gain knowledge and information about competing brands, but the salesperson in an electronics store may be the one who actually encourages the buyer to decide a particular brand is the best choice. The salesperson also has the advantage of having the computer physically there to demonstrate its capabilities to the buyer.

Public relations has its greatest impact in gaining attention for a company, good, or service. Many companies can attract attention and build goodwill by sponsoring community events that benefit a worthy cause such as antidrug and antigang programs. Such sponsorships project a positive image of the firm and

Exhibit 12.6

When the Elements of Promotion Are Most Useful

	Attention	Interest	Desire	Action
Advertising	Very effective	Very effective	Somewhat effective	Not effective
Public Relations	Very effective	Very effective	Very effective	Not effective
Sales Promotion	Somewhat effective	Somewhat effective	Very effective	Somewhat effective
Personal Selling	Somewhat effective	Very effective	Very effective	Very effective

its products into the minds of consumers and potential consumers. Good publicity can also help develop consumer desire for a product. When Hasbro's Tiger Electronics wanted to launch its new line of toys—robotic dogs—the company arranged for Iditarod winner Doug Swingley to deliver the first litter of Poo-Chis to New York's FAO Schwarz via his winning dogsled team. NBC's *Today Show* picked up the publicity stunt and more than a thousand robotic dogs were sold in the store's opening hours.[23] Book publishers push to get their titles on the best-seller lists of major publications, such as *Publishers Weekly* or the *New York Times*. Book authors also make appearances on talk shows and at bookstores to personally sign books and speak to fans. Similarly, movie marketers use prerelease publicity to raise the profile of their movies and to increase initial box-office sales. For example, most major motion picture studios have their own Web sites with multimedia clips and publicity photos of their current movies to attract viewers. Furthermore, movie promoters will include publicity gained from reviewers' quotes and Academy Award nominations in their advertising.

Sales promotion's greatest strength is in creating strong desire and purchase intent. Coupons and other price-off promotions are techniques used to persuade customers to buy new products. Frequent buyer sales promotion programs, popular among retailers, allow consumers to accumulate points or dollars that can later be redeemed for goods. Frequent buyer programs tend to increase purchase intent and loyalty and encourage repeat purchases. While many supermarket chains have developed loyalty programs patterned after the frequent flyer programs started by airlines, Safeway actually partnered with United Airlines to launch a program called "Grocery Miles." This program allows customers to earn frequent flyer miles for their supermarket purchases. To take part, customers must be members of United's Mileage Plus frequent flyer program and the Safeway Club. Then, once enrolled in Grocery Miles, shoppers earn 125 miles for every $250 they spend through a specified time period.[24]

Factors Affecting the Promotional Mix

7

Describe the factors that affect the promotional mix

Promotional mixes vary a great deal from one product and one industry to the next. Normally, advertising and personal selling are used to promote goods and services, supported and supplemented by sales promotion. Public relations helps develop a positive image for the organization and the product line. However, a firm may choose not to use all four promotional elements in its promotional mix, or it may choose to use them in varying degrees. The particular promotional mix chosen by a firm for a product or service depends on several factors: the nature of the product, the stage in the product life cycle, target market characteristics, the type of buying decision, funds available for promotion, and whether a push or a pull strategy will be used.

Nature of the Product

Characteristics of the product itself can influence the promotional mix. For instance, a product can be classified as either a business product or a consumer product (refer to Chapter 8). As business products are often custom-tailored to the buyer's exact specifications, they are often not well suited to mass promotion. Therefore, producers of most business goods, such as computer systems or industrial machinery, rely more heavily on personal selling than on advertising. Informative personal selling is common for industrial installations, accessories, and component parts and materials. Advertising, however, still serves a purpose in promoting business goods. Advertisements in trade media may be used to create general buyer awareness and interest. Moreover, advertising can help locate potential customers for the sales force. For example, print media advertising often includes coupons soliciting the potential customer to "fill this out for more detailed information."

In contrast, because consumer products generally are not custom-made, they do not require the selling efforts of a company representative who can tailor them to the user's needs. Thus, consumer goods are promoted mainly through advertising to create brand familiarity. Broadcast advertising, newspapers, and consumer-oriented magazines are used extensively to promote consumer goods, especially nondurables. Sales promotion, the brand name, and the product's packaging are about twice as important for consumer goods as for business products. Persuasive personal selling is important at the retail level for shopping goods such as automobiles and appliances.

The costs and risks associated with a product also influence the promotional mix. As a general rule, when the costs or risks of using a product increase, personal selling becomes more important. Items that are a small part of a firm's budget (supply items) or of a consumer's budget (convenience products) do not require a salesperson to close the sale. In fact, inexpensive items cannot support the cost of a salesperson's time and effort unless the potential volume is high. On the other hand, expensive and complex machinery, new buildings, cars, and new homes represent a considerable investment. A salesperson must assure buyers that they are spending their money wisely and not taking an undue financial risk.

Social risk is an issue as well. Many consumer goods are not products of great social importance because they do not reflect social position. People do not experience much social risk in buying a loaf of bread or a candy bar. However, buying some shopping products and many specialty products such as jewelry and clothing does involve a social risk. Many consumers depend on sales personnel for guidance and advice in making the "proper" choice.

Stage in the Product Life Cycle

The product's stage in its life cycle is a big factor in designing a promotional mix (see Exhibit 12.7). During the *introduction stage*, the basic goal of promotion is to inform the target audience that the product is available. Initially, the emphasis is on the general product class—for example, personal computer systems. This emphasis gradually changes to gaining attention for a specific brand, such as IBM,

Product Life Cycle and the Promotional Mix   **Exhibit 12.7**

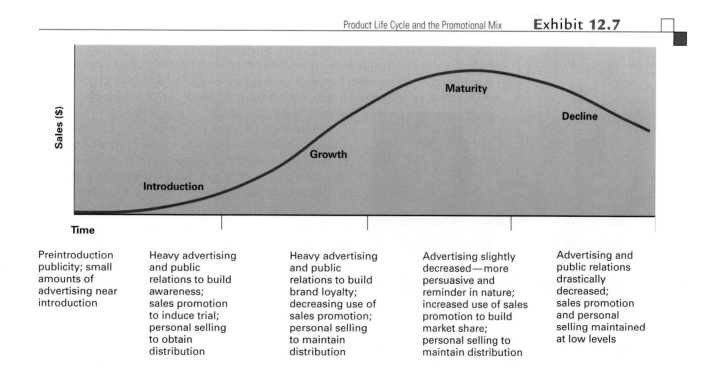

| Preintroduction publicity; small amounts of advertising near introduction | Heavy advertising and public relations to build awareness; sales promotion to induce trial; personal selling to obtain distribution | Heavy advertising and public relations to build brand loyalty; decreasing use of sales promotion; personal selling to maintain distribution | Advertising slightly decreased—more persuasive and reminder in nature; increased use of sales promotion to build market share; personal selling to maintain distribution | Advertising and public relations drastically decreased; sales promotion and personal selling maintained at low levels |

Apple, and Compaq. Typically, both extensive advertising and public relations inform the target audience of the product class or brand and heighten awareness levels. Sales promotion encourages early trial of the product, and personal selling gets retailers to carry the product.

When the product reaches the *growth stage* of the life cycle, the promotion blend may shift. Often a change is necessary because different types of potential buyers are targeted. Although advertising and public relations continue to be major elements of the promotional mix, sales promotion can be reduced because consumers need fewer incentives to purchase. The promotional strategy is to emphasize the product's differential advantage over the competition. Persuasive promotion is used to build and maintain brand loyalty to support the product during the growth stage. By this stage, personal selling has usually succeeded in getting adequate distribution for the product.

As the product reaches the *maturity stage* of its life cycle, competition becomes fiercer, and thus persuasive and reminder advertising are more strongly emphasized. Sales promotion comes back into focus as product sellers try to increase their market share.

All promotion, especially advertising, is reduced as the product enters the *decline stage*. Nevertheless, personal selling and sales promotion efforts may be maintained, particularly at the retail level.

Target Market Characteristics

A target market characterized by widely scattered potential customers, highly informed buyers, and brand-loyal repeat purchasers generally requires a promotional mix with more advertising and sales promotion and less personal selling. Sometimes, however, personal selling is required even when buyers are well informed and geographically dispersed. Although industrial installations and component parts may be sold to extremely competent people with extensive education and work experience, salespeople must still be present to explain the product and work out the details of the purchase agreement.

Often firms sell goods and services in markets where potential customers are hard to locate. Print advertising can be used to find them. The reader is invited to call for more information or to mail in a reply card for a detailed brochure. As the calls or cards are received, salespeople are sent to visit the potential customers.

Type of Buying Decision

The promotional mix also depends on the type of buying decision—for example, a routine decision or a complex decision. For routine consumer decisions like buy-

Consumers making complex buying decisions often depend on the salesperson to provide important product information. Purchasing a car is one such example. Can you think of others?

ing toothpaste or soft drinks, the most effective promotion calls attention to the brand or reminds the consumer about the brand. Advertising and, especially, sales promotion are the most productive promotion tools to use for routine decisions.

If the decision is neither routine nor complex, advertising and public relations help establish awareness for the good or service. Suppose a man is looking for a bottle of wine to serve to his dinner guests. As a beer drinker, he is not familiar with wines, yet he has seen advertising for Sutter Home wine and has also read an article in a popular magazine about the Sutter Home winery. He may be more likely to buy this brand because he is already aware of it.

In contrast, consumers making complex buying decisions are more extensively involved. They rely on large amounts of information to help them reach a purchase decision. Personal selling is most effective in helping these consumers decide. For example, consumers thinking about buying a car usually depend on a salesperson to provide the information they need to reach a decision. Print advertising may also be used for high-involvement purchase decisions because it can often provide a large amount of information to the consumer.

Available Funds

Money, or the lack of it, may easily be the most important factor in determining the promotional mix. A small, undercapitalized manufacturer may rely heavily on free publicity if its product is unique. If the situation warrants a sales force, a financially strained firm may turn to manufacturers' agents, who work on a commission basis with no advances or expense accounts. Even well-capitalized organizations may not be able to afford the advertising rates of publications like *Better Homes and Gardens, Reader's Digest,* and the *Wall Street Journal.* The price of a high-profile advertisement in these media could support a salesperson for a year.

When funds are available to permit a mix of promotional elements, a firm will generally try to optimize its return on promotion dollars while minimizing the *cost per contact,* or the cost of reaching one member of the target market. In general, the cost per contact is very high for personal selling, public relations, and sales promotions like sampling and demonstrations. On the other hand, for the number of people national advertising reaches, it has a very low cost per contact.

Usually, there is a trade-off among the funds available, the number of people in the target market, the quality of communication needed, and the relative costs of the promotional elements. A company may have to forgo a full-page, color advertisement in *People* magazine in order to pay for a personal selling effort. Although the magazine ad will reach more people than personal selling, the high cost of the magazine space is a problem.

Push and Pull Strategies

The last factor that affects the promotional mix is whether a push or a pull promotional strategy will be used. Manufacturers may use aggressive personal selling and trade advertising to convince a wholesaler or a retailer to carry and sell their merchandise. This approach is known as a **push strategy** (see Exhibit 12.8). The wholesaler, in turn, must often push the merchandise forward by persuading the retailer to handle the goods. The retailer then uses advertising, displays, and other forms of promotion to convince the consumer to buy the "pushed" products. This concept also applies to services. For example, the Jamaican Tourism Board targets promotions to travel agencies, which, in turn, tell their customers about the benefits of vacationing in Jamaica.

At the other extreme is a **pull strategy**, which stimulates consumer demand to obtain product distribution. Rather than trying to sell to the wholesaler, the manufacturer using a pull strategy focuses its promotional efforts on end consumers or opinion leaders. For example, to prolong demand for his books, author James

push strategy
A marketing strategy that uses aggressive personal selling and trade advertising to convince a wholesaler or a retailer to carry and sell particular merchandise.

pull strategy
A marketing strategy that stimulates consumer demand to obtain product distribution.

Exhibit 12.8   Push Strategy versus Pull Strategy

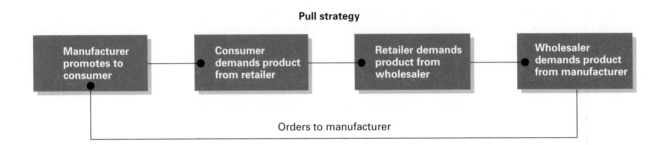

Push strategy

Manufacturer promotes to wholesaler → Wholesaler promotes to retailer → Retailer promotes to consumer → Consumer buys from retailer

Orders to manufacturer

Pull strategy

Manufacturer promotes to consumer → Consumer demands product from retailer → Retailer demands product from wholesaler → Wholesaler demands product from manufacturer

Orders to manufacturer

Patterson, a veteran advertising executive, insists that his publisher begin a second wave of marketing two months after one of his books is released. By doing so he prevents booksellers from moving the book to the back of the store after six to eight weeks, as is standard practice in the bookselling business.[25] As consumers begin demanding the product, the retailer orders the merchandise from the wholesaler. The wholesaler, confronted with rising demand, then places an order for the "pulled" merchandise from the manufacturer. Consumer demand pulls the product through the channel of distribution (see Exhibit 12.8). Heavy sampling, introductory consumer advertising, cents-off campaigns, and couponing are part of a pull strategy. For example, Smirnoff Ice sold almost eleven million cases in its first six months of national distribution. Contributing to those unprecedented numbers were extensive sampling, on-premise promotions, and $25 million in advertising.[26]

Rarely does a company use a pull or a push strategy exclusively. Instead, the mix will emphasize one of these strategies. For example, pharmaceutical companies generally use a push strategy, through personal selling and trade advertising, to promote their drugs and therapies to physicians. Sales presentations and advertisements in medical journals give physicians the detailed information they need to prescribe medication to their patients. Most pharmaceutical companies supplement their push promotional strategy with a pull strategy targeted directly to potential patients through advertisements in consumer magazines and on television.

Personal Selling

Describe personal selling

As mentioned at the beginning of the chapter, personal selling is direct communication between a sales representative and one or more prospective buyers in an attempt to influence each other in a purchase situation.

In a sense, all businesspeople are salespeople. An individual may become a plant manager, a chemist, an engineer, or a member of any profession and yet still have to sell. During a job search, applicants must "sell" themselves to prospective employers in an interview. To reach the top in most organizations, individuals need to sell ideas to peers, superiors, and subordinates. Most important, people must sell themselves and their ideas to just about everyone with whom they have a continuing relationship and to many other people they see only once or twice. Chances are that students majoring in business or marketing will start their professional careers in sales. Even students in nonbusiness majors may pursue a sales career.

Personal selling offers several advantages over other forms of promotion:

- Personal selling provides a detailed explanation or demonstration of the product. This capability is especially needed for complex or new goods and services.

- The sales message can be varied according to the motivations and interests of each prospective customer. Moreover, when the prospect has questions or raises objections, the salesperson is there to provide explanations. In contrast, advertising and sales promotion can only respond to the objections the copywriter thinks are important to customers.

- Personal selling can be directed only to qualified prospects. Other forms of promotion include some unavoidable waste because many people in the audience are not prospective customers.

- Personal selling costs can be controlled by adjusting the size of the sales force (and resulting expenses) in one-person increments. On the other hand, advertising and sales promotion must often be purchased in fairly large amounts.

- Perhaps the most important advantage is that personal selling is considerably more effective than other forms of promotion in obtaining a sale and gaining a satisfied customer.

Personal selling might work better than other forms of promotion given certain customer and product characteristics. Generally speaking, personal selling becomes more important as the number of potential customers decreases, as the complexity of the product increases, and as the value of the product grows (see Exhibit 12.9). When there are relatively few potential customers and the value of the good or service is relatively sufficient, the time and travel costs of personally visiting each prospect are justifiable. For highly complex goods, such as business jets or private communication systems, a salesperson is needed to determine the prospective customer's needs, explain the product's basic advantages, and propose the exact features and accessories that will meet the client's needs.

Exhibit 12.9

Comparison of Personal Selling and Advertising/Sales Promotion

Personal selling is more important if . . .	Advertising and sales promotion are more important if . . .
The product has a high value.	The product has a low value.
It is a custom-made product.	It is a standardized product.
There are few customers.	There are many customers.
The product is technically complex.	The product is easy to understand.
Customers are concentrated.	Customers are geographically dispersed.
Examples: insurance policies, custom windows, airplane engines	**Examples:** soap, magazine subscriptions, cotton T-shirts

Relationship Selling

Until recently, marketing theory and practice concerning personal selling focused almost entirely on a planned presentation to prospective customers for the sole purpose of making the sale. Marketers were most concerned with making a one-time sale and then moving on to the next prospect. Whether the presentation took place face-to-face during a personal sales call or over the telephone (telemarketing), traditional personal selling methods attempted to persuade the buyer to accept a point of view or convince the buyer to take some action. Once the customer was somewhat convinced, then the salesperson used a variety of techniques in an attempt to elicit a purchase. Frequently, the objectives of the salesperson were at the expense of the buyer, creating a win-lose outcome. Although this type of sales approach has not disappeared entirely, it is being used less and less often by professional salespeople.

relationship selling (consultative selling)
A sales practice that involves building, maintaining, and enhancing interactions with customers in order to develop long-term satisfaction through mutually beneficial partnerships.

In contrast, modern views of personal selling emphasize the relationship that develops between a salesperson and a buyer. **Relationship selling**, or **consultative selling**, is a multistage process that emphasizes personalization and empathy as key ingredients in identifying prospects and developing them as long-term, satisfied customers. The old way was to sell a product, but with relationship selling, the objective is to build long-term branded relationships with consumers/buyers.[27] Thus, the focus is on building mutual trust between the buyer and seller through the delivery of anticipated, long-term, value-added benefits to the buyer. Relationship or consultative sales-people, therefore, become consultants, partners, and problem solvers for their customers. They strive to build long-term relationships with key accounts by developing trust over time. The emphasis shifts from a one-time sale to a long-term relationship in which the salesperson works with the customer to develop solutions for enhancing the customer's bottom line. Moreover, research has shown that a positive customer-salesperson relationship contributes to trust, increased customer loyalty, and the intent to continue the relationship with the salesperson.[28] Thus, relationship selling promotes a win-win situation for both buyer and seller.

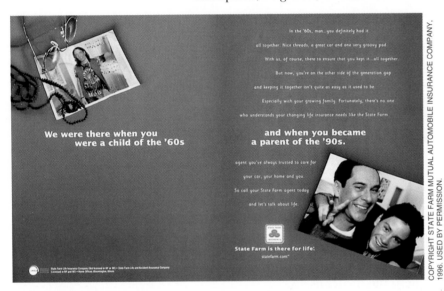

We were there when you were a child of the '60s

and when you became a parent of the '90s.

State Farm is there for life.
statefarm.com®

COPYRIGHT STATE FARM MUTUAL AUTOMOBILE INSURANCE COMPANY, 1996. USED BY PERMISSION.

Relationship selling emphasizes personalization and empathy in the process of developing long-term customers. This ad for State Farm showcases the commitment of the company to its customers throughout their various life stages.

The end result of relationship selling tends to be loyal customers who purchase from the company time after time. A relationship selling strategy focused on retaining customers costs a company less than if it were constantly prospecting and selling to new customers. Companies that focus on customer retention through high customer service gain 6 percent market share per year, while companies that offer low customer service lose 2 percent market share per year.[29] In fact, it costs businesses six times more to gain a new customer than to retain a current one.[30]

Relationship selling is more typical with selling situations for industrial-type goods, such as heavy machinery or computer systems, and services, such as airlines and insurance, than for consumer goods. For example, Kinko's has built a long-term business relationship with PeopleSoft. The software maker now gives many of its training and educational materials printing jobs to Kinko's—a deal worth close to $5 million in revenues. Kinko's has forged such a close relationship with the company that Kinko's representatives are even invited to sit in on internal planning meetings in PeopleSoft's human resources department at the company's headquarters.[31]

Exhibit 12.10 lists the key differences between traditional personal selling and relationship or consultative selling. These differences will become more apparent as we explore the personal selling process later in the chapter.

Traditional Personal Selling	Relationship or Consultative Selling
Sell products (goods and services)	Sell advice, assistance, and counsel
Focus on closing sales	Focus on improving the customer's bottom line
Limited sales planning	Consider sales planning as top priority
Spend most contact time telling customers about product	Spend most contact time attempting to build a problem-solving environment with the customer
Conduct "product-specific" needs assessment	Conduct discovery in the full scope of the customer's operations
"Lone wolf" approach to the account	Team approach to the account
Proposals and presentations based on pricing and product features	Proposals and presentations based on profit-impact and strategic benefits to the customer
Sales follow-up is short term, focused on product delivery	Sales follow-up is long term, focused on long-term relationship enhancement

SOURCE: Robert M. Peterson, Patrick L. Schul, and George H. Lucas, Jr., "Consultative Selling: Walking the Walk in the New Selling Environment," National Conference on Sales Management, *Proceedings,* March 1996.

Steps in the Selling Process

List the steps in the selling process

sales process (sales cycle)
The set of steps a salesperson goes through in a particular organization to sell a particular product or service.

Although personal selling may sound like a relatively simple task, completing a sale actually requires several steps. The **sales process**, or **sales cycle**, is simply the set of steps a salesperson goes through to sell a particular product or service. The sales process or cycle can be unique for each product or service, depending on the features of the product or service, characteristics of customer segments, and internal processes in place within the firm, such as how leads are gathered.

Some sales take only a few minutes, but others may take months or years to complete, especially when selling customized goods or services. The typical sale for Eastman Kodak's line of high-speed motion analysis cameras takes anywhere from nine to eighteen months to close.[32] On the other end of the spectrum, sales of its more basic cameras to retailers are generally more routine and may take only a few days. Whether a salesperson spends a few minutes or a few years on a sale, these are the seven basic steps in the personal selling process:

1. Generating leads
2. Qualifying leads
3. Approaching the customer and probing needs
4. Developing and proposing solutions
5. Handling objections
6. Closing the sale
7. Following up

Like other forms of promotion, these steps follow the AIDA concept discussed earlier in the chapter. Once a salesperson has located a prospect with the authority to buy, he or she tries to get the prospect's attention. A thorough needs assessment turned into an effective sales proposal and presentation should generate interest. After developing the customer's initial desire (preferably during the presentation of the sales proposal), the salesperson seeks action in the close by trying to get an agreement to buy. Follow-up after the sale, the final step in the selling process, not only lowers cognitive dissonance (refer to Chapter 4) but also may open up opportunities to discuss future sales. Effective follow-up will also lead to repeat business in which the process may start all over again at the needs assessment step.

Traditional selling and relationship selling follow the same basic steps, but they differ in the relative importance placed on key steps in the process (see Exhibit 12.11). Traditional selling efforts are transaction oriented, focusing on generating as many leads as possible, making as many presentations as possible, and closing as many sales as possible. Minimal effort is placed on asking questions to identify customer needs and wants or matching these needs and wants to the benefits of the product or service. In contrast, the salesperson practicing relationship selling emphasizes an up-front investment in the time and effort needed to uncover each customer's specific needs and wants and matching to them, as closely as possible, the product or service offering. By doing the homework up front, the salesperson creates the conditions necessary for a relatively straightforward close.[33] Let's look at each step of the selling process individually.

Generating Leads

lead generation (prospecting)
Identification of those firms and people most likely to buy the seller's offerings.

Initial groundwork must precede communication between the potential buyer and the salesperson. **Lead generation**, or **prospecting**, is the identification of those firms and people most likely to buy the seller's offerings. These firms or people become "sales leads" or "prospects."

Sales leads can be secured in various ways, most notably through advertising, trade shows and conventions, or direct-mail and telemarketing programs. Favorable publicity also helps to create leads. Company records of past client purchases are another excellent source of leads. Many sales professionals are also securing valuable leads from their firm's Internet Web site. For example, Ford Motor Company's drive to reach consumers on-line is paying off. Recently, the company's combination of Web sites and other on-line ventures sent an estimated half-million leads—60 percent of them in the United States—to its dealers.[34] In the future, more than half of all sales leads likely will come from the Internet.

referral
A recommendation to a salesperson from a customer or business associate.

Another way to gather a lead is through a **referral**—a recommendation from a customer or business associate. The advantages of referrals over other forms of prospecting include highly qualified leads, higher closing rates, larger initial transactions, and shorter sales cycles. Simply put, the salesperson and the company can earn more money in less time when prospecting using referrals. To increase the number of referrals they receive, some companies even pay or send small gifts to customers or suppliers who provide referrals. Research has suggested that one referral is as valuable as up to twelve cold calls. However, although 80 percent of clients would be willing to give referrals, only 20 percent are ever asked.[35]

networking
A process of finding out about potential clients from friends, business contacts, coworkers, acquaintances, and fellow members in professional and civic organizations.

Networking is the related method of using friends, business contacts, coworkers, acquaintances, and fellow members in professional and civic organizations to find out about potential clients. Indeed, a number of national networking clubs have recently been started for the sole purpose of generating leads and providing valuable business advice. The networking clubs usually have between fifteen and thirty members in noncompeting business categories. During weekly breakfast or lunch meet-

Key Selling Steps	Traditional Selling	Relationship/Consultative Selling
Generating leads	High	Low
Qualifying leads	Low	High
Approaching the customer and probing needs	Low	High
Developing and proposing solutions	Low	High
Handling objections	High	Low
Closing the sale	High	Low
Following up	Low	High

ings, each member is allotted a period of time to talk about the company he or she represents. Then members exchange lead cards. Research suggests that, on average, chapter members see an increase in business volume of between 16 and 25 percent after they've been with their group for three to six months.[36]

Before the advent of more sophisticated methods of lead generation, such as direct mail and telemarketing, most prospecting was done through **cold calling**—a form of lead generation in which the salesperson approaches potential buyers without any prior knowledge of the prospects' needs or financial status. Although this method is still used, many sales managers have realized the inefficiencies of having their top salespeople use their valuable selling time searching for the proverbial "needle in a haystack." Passing the job of cold calling to a lower-cost employee, typically an internal sales support person, allows salespeople to spend more time and use their relationship-building skills on prospects who have already been identified. Sales experts note that the days of cold calls and unannounced office visits have given way to referral-based and relationship selling.[37]

Qualifying Leads

When a prospect shows interest in learning more about a product, the salesperson has the opportunity to follow up, or qualify, the lead. Personally visiting unqualified prospects wastes valuable salesperson time and company resources. Often many leads go unanswered because salespeople are given no indication as to how qualified the leads are in terms of interest and ability to purchase. One study that surveyed four hundred marketers whose companies advertise in trade publications found that almost 40 percent of the leads generated went completely unanswered, most likely due to the fact that they were unqualified.[38]

Lead qualification consists of determining whether the prospect has three things:[39]

- *A recognized need:* The most basic criterion for determining whether someone is a prospect for a product is a need that is not being satisfied. The salesperson

cold calling
A form of lead generation in which the salesperson approaches potential buyers without any prior knowledge of the prospects' needs or financial status.

lead qualification
Determination of a sales prospect's (1) recognized need, (2) buying power, and (3) receptivity and accessibility.

should first consider prospects who are aware of a need but should not discount prospects who have not yet recognized that they have one. With a little more information about the product, they may decide they do have a need for it. Preliminary interviews and questioning can often provide the salesperson with enough information to determine whether there is a need.

- *Buying power:* Buying power involves both authority to make the purchase decision and access to funds to pay for it. To avoid wasting time and money, the salesperson needs to identify the purchasing authority and the ability to pay before making a presentation. Organizational charts and information about a firm's credit standing can provide valuable clues.

- *Receptivity and accessibility:* The prospect must be willing to see the salesperson and be accessible to the salesperson. Some prospects simply refuse to see salespeople. Others, because of their stature in their organization, will see only a salesperson or sales manager with similar stature.

Often the task of lead qualification is handled by a telemarketing group or a sales support person who *prequalifies* the lead for the salesperson. Prequalification systems free sales representatives from the time-consuming task of following up on leads to determine need, buying power, and receptiveness. Prequalification systems may even set up initial appointments with the prospect for the salesperson. The result is more time for the sales force to spend in front of interested customers. Protocol, an integrated direct marketing services company, helps clients with follow-up by loading lead information into a high-yield database. Protocol contacts trade show attendees and qualifies them using a scripting process based on input from the company for which it is working. After qualification, Protocol distributes A- and B-level leads to the client.[40]

With more and more companies setting up Web sites on the Internet, qualifying on-line leads has also received some attention. The object of a company's Web site should be to get visitors to register, indicate what products they are interested in, and offer up some information on their time frame and resources. Leads from the Internet can then be prioritized (those indicating a short time frame, for instance, given a higher priority) and then transferred to salespeople. Often Web site visitors can be enticed to answer questions with offers of free merchandise or information. Enticing visitors to register also allows companies to customize future electronic interactions—for example, by giving prospects who visit the Web site their choice from a menu of products tailored specifically to their needs.[41]

Approaching the Customer and Probing Needs

Prior to approaching the customer, the salesperson should learn as much as possible about the prospect's organization and its buyers. This process, called the **preapproach**, describes the "homework" that must be done by the salesperson before contacting the prospect. This may include consulting standard reference sources, such as Moody's, Standard & Poor's, or Dun & Bradstreet, or contacting acquaintances or others who may have information about the prospect. Another preapproach task is to determine whether the actual approach should be a personal visit, a phone call, a letter, or some other form of communication.

During the sales approach, the salesperson either talks to the prospect or secures an appointment for a future time in which to probe the prospect further as to his or her needs. Relationship selling theorists suggest that salespeople should begin developing mutual trust with their prospect during the approach. Salespeople should use the approach as a way of introducing themselves and their company and products. They must sell themselves before they can sell the product. Small talk that introduces sincerity and some suggestion of friendship is encouraged to build rapport with the prospect, but remarks that could be construed as insincere should be avoided.[42] Harvey Saltzman, owner of Triangle Printers, Inc.,

preapproach
A process that describes the "homework" that must be done by a salesperson before he or she contacts a prospect.

expanded his local customer base by drafting letters introducing himself and his company to other businesses in Skokie, Illinois. His letter pointed out that Triangle Printers was their neighbor. As a result, he captured twenty new customers worth approximately $200,000 in revenue.[43]

The salesperson's ultimate goal during the approach is to conduct a **needs assessment** to find out as much as possible about the prospect's situation. This involves interviewing the customer to determine his or her specific needs and wants and the range of options the customer has for satisfying them. The salesperson should be determining how to maximize the fit between what he or she can offer and what the prospective customer wants. As part of the needs assessment, the consultative salesperson must know everything there is to know about the following:[44]

- *The product or service:* Product knowledge is the cornerstone for conducting a successful needs analysis. The consultative salesperson must be an expert on his or her product or service, including technical specifications, the product's features and benefits, pricing and billing procedures, warranty and service support, performance comparisons with the competition, other customers' experiences with the product, and current advertising and promotional campaign messages.

- *Customers and their needs:* The salesperson should know more about customers than they know about themselves such that he or she acts not only as a supplier of products and services but also as a trusted consultant and adviser. The professional salesperson brings to each client business-building ideas and solutions to problems. For the customer, consulting a professional salesperson is like having another vital person on the team at no cost.

- *The competition:* The salesperson must know as much about competitors and their products as he or she knows about his or her own company, including who the competitors are and what is known about them; how their products and services compare; advantages and disadvantages; and strengths and weaknesses.

- *The industry:* Knowing the industry involves active research on the part of the salesperson. This means attending industry and trade association meetings, reading articles published in industry and trade journals, keeping track of legislation and regulation that affect the industry, awareness of product alternatives and innovations from domestic and foreign competition, and having a feel for economic and financial conditions that may affect the industry.

Creating a *customer profile* during the approach helps salespeople optimize their time and resources. This profile is then used to help develop an intelligent analysis of the prospect's needs in preparation for the next step, developing and proposing solutions. Customer profile information is typically stored and manipulated using sales force automation software packages designed for use on laptop computers. Such software provides sales reps with a computerized and efficient method of collecting customer information for use during the entire sales process. Further, customer and sales data stored in a computer database can be easily shared among sales team members. The information can also be appended with industry statistics, sales or meeting notes, billing data, and other information that may be pertinent to the prospect or the prospect's company. The more salespeople know about their prospects, the better they can meet their needs.

Salespeople should wrap up their sales approach and need-probing mission by summarizing the prospect's need, problem, and interest. The salesperson should also get a commitment from the customer to some kind of action, whether it's reading promotional material or agreeing to a demonstration. This commitment helps qualify the prospect further and justify additional time invested by the salesperson. The salesperson should reiterate the action he or she promises to take, such as sending information or calling back to provide answers to questions. The

needs assessment
A determination of the customer's specific needs and wants and the range of options the customer has for satisfying them.

date and time of the next call should be set at the conclusion of the sales approach as well as an agenda for the next call in terms of what the salesperson hopes to accomplish, such as providing a demonstration or presenting a solution.[45]

Developing and Proposing Solutions

Once the salesperson has gathered the appropriate information about the client's needs and wants, the next step is to determine whether his or her company's products or services match the needs of the prospective customer. The salesperson then develops a solution, or possibly several solutions, in which the salesperson's product or service solves the client's problems or meets a specific need.

These solutions are typically presented to the client in the form of a sales proposal presented at a sales presentation. A **sales proposal** is a written document or professional presentation that outlines how the company's product or service will meet or exceed the client's needs. The **sales presentation** is the formal meeting in which the salesperson has the opportunity to present the sales proposal. The presentation should be explicitly tied to the prospect's expressed needs. Further, the prospect should be involved in the presentation by being encouraged to participate in demonstrations or by exposure to computer exercises, slides, video or audio, flipcharts, photographs, and so on.[46]

Because the salesperson often has only one opportunity to present solutions, the quality of both the sales proposal and presentation can make or break the sale. Salespeople must be able to present the proposal and handle any customer objections confidently and professionally. For a powerful presentation, salespeople must be well prepared, use direct eye contact, ask open-ended questions, be poised, use hand gestures and voice inflection, focus on the customer's needs, incorporate visual elements that impart valuable information, know how to operate the audio/visual or computer equipment being used for the presentation, make sure the equipment works, and practice, practice, practice.[47] Nothing dies faster than a boring presentation. If the salesperson doesn't have a convincing and confident manner, then the prospect will very often forget the information. Prospects take in body language, voice patterns, dress, and body type. Often customers are more likely to remember how salespeople present themselves than what salespeople say.

Handling Objections

Rarely does a prospect say "I'll buy it" right after a presentation. Instead, the prospect often raises objections or asks questions about the proposal and the product. The potential buyer may insist that the price is too high, that he or she does not have enough information to make a decision, or that the good or service will not satisfy the present need. The buyer may also lack confidence in the seller's organization or product.

One of the first lessons that every salesperson learns is that objections to the product should not be taken personally as confrontations or insults. Rather, a salesperson should view objections as requests for information. A good salesperson considers objections a legitimate part of the purchase decision. To handle objections effectively, the salesperson should anticipate specific objections such as concerns about price, fully investigate the objection with the customer, be wary of what the competition is offering, and, above all, stay calm. Before a crucial sales presentation with an important prospect, for example, Dell Computer salespeople anticipated that the customer would have doubts as to whether Dell's direct selling model would provide the same level of service and dedication as a reseller would. Being prepared helped Dell win the contract.[48]

Often the salesperson can use the objection to close the sale. If the customer tries to pit suppliers against each other to drive down the price, the salesperson should be prepared to consider the competitor's offer and then identify value-added services that the competitor's deal lacks. Finally, the revised contract should be differentiated making it more difficult for comparisons.[49]

sales proposal
A formal written document or professional presentation that outlines how the salesperson's product or service will meet or exceed the prospect's needs.

sales presentation
A formal meeting in which the salesperson presents a sales proposal to a prospective buyer.

Closing the Sale

At the end of the presentation, the salesperson should ask the customer how he or she would like to proceed. If the customer exhibits signs that he or she is ready to purchase and all questions have been answered and objections have been met, then the salesperson can try to close the sale. Customers often give signals during or after the presentation that they are ready to buy or are not interested. Examples include changes in facial expressions, gestures, and questions asked. The salesperson should look for these signals and respond appropriately.

Closing requires courage and skill. Naturally, the salesperson wants to avoid rejection, and asking for a sale carries with it the risk of a negative answer. A salesperson should keep an open mind when asking for the sale and be prepared for either a yes or a no. Rarely is a sale closed on the first call. In fact, the typical salesperson averages about 765 sales calls a year, many of which are repeat calls to the same client in an attempt to make the sale.[50] Some salespeople may negotiate with large accounts for several years before closing a sale. As you can see, building a good relationship with the customer is very important. Often, if the salesperson has developed a strong relationship with the customer, only minimal efforts are needed to close a sale.

Negotiation often plays a key role in the closing of the sale. **Negotiation** is the process during which both the salesperson and the prospect offer special concessions in an attempt to arrive at a sales agreement. For example, the salesperson may offer a price cut, free installation, free service, or a trial order. Effective negotiators, however, avoid using price as a negotiation tool because cutting price directly affects a company's profitability. Because companies spend millions on advertising and product development to create value, when salespeople give in to price negotiations too quickly, it decreases the value of the product. Instead, effective salespeople should emphasize value to the customer, rendering price a nonissue. Salespeople should also be prepared to ask for trade-offs and try to avoid giving unilateral concessions. If you're making only a 50 percent margin on a product, and you need at least a 60 percent margin, raise your prices or drop the product.[51] Moreover, if the customer asks for a 5 percent discount, the salesperson should ask for something in return, such as higher volume or more flexibility in delivery schedules.

 More and more U.S. companies are expanding their marketing and selling efforts into global markets. Salespeople selling in foreign markets should tailor their presentation and closing styles to each market. Different personalities and skills will be successful in some countries and absolute failures in others. For instance, a salesperson who is an excellent closer and always focuses on the next sale might have difficulty doing business in Latin America where people want to take a long time building a personal relationship with their suppliers.[52]

Following Up

Unfortunately, many salespeople think that making the sale is all that's important. Once the sale is made, they can forget about their customers. They are wrong. Salespeople's responsibilities do not end with making the sales and placing the orders. One of the most important aspects of their jobs is **follow-up**—the final step in the delivery process, in which they must ensure that delivery schedules are met, that the goods or services perform as promised, and that the buyers' employees are properly trained to use the products.

Whereas the traditional sales approach's extent of follow-up with the customer is generally limited to successful product delivery and performance, a basic goal of relationship selling is to motivate customers to come back, again and again, by developing and nurturing long-term relationships. Most businesses depend on repeat sales, and repeat sales depend on thorough and continued follow-up by the salesperson. Finding a new customer is far more expensive than retaining an exist-

negotiation
The process during which both the salesperson and the prospect offer special concessions in an attempt to arrive at a sales agreement.

follow-up
The final step of the selling process, in which the salesperson ensures that delivery schedules are met, that the goods or services perform as promised, and that the buyers' employees are properly trained to use the products.

ing customer. When customers feel abandoned, cognitive dissonance arises and repeat sales decline. Today, this issue is more pertinent than ever because customers are far less loyal to brands and vendors. Buyers are more inclined to look for the best deal, especially in the case of poor after-the-sale follow-up. More and more buyers favor building a relationship with sellers.

 Automated e-mail follow-up marketing—a combination of sales automation and Internet technology—is enhancing customer satisfaction as well as bringing in more business for some marketers. Here's how it works: After the initial contact with a prospect, a software program automatically sends a series of personalized e-mail over a period of time. For example, CollegeRecruiter.com posts ads for businesses recruiting recent college graduates on its Web site and has seen phenomenal results from autoresponse marketing. Prospects start receiving a series of e-mails once they have visited the site and requested advertising rates. The first message goes out immediately. The next two go out in four to eleven days. From there, e-mails go out monthly. The average sale for CollegeRecruiter.com is $375, and the company gets $4,000 to $5,000 in additional sales from new customers each month just from the automated follow-ups.[53]

Sales Management

11

Describe the functions of sales management

There is an old adage in business that nothing happens until a sale is made. Without sales there is no need for accountants, production workers, or even a company president. Sales provide the fuel that keeps the corporate engines humming. Companies like Cisco Systems, International Paper, and Johnson Controls, and several thousand other manufacturers would cease to exist without successful salespeople. Even companies like Procter & Gamble and Kraft General Foods that mainly sell consumer goods and use extensive advertising campaigns still rely on salespeople to move products through the channel of distribution. Thus, sales management is one of marketing's most critical specialties. Effective sales management stems from a highly success-oriented sales force that accomplishes its mission economically and efficiently. Poor sales management can lead to unmet profit objectives or even to the downfall of the corporation.

Just as selling is a personal relationship, so is sales management. Although the sales manager's basic job is to maximize sales at a reasonable cost while also maximizing profits, he or she also has many other important responsibilities and decisions:

1. Defining sales goals and the sales process

2. Determining the sales force structure

3. Recruiting and training the sales force

4. Compensating and motivating the sales force

5. Evaluating the sales force

Defining Sales Goals and the Sales Process

Effective sales management begins with a determination of sales goals. Without goals to achieve, salesperson performance would be mediocre at best, and the company would likely fail. Like any marketing objective, sales goals should be stated in clear, precise, and measurable terms and should always specify a time frame for their fulfillment. Overall sales force goals are usually stated in terms of desired dollar sales volume, market share, or profit level. For example, a life insurance company may have a goal to sell $50 million in life insurance policies annually, to attain a 12 percent market share, or to achieve $1 million in profits. Individual salespeople are also assigned goals in the form of quotas. A **quota** is simply a statement of the salesperson's sales goals, usually based on sales volume alone but sometimes including key accounts (those with greatest potential), new accounts, repeat sales, and specific products.

quota
A statement of the individual salesperson's sales objectives, usually based on sales volume alone but sometimes including key accounts (those with greatest potential), new accounts, repeat sales, and specific products.

Great sales managers focus not only on sales goals but also on the entire process that drives their sales organizations to reach those goals. Without a keen understanding of the sales process, a manager will never be successful—no matter how defined the sales goals or how great the sales reps. An important responsibility of the sales manager, therefore, is to determine the most effective and efficient sales process to follow in selling each different product and service. Although the basic steps of the sales process are the same as discussed earlier in the chapter (i.e., lead generation and qualification, approach and needs assessment, proposal creation and presentation, handling objections, closing, and follow-up), a manager must formally define the specific procedures salespeople go through to do their jobs—for example, where leads are generated, how they are qualified, what the best way is to approach potential clients, and what terms can be negotiated during closing.

Determining the Sales Force Structure

Because personal selling is so costly, no sales department can afford to be disorganized. Proper design helps the sales manager organize and delegate sales duties and provide direction for salespeople. Sales departments are most commonly organized by geographic regions, by product line, by marketing function performed (such as account development or account maintenance), by market or industry, or by individual client or account. The sales force for IBM could be organized into sales territories covering New England, the Midwest, the South, and the West Coast or could be organized into distinct groups selling personal computer systems and mainframe computer systems. IBM salespeople may also be assigned to a specific industry or market, for example, the telecommunications industry, or to key clients such as AT&T and Sprint.

Market- or industry-based structures and key account structures are gaining popularity in today's competitive selling environment, especially with the emphasis on relationship selling. Being familiar with one industry or market allows sales reps to become experts in their fields and thereby offer better solutions and service. Further, by organizing the sales force around specific customers, many companies hope to improve customer service, encourage collaboration with other arms of the company, and unite salespeople in customer-focused sales teams. Clear Channel Communications, for example, which offers radio programming, outdoor advertising (billboards), and sponsorship of live entertainment, organizes its sales team by product. The company recently added a sales team dedicated to selling all three products as one package to make easier for large clients by offering them a single point of contact.[54]

Recruiting and Training the Sales Force

Sales force recruitment should be based on an accurate, detailed description of the sales task as defined by the sales manager. Aside from the usual characteristics such as level of experience or education, what traits should sales managers look for in applicants? One of the most important traits of top performers is ego strength, or having a

Motivating the sales force is one of the sales manager's toughest jobs. At Wal-Mart Home Office in Bentonville, Arkansas, associates attend a weekly sales meeting that brings executives, management, and associates together in an informal setting.

AP/WIDE WORLD PHOTOS

strong, healthy self-esteem and the ability to bounce back from rejection. Great salespeople also have a sense of urgency and competitiveness that pushes their sales to completion. Moreover, they have a desire to persuade people and close the sale. Effective salespeople are also assertive; they have the ability to be firm in one-to-one negotiations, to lead the sales process, and to get their point across confidently, without being overbearing or aggressive. They are sociable, willing to take risks, and capable of understanding complex concepts and ideas. Additionally, great salespeople are creative in developing client solutions, and they possess empathy—the ability to place oneself in someone else's shoes. Not surprisingly, in a recent study of top salespeople, almost 95 percent claim their sales style is relationship oriented rather than transaction oriented.[55]

After the sales recruit has been hired and given a brief orientation, training begins. A new salesperson generally receives instruction in company policies and practices, selling techniques, product knowledge, industry and customer characteristics, and nonselling duties such as filling out sales and market information reports or using a sales automation computer program. Firms that sell complex products generally offer the most extensive training programs. Pharmaceutical giant Merck, for example, takes a highly scientific approach to its market and trains its reps to understand the science of the medicine it sells so that they can maintain a peer-to-peer discussion with the physicians they call upon.[56]

Most successful sales organizations have learned that training is not just for newly hired salespeople. Instead, training is offered to all salespeople in an ongoing effort to hone selling skills and relationship building. In pursuit of solid salesperson-client relationships, training programs now seek to improve salespeople's consultative selling and listening skills and to broaden their product and customer knowledge. In addition, training programs stress the interpersonal skills needed to become the contact person for customers. Because negotiation is increasingly important in closing a sale, salespeople are also trained to negotiate effectively without risking profits. Corel Corporation started an on-line training program to educate its own salespeople. The on-line training has been so successful that it recently was expanded to include customers using Corel products.[57]

Compensating and Motivating the Sales Force

Compensation planning is one of the sales manager's toughest jobs. Only good planning will ensure that compensation attracts, motivates, and retains good salespeople. Generally, companies and industries with lower levels of compensation suffer higher turnover rates, which increase costs and decrease effectiveness. Therefore, compensation needs to be competitive enough to attract and motivate the best salespeople.

The three basic compensation methods for salespeople are commission, salary, and combination plans. A typical commission plan gives salespeople a specified percentage of their sales revenue. A **straight commission** system compensates the salesperson only when a sale is made. On the other end of the spectrum, a **straight salary** system compensates a salesperson with a stated salary regardless of sales productivity. Most companies, however, offer a compromise between straight commission and straight salary plans. A **combination system** offers a base salary plus an incentive—usually a commission or a bonus. Combination systems have benefits for both the sales manager and the salesperson. The salary portion of the plan helps the manager control the sales force; the incentive provides motivation. For the salesperson, a combination plan offers an incentive to excel while minimizing the extremely wide swings in earnings that may occur when the economy surges or contracts too much.

Firms sometimes take profit into account when developing their compensation plans. Instead of paying salespeople on overall volume, they pay according to the profitability achieved from selling each product. Still other companies tie a part of the salesperson's total compensation to customer satisfaction assessed through periodic customer surveys. As the emphasis on relationship selling in-

straight commission
A method of compensation in which the salesperson is paid some percentage when a sale is made.

straight salary
A method of compensation in which the salesperson receives a salary regardless of sales productivity.

combination system
A method of compensation in which the salesperson receives a base salary and an incentive.

creases, many sales managers feel that the latter encourages relationship building. Sales managers can survey clients on a salesperson's ability to create realistic expectations and his or her responsiveness to customer needs.[58] At PeopleSoft, structure, culture, and strategies are built around customer satisfaction. Sales force compensation is tied to both sales quotas and a satisfaction metric that allows clients to voice their opinions on the service given.[59]

Although the compensation plan motivates a salesperson to sell, sometimes it is not enough to produce the volume of sales or the profit margin required by sales management. Sales managers, therefore, often offer rewards or incentives, such as recognition at ceremonies, plaques, vacations, merchandise, and pay raises or cash bonuses. For example, Lorry I. Lokey, president and CEO of Business Wire, invites employees from one of the company's twenty-six offices nationwide to join him on a free trip to a predetermined location, usually overseas. To qualify, employees must have celebrated their five-year anniversary with the company.[60] But, of course, the most popular incentives are cash rewards, used by 64 percent of sales organizations polled in a recent survey.[61] Rewards may help increase overall sales volume, add new accounts, improve morale and goodwill, move slow items, and bolster slow sales. They can be used to achieve long-term or short-term objectives, such as unloading overstocked inventory and meeting a monthly or quarterly sales goal.

Motivation also takes the form of effective sales leadership on the part of the sales manager. An effective sales manager is inspirational to his or her salespeople, encouraging them to achieve their goals through clear and enthusiastic communications. He or she has a clear vision and commitment to the mission of the organization and the ability to instill pride and earn the respect of employees. Effective sales leaders continuously increase their knowledge and skill base while also encouraging others to do so. A recent study that assessed the attributes of sales leaders found that the best sales leaders share a number of key personality traits (see Exhibit 12.12),

Exhibit 12.12

Seven Key Leadership Traits of Effective Sales Leaders

Effective sales leaders . . .	
Are assertive	Assertive sales leaders know when and how to get tough and how to assert their authority.
Possess ego drive	Sales leaders with ego drive have the desire and ability to persuade their reps to take action.
Possess ego strength	Sales leaders with ego strength are able to make sure not only that they bounce back from rejection but also that their reps rebound, too.
Take risks	Risk-taking sales leaders are willing to go out on a limb in an effort to make a sale or enhance a relationship.
Are innovative	Innovative sales leaders stay open to new ideas and new ways of conducting business.
Have a sense of urgency	Urgent sales leaders understand that getting things done now is critical to winning and keeping business.
Are empathetic	Empathetic sales leaders help their reps grow by listening and understanding.

SOURCE: Table adapted from "The 7 Traits of Great Sales Leaders" by Geoffrey Brewer, *Sales & Marketing Management*, July 1997, 38–46. Reprinted with permission.

such as a sense of urgency, openness to new ideas, and a desire to take risks. These traits separate motivational sales leaders from mere sales managers.

Evaluating the Sales Force

The final task of sales managers is evaluating the effectiveness and performance of the sales force. To evaluate the sales force, the sales manager needs feedback—that is, regular information from salespeople. Typical performance measures include sales volume, contribution to profit, calls per order, sales or profits per call, or percentage of calls achieving specific goals such as sales of products that the firm is heavily promoting.

Performance information helps the sales manager monitor a salesperson's progress through the sales cycle and pinpoint where breakdowns may be occurring. For example, by knowing the number of prospects an individual salesperson has in each step of the sales cycle process and determining where prospects are falling out of the sales cycle, a manager can determine how effective a salesperson may be at lead generation, needs assessment, proposal generation, presenting, closing, and follow-up stages. This information can then tell a manager what sales skills may need to be reassessed or retrained. For example, if a sales manager notices that a sales rep seems to be letting too many prospects slip away after presenting proposals, it may mean he or she needs help with developing proposals, handling objections, or closing sales.

The Impact of Technology on Personal Selling

Will the increasingly sophisticated technology now available at marketers' fingertips eliminate the need for salespeople? Experts agree that a relationship between the salesperson and customer will always be necessary. Technology, however, can certainly help to improve that relationship.[62] Cellphones, laptops, pagers, e-mail, and electronic organizers allow salespeople to be more accessible to both clients and the company. Moreover, the Internet provides salespeople with vast resources of information on clients, competitors, and the industry. In fact, many companies are utilizing technology to stay more in touch with their own employees. For instance, IBM invited 320,000 employees to an electronic brainstorming session. A total of 52,600 employees logged on to the event to discuss issues of employee retention, work efficiency, quality, and teamwork.[63]

E-business, or buying, selling, marketing, collaborating with partners, and servicing customers electronically using the Internet, is also having a significant impact on personal selling. For customers, the Web has become a powerful tool to get accurate and up-to-date information on products, pricing, and order status. For example, Dell Computer uses the Internet to offer customized services for its large clients and generates more than $50 million in online sales annually. The company believes that by using technology to provide information, it creates stronger relationships with its customers.[64] The Internet also cost-effectively processes orders and services requests. Although on the surface the Internet might look like a threat to the job security of salespeople, the Web is actually freeing sales reps from tedious administrative tasks, like shipping catalogs, placing routine orders, or tracking orders. This leaves them more time to focus on the needs of their clients. Similarly, Carlson Wagonlit Travel has moved sales of routine products like shuttle flights to the Internet, allowing travel agents to focus on selling to high-potential customers.[65]

The publishers of *Maxim* employ many different elements of the promotional mix to promote the magazine to its readers. Guerrilla marketing tactics, public relations, and publicity are important elements of their plan. *Maxim*'s integrated promotional plan conveys a consistent and clear message of the magazine's image and has been crucial to the company's success in the men's magazine industry. As you read the next chapter, keep in mind that marketers try to choose the mix of promotional elements that will best promote their good or service. Rarely will a marketer rely on just one method of promotion.

USE IT

Learn a New Form of Communication
ON LINE Learn American Sign Language and communicate through your hands, gestures, and body movements. Visit HandSpeak at **http://www.handspeak.com** for a practical visual dictionary of sign language for everyday life. More information is available at **http://www.deafresources.com**.

Become a Marketing Guerrilla
ON LINE Entrepreneurs and small businesses don't always have big promotional budgets. For hundreds of low-cost promotional ideas, turn to the Guerrilla Marketing Web page at **http://www.gmarketing.com**. Find out how to promote effectively for a fraction of what the big guys spend.

REVIEW IT

(1) Discuss the role of promotion in the marketing mix. Promotion is communication by marketers that informs, persuades, and reminds potential buyers of a product in order to influence an opinion or elicit a response. Promotional strategy is the plan for using the elements of promotion—advertising, public relations, sales promotion, and personal selling—to meet the firm's overall objectives and marketing goals. Based on these objectives, the elements of the promotional strategy become a coordinated promotion plan. The promotion plan then becomes an integral part of the total marketing strategy for reaching the target market along with product, distribution, and price.

1.1 What is a promotional strategy? Explain the concept of a competitive advantage in relation to promotional strategy.

(2) Discuss the elements of the promotional mix. The elements of the promotional mix include advertising, public relations, sales promotion, and personal selling. Advertising is a form of impersonal, one-way mass communication paid for by the source. Public relations is the function of promotion concerned with a firm's public image. Firms can't buy good publicity, but they can take steps to create a positive company image. Sales promotion is typically used to back up other components of the promotional mix by stimulating immediate demand. Finally, personal selling typically involves direct communication, in person or by telephone; the seller tries to initiate a purchase by informing and persuading one or more potential buyers.

2.1 WRITING As the promotional manager for a new line of cosmetics targeted to preteen girls, you have been assigned the task of deciding which promotional mix elements—advertising, public relations, sales promotion, and personal selling—should be used in promoting it. Your budget for promoting the preteen cosmetics line is limited. Write a promotional plan explaining your choice of promotional mix elements given the nature of the product, the stage in the product life cycle, the target market characteristics, the type of buying decision, available funds, and the use of a pull or push strategy.

(3) Discuss the concept of integrated marketing communications. Integrated marketing communications is the careful coordination of all promotional messages for a product or service to assure the consistency of messages at every contact point where a company meets the consumer—advertising, sales promotion, personal selling, public relations, as well as direct marketing, packaging, and other forms of communication. Marketing managers carefully coordinate all promotional activities to ensure that consumers see and hear one message. Integrated marketing communications has received more attention in recent years due to the proliferation of media choices, the fragmentation of mass markets into more segmented niches, and the decrease in advertising spending in favor of promotional techniques that generate an immediate sales response.

3.1 Discuss the importance of integrated marketing communications. Give some current examples of companies that are and are not practicing IMC.

(4) Describe the communication process. The communication process has several steps. When an individual or organization has a message it wishes to convey to a target audience, it encodes that message using language and symbols familiar to the intended receiver and sends the message through a channel of communication. Noise in the transmission channel distorts the source's intended message. Reception occurs if the message falls within the receiver's frame of reference. The receiver decodes the message and usually provides feedback to the source. Normally, feedback is direct for interpersonal communication and indirect for mass communication.

4.1 Why is understanding the target market a crucial aspect of the communication process?

(5) Explain the goals and tasks of promotion. The fundamental goals of promotion are to induce, modify, or reinforce behavior by informing, persuading, and reminding. Informative promotion explains a good's or service's purpose and benefits. Promotion that informs the consumer is typically used to increase demand for a general product category or to introduce a new good or service. Persuasive promotion is designed to stimulate a purchase or an action. Promotion that persuades the consumer to buy is essential during the growth stage of the product life cycle, when competition becomes fierce. Reminder promotion is used to keep the product and brand name in the public's mind. Promotions that remind are generally used during the maturity stage of the product life cycle.

5.1 Why might a marketing manager choose to promote his or her product using persuasion? Give some current examples of persuasive promotion.

5.2 Choose a partner from class and go together to interview the owners or managers of several small businesses in your city. Ask them what their promotional objectives are and why. Are they trying to inform, persuade, or remind customers to do business with them? Also determine whether they believe they have an awareness problem or whether they need to persuade customers to come to them instead of to competitors. Ask them to list the characteristics of their primary market, the strengths and weaknesses of their direct competitors, and how they are positioning their store to compete. Prepare a report to present in class summarizing your findings.

(6) Discuss the AIDA concept and its relationship to the promotional mix. The AIDA model outlines the four basic stages in the purchase decision-making process, which are initiated and propelled by promotional activities: (1) attention, (2) interest, (3) desire, and (4) action. The components of the promotional mix have varying levels of influence at each stage of the AIDA model. Advertising is a good tool for increasing awareness and knowledge of a good or service. Sales promotion is effective when consumers are at the purchase stage of the decision-making process. Personal selling is most effective in developing customer interest and desire.

6.1 Discuss the AIDA concept. How do these different stages of consumer involvement affect the promotional mix?

6.2 What role can the Internet play in the AIDA concept? Consider Exhibit 12.6. Recreate the table by deciding how effective you think the Internet would be as an advertising tool to create attention, interest, desire, and action. Continue to evaluate the Internet as a public relations tool, sales promotion tool, and personal selling tool.

(7) **Describe the factors that affect the promotional mix.** Promotion managers consider many factors when creating promotional mixes. These factors include the nature of the product, product life-cycle stage, target market characteristics, the type of buying decision involved, availability of funds, and feasibility of push or pull strategies. Because most business products tend to be custom-tailored to the buyer's exact specifications, the marketing manager may choose a promotional mix that relies more heavily on personal selling. On the other hand, consumer products are generally mass produced and lend themselves more to mass promotional efforts such as advertising and sales promotion. As products move through different stages of the product life cycle, marketers will choose to use different promotional elements. For example, advertising is emphasized more in the introductory stage of the product life cycle than in the decline stage. Characteristics of the target market, such as geographic location of potential buyers and brand loyalty, influence the promotional mix as does whether the buying decision is complex or routine. The amount of funds a firm has to allocate to promotion may also help determine the promotional mix. Small firms with limited funds may rely more heavily on public relations, whereas larger firms may be able to afford broadcast or print advertising. Last, if a firm uses a push strategy to promote the product or service, the marketing manager may choose to use aggressive advertising and personal selling to wholesalers and retailers. If a pull strategy is chosen, then the manager often relies on aggressive mass promotion, such as advertising and sales promotion, to stimulate consumer demand.

7.1 Explain the difference between a "pull" and a "push" promotional strategy. Under what conditions should each strategy be used?

7.2 *INFOTRAC COLLEGE EDITION* **WRITING** Choose two companies, one a consumer-products company and the other an on-line retailer. Conduct some research on these two companies in terms of their promotional practices by observation (such as looking in magazines, the newspaper, television, Web site, etc.) and searching at your campus library. You may also use InfoTrac (**http://www.infotrac-college.com**) to locate any articles written on the promotional activities of the companies you select. Describe some of the types of promotions that these companies have engaged in during the last year—for example, ran television ads, sponsored an event, held a sweepstakes, or expanded sales force. To the best of your abilities, determine the objective of each promotion in relation to the AIDA model. For example, the objective of a magazine ad might be to gain attention or to create interest, while the objective of a coupon might be to stimulate the action of purchase. Also note if the companies' promotions are integrated or not.

7.3 **ON LINE** Visit **http://www.teenresearch.com**. What research can this company offer about the size and growth of the teen market, the buying power of teenagers, and their buying habits? Why might these statistics be important to a company targeting teenagers in terms of marketing communications and promotion strategy?

(8) **Describe personal selling.** Personal selling is direct communication between a sales representative and one or more prospective buyers in an attempt to influence each other in a purchase situation. Broadly speaking, all businesspeople use personal selling to promote themselves and their ideas. Personal selling offers several advantages over other forms of promotion. Personal selling allows salespeople to thoroughly explain and demonstrate a product. Salespeople have the flexibility to tailor a sales proposal to the needs and preferences of individual customers. Personal selling is more efficient than other forms of promotion because salespeople target qualified prospects and avoid wasting efforts on unlikely buyers. Personal selling affords greater managerial control over promotion costs. Finally, personal selling is the most effective method of closing a sale and producing satisfied customers.

8.1 Discuss the role of personal selling in promoting products. What advantages does personal selling offer over other forms of promotion?

(9) **Discuss the key differences between relationship selling and traditional selling.** Relationship selling is the practice of building, maintaining, and enhancing interactions with customers in order to develop long-term satisfaction through mutually beneficial partnerships. Traditional selling, on the other hand, is transaction focused. That is, the salesperson is most concerned with making one-time sales and moving on to the next prospect. Salespeople practicing relationship selling spend more time understanding a prospect's needs and developing solutions to meet those needs.

9.1 What are the key differences between relationship selling and traditional methods of selling? What types of products or services do you think would be conducive to relationship selling?

(10) **List the steps in the selling process.** The selling process is composed of seven basic steps: (1) generating leads, (2) qualifying leads, (3) assessing approach and needs, (4) developing and proposing solutions, (5) handling objections, (6) closing the sale, and (7) following up.

10.1 **WRITING** You are a new salesperson for a well-known medical software company, and one of your clients is a large group of physicians. You have just arranged an initial meeting with the office manager. Develop a list of questions you might ask at this meeting to uncover the group's specific needs.

10.2 What does sales follow-up entail? Why is it an essential step in the selling process, particularly from the perspective of relationship selling? How does it relate to cognitive dissonance?

(11) **Describe the functions of sales management.** Sales management is a critical area of marketing that performs several important functions. Sales managers set overall company sales goals and define the sales process most effective for achieving those goals. They determine sales force structure based on geographic, product, functional, or customer variables. Managers develop the sales force through recruiting and training. Sales management motivates the sales force through compensation planning, motivational tools, and effective sales leadership. Finally, sales managers evaluate the sales force through salesperson feedback and other methods of determining their performance.

11.1 *INFOTRAC COLLEGE EDITION* Managing a sales force in today's e-business environment can be difficult, especially with the Internet perceived as a threat to job security. Use InfoTrac (**http://www.infotrac-college.com**) to locate an article in *Electronic News* titled, "Creating a Web-Savvy Sales Force" by Wally York. Read the article and list York's key elements. How does this tie in with what you read in the chapter?

11.2 **TEAM** With two classmates, select a company or business near campus that has a sales force. Using York's article (from question 11.1) as a starting point, list all the things the company would need to do to create an e-savvy sales force.

11.3 *INFOTRAC COLLEGE EDITION* Without revenue, a company cannot survive, and sales is the means to that end. How important is the effectiveness of a company's sales force? Use InfoTrac (**http://www.infotrac-college.com**) to run a keyword search for "sales force" or "sales force automation." Skim six to ten articles and write down all the automation tools (software and hardware) that you discover.

DEFINE IT

APPLY IT

Application for Entrepreneurs

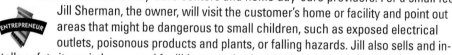

Be Safe is a small, independent business that markets child-proofing services to parents with small children and to day-care centers and home day-care providers. For a small fee, Jill Sherman, the owner, will visit the customer's home or facility and point out areas that might be dangerous to small children, such as exposed electrical outlets, poisonous products and plants, or falling hazards. Jill also sells and installs safety items in homes and facilities to make them safer for children. Currently, most of her business comes through referrals or the Yellow Pages, but she would like to increase her business through some form of promotion, although her budget to do so will be small. She has noticed that many of her clients, especially new parents, don't know much about child safety in the home or about the products that can help prevent child injuries. Other clients, especially day-care centers, know about child safety but often install the wrong products or don't maintain a safe environment at all times, exposing children to danger.

Questions

1. What goals should Be Safe's promotional efforts try to achieve? How will these goals differ by target market?

2. How might the type of buying decision and the nature of this service influence the promotional mix?

3. Given Be Safe's small budget, what types of promotional methods would you suggest?

THINK ABOUT IT

Ethics Exercise 1

Integrated Marketing Solutions is a consumer products marketing services firm. Currently, the firm is handling the launch of a new book for one of its publishing clients. The campaign includes advance review copies for key book reviewers, "Coming Soon" posters for booksellers, an author book-signing tour, and several television interviews. Everything has been produced and scheduled for release next week. Today, Jane Kershaw, the account executive, learned that although the book received numerous favorable reviews, the book review quoted on all of the promotional materials is fabricated.

Questions

1. What should Jane do?

2. What does the AMA Code of Ethics say about accuracy in promotional materials? Go to **http://www.marketingpower.com** and review the code. Then, write a brief paragraph describing how the AMA Code of Ethics relates to this issue.

Ethics Exercise 2

Bruce Jackson sells air conditioners for Comfort Heating and Air Conditioning. He is having a very good year and hopes to win the incentive trip his company awards the top salesperson each year. With one quarter in the year left to go, Bruce learns that another salesperson has slightly higher sales. He also learns that the other salesperson is exaggerating product benefits in his sales pitch but company officials seem to be looking the other way.

Questions

1. What should Bruce do?

2. Does the AMA Code of Ethics address this issue? Go to **http://www.marketingpower. com** and review the code. Then, write a brief paragraph describing how the AMA Code of Ethics relates to this issue.

TRY IT

Entrepreneurship Case

Varsity Group: The Campus Bookstore Alternative

The U.S. market for educational textbooks is roughly an $8 billion industry, with U.S. college students spending $4–5 billion each year purchasing over seventy million textbooks needed for classes. With the industry averaging 7 percent annual growth, the marketing implications—and opportunities—can be huge, but so can the challenges. Varsity Group knows this probably better than most.

The company burst onto the college campus scene in 1998 ready to turn what is now a $10 billion-a-year campus store retail business on its ear by providing an on-line store where college students could buy their books and supplies at a discount. When the company first launched its on-line storefront, VarsityBooks.com, only about 1 percent of college textbooks were sold via the Web. But with close to 100 percent of college students using the Internet and over 70 percent logging on daily, the potential for Varsity Group and other on-line textbook retailers to make it big was enormous. On-line textbook retailers offered all the conveniences of Internet shopping, such as round-the-clock service and a wider selection than the campus bookstore could offer. And because Varsity Group had no brick-and-mortar storefront and few storage costs, it could sell some textbooks for as much as 40 percent less than traditional textbook sellers.

Initially, Varsity Group succeeded in the on-line textbook market because of its highly creative, albeit unusual, promotional tactics. Instead of putting its entire promotional budget into buying ads in the campus newspaper or on local radio stations, Varsity Group would recruit college students to help promote its Web site on college campuses and to persuade their classmates to purchase their textbooks from the company's Web site instead of at inconvenient campus bookstores where prices are higher. At one point, close to three thousand students on six hundred U.S. campuses signed on to become representatives for Varsity Group. Campus reps received hourly and commission-based wages and the freedom to execute their own campaigns. Lead campus reps enjoyed business cards, stock options, a PalmPilot, and a flexible budget. Student reps also attended biannual training programs to listen to speakers on marketing best practices, case studies, codes of conduct, and team management skills.

Some of the more interesting grassroots promotional and sales techniques to student reps used to promote VarsityBooks.com included sponsoring parties, dressing local bands in VarsityBooks.com t-shirts, and handing out candy bars, granola bars, and lollipops with

VarsityBooks.com coupons. At Florida State University, campus reps used sidewalk chalk to pen messages such as "Smashing Savings" on sidewalks around campus. At Stanford University, Varsity reps passed out coupons at a nearby movie theater. Other reps distributed price comparison flyers for particular courses at classroom doorways.

Immediately, there was a high level of interest from students nationwide, forcing college bookstores to respond quickly and become more competitive on prices and improve their service levels. With these enhancements made at the nearby college bookstore, students could generally get their textbooks more quickly and easily on campus. Within two years, Varsity Group was changing its business model to address the new marketplace. Confident that there was still a role for an on-line campus bookstore, the company shifted its focus from selling textbooks directly to students to a more institutional approach that offered an on-line bookstore solution for private secondary schools and colleges. Rather than an army of student sales reps, Varsity Groups now employs an in-house sales force dedicated to the entire sales process.

For roughly six months out of the year, in-house account managers work to generate leads about educational institutions in need of a viable bookstore option. Managers are looking for the many smaller, private schools and colleges that are no longer able to underwrite the expense of an independent campus bookstore or that no longer want the hassle of managing one. Through its eduPartners program, Varsity Group enrolled over one hundred and forty such institutions in 2002.

Once account managers have identified schools that would be good candidates for the eduPartners program, senior sales representatives take over to complete the sales process. This includes visiting the campus and assessing the full needs of the potential client. This process can take anywhere from one month to one year, and schools that join typically start using VarsityBooks the following semester, so Varsity Group now has a sales cycle that could stretch to twelve months or longer. Since the target customer has changed from the student buying the book to the school providing the service of a bookstore, the sales force has taken a more consultative approach to its sales strategy. That is, the student reps spent a great deal of time in designing and implementing creative promotional strategies to attract student customers. Now, the in-house sales reps spend more time building relationships with Varsity Group's eduPartners, listening to their needs and developing solutions to match them: eduPartners receive a high level of service at a reasonable price and lose all the hassles of managing and financing a campus store.

Although Varsity Group has changed its sales strategy from a customer focus to an institutional focus, the company continues to look for unique market segments and opportunities by leveraging a novel approach in its marketing efforts. The student reps were the first way the company did this; being the first on-line bookstore solution for smaller schools is the current way the company is doing this.

Questions

1. What can you deduce about the textbook market from Varsity Group's new sales strategy?

2. What can you deduce about Varsity Group's promotional goals from the changes it has made to its business model?

3. You are a sales rep for Varsity Group and are working with potential clients, who are not entirely convinced that eduPartners will work for their campus. Anticipate objections that they may raise and address them positively. You may consult the VarsityBooks.com Web site at **http://www.varsitybooks.com** as a resource.

WATCH IT

Short

The *Essentials of Marketing* PowerPoint CD-ROM has five video ad clips embedded in the Chapter 12 slide presentation. After watching the three Pepsi ads, determine how consistent the marketing message was. What communication function do the Dodge and Taco Bell ads convey?

Medium

Licensing is a popular way to expand the potential of a brand. This CNN clip takes you to a licensing trade show to see how cartoon characters are licensed and promoted. Is this a typical trade show? What brands (i.e., characters) do you recognize? Recall information from Chapter 3 as you view the clip.

When the outside auditor of McDonald's popular Monopoly givaway game was charged with fraud, the fast-food giant had a serious communication problem on its hands. Watch the clip on the scandal and determine how well McDonald's communicated with its customers during and after the game was compromised. This segment is also relevant for Chapter 13.

Long

For Chapter 12, Small Business School takes you inside the world of Ann and Michael McGilvray, founders of AMCI, a sales agency with over ninety sales reps covering twenty-two states. Have you ever bought a rubber bug? It may very well have been sold to the store where you bought it by Ann McGilvray or one of her reps. Let's see what the woman who has sold everything from greeting cards to glow-in-the-dark cockroaches has to say about personal selling and sales management. AMCI also offers a great example of sales management as well as marketing channels. So recall the material you learned in Chapter 10 as you turn your attention to the AMCI Master Class.

FLIP IT

Flip to Chapter 12 in your *Grademaker Study Guide* for more review opportunities, including the pretest, vocabulary review, Internet activities, study test questions, and an application exercise based on promotion and personal selling concepts. Can you close your book and diagram the communication process? What about describing the difference between push and pull strategies? Do you know the difference between traditional selling and relationship selling? If not, pick up your *Grademaker* and review.

CLICK IT

The *Essentials of Marketing* Web site links you to all the Internet-based activities in this chapter, like the "Use It," "Review It" questions 7.2, 7.3, 11.1, and 11.3, "Think About It," and the On-Line exercises in the chapter margins. As a review, do the Chapter 12 quiz and crossword puzzle. And don't forget the Career Exersite that gives you resources for exploring marketing career opportunities in promotions. Review the main concepts in the PowerPoint presentation for Chapter 12, too. Go to **http://lamb.swlearning.com**, read the material, and follow the links right from the site.

Surf Xtra! to test your understanding of the promotion concepts in the chapter by completing the worksheets for Exhibits 12.1 and 12.3 through 12.12. If your instructor has assigned a marketing plan project, worksheets on Xtra! can help you organize your work. In addition to the quiz on the Web site, there's another quiz on the Xtra!, plus video of the authors answering frequently asked questions about promotion topics, such as, "Which factors influence the promotional mix and how?" and "How do businesses tell customers about their products and services?"

Still Shaky? Here's a Tip.

Use the learning objectives list on page 402 as a study tool. After reading the whole chapter, return to the beginning and write the summary for each objective. Check your work by reading the actual summary points on pages 437–440.

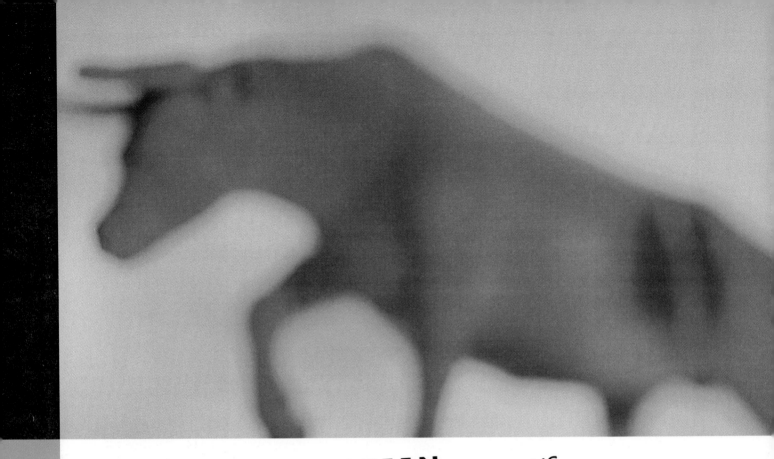

CHAPTER THIRTEEN
ADVERTISING, PUBLIC RELATIONS, AND SALES PROMOTIONS

Learning Objectives

1 Discuss the effects of advertising on market share and consumers

2 Identify the major types of advertising

3 Discuss the creative decisions in developing an advertising campaign

4 Describe media evaluation and selection techniques

5 Discuss the role of public relations in the promotional mix

6 Define and state the objectives of sales promotion

7 Discuss the most common forms of consumer sales promotion

8 List the most common forms of trade sales promotion

It's after midnight and the dance clubs are jumping—music is pulsating, lights are flashing, people are dancing, and the bar is littered with little silver and blue cans. Yes, Red Bull is in the house—and has absolutely no intention of leaving the party.

Red Bull, exported from Austria, has created and dominated the energy drink category with marketing savvy, guerrilla tactics, and unusual distribution methods. Dietrich Mateschitz, the owner of Red Bull International, created the caffeine-charged beverage in 1987, based on a popular health tonic he discovered in Thailand. After spreading into neighboring countries including Hungary, Slovenia, Germany, and Switzerland, Red Bull charged into the U.S. market, virtually creating the energy drink market and taking it by the horns.

Initially, Red Bull was the drink of choice for extreme athletes and all-night ravers, but the taurine-based energy drink has gained a larger following and can now be found on supermarket shelves in almost every state. According to Red Bull's Web site at (**http://www. redbull.com**), "Taurine is a conditionally essential amino acid, which naturally occurs in the body. But in times of extreme physical exertion, the body no longer produces the required amounts and a relative deficiency results." Hence, a need is identified and Red Bull races to fill it.

In less than three years, Red Bull has spawned a hot new beverage category and boosted sales from a base of $12 million to $42 million in 1998 and $75 million in 1999, according to Beverage Marketing Corporation. Now Coke, Anheuser-Busch, and Pepsi are looking to get a piece of the action, and some predict that sales of energy drinks in the United States could top $500 million in the next few years.

But with 70 percent of the market share, Red Bull executives feel confident that they can continue leading the category by employing the same marketing techniques that put them on the map in the first place.

The company's consistent strategy has been to "open up" a market by securing unusual distribution channels. Red Bull initially began its U.S. charge in Santa Monica, California, by piggybacking with established distributors that deliver a number of brands. As the drink became more popular, Red Bull narrowed its distribution methods by contacting smaller distributors and insisting that they sell only Red Bull. Otherwise, Red Bull sets up warehouses and hires college students to deliver its product. Results have been incredible—in a new market, Red Bull generally breaks even within the first three months and shows a profit after six.

Another tactic that Red Bull employs is hiring hip locals "who embody the spirit of Red Bull" in target areas to drive around in a Red Bull logoed car, hand out samples, and educate consumers about the product.

Sales teams also visit targeted on-site accounts—trendy nightclubs and bars. After an initial purchase of a few cases, Red Bull supplies the bar with a branded cooler and other POP (Point-of-Purchase) items. The sales teams also work to get the drink into convenience stores near colleges, gyms, health-food stores, and supermarkets.

While Red Bull relies heavily on sampling events at bars and nightclubs, alternative sports have proved to be a natural fit for the product. Red Bull underwrites a number of extreme sports competitions and sponsors about three dozen athletes like kayaker Tao Berman, who set a world record by paddling over a 98-foot waterfall. Another unique event Red Bull sponsors is a DJ Academy. The latest one, held in New York City and taught by such mix masters as MJ Cole and Shadow Boy, was offered to sixty aspiring DJs from around the world.

Once established in a market, Red Bull employs more traditional advertising. Current ads portray an animated bull character and carry the tag "Red Bull Gives You Wings." The ads run on late-night TV and on popular alternative radio shows.[1]

How do marketers like Red Bull decide what type of advertising message should be conveyed to prospective consumers? How do marketers decide which media to use? How do public relations and publicity benefit a marketer's promotional plan? Answers to these questions and many more will be found as you read through this chapter.

The Effects of Advertising

1

Discuss the effects of advertising on market share and consumers

Advertising was defined in Chapter 12 as any form of impersonal, paid communication in which the sponsor or company is identified. It is a popular form of promotion, especially for consumer packaged goods and services. Advertising spending generally increases annually, with estimated U.S. advertising expenditures now exceeding $230 billion per year.[2]

Although total advertising expenditures seem large, the industry itself is very small. Only about 284,000 people are employed in the advertising departments of manufacturers, wholesalers, and retailers and in the 13,000 or so advertising agencies.[3] This figure also includes people working in media services, such as radio and television, magazines and newspapers, and direct-mail firms.

The amount of money budgeted for advertising by some firms is staggering (see Exhibit 13.1). General Motors, Procter & Gamble, Ford Motor Company, PepsiCo, and Pfizer each spend over $2 billion annually on national advertising alone. That's $6 million or more a day by each company. If public relations and sales promotion are included, this figure rises even higher. Over ninety additional companies spend over $200 million each.

Spending on advertising varies by industry. For example, the game and toy industry has one of the highest ratios of advertising dollars to sales. For every $1.00 of merchandise sold in the toy industry, about 12¢ to 15¢ is spent on advertising the toy to consumers. Similarly, candy makers spend almost 16¢ on advertising for every $1.00 of candy sales. In contrast, automobile dealers spend only about 1¢ per

Exhibit 13.1

Top Ten Leaders by U.S. Advertising Spending

Rank	Advertiser	Total U.S. Ad Spending In 2001 (in millions)	Average Ad Spending per Day in 2001
1	General Motors	$3,374.4	$9,244,923
2	Procter & Gamble	$2,540.6	$6,960,548
3	Ford Motor Company	$2,408.2	$6,597,808
4	PepsiCo	$2,210.4	$6,055,890
5	Pfizer	$2,189.5	$5,998,630
6	DaimlerChrysler	$1,985.3	$5,439,178
7	AOL Time Warner	$1,885.3	$5,165,205
8	Phillip Morris Cos.	$1,815.7	$4,974,521
9	Walt Disney Co.	$1,757.3	$4,814,521
10	Johnson & Johnson	$1,618.1	$4,433,151

SOURCE: Computed from data obtained from "100 Leading National Advertisers," http://www.adage.com/datacenter/marketing, 2002.

$1.00 of sales. Other industries that spend heavily on advertising in relation to total sales include amusement parks, loan brokers, mailing and copy services, and wine and liquor makers.[4]

Advertising and Market Share

Today's most successful brands of consumer goods, like Ivory soap and Coca-Cola, were built by heavy advertising and marketing investments long ago. Today's advertising dollars are spent on maintaining brand awareness and market share.

New brands with a small market share tend to spend proportionately more for advertising and sales promotion than those with a large market share, typically for two reasons. First, beyond a certain level of spending for advertising and sales promotion, diminishing returns set in. That is, sales or market share begins to decrease no matter how much is spent on advertising and sales promotion. This phenomenon is called the **advertising response function**. Understanding the advertising response function helps marketers use budgets wisely. For example, PepsiCo may spend proportionately less on advertising a market leader like Pepsi than on a new brand like Sierra Mist. PepsiCo spends more on Sierra Mist in an attempt to increase awareness and market share, whereas with Pepsi it spends only as much as is needed to maintain market share; anything more would likely reap diminishing benefits. Because Pepsi has already captured the attention of the majority of the target market, PepsiCo needs mostly to remind customers of its product.

The second reason that new brands tend to require higher spending for advertising and sales promotion is that a certain minimum level of exposure is needed to measurably affect purchase habits. If PepsiCo advertised Sierra Mist in only one or two publications and bought only one or two television spots, it certainly would not achieve the exposure needed to penetrate consumers' perceptual defenses, obtain awareness and comprehension, and ultimately affect their purchase intentions. Instead, PepsiCo launched Sierra Mist with an aggressive marketing campaign that began with heavy advertising during Super Bowl XXXVII.[5]

The Effects of Advertising on Consumers

Advertising affects consumers' daily lives, informing them about products and services and influencing their attitudes, beliefs, and ultimately their purchases. The average U.S. citizen is exposed to hundreds of advertisements a day from all types of advertising media. In the television medium alone, researchers estimate that the average viewer watches at least six hours of commercial messages a week. This estimate of media exposure does not include the countless print ads and promotional messages seen in other places.[6] Advertising affects the TV programs people watch, the content of the newspapers they read, the politicians they elect, the medicines they take, and the toys their children play with. Consequently, the influence of advertising on the U.S. socioeconomic system has been the subject of extensive debate among economists, marketers, sociologists, psychologists, politicians, consumerists, and many others.

While advertising cannot change consumers' deeply rooted values and attitudes, advertising may succeed in transforming a person's negative attitude toward a product into a positive one. For instance, serious or dramatic advertisements are more effective at changing consumers' negative attitudes. Humorous ads, on the other hand, have been shown to be more effective at shaping attitudes when consumers already have a positive image of the advertised brand.[7] For this reason, beer marketers often use humorous ads to communicate with their core market of young adults.

Advertising also reinforces positive attitudes toward brands. When consumers have a neutral or favorable frame of reference toward a product or brand,

advertising response function
A phenomenon in which spending for advertising and sales promotion increases sales or market share up to a certain level but then produces diminishing returns.

COURTESY OF AMERICAN ADVERTISING FEDERATION

Advertising investments undeniably help build a brand. The American Advertising Federation reminds companies of this through its Great Brands campaign. Intel Corporation gave permission to modify its logo for use in this campaign.

advertising often positively influences them. When consumers are already highly loyal to a brand, they may buy more of it when advertising and promotion for that brand increase.[8] This is why market leaders like General Motors and Procter & Gamble spend billions of dollars annually to reinforce and remind their loyal customers about the benefits of their cars and household products.

Further, advertising can affect the way consumers rank a brand's attributes, such as color, taste, smell, and texture. For example, in years past, car ads emphasized such brand attributes as roominess, speed, and low maintenance. Today, however, car marketers have added safety to the list. Safety features like antilock brakes, power door locks, and air bags are now a standard part of the message in many carmakers' ads.

Major Types of Advertising

Identify the major types of advertising

institutional advertising
A form of advertising designed to enhance a company's image rather than promote a particular product.

product advertising
A form of advertising that touts the benefits of a specific good or service.

The firm's promotional objectives determine the type of advertising it uses. If the goal of the promotion plan is to build up the image of the company or the industry, **institutional advertising** may be used. In contrast, if the advertiser wants to enhance the sales of a specific good or service, **product advertising** is used.

Institutional Advertising

Advertising in the United States has historically been product oriented. However, modern corporations market multiple products and need a different type of advertising. Institutional advertising, or corporate advertising, promotes the corporation as a whole and is designed to establish, change, or maintain the corporation's identity. It usually does not ask the audience to do anything but maintain a favorable attitude toward the advertiser and its goods and services. Following its acquisition of Compaq, Hewlett-Packard launched a major advertising campaign to rebuild the company's positive image and reposition H-P as a broad technology company instead of as a maker of printers and PCs. The "H-P makes more things possible" campaign highlights a wide range of H-P products and technologies and high-profile clients such as DreamWorks and NASA that use them. The campaign attempts to make consumers feel good about their own choice to use H-P products." [9]

advocacy advertising
A form of advertising in which an organization expresses its views on controversial issues or responds to media attacks.

A form of institutional advertising called **advocacy advertising** is typically used to safeguard against negative consumer attitudes and to enhance the company's credibility among consumers who already favor its position. Often corporations use advocacy advertising to express their views on controversial issues. At other times, firms' advocacy campaigns react to criticism or blame, some in direct response to criticism by the media. Other advocacy campaigns may try to ward off increased regulation, damaging legislation, or an unfavorable outcome in a lawsuit. For example, Harrah's Entertainment recently ran a "responsible gambling" campaign. Though the campaign encourages casino patrons to be smart about their gambling, its main objective is to convince the larger public, including voters and politicians, that Harrah's is a good corporate citizen. In fact, in Missouri, where the company had experienced public resistance to its casinos, the advertisements increased the company's "favorability" scores from 45 percent to 58 percent.[10] In another instance, Philip Morris added a leaflet to packaging for its "light" and "ultra light" cigarettes telling smokers that those cigarettes are not safer than regular cigarettes. The company decided to include the leaflet to make it more difficult for public-health advocates to push for more stringent controls of its marketing efforts.[11]

Product Advertising

Unlike institutional advertising, product advertising promotes the benefits of a specific good or service. The product's stage in its life cycle often determines which type of product advertising is used: pioneering advertising, competitive advertising, or comparative advertising.

Pizza Hut
Papa John's
Can you find evidence of comparative advertising on either Pizza Hut's or Papa John's Web site?
http://www.pizzahut.com
http://www.papajohns.com

On Line

Pioneering Advertising

Pioneering advertising is intended to stimulate primary demand for a new product or product category. Heavily used during the introductory stage of the product life cycle, pioneering advertising offers consumers in-depth information about the benefits of the product class. Pioneering advertising also seeks to create interest. Microsoft used pioneering advertising to introduce its new Windows and Office software products. In a move to reposition the products as more "user-friendly," the software giant renamed its flagship products by adding "XP"—short for "Experience"—to the Windows and Office upgrades.[12] Microsoft's $200 million four-month launch phase kicked off with two fifteen-second TV teaser spots, plus one sixty-second and two thirty-second TV spots that featured the Madonna song "Ray of Light." The print, outdoor, TV, and on-line campaign carries the tagline "Yes, you can" and features XP's signature look—blue skies with white clouds over a green field. The goal of Microsoft's pioneering campaign was to convince PC users to buy the upgrade because of the more intuitive interfaces and abilities to work seamlessly and easily with digital photographs, music files, and video.[13]

pioneering advertising
A form of advertising designed to stimulate primary demand for a new product or product category.

Competitive Advertising

Firms use competitive or brand advertising when a product enters the growth phase of the product life cycle and other companies begin to enter the marketplace. Instead of building demand for the product category, the goal of **competitive advertising** is to influence demand for a specific brand. Often promotion becomes less informative and appeals more to emotions during this phase. Advertisements may begin to stress subtle differences between brands, with heavy emphasis on building recall of a brand name and creating a favorable attitude toward the brand. Automobile advertising has long used very competitive messages, drawing distinctions based on such factors as quality, performance, and image.

competitive advertising
A form of advertising designed to influence demand for a specific brand.

Comparative Advertising

Comparative advertising directly or indirectly compares two or more competing brands on one or more specific attributes. Some advertisers even use comparative advertising against their own brands. Products experiencing sluggish growth or those entering the marketplace against strong competitors are more likely to employ comparative claims in their advertising. For instance, Apple Computer launched a multimillion dollar advertising campaign called "Real People," aimed at enticing Microsoft Windows PC users to switch to Apple's Macintosh computers. The goal of the campaign was to increase Apple's market share, which had been stuck at about 5 percent.[14] Similarly, Procter & Gamble employed the same kind of comparative advertising the company traditionally uses to sell laundry detergent to sell its beauty products when it decided to go after market leader L'Oreal's customers. For example, one of P&G's ads for Olay Total Effects Night Firming Cream claimed the Olay product worked better than the leading department store brands including two products from L'Oreal's Lancôme brand.[15]

comparative advertising
A form of advertising that compares two or more specifically named or shown competing brands on one or more specific attributes.

Before the 1970s, comparative advertising was allowed only if the competing brand was veiled and unidentified. In 1971, however, the Federal Trade Commission (FTC) fostered the growth of comparative advertising by saying that it provided information to the customer and that advertisers were more skillful than the government in communicating this information. Federal rulings prohibit advertisers from falsely describing competitors' products and allow competitors to sue if ads show their products or mention their brand names in an incorrect or false manner. For instance, Target Corporation initiated a legal challenge to force Kmart to discontinue its "Dare to Compare" in-store advertising program. The campaign boasted that Kmart's prices on certain items beat the prices at competing stores, including Target. Target provided an audit, which showed that 74 percent of the signage surveyed listed the wrong Kmart or Target price and compared items that the nearest Target didn't even sell. Target withdrew its motion for a temporary restraining order after Kmart permanently removed the "Dare to Compare" signage in all its U.S. stores.[16]

 FTC rules also apply to advertisers making false claims about their own products. To settle a lawsuit filed by one of its competitors, Duracell agreed to add a disclaimer to its "Mr. Quackers's" television commercial. In the commercial, Duracell claimed that its Coppertop batteries are longer lasting than "heavy-duty" competitors. Although the statement is true, competitors argued that the advertisement was misleading because all alkaline batteries, including those produced by the competitors, last longer then "heavy-duty" batteries, a term used in the industry to describe inexpensive, zinc batteries.[17]

 Companies must be careful with comparative advertising approaches in other countries as well. Germany, Italy, Belgium, and France, for example, do not permit advertisers to claim that their products are best or better than competitors' products, which are common claims in the United States. In the Netherlands, car manufacturers cannot make claims in their advertising about the fuel consumption or environmental aspects of the car. Similarly, Lands' End ran afoul of a German law prohibiting lifetime guarantee claims, which happen to be one of Lands' End's guiding principles. The law is making it difficult for the direct retailer to sell its products and advertise its lifetime guarantee through the Internet and direct mail. In Italy, Absolut ran an ad claiming that it was the only vodka made from grain, which is perceived to produce a higher quality vodka than that made from potatoes. Rival distributor Aosta Company, noting that two of its products were made from grain, filed a complaint against Absolut's Italian distributor, Seagram Italia.[18] Although comparative advertising has been legal in Italy since 1999, ads cannot make unsubstantiated claims. So authorities ordered the campaign stopped and Seagram Italia had to pull all ads. Finally, in South Korea, where comparative advertising is banned, ads for the domestic search engine Empas proclaim, "Empas Is No. 1, Yahoo! Is No. 6," and "If you can't find it with Yahoo!, try Empas." Yahoo! filed a complaint with Korea's Fair Trade Commission requesting that the ads be stopped.[19]

In other countries, hard-hitting comparative advertising will not be effective because it offends cultural values. For example, Arabic culture generally encourages people not to compete with one another, and the sharing of wealth is common practice. Therefore, comparative advertising is not consistent with social values in these countries.[20] Japanese advertisers are also reluctant to use comparative advertising because it is considered confrontational and doesn't promote the respectful treatment of consumers or portray a company in a respectful light. Nevertheless, although the Japanese have traditionally favored soft-sell advertising approaches, consumers are witnessing a trend toward comparative ads. Even in Mexico, where comparative advertising claims have sometimes been exaggerated, there is growing resistance. Wal-Mart recently resigned from Mexico's Retailers Association when the organization passed a code prohibiting members from using comparative advertising that could harm the business of other retailers or the retail industry.[21]

Creative Decisions in Advertising

3

Discuss the creative decisions in developing an advertising campaign

Advertisements that are seen on television, in magazines, and on the Internet are typically the result of an **advertising campaign**—a series of related advertisements focusing on a common theme, slogan, and set of advertising appeals. It is a specific advertising effort for a particular product that extends for a defined period of time. For example, Coca-Cola recently launched a new advertising campaign with the tagline "Coca-Cola Real." The camapign, which features celebrities like Courtney Cox and Penelope Cruz as well as unknown teens, is designed to catch the attention of young consumers. The various spots are all tied together by the campaign tagline.[22]

Before any creative work can begin on an advertising campaign, it is important to determine what goals or objectives the advertising should achieve. An **advertising objective** identifies the specific communication task that a campaign should accomplish for a specified target audience during a specified period. The objectives of a specific advertising campaign often depend on the overall corporate objectives and the product being advertised. For instance, the objective of Intel's "Yes" campaign was to show how the company's technology has changed people's lifestyles. The ads feature young people using digital photography, videos, music, and wireless messaging. Each ad ends with the question, "Can a better computer really change your life? Yes."[23]

The DAGMAR approach (Defining Advertising Goals for Measured Advertising Results) is one method of setting objectives. According to this method, all advertising objectives should precisely define the target audience, the desired percentage change in some specified measure of effectiveness, and the time frame in which that change is to occur. For example, the objectives of the Sierra Mist advertising campaign might be to achieve a 50 percent product trial rate within the first six months of introduction as a result of the advertising campaign.

Once objectives are defined, creative work can begin on the advertising campaign. Advertising campaigns often follow the AIDA model, which was discussed in Chapter 12. Depending on where consumers are in the AIDA process, the creative development of an advertising campaign might focus on creating attention, arousing interest, stimulating desire, or ultimately leading to the action of buying the product. Specifically, creative decisions include identifying product benefits, developing and evaluating advertising appeals, executing the message, and evaluating the effectiveness of the campaign.

Identifying Product Benefits

A well-known rule of thumb in the advertising industry is "Sell the sizzle, not the steak"—that is, in advertising the goal is to sell the benefits of the product, not its attributes. An attribute is simply a feature of the product such as its easy-open package or special formulation. A benefit is what consumers will receive or achieve by using the product. A benefit should answer the consumer's question "What's in it for me?" Benefits might be such things as convenience, pleasure, savings, or relief. A quick test to determine whether you are offering attributes or benefits in your advertising is to ask "So?" Consider this example:

> *Attribute:* The Electrasol Gelpac is the first automatic liquid dish detergent packaged in premeasured individual load-sized packs.
> So . . . ?"
> *Benefit:* No more carrying heavy liquid detergent bottles and measuring to get the correct amount. The campaign tagline is "Dishwashing for the 21st Century."[24]

Marketing research and intuition are usually used to unearth the perceived benefits of a product and to rank consumers' preferences for these benefits. The advertising campaign for the new Electrasol Geltabs taps into the trend for consumers to spend less and less time on household chores.[25]

Developing and Evaluating Advertising Appeals

An **advertising appeal** identifies a reason for a person to buy a product. Developing advertising appeals, a challenging task, is typically the responsibility of the creative people in the advertising agency. Advertising appeals typically

advertising campaign
A series of related advertisements focusing on a common theme, slogan, and set of advertising appeals.

advertising objective
A specific communication task that a campaign should accomplish for a specified target audience during a specified period.

advertising appeal
A reason for a person to buy a product.

play off of consumers' emotions, such as fear or love, or address some need or want the consumer has, such as a need for convenience or the desire to save money.

Advertising campaigns can focus on one or more advertising appeals. Often the appeals are quite general, thus allowing the firm to develop a number of sub-themes or minicampaigns using both advertising and sales promotion. Several possible advertising appeals are listed in Exhibit 13.2.

Choosing the best appeal from those developed normally requires market research. Criteria for evaluation include desirability, exclusiveness, and believability. The appeal first must make a positive impression on and be desirable to the target market. It must also be exclusive or unique; consumers must be able to distinguish the advertiser's message from competitors' messages. Most important, the appeal should be believable. An appeal that makes extravagant claims not only wastes promotional dollars but also creates ill will for the advertiser.

The advertising appeal selected for the campaign becomes what advertisers call its **unique selling proposition**. The unique selling proposition usually becomes the campaign's slogan. Electrasol's advertising campaign, which features "The Jetsons" theme song, brags that the new product is "an advanced gel detergent years ahead of its time." This is also the product's unique selling proposition, implying that the product represents an important innovation and is the wave of the future.[26]

Effective slogans often become so ingrained that consumers can immediately conjure up images of the product just by hearing the slogan. For example, most consumers can easily name the companies and products behind these memorable slogans or even hum the jingle that goes along with some of them: "Have it your way," "Tastes great, less filling," "Ring around the collar," and "Tum te Tum Tum." Advertisers often revive old slogans or jingles in the hope that the nostalgia will create good feelings with consumers. American Motors brought back Joe Isuzu after an eleven-year absence because research showed that during the initial four-year campaign the brand's awareness was at an all-time high. Maytag Corporation refreshed its campaign featuring its appliance pitchman by changing the actor who plays him—the second change since the ads originated in 1967. And Hershey Foods' Kit Kat bar's ten-year old jingle "Gimme a Break" is so etched in consumers' minds that recently the agency hired a film crew to walk around and ask people on the street to sing the jingle for use in future spots.[27]

Executing the Message

Message execution is the way an advertisement portrays its information. In general, the AIDA (see Chapter 12) plan is a good blueprint for executing an advertising message. Any ad should immediately draw the reader's, viewer's, or listener's attention. The advertiser must then use the message to hold consumers' interest, create desire for the good or service, and ultimately motivate action—a purchase.

The style in which the message is executed is one of the most creative elements of an advertisement. Exhibit 13.3 on page 456 lists some examples of executional styles used by advertisers. Executional styles often dictate what type of media is to be employed to convey the message. Scientific executional styles lend themselves well to print advertising where more information can be conveyed. On the other hand, demonstration and musical styles are more likely found in broadcast advertising.

Injecting humor into an advertisement is a popular and effective executional style. Humorous executional styles are more often used in radio and television advertising than in print or magazine advertising where humor is less easily communicated. Humorous ads typically are used for lower risk, routine purchases such as candy and soft drinks. But recently they are increasingly being used for more expensive products and services. For example, Sears has begun using humor in its

unique selling proposition
A desirable, exclusive, and believable advertising appeal selected as the theme for a campaign.

Exhibit 13.2

Common Advertising Appeals

Profit	Lets consumers know whether the product will save them money, make them money, or keep them from losing money
Health	Appeals to those who are body-conscious or who want to be healthy
Love or Romance	Is used often in selling cosmetics and perfumes
Fear	Can center around social embarrassment, growing old, or losing one's health; because of its power, requires advertiser to exercise care in execution
Admiration	Is the reason that celebrity spokespeople are used so often in advertising
Convenience	Is often used for fast-food restaurants and microwave foods
Fun and Pleasure	Are the key to advertising vacations, beer, amusement parks, and more
Vanity and Egotism	Are used most often for expensive or conspicuous items such as cars and clothing
Environmental Consciousness	Centers around protecting the environment and being considerate of others in the community

advertisements for appliances. In an advertisement for Sears' refrigerators, a husband and wife are seen in their kitchen first thing in the morning. The wife leisurely reads the newspaper, while the husband sneaks a sip of milk out of the milk carton. As he spews milk across the room, he casually mentions that the refridgerator is broken. In another spot for treadmills, a young boy looks back and forth from his pregnant mother to his father before asking, "Dad are you pregnant, too?" Similarly, H&R Block recently developed a humerous ad campaign featuring country music singer Willie Nelson to promote its tax services (Willie Nelson was found guilty of tax evasion by the IRS).[28]

Executional styles for foreign advertising are often quite different from those we are accustomed to in the United States. Sometimes they are sexually oriented or aesthetically imaginative. For example, European advertising avoids the direct-sell approaches common in U.S. ads and instead is more indirect, more symbolic, and, above all, more visual. Nike, known in the United States for "in-your-face" advertising and irreverent slogans such as "Just Do It," discovered that its brash advertising did not appeal to Europeans. A television commercial of Satan and his demons playing soccer against a team of Nike endorsers was a hit in America. Many European stations refused to run it, however, saying it was too scary and offensive to show in prime time, when kids were watching.[29]

German advertising is known for its no nonsense, just the facts approach. For example, the copy for a German advertisement for Exquisa low-fat cheese reads "Exquisa fit-line fulfills your wishes for a healthy and easy-to-digest bread spread with only 2% fats and lots of biological high protein." Similarly, while beer ads in the United States are known for their humor, a German print ad for Beck's reads "Pure taste of Pils beer. Limitlessly fresh. Also available alcohol free.[30]

Exhibit 13.3

Slice-of-Life	Depicts people in normal settings, such as at the dinner table or in their car. McDonald's often uses slice-of-life styles showing youngsters munching french fries and Happy Meals on family outings.
Lifestyle	Shows how well the product will fit in with the consumer's lifestyle. As their Volkswagen Jetta moves through the streets of the French Quarter, the Gen X drivers plug in a techno music CD and marvel at how the rhythms of the world mimic the ambient vibe inside their vehicle.
Spokesperson/ Testimonial	Can feature a celebrity, company official, or typical consumer making a testimonial or endorsing a product. Sarah Michelle Gellar, star of *Buffy the Vampire Slayer,* endorses Maybelline cosmetics while country singer Shania Twain introduced Revlon's ColorStay Liquid Lip. Dell Computer founder Michael Dell touts his vision of the customer experience via Dell in television ads.
Fantasy	Creates a fantasy for the viewer built around use of the product. Carmakers often use this style to let viewers fantasize about how they would feel speeding around tight corners or down long country roads in their cars.
Humorous	Advertisers often use humor in their ads, such as Snickers' "Not Going Anywhere for a While" campaign featuring hundreds of souls waiting, sometimes impatiently, to get into heaven.
Real/Animated Product Symbols	Creates a character that represents the product in advertisements, such as the Energizer bunny, Starkist's Charlie the Tuna, or General Mills' longtime icon, Betty Crocker, redesigned for the new millennium.
Mood or Image	Builds a mood or image around the product, such as peace, love, or beauty. DeBeers ads depicting shadowy silhouettes wearing diamond engagement rings and diamond necklaces portray passion and intimacy while extolling that a "diamond is forever."
Demonstration	Shows consumers the expected benefit. Many consumer products use this technique. Laundry-detergent spots are famous for demonstrating how their product will clean clothes whiter and brighter. Fort James Corporation recently demonstrated in television commercials how its Dixie Rinse & ReUse disposable stoneware product line can stand up to the heat of a blowtorch and survive a cycle in a clothes washer.
Musical	Conveys the message of the advertisement through song. For example, Nike's recent ads depicting a marathoner's tortured feet, skier Picabo Street's surgery-scarred knee, and a surfer's thigh scarred by a shark attack while strains of Joe Cocker's "You Are So Beautiful" are heard in the background.
Scientific	Uses research or scientific evidence to give a brand superiority over competitors. Pain relievers like Advil, Bayer, and Excedrin use scientific evidence in their ads.

Postcampaign Evaluation

Evaluating an advertising campaign can be the most demanding task facing advertisers. How do advertisers know whether the campaign led to an increase in sales or market share or elevated awareness of the product? Most advertising campaigns aim to create an image for the good or service instead of asking for action, so their real effect is unknown. So many variables shape the effectiveness of an ad that, in many cases, advertisers must guess whether their money has been well spent. Despite this gray area, marketers spend a considerable amount of time studying advertising effectiveness and its probable impact on sales, market share, or awareness.

Testing ad effectiveness can be done either before or after the campaign. Before a campaign is released, marketing managers use pretests to determine the best advertising appeal, layout, and media vehicle. After advertisers implement a campaign, they often conduct tests to measure its effectiveness. Several monitoring techniques can be used to determine whether the campaign has met its original goals. Even if a campaign has been highly successful, advertisers still typically do a postcampaign analysis. They assess how the campaign might have been more efficient and what factors contributed to its success.

AP/WIDE WORLD PHOTOS

Using a spokesperson is a common executional style. The Maytag Man may be the most well-known spokesperson, revived in the past decade by Gordon Jump, who starred in the 1970s sit-com *WKRP in Cincinnati.*

Media Decisions in Advertising

A major decision for advertisers is the choice of **medium**—the channel used to convey a message to a target market. **Media planning**, therefore, is the series of decisions advertisers make regarding the selection and use of media, allowing the marketer to optimally and cost-effectively communicate the message to the target audience.[31] Specifically, advertisers must determine which types of media will best communicate the benefits of their product or service to the target audience and when and for how long the advertisement will run.

Promotional objectives and the appeal and executional style of the advertising strongly affect the selection of media. It is important to understand that both creative and media decisions are made at the same time. Creative work cannot be completed without knowing which medium will be used to convey the message to the target market. For instance, creative planning will likely differ for an ad to be displayed on an outdoor billboard versus that placed in a print medium, such as a newspaper or magazine. In many cases, the advertising objectives dictate the medium and the creative approach to be used. For example, if the objective is to demonstrate how fast a product operates, a TV commercial that shows this action may be the best choice.

As mentioned at the beginning of this chapter, U.S. advertisers spend over $230 billion on media advertising annually. About 47 percent, or $109 billion, is spent on media monitored by national reporting services—newspapers, magazines, Yellow Pages, Internet, radio, television, and outdoor media. The remaining 53 percent, or $122 billion, is spent on unmonitored media, such as direct mail, trade exhibits, cooperative advertising, brochures, coupons, catalogs, and special events.[32] Exhibit 13.4 breaks down the spending on monitored and unmonitored advertising by media type. As you can see, almost a quarter of every dollar spent goes toward the purchase of TV ads.

4

Describe media evaluation and selection techniques

medium
The channel used to convey a message to a target market.

media planning
The series of decisions advertisers make regarding the selection and use of media, allowing the marketer to optimally and cost-effectively communicate the message to the target audience.

Exhibit 13.4

Domestic Advertising Spending in
Monitored and Unmonitored Media
for 2001

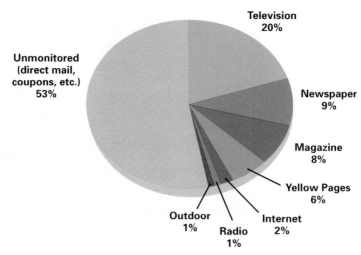

SOURCE: "Domestic Advertising Spending Totals," http://www.adage.com/datacenter.

Media Types

Advertising media are channels that advertisers use in mass communication.
The seven major advertising media are newspapers, magazines, radio, television,
outdoor media, Yellow Pages, and the Internet. Exhibit 13.5 summarizes the
advantages and disadvantages of these major channels. In recent years, however,
alternative media vehicles have emerged that give advertisers innovative ways to
reach their target audience and avoid advertising clutter.

Newspapers

The advantages of newspaper advertising include geographic flexibility and timeliness. Because copywriters can usually prepare newspaper ads quickly and at a reasonable cost, local merchants can reach their target market almost daily. Because
newspapers are generally a mass-market medium, however, they may not be the
best vehicle for marketers trying to reach a very narrow market. For example, local
newspapers are not the best media vehicles for reaching purchasers of specialty
steel products or even tropical fish. These target consumers make up very small,
specialized markets. Newspaper advertising also encounters a lot of distractions
from competing ads and news stories; thus, one company's ad may not be particularly visible.

    The main sources of newspaper ad revenue are local retailers, classified ads,
and cooperative advertising. In **cooperative advertising**, the manufacturer and the
retailer split the costs of advertising the manufacturer's brand. One reason manufacturers use cooperative advertising is the impracticality of listing all their dealers
in national advertising. Also, co-op advertising encourages retailers to devote more
effort to the manufacturer's lines.

cooperative advertising
An arrangement in which the
manufacturer and the retailer
split the costs of advertising the
manufacturer's brand.

Magazines

Compared to the cost of other media, the cost per contact in magazine advertising
is usually high. The cost per potential customer may be much lower, however, because magazines are often targeted to specialized audiences and thus reach more
potential customers. The types of products most frequently advertised in magazines include automobiles, apparel, computers, and cigarettes.

    One of the main advantages of magazine advertising is its market selectivity.
Magazines are published for virtually every market segment. For instance, take a
look at the variety of magazines that are attracting top advertising dollars. *Fitness*

is a leading women's health magazine; *Transworld Skateboarding* is aimed at younger boys; *Lucky* is aimed at women who like to shop but don't take fashion too seriously; *Newsweek* is a popular news weekly aimed at newshounds; *Marketing News* is a trade publication for marketing professionals.[33]

Radio

Radio has several strengths as an advertising medium: selectivity and audience segmentation, a large out-of-home audience, low unit and production costs, timeliness, and geographic flexibility. Local advertisers are the most frequent users of radio advertising, contributing over three-quarters of all radio ad revenues. Like newspapers, radio also lends itself well to cooperative advertising.

Exhibit 13.5

Advantages and Disadvantages of Major Advertising Media

Medium	Advantages	Disadvantages
Newspapers	Geographic selectivity and flexibility; short-term advertiser commitments; news value and immediacy; year-round readership; high individual market coverage; co-op and local tie-in availability; short lead time	Little demographic selectivity; limited color capabilities; low pass-along rate; may be expensive
Magazines	Good reproduction, especially for color; demographic selectivity; regional selectivity; local market selectivity; relatively long advertising life; high pass-along rate	Long-term advertiser commitments; slow audience buildup; limited demonstration capabilities; lack of urgency; long lead time
Radio	Low cost; immediacy of message; can be scheduled on short notice; relatively no seasonal change in audience; highly portable; short-term advertiser commitments; entertainment carryover	No visual treatment; short advertising life of message; high frequency required to generate comprehension and retention; distractions from background sound; commercial clutter
Television	Ability to reach a wide, diverse audience; low cost per thousand; creative opportunities for demonstration; immediacy of messages; entertainment carryover; demographic selectivity with cable stations	Short life of message; some consumer skepticism about claims; high campaign cost; little demographic selectivity with network stations; long-term advertiser commitments; long lead times required for production; commercial clutter
Outdoor media	Repetition; moderate cost; flexibility; geographic selectivity	Short message; lack of demographic selectivity; high "noise" level distracting audience
Internet	Fastest growing medium; ability to reach a narrow target audience; relatively short lead time required for creating Web-based advertising; moderate cost	Difficult to measure ad effectiveness and return on investment; ad exposure relies on "click-through" from banner ads; not all consumers have access to the Internet

Long merely an afterthought to many advertisers, radio advertising is enjoying a resurgence in popularity. As Americans become more mobile and pressed for time, other media such as network television and newspapers struggle to retain viewers and readers. Radio listening, however, has grown in step with population increases mainly because its immediate, portable nature meshes so well with a fast-paced lifestyle. The ability to target specific demographic groups is also a major selling point for radio stations, attracting advertisers who are pursuing narrowly defined audiences that are more likely to respond to certain kinds of ads and products. Moreover, radio listeners tend to listen habitually and at predictable times, with the most popular being "drive time," when commuters form a vast captive audience.[34]

Television

Because television is an audiovisual medium, it provides advertisers with many creative opportunities. Television broadcasters include network television, independent stations, cable television, and a relative newcomer, direct broadcast satellite television. ABC, CBS, NBC, and the Fox Network dominate network television, which reaches a wide and diverse market. Conversely, cable television and direct broadcast satellite systems, such as DirecTV and PrimeStar, offer consumers a multitude of channels devoted exclusively to particular audiences—for example, women, children, African Americans, nature lovers, senior citizens, Christians, Hispanics, sports fans, fitness enthusiasts. Because of its targeted channels, cable television is often characterized as "narrowcasting" by media buyers. More businesses are including cable buys in their marketing mix. For instance, Novell, a marketer of Internet software, found that consumers who were exposed to its ads several times on cable were more familiar with its story and had an increasingly favorable view of the company. Even better, viewers of its spots on cable were found to be more likely to buy or recommend a Novell product.[35]

Advertising time on television can be very expensive, especially for network stations and popular cable stations. First-run prime-time shows and special events command the highest rates. Advertisers spend about $439,000 for a thirty-second spot during NBC's *ER*, for example, and about $482,000 for one during CBS's *Survivor*. The same length spot costs about $377,000 on *Will & Grace*. Spots during *Monday Night Football* cost about $298,000.[36] Spots during the Super Bowl are particularly expensive. One thirty-second spot during the 2003 Super Bowl telecast cost advertisers an average of $2.2 million.[37]

infomercial
A thirty-minute or longer advertisement that looks more like a TV talk show than a sales pitch.

A relatively new form of television advertising is the **infomercial**, a thirty-minute or longer advertisement. Infomercials are an attractive advertising vehicle for many marketers because of the cheap air time and the relatively small production cost. Advertisers say the infomercial is an ideal way to present complicated information to potential customers, which other advertising vehicles typically don't allow time to do. Infomercials are rapidly gaining favor with some of the more mainstream marketers. In the last few years, several companies including AOL, Philips Electronics, Apple, Nissan, Mercedes, Nikon, and Micro-soft have bought infomercial airtime. And a growing number of businesses are adding to the legitimacy of the medium by producing infomercials with a more polished look. For example, Callaway Golf used an infomercial to pitch its expensive new Rule 35 ball to upscale golfers. A higher production budget was established to allow for a lot of graphic detail with a rich feel to enhance the perceived quality of the product and the medium. Hollywood is even cashing in on infomercials. Universal Pictures recently released a thirty-minute infomercial for its Jurassic Park franchise hosted by E! Entertainment's Steve Kmetko. The actual offer—a boxed DVD/video set of the movie's first two installments—airs periodically during the glossy, behind-the-scenes footage, which includes interviews with the stars of the latest flick, *Jurassic Park III*. With the polished look of a behind-the-scenes special, it feels more like thirty minutes of programming than an infomercial.[38]

Outdoor Media

Outdoor or out-of-home advertising is a flexible, low-cost medium that may take a variety of forms. Examples include billboards, skywriting, giant inflatables, minibillboards in malls and on bus stop shelters, signs in sports arenas, lighted moving signs in bus terminals and airports, and ads painted on the sides of cars, trucks, buses, or even water towers. Marketers have even begun utilizing the plywood scaffolding that often rings downtown construction sites. Manhattan's Times Square, with an estimated 1.5 million daily pedestrians and recent construction projects, for example, has been a popular area for outdoor advertising using scaffolding.[39]

Outdoor advertising reaches a broad and diverse market and is, therefore, ideal for promoting convenience products and services as well as directing consumers to local businesses. The FBI recently turned to billboards as part of its ongoing efforts to improve recruiting, especially among minorities. According to an FBI spokesperson, the billboard campaign, which features photos of a diverse group of FBI employees, allows the bureau to position the FBI as a diverse workplace while encouraging viewers to consider "A Career with America's Finest."[40] One of outdoor's main advantages over other media is that its exposure frequency is very high, yet the amount of clutter from competing ads is very low. Outdoor advertising also has the ability to be customized to local marketing needs. For these reasons, local business establishments, such as local services and amusements, retailers, public transportation, and hotels and restaurants, are the leading outdoor advertisers.[41]

Outdoor advertising is becoming increasingly innovative and three-dimensional. Delta's living billboard is an example of how far you can go with outdoor media.

Though outdoor advertising has been growing in the United States for the past several years, the industry is facing some tough challenges in other countries. For instance, in Poland, a recent ban on tobacco and beer advertising eliminated close to 40 percent of the country's outdoor market.[42] Changes in government regulations also threaten the outdoor advertising in France, where outdoor advertising has traditionally accounted for a large percentage of total ad spending. In this case, the government is considering lifting a ban on retailers using television advertising. If the government lifts the ban, many retailers plan to move a large portion of their ad budget from outdoor media to television.[43]

Outdoor advertising continues to become more innovative. For instance, Absolut Vodka teamed up with Ikea furniture to produce a 19-by-49-foot billboard in Manhattan's SoHo district. The billboard shows a life-size studio apartment in the shape of an Absolut bottle that is filled with furniture from Ikea. The billboard is basically a fully furnished apartment with everything glued to the board and then turned on its side.[44]

The Internet

The World Wide Web and the Internet have undoubtedly shaken up the advertising world. With ad revenues near $6 billion in 2001, the Internet has established itself as a solid advertising medium.[45] On-line advertising has made significant gains since the early 1990s and is making up an ever-larger portion of companies' total advertising budgets. According to Forrester Research, companies currently send consumers more than 430 billion e-mail advertisements a year, and that number is expected to reach more than 960 million by 2006. Popular Internet sites and search engines like MSN.com and Yahoo!, as well as on-line service providers like America Online, generally sell advertising space, called "banners," to marketers to promote their goods and services.[46] Internet surfers click on these banners to be linked to more information about the advertised product or service.

Advertising executives and academicians have hotly debated the effectiveness of banner ads. Although research has shown that banner ads are effective, many marketers continue to debate their value. For

On Line

example, according to the research firm eMarketer, average click-through rates in 2002 were only 1.8 percent. As a result, many marketers continue to look for innovative ways to make on-line advertising stand out. The Interactive Advertising Bureau, for example, recently recommended that advertisers move away from traditional banner ads to large ads that are harder for consumers to ignore. Other advertisers are using full video and audio in their ads. A recent Anheuser-Busch on-line advertising campaign even allowed consumers to insert their own faces into Bud light ads and e-mail them to their friends. Early indications, however, are that these ads do not have higher click-through rates than traditional banner ads. Inspite of the challenges, on-line advertising continues to be an attractive media choice because the average cost to reach 1,000 consumers is about $5 compared to $500 to $700 for direct mail.[47]

Marketing on the Internet and World Wide Web is discussed in more detail in Chapter 14.

Alternative Media

To cut through the clutter of traditional advertising media, advertisers are creating new media vehicles to advertise their products, some ordinary and others quite innovative. Alternative media vehicles can include shopping carts in grocery stores, computer screen savers, CD-ROMs, interactive kiosks in department stores, and advertisements run before movies at the cinema and on rented videocassettes. To promote the Xbox in Europe, Microsoft recently gave away two million interactive DVDs, and Regal Entertainment's movie theaters are developing twenty-minute premovie digital programming that will target ads by film or theater.[48] In fact, just about anything can become a vehicle for displaying advertising. For instance, marketers in the United States have placed ads on everything from urinals to the inside of golf holes and are showing commercials on televisions in taxicabs.[49] Video Venue recently unveiled plans to install ten-inch, wireless, high-resolution screens at gas pumps to run six-minute cycles of full-motion video and sound ads. Marketers are hoping to capitalize on the four to six minutes it takes for consumers to pump gas and will advertise products available right there in the store.[50] Marketers are also looking for more innovative ways to reach captive and often bored commuters. For instance, subway systems are now showing ads via lighted boxes installed along tunnel walls. As a train passes through the tunnel, the passengers view the illuminated boxes, which create the same kind of illusion as a child's flip book, in which the images appear to move as the pages are flipped rapidly.[51] In Europe, there has even been a fad of painting ad slogans on live cows and baby strollers.[52]

As marketers keep looking for innovative ways to get noticed, some are using shocking images in their advertising in hopes of capturing attention. Read more about this issue in the "Ethics in Marketing" box.

Sex Sells—But at What Price?

Housewives in Scotland are plastering their kitchens with posters of the new Scottish beefcake hocking the virtues of Scottish beef. Print ads selling shoes show leather-clad dominatrix models. Lap dances seem to go hand in hand with liquor ads. Even yogurt is getting naughty with a television spot showing a woman—dressed in only a French maid's costume and a bad accent—spoon feeding the wholesome goodness to her husband. Yes, in the land of *Sex in the City* and political sex scandals, it seems anything goes. But are marketers pushing the envelope when it comes to using sex in advertising?

Since the 1950s, sex has been used to sell products like beer, cars, and jeans. But these days, sex is being used to peddle everything from tea to shampoo. Some marketers contend that ads with shock value may be the only way to reach a public desensitized by the likes of Howard Stern, *The Man Show,* and Jerry Springer. But many companies are crossing the line in their advertising and targeting a much younger audience. For example, Abercrombie & Fitch, a popular clothing line for teens, offered a "Naughty & Nice" catalog that caused four states to threaten legal action. The catalog featured "various models in states of undress, sex tips from porn star Jenna Jameson, and a cartoon of Santa and Mrs. Claus enjoying a little S&M." Similarly, Nike took its "Just Do It" slogan to a whole new level with sports bra ads showing nothing but breasts—some covered with hands, some bare.

But some ad campaigns are causing much more of a stir than companies bargained for. The French Connection has had several print and television spots banned by the United Kingdom's Advertising Standards Authority. Five employees lost their jobs at InfoUSA when the CEO found out they had approved an ad featuring "a blond woman wearing black leather, a mask, and a dog collar." And, after receiving a signed complaint from approximately forty-five high school librarians, *Seventeen* magazine pulled a Candie's fragrance ad featuring a young woman sitting on a sink with her legs wrapped suggestively around a male model.

Other countries are also cracking down on sexually explicit advertising. In France, advertising authorities have set up standards on how the body may be portrayed to sell products. Advertising watchdogs in Germany and Italy have denounced ads deemed humiliating to women, and the European Union is discussing whether to place more severe restrictions on television commercials aimed at children.[53]

Overall, ad professionals claim to have little respect for sexual appeals that are used just to get attention. But sexual imagery will be used to sell products as long as people keep buying. How far is too far in terms of sexually explicit advertising? Do marketers have a moral responsibility to the public when it comes to advertising? How might consumer backlash over an ad campaign adversely affect a company's corporate reputation?

Media Selection Considerations

An important element in any advertising campaign is the **media mix**, the combination of media to be used. Media mix decisions are typically based on several factors: cost per contact, reach, frequency, target audience considerations, flexibility of the medium, noise level, and the life span of the medium.

Cost per contact is the cost of reaching one member of the target market. Naturally, as the size of the audience increases, so does the total cost. Cost per contact enables an advertiser to compare media vehicles, such as television versus radio or magazine versus newspaper, or more specifically *Newsweek* versus *Time.* An advertiser debating whether to spend local advertising dollars for TV spots or radio spots could consider the cost per contact of each. The advertiser might then pick the vehicle with the lowest cost per contact to maximize advertising punch for the money spent.

Reach is the number of different target consumers who are exposed to a commercial at least once during a specific period, usually four weeks. Media plans for product introductions and attempts at increasing brand awareness usually emphasize reach. For example, an advertiser might try to reach 70 percent of the target audience during the first three months of the campaign. Reach is related to a medium's ratings, generally referred to in the industry as *gross ratings points,* or GRP. A television program with a higher GRP means that more people are tuning in to the show and the reach is higher. Accordingly, as GRP increases for a particular medium, so does cost per contact.

Because the typical ad is short-lived and because often only a small portion of an ad may be perceived at one time, advertisers repeat their ads so that consumers

media mix
The combination of media to be used for a promotional campaign.

cost per contact
The cost of reaching one member of the target market.

reach
The number of target consumers exposed to a commercial at least once during a specific period, usually four weeks.

Exhibit 13.6

Exposure and Frequency of
Top TV Advertisers*

Advertised Brand	Household Exposures (in millions)**	Number of Times Ad Aired
Burger King	285.8	57
JCPenney	181.6	31
Pontiac Grand Am	173.3	25
Boston Market	166.1	27
Ford autos and trucks	162.5	21
Honda Accord	152.4	23
Nissan Altima	150.7	14
AT&T	143.4	22
Wendy's	137.0	26
Miller Lite	131.8	12

*Advertisers getting the most exposure during prime-time TV on ABC, CBS, NBC, Fox, UPN, and WB networks
**One household might be exposed to several ads each day.
SOURCES: "Nielsen's Top TV Advertisers," *USA Today*, June 15, 1998, 8B; Nielsen Media Research, Monitor Plus Service.

frequency
The number of times an individual is exposed to a given message during a specific period.

audience selectivity
The ability of an advertising medium to reach a precisely defined market.

will remember the message. **Frequency** is the number of times an individual is exposed to a message during a specific period. Advertisers use average frequency to measure the intensity of a specific medium's coverage. For example, Coca-Cola might want an average exposure frequency of five for its Powerade television ads. That means that each of the television viewers who saw the ad saw it an average of five times. Exhibit 13.6 provides a glimpse at exposure and frequency rates for some of today's top brands.

Media selection is also a matter of matching the advertising medium with the product's target market. If marketers are trying to reach teenage females, they might select *Seventeen* magazine. If they are trying to reach consumers over fifty years old, they may choose *Modern Maturity* magazine. A medium's ability to reach a precisely defined market is its **audience selectivity**. Some media vehicles, like general newspapers and network television, appeal to a wide cross section of the population. Others—such as *Brides, Popular Mechanics, Architectural Digest*, MTV, ESPN, and Christian radio stations—appeal to very specific groups. Viewer profiles for a sampling of popular cable networks are presented in Exhibit 13.7.

The *flexibility* of a medium can be extremely important to an advertiser. In the past, because of printing timetables, pasteup requirements, and so on, some magazines required final ad copy several months before publication. Therefore, magazine advertising traditionally could not adapt as rapidly to changing market conditions. While this is fast changing due to computer technology that creates electronic ad images and layouts, the lead time for magazine advertising is still considerably longer. Radio and Internet advertising, on the other hand, provide maximum flexibility. Usually, the advertiser can change a radio ad on the day it is

Exhibit 13.7

Selected Cable Television Network
Viewer Profiles

BET	Targeted to African Americans aged 18 to 49.
CNBC	*Business Day* viewers have a median household net worth of over $1 million; 98% are college educated; 80% use their computer daily; 69% connect to the Internet daily.
Discovery Channel	Appeals to adults aged 25 to 54 with household incomes over $75,000.
ESPN Classic	Delivers a higher concentration of men aged 18 to 49 than the ten most widely distributed cable networks.
House & Garden Television (HGTV)	Appeals strongly to men and women who own their own homes with incomes of $75,000 or more; most likely to be in professional or managerial position.
Lifetime Network	Top cable network aimed at working women.
MTV	Number one rated cable network for 12- to 24-year-olds; Watched by over 305 million households in 87 territories around the globe.

SOURCE: "2002 Cable Programming Guide," reprinted with permission from the June 5, 2002 issue of *Advertising Age.* Copyright Crain Communications, Inc., 2002.

aired, if necessary. Similarly, advertisements on the Internet can be changed in minutes with the click of a few buttons.

Noise level is the level of distraction to the target audience in a medium. For example, to understand a televised promotional message, viewers must watch and listen carefully. But they often watch television with others, who may well provide distractions. Noise can also be created by competing ads, as when a street is lined with billboards or when a television program is cluttered with competing ads. About two-thirds of a newspaper's pages are now filled with advertising. A recent Sunday issue of the *Los Angeles Times* contained over one thousand ads, not counting the small classifieds. Even more space is dedicated to ads in magazines. For example, 85 percent of the space in the February/March issue of *Brides* magazine is typically devoted to advertisements. In contrast, direct mail is a private medium with a low noise level. Typically, no other advertising media or news stories compete for direct-mail readers' attention.

Media have either a short or long life span. *Life span* means that messages can either quickly fade or persist as tangible copy to be carefully studied. For example, a radio commercial may last less than a minute. Listeners can't replay the commercial unless they have recorded the program. One way advertisers overcome this problem is by repeating radio ads often. In contrast, a magazine has a relatively long life span. A person may read several articles, put the magazine down, and pick it up a week later to continue reading. In addition, magazines often have a high pass-along rate. That is, one person will read the publication and then give it to someone else to read.

Media planners have traditionally relied upon the above factors for selecting an effective media mix, with reach, frequency, and cost often the overriding criteria. Some recent studies, however, question the reliance media planners have traditionally placed on reach and frequency. For instance, one recent study suggests that well-established brands with familiar messages may need fewer exposures to be effective, while newer brands or brands with unfamiliar messages may need more exposures to become familiar.[54]

Laundry detergent is a product in the mature stage of the product life cycle. As such, companies like Procter & Gamble use a continuous media schedule to remind consumers to chose Tide over the competition.

Additionally, media planners have hundreds more media options today than they had forty years ago when network television reigned. For instance, there are over 1,600 television stations across the country. In the Los Angeles market alone, there are now seventy-nine radio stations, seven offering an "adult contemporary" format. The number of unique magazine titles has more than doubled over the last decade, with publications now targeting every target market possible. Satellite television can now bring hundreds of channels into viewers' homes. The Internet provides media planners with even more targeted choices in which to send their messages. And alternative media choices are popping up in some very unlikely places. *Media fragmentation* is forcing media planners to pay as much attention to where they place their advertising, as to how often the advertisement is repeated. New research suggests evaluating reach along with frequency in assessing the effectiveness of advertising. That is, it may be more important to reach as many consumers in as many media vehicles as possible than to achieve a certain number of exposures in any one particular medium.[55] In evaluating reach versus frequency, therefore, the media planner ultimately must select an approach that is most likely to result in the ad being understood and remembered when a purchase decision is being made.

Advertising researchers are also discussing the qualitative factors that should be present during media selection. These qualitative factors include such things as attention to the commercial and the program, involvement, program liking, lack of distractions, and other audience behaviors that affect the likelihood that a commercial message is being seen and, hopefully, absorbed. While advertisers can advertise their product in as many media as possible and repeat the ad as many times as they like, the ad still may not be effective if the audience is not paying attention.[56] Recent research into audience attentiveness for television, for example, shows that the longer viewers stay tuned to a particular program, the more memorable they find the commercials. The study suggests that "holding power," is more important than ratings (the number of people tuning in to any part of the program) when selecting media vehicles, challenging the long-held assumption that the higher the rating of a program, the higher the cost to advertise during the program. For instance, the television program *ER*, which is one of the top-rated shows among twenty-five- to fifty-four-year-olds and costs over $400,000 for a thirty-second spot, measures relatively lower for holding power than the low-rated program *Candid Camera*, which ranks high in holding power, but costs only $55,000 for a thirty-second spot.[57]

Media Scheduling

After choosing the media for the advertising campaign, advertisers must schedule the ads. A **media schedule** designates the medium or media to be used (such as magazines, television, or radio), the specific vehicles (such as *People* magazine, *The West Wing* TV show, or Howard Stern's national radio program), and the insertion dates of the advertising.

There are three basic types of media schedules:

- Products in the latter stages of the product life cycle, which are advertised on a reminder basis, use a **continuous media schedule**. A continuous schedule allows the advertising to run steadily throughout the advertising period. Examples include Ivory soap, Coca-Cola, and Marlboro cigarettes.

media schedule
Designation of the media, the specific publications or programs, and the insertion dates of advertising.

continuous media schedule
A media scheduling strategy in which advertising is run steadily throughout the advertising period; used for products in the latter stages of the product life cycle.

- With a **flighted media schedule**, the advertiser may schedule the ads heavily every other month or every two weeks to achieve a greater impact with an increased frequency and reach at those times. Movie studios might schedule television advertising on Wednesday and Thursday nights, when moviegoers are deciding which films to see that weekend. A variation is the **pulsing media schedule**, which combines continuous scheduling with flighting. Continuous advertising is simply heavier during the best sale periods. A retail department store may advertise on a year-round basis but place more advertising during certain sale periods such as Thanksgiving, Christmas, and back-to-school.

- Certain times of the year call for a **seasonal media schedule**. Products like Contac cold tablets and Coppertone suntan lotion, which are used more during certain times of the year, tend to follow a seasonal strategy. Advertising for champagne is concentrated during the weeks of Christmas and New Year's, whereas health clubs concentrate their advertising in January to take advantage of New Year's resolutions.

New research comparing continuous media schedules versus flighted ones finds that continuous schedules for television advertisements are more effective than flighting in driving sales. The research suggests that it may be more important to get exposure as close as possible to the time when someone is going to make a purchase. For example, if a consumer shops on a weekly basis, the best time to reach that person is right before he or she shops. Therefore, the advertiser should maintain a continuous schedule over as long a period of time as possible.[58] Often called *recency planning*, this new theory of scheduling is now commonly used for scheduling television advertising for frequently purchased products, such as Coca-Cola or Tide detergent. Recency planning's main premise is that advertising works by influencing the brand choice of people who are ready to buy.[59]

flighted media schedule
A media scheduling strategy in which ads are run heavily every other month or every two weeks, to achieve a greater impact with an increased frequency and reach at those times.

pulsing media schedule
A media scheduling strategy that uses continuous scheduling throughout the year coupled with a flighted schedule during the best sales periods.

seasonal media schedule
A media scheduling strategy that runs advertising only during times of the year when the product is most likely to be used.

Public Relations

Public relations is the element in the promotional mix that evaluates public attitudes, identifies issues that may elicit public concern, and executes programs to gain public understanding and acceptance. Like advertising and sales promotion, public relations is a vital link in a progressive company's marketing communication mix. Marketing managers plan solid public relations campaigns that fit into overall marketing plans and focus on targeted audiences. These campaigns strive to maintain a positive image of the corporation in the eyes of the public. Before launching public relations programs, managers evaluate public attitudes and company actions. Then they create programs to capitalize on the factors that enhance the firm's image and minimize the factors that could generate a negative image.

Many people associate public relations with publicity. *Publicity* is the effort to capture media attention—for example, through articles or editorials in publications or through human-interest stories on radio or television programs. Corporations usually initiate publicity through a press release that furthers their public relations plans. A company about to introduce a new product or open a new store may send press releases to the media in the hope that the story will be published or broadcast. Savvy publicity can often create a buzz overnight. For example, because consumers look forward to Super Bowl commercials, many advertisers hire public relations firms to build excitement around their Super Bowl ads. In 2003, Trident sent out blue tote bags with a toy squirrel, a football, two packs of Trident gum, and a videotape of its television ad to major media outlets like *The David Letterman Show* and *Late Nite with Conan O'Brien*. PepsiCo created a Web site where consumers could view one of its Super Bowl ads and select

5
Discuss the role of public relations in the promotional mix

the ending they would like to see. And H&R Block hired four full-time public relations professionals to promote its ads featuring Willie Nelson.[60]

Corporate donations and sponsorships can also create favorable publicity. When two high school seniors wanted to go to college in California, but couldn't afford the tuition, they set out to find corporate sponsors to pay for their education. The young entrepreneurs set up a Web site offering their services as "spokesguys" and posted photos of themselves wearing T-shirts and carrying surfboards inscribed with the message YOUR LOGO HERE. They got the attention of First USA, the country's largest Visa issuer, which decided to lend a hand. In exchange for the boys promoting fiscal responsibility to other college kids, First USA paid for their tuition and room and board. As a public relations investment, it's already paid off with the kind of publicity that money can't buy, including a story in the *New York Times*.[61]

Public relations departments may perform any or all of the following functions:

- *Press relations:* placing positive, newsworthy information in the news media to attract attention to a product, a service, or a person associated with the firm or institution

- *Product publicity:* publicizing specific products or services

- *Corporate communication:* creating internal and external messages to promote a positive image of the firm or institution

- *Public affairs:* building and maintaining national or local community relations

- *Lobbying:* influencing legislators and government officials to promote or defeat legislation and regulation

- *Employee and investor relations:* maintaining positive relationships with employees, shareholders, and others in the financial community

- *Crisis management:* responding to unfavorable publicity or a negative event

Major Public Relations Tools

Public relations professionals commonly use several tools, including new-product publicity, product placement, consumer education, event sponsorship, and issue sponsorship. A relatively new tool public relations professionals are using in increasing numbers is a Web site on the Internet. Although many of these tools require an active role on the part of the public relations professional, such as writing press releases and engaging in proactive media relations, many of these techniques create their own publicity.

New-Product Publicity

Publicity is instrumental in introducing new products and services. Publicity can help advertisers explain what's different about their new product by prompting free news stories or positive word of mouth about it. During the introductory period, an especially innovative new product often needs more exposure than conventional, paid advertising affords. Public relations professionals write press releases or develop videos in an effort to generate news about their new product. They also jockey for exposure of their product or service at major events, on popular television and news shows, or in the hands of influential people. When Heinz released its "Funky Purple" ketchup, its public relations firm built excitement through a series of news releases. The first release, headlined "Grab Your Buns and Brace Yourself," announced plans for a new color but kept the color choice a secret. These releases were followed by a new kit with product photos, bottles of both "Funky Purple" and original red ketchup, and dip cups and bags of chips that reporters could use to conduct their own taste tests. As a result of the public relations campaign, Heinz received more than two thousand news stories valued at roughly $6.4 million for a $100,600 budget.[62]

Product Placement

Marketers can also garner publicity by making sure their products appear at special events or in movies or television shows. In fact, more and more marketers are turning to product placement to get their products in front of television viewers who are increasingly skipping over traditional ads. For instance, Fox's *The Best Damn Sports Show Period* has product placement deals with Ford Motor Comany and Labatt USA, the parent company of Rolling Rock, Labatt Blue, and Dos Equis brands. Under the agreement, the hosts are seen driving Ford's Lincoln Aviator, and the show's set includes a bar with keg spouts and neon beer signs. Similarly, CBS's *The Amazing Race* has product palcement deals with T-mobile, Kodak, and Royal Caribbean.[63]

Product placements are also playing a larger role in movies. For example, in *Die Another Day* Pierce Brosnan's James Bond is seen checking his Omega Seamaster watch, drinking a Finlandia martini, and shaving with a Norelco Spectra razor. Similarly, his costar Halle Berry sports Revlon products.[64]

Product placement is also catching on in other countries. Read the "Global Perspectives" box to find out how marketers are placing their products in Chinese soap operas.

Companies reap invaluable product exposure through product placement, usually at a fraction of the cost of paid-for advertising. Often the fee for exposure is in merchandise. Fashion designer Georgio Armani, for example, uses celebrities to burnish his brand in the eyes of the public. Armani clothed Samuel L. Jackson for his role in the movie *Shaft*. The designer then marketed a line of *Shaft*-inspired clothes and featured Jackson in fashion shows in Milan, Italy. Armani also provides select Hollywood stars and celebrities like Ricky Martin and Lauryn Hill with free gowns and tuxedos for personal appearances.[65]

Consumer Education

Some major firms believe that educated consumers are better, more loyal customers. Financial planning firms often sponsor free educational seminars on money management, retirement planning, and investing in the hope that the seminar participants will choose the sponsoring organization for their future financial needs. Likewise, computer hardware and software firms, realizing that many consumers feel intimidated by new technology and recognizing the strong relationship between learning and purchasing patterns, sponsor computer seminars and free in-store demonstrations. Hospitals and drug companies frequently team up with health associations like the American Cancer Society or the Arthritis Foundation to launch public-health campaigns. For example, Aventis, a French drug company, recently teamed up with a coalition of diabetes associations to create a public awareness campaign about Type 2 diabetes and the new A1C test, which measures a person's glucose level and warns diabetics if their glucose levels are too high.[66]

Event Sponsorship

Public relations managers can sponsor events or community activities that are sufficiently newsworthy to achieve press coverage; at the same time, these events also reinforce brand identification. Although many are now turning to more specialized events such as tie-ins with schools, charities, and other community service organizations, sporting, music, and arts events remain the most popular choices of events sponsors. For example, Coca-Cola, Adidas, and Royal Philips Electronics are global brands that pay approximately $40 million each to sponsor the World Cup soccer games. And although Anheuser-Busch is the official Super Bowl sponsor, its rivals Coors and Miller both host Super Bowl–related events and parties for their customers.[67]

Product Placement in Chinese Soap Opera

To the delight of marketers, soap is suddenly showing up on the set of China's popular soap opera *Love Talks*, one of the first television series in China engineered by advertisers. Set in a fictitious Shanghai ad agency, the soap opera features the budding romance between a veteran male account director and a novice account executive. The unique aspect of this show is the obvious placement of brand-name products visible throughout the show. For example, one scene shows the soap's star Qu Ying, rushing to work, leaving an important folder at home. The camera zooms in on the forgotten folder, which just happens to be sitting next to a big tube of Pond's Vaseline Intensive Care lotion. The scene then cuts to Ms. Qu in a cab where she is applying Maybelline lipstick, when she notices the missing folder—oh no! Quickly, she borrows a Motorola mobile phone from a handsome stranger in another car.

Marketers, such as Unilever, Motorola, Maybelline, Duracell, and General Electric, have already signed up as sponsors of *Love Talks*. Other brands, such as Braun and Nike, have also cashed in on sponsorships, promotion, and product placement opportunities with the Chinese soap opera. Show sponsorships cost $240,000 to $360,000. Television in China is still under strict government control, but shows such as *Love Talks* are demonstrating new opportunities for advertisers.

While paying to have a product appear in movies or television shows is old hat in the United States and other countries, the concept is revolutionary in China. Most commercials on Chinese state-run television are run in back-to-back, ten-minute-long "bricks," or segments. Due to the large number of commercials that run during each brick, it's difficult for any one advertiser to attract viewers' attention with just a thirty-second ad. Product placement, therefore, provides an innovative way for a product to get noticed. Advertisers are also attracted to the drama since its viewers represent a burgeoning middle class in the world's most populous country.

Love Talks, produced by United Media, now airs on 128 of China's 800 television stations. The show has been so popular with viewers that the production company has begun developing two more series—one about an architect's family life, called *Home*, and another about a modeling agency, called *Model*. The original *Love Talks* series has also been syndicated to broadcasters in Taiwan, Hong Kong, Thailand, Malaysia, and Singapore.[68]

Can you recall any name-brand products that you saw in a television series or a motion picture? How did this affect your perception of the brand?

Marketers can also create their own events tied around their product. For instance, to promote the Volkswagen Beetle, the company held car-washing events and handed out its "Drivers Wanted" posters.[69] Similarly, Brown-Forman sponsors "Forester Football" nights at sports bars throughout football season to promote its Old Forester bourbon.[70]

Issue Sponsorship

Corporations can build public awareness and loyalty by supporting their customers' favorite issues. Education, health care, and social programs get the largest share of corporate funding. Firms often donate a percentage of sales or profits to a worthy cause that their target market is likely to favor. When Nordstrom's opened its first store in Houston, the retailer hosted a gala shopping event with fashion shows, gourmet food, and live entertainment to introduce the department store to Houston shoppers. The event, with ticket prices starting at $150, was also a benefit for Houston's M. D. Anderson Cancer Center.

"Green marketing" has also become an important way for companies to build awareness and loyalty by promoting a popular issue. By positioning their brands as ecologically sound, marketers can convey concern for the environment and society as a whole. Burger King and McDonald's no longer use styrofoam cartons to package their burgers in an effort to decrease waste in landfills. In a similar effort, Toyota is working with the Japanese government to implement a program where people purchase "transportation" without owning a car. Consumers can buy access to Toyota's electronic fleet of automobiles to travel for short distances. Thus, Toyota is both establishing itself as the leader in electronic-combustion automobiles and reducing a negative environmental impact.[71]

Internet Web Sites

Public relations professionals are increasingly using their Internet Web sites as a vehicle to post news releases on products, product enhancements, strategic relationships, and financial earnings. Corporate press releases, technical papers and articles, and product news help inform the press, customers, prospects, industry analysts, stockholders, and others of the firm's products and services and their applications. The Web site can also be an open forum for new-product ideas, product improvements, and customer feedback. On-line reviews from opinion leaders and other consumers also help marketers sway shopping decisions in their favor. When Sony redesigned Playstation.com, it incorporated message boards where its game-playing community could post notes. Players discuss techie topics like "Desperately Seeking Playstation2," review and exchange tips on games, and even vote on lifestyle issues such as music and personal taste.[72]

Several marketers also use the Web to try new products and gather more consumer data. Through research, Volkswagen knew that 60 percent of its customers use the Internet. So, when the company wanted to attract a different, "funkier" audience for its new Beetle and test out new car colors, it employed a special on-line marketing promotion. Volkswagen made a limited-edition model of its Beetle available exclusively on-line, in two limited-edition colors: Vapor Blue and Reflex Yellow. The company got the word out about the promotion through traditional advertising methods. After experiencing print, TV, or radio advertisements, consumers signed up to learn more via e-mail. On being admitted to a special section of the VW site, consumers learned more about the car, viewed photos, checked the availability, picked a dealer, and considered financing and a purchase date. The on-line promotion was a huge success, and Volkswagen sold out of all four thousand limited-edition Beetles.[73]

BMW
Find out more about BMW films starring Clive Owen. Do these films, directed by award-winning directors, do a good job promoting BMW cars?
http://www.bmwfilms.com

On Line

Managing Unfavorable Publicity

Although the majority of marketers try to avoid unpleasant situations, crises do happen. Intel faced this reality after consumers became aware of an obscure flaw in its Pentium chip. In our free-press environment, publicity is not easily controlled, especially in a crisis. **Crisis management** is the coordinated effort to handle the effects of unfavorable publicity, ensuring fast and accurate communication in times of emergency.

A good public relations staff is perhaps more important in bad times than in good. Companies must have a communication policy firmly in hand before a disaster occurs, because timing is uncontrollable. Following September 11, American Airlines had to deal not only with the loss of employees, passengers, and two airplanes, but also with the questions raised by the media about its security. To make matters worse, because of an FBI news blackout, the company could not implement a large part of its crisis communications plan. Because the plan was comprehensive, however, the company was able to communicate internally with its employees via an employee hotline, which the media also check regularly. The airline also had positive relationships with many of the airline security experts being interviewed and was able to pass on its messages through them. As a result, the media's focus quickly shifted away from the airline, minimizing the negative impact on the company.[74]

Internet auctioneer eBay used effective crisis management to climb its way out of a public relations mess after a computer crash halted its bidding operations for twenty-two hours. The outage left nearly 2.3 million auctions stranded in the middle of bids, infuriating customers and sellers. To soothe users' frustrations, eBay sent messages apologizing for the disruption and promising to aggressively hire more computer-network experts. The company also refunded users' listing fees totaling close to $5 million.[75]

crisis management
A coordinated effort to handle the effects of unfavorable publicity or of another unexpected, unfavorable event.

Sales Promotion

6

Define and state the objectives of sales promotion

consumer sales promotion
Sales promotion activities targeting the ultimate consumer.

trade sales promotion
Sales promotion activities targeting a channel member, such as a wholesaler or retailer.

In addition to using advertising, public relations, and personal selling, marketing managers can use sales promotion to increase the effectiveness of their promotional efforts. *Sales promotion* is marketing communication activities, other than advertising, personal selling, and public relations, in which a short-term incentive motivates consumers or members of the distribution channel to purchase a good or service immediately, either by lowering the price or by adding value.

Advertising offers the consumer a reason to buy; sales promotion offers an incentive to buy. Both are important, but sales promotion is usually cheaper than advertising and easier to measure. A major national TV advertising campaign may cost over $2 million to create, produce, and place. In contrast, a newspaper coupon campaign or promotional contest may cost only about half as much. It is also hard to calculate exactly how many people buy a product as a result of seeing a TV ad. With sales promotion, however, marketers know the precise number of coupons redeemed or the number of contest entries.

Sales promotion is usually targeted toward either of two distinctly different markets. **Consumer sales promotion** is targeted to the ultimate consumer market. **Trade sales promotion** is directed to members of the marketing channel, such as wholesalers and retailers. Sales promotion has become an important element in a marketer's integrated marketing communications program (see Chapter 12). Sales promotion expenditures have been steadily increasing over the last several years as a result of increased competition, the ever-expanding array of available media choices, consumers and retailers demanding more deals from manufacturers, and the continued reliance on accountable and measurable marketing strategies. In addition, product and service marketers that have traditionally ignored sales promotion activities, such as power companies and restaurants, have discovered the marketing power of sales promotion. In fact, *PROMO Magazine* estimates that promotion marketing in the United States now exceeds $100 billion a year.[76]

The Objectives of Sales Promotion

Sales promotion usually has more effect on behavior than on attitudes. Immediate purchase is the goal of sales promotion, regardless of the form it takes. Therefore, it seems to make more sense when planning a sales promotion campaign to target customers according to their general behavior. For instance, is the consumer loyal to your product or to your competitor's? Does the consumer switch brands readily in favor of the best deal? Does the consumer buy only the least expensive product, no matter what? Does the consumer buy any products in your category at all?

The objectives of a promotion depend on the general behavior of target consumers (see Exhibit 13.8). For example, marketers who are targeting loyal users of their product actually don't want to change behavior. Instead, they need to reinforce existing behavior or increase product usage. An effective tool for strengthening brand loyalty is the *frequent buyer program* that rewards consumers for repeat purchases. Other types of promotions are more effective with customers prone to brand switching or with those who are loyal to a competitor's product. A cents-off coupon, free sample, or eye-catching display in a store will often entice shoppers to try a different brand. Consumers who do not use the product may be enticed to try it through the distribution of free samples.

Once marketers understand the dynamics occurring within their product category and have determined the particular consumers and consumer behaviors they want to influence, they can then go about selecting promotional tools to achieve these goals.

Types of Consumers and Sales Promotion Goals **Exhibit 13.8**

Type of Buyer	Desired Results	Sales Promotion Examples
Loyal customers People who buy your product most or all of the time	Reinforce behavior, increase consumption, change purchase timing	• Loyalty marketing programs, such as frequent buyer cards or frequent shopper clubs • Bonus packs that give loyal consumers an incentive to stock up or premiums offered in return for proofs of purchase
Competitor's customers People who buy a competitor's product most or all of the time	Break loyalty, persuade to switch to your brand	• Sampling to introduce your product's superior qualities compared to their brand • Sweepstakes, contests, or premiums that create interest in the product
Brand switchers People who buy a variety of products in the category	Persuade to buy your brand more often	• Any promotion that lowers the price of the product, such as coupons, price-off packages, and bonus packs • Trade deals that help make the product more readily available than competing products
Price buyers People who consistently buy the least expensive brand	Appeal with low prices or supply added value that makes price less important	• Coupons, price-off packages, refunds, or trade deals that reduce the price of the brand to match that of the brand that would have been purchased

SOURCE: From *Sales Promotion Essentials*, 2nd ed., by Don E. Schultz, William A. Robinson, and Lisa A. Petrison. Reprinted by permission of NTC Publishing Group, 4255 Touhy Ave., Lincolnwood, IL 60048.

Tools for Consumer Sales Promotion

Marketing managers must decide which consumer sales promotion devices to use in a specific campaign. The methods chosen must suit the objectives to ensure success of the overall promotion plan. Popular tools for consumer sales promotion are coupons and rebates, premiums, loyalty marketing programs, contests and sweepstakes, sampling, and point-of-purchase promotion. Consumer sales promotion tools have also been easily transferred to on-line versions to entice Internet users to visit sites, purchase products, or use services on the Web.

Discuss the most common forms of consumer sales promotion

Coupons and Rebates

A **coupon** is a certificate that entitles consumers to an immediate price reduction when they buy the product. Coupons are a particularly good way to encourage product trial and repurchase. They are also likely to increase the amount of a product bought.

Coupon distribution has been steadily declining in recent years as packaged-goods marketers attempt to wean consumers off coupon clipping. In fact, average

coupon
A certificate that entitles consumers to an immediate price reduction when they buy the product.

coupon redemption rates have fallen to 1.7 percent.[77] Part of the problem is that coupons are often wasted on consumers who have no interest in the product, such as pet food or feminine products coupons that reach the petless or men. This is due mainly to the typical distribution of coupons in mass-media newspaper Sunday inserts. Additionally, coupons are more likely to encourage repeat purchase by regular users, customers who would have purchased the product regardless, than to stimulate product trial by nonusers.

Because of their high cost and disappointing redemption rates, many marketers are reevaluating their use of coupons. By shortening the time the coupon can be redeemed, some marketers have increased redemption rates by creating a greater sense of urgency to redeem the coupon. Other marketers are deemphasizing their use of coupons in favor of everyday low pricing, while others are distributing single, all-purpose coupons that can be redeemed for several brands. For example, Procter & Gamble recently canceled coupons for its Luvs diaper brand because they had a redemption rate of less than 1 percent. The company explained to consumers who compalined that by saving the expense of producing the coupons it could reduce the cost of the product.[78]

Instant coupons on product packages, coupons distributed from on-shelf coupon-dispensing machines, and electronic coupons issued at the checkout counter are achieving much higher redemption rates. Indeed, instant coupons are redeemed more than fifteen times more frequently than traditional newspaper coupons, indicating that consumers are making more in-store purchase decisions. As marketing tactics grow more sophisticated, coupons are no longer being viewed as a stand-alone tactic, but as an integral component of a larger promotional campaign. For example, Dr. Pepper/Seven Up kicked off its sponsorship of the Grammys with a "Sit On Your Can at the Grammys" under-the-cap game and included a 55¢ coupon on-pack to encourage buying the brand.[79]

Rebates are similar to coupons in that they offer the purchaser a price reduction; however, because the purchaser must mail in a rebate form and usually some proof of purchase, the reward is not as immediate. Traditionally used by food and cigarette manufacturers, rebates now appear on all types of products, from computers and software to film and baby seats. Consumers purchasing Earth's Best baby foods, for example, received a $2 rebate when they also bought the children's music CD "More Songs from Pooh Corner" by singer Kenny Loggins. In exchange, Earth's Best got to place its own coupons inside the Sony CD package.[80]

Manufacturers prefer rebates for several reasons. Rebates allow manufacturers to offer price cuts to consumers directly. Manufacturers have more control over rebate promotions because they can be rolled out and shut off quickly. Further, because buyers must fill out forms with their names, addresses, and other data, manufacturers use rebate programs to build customer databases. Perhaps the best reason of all to offer rebates is that although rebates are particularly good at enticing purchase, most consumers never bother to redeem them. Studies have found that as few as 2 percent of consumers eligible for rebates apply for them.[81]

Premiums

A **premium** is an extra item offered to the consumer, usually in exchange for some proof that the promoted product has been purchased. Premiums reinforce the consumer's purchase decision, increase consumption, and persuade nonusers to switch brands. Premiums like telephones, tote bags, and umbrellas are available when consumers buy cosmetics, magazines, bank services, rental cars, and so on. Probably the best example of the use of premiums is the McDonald's Happy Meal that rewards children with a small toy in the meal. The fast-food marketer's lucrative pacts with Ty, Inc., marketer of Beanie Babies, and Disney puts its Happy Meals in high demand with children. And recently, McDonald's teamed up with Toys "R" Us for a holiday program that made the most of cross-promotion for both companies. During the Christmas holidays, Happy Meals

rebate
A cash refund given for the purchase of a product during a specific period.

premium
An extra item offered to the consumer, usually in exchange for some proof of purchase of the promoted product.

featured one of eight miniature premiums based on Paramus, the Toys "R" Us private-label plush line. The toys were poly-bagged with a miniature twenty-page version of the Big Toy Book, the chain's annual holiday megacircular. The mini-books contained $100 in Toys "R" Us coupons for McDonald's customers. The campaign marks the first time McDonald's has let a retailer tie into Happy Meals on such a grand scale.[82]

Premiums can also include more product for the regular price, such as two-for-the-price-of-one bonus packs or packages that include more of the product. Kellogg's, for instance, added two more pastries and waffles to its Pop Tarts and Eggo packages without increasing the price in an effort to boost market share lost to private-label brands and new competitors. The promotion was so successful the company decided to keep the additional product in its regular packaging.

Loyalty Marketing Programs

Loyalty marketing programs, or **frequent buyer programs**, reward loyal consumers for making multiple purchases. Popularized by the airline industry in the mid-1980s through frequent flyer programs, loyalty marketing enables companies to strategically invest sales promotion dollars in activities designed to capture greater profits from customers already loyal to the product or company.[83] One study concluded that if a company retains an additional 5 percent of its customers each year, profits will increase by at least 25 percent. What's more, improving customer retention by a mere 2 percent can decrease costs by as much as 10 percent.[84] The Phoenix Suns and Cleveland Cavaliers, for example, have both recently installed loyalty marketing programs that team officials say attracted seven thousand fans in the first month of the season.[85]

The objective of loyalty marketing programs is to build long-term, mutually beneficial relationships between a company and its key customers. Frequent shopper card programs offered by many supermarkets and other retailers have become so popular that almost half of all American households now belong to one. For example, Neiman Marcus created InCircle as a way to cater to its best customers. InCircle members can cash in points—one point is earned for each dollar spent—for a snakeskin-patterned Nokia phone cover, a trip to Los Angeles for a movie premiere with *InStyle* magazine, or a photo shoot with celebrity photographer Annie Leibovitz.[86] Through loyalty programs, shoppers receive discounts, alerts on new products, and other types of enticing offers. In exchange, retailers are able to build customer databases that help them better understand customer preferences.

loyalty marketing program
A promotional program designed to build long-term, mutually beneficial relationships between a company and its key customers.

frequent buyer program
A loyalty program in which loyal consumers are rewarded for making multiple purchases of a particular good or service.

Contests and Sweepstakes

Contests and sweepstakes are generally designed to create interest in a good or service, often to encourage brand switching. *Contests* are promotions in which participants use some skill or ability to compete for prizes. A consumer contest usually requires entrants to answer questions, complete sentences, or write a paragraph about the product and submit proof of purchase. Winning a *sweepstakes*, on the other hand, depends on chance or luck,

Although it seems that loyalty marketing programs are a recent trend, they date back quite a while. General Mills' Betty Crocker coupon program is entering its seventh decade and is among the longest-running loyalty marketing programs in the United States. Customers collect points from the packaging of General Mills products and then redeem the accumulated points for various products.

AP/WIDE WORLD PHOTOS

Sweepstakes Online

How do on-line sweepstakes sites compare to the kind of sweepstakes entries you receive in the mail? Visit the popular sweepstakes site Sweepstakesonline.com. Do any of the contests interest you? Do you think the pitches on-line are ethical? Why or why not?

http://www.sweepstakesonline.com

On Line

and participation is free. Sweepstakes usually draw about ten times more entries than contests do.

While contests and sweepstakes may draw considerable interest and publicity, generally they are not effective tools for generating long-term sales. To increase their effectiveness, sales promotion managers must make certain the award will appeal to the target market.[87] For example, Home & Garden Television Network's annual "Dream Home Giveaway" sweepstakes awards a fully furnished, custom-built home to one lucky viewer. The promotion is cosponsored by Sears, which stocks the home with Kenmore appliances, a Craftsman workshop, home fashions, lawn and garden equipment, and home electronics, and General Motors, which fills the garage with a new sport utility vehicle. The annual sweepstakes typically draws over four million entries.[88] But offering several smaller prizes to many winners instead of one huge prize to just one person often will increase the effectiveness of the promotion. A recent trend in sweepstakes is to combine on-pack and on-line promotions such as Kraft Foods' Game of Life (get the game piece on the packaging and check on-line to see if you're a winner). Such sweepstakes not only drive site traffic, but also save money on postage, seeding, and security. On-line sweepstakes can also require consumers to divulge information before entering—a plus for databases. And companies are offering extra entries as perks for supplying information. For example, Kellogg's "Be the Ultimate Pokémon Master" sweepstakes gave kids an extra entry for each e-card they sent to friends. And Gillette's launch of the Venus razor included an on-line sweepstakes offering extra entries for serving up friends' e-mail addresses.[89]

Sampling

sampling
A promotional program that allows the consumer the opportunity to try a product or service for free.

Consumers generally perceive a certain amount of risk in trying new products. Many are afraid of trying something they will not like (such as a new food item) or spending too much money and getting little reward. **Sampling** allows the customer to try a product risk-free. Sampling can increase retail sales by as much as 40 percent.[90] It is no surprise, therefore, that product sampling has increased 8.2 percent annually in recent years and that spending on sampling is projected to reach $1.8 billion by 2005.[91]

Selecting the right delivery method is important when planning a sampling campaign. Sampling can be accomplished in various ways including directly mailing the sample to the consumer, delivering the sample door-to-door, packaging the sample with another product, or demonstrating the product at a retail store. In other cases, the appeal may be less direct. For example, to encourage consumers to sample its subscription-based media service, RealNetworks used print and on-line advertising to encourage the "first 300 million" consumers to try the serviice free for two days.[92]

In some foreign countries, marketers are trying new methods of distributing their samples. For instance, in Brazil, many multinational companies have started to distribute samples through local gas company representatives who call door-to-door on housewives to deliver tanks of gas. The gas company reps present the samples to the women as a "gift of appreciation" for their best customers. The system is effective because the marketers do not have to create their own delivery system and the consumer

Distributing samples can often mitigate the risks consumers perceive in trying a new product. As part of its global marketing strategy, Starbucks has aggressively expanded into Asia. A woman in Hong Kong samples of cup of coffee from "Mercury Man," a Starbucks employee who walks around with a pot of coffee on his back.

© AFP/CORBIS

already has a relationship with the gas company reps. In one case, Colgate-Palmolive saw product sales increase threefold after beginning the program.[93]

Sampling at special events is a popular, effective, and high-profile distribution method that permits marketers to piggyback onto fun-based consumer activities—including sporting events, college fests, fairs and festivals, beach events, and chili cook-offs. To help demonstrate Sprint PCS wireless telecommunications products in Los Angeles, Sprint hired a local high school track team to run alongside Los Angeles Marathon competitors so that runners could call friends and family free while running. Sprint also supplied phones to moviegoers for free calls while waiting in line. Similarly, product sampling during tailgating at college and professional football stadiums allows marketers to reach anywhere from 10,000 to 50,000 consumers in a single afternoon. For example, H. J. Heinz is now testing products such as new barbecue sauces and ketchups to get immediate feedback about what consumers like and dislike about the products.[94]

Distributing samples to specific location types where consumers regularly meet for a common objective or interest, such as health clubs, churches, or doctors' offices, is one of the most efficient methods of sampling. What better way to get consumers to try a product than to offer a sample exactly when it is needed most? Marketers agree that companies must be much more precise in what, where, and how samples are delivered. If someone visits a health club regularly, chances are he or she is a good prospect for a health-food product or vitamin supplement. Health club instructors are handing out not only these products but also body wash, deodorant, and face cloths to sweating participants at the end of class, and makers of stain removers and hand cleansers are giving away samples in mall food courts and petting zoos. This method of distributing samples is working. In fact, one recent study found that sampling events produced an average 36 percent increase in sales soon afterward.[95]

Likewise, pharmaceutical companies offer free samples of new and expensive drugs as a tactic to entice doctors and consumers to become loyal to a product. Marketing practices for the pharmaceutical industry as a whole, however, are coming under increased scrutiny. Read about this issue in the "Ethics in Marketing" box.

Point-of-Purchase Promotion

Point-of-purchase (P-O-P) promotion includes any promotional display set up at the retailer's location to build traffic, advertise the product, or induce impulse buying. Point-of-purchase promotions include shelf "talkers" (signs attached to store shelves), shelf extenders (attachments that extend shelves so products stand out), ads on grocery carts and bags, end-aisle and floor-stand displays, television monitors at supermarket checkout counters, in-store audio messages, and audiovisual displays. One big advantage of P-O-P promotion is that it offers manufacturers a captive audience in retail stores. Another advantage is that between 70 and 80 percent of all retail purchase decisions are made in-store, so P-O-P promotions can be very effective. A recent study found that properly displayed P-O-P promotions boosted sales anywhere from 2 to 65 percent, depending on the brand and P-O-P mix. Signs such as header or riser cards increased weekly store sales 6 percent for one brand; base or case wraps boosted total sales 12 percent; standees, 2 percent; inflatable or mobile displays, 40 percent; and signs that advertised a brand's sports, movie, or charity tie-in, 65 percent.[96]

Corporations are cashing in on in-store purchasing decisions through more sophisticated P-O-P promotions. For example, MasterCard International sent 300,000 of its merchant and restaurant partners across the country P-O-P kits containing window clings, tent cards, employee buttons, register decals, coupons, and check presenter inserts customized by retail category. The promotion program, called Priceless P-O-P, awarded one cardholder five "prizes of a lifetime": an African safari, a visit from a celebrity chef, a behind-the-scenes tour of Space Center Houston, a trip to a racing school in England, and VIP passes to the My VH-1 Music Awards. MasterCard encouraged compliance among retailers with a mystery shopper program that sent teams into stores to award $50 gift cards to store

point-of-purchase display
A promotional display set up at the retailer's location to build traffic, advertise the product, or induce impulse buying.

Pharmaceutical Sales—Just What the Doctor Ordered?

In recent years, the $120 billion-a-year pharmaceutical industry has been highly criticized for its sales and marketing practices, and many physicians are concerned that the increasingly lavish spending on the part of drug companies is undermining the integrity of the profession. Other doctors reject the idea that receiving gifts ranging from pens and note cards to free meals and travel would affect their prescribing habits.

Either way, pharmaceutical selling is quickly becoming a daily exercise in ethical judgment. Why? There's a fine line between the common practice of buying a prospect's time with a free meal and bribing doctors to prescribe a manufacturer's drug. Although some supporters of incentives and samples may feel bribery is too strong a word, a recent industry estimate shows that pharmaceutical promotional spending has reached nearly $14 billion. In addition, the collective pharmaceutical sales force has grown to more than 56,000 people, or one sales rep and

almost $10,000 per practicing physician in the United States.

While most physicians agree that pharmaceutical reps provide much-needed information and education through brochures, article reprints, and presentations, the sales push rarely stops there. Office visits are often followed by meals at expensive restaurants, meetings in exotic locales, and a deluge of promotional specialty items for reps to leave behind.

This is not a new phenomenon. Drugmakers have been "wining and dining" physicians for years—and this practice has aroused enough controversy to bring about periodic reviews by Congress and the American Medical Association (AMA). According to current guidelines in the AMA's Code of Ethics, doctors are supposed to limit gifts they receive from pharmaceutical companies to $100. However, both drug manufacturers and physicians can easily get around these guidelines. Doctors are allowed to receive honoraria for "advising" drug compa-

nies for just a couple of hours. Training seminars held at vacation destinations, dinner parties with featured guest lecturers, and golf excursions are all ways to buy time with doctors. In fact, recent figures show that physicians received invitations to 225,000 pharmaceutical events in one year.

Although many doctors deny that the marketing practices employed by the pharmaceutical industry influence their prescription decisions, research shows the contrary. Studies have shown that after doctors participate in industry-sponsored events, they write more prescriptions and are more likely to prescribe expensive, brand-name medications than generic drugs.[97]

Should pharmaceutical companies be able to spend so much to entertain and provide gifts to physicians? How much is too much to spend on physicians in an attempt to market a particular drug? What effect do these marketing practices have on the patient?

---

employees whenever they encountered a Priceless P-O-P. Five random participants won $2,500 gift cards, and the staff at the store that produced the grand-prize winner earned a Major League Baseball prize package.[98]

On-line Sales Promotion

On-line sales promotions have been booming in recent years due to the overwhelming popularity of the Internet. Marketers funneled over $1.5 billion into on-line sales promotions in 2002. Marketers are finding that sales promotion on the Internet is most effective as part of an integrated marketing plan.[99] For example, Frito-Lay recently shifted the majority of its marketing budget for Doritos to Doritos.com. The company uses television and print advertising and product packaging to drive traffic to the Web site. The Web site offers consumers a chance to view commercials before they air and offer feedback. The site also features contests and sweepstakes such as an Austin Powers instant-win game and an MTV Spring Break sweepstakes. By offering the promotions through its Web site, Frito-Lay was able to build a database of almost 350,000 names the company plans to engage in one-to-one communications. Since initiating the new strategy, Doritos' sales have increased 5 percent.[100]

Eager to boost traffic, Internet retailers often run on-line promotions to lure consumers to their Web sites. For example, Gap.com frequently offers free shipping on orders over a minimum amount. Eddie Bauer offers on-line shoppers special sales. And eDiets offers special rates.

After several years of declining coupon distribution due to high cost and low redemption rates, many marketers have begun experimenting with distributing coupons on-line. One recent study found that nearly 30 percent of all Web surfers clip virtual coupons. Although e-coupons make up less than 1 percent of the 248 billion coupons distributed yearly in the United States, almost 57 percent of those who click on e-coupons or get them via e-mail redeem them, compared with the 1.2 percent of Sunday paper coupons that are redeemed. In addition, e-coupons can help marketers lure new customers. For example, Staples.com jumped from 23rd to 14th among retail Web sites with the most buyers through an e-coupon promotion that offered $25 off on purchases of $75 or more.[101]

On-line versions of loyalty programs are also popping up. Burger King is rewarding its loyal Whopper fans with the fast-food version of frequent flyer miles they can cash in on the Internet. In one program, customers were able to use points earned with fast-food purchases to bid on compact discs, tickets, and other rewards with on-line auctioneer eBay.[102]

Upromote.com

How can Upromote.com help you with your sales promotions efforts? What kind of marketing budget would you need to take advantage of its services? What kind of company would be best served by Upromote.com?

http://www.upromote.com

On Line

Tools for Trade Sales Promotion

Whereas consumer promotions *pull* a product through the channel by creating demand, trade promotions *push* a product through the distribution channel (see Chapter 10). When selling to members of the distribution channel, manufacturers use many of the same sales promotion tools used in consumer promotions—such as sales contests, premiums, and point-of-purchase displays. Several tools, however, are unique to manufacturers and intermediaries:

List the most common forms of trade sales promotion

- *Trade allowances:* A **trade allowance** is a price reduction offered by manufacturers to intermediaries such as wholesalers and retailers. The price reduction or rebate is given in exchange for doing something specific, such as allocating space for a new product or buying something during special periods. For example, a local dealer could receive a special discount for running its own promotion on GE telephones.

trade allowance
A price reduction offered by manufacturers to intermediaries, such as wholesalers and retailers.

- *Push money:* Intermediaries receive **push money** as a bonus for pushing the manufacturer's brand through the distribution channel. Often the push money is directed toward a retailer's salespeople. LinoColor, the leading high-end scanner company, produces a Picture Perfect Rewards catalog filled with merchandise retailers can purchase with points accrued for every LinoColor scanner they sell. The cover of the catalog features a wave runner that was brought to three industry trade shows and given away in a sweepstakes to one of the dealers who had visited all the product displays and passed a quiz. The program resulted in a 26 percent increase in LinoColor sales, and the manufacturer recruited thirty-two new dealers to carry the product line.[103]

push money
Money offered to channel intermediaries to encourage them to "push" products—that is, to encourage other members of the channel to sell the products.

- *Training:* Sometimes a manufacturer will train an intermediary's personnel if the product is rather complex—as frequently occurs in the computer and telecommunication industries. For example, if a large department store purchases an NCR computerized cash register system, NCR may provide free training so the salespeople can learn how to use the new system.

- *Free merchandise:* Often a manufacturer offers retailers free merchandise in lieu of quantity discounts. For example, a breakfast cereal manufacturer may throw in one case of free cereal for every twenty cases ordered by the retailer. Occasionally, free merchandise is used as payment for trade allowances normally provided through other sales promotions. Instead of giving a retailer a price reduction for buying a certain quantity of merchandise, the manufacturer may throw in extra merchandise "free" (that is, at a cost that would equal the price reduction).

- *Store demonstrations:* Manufacturers can also arrange with retailers to perform an in-store demonstration. Food manufacturers often send representatives to grocery stores and supermarkets to let customers sample a product while shopping. Cosmetic companies also send their representatives to department stores to promote their beauty aids by performing facials and makeovers for customers.

Store demonstrations are not limited to trade sales promotion. The Bath and Body Works in Columbus, Ohio, gives customers free samples of massages, manicures, and sugar scrubs to create a stress-free shopping experience.

- *Business meetings, conventions, and trade shows:* Trade association meetings, conferences, and conventions are an important aspect of sales promotion and a growing, multibillion-dollar market. At these shows, manufacturers, distributors, and other vendors have the chance to display their goods or describe their services to customers and potential customers. A recent study reported that, on average, it costs 56 percent less to close a lead generated at an exhibition than a lead generated in the field—$625 versus $1,117.[104] Trade shows have been uniquely effective in introducing new products; they can establish products in the marketplace more quickly than can advertising, direct marketing, or sales calls. Companies participate in trade shows to attract and identify new prospects, serve current customers, introduce new products, enhance corporate image, test the market response to new products, enhance corporate morale, and gather competitive product information.

Trade promotions are popular among manufacturers for many reasons. Trade sales promotion tools help manufacturers gain new distributors for their products, obtain wholesaler and retailer support for consumer sales promotions, build or reduce dealer inventories, and improve trade relations. Car manufacturers annually sponsor dozens of auto shows for consumers. Many of the displays feature interactive computer stations where consumers enter vehicle specifications and get a printout of prices and local dealer names. In return, the local car dealers get the names of good prospects. The shows attract millions of consumers, providing dealers with increased store traffic as well as good leads.

CONNECT IT

As you finish reading this chapter, think back to the opening story about how Red Bull created and continues to dominate the energy drink category with marketing savvy, guerrilla tactics, and unusual distribution methods. To advertise its products, Red Bull's promotional team went through the same creative steps as other marketers—from determining what appeal to use to choosing the appropriate executional style. Great effort was also expended in deciding which medium would best reach the desired target market. Public relations and publicity also played a significant role in the success Red Bull has achieved.

USE IT

Becoming a Media Expert
Find the perfect magazine to advertise your product or service. Visit the Media-Finder Web site at **http://www.mediafinder.com**. The site has a searchable database of thousands of magazines. Or visit Channel Seven at **http://www.channelseven.com** to find news and views on hot new advertising mediums.

Ticked Off about That Ad?
File a complaint with the Better Business Bureau. See which companies get the most complaints about their advertising at the Better Business Bureau's Web site at **http://www.bbb.org**. Want to avoid legal problems with your advertising campaign? Find detailed information about advertising law and Federal Trade Commission regulations at **http://www.advertisinglaw.com**.

Get Free Product Samples On-line
Receive free samples of consumer products by registering on-line at **http://www.FreeSamples.com** and **http://www.StartSampling.com**. There you can choose from a variety of free products, such as beauty aids, pet food, and new food products. In exchange, you provide marketers with feedback on what you liked and didn't like about the product.

Looking for a Sales Job?
Find job leads in the *Sales & Marketing Management* magazine careers section at **http://www.salesandmarketing.com**. Or visit popular employment site Monster.com (**http://www.monster.com**) and use its searchable database to search for sales opportunities in a specific geographic area. You can also post your résumé at these and a number of other employment sites.

(1) **Discuss the effects of advertising on market share and consumers.** Advertising helps marketers increase or maintain brand awareness and, subsequently, market share. Typically, more is spent to advertise new brands with a small market share than to advertise older brands. Brands with a large market share use advertising mainly to maintain their share of the market. Advertising affects consumers' daily lives as well as their purchases. Although advertising can seldom change strongly held consumer attitudes and values, it may transform a consumer's negative attitude toward a product into a positive one. Additionally, when consumers are highly loyal to a brand, they may buy more of that brand when advertising is increased. Last, advertising can also change the importance of a brand's attributes to consumers. By emphasizing different brand attributes, advertisers can change their appeal in response to consumers' changing needs or try to achieve an advantage over competing brands.

1.1 Discuss the reasons why new brands with a smaller market share spend proportionately more on advertising than brands with a larger market share.

1.2 **TEAM** Form a three-person team. Divide the responsibility for getting newspaper advertisements and menus for several local restaurants. While you are at the restaurants to obtain copies of their menus, observe the atmosphere and interview the manager to determine what he or she believes are the primary reasons people choose to dine there. Pool your information and develop a table comparing the restaurants in terms of convenience of location, value for the money, food variety and quality, atmosphere, and so on. Rank the restaurants in terms of their appeal to college students. Explain the basis of your rankings. What other market segment would be attracted to the restaurants and why? Do the newspaper advertisements emphasize the most effective appeal for a particular restaurant? Explain.

(2) **Identify the major types of advertising.** Advertising is any form of nonpersonal, paid communication in which the sponsor or company is identified. The two major types of advertising are institutional advertising and product advertising. Institutional advertising is not product oriented; rather, its purpose is to foster a positive company image among the general public, investment community, customers, and employees. Product advertising is designed mainly to promote goods and services, and it is classified into three main categories: pioneering, competitive, and comparative. A product's place in the product life cycle is a major determinant of the type of advertising used to promote it.

2.1 At what stage in a product's life cycle are pioneering, competitive, and comparative advertising most likely to occur? Give a current example of each type of advertising.

(3) **Discuss the creative decisions in developing an advertising campaign.** Before any creative work can begin on an advertising campaign, it is important to determine what goals or objectives the advertising should achieve. The objectives of a specific advertising campaign often depend on the overall corporate objectives and the product being advertised. Once objectives are defined, creative work can begin on the advertising campaign. Creative decisions include identifying the product's benefits, developing possible advertising appeals, evaluating and selecting the advertising appeals, executing the advertising message, and evaluating the effectiveness of the campaign.

3.1 What is an advertising appeal? Give some examples of advertising appeals you have observed recently in the media.

3.2 **WRITING** Design a full-page magazine advertisement for a new brand of soft drink. The name of the new drink, as well as package design, is at your discretion. On a separate sheet, specify the benefits stressed or appeals made in the advertisement.

④ **Describe media evaluation and selection techniques.** Media evaluation and selection make up a crucial step in the advertising campaign process. Major types of advertising media include newspapers, magazines, radio, television, outdoor advertising such as billboards and bus panels, and the Internet. Recent trends in advertising media include fax, video shopping carts, computer screen savers, and cinema and video advertising. Promotion managers choose the advertising campaign's media mix on the basis of the following variables: cost per contact, reach, frequency, characteristics of the target audience, flexibility of the medium, noise level, and the life span of the medium. After choosing the media mix, a media schedule designates when the advertisement will appear and the specific vehicles it will appear in.

4.1 What are the advantages of radio advertising? Why is radio expanding as an advertising medium?

4.2 **WRITING** You are the advertising manager of a sailing magazine, and one of your biggest potential advertisers has questioned your rates. Write the firm a letter explaining why you believe your audience selectivity is worth the extra expense for advertisers.

4.3 Identify an appropriate media mix for the following products:

a. Chewing tobacco

b. *People* magazine

c. Weed-Eaters

d. Foot odor killers

e. "Drink responsibly" campaigns by beer brewers

⑤ **Discuss the role of public relations in the promotional mix.** Public relations is a vital part of a firm's promotional mix. A company fosters good publicity to enhance its image and promote its products. Popular public relations tools include new-product publicity, product placement, consumer education, event sponsorship, issue sponsorship, and Internet Web sites. An equally important aspect of public relations is managing unfavorable publicity in a way that is least damaging to a firm's image.

5.1 How can advertising and publicity work together? Give an example.

5.2 **WRITING** As the new public relations director for a sportswear company, you have been asked to set public relations objectives for a new line of athletic shoes to be introduced to the teen market. Draft a memo outlining the objectives you propose for the shoe's introduction and your reasons for them.

5.3 **WRITING** Reports have just surfaced that your company, a fast-food chain, sold contaminated food products that have made several people seriously ill. As your company's public relations manager, devise a plan to handle the crisis.

5.4 **WRITING** *INFOTRAC® COLLEGE EDITION* The Ford/Firestone tire recall of 2000 was one of the biggest public relations nightmares of recent memory. How well did the companies handle the situation? Use InfoTrac (**http://www.infotrac-college.com**) to run a keyword search on "Ford public relations." Read a selection of the articles, and then write an analysis of CEO Jacques Nasser's performance in the face of this crisis. What did he do well? What could he have done better? Evaluate his solution to the problem. Has Ford recovered from the recall? What about Firestone?

⑥ **Define and state the objectives of sales promotion.** Sales promotion consists of those marketing communication activities, other than advertising, personal selling, and public relations, in which a short-term incentive motivates consumers or members of the distribution channel to purchase a good or service immediately, either by lowering the price or by adding value. The main objectives of sales promotion are to increase trial purchases, consumer inventories, and repeat purchases. Sales promotion is also used to encourage brand switching and to build brand loyalty. Sales promotion supports advertising activities.

6.1 **WRITING** You have recently been assigned the task of developing promotional techniques to introduce your company's new product, a Cajun chicken sandwich. Advertising spending is limited, so the introduction will include only some low-budget sales promotion techniques. Write a sales promotion plan that will increase awareness of your new sandwich and allow your customer base to try it risk-free.

7 **Discuss the most common forms of consumer sales promotion.** Consumer forms of sales promotion include coupons and rebates, premiums, loyalty marketing programs, contests and sweepstakes, sampling, and point-of-purchase displays. Coupons are certificates entitling consumers to an immediate price reduction when they purchase a product or service. Coupons are a particularly good way to encourage product trial and brand switching. Similar to coupons, rebates provide purchasers with a price reduction, although it is not immediate. To receive a rebate, consumers generally must mail in a rebate form with a proof of purchase. Premiums offer an extra item or incentive to the consumer for buying a product or service. Premiums reinforce the consumer's purchase decision, increase consumption, and persuade nonusers to switch brands. Rewarding loyal customers is the basis of loyalty marketing programs. Loyalty programs are extremely effective at building long-term, mutually beneficial relationships between a company and its key customers. Contests and sweepstakes are generally designed to create interest, often to encourage brand switching. Because consumers perceive risk in trying new products, sampling is an effective method for gaining new customers. Finally, point-of-purchase displays set up at the retailer's location build traffic, advertise the product, and induce impulse buying.

7.1 Discuss how different forms of sales promotion can erode or build brand loyalty. If a company's objective is to enhance customer loyalty to its products, what sales promotion techniques will be most appropriate?

7.2 What forms of consumer sales promotion might induce impulse purchases? What forms of sales promotion are more effective at persuading consumers to switch brands?

7.3 **TEAM** Form a three-person team. Go to the local grocery store and write down all of the forms of sales promotion you see, including company name, product being promoted, form of promotion, and objective. Also, make a note of the sales promotion's message or offer, such as "two-for-one" or "cents off." Create a table that lists this information; then rate the effectiveness of each one, in your opinion, on a scale from 1 to 5 where 1 is "poor" and 5 is "excellent." Present a summary of your findings to the class. What kind of conclusions can you draw about product type and promotion?

7.4 **ON LINE** Visit the site **http://www.ci.cendant.com**. How does this company help on-line businesses conduct loyalty marketing programs? Present some examples.

7.5 **ON LINE** Not everyone thinks supermarket shopper cards are a bargain. Go to **http://www.nocards.org**. and read several pages. Is the information on the site compelling? What do you think of shopper cards? You may want to use the Internet to research shopper cards in more detail before forming an opinion.

8 **List the most common forms of trade sales promotion.** Manufacturers use many of the same sales promotion tools used in consumer promotions, such as sales contests, premiums, and point-of-purchase displays. In addition, manufacturers and channel intermediaries use several unique promotional strategies: trade allowances, push money, training programs, free merchandise, store demonstrations, and meetings, conventions, and trade shows.

8.1 How does trade sales promotion differ from consumer sales promotion? How is it the same?

8.2 Form a team of three to five students. As marketing managers, you are in charge of selling Dixie cups. Design a consumer sales promotion plan and trade sales promotion plan for your product. Incorporate at least three different promotion tools into each plan. Share your results with the other teams in the class.

DEFINE IT

APPLY IT

Application for Entrepreneurs

 Quality of service is increasingly the basis for deciding where to do business. Customers are five times more likely to return to a particular business if they perceive that it is providing higher quality service than the competition.

The Student Copy Center is a local business competing with Kinko's and a couple of other national franchise copy centers. Its owner, Mack Bayles, just attended a Small Business Administration workshop on customer service. He learned that when people say they expect good customer service, they most often mean they want prompt and accurate service from friendly, knowledgeable, and courteous employees. The presenter also emphasized that all market segments, even the most price conscious, expect good customer service. Mack wants to use this knowledge to develop an effective advertising campaign.

Mack has no idea what his customers think about either his copy business or that of his competitors. He decides, therefore, to ask his customers to complete a brief survey while in his store. From his survey he learns that Student Copy Center is considered friendlier and more courteous than the major competitors but is rated lower on speed of service.

Questions

1. What should Mack do before developing his advertising campaign?

2. Should Mack use comparative ads? Explain your choice.

3. What advertising appeal would be most effective for Mack? Why?

4. Should Mack consider Internet advertising? If so, what kind?

Ethics Exercise

Creative Advertising Agency has been asked to help its largest client improve its corporate image after a highly publicized product recall. The client requests a television advertisement highlighting the company's generous donation of products to low-income families. The only such donation the company has made, however, is a donation of the recalled products. The account executive fears promoting the donation could cause further consumer backlash, but the client continues to press for the spot.

Questions

1. Should Creative Advertising meet the client's expectations (i.e., create the promotional spot) or risk losing the account? Explain your reasoning.

2. What does the AMA Code of Ethics say about truth in advertising? Go to **http://www. marketingpower.com** and review the code. Then, write a brief paragraph describing how the AMA Code of Ethics relates to this issue.

TRY IT

Entrepreneurship Case

The Move from TV to TiVo

In the late 1990s, Silicon Graphics, Inc., employees Mike Ramsay and Jim Barton were working together on the *Full-Service Network Project* in Orlando, Florida, a joint venture between then Time Warner and Silicon Graphics to create the first large-scale interactive television system, when they hit upon an idea. They could build a system that would give viewers control over their television programming and their time, but with far greater intelligence and ease-of-use than anything previously designed at a price the average customer could afford.

Their idea was the genesis of TiVo, a revolutionary new service that puts viewers in control of their television-viewing experience in a way never before possible. TiVo's service uses an electronic device called a digital video recorder (DVR). Its newest set top box, the Series2, can digitally save up to 60 hours of television programs to its hard disk. But instead of punching in times and channels one at a time to record a show on a video cassette tape, like with a VCR, the DVR uses a telephone connection to download television program schedules that pop up on the TV screen. TiVo subscribers then click on any shows they want to select and digitally record them. What's more, the Series2 has the ability to deliver digital music and photo files, video party games, Internet radio, and broadband video.

With TiVo, viewers get more control than ever over what they want to watch on television. Subscribers can digitally record their favorite shows, creating and organizing their own programming schedule to watch when they want, not bound by the timetable of any network schedule. Some of TiVo's television network partners even allow subscribers to select shows as they are advertised in televised promotions. For instance, if a subscriber sees a promo for an upcoming show to be aired on Showtime, she can click the remote when a small icon appears in the corner of her television screen during the promo to automatically record it when the program is aired. No longer do viewers have to remember when the desired show will come on in order to watch it—TiVo records properly even if the network changes its schedule! TiVo can also automatically record subscribers' favorite shows every week or suggest other shows that they might want to see based on what they've recorded in the past.

Ranging in cost from $299 for the 40-hour version available for AT&T Broadband customers to $399 for the 60-hour version, the digital video recorders provide several features that are superior to a conventional VCR and its limited recording capabilities. During live programs, for example, viewers can pause during a broadcast while the DVR keeps recording. DVRs can also provide instant replay and slow motion features so avid sports fans will never miss a play again. Additionally, TiVo DVRs include a fast-forward button so viewers can bypass television commercials or catch up with live programming that they have paused.

TiVo, based in Alviso, California, currently has over 422,000 subscribers, with projections of continued growth. While analysts expect DVRs to take several years to reach the market penetration of the ubiquitous VCR, DVRs are projected to be in 14 million homes by 2005, possibly making them the fastest-growing consumer electronics product in history. If this prediction pans out, the impact on television from DVRs and TiVo-like services could be enormous. For instance, since TiVo subscribers can create their own programming schedule, prime time could become increasingly irrelevant as more shows get recorded for later viewing. Additionally, viewers armed with the ability to fast-forward through commercials will see less of them; analysts are estimating that the viewing of commercials will decrease by 50 percent by 2009 with increased market penetration of DVRs.

Not surprisingly, TiVo and DVRs have most advertising and television executives watching carefully to see how the technology emerges. TiVo believes its technology is actually an opportunity for advertisers to target their audiences more directly. Best Buy was the first consumer electronics retailer to work with TiVo to deliver customized advertising to TiVo subscribers. As an extension of their national "Go Mobile" advertising campaign, Best Buy provided an electronic tag for commercials that appeared to TiVo subscribers. Simply clicking their remote control while the ads were on their television screen transported TiVo subscribers to a "Video Showcase" area where they could view innovative Best Buy branded entertainment.

For the TiVo portion of this campaign, Best Buy filmed an exclusive "behind the scenes" jam session with artist Sheryl Crow featuring two singles from her latest album. In addition to the Sheryl Crow content, TiVo viewers also saw branded entertainment vignettes that offered fun, tongue-in-cheek tips for achieving "Electronic Feng Shui" with Best Buy's mobile products. While viewers watched the Best Buy branded advertainment, TiVo paused the program they were watching so they could return immediately to the programming, whether live or recorded, without missing a moment of their show.

Another feature Best Buy took advantage of was TiVo's lead generation and request-for-information capabilities. To test this feature, Best Buy gave TiVo subscribers a chance to receive a free Sheryl Crow CD. Using their remote control, the first two thousand TiVo subscribers to opt-in received the CD from Best Buy.

Lastly, but perhaps most importantly, the feature that advertisers may look forward to the most is the ability to measure audience exposure in real time. For the first time ever, companies can accurately track their return-on-advertising. TiVo can provide deep information on how anonymous users interacted with the entertainment including when it was viewed and how often, giving brand marketers new tools for maximizing the effectiveness of their television campaigns.

For now, many in the entertainment industry have decided it's better to join than oppose digital video recording services. Entertainment giants like AOL Time Warner, DIRECTV, AT&T, RealNetworks, Blockbuster, Cox Communications, Showtime Networks, Home Box Office, and others have partnered with TiVo to develop programming and advertising solutions. Additionally, entertainment companies including Interscope Geffen A&M, New Line Cinema, Sony Pictures and PBS have partnered with TiVo to produce entertainment Showcases similar to the Best Buy campaign that will extend their advertising campaigns and appeal to the entertainment enthusiasts within TiVo's subscriber base.

Questions

1. If the majority of TiVo viewers fast-forward through commercials, advertisers will be essentially wasting the millions of dollars they spend on them. What solutions might you suggest to advertisers as TiVo gains in popularity?

2. How might TiVo and DVRs affect traditional television networks that rely on advertising revenue to support original programming?

3. How might the popularity of TiVo's service affect traditional media selection criteria like reach and frequency?

WATCH IT

Short

The *Essentials of Marketing* PowerPoint CD-ROM has five video ad clips embedded in the Chapter 13 slide presentation. Ads for Pizza Hut, e*Trade, Chrysler, Dockers, and Goodyear illustrate the concepts of event sponsorship, institutional advertising, executional styles, and sampling. List all the concepts you see working in the ads, then identify the executional styles for each.

Medium

A new trend in advertising is called *advertainment*, or using entertainment as a medium for advertising. Several companies have put specialized movies on their Web sites as a means to pull customers to their sites. Perhaps the best known are the BMW films directed by Oscar-winning directors. Watch the CNN clip on Internet movies and evaluate advertainment.

Long SmallBusinessSchool
the Series on PBS stations and the Web

To give you insights into Chapter 13, Small Business School introduces you to Tere Zubizarreta, founder and CEO of Zubi Advertising. Based in Miami, Zubi Advertising specializes in creating advertising for the entire Hispanic American market. Tere Zubizarreta, also called Mama Zubi, knows how to sell everything from car wax to airline tickets to the men and women who grew up speaking Spanish at home, or who call Spanish their first language. Join Mama Zubi for a look inside the advertising world and the Hispanic target market.

FLIP IT

Flip to Chapter 13 in your *Grademaker Study Guide* for more review opportunities, including the pretest, vocabulary review, Internet activities, study test questions, and an application exercise based on advertising concepts. What are the major types of advertising? How do you decide where to advertise your message? Can you close your book and list several advertising appeals and executional styles? If not, then pick up your *Grademaker* and review.

CLICK IT

The *Essentials of Marketing* Web site links you to all the Internet-based activities in this chapter, like the "Use It," "Review It" questions 5.4, 7.4, and 7.5, and the On-Line exercises in the chapter margins. As a review, do the Chapter 13 quiz and crossword puzzle. And don't forget the Career Exersite that gives you resources for exploring marketing career opportunities in advertising and public relations. Review the main concepts in the PowerPoint presentation for Chapter 13, too. Go to **http://lamb.swlearning.com**, read the material, and follow the links right from the site.

Surf to Xtra! to test your understanding of the advertising concepts in the chapter by completing the worksheets for Exhibits 13.2, 13.3, 13.5, and 13.8. If your instructor has assigned a marketing plan project, worksheets on Xtra! can help you organize your work. In addition to the quiz on the Web site, there's another quiz on Xtra!, plus video of the authors answering frequently asked questions about advertising topics, such as "How do businesses know how much to advertise?"

CHAPTER FOURTEEN
INTERNET MARKETING

Learning Objectives

1 Explain how the Internet affects the traditional marketing mix

2 Describe how marketers are leveraging the power of on-line technology

3 Discuss the legal and privacy issues surrounding Internet-based commerce

4 Name the critical factors marketers face when measuring on-line success

5 Discuss the effects of the Internet on marketing objectives and strategy

14

1 **The Internet's Impact on the Traditional Marketing Mix**
Product
Promotion
Price
Place
Integrating conventional and Internet marketing strategies

2 **Leveraging the Power of On-Line Technology**
Internet demographics and trends
Interactivity: the voice of the customer
Maximizing CRM
Search-engine maximization

3 **Legal and Privacy Issues**
Cookies
Not-so-private e-mail
Spam
Identity theft
Transaction fraud
Cyberstalking
Website (in)security
Conflicting legislation
Trust for sale?

4 **Measuring On-Line Success**
Web measurement issues
Metrics that work

5 **Internet Marketing Objectives and Strategy**
Porter's Five Forces on-line
Back to basics

Find the whole chapter on-line at
http://lamb.swlearning.com

CHAPTER FIFTEEN
PRICING CONCEPTS

Learning Objectives

1 Discuss the importance of pricing decisions to the economy and to the individual firm

2 List and explain a variety of pricing objectives

3 Explain the role of demand in price determination

4 Understand the concept of yield management systems

5 Describe cost-oriented pricing strategies

6 Demonstrate how the product life cycle, competition,

distribution and promotion strategies, customer demands, the Internet and extranets, and perceptions of quality can affect price

7 Describe the procedure for setting the right price

8 Identify the legal and ethical constraints on pricing decisions

9 Explain how discounts, geographic pricing, and other special pricing tactics can be used to fine-tune the base price

Major League Baseball is banking on fan loyalty in a new way. It is charging a fee for searchable video highlights and live radio feeds of games broadcast over the Internet.

The Internet arm of Major League Baseball is streaming video highlights of nearly all games over the Net. The video is available on **Mlb.com** and individual team sites an hour after each game. Major League Baseball Advanced Media is using Virage, Inc.'s video-serving technology, which breaks up video clips pitch-by-pitch and makes them searchable. Fans can download the clips at 56 Kbps or 300 Kbps. Major League Baseball officials hope such capabilities will persuade fans to log on, even though they'll have to pay a small monthly fee, less than $10, for the video clip–search service.

Virage CEO Paul Lego says the service is worth the price. "It's the biggest video product on the Web today," he says. "There's no reason Internet content shouldn't be able to command the same types of deals as TV content."

That philosophy is extending to Internet radio broadcasts as well. Baseball cut a deal with RealNetworks, Inc., that ends free Internet radio broadcasts of major league games. The broadcasts cost $10 per year, though subscribers get a $10 gift certificate from Mlb.com's online store.

Ultimately, Major League Baseball wants to show live videocasts of games over the Net, says Bob Bowman, CEO of MLB Advanced Media, a company jointly owned by the thirty major league franchises, though he declined to predict a date. Baseball is prevented from televising local games on the Net under existing TV contracts. "Sports helped make the cable industry," Bowman says. "They're going to help make the Internet as well."[1]

Major League Baseball is counting on significant demand for its Internet video highlights. How are demand, costs, and profits related? Will the Internet have a major impact on pricing in general? What role are yield management systems playing in increased profitability? Can price influence the perceived quality of a product?

The Importance of Price

Discuss the importance of pricing decisions to the economy and to the individual firm

Price means one thing to the consumer and something else to the seller. To the consumer, it is the cost of something. To the seller, price is revenue, the primary source of profits. In the broadest sense, price allocates resources in a free-market economy. With so many ways of looking at price, it's no wonder that marketing managers find the task of setting prices a challenge.

What Is Price?

price
That which is given up in an exchange to acquire a good or service.

Price is that which is given up in an exchange to acquire a good or service. Price is typically the money exchanged for the good or service. It may also be time lost while waiting to acquire the good or service. Standing in long lines at the airport first to check in and then to get through the new security checkpoint procedures is a cost. In fact, these delays are one reason more people are selecting alternative modes of transportation for relatively short trips. Price might also include "lost dignity" for individuals who lose their jobs and must rely on charity to obtain food and clothing.

Consumers are interested in obtaining a "reasonable price." "Reasonable price" really means "perceived reasonable value" at the time of the transaction. One of the authors of this textbook bought a fancy European-designed toaster for about $45. The toaster's wide mouth made it possible to toast a bagel, warm a muffin, and, with a special $15 attachment, make a grilled sandwich. The author felt that a toaster with all these features surely must be worth the total price of $60. But after three months of using the device, toast burned around the edges and raw in the middle lost its appeal. The disappointed buyer put the toaster in the attic. Why didn't he return it to the retailer? Because the boutique had gone out of business, and no other local retailer carried the brand. Also, there was no U.S. service center. Remember, the price paid is based on the satisfaction consumers *expect* to receive from a product and not necessarily the satisfaction they *actually* receive.

Price can relate to anything with perceived value, not just money. When goods and services are exchanged, the trade is called *barter*. For example, if you exchange this book for a chemistry book at the end of the term, you have engaged in barter. The price you paid for the chemistry book was this textbook.

The Importance of Price to Marketing Managers

revenue
The price charged to customers multiplied by the number of units sold.

profit
Revenue minus expenses.

Prices are the key to revenues, which in turn are the key to profits for an organization. **Revenue** is the price charged to customers multiplied by the number of units sold. Revenue is what pays for every activity of the company: production, finance, sales, distribution, and so on. What's left over (if anything) is **profit**. Managers usually strive to charge a price that will earn a fair profit.

To earn a profit, managers must choose a price that is not too high or too low, a price that equals the perceived value to target consumers. If, in consumers' minds, a price is set too high, the perceived value will be less than the cost, and sales opportunities will be lost. Many mainstream purchasers of cars, sporting goods, CDs, tools, wedding gowns, and computers are buying "used or preowned" items to get a better deal. Pricing a new product too high may give some shoppers an incentive to go to a "preowned" or consignment retailer.[2]

Lost sales mean lost revenue. Conversely, if a price is too low, it may be perceived as a great value for the consumer, but the firm loses revenue it could have earned. Setting prices too low may not even attract as many buyers as managers might think. One study surveyed over two thousand shoppers at national chains around the country and found that over 60 percent intended to buy full-price items only.[3] Retailers that place too much emphasis on discounts may not be able to meet the expectations of full-price customers.

Trying to set the right price is one of the most stressful and pressure-filled tasks of the marketing manager, as trends in the consumer market attest:

- Confronting a flood of new products, potential buyers carefully evaluate the price of each one against the value of existing products.

- The increased availability of bargain-priced private and generic brands has put downward pressure on overall prices.

- Many firms are trying to maintain or regain their market share by cutting prices. For example, Dell has gained PC market share by aggressively cutting prices.

- With the general decline in consumer confidence after the terrorist attacks of 2001, some consumers were reluctant to spend.

 In the organizational market, where customers include both governments and businesses, buyers are also becoming more price sensitive and better informed. In the consumer market, consumers are using the Internet to make wiser purchasing decisions. Computerized information systems enable the organizational buyer to compare price and performance with great ease and accuracy. Improved communication and the increased use of telemarketing and computer-aided selling have also opened up many markets to new competitors. Finally, competition in general is increasing, so some installations, accessories, and component parts are being marketed like indistinguishable commodities.

Setting the right price on a product is extremely critical and so is a source of much stress for the marketing manager. Part of the reason is the continuous flood of new products that encourages shoppers to carefully compare prices.

Pricing Objectives

To survive in today's highly competitive marketplace, companies need pricing objectives that are specific, attainable, and measurable. Realistic pricing goals then require periodic monitoring to determine the effectiveness of the company's strategy. For convenience, pricing objectives can be divided into three categories: profit oriented, sales oriented, and status quo.

List and explain a variety of pricing objectives

Profit-Oriented Pricing Objectives

Profit-oriented objectives include profit maximization, satisfactory profits, and target return on investment. A brief discussion of each of these objectives follows.

Profit Maximization

Profit maximization means setting prices so that total revenue is as large as possible relative to total costs. (A more theoretically precise definition and explanation of profit maximization appear later in the chapter.) Profit maximization does not always signify unreasonably high prices, however. Both price and profits depend on the type of competitive environment a firm faces, such as whether it is in a monopoly position (being the only seller) or in a much more competitive situation. Also, remember that a firm cannot charge a price higher than the product's perceived value. Many firms do not have the accounting data they need for maximizing profits. It is easy to say that a company should keep producing and selling goods or services as long as revenues exceed costs. Yet it is often hard to set up an accounting system that can accurately determine the point of profit maximization.

Sometimes managers say that their company is trying to maximize profits—in other words, trying to make as much money as possible. Although this goal may sound impressive to stockholders, it is not good enough for planning. The statement

"We want to make all the money we can" is vague and lacks focus. It gives management license to do just about anything it wants to do.

Satisfactory Profits

Satisfactory profits are a reasonable level of profits. Rather than maximizing profits, many organizations strive for profits that are satisfactory to the stockholders and management—in other words, a level of profits consistent with the level of risk an organization faces. In a risky industry, a satisfactory profit may be 35 percent. In a low-risk industry, it might be 7 percent. To maximize profits, a small-business owner might have to keep his or her store open seven days a week. However, the owner might not want to work that hard and might be satisfied with less profit.

Target Return on Investment

return on investment (ROI)
Net profit after taxes divided by total assets.

The most common profit objective is a target **return on investment (ROI)**, sometimes called the firm's return on total assets. ROI measures management's overall effectiveness in generating profits with the available assets. The higher the firm's return on investment, the better off the firm is. Many companies—including DuPont, General Motors, Navistar, ExxonMobil, and Union Carbide—use target return on investment as their main pricing goal.

Return on investment is calculated as follows:

$$\text{Return on investment} = \frac{\text{Net profits after taxes}}{\text{Total assets}}$$

Assume that in 2004 Johnson Controls had assets of $4.5 million, net profits of $550,000, and a target ROI of 10 percent. This was the actual ROI:

$$\text{ROI} = \frac{550,000}{4,500,000}$$

$$= 12.2 \text{ percent}$$

As you can see, the ROI for Johnson Controls exceeded its target, which indicates that the company prospered in 2004.

Comparing the 12.2 percent ROI with the industry average provides a more meaningful picture, however. Any ROI needs to be evaluated in terms of the competitive environment, risks in the industry, and economic conditions. Generally speaking, firms seek ROIs in the 10 to 30 percent range. For example, General Electric seeks a 25 percent ROI, whereas Alcoa, Rubbermaid, and most major pharmaceutical companies strive for a 20 percent ROI. In some industries such as the grocery industry, however, a return of under 5 percent is common and acceptable.

A company with a target ROI can predetermine its desired level of profitability. The marketing manager can use the standard, such as 10 percent ROI, to determine whether a particular price and marketing mix are feasible. In addition, however, the manager must weigh the risk of a given strategy even if the return is in the acceptable range.

Sales-Oriented Pricing Objectives

Sales-oriented pricing objectives are based either on market share or on dollar or unit sales. The effective marketing manager should be familiar with these pricing objectives.

Market Share

market share
A company's product sales as a percentage of total sales for that industry.

Market share is a company's product sales as a percentage of total sales for that industry. Sales can be reported in dollars or in units of product. Many companies believe that maintaining or increasing market share is an indicator of the effectiveness of their marketing mix. Larger market shares have indeed often meant higher profits, thanks to greater economies of scale, market power, and ability to compensate top-quality management. Conventional wisdom also says that market share and return on investment are strongly related. For the most part they are; however, many companies with low market share survive and even prosper. To succeed with a low market share, companies need to compete in industries with slow growth and few product changes—for instance, industrial component parts and supplies. Otherwise, they must vie in an industry that makes frequently bought items, such as consumer convenience goods.

Research organizations like A. C. Nielsen and Information Resources, Inc., provide excellent market share reports for many different industries. These reports enable companies to track their performance in various product categories over time.

Sales Maximization

Rather than strive for market share, sometimes companies try to maximize sales. A firm with the objective of maximizing sales ignores profits, competition, and the marketing environment as long as sales are rising.

If a company is strapped for funds or faces an uncertain future, it may try to generate a maximum amount of cash in the short run. Management's task when using this objective is to calculate which price–quantity relationship generates the greatest cash revenue. Sales maximization can also be effectively used on a temporary basis to sell off excess inventory. It is not uncommon to find Christmas cards, ornaments, and so on discounted at 50 to 70 percent off retail prices after the holiday season. In addition, management can use sales maximization for year-end sales to clear out old models before introducing the new ones.

Maximization of cash should never be a long-run objective because cash maximization may mean little or no profitability. Without profits, a company cannot survive.

Status Quo Pricing Objectives

Status quo pricing seeks to maintain existing prices or to meet the competition's prices. This third category of pricing objectives has the major advantage of requiring little planning. It is essentially a passive policy.

Often firms competing in an industry with an established price leader simply meet the competition's prices. These industries typically have fewer price wars than those with direct price competition. In other cases, managers regularly shop competitors' stores to ensure that their prices are comparable. Target's middle managers must visit competing Sears stores weekly to compare prices and then make adjustments.

status quo pricing
A pricing objective that maintains existing prices or meets the competition's prices.

The Demand Determinant of Price

After marketing managers establish pricing goals, they must set specific prices to reach those goals. The price they set for each product depends mostly on two factors: the demand for the good or service and the cost to the seller for that good or service. When pricing goals are mainly sales oriented, demand considerations usually dominate. Other factors, such as distribution and promotion strategies, perceived quality, demands of large customers, the Internet, and stage of the product life cycle, can also influence price.

The Nature of Demand

Demand is the quantity of a product that will be sold in the market at various prices for a specified period. The quantity of a product that people will buy depends on its

Explain the role of demand in price determination

demand
The quantity of a product that will be sold in the market at various prices for a specified period.

supply
The quantity of a product that will be offered to the market by a supplier at various prices for a specified period.

price. The higher the price, the fewer goods or services consumers will demand. Conversely, the lower the price, the more goods or services they will demand.

Supply is the quantity of a product that will be offered to the market by a supplier or suppliers at various prices for a specified period. At higher prices, manufacturers will obtain more resources and produce more goods.

Elasticity of Demand

elasticity of demand
Consumers' responsiveness or sensitivity to changes in price.

elastic demand
A situation in which consumer demand is sensitive to changes in price.

inelastic demand
A situation in which an increase or a decrease in price will not significantly affect demand for the product.

To appreciate demand analysis, you should understand the concept of elasticity. **Elasticity of demand** refers to consumers' responsiveness or sensitivity to changes in price. **Elastic demand** occurs when consumers buy more or less of a product when the price changes. Conversely, **inelastic demand** means that an increase or a decrease in price will not significantly affect demand for the product.

Several factors affect elasticity of demand, including the following:

- *Availability of substitutes:* When many substitute products are available, the consumer can easily switch from one product to another, making demand elastic. The same is true in reverse: A person with complete renal failure will pay whatever is charged for a kidney transplant because there is no substitute.

- *Price relative to purchasing power:* If a price is so low that it is an inconsequential part of an individual's budget, demand will be inelastic. For example, if the price of salt doubles, consumers will not stop putting salt and pepper on their eggs because salt is cheap anyway.

- *Product durability:* Consumers often have the option of repairing durable products rather than replacing them, thus prolonging their useful life. If a person had planned to buy a new car and prices suddenly began to rise, he or she might elect to fix the old car and drive it for another year. In other words, people are sensitive to the price increase, and demand is elastic.

- *A product's other uses:* The greater the number of different uses for a product, the more elastic demand tends to be. If a product has only one use, as may be true of a new medicine, the quantity purchased probably will not vary as price varies. A person will consume only the prescribed quantity, regardless of price. On the other hand, a product like steel has many possible applications. As its price falls, steel becomes more economically feasible in a wider variety of applications, thereby making demand relatively elastic.

The Power of Yield Management Systems

Understand the concept of yield management systems

yield management systems (YMS)
A technique for adjusting prices that uses complex mathematical software to profitably fill unused capacity by discounting early purchases, limiting early sales at these discounted prices, and overbooking capacity.

When competitive pressures are high, a company must know when it can raise prices to maximize its revenues. More and more companies are turning to yield management systems to help adjust prices. First developed in the airline industry, **yield management systems** (**YMS**) use complex mathematical software to profitably fill unused capacity. The software employs techniques such as discounting early purchases, limiting early sales at these discounted prices, and overbooking capacity. YMS now are appearing in other services such as lodging, other transportation forms, rental firms, and even hospitals.[4]

Yield management systems are spreading beyond service industries as their popularity increases. The lessons of airlines and hotels aren't entirely applicable to other industries, however, because plane seats and hotel beds are perishable—if they go empty, the revenue opportunity is lost forever. So it makes sense to slash prices to move toward capacity if it's possible to do so without reducing the prices that other customers pay. Cars and steel aren't so perishable. Still, the capacity to make these goods is perishable. An underused factory or mill is a lost revenue opportunity. So it makes sense to cut prices to use up capacity if it's possible to do so while getting other customers to pay full price.

ProfitLogic has helped customers such as JCPenney, Gymboree, Ann Taylor, and Gap determine the best markdown price. The software has boosted profit margins from 5 to 18 percent. KhiMetrics, used by Buy.com and others, analyzes dozens of factors such as a product's life cycle, competitors' prices, and past sales data at various price points before churning out a list of possible prices and calculating the best ones. New sales data are fed back into the formulae daily to refine the process. Systems such as this aren't cheap, however, costing from $200,000 to $500,000.[5]

Some companies, such as American Airlines and Omni Hotels, are creating their own YMS software. Omni Charm (Centralized Hotel Automated Revenue Management), created by Omni Hotels, predicts demand and indicates when to discount rooms and when to charge the maximum. Marriott, with a similar system, earns an additional estimated $400 million per year.[6]

COURTESY OF OMNI HOTELS

Although yield management is being implemented across diverse and multiple industries, it is the hallmark of the travel industry. Often hotels like Omni offer different weekend specials each week to encourage the kind of spontaneous travel that will maximize company revenues.

The Cost Determinant of Price

Sometimes companies minimize or ignore the importance of demand and decide to price their products largely or solely on the basis of costs. Prices determined strictly on the basis of costs may be too high for the target market, thereby reducing or eliminating sales. On the other hand, cost-based prices may be too low, causing the firm to earn a lower return than it should. Nevertheless, costs should generally be part of any price determination, if only as a floor below which a good or service must not be priced in the long run.

The idea of cost may seem simple, but it is actually a multifaceted concept, especially for producers of goods and services. A **variable cost** is a cost that varies with changes in the level of output; an example of a variable cost is the cost of materials. In contrast, a **fixed cost** does not change as output is increased or decreased. Examples include rent and executives' salaries.

Markup Pricing

Markup pricing, the most popular method used by wholesalers and retailers to establish a selling price, does not directly analyze the costs of production. Instead, **markup pricing** uses the cost of buying the product from the producer, plus amounts for profit and for expenses not otherwise accounted for. The total determines the selling price.

A retailer, for example, adds a certain percentage to the cost of the merchandise received to arrive at the retail price. An item that costs the retailer $1.80 and is sold for $2.20 carries a markup of 40¢, which is a markup of 22 percent of the cost (40¢ ÷ $1.80). Retailers tend to discuss markup in terms of its percentage of the retail price—in this example, 18 percent (40¢ ÷ $2.20). The difference between the retailer's cost and the selling price (40¢) is the gross margin, as Chapter 11 explained.

The biggest advantage of markup pricing is its simplicity. The primary disadvantage is that it ignores demand and may result in overpricing or underpricing the merchandise.

High profits from unhealthy products such as cigarettes can raise ethical questions. So can governments' addictions to cigarette revenue, as discussed in the "Ethics in Marketing" box.

Describe cost-oriented pricing strategies

variable cost
A cost that varies with changes in the level of output.

fixed cost
A cost that does not change as output is increased or decreased.

markup pricing
The cost of buying the product from the producer plus amounts for profit and for expenses not otherwise accounted for.

Many Governments Are Hooked on Tobacco Revenue

Four million people will die this year from lung cancer and other smoking-related diseases, according to the World Health Organization. By 2030, the agency predicts, the annual loss of life will more than double, making cigarettes the leading cause of premature death around the globe, outstripping malaria, AIDS, and other scourges.

Yet, some countries make more money from a pack of smokes than do the tobacco companies. More than 70 percent of the average retail price of Marlboro cigarettes in the European Union goes into governments' pockets. In Brazil, the government's take is about 65 percent. Tobacco taxes account for about 6 percent of federal government tax revenue in Germany. For the roughly two dozen governments that still manufacture cigarettes, dependence on tobacco revenue can be even higher. China, whose government is the world's largest cigarette maker, derives about 13 percent of its annual income from tobacco sales and taxes.

All that can make governments reluctant to take aggressive action against smoking. In Japan, where the government owns two-thirds of the country's largest cigarette maker, Japan Tobacco, Inc., the Health Ministry dropped plans for specific targets to reduce tobacco use after complaints from tobacco interests.

Because smokers are hooked on cigarettes, they are less responsive to price increases than consumers of many other goods. That means that in the short to medium term, tax revenue would increase as consumption declines. In the United States, a 10 percent increase in cigarette prices translates into a 4 percent drop in consumption. In developing countries, where people have less disposable income, the World Bank estimates that a 10 percent price increase would reduce consumption by about 8 percent, on average.

A study by Teh-wei Hu, a health economist at the University of California at Berkeley, and Zhengzhong Mao, of the West China University of Medical Sciences, concludes that a 25 percent cigarette-tax increase in China would reduce consumption there by 4.57 billion packs and boost central-government revenue by 24.74 billion yuan.

Worldwide, the public-health benefits of tax increases would be significant, the World Bank says. A recent bank report estimates that a sustained 10 percent increase in the real price of cigarettes around the globe would prompt 40 million people to quit and deter many others from starting to smoke, saving about 10 million lives while, at the same time, boosting government revenue by an average of 7 percent.[7]

Should governments get out of the tobacco business? Why or why not? Do you think that the U.S. government should increase taxes on cigarettes 100 percent or more? Why or why not? Consider the 2002 tax increase in New York City. A more direct alternative is to ban smoking altogether. Is this feasible?

Break-Even Pricing

break-even analysis
A method of determining what sales volume must be reached before total revenue equals total costs.

Now let's take a closer look at the relationship between sales and cost. **Break-even analysis** determines what sales volume must be reached before the company breaks even (its total costs equal total revenue) and no profits are earned.

The typical break-even model assumes a given fixed cost. Suppose that Universal Sportswear, a hypothetical firm, has fixed costs of $2,000 and that the cost of labor and materials for each unit produced is 50¢. Assume that it can sell up to 6,000 units of its product at $1 without having to lower its price.

Exhibit 15.1 illustrates Universal Sportswear's break-even point. Universal Sportswear's total variable costs increase by 50¢ every time a new unit is produced, and total fixed costs remain constant at $2,000 regardless of the level of output. Therefore, for 4,000 units of output, Universal Sportswear has $2,000 in fixed costs and $2,000 in total variable costs (4,000 units × 50¢), or $4,000 in total costs.

Revenue is also $4,000 (4,000 units × $1), giving a net profit of zero dollars at the break-even point of 4,000 units. Notice that once the firm gets past the break-even point, the gap between total revenue and total costs gets wider and wider because both functions are assumed to be linear.

The advantage of break-even analysis is that it provides a quick estimate of how much the firm must sell to break even and how much profit can be earned if a higher sales volume is obtained. If a firm is operating close to the break-even point, it may want to see what can be done to reduce costs or increase sales.

Break-even analysis is not without several important limitations. Sometimes it is hard to know whether a cost is fixed or variable. If labor wins a tough guaranteed-

Exhibit 15.1

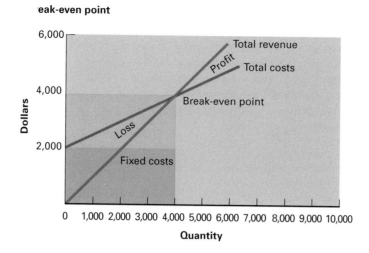

employment contract, are the resulting expenses a fixed cost? Are middle-level executives' salaries fixed costs? More important than cost determination is the fact that simple break-even analysis ignores demand. How does Universal Sportswear know it can sell 4,000 units at $1? Could it sell the same 4,000 units at $2 or even $5? Obviously, this information would profoundly affect the firm's pricing decisions.

Other Determinants of Price

Other factors besides demand and costs can influence price. For example, the stages in the product life cycle, the competition, and the product distribution strategy, promotion strategy, and perceived quality can all affect pricing.

Stages in the Product Life Cycle

As a product moves through its life cycle (see Chapter 9), the demand for the product and the competitive conditions tend to change:

Demonstrate how the product life cycle, competition, distribution, the Internet and extranets, promotion, demands of large customers, and perceptions of quality can affect price

- *Introductory stage:* Management usually sets prices high during the introductory stage. One reason is that it hopes to recover its development costs quickly. In addition, demand originates in the core of the market (the customers whose needs ideally match the product's attributes) and thus is relatively inelastic. On the other hand, if the target market is highly price sensitive, management often finds it better to price the product at the market level or lower. For example, when Kraft General Foods brought out Country Time lemonade, it was priced like similar products in the highly competitive beverage market because the market was price sensitive.

- *Growth stage:* As the product enters the growth stage, prices generally begin to stabilize for several reasons. First, competitors have entered the market, increasing the available supply. Second, the product has begun to appeal to a broader market, often lower income groups. Finally, economies of scale are lowering costs, and the savings can be passed on to the consumer in the form of lower prices.

- *Maturity stage:* Maturity usually brings further price decreases as competition increases and inefficient, high-cost firms are eliminated. Distribution channels become a significant cost factor, however, because of the need to offer wide product lines for highly segmented markets, extensive service requirements, and the sheer number of dealers necessary to absorb high-volume production. The manufacturers that remain in the market toward the end of the maturity stage typically offer similar prices. Usually, only the most efficient remain, and they have comparable costs. At this stage, price increases are usually cost initiated, not demand initiated. Nor do price reductions in the late phase of maturity stimulate much demand. Because demand is limited and producers have similar cost structures, the remaining competitors will probably match price reductions.

- *Decline stage:* The final stage of the life cycle may see further price decreases as the few remaining competitors try to salvage the last vestiges of demand. When only one firm is left in the market, prices begin to stabilize. In fact, prices may eventually rise dramatically if the product survives and moves into the specialty goods category, as horse-drawn carriages and vinyl records have.

The Competition

Competition varies during the product life cycle, of course, and so at times it may strongly affect pricing decisions. Although a firm may not have any competition at first, the high prices it charges may eventually induce another firm to enter the market. Several Internet auto sellers, such as Autobytel.com, have sprung up in response to the perceived high profit margins earned by car dealers.

Distribution Strategy

An effective distribution network can often overcome other minor flaws in the marketing mix.[8] For example, although consumers may perceive a price as being slightly higher than normal, they may buy the product anyway if it is being sold at a convenient retail outlet.

Adequate distribution for a new product can often be attained by offering a larger-than-usual profit margin to distributors. A variation on this strategy is to give dealers a large trade allowance to help offset the costs of promotion and further stimulate demand at the retail level.

The Impact of the Internet and Extranets

The Internet, corporate networks, and wireless setups are linking people, machines, and companies around the globe—and connecting sellers and buyers as never before. This link is enabling buyers to quickly and easily compare products and prices, putting them in a better bargaining position. At the same time, the technology allows sellers to collect detailed data about customers' buying habits, preferences, and even spending limits so that they can tailor their products and prices. For a time, all of these developments raised hopes of a more efficient marketplace.

Unfortunately, the promise of pricing efficiencies for Internet retailers and lower costs for consumers has run headlong into reality. Flawed pricing strategies have taken much of the blame for the continuing implosion of dot-coms. Too many merchants offered deep discounts that made profits all but impossible to achieve. Other e-retailers have felt the consumer backlash against price discrimination, as the Internet has given shoppers the ability to better detect price discrepancies and bargains. The dot-com survivors must now figure out if it is even possible to take advantage of the Internet's unique capabilities to set dynamic prices, which would better reflect a customer's willingness to pay more under different circumstances.

"Before the Internet existed, retail was a very competitive, difficult, low-margin business," says Austan Goolsbee, an economist at the University of Chicago. "With the advent of Internet retailers, there was a brief moment in which they and others believed they had broken the iron chain of low margins and high competition in retail by introducing the Internet. Now, retail on-line is starting to look like retail off-line—very competitive, profit margins squeezed. In all, a very tough place to be."[9]

Setting prices on the Internet was expected to offer retailers a number of advantages. To begin with, it would be far easier to raise or lower prices in response to demand, without the need for a clerk to run through a store with a pricing gun. On-line prices could be changed in far smaller increments—even by just a penny or two—as frequently as a merchant desired, making it possible to fine-tune pricing strategies.

But the real payoff was supposed to be better information on exactly how price-conscious customers are. For instance, knowing that customer A doesn't care whether an Oscar-nominated DVD in her shopping basket costs $21.95 or $25.95 would leave an enterprising merchant free to charge the higher price on the spot. By contrast, knowing that customer B is going to put author John Le Carre's latest thriller back on the shelf unless it's priced at $20, instead of $28, would open an opportunity for a bookseller to make the sale by cutting the price in real time.

AP/WIDE WORLD PHOTOS

Competition can be a significant factor in pricing. Microsoft's Xbox and Sony's PlayStation are continuing to go head-to-head, much like Coke and Pepsi. Such intense competition has a definite impact on pricing, which in turn affects revenue.

The idea was to charge exactly what the market will bear. But putting this into practice on-line has turned out to be exceptionally difficult, in part because the Internet has also empowered consumers to compare prices to find out if other merchants are offering a better deal or if other consumers are getting a bigger break. And the Internet has also made it easier for consumers to complain.

For example, Amazon.com faced a problem when customers learned they had paid different prices for the same DVD movies as a result of a marketing test in which the retailer varied prices to gauge the effect on demand. After complaints from irate consumers, who learned from on-line chat boards that they had paid higher prices, Amazon announced it would refund the difference between the highest and lowest prices in the test.

While the Internet helps drive down prices by making it easier for consumers to shop for the best bargain, it also makes it possible for on-line merchants to monitor each other's prices—whether higher or lower—and to adjust them in concert without overtly colluding. As long as the number of retailers in a given market is relatively small, it is now much simpler for merchants to signal each other by changing prices for short periods—long enough for their competitors to notice, but not so long that consumers do. Airlines have long used on-line reservation systems to signal fare changes to each other.

"On-line markets may not be as cutthroat as is commonly expected," says Hal Varian, dean of the school of information management and systems at the University of California at Berkeley. "The only check on this upward drift in prices comes from competitive suppliers such as local [bricks-and-mortar] merchants who may find it more difficult to change prices so rapidly."[10] Recent research has supported the notion that on-line merchants can find ways to raise prices. One study looked at the on-line pricing of books at Amazon.com and its two closest competitors: Borders.com and Barnes & Noble.com. The researchers found that for over half the items studied, all three retailers charged virtually the same price, differing at most by five cents. What's more, those prices were substantially higher than the lowest prices offered by other on-line retailers.[11] That runs against early conventional wisdom of Internet shopping—that consumers were only a click away from lower prices offered by a competing merchant.

On-line price-comparison engines, known as shopbots, were supposed to make it easy for consumers to find the lowest prices for any goods. But making effective use of competitive price information has been more difficult for consumers than

extranet
A private electronic network that links a company with its suppliers and customers.

retailers and economists originally thought. For one thing, price comparisons, which must include a range of shipping options and fees, state-based sales taxes, and any special offers from individual merchants, are far from straightforward. And the time it takes to look up the best prices for a collection of items—say, books or DVDs—can outweigh price savings of a dollar or two.

"Shopbots are tedious to use," says Karen Clay, a Carnegie Mellon economist, who notes that consumers also tend to be willing to pay more for goods from familiar on-line retailers. Since trying a new retailer always involves uncertainty as to whether goods will arrive on time, whether customer service is satisfactory, and even whether the merchant has honestly posted its prices, she says, "that uncertainty can easily outweigh what you could save by shopping somewhere else."[12]

One area where the Internet is having, and will continue to have, a major impact on pricing is the bargaining power between buyers and sellers. For example, a group of forty-plus retailers, with nearly three and a half times the buying power of Wal-Mart, have formed the WorldWide Retail Exchange. On the manufacturing side, Procter & Gamble, Kraft Foods, and others have invested more than $250 million to build business-to-business (B2B) megamarket Transora. Whatever the outcome of these markets, suppliers will soon be facing a world in which there are no more weak customers. Every buyer will wield Wal-Mart's bargaining power.[13]

As bargaining power evens out, companies are reaching price agreements more quickly and then disseminating this information throughout the channel of distribution. Manufacturers are creating private networks, or **extranets,** that link them with their suppliers and customers. These systems make it possible to get a precise handle on inventory, costs, and demand at any given moment—and, after bargaining with suppliers, adjust prices instantly. In the past, a significant cost, known as the "menu cost," was associated with changing prices. For a company with a large product line, it could take months for price adjustments to filter down to distributors, retailers, and salespeople. Streamlined networks reduce menu cost and time to near zero.

Internet Auctions

The Internet auction business is huge. Part of the lure of buying on-line is that shoppers don't have to go to a flea market or use up a coveted weekend day or worry about the weather. Plus, bidding itself can be fun and exciting. A few of the most popular consumer auction sites are the following

- **http://www.ebay.com:** The most popular auction site.
- **http://www.auctions.amazon.com:** Not as extensive as e-bay, but still a wide variety.
- **http://www.auctions.yahoo.com:** Free listings and numerous selling categories including international auctions.

Even though consumers are spending billions on Internet auctions, B2B auctions are likely to be the dominant form in the future. FreeMarkets, Inc., a publicly traded B2B exchange based in Pittsburgh, has hosted on-line reverse auctions—in which suppliers bid for a factory's component order—involving $5.4 billion of transactions. Among the companies using FreeMarkets are Owens Corning, GlaxoSmithKline PLC, and Visteon Corporation, the auto-parts unit spun off by Ford Motor Company.[14] As an example of the benefits of using FreeMarkets.com, a company paid $175,000 for the last batch of plastic auto parts—before using auctions. This time, in thirty-three minutes of frenzied bidding by twenty-five competing suppliers, the price comes down to $118,000.[15]

FreeMarkets has quickly moved beyond selling metal and plastic parts and is auctioning tax preparation services, relocation services, temporary help, and other services. And it's just getting started. Ford, General Motors, and DaimlerChrysler have created an exchange called Covisint (competing with FreeMarkets) to buy huge quantities of parts; retailers have created the Worldwide Retail Exchange and Global Net Xchange; and dozens of similar services are running or in the works.

Promotion Strategy

Price is often used as a promotional tool to increase consumer interest. The weekly flyers sent out by grocery stores in the Sunday newspaper, for instance, advertise many products with special low prices. Crested Butte Ski Resort in Colorado tried a unique twist on price promotions. It made the unusual offer of free skiing between Thanksgiving and Christmas. Its only revenues were voluntary contributions from lodging and restaurant owners who benefited from the droves of skiers taking advantage of the promotion. Lodging during the slack period is now booked solid, and on the busiest days nine thousand skiers jam slopes designed for about sixty-five hundred. Crested Butte Resort no longer loses money during this time of the year.

Pricing can be a tool for trade promotions as well. For example, Levi's Dockers (casual men's pants) are very popular with white-collar men ages twenty-five to forty-five, a growing and lucrative market. Sensing an opportunity, rival pants-maker Bugle Boy began offering similar pants at cheaper wholesale prices, which gave retailers a bigger gross margin than they were getting with Dockers. Levi Strauss had to either lower prices or risk its $400 million annual Docker sales. Although Levi Strauss intended its cheapest Dockers to retail for $35, it started selling Dockers to retailers for $18 a pair. Retailers could then advertise Dockers at a very attractive retail price of $25.

Demands of Large Customers

Large customers of manufacturers such as Wal-Mart, JCPenney, and other department stores often make specific pricing demands that the suppliers must agree to. Department stores are making greater-than-ever demands on their suppliers to cover the heavy discounts and markdowns on their own selling floors. They want suppliers to guarantee their stores' profit margins, and they insist on cash rebates if the guarantee isn't met. They are also exacting fines for violations of ticketing, packing, and shipping rules. Cumulatively, the demands are nearly wiping out profits for all but the very biggest suppliers, according to fashion designers and garment makers.

Few stores ask for stiffer margin guarantees than May's Lord & Taylor chain.[16] Makers of moderate-priced dresses say Lord & Taylor is the entry point for vendors hoping to do business with other May department store chains like Hecht's and Foley's. May sets the profitability bar high, insisting on a guaranteed profit margin as high as 48 percent in some cases, according to Beau Baker, former chief executive officer of Beau David, Inc., a small dress company.

In the past when a garment maker sold to a store, the two parties would agree on a retail price, and at the end of the season, the supplier would rebate some of the cost of markdowns. Discounts and markdowns were far rarer then than they are today: Department stores could afford plenty of sales help to push products. As stores cut labor costs, however, they came to rely on promotional markdowns and sales to move goods—with suppliers covering profit-margin shortfalls.

The Relationship of Price to Quality

When a purchase decision involves great uncertainty, consumers tend to rely on a high price as a predictor of good quality. In the absence of other information, people typically assume that prices are higher because the products contain better materials, because they are made more carefully, or, in the case of professional services, because the provider has more expertise. In other

Hair-care products benefit from the customer perception that higher prices mean higher quality. Salon products, like Bed Head and Paul Mitchell, convey the message of quality through high prices and exclusive distribution. In fact, customers may assume that the products are better because of the expertise of the hairdresser in whose salon the products are sold.

COURTESY OF TIGI

prestige pricing
Charging a high price to help promote a high-quality image.

words, consumers assume that "You get what you pay for." Knowledgeable merchants take these consumer attitudes into account when devising their pricing strategies. **Prestige pricing** is charging a high price to help promote a high-quality image.

How to Set a Price on a Product

 7

Describe the procedure for setting the right price

Setting the right price on a product is a four-step process (see Exhibit 15.2):

1. Establish pricing goals.
2. Estimate demand, costs, and profits.
3. Choose a price strategy to help determine a base price.
4. Fine-tune the base price with pricing tactics.

The first three steps are discussed next; the fourth step is discussed later in the chapter.

Establish Pricing Goals

The first step in setting the right price is to establish pricing goals. Recall that pricing objectives fall into three categories: profit oriented, sales oriented, and status quo. These goals are derived from the firm's overall objectives.

All pricing objectives have trade-offs that managers must weigh. A profit maximization objective may require a bigger initial investment than the firm can commit or wants to commit. Reaching the desired market share often means sacrificing short-term profit because without careful management, long-term profit goals may not be met. Meeting the competition is the easiest pricing goal to implement.

Exhibit 15.2

Steps in Setting the Right Price on a Product

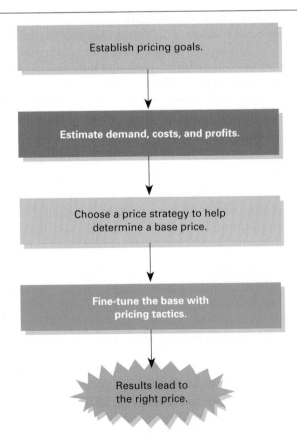

But can managers really afford to ignore demand and costs, the life-cycle stage, and other considerations? When creating pricing objectives, managers must consider these trade-offs in light of the target customer and the environment.

Estimate Demand, Costs, and Profits

Earlier we explained that total revenue is a function of price and quantity demanded and that quantity demanded depends on elasticity. After establishing pricing goals, managers should estimate total revenue at a variety of prices. Next, they should determine corresponding costs for each price. They are then ready to estimate how much profit, if any, and how much market share can be earned at each possible price. These data become the heart of the developing price policy. Managers can study the options in light of revenues, costs, and profits. In turn, this information can help determine which price can best meet the firm's pricing goals.

Choose a Price Strategy

The basic, long-term pricing framework for a good or service should be a logical extension of the pricing objectives. The marketing manager's chosen **price strategy** defines the initial price and gives direction for price movements over the product life cycle.

The price strategy sets a competitive price in a specific market segment, based on a well-defined positioning strategy. Changing a price level from premium to superpremium may require a change in the product itself, the target customers served, the promotional strategy, or the distribution channels. Thus, changing a price strategy can require dramatic alterations in the marketing mix. A carmaker cannot successfully compete in the superpremium category if the car looks and drives like an economy car.

A company's freedom in pricing a new product and devising a price strategy depends on the market conditions and the other elements of the marketing mix. If a firm launches a new item resembling several others already on the market, its pricing freedom will be restricted. To succeed, the company will probably have to charge a price close to the average market price. In contrast, a firm that introduces a totally new product with no close substitutes will have considerable pricing freedom.

Companies that do serious planning for creating a price strategy can select from three basic approaches: price skimming, penetration pricing, and status quo pricing. A discussion of each type follows.

Price Skimming

Price skimming is sometimes called a "market-plus" approach to pricing because it denotes a high price relative to the prices of competing products. Radius Corporation produces unique oval-headed toothbrushes made of black neoprene that look like a scuba-diving accessory. Radius uses a skimming policy, pricing the toothbrushes at $9.95, compared to around $2.00 for a regular toothbrush.

The term **price skimming** is derived from the phrase "skimming the cream off the top." Companies often use this strategy for new products when the product is perceived by the target market as having unique advantages. For example, Caterpillar sets premium prices on its construction equipment to support and capture its high perceived value. Genzyme Corporation

price strategy
A basic, long-term pricing framework, which establishes the initial price for a product and the intended direction for price movements over the product life cycle.

price skimming
A pricing policy whereby a firm charges a high introductory price, often coupled with heavy promotion.

SEND THE KIDS TO YOUR ROOM!

Introducing Ceiva. The digital picture frame that lets you share photos over the internet. It's easy to set up. Easy to use. You don't even need a computer to receive photos. And anyone you want can send photos to your Ceiva frame from just about anywhere. Set your sights on one. And get one for your parents. So you can send the kids to their house whenever you want. **SHARE** photos **EVERYDAY**

ceiva.com

COURTESY OF CEIVA LOGIC, INC.

New products with no close substitutes are less restricted in the pricing strategies they can pursue. How do you think Ceiva will price this Internet-connected digital picture frame? Keep in mind that other factors besides novelty may affect the pricing strategy.

introduced Ceredase as the first effective treatment for Gaucher's disease. The pill allows patients to avoid years of painful physical deterioration and lead normal lives. A year's supply for one patient can exceed $300,000.

As a product progresses through its life cycle, the firm may lower its price to successfully reach larger market segments. Economists have described this type of pricing as "sliding down the demand curve." Not all companies slide down the curve. Genentech's TPA, a drug that clears blood clots, was still priced at $2,200 a dose four years after its introduction, despite competition from a much lower priced competitor.

Price skimming works best when the market is willing to buy the product even though it carries an above-average price. If, for example, some purchasing agents feel that Caterpillar equipment is far superior to competitors' products, then Caterpillar can charge premium prices successfully. Firms can also effectively use price skimming when a product is well protected legally, when it represents a technological breakthrough, or when it has in some other way blocked the entry of competitors. Managers may follow a skimming strategy when production cannot be expanded rapidly because of technological difficulties, shortages, or constraints imposed by the skill and time required to produce a product. As long as demand is greater than supply, skimming is an attainable strategy.

A successful skimming strategy enables management to recover its product development or "educational" costs quickly. (Often consumers must be "taught" the advantages of a radically new item, such as high-definition TV.) Even if the market perceives an introductory price as too high, managers can easily correct the problem by lowering the price. Firms often feel it is better to test the market at a high price and then lower the price if sales are too slow. They are tacitly saying, "If there are any premium-price buyers in the market, let's reach them first and maximize our revenue per unit." Successful skimming strategies are not limited to products. Well-known athletes, entertainers, lawyers, and hairstylists are experts at price skimming. Naturally, a skimming strategy will encourage competitors to enter the market.

Penetration Pricing

penetration pricing
A pricing policy whereby a firm charges a relatively low price for a product initially as a way to reach the mass market.

Penetration pricing is at the opposite end of the spectrum from skimming. **Penetration pricing** means charging a relatively low price for a product as a way to reach the mass market. The low price is designed to capture a large share of a substantial market, resulting in lower production costs. If a marketing manager has made obtaining a large market share the firm's pricing objective, penetration pricing is a logical choice.

Penetration pricing does mean lower profit per unit, however. Therefore, to reach the break-even point, it requires a higher volume of sales than would a skimming policy. If reaching a high volume of sales takes a long time, then the recovery of product development costs will also be slow. As you might expect, penetration pricing tends to discourage competition.

The big advantage of penetration pricing is that it typically discourages or blocks competition from entering a market. The disadvantage is that penetration means gearing up for mass production to sell a large volume at a low price. What if the volume fails to materialize? The company will face huge losses from building or converting a factory to produce the failed product. Skimming, in contrast, lets a firm "stick its toe in the water" and see if limited demand exists at the high price. If not, the firm can simply lower the price. Skimming lets a company start out with a small production facility and expand it gradually as price falls and demand increases.

Penetration pricing can also prove disastrous for a prestige brand that adopts the strategy in an effort to gain market share and fails. When Omega—once a more prestigious brand than Rolex—was trying to improve the market share of its watches, it adopted a penetration pricing strategy that succeeded in destroying the watches' brand image by flooding the market with lower priced products. Omega never gained sufficient share on its lower priced/lower image competitors to justify destroying its brand image and high-priced position with upscale buyers. The

Irish Airline Flies High Just Like Southwest Airlines

Europe's grand old airlines have hit a rough patch of air these days, and Michael O'Leary is proud to be a big part of their problem.

The chief executive of Ryanair Holdings didn't set out to rattle the once cozy world of European aviation. Ten years ago, when he was financial adviser to Irish tycoon Tony Ryan, he was asked by Ryan for some thoughts on fixing the struggling family-owned carrier. O'Leary's advice: "Shut the bloody thing down."

Instead, Ryan persuaded O'Leary to visit Southwest Airlines in Dallas and learn how the pioneer of low-cost air travel makes a big profit. There, under the Texas sun, O'Leary found cut-price religion. He agreed to run Ryanair, in the process taking on some of the biggest names in aviation.

Today, Ryanair stands foremost among a handful of European budget airlines, rewriting the rules and battering venerable flag carriers. Passengers grumble that flying Ryanair is like riding a bus, but they are doing it by the bus-load. Ryanair carries seven million passengers in eleven countries each year—Britain, France, and Italy, among them—ranking its traffic volume above that of Ireland's state-owned Aer Lingus. That makes Ryanair Europe's first start-up to surpass a national carrier.

Ryanair's rise from Irish puddle-jumper to continental contender is more than one airline's growth story. The Gaelic upstart and its followers such as London-based EasyJet are fundamentally shifting the economics of flying around Europe. Some promotional Ryanair fares are as cheap as £1 ($1.45) to fly from one European city to another; the majority of the carrier's tickets are in the same price range as old-line carriers' bargain fares. But while major airlines make most of their money from premium travelers and offer discounts mainly to fill unsold seats, Ryanair is able to turn a profit at discount-fare levels.

The carrier, which today bases most of its flights in London, can make money on bargain fares be-cause it pares costs to the bone and then keeps cutting. Frequent flyer plan? Forget about it. Want a snack or drink on board? You buy it. And Ryanair won't serve peanuts, because prying them out from between the seat cushions takes too long (and hence, costs too much money). In its no-frills fervor, Ryanair even refuses to use those extendable boarding corridors at airports because it's quicker to park a plane at the gate, roll stairs up to the front and back doors, and let passengers hustle across the tarmac. The result: Ryanair can break even with its planes almost half empty—although its average flight is 75 percent full, better than most major European carriers.[17]

What type of pricing strategy is Ryanair following? What might Europe's traditional airlines, like British Airways and Lufthansa, do to counteract Ryanair's success? What other problems might Ryanair face in following this pricing strategy?

Cadillac Cimarron and Lacoste clothing experienced similar outcomes from a penetration pricing strategy.

Sometimes marketers in other countries see the success of American companies' price strategies and decide to emulate them. Such was the case of Ryanair as explained in the "Global Perspectives" box.

Status Quo Pricing

The third basic price strategy a firm may choose is status quo pricing, or meeting the competition. It means charging a price identical to or very close to the competition's price. JCPenney, for example, makes sure it is charging comparable prices by sending representatives to shop at Sears stores.

Although status quo pricing has the advantage of simplicity, its disadvantage is that the strategy may ignore demand or cost or both. If the firm is comparatively small, however, meeting the competition may be the safest route to long-term survival.

The Legality and Ethics of Price Strategy

As we mentioned in Chapter 2, some pricing decisions are subject to government regulation. Before marketing managers establish any price strategy, they should know the laws that limit their decision making. Among the issues that fall into this

Identify the legal and ethical constraints on pricing decisions

unfair trade practice acts
Laws that prohibit wholesalers and retailers from selling below cost.

price fixing
An agreement between two or more firms on the price they will charge for a product.

In a scandal that rocked the art world, Sotheby's and Christie's, two of the industry's most venerable auction houses, were caught in a price-fixing scheme. The CEOs of both companies received substantial fines and prison time.

category are unfair trade practices, price fixing, price discrimination, and predatory pricing.

Unfair Trade Practices

In over half the states, **unfair trade practice acts** put a floor under wholesale and retail prices. Selling below cost in these states is illegal. Wholesalers and retailers must usually take a certain minimum percentage markup on their combined merchandise cost and transportation cost. The most common markup figures are 6 percent at the retail level and 2 percent at the wholesale level. If a specific wholesaler or retailer can provide "conclusive proof" that operating costs are lower than the minimum required figure, lower prices may be allowed.

The intent of unfair trade practice acts is to protect small local firms from giants like Wal-Mart and Target, which operate very efficiently on razor-thin profit margins. State enforcement of unfair trade practice laws has generally been lax, however, partly because low prices benefit local consumers.

Price Fixing

Price fixing is an agreement between two or more firms on the price they will charge for a product. Suppose two or more executives from competing firms meet to decide how much to charge for a product or to decide which of them will submit the lowest bid on a certain contract. Such practices are illegal under the Sherman Act and the Federal Trade Commission Act. Offenders have received fines and sometimes prison terms. Price fixing is one area where the law is quite clear, and the Justice Department's enforcement is vigorous.

In the past several years, the Justice Department has vigorously pursued price-fixing cases. In late 2001, A. Alfred Taubman, chairman of Sotheby's Holdings, the global auction house giant, was found guilty of price fixing. The jury determined that Taubman had conspired with the former chairman of rival Christie's International to fix fees charged to art clients.[18] He was later sentenced to a year and a day in prison and a $7.5 million fine.

Price Discrimination

The Robinson-Patman Act of 1936 prohibits any firm from selling to two or more different buyers, within a reasonably short time, commodities (not services) of like grade and quality at different prices where the result would be to substantially lessen competition. The act also makes it illegal for a seller to offer two buyers different supplementary services and for buyers to use their purchasing power to force sellers into granting discriminatory prices or services.

The Robinson-Patman Act provides three defenses for the seller charged with price discrimination (in each case the burden is on the defendant to prove the defense):

AP/WIDE WORLD PHOTOS

- *Cost:* A firm can charge different prices to different customers if the prices represent manufacturing or quantity discount savings.

- *Market conditions:* Price variations are justified if designed to meet fluid product or market conditions. Examples include the deterioration of perishable goods, the obsolescence of seasonal products, a distress sale under court order, and a legitimate going-out-of-business sale.

- *Competition:* A reduction in price may be necessary to stay even with the competition. Specifically, if a competitor undercuts the price quoted by a seller to a buyer, the law authorizes the seller to lower the price charged to the buyer for the product in question.

Predatory Pricing

Predatory pricing is the practice of charging a very low price for a product with the intent of driving competitors out of business or out of a market. Once competitors have been driven out, the firm raises its prices. This practice is illegal under the Sherman Act and the Federal Trade Commission Act. Proving the use of the practice is difficult and expensive, however. The Justice Department must show that the predator, the destructive company, explicitly tried to ruin a competitor and that the predatory price was below the predator's average variable cost.

predatory pricing
The practice of charging a very low price for a product with the intent of driving competitors out of business or out of a market.

Tactics for Fine-Tuning the Base Price

Explain how discounts, geographic pricing, and other special pricing tactics can be used to fine-tune the base price

After managers understand both the legal and the marketing consequences of price strategies, they should set a **base price**, the general price level at which the company expects to sell the good or service. The general price level is correlated with the pricing policy: above the market (price skimming), at the market (status quo pricing), or below the market (penetration pricing). The final step, then, is to fine-tune the base price.

Fine-tuning techniques are short-run approaches that do not change the general price level. They do, however, result in changes within a general price level. These pricing tactics allow the firm to adjust for competition in certain markets, meet ever-changing government regulations, take advantage of unique demand situations, and meet promotional and positioning goals. Fine-tuning pricing tactics include various sorts of discounts, geographic pricing, and special pricing tactics.

base price
The general price level at which the company expects to sell the good or service.

Discounts, Allowances, Rebates, and Value-Based Pricing

A base price can be lowered through the use of discounts and the related tactics of allowances, rebates, low or zero percent financing, and value-based pricing. Managers use the various forms of discounts to encourage customers to do what they would not ordinarily do, such as paying cash rather than using credit, taking delivery out of season, or performing certain functions within a distribution channel. The following are of the most common tactics:

- *Quantity discounts:* When buyers get a lower price for buying in multiple units or above a specified dollar amount, they are receiving a **quantity discount**. A **cumulative quantity discount** is a deduction from list price that applies to the buyer's total purchases made during a specific period; it is intended to encourage customer loyalty. In contrast, a **noncumulative quantity discount** is a deduction from list price that applies to a single order rather than to the total volume of orders placed during a certain period. It is intended to encourage orders in large quantities.

- *Cash discounts:* A **cash discount** is a price reduction offered to a consumer, an industrial user, or a marketing intermediary in return for prompt payment of a bill. Prompt payment saves the seller carrying charges and billing expenses and allows the seller to avoid bad debt.

- *Functional discounts:* When distribution channel intermediaries, such as wholesalers or retailers, perform a service or function for the manufacturer, they must be compensated. This compensation, typically a percentage discount from the base price, is called a **functional discount** (or **trade discount**). Functional discounts vary greatly from channel to channel, depending on the tasks performed by the intermediary.

- *Seasonal discounts:* A **seasonal discount** is a price reduction for buying merchandise out of season. It shifts the storage function to the purchaser. Seasonal discounts also enable manufacturers to maintain a steady production schedule year-round.

quantity discount
A price reduction offered to buyers buying in multiple units or above a specified dollar amount.

cumulative quantity discount
A deduction from list price that applies to the buyer's total purchases made during a specific period.

noncumulative quantity discount
A deduction from list price that applies to a single order rather than to the total volume of orders placed during a certain period.

cash discount
A price reduction offered to a consumer, an industrial user, or a marketing intermediary in return for prompt payment of a bill.

functional discount (trade discount)
A discount to wholesalers and retailers for performing channel functions.

seasonal discount
A price reduction for buying merchandise out of season.

promotional allowance (trade allowance)
A payment to a dealer for promoting the manufacturer's products.

rebate
A cash refund given for the purchase of a product during a specific period.

value-based pricing
Setting the price at a level that seems to the customer to be a good price compared to the prices of other options.

FOB origin pricing
A price tactic that requires the buyer to absorb the freight costs from the shipping point ("free on board").

uniform delivered pricing
A price tactic in which the seller pays the actual freight charges and bills every purchaser an identical, flat freight charge.

zone pricing
A modification of uniform delivered pricing that divides the United States (or the total market) into segments or zones and charges a flat freight rate to all customers in a given zone.

- *Promotional allowances:* A **promotional allowance** (also known as a **trade allowance**) is a payment to a dealer for promoting the manufacturer's products. It is both a pricing tool and a promotional device. As a pricing tool, a promotional allowance is like a functional discount. If, for example, a retailer runs an ad for a manufacturer's product, the manufacturer may pay half the cost. If a retailer sets up a special display, the manufacturer may include a certain quantity of free goods in the retailer's next order.

- *Rebates:* A **rebate** is a cash refund given for the purchase of a product during a specific period. The advantage of a rebate over a simple price reduction for stimulating demand is that a rebate is a temporary inducement that can be taken away without altering the basic price structure. A manufacturer that uses a simple price reduction for a short time may meet resistance when trying to restore the price to its original, higher level.

- *Zero percent financing:* After the terrorist attacks on September 11, 2001, new-car sales plummeted. To get people back into the automobile showrooms, manufacturers offered zero percent financing, which enabled purchasers to borrow money to pay for new cars with no interest charge. The tactic created a huge increase in sales but not without cost to the manufacturers. A five-year interest-free car loan represented a cost of over $3,000 on a typical vehicle sold during the zero percent promotion. And several automakers were still offering such incentives over a year later!

Value-Based Pricing

Value-based pricing (also called *value pricing*) is a pricing strategy that has grown out of the quality movement. Instead of figuring prices based on costs or competitors' prices, it starts with the customer, considers the competition, and then determines the appropriate price. The basic assumption is that the firm is customer driven, seeking to understand the attributes customers want in the goods and services they buy and the value of that bundle of attributes to customers. Because very few firms operate in a pure monopoly, however, a marketer using value-based pricing must also determine the value of competitive offerings to customers. Customers determine the value of a product (not just its price) relative to the value of alternatives. In value-based pricing, therefore, the price of the product is set at a level that seems to the customer to be a good price compared with the prices of other options.

Geographic Pricing

Because many sellers ship their wares to a nationwide or even a worldwide market, the cost of freight can greatly affect the total cost of a product. Sellers may use several different geographic pricing tactics to moderate the impact of freight costs on distant customers. The following methods of geographic pricing are the most common:

- *FOB origin pricing:* **FOB origin pricing**, also called FOB factory or FOB shipping point, is a price tactic that requires the buyer to absorb the freight costs from the shipping point ("free on board"). The farther buyers are from sellers, the more they pay, because transportation costs generally increase with the distance merchandise is shipped.

- *Uniform delivered pricing:* If the marketing manager wants total costs, including freight, to be equal for all purchasers of identical products, the firm will adopt uniform delivered pricing, or "postage stamp" pricing. With **uniform delivered pricing**, the seller pays the actual freight charges and bills every purchaser an identical, flat freight charge.

- *Zone pricing:* A marketing manager who wants to equalize total costs among buyers within large geographic areas—but not necessarily all of the seller's market area—may modify the base price with a zone-pricing tactic. **Zone pricing** is a modification of uniform delivered pricing. Rather than placing the entire United States (or its total market) under a uniform freight rate, the firm divides it into segments or zones and charges a flat freight rate to all customers in a given zone. The U.S. Postal Service's parcel post rate structure is probably the best-known zone-pricing system in the country.

- *Freight absorption pricing:* In **freight absorption pricing**, the seller pays all or part of the actual freight charges and does not pass them on to the buyer. The manager may use this tactic in intensely competitive areas or as a way to break into new market areas.

- *Basing-point pricing:* With **basing-point pricing**, the seller designates a location as a basing point and charges all buyers the freight cost from that point, regardless of the city from which the goods are shipped. Thanks to several adverse court rulings, basing-point pricing has waned in popularity. Freight fees charged when none were actually incurred, called *phantom freight*, have been declared illegal.

Special Pricing Tactics

Unlike geographic pricing, special pricing tactics are unique and defy neat categorization. Managers use these tactics for various reasons—for example, to stimulate demand for specific products, to increase store patronage, and to offer a wider variety of merchandise at a specific price point. Special pricing tactics include a single-price tactic, flexible pricing, professional services pricing, leader pricing, bait pricing, odd–even pricing, price bundling, and two-part pricing. A brief overview of each of these tactics follows, along with a manager's reasons for using that tactic or a combination of tactics to change the base price.

Single-Price Tactic

A merchant using a **single-price tactic** offers all goods and services at the same price (or perhaps two or three prices). Retailers using this tactic include One Price Clothing Stores, Dre$$ to the Nine$, Your $10 Store, and Fashions $9.99. One Price Clothing Stores, for example, tend to be small, about three thousand square feet. Their goal is to offer merchandise that would sell for at least $15 to $18 in other stores. The stores carry pants, shirts, blouses, sweaters, and shorts for juniors, misses, and large-sized women. The stores do not feature any seconds or irregular items, and everything is sold for $6.

Single-price selling removes price comparisons from the buyer's decision-making process. The consumer just looks for suitability and the highest perceived quality. The retailer enjoys the benefits of a simplified pricing system and minimal clerical errors. However, continually rising costs are a headache for retailers following this strategy. In times of inflation, they must frequently raise the selling price.

Flexible Pricing

Flexible pricing (or **variable pricing**) means that different customers pay different prices for essentially the same merchandise bought in equal quantities. This tactic is often found in the sale of shopping goods, specialty merchandise, and most industrial goods except supply items. Car dealers, many appliance retailers, and manufacturers of industrial installations, accessories, and component parts commonly follow the practice. It allows the seller to adjust for competition by meeting another seller's price. Thus, a marketing manager with a status quo pricing objective might readily adopt the tactic. Flexible pricing also enables the seller to close a sale with price-conscious consumers. If buyers show promise of becoming large-volume shoppers, flexible pricing can be used to lure their business.

The obvious disadvantages of flexible pricing are the lack of consistent profit margins, the potential ill will of high-paying purchasers, the tendency for salespeople to automatically lower the price to make a sale, and the possibility of a price war among sellers. The disadvantages of flexible pricing have led the automobile industry to experiment with one price for all buyers. General Motors uses a one-price tactic for some of its models, including the Saturn and the Buick Regal.

freight absorption pricing
A price tactic in which the seller pays all or part of the actual freight charges and does not pass them on to the buyer.

basing-point pricing
A price tactic that charges freight from a given (basing) point, regardless of the city from which the goods are shipped.

single-price tactic
A price tactic that offers all goods and services at the same price (or perhaps two or three prices).

flexible pricing (variable pricing)
A price tactic in which different customers pay different prices for essentially the same merchandise bought in equal quantities.

Professional Services Pricing

Professional services pricing is used by people with lengthy experience, training, and often certification by a licensing board—for example, lawyers, physicians, and family counselors. Professionals sometimes charge customers at an hourly rate, but sometimes fees are based on the solution of a problem or performance of an act (such as an eye examination) rather than on the actual time involved. A surgeon may perform a heart operation and charge a flat fee of $5,000. The operation itself may require only four hours, resulting in a hefty $1,250 hourly rate. The physician justifies the fee because of the lengthy education and internship required to learn the complex procedures of a heart operation. Lawyers also sometimes use flat-rate pricing, such as $500 for completing a divorce and $50 for handling a traffic ticket.

Those who use professional pricing have an ethical responsibility not to over-charge a customer. Because demand is sometimes highly inelastic, such as when a person requires heart surgery or a daily insulin shot to survive, there may be a temptation to charge "all the traffic will bear."

Leader Pricing

Leader pricing (or **loss-leader pricing**) is an attempt by the marketing manager to attract customers by selling a product near or even below cost in the hope that shoppers will buy other items once they are in the store. This type of pricing appears weekly in the newspaper advertising of supermarkets, specialty stores, and department stores. Leader pricing is normally used on well-known items that consumers can easily recognize as bargains at the special price. The goal is not necessarily to sell large quantities of leader items, but to try to appeal to customers who might shop elsewhere.

Leader pricing is not limited to products. Health clubs offer a one-month free trial as a loss leader. Lawyers give a free initial consultation. And restaurants distribute two-for-one coupons and "welcome to the neighborhood" free meal coupons.

Bait Pricing

In contrast to leader pricing, which is a genuine attempt to give the consumer a reduced price, bait pricing is deceptive. **Bait pricing** tries to get the consumer into a store through false or misleading price advertising and then uses high-pressure selling to persuade the consumer to buy more expensive merchandise. You may have seen this ad or a similar one:

> REPOSSESSED . . . Singer slant-needle sewing machine . . . take over 8 payments of $5.10 per month . . . ABC Sewing Center.

This is bait. When a customer goes in to see the machine, a salesperson says that it has just been sold or else shows the prospective buyer a piece of junk no one would buy. Then the salesperson says, "But I've got a really good deal on this fine new model." This is the switch that may cause a susceptible consumer to walk out with a $400 machine. The Federal Trade Commission considers bait pricing a deceptive act and has banned its use in interstate commerce. Most states also ban bait pricing, but sometimes enforcement is lax.

Odd–Even Pricing

Odd–even pricing (or **psychological pricing**) means pricing at odd-numbered prices to connote a bargain and pricing at even-numbered prices to imply quality. For years, many retailers have priced their products in odd numbers—for example, $99.95 or $49.95—to make consumers feel they are paying a lower price for the product.

Some retailers favor odd-numbered prices because they believe that $9.99 sounds much less imposing to customers than $10.00. Other retailers believe that an odd-numbered price signals to consumers that the price is at the lowest level possible, thereby encouraging them to buy more units. Neither theory has ever been conclusively proved, although one study found that consumers perceive odd-priced products as being on sale.[19] The most recent research shows that consumers do purchase more at odd prices.[20]

Even-numbered pricing is sometimes used to denote quality. Examples include a fine perfume at $100 a bottle, a good watch at $500, or a mink coat at $3,000. The demand curve for such items would also be sawtoothed, except that the outside edges would represent even-numbered prices and, therefore, elastic demand.

Price Bundling

Price bundling is marketing two or more products in a single package for a special price. Examples include the sale of maintenance contracts with computer hardware and other office equipment, packages of stereo equipment, packages of options on cars, weekend hotel packages that include a room and several meals, and airline vacation packages. Microsoft offers "suites" of software that bundle spreadsheets, word processing, graphics, electronic mail, Internet access, and groupware for networks of microcomputers. Price bundling can stimulate demand for the bundled items if the target market perceives the price as a good value.[21]

A related price tactic is **unbundling**, or reducing the bundle of services that comes with the basic product. Rather than raise the price of hotel rooms, some hotel chains have started charging registered guests for parking. To help hold the line on costs, some stores require customers to pay for gift wrapping.

Two-Part Pricing

Two-part pricing means establishing two separate charges to consume a single good or service. Tennis clubs and health clubs charge a membership fee and a flat fee each time a person uses certain equipment or facilities. In other cases they charge a base rate for a certain level of usage, such as ten racquetball games per month, and a surcharge for anything over that amount.[22]

Consumers sometimes prefer two-part pricing because they are uncertain about the number and the types of activities they might use at places like an amusement park. Also, the people who use a service most often pay a higher total price. Two-part pricing can increase a seller's revenue by attracting consumers who would not pay a high fee even for unlimited use. For example, a health club might be able to sell only 100 memberships at $700 annually with unlimited use of facilities, for total revenue of $70,000. However, perhaps it could sell 900 memberships at $200 with a guarantee of using the racquetball courts ten times a month. Every use over ten would require the member to pay a $5 fee. Thus, membership revenue would provide a base of $180,000, with some additional usage fees coming in throughout the year.

Consumer Penalties

More and more businesses are adopting **consumer penalties**—extra fees paid by consumers for violating the terms of a purchase agreement.

Businesses impose consumer penalties for two reasons: They will allegedly (1) suffer an irrevocable revenue loss

COURTESY OF CLUB MED

Club Med advertises an all-inclusive vacation for one from $899 in this humorous ad. Included in the price are the room, airfare, meals, sports, and children's clubs. However, several contingencies are placed on this bundled vacation—listed in the ad's fine print.

and/or (2) incur significant additional transaction costs should customers be unable or unwilling to complete their purchase obligations. For the company, these customer payments are part of doing business in a highly competitive marketplace. With profit margins in many companies increasingly coming under pressure, organizations are looking to stem losses resulting from customers not meeting their obligations. However, the perceived unfairness of a penalty may affect some consumers' willingness to patronize a business in the future.

One study found that most consumers (53 percent) had paid a price penalty in the past year. A "fair" penalty exists when consumers believe that they are reimbursing the seller for actual lost revenue and not simply enabling the seller to make extra profit.[23]

CONNECT IT

Look back at the story at the beginning of this chapter on how Major League Baseball is charging fees for Internet video clips. Costs, revenues, and profits are directly related. Revenue minus costs equals profits. Profits can be increased by increasing revenues, lowering costs, or both. The Internet is already having a major impact on pricing. Consumers are finding better deals and making better decisions by comparing prices. Old-line manufacturers face the dilemma of competing directly with their channel members if the manufacturer sells through its own Web site.

Yield management systems will help boost revenues of not only service businesses but old-line manufacturers as well. This in turn will mean increased profits for the organization.

Price can have an impact on perceived quality, depending on a number of issues, such as the type of product, advertising, and the consumer's personality. For durable goods, price plays a key role in determining quality if consumers are focusing on prestige and/or durability as determinants of quality.

USE IT

Auctions accounted for 29 percent of all e-commerce, or $129 billion, in 2002.[24] Why not join the crowd? You must, however, avoid the "winner's curse"—that is, overestimating the value of an item and bidding too much. The best way to avoid this is to be informed. On eBay (http://www.ebay.com), bidders can study past auctions of similar items and also read feedback about sellers.

Although using on-line auctions is increasingly easy—and popular—, sometimes the auction process leaves customers dissatisfied. If you've ever had a problem with an on-line auction, you should know about auction dispute resolution services, like **SquareTrade.com, Tradiator.com,** and **eSpute.com.** These sites help auction buyers and sellers settle disputes on neutral ground, with a third party as referee or mediator. Square Trade also allows sellers to subscribe to its services as a way to assure buyers of their honesty. Subscribers can post a Square Trade icon on their auction pages. Another site, **www.odrnews.com** distributes news about on-line dispute resolution.

You can also save some money by using coupons. Whether you're shopping on-line or heading to the mall, make a pit stop at Ultimate-Coupons.com. The site features coupons from more than a hundred major retailers (mostly on the Web) in categories such as groceries and electronics. It also searches through offers on other coupon Web sites, so you'll get the best deals. One recent bargain: Save $10 when you spend $75 or more at Amazon.com. Printable coupons are available for brick-and-mortar stores; discount codes are provided for orders at e-tailers. Some stores, however, won't accept computer-printed coupons, so check before you shop.

Compare prices before you buy. Rely on price comparison services like My Simon (**http://www.mysimon.com**) or Price Scan (**http://www.pricescan.com**).

(1) Discuss the importance of pricing decisions to the economy and to the individual firm. Pricing plays an integral role in the U.S. economy by allocating goods and services among consumers, governments, and businesses. Pricing is essential in business because it creates revenue, which is the basis of all business activity. In setting prices, marketing managers strive to find a level high enough to produce a satisfactory profit.

1.1 Why is pricing so important to the marketing manager?

(2) List and explain a variety of pricing objectives. Establishing realistic and measurable pricing objectives is a critical part of any firm's marketing strategy. Pricing objectives are commonly classified into three categories: profit oriented, sales oriented, and status quo. Profit-oriented pricing is based on profit maximization, a satisfactory level of profit, or a target return on investment. The goal of profit maximization is to generate as much revenue as possible in relation to cost. Often, a more practical approach than profit maximization is setting prices to produce profits that will satisfy management and stockholders. The most common profit-oriented strategy is pricing for a specific return on investment relative to a firm's assets. The second type of pricing objective is sales oriented, and it focuses on either maintaining a percentage share of the market or maximizing dollar or unit sales. The third type of pricing objective aims to maintain the status quo by matching competitors' prices.

2.1 Give an example of each major type of pricing objective.

(3) Explain the role of demand in price determination. Demand is a key determinant of price. When establishing prices, a firm must first determine demand for its product. A typical demand schedule shows an inverse relationship between quantity demanded and price: When price is lowered, sales increase; and when price is increased, the quantity demanded falls. For prestige products, however, there may be a direct relationship between demand and price: The quantity demanded will increase as price increases.

Marketing managers must also consider demand elasticity when setting prices. Elasticity of demand is the degree to which the quantity demanded fluctuates with changes in price. If consumers are sensitive to changes in price, demand is elastic; if they are insensitive to price changes, demand is inelastic. Thus, an increase in price will result in lower sales for an elastic product and little or no loss in sales for an inelastic product.

3.1 Explain the role of supply and demand in determining price.

3.2 If a firm can increase its total revenue by raising its price, shouldn't it do so?

3.3 Explain the concepts of elastic and inelastic demand. Why should managers understand these concepts?

(4) Understand the concept of yield management systems. Yield management systems use complex mathematical software to profitably fill unused capacity. The software uses techniques such as discounting early purchases, limiting early sales at these discounted prices, and overbooking capacity. These systems are primarily used in service businesses and are substantially raising revenues.

4.1 Why are so many companies adopting yield management systems?

4.2 *INFOTRAC* COLLEGE EDITION How is yield management helping companies achieve competitive advantage? Use InfoTrac to find out (**http://www.infotrac-college.com**). Run a keyword search for "yield management" and read through the headlines to see what industries are profiled most often. Then read the article from *Computerworld* titled "Software Fills Trucks, Maximizes Revenue; Sitton Motor Lines

Takes Lead in Applying Analysis Tool Outside the Travel Industry" by Matthew Schwartz. Answer the following questions:

- How is Sitton Motor Lines using yield management principles and software?
- Describe the implementation of the new software.
- What other industries are cited as good candidates for yield management?

(5) **Describe cost-oriented pricing strategies.** The other major determinant of price is cost. Marketers use several cost-oriented pricing strategies. To cover their own expenses and obtain a profit, wholesalers and retailers commonly use markup pricing: They tack an extra amount onto the manufacturer's original price. Another pricing strategy determines how much a firm must sell to break even and uses this amount as a reference point for adjusting price.

5.1 **WRITING** Your firm has based its pricing strictly on cost in the past. As the newly hired marketing manager, you believe this policy should change. Write the president a memo explaining your reasons.

5.2 Why is it important for managers to understand the concept of break-even points? Are there any drawbacks?

(6) **Demonstrate how the product life cycle, competition, distribution, the Internet and extranets, promotion, demands of large customers, and perceptions of quality can affect price.** The price of a product normally changes as it moves through the life cycle and as demand for the product and competitive conditions change. Management often sets a high price at the introductory stage, and the high price tends to attract competition. The competition usually drives prices down because individual competitors lower prices to gain market share.

Adequate distribution for a new product can sometimes be obtained by offering a larger-than-usual profit margin to wholesalers and retailers. The Internet enables consumers to compare products and prices quickly and efficiently. Extranets help control costs and lower prices. Price is also used as a promotional tool to attract customers. Special low prices often attract new customers and entice existing customers to buy more. Demands of large customers can squeeze the profit margins of suppliers.

Perceptions of quality can also influence pricing strategies. A firm trying to project a prestigious image often charges a premium price for a product. Consumers tend to equate high prices with high quality.

6.1 **TEAM** Divide the class into teams of five. Each team will be assigned a different grocery store from a different chain. (An independent is fine.) Appoint a group leader. The group leaders should meet as a group and pick fifteen nationally branded grocery items. Each item should be specifically described as to brand name and size of the package. Each team will then proceed to its assigned store and collect price data on the fifteen items. The team should also gather price data on fifteen similar store brands and fifteen generics, if possible.

Each team should present its results to the class and discuss why there are price variations between stores, national brands, store brands, and generics.

As a next step, go back to your assigned store and share the overall results with the store manager. Bring back the manager's comments and share them with the class.

6.2 How does the stage of a product's life cycle affect price? Give some examples.

6.3 Go back to Priceline.com. Can you research a ticket's price before purchasing it? What products and services are available for purchasing? How comfortable are you with naming your own price? Relate the supply and demand curves to customer-determined pricing.

Go to one of the Internet auction sites listed in this chapter. Report to the class on how the auction process works and the items being auctioned.

6.4 *INFOTRAC COLLEGE EDITION* How important is pricing when a company is entering new markets? The article in *Across the Board* titled "Is the Price Right?" by Peter Meyer can tell you. Print out the article using InfoTrac (**http://www.infotrac-college.com**) and then underline all of the chapter concepts that it discusses. What issues does the article address that the chapter does not? What issues does the chapter address that are not included in the article?

(7) Describe the procedure for setting the right price. The process of setting the right price on a product involves four major steps: (1) establishing pricing goals; (2) estimating demand, costs, and profits; (3) choosing a price policy to help determine a base price; and (4) fine-tuning the base price with pricing tactics.

A price strategy establishes a long-term pricing framework for a good or service. The three main types of price policies are price skimming, penetration pricing, and status quo pricing. A price-skimming policy charges a high introductory price, often followed by a gradual reduction. Penetration pricing offers a low introductory price to capture a large market share and attain economies of scale. Finally, status quo pricing strives to match competitors' price.

7.1 A manufacturer of office furniture decides to produce antique-style rolltop desks reconfigured to accommodate personal computers. The desks will have built-in surge protectors, a platform for raising or lowering the monitor, and a number of other features. The quality, solid-oak desks will be priced far below comparable products. The marketing manager says, "We'll charge a low price and plan on a high volume to reduce our risks." Comment.

7.2 Janet Oliver, owner of a mid-priced dress shop, notes, "My pricing objectives are simple: I just charge what my competitors charge. I'm happy because I'm making money." React to Janet's statement.

7.3 What is the difference between a price policy and a price tactic? Give an example.

7.4 *TEAM* Divide into teams of four persons. Each team should choose one of the following topics: skimming, penetration pricing, status quo pricing, price fixing, geographic pricing, adopting a single-price tactic, flexible pricing, or professional services pricing. Each team should then pick a retailer that it feels most closely follows the team's chosen pricing strategy. Go to the store and write down examples of the strategy. Interview the store manager and get his or her views on the advantages and disadvantages of the strategy. Each team should then make an oral report in class.

(8) Identify the legal and ethical constraints on pricing decisions. Government regulation helps monitor four major areas of pricing: unfair trade practices, price fixing, predatory pricing, and price discrimination. Many states have enacted unfair trade practice acts that protect small businesses from large firms that operate efficiently on extremely thin profit margins; the acts prohibit charging below-cost prices. The Sherman Act and the Federal Trade Commission Act prohibit both price fixing, which is an agreement between two or more firms on a particular price, and predatory pricing, in which a firm undercuts its competitors with extremely low prices to drive them out of business. Finally, the Robinson-Patman Act makes it illegal for firms to discriminate between two or more buyers in terms of price.

8.1 *INFOTRAC COLLEGE EDITION* What kind of factors can push a respectable firm to enter a price-fixing arrangement with a competitor? Using InfoTrac (**http://www.infotrac-college.com**), read about the price-fixing scandals that rocked the art auction industry or the Hollywood movie studios and Blockbuster Video during 2001 and 2002. If there are more current scandals, read a selection of articles on a particular industry. Then compile a list of business practices and pricing issues that are present in the reports of each scandal. Is each scandal unique, or are there overlapping characteristics? What conclusion can you draw about price fixing from the articles you read? How does the federal government deal with price fixing?

9 **Explain how discounts, geographic pricing, and other special pricing tactics can be used to fine-tune the base price.** Several techniques enable marketing managers to adjust prices within a general range in response to changes in competition, government regulation, consumer demand, and promotional and positioning goals. Techniques for fine-tuning a price can be divided into three main categories: discounts, allowances, rebates, and value-based pricing; geographic pricing; and special pricing tactics.

The first type of tactic gives lower prices to those that pay promptly, order a large quantity, or perform some function for the manufacturer. Value-based pricing starts with the customer, considers the competition and costs, and then determines a price. Other tactics in this category include seasonal discounts, promotion allowances, and rebates (cash refunds).

Geographic pricing tactics—such as FOB origin pricing, uniform delivered pricing, zone pricing, freight absorption pricing, and basing-point pricing—are ways of moderating the impact of shipping costs on distant customers.

A variety of special pricing tactics stimulate demand for certain products, increase store patronage, and offer more merchandise at specific prices.

More and more customers are paying price penalties, which are extra fees for violating the terms of a purchase contract. The perceived fairness or unfairness of a penalty may affect some consumers' willingness to patronize a business in the future.

9.1 **WRITING** You are contemplating a price change for an established product sold by your firm. Write a memo analyzing the factors you need to consider in your decision.

9.2 Columnist Dave Barry jokes that federal law requires this message under the sticker price of new cars: "Warning to stupid people: Do not pay this amount." Discuss why the sticker price is generally higher than the actual selling price of a car. Tell how you think car dealers set the actual prices of the cars they sell.

9.3 Explain the difference between freight absorption pricing and uniform delivered pricing. When would it be appropriate to use each?

9.4 The U.S. Postal Service regularly raises the price of a first-class stamp but continues to operate in the red year after year. Is uniform delivered pricing the best choice for first-class mail? Explain your reasoning?

9.5 How is the "information age" changing the nature of pricing?

9.6 Have you ever paid a price penalty? How did it affect your attitude toward that company?

DEFINE IT

Application for Entrepreneurs

RoseAnn decided that time is, indeed, money. So she opened a Chinese buffet in Arlington, Texas. The new twist is that you pay by the minute. The restaurant, known as Rose's Chinese Buffet, is all-you-can-eat-by-the-minute.* The buffet table is piled with delectable seafood and steaming stir-fried dishes. Diners rush to their tables and wolf down spring rolls, fried noodles, fried rice, and other goodies. RoseAnn allows only the first thirty customers at lunch and dinner to pay by the minute. The rest must order from a traditional menu or pay the normal buffet price. By-the-minute lunch customers pay 30¢ a minute.

*Such restaurants do exist in Japan.

Questions

1. RoseAnn concedes that she only breaks even on her by-the-minute customers. Should she drop the concept?

2. What pricing tactics is she using?

3. Would such a restaurant be successful in your community?

Ethics Exercise

People feel better when they think that they are getting a great bargain when they shop. Knowing this, some retailers mark up items above the traditional retail price and then offer a 60 percent discount. If they had simply discounted the normal retail price by 20 percent the resulting "sale price" would have been the same. One retailer says that he is just making shoppers happy that they got a great deal when he inflates the retail price before discounting.

Questions

1. What do you think?

2. Does the AMA Code of Ethics address this issue? Go to **http://www.marketingpower. com** and review the code. Then, write a brief paragraph summarizing what the AMA Code of Ethics contains that relates to retail pricing.

Entrepreneurship Case
Setting the Right Price for a Special ISP

With only twenty-two thousand residents, Mercer Island is small enough to avoid recognition as a major market for anything. The affluent community, however, is situated on a small strip of land in the middle of Lake Washington on Seattle's western border. That means the community has major market needs and the means to fulfill them, but a group of ambitious entrepreneurs from the island's high school hopes to outdo Seattle when it comes to providing the island's Internet service.

At Mercer Island High School, information-technology teacher John Davis heads a team of students seeking to become the island's sole Internet service provider. He and his band of students call their nonprofit company IslanderISP, and together they hope that the profits from the business can be dedicated to funding the Mercer Island School District's technology needs.

The group hopes that it can prove to the world that it isn't necessary to have hundreds of thousands or millions of dollars in seed money from a venture capitalist to start a successful technology company. Having worked for the Navy, IBM, and Hewlett-Packard, Davis has the experience to lead his youthful partners. He sees the start-up as a means to developing more mature, experienced, and job-ready students in an increasingly competitive world. He plans to bolster his time-strapped staff by recruiting college students and retired teachers to work for them.

After incorporating as a nonprofit, staff members approached school officials about locating headquarters on high school property. They also contacted Qwest, which will provide them with connectivity to the Internet and advice on modem quantities and server locations. Qwest will also house IslanderISP's e-mail and Web servers, an arrangement that will give IslanderISP an advantage over most dial-up services by greatly reducing the time it will take for its customers to dial in to the information superhighway.

On campus, the young entrepreneurs are generating buzz through word of mouth and by handing out brochures at school sporting events. David Booth, a senior and public relations officer for the company, is pushing the school radio station and the local newspapers for exposure, as he hopes to benefit from the close-knit community and progressive atmosphere on the island. Between residences and businesses, the would-be ISP identifies ten thousand potential customers it hopes to sign to service subscriptions.

A subscription costs $22.50 per month. Customers who pay in full and up-front for the year receive one month free and pay only $247.50 for twelve months of service. Those who sign for a three-year subscription pay just $675, a discount equaling six months of free service at the introductory price. If it achieves 100 percent market penetration, IslanderISP projects a $2 million annual profit above the $400,000 to $500,000 incurred in maintenance, salary, rent, and Qwest service expenses.

With a dozen residents already signed, the students need to close eighty-eight more sales before activating the service. If the business fails to reach a hundred customers, the service agreements of the charter customers provide that the money they paid will be donated to Mercer Island School Foundation, a school system fund-raising entity.

Questions

1. Did IslanderISP thoroughly follow the procedure for setting the right price? Explain and critique.

2. What type of pricing strategy do you think would work best for IslanderISP?

3. Explain the special pricing tactics IslanderISP used in fine-tuning its base price.

4. If the company incurs $500,000 in expenses, how many one-year subscriptions (at $247.50) will it need to sell to break even? Do you think that is realistic? Explain.

 **WATCH IT**

Short  **SUPERBOWL**

The *Essentials of Marketing* PowerPoint CD-ROM contains four video ad clips embedded in the Chapter 15 slide presentation. How do Chrysler and Saturn advertise the ways that they fine-tune the base price of their cars? Are any special pricing strategies highlighted by the ads? What chapter concepts do the ads for TacoBell and NFL.com illustrate?

Medium **VIDEO**

Luxury products are typically insulated from the impact of an economic downturn. Watch a CNN report on the boom in yacht sales during the economic uncertainties of the past few years. Could yacht manufacturers use any pricing strategies to increase their sales even more without compromising the luxury of their products?

For Chapter 15, Small Business School takes you to Nicole Miller Fashion House in New York City. When you see the video, focus on how Nicole Miller used price to create her niche and how she establishes a price-quality relationship. Watch the segment and think about the kind of pricing strategy Nicole Miller uses for her products and her distribution channels.

FLIP IT

 Flip to Chapter 15 in your *Grademaker Study Guide* for more review opportunities, including the pretest, vocabulary review, Internet activities, study test questions, and an application exercise based on pricing concepts. How do marketers set the right price? What government regulations constrain pricing decisions? Can you shut your book and list the ways that marketers can fine-tune the base price of their product or service? If not, then open your *Grademaker* and review.

CLICK IT

The *Essentials of Marketing* Web site links you to all the Internet-based activities in this chapter, like the "Use It," "Review It" questions 4.2, 6.3, 6.4, and 8.1, "Think About It," and the On-Line exercises in the chapter margins. As a review, do the Chapter 15 quiz and crossword puzzle. And don't forget the Career Exersite that shows you resources for exploring marketing career opportunities in pricing. Review the main concepts in the Power-Point presentation for Chapter 15, too. Go to **http://lamb.swlearning.com**, read the material, and follow the links right from the site.

Surf to Xtra! to test your understanding of the pricing concepts in the chapter by completing the worksheets for Exhibit 15.2. If your instructor has assigned a marketing plan project, templates on Xtra! can help you organize your work. In addition to the quiz on the Web site, there's another quiz on Xtra!, plus video of the authors answering frequently asked questions about pricing topics, such as "What can managers do to get back some pricing control?" and "What is the importance of setting a base price?"

Still Shaky? Here's a Tip.

Chapter 15 is a good place to revisit study tips from Chapters 4, 6, and 10 (pages 154, 213, and 351). Try to find additional examples for each pricing technique described in the chapter. Associate a pricing strategy with each of your personal belongings (furniture, clothing, toiletries, electronics, bike, books, car, etc.).

MARKETING MISCUES

Duracell's Duck Is Turned Off

The Duracell division of The Gillette Company is a worldwide leader in the manufacturing and marketing of high-performance alkaline batteries; its Duracell Coppertop battery is one of the most popular alkaline batteries in the world. In June 2001, Duracell introduced an improved line of Duracell Coppertop alkaline batteries. In November 2001, the company announced the debut of "Mr. Quackers" as the star of a new television advertising campaign. By early 2002, however, the company had to stop running the ad. Battery competitor Energizer had accused Duracell of false and misleading advertising.

Founded in 1901, Gillette is a world-renowned consumer-products company. It operates in three major consumer businesses: grooming, portable power, and oral care. Skillful marketing and superior technology are hallmarks of Gillette's success. The company's vision focuses on building its brands by delivering consumer value faster and better than its competition. The company's success at achieving its vision is reflected in the fact that more than one billion people around the world use one or more Gillette products daily. All three of the company's major businesses within Gillette are world leaders in their markets.

With the proliferation of portable electronic devices, the premium battery market in the United States had become a $2.5 billion segment by 2001. The two market leaders were Duracell and Energizer. Though Energizer, long known for its Energizer bunny, held a sizable share of this premium segment, Duracell was, by far, the market share leader with almost 50 percent share of the U.S. alkaline battery market. Nevertheless, 75 percent of the world's battery consumers still used the less costly zinc carbon battery, a lower performing battery. Hence, a huge market opportunity existed if consumers could be persuaded to switch from zinc carbon to alkaline batteries.

Recognizing this vast market potential, both Duracell and Energizer decided to refocus their 2001 promotional efforts on their flagship brands. For Duracell, this meant focusing on the new and improved version of its flagship Coppertop brand, which incor-

porated the company's revolutionary M3 technology—more fuel, more efficiency, and more power. The battery line consisted of AA, AAA, C, D, and 9-volt sizes. Additionally, Duracell offered a line of specialty batteries for use in items such as cameras, hearing aids, and watches.

New York–based BBDO created "Mr. Quackers" to star in Duracell's new television advertising campaign for the improved battery. Mr. Quackers was a cute little robotic duck whose alkaline power outlasted that of three remote-controlled villains (Dr. Shred, The Incinerator, and The Black Widow) who were powered by heavy-duty batteries. The ad closed with the claim that Duracell Coppertop batteries lasted up to three times longer than heavy-duty or super heavy-duty batteries. The commercial, part of a $100 million global ad and marketing campaign, was targeted to air during prime-time, daytime, late-night, syndicated, cable, and Hispanic programming in North America.

With such an unassuming star in the ad, Gillette, Duracell, and BBDO were surprised when Energizer filed a lawsuit alleging false and misleading advertising. Gillette's ad touted the durability of its Duracell Coppertop battery over zinc. Energizer felt that the commercials led consumers to believe that only Duracell alkaline batteries were more durable than zinc batteries, when, in fact, all alkaline batteries (including those made by Energizer) outperform zinc batteries.

Questions

1. What were the goals of the "Mr. Quackers" ad?
2. Why was Duracell using this form of comparative advertising?

CRITICAL THINKING CASE

Apple Bites Into On-Line Music Sales

Based in Cupertino, California, Apple has been at the forefront in innovative computer design. The company ignited the computer revolution in the 1970s with the Apple II and then reenergized the personal computer market in the 1980s with the Macintosh. Now, in the twenty-first century, Apple is emerging as a leading innovator in the music industry with its iTunes music store.

Like most Apple product launches, iTunes was rolled out in spectacular fashion. Taking the stage at San Francisco's Moscone Center to the sound of David Bowie's "Changes," Apple CEO Steve Jobs announced the iTunes music store, along with improvements to the company's iTunes software and iPod personal music player. Apple has managed to fashion a near-perfect retail outlet on the Web, clearly taking cues from Amazon and, more subtly, from Starbucks, Crate & Barrel, and a few other vanguard retailers. A multimillion dollar television advertising campaign followed the iTunes store launch. Chiat-Day created ads that featured unknowns warbling hit songs while listening to their iPods with the tag line, "Your favorite songs. 99 cents."

iTunes does what Napster and Kazaa were unable to do: legally distribute music electronically. After numerous meetings with over 150 music label executives, Jobs assembled a database of around 250,000 songs from all five major record labels, including some artists who had previously resisted on-line distribution, such as Eminem, U2, and the Eagles. Music lovers can easily search iTunes' broad catalog of songs and then listen to a thirty-second clip before deciding whether to buy the track. On average, people listen to about ten sample clips before buying a single track. After making a selection (or selections), a customer can download singles—or entire albums—at the price of 99 cents per track with no subscription fee, and the cover art is included. Once

downloaded, the AAC file format song is automatically stored in the iTunes library on the customer's Macintosh computer. Purchased tracks are the permanent property of the customer. They can be shared among as many as three other Macs, transferred onto an Ipod, or burned to CD. The only restriction is that each playlist can be burned no more than ten times.

Initially, only users of Apple's Mas OS X operating system could shop at the store. Even with the small (some would say minuscule) market, iTunes sold over 5 million songs in its first eight weeks, and over 80 percent of the songs in the database were purchased at least once. Surprisingly, 45 percent of all songs are purchased as part of an album, not as single tracks. The initial success of iTunes signals the likelihood of a shootout over the real money—the much bigger Microsoft-driven PC market. As existing and upstart competitors begin to capitalize on Apple's success, a floodgate could open for new sales, as thousands of previously unavailable songs go on-line legally.

Despite the healthy start, industry analysts are concerned about the 99-cent price. Major labels are charging Apple approximately 70 cents per download, so launching at a lower price is not a viable option. Considering the other costs associated with individual transactions, not to mention maintaining the site, Apple is making only cents on the dollar from iTunes.

Questions

1. Will iTunes change the way major record labels promote their music? How?

2. How does the supply and demand relationship work in Apple's iTune model?

3. What is Apple's pricing strategy with iTunes? How can it fine-tune its base price of 99 cents per song?

MARKETING PLANNING ACTIVITIES

To complete all eleven promotion activities, eight pricing activities, and ten Internet marketing activities, use the Part 4 Marketing Planning Worksheets on Xtra! If you need a company for the basis of your work, follow the "Marketing Plan Project" link on the *Essentials of Marketing* Web site (**http://lamb. swlearning.com**).

Promotion Decisions

For continued general assistance on business plans and marketing plans, visit **http://www.bplans.com**

or **http://www.businessplans.org**. For electronic sources of information, search on the Electric Library at **http://wwws.elibrary.com** or the Internet Public Library at **http://www.ipl.org**. Another excellent source of information is the Sales and Marketing Executives Marketing Library at **http://www. smei.org**.

You began your strategic marketing plan by stating your business mission and objectives and conducting a detailed SWOT analysis. In the second part of the plan, you identified and described target market segments and identified sources of competitive intelligence and the need for further marketing research. Next, you began the process of defining the marketing mix, starting with the components of product and distribution.

The next stage of the strategic planning process continues the task of defining the elements of the marketing mix, and this section focuses on promotions. If you are working with an electronic offering, integrating promotional communications seamlessly presents unique challenges for the marketer because Web-based strategies are so different from traditional media. Even so, it is important to consider all parts of the promotion mix, including advertising, public relations, sales promotion, and personal selling. An excellent on-line resource with many links to promotion sites is **http://advertising.utexas.edu/world**.

Use the following exercises to guide you through the promotions part of your strategic marketing plan:

1. Define your promotional objectives. What specific results do you hope to accomplish, and which promotional tools will be responsible? How will you use promotions to differentiate yourself from your competition? Remember that promotions cannot be directly tied to sales because too many other factors (competition, environment, price, distribution, product, customer service, company reputation, and so on) affect sales. State specific objectives that can be tied directly to the result of promotional activities—for example, number of people redeeming a coupon, share of audience during a commercial, percentage attitude change after a telemarketing campaign, or number of people calling a toll-free information hotline. Remember to have off-line promotions drive on-line traffic as well.

2. Design a promotional message or theme. Does this message inform, remind, persuade, or educate the target market? Make sure this message will work across both traditional and electronic media. How is your promotional message consistent with your branding? Is this message or slogan unique and important enough to be copyrighted? Check with the U.S. Copyright Office at **http://lcweb.loc.gov/copyright**.

3. Will you be designing and producing all your promotional tools in-house, or do you need to find an agency? What are the advantages of designing promotional tools in-house? Disadvantages? Try **http://www.agencyfinder.com** for assistance with your decision or investigate **http://pwr.com/ creative** to find additional creative talent to enhance your own work.

4. Investigate different media placement rates (such as for a school newspaper, local newspaper, national newspaper, local radio station, local TV sta-

tion, general or specialty interest magazine, local billboard, transit advertising, or the Internet). You can either call local media or consult *Standard Rate and Data Services (SRDS)*. Which media should your firm use? Which media can your firm afford? When should media be used? To request on-line media kits from both traditional and electronic media sources, go to the Kit Director at **http://www.mediadirector.com**.

5. Do an Internet-only firm and a firm with an established brick-and-mortar presence have different advertising concerns? If so, what are they? Design the advertising for each medium selected in question 4. Do all advertising pieces carry a uniform theme and style? Is there sufficient information about benefits offered to consumers? Do customers have an option for obtaining further information?

6. List the public relations activities that your company should do. Be sure to make them consistent with your branding and other promotions. In addition, write a plan for handling bad publicity. Bad publicity travels at light speed over the Internet and is much more of a challenge to an e-marketer. Check out **http://urbanlegends.about.com** to see how misinformation can travel the Internet and cause public relations nightmares for companies. Think about using a news clipping service for your company (such as the one you hired to gather competitive intelligence earlier). For further public relations resources, visit **http://www.aboutpr. com**.

7. Evaluate or create printed materials for your chosen company (such as data sheets, brochures, stationery, or rate cards). Does the literature sufficiently answer questions? Provide enough information for further contact? Effectively promote product features and customer service? Note a competitive advantage?

8. Think about ways your promotions could turn a first-time customer or deal-hunter into a repeat, loyal customer. Which sales promotion tools should your company use? What trade shows could your firm attend? Search the *Eventline* database for trade shows appropriate to your firm. Order media kits and explore the feasibility and costs of attending those trade shows. For a listing of trade shows, go to **http://www. exhibitornet.com** and look for the directory of shows, or the Trade Show News Network at **http://www.tsnn.com**. What about on-line coupons? There are dozens of on-line coupon sites that you can find with any search engine. What about promotional products?

9. What other sales promotion tools could your firm use? What are the costs? What is the impact of using these methods on pricing?

10. Will you need a sales force? Identify and justify the best type (internal or external) and structure (product, customer, geographic, etc.) for your firm's sales force. You may find that in e-marketing, a sales force is more of a customer service and customer relations management tool. True selling activities may be limited to selling and buying on-line media space and links. In many circumstances, strategic partnerships and distribution deals have replaced traditional sales in the Internet space. What types of alliances and partnerships will you pursue? Will you work with other on-line firms, off-line firms, or both?

11. Explore the Internet to research your company, its competition, and the industry in general. How are advertising and promotion being handled in this medium?

Pricing Decisions

The next stage of the strategic planning process—pricing—completes the elements of the marketing mix. Pricing is a special challenge to the e-marketer because prices can be quickly and easily compared on the Internet. In any case, your goal should be to make pricing competitive and value driven, as well as to have it cover costs. Other features and benefits of your offering are likely to be more important than price.

Use the following exercises to guide you through the pricing part of your strategic marketing plan:

1. List possible pricing objectives for your chosen firm. How might adopting different pricing objectives change the behavior of the firm and its marketing plans?

2. Gather information on the tactics you selected for the first parts of your marketing plan. What costs are associated with those decisions? Will you incur more or fewer costs by selling on-line? Will your marketing costs increase or decrease? Why? Calculate the break-even point for selling your offering. Can you sell enough to cover your costs? Use the Internet to find a break-even analysis tool to help with your calculations.

3. Pricing is an integral component of marketing strategy. Discuss how your firm's pricing can affect or be affected by competition, the economic environment, government regulations, product features, extra customer service, changes in distribution, or changes in promotion.

4. Is demand elastic or inelastic for your company's product or service? Why? What is the demand elasticity for your offering in an off-line world? Whatever the level, it is likely to be *more* elastic on-line. What tactics can you use to soften or reduce this on-line price sensitivity?

5. What price policy should your firm use? Are there any legal implications of this choice? Will there be differences in on-line versus off-line pricing policies? Are these differences related to your cost structure in the on-line environment? Why? Are these differences legal?

6. Note how easy it is to compare prices on the Internet. Check out price comparison sites such as **http://www.pricescan.com**, **http://www.mysimon.com**, and **http://www.bizrate.com**. Given how products and prices are displayed, how can your offering show a competitive advantage if there is a price difference? As prices reach parity on the Internet, how else will you differentiate your products or services?

7. What kinds of price discounts can your company offer? Should on-line buyers be offered discounted prices that off-line buyers do not receive? Why might you charge your on-line customers less than your off-line customers?

8. As you work on the Internet component of your marketing plan, you must decide how to set geographic pricing policies. Will you appear as a non-geographic specific Internet provider and offer the same shipping costs to all, or will you have to charge more for longer distances? Will you market your product or services locally, regionally, or nationally? Just because you are on the Internet, does that mean you have to try to serve all markets? To check out how distances and even global transportation can affect your price, go to the United Parcel Rate Calculator at **http://www.ups.com**.

Internet Marketing

Now you must clearly identify the ways in which your company will leverage the capabilities of the Internet in product, distribution, promotion, and pricing decisions.

Use the following exercises to guide you through the additional technology aspects of a strategic marketing plan:

1. Assume your company is or will be marketing its products and/or services over the Internet. How should your company enter this electronic marketplace? How will technology issues affect your firm?

2. How will marketing over the Internet modify your target market segment(s)? Redefine the demographics, psychographics, geographics, economic factors, size, growth rate, trends, and any other applicable qualities of the target segment(s) you intend to reach through the Internet. How do your potential on-line customers compare with off-line customers? For customer profiles visit **http://www.cc.gatech.edu/gvu/user_surveys**. Other information about on-line users is at **http://www.survey.net**.

3. One of the most important aspects of having an e-marketing offering is to select the right Internet

service provider (ISP). Different ISPs offer different prices and services. Checking up on e-commerce capabilities for secure on-line transactions will be particularly important. To find and compare ISPs and Web hosts, go to **http://thelist.internet.com**. For a comprehensive list of Web design firms, go to **http://www.firmlist.com/main.shtml**.

4. Choosing a domain name that is easy to remember and spell, as well as one that uniquely identifies your firm, is an important challenge. Does your domain name have to be the same as your company name? To see if your desired domain name is already being used, go to **http://411direct.com/domainnamereg.htm**. Or check the "Who Is" area of **http://www.networksolutions.com**.

5. Web site development is a key tool to identify your offering, brand, and company. Development of a unique, secure, and user-friendly site will take time and money. Should you legally protect the contents of your site? Check out **http://www.benedict.com** to check on copyright issues for your Web site contents. Internet patent and trademark information is shown on **http://www.micropat.com**.

6. What kinds of consumer or business product or service is your firm planning to market over the Internet? Identify ways that marketing over the Internet will change the basic design of your core product or service. How will modification of the product or service affect your costs? Identify any modification to your return policies that will need to be made to address new Internet customers.

7. Discuss the implications of adding the Internet as a channel to your already developed distribution network. How will this affect channel relationships? The final price offered to Internet customers? Any promotional efforts launched over the Internet?

8. How can e-mail newsletters be a beneficial marketing tool? Should your company create and distribute one? If so, who will create the content, and what will the content be?

9. Should your company participate in, monitor, or sponsor a mailing or on-line discussion list? One of the hottest topics in Internet marketing is how to build a "sticky" on-line community at e-commerce sites—in other words, a community that keeps visitors at the site for a long time. Would your site benefit from having community resources? Why or why not? If so, what features would you add to build a community presence? How will you make it "sticky"? To search for lists in your company's area of interest, go to **http://www.liszt.com**.

10. Investigate the expansion of your marketing efforts to include a one-to-one database marketing program. How will you collect data? How will you use the data? What effect will the creation of the database have on your diverse marketing methods (mailings, catalogs, e-mailings, coupon distribution, product sample distribution, and so on)? Write your on-line privacy policy. Consult the AMA Code of Ethics for information on privacy (**http://www.marketingpower.com**).

Implementation

The last and concluding part of a strategic marketing plan deals with implementation, evaluation, and control. A strategic plan is effective only when it is acted upon, so implementation guidelines should list specific action plans and a recommended time frame. Evaluation is needed to see if actual marketing activities are resulting in expected objectives. If not, control measures will need to take place.

Use the following exercises to conclude your strategic marketing plan with implementation, evaluation, and control:

1. Project management tools are the best way to set up your implementation, evaluation, and control program. For a free timeline utility tool, visit **http://www.smartdraw.com**. Decide whether the marketing or operations department will manage the implementation and control of the plan.

2. Make sure performance standards are set for each area of the marketing plan. Because **performance** will be compared against objectives, the objectives must be stated in numerical terms. What will your objectives be in terms of traffic (hits), sales, page views, visits per customer, and length of average visit (in minutes)? Which measurement is most important? Why?

3. What is the financial impact on the plan if performance standards are met? How long can you last if they are not met? For on-line extensions of off-line businesses, how many resources should the off-line business put behind its on-line counterpart? Use financial spreadsheet software to set up a calendar-based pro-forma statement outlining expected sales and costs over the course of the marketing cycle.

4. Using additional spreadsheets, compare actual versus expected performance. Where actuals exceed expectations, what are the sources of success that should be further capitalized on? When actuals fail to meet expectations, what are the sources of the problems, and how can they be corrected? Are the sources directly related to doing business on-line?

5. What other marketing research is needed to assist in the evaluation and modification of your strategic marketing plan? Looking back over your now complete marketing plan, do marketing costs appear to be more or less intensive in the on-line business environment than in the traditional one?

CROSS-FUNCTIONAL CONNECTIONS SOLUTIONS

**Understanding Marketing Communications'
Contribution to Firm Value**

Questions

1. Why is a company's marketing communications of particular concern to R&D and manufacturing?

   Marketers have a tendency to refer to product quality in their communications with potential customers. However, it is not the marketing department that develops and produces the actual product. The R&D and manufacturing groups provide the physical product that marketing presents to customers. If a customer is dissatisfied with the product's quality, then it is typically the "hands-on" groups that are blamed for the low-quality product.

2. Why do financial managers view advertising and promotional expenditures as costs?

   Financial managers believe there is a direct correlation between advertising and promotional expenditures and sales. In recognizing this relationship, financial managers view these expenditures as variable costs, thinking that one directly affects the other. Financial analysts are result oriented and ultimately will base their allocation of funds on whether or not the product is selling; they view an increase in sales as "money well spent." Unfortunately, viewing this relationship as such can be detrimental to the product; advertising budgets may be cut, based on low sales numbers, when they are needed most. These expenditures should be viewed as fixed costs, unrelated to sales increases or decreases.

3. How has personal selling become functionally integrated?

   Personal selling has become functionally integrated in many ways. One major change in the salesperson's skill set has become the need to possess intimate knowledge of the products being presented to a customer. It is no longer sufficient to have great personal interacting skills—the salesperson has to clearly understand the products he or she is presenting. Another major area of integration has been the involvement of R&D and manufacturing in customer visits. Finance, accounting, and human resources are taking a much stronger role in the sales process with regard to compensation systems, cross selling, and teamwork.

Suggested Readings

Bob Donath, "Tell Bean Counters Your Variable Is Fixed," *Marketing News*, June 19, 2000, 14.

Erin Strout, "Planning to Profit from National Accounts," *Sales and Marketing Management*, October 1999, 107.

Careers Appendix

CAREERS IN MARKETING

One of the most important decisions in your life is deciding on your career. Not only will a career choice affect your income and lifestyle, but it also will have a major impact on your happiness and self-fulfillment. Probably the most difficult part of job hunting is deciding exactly what type of work you would like. Many students have had no working experience other than summer jobs, so they are not sure what career to pursue. Too often, college students and their parents rush toward occupational fields that seem to offer the highest monetary payoff or are currently "hot," instead of looking at the long run over a forty- to fifty-year working life.

In order to help you as you begin thinking about career goals and job hunting, the *Essentials of Marketing* Web site contains an appendix titled "Careers in Marketing." Not only can it inform you about career opportunities in the marketing field, it also provides a wealth of information to help you at each stage of your job search:

- A self-assessment tool
- Career listings with compensation ranges
- Features-advantages-benefits model to help you determine job fit
- Resources for job prospecting
- How to write your résumé
- How to write a professional cover letter
- Self-preparedness test to determine readiness to interview
- Pre-interview checklist
- Tips to keep in mind while preparing for an interview
- More than seventy frequently asked job interview questions
- Questions to ask an interviewer
- How to conduct yourself during an interview
- How to handle objections raised by an interviewer
- Tips on following up after an interview
- How to write a letter accepting a job offer
- How to write a letter declining a job offer

Visit **http://lamb.swlearning.com** to find out how to market yourself to the marketing industry.

GETTING STARTED

Getting started can be the toughest part of job hunting, especially if you are uncertain about what career you want to pursue. The careers appendix can help you in this initial stage with its self-assessment tool, career and compensation lists, features-advantages-benefits (FAB) matrix, and listing of resources for job prospecting.

A self-assessment tool can help you identify your personal needs, capabilities, characteristics, strengths, weaknesses, and desires. The on-line careers appendix includes a thirteen-question assessment tool that can help you begin to analyze what is important to you in choosing the kind of work you will do and the kind of employer for whom you will work. There is also a complete listing of careers available in the marketing industry, with compensation figures for each. This information can help you determine what marketing fields interest you and meet your income needs. Using the FAB matrix, you can plot your abilities and skills against the employer's job requirements. Once you complete the model, you will have a better idea of what you have to sell a potential employer. If you have identified a career that suits you but are having trouble finding an employer that offers that particular career opportunity, the on-line careers appendix can help. It provides a list of resources that can be useful when prospecting for an employer. Information on where to locate and how to use the various resources is also included.

ARE YOU READY TO INTERVIEW?

Once you have moved through the initial phase of your job search, the on-line careers appendix can still help you. It shows you how to write your résumé and cover letter so that you convey a positive and professional attitude. The information in the appendix can also help you determine how ready you are for a job interview. It provides you with a self-preparedness test, a pre-interview checklist, and a list of considerations to keep in mind when preparing for your interview.

Since interviewing can often be a source of nervousness and anxiety, the on-line careers appendix gives you tools you can use to feel calm and prepared during an interview. A list of over seventy frequently asked job interview questions is provided along with a list of questions for you to ask the interviewer. You can receive guidance on how to conduct yourself professionally during the interview and how to handle objections raised by the interviewer. You can also find tips on following up after the interview and on accepting or declining a job offer.

GO ON-LINE!

Many of the basic concepts of marketing introduced in this book can be used to help you get the career you want by marketing yourself. This complete on-line appendix, "Careers in Marketing," is designed to help you do just that. In addition to this appendix, specially designed career activities and resources, called Career Exersites, are locatd on the Web site. There is one exersite per chapter, so you can explore different career possibilities for the various marketing areas discussed in this textbook. Visit **http://lamb.swlearning.com** to explore marketing careers and begin learning how to successfully market yourself to prospective employers!

Glossary

accessory equipment Goods, such as portable tools and office equipment, that are less expensive and shorter-lived than major equipment.

adopter A consumer who was happy enough with his or her trial experience with a product to use it again.

advertising Impersonal, one-way mass communication about a product or organization that is paid for by a marketer.

advertising appeal Reason for a person to buy a product.

advertising campaign Series of related advertisements focusing on a common theme, slogan, and set of advertising appeals.

advertising objective Specific communication task a campaign should accomplish for a specified target audience during a specified period.

advertising response function Phenomenon in which spending for advertising and sales promotion increases sales or market share up to a certain level but then produces diminishing returns.

advocacy advertising Form of advertising in which an organization expresses its views on controversial issues or responds to media attacks.

agents and brokers Wholesaling intermediaries who facilitate the sale of a product from producer to end user by representing retailers, wholesalers, or manufacturers and who do not take title to the product.

AIDA concept Model that outlines the process for achieving promotional goals in terms of stages of consumer involvement with the message; the acronym stands for Attention, Interest, Desire, and Action.

applied research Attempts to develop new or improved products.

Asia-Pacific Economic Cooperation (APEC) A trade agreement that includes most ASEAN countries plus eleven other nations.

aspirational reference group Group that someone would like to join.

Association of Southeast Asian Nations (ASEAN) A trade agreement among ten Asian nations.

atmosphere The overall impression conveyed by a store's physical layout, decor, and surroundings.

attitude Learned tendency to respond consistently toward a given object.

audience selectivity Ability of an advertising medium to reach a precisely defined market.

automatic vending The use of machines to offer goods for sale.

baby boomers People born between 1946 and 1964.

bait pricing Price tactic that tries to get consumers into a store through false or misleading price advertising and then uses high-pressure selling to persuade consumers to buy more expensive merchandise.

base price The general price level at which the company expects to sell the good or service.

basic research Pure research that aims to confirm an existing theory or to learn more about a concept or phenomenon.

basing-point pricing Price tactic that charges freight from a given (basing) point, regardless of the city from which the goods are shipped.

BehaviorScan Scanner-based research program that tracks the purchases of three thousand households through store scanners.

belief Organized pattern of knowledge that an individual holds as true about his or her world.

benefit segmentation The process of grouping customers into market segments according to the benefits they seek from the product.

brainstorming Getting a group to think of unlimited ways to vary a product or solve a problem.

brand A name, term, symbol, design, or combination thereof that identifies a seller's products and differentiates them from competitors' products.

brand equity The value of company and brand names.

brand loyalty A consistent preference for one brand over all others.

brand mark The elements of a brand that cannot be spoken.

brand name That part of a brand that can be spoken, including letters, words, and numbers.

break-even analysis Method of determining what sales volume must be reached before total revenue equals total costs.

business analysis The second stage of the screening process, at which time preliminary figures for demand, cost, sales, and profitability are calculated.

business marketing The marketing of goods and services to individuals and organizations for purposes other than personal consumption.

business product (industrial product) Product used to manufacture other goods or services, to facilitate an organization's operations, or to resell to other customers.

business services Expense items that do not become part of a final product.

buyer Department head who selects the merchandise for his or her department and may also be responsible for promotion and personnel.

buyer for export Intermediary in the global market that assumes all ownership risks and sells globally for its own account.

buying center All those persons in an organization who become involved in the purchase decision.

cannibalization Situation that occurs when sales of a new product cut into sales of a firm's existing products.

cash discount A price reduction offered to a consumer, an industrial user, or a marketing intermediary in return for prompt payment of a bill.

category killers Term often used to describe specialty discount stores because they so heavily dominate their narrow merchandise segment.

central-location telephone (CLT) facility A specially designed phone room used to conduct telephone interviewing.

chain stores Stores owned and operated as a group by a single organization.

channel Medium of communication—such as a voice, radio, or newspaper—for transmitting a message.

channel conflict Clash of goals and methods between distribution channel members.

channel control Situation that occurs when one marketing channel member intentionally affects another member's behavior.

channel leader (channel captain) Member of a marketing channel that exercises authority and power over the activities of other channel members.

channel members All parties in the marketing channel that negotiate with one another, buy and sell products, and facilitate the change of ownership between buyer and seller in the course of moving the product from the manufacturer into the hands of the final consumer.

channel partnering (channel cooperation) The joint effort of all channel members to create a supply chain that serves customers and creates a competitive advantage.

channel power Capacity of a particular marketing channel member to control or influence the behavior of other channel members.

closed-ended question An interview question that asks the respondent to make a selection from a limited list of responses.

CLT. *See* **central-location telephone facility.**

cobranding Placing two or more brand names on a product or its package.

code of ethics A guideline to help marketing managers and other employees make better decisions.

cognitive dissonance Inner tension that a consumer experiences after recognizing an inconsistency between behavior and values or opinions.

cold calling Form of lead generation in which the salesperson approaches potential buyers without prior knowledge of the prospects' needs or financial status.

combination system A method of compensation in which the salesperson receives a base salary and an incentive.

commercialization The decision to market a product.

communication Process by which we exchange or share meanings through a common set of symbols.

comparative advertising Form of advertising that compares two or more specifically named or shown competing brands on one or more specific attributes.

competitive (differential) advantage The set of unique features of a company and its products that are perceived by the target market as significant and superior to the competition.

competitive advertising Form of advertising designed to influence demand for a specific brand.

competitive intelligence An intelligence system that helps managers assess their competition and their vendors in order to become more efficient and effective competitors.

component lifestyles Practice of choosing goods and services that meet one's diverse needs and interests rather than conforming to a single, traditional lifestyle.

component parts Either finished items ready for assembly or products that need very little processing before becoming part of some other product.

computer-assisted personal interviewing Interviewing method in which the interviewer reads the questions from a computer screen and enters the respondent's data directly into the computer.

computer-assisted self-interviewing Interviewing method in which a mall interviewer intercepts and directs willing respondents to a nearby computer where the respondent reads questions off the computer screen and directly keys his or her answers into the computer.

concentrated targeting strategy A strategy used to select one segment of a market or targeting marketing efforts.

concept test Test to evaluate a new product idea, usually before any prototype has been created.

consumer behavior Processes a consumer uses to make purchase decisions as well as to use and dispose of purchased goods or services; also includes factors that influence purchase decisions and the use of products.

consumer decision-making process A five step process used by consumers when buying goods or services.

consumer penalty An extra fee paid by the consumer for violating the terms of the purchase agreement.

consumer product Product bought to satisfy an individual's personal wants.

Consumer Product Safety Commission (CPSC) A federal agency established to protect the health and safety of consumers in and around their homes.

consumer sales promotion Sales promotion activities targeting the ultimate consumer.

continuous media schedule Media scheduling strategy, used for products in the latter stages of the product life cycle, in which advertising is run steadily throughout the advertising period.

contract manufacturing Private label manufacturing by a foreign company.

convenience product A relatively inexpensive item that merits little shopping effort.

convenience sample A form of nonprobability sample using respondents who are convenient or readily accessible to the researcher, for example, employees, friends, or relatives.

convenience store A miniature supermarket, carrying only a limited line of high-turnover convenience goods.

cooperative advertising Arrangement in which the manufacturer and the retailer split the costs of advertising the manufacturer's brand.

cost per contact The cost of reaching one member of the target market.

countertrade A form of trade in which all or part of the payment for goods or services is in the form of other goods or services.

coupon Certificate that entitles consumers to an immediate price reduction when they buy the product.

credence quality A characteristic that consumers may have difficulty assessing even after purchase because they do not have the necessary knowledge or experience.

crisis management Coordinated effort to handle the effects of unfavorable publicity or of another unexpected, unfavorable event.

cross-tabulation A method of analyzing data that lets the analyst look at the responses to one question in relation to the responses to one or more other questions.

culture Set of values, norms, attitudes, and other meaningful symbols that shape human behavior and the artifacts, or products, of that behavior as they are transmitted from one generation to the next.

cumulative quantity discount A deduction from list price that applies to the buyer's total purchases made during a specific period.

customer satisfaction The feeling that a product has met or exceeded the customer's expectations.

customer value The ratio of benefits to the sacrifice necessary to obtain those benefits.

database marketing The creation of a large computerized file of customers' and potential customers' profiles and purchase patterns.

decision support system (DSS) An interactive, flexible computerized information system that enables managers to obtain and manipulate information as they are making decisions.

decline stage A long-run drop in sales.

decoding Interpretation of the language and symbols sent by the source through a channel.

demand The quantity of a product that will be sold in the market at various prices for a specified period.

demographic segmentation Segmenting markets by age, gender, income, ethnic background, and family life cycle.

demography The study of people's vital statistics, such as their age, race and ethnicity, and location.

department store A store housing several departments under one roof.

derived demand The demand for business products.

development Stage in the product development process in which a prototype is developed and a marketing strategy is outlined.

diffusion The process by which the adoption of an innovation spreads.

direct channel Distribution channel in which producers sell directly to consumers.

direct foreign investment Active ownership of a foreign company or of overseas manufacturing or marketing facilities.

direct marketing (direct-response marketing) Techniques used to get consumers to make a purchase from their home, office, or other nonretail setting.

direct retailing The selling of products door-to-door, office-to-office, or at home parties by representatives.

discount store A retailer that competes on the basis of low prices, high turnover, and high volume.

discrepancy of assortment Lack of all the items a customer needs to receive full satisfaction from a product or products.

discrepancy of quantity Difference between the amount of product produced and the amount a customer wants to buy.

distribution resource planning (DRP) Inventory control system that manages the replenish-ment of goods from the manufacturer to the final consumer.

DRP. *See* **distribution resource planning.**

drugstore A retail store that stocks pharmacy-related products and services as its main draw.

DSS. *See* **decision support system.**

dual distribution (multiple distribution) Use of two or more channels to distribute the same product to target markets.

dumping The sale of an exported product at a price lower than that charged for the same or a like product in the "home" market of the exporter.

EDI. *See* **electronic data interchange.**

80/20 principle Principle that holds that 20 percent of all customers generate 80 percent of the demand.

elastic demand Situation in which consumer demand is sensitive to changes in price.

elasticity of demand Consumers' responsiveness or sensitivity to changes in price.

electronic data interchange (EDI) Information technology that replaces the paper documents that usually accompany business transactions, such as purchase orders and invoices, with electronic transmission of the needed information to reduce inventory levels, improve cash flow, streamline operations, and in-crease the speed and accuracy of information transmission.

electronic distribution Distribution technique that includes any kind of product or service that can be distributed electronically, whether over traditional forms such as fiber-optic cable or through satellite transmission of electronic signals.

empowerment Delegation of authority to solve customers' problems quickly—usually by the first person that the customer notifies regarding a problem.

encoding Conversion of the sender's ideas and thoughts into a message, usually in the form of words or signs.

environmental management When a company implements strategies that attempt to shape the external environment within which it operates.

environmental scanning Collection and interpretation of information about forces, events, and relationships in the external environment that may affect the future of the organization or the implementation of the marketing plan.

ethics The moral principles or values that generally govern the conduct of an individual.

evaluation Gauging the extent to which the marketing objectives have been achieved during the specified time period.

evoked set (consideration set) Group of brands, resulting from an information search, from which a buyer can choose.

exchange The idea that people give up something to receive something they would rather have.

exclusive distribution Form of distribution that establishes one or a few dealers within a given area.

executive interviews A type of survey that involves interviewing businesspeople at their offices concerning industrial products or services.

experience quality A characteristic that can be assessed only after use.

experiment Method a researcher uses to gather primary data.

export agent Intermediary who acts like a manufacturer's agent for the exporter. The export agent lives in the foreign market.

export broker Intermediary who plays the traditional broker's role by bringing buyer and seller together.

exporting Selling domestically produced products to buyers in another country.

express warranty A written guarantee.

extensive decision making Most complex type of consumer decision making, used when buying an unfamiliar, expensive product or an infrequently bought item; requires use of several criteria for evaluating options and much time for seeking information.

external information search Process of seeking information in the outside environment.

extranet A private network that uses Internet technology and a browser interface, also a network that links a company with its suppliers and customers.

factory outlet An off-price retailer that is owned and operated by a manufacturer.

family brand The marketing of several different products under the same brand name.

family life cycle (FLC) A series of stages determined by a combination of age, marital status, and the presence or absence of children.

Federal Trade Commission (FTC) A federal agency empowered to prevent persons or corporations from using unfair methods of competition in commerce.

feedback Receiver's response to a message.

field service firm A firm that specializes in interviewing respondents on a subcontracted basis.

fixed cost Cost that does not change as output is increased or decreased.

FLC. *See* **family life cycle.**

flexible pricing (variable pricing) Price tactic in which different customers pay different prices for essentially the same merchandise bought in equal quantities.

flighted media schedule Media scheduling strategy in which ads are run heavily every other month or every two weeks, to achieve a greater impact with an increased frequency and reach at those times.

FOB origin pricing Price tactic that requires the buyer to absorb the freight costs from the shipping point ("free on board").

focus group Seven to ten people who participate in a group discussion led by a moderator.

follow-up Final step of the selling process, in which the salesperson ensures that delivery schedules are met, that the goods or services perform as promised, and that the buyers' employees are properly trained to use the products.

Food and Drug Administration (FDA) A federal agency charged with enforcing regulations against selling and distributing adulterated, misbranded, or hazardous food and drug products.

four Ps Product, place, promotion, and price, which together make up the marketing mix.

frame error Error that occurs when a sample drawn from a population differs from the target population.

franchise The right to operate a business or to sell a product.

franchisee Individual or business that is granted the right to sell another party's product.

franchiser Originator of a trade name, product, methods of operation, and so on, that grants operating rights to another party to sell its product.

Free Trade Agreement of the Americas (FTAA) A regional trade agreement that, when signed, will create a regional trading zone encompassing 36 countries in North and South America.

freight absorption pricing Price tactic in which the seller pays all or part of the actual freight charges and does not pass them on to the buyer.

frequency Number of times an individual is exposed to a given message during a specific period.

frequent buyer program A loyalty program in which loyal consumers are rewarded for making multiple purchases of a particular good or service.

full-line discount store A retailer that offers consumers very limited service and carries a broad assortment of well-known, nationally branded "hard goods."

fully industrialized society The fifth stage of economic development, a society that is an exporter of manufactured products, many of which are based on advanced technology.

functional discount (trade discount) Discount to wholesalers and retailers for performing channel functions.

General Agreement on Tariffs and Trade (GATT) Agreement that provided loopholes that enabled countries to avoid trade-barrier reduction agreements.

Generation X People born between the years 1965 and 1978.

Generation Y People born between the years 1979 and 1994.

generic product A no-frills, no-brand-name, low-cost product that is simply identified by its product category.

generic product name Name that identifies a product by class or type and that cannot be trademarked.

geodemographic segmentation Segmenting potential customers into neighborhood lifestyle categories.

global brand A brand where at least 20 percent of the product is sold outside its home country or region.

global marketing Marketing to target markets throughout the world.

global marketing standardization Production of uniform products that can be sold the same way all over the world.

global vision Recognizing and reacting to international marketing opportunities, being aware of threats from foreign competitors in all markets, and effectively using international distribution networks.

gross margin Amount of money the retailer makes as a percentage of sales after the cost of goods sold is subtracted.

group dynamics Interaction essential to the success of focus group research.

growth stage The second stage of the product life cycle when sales typically grow at an increasing rate, many competitors enter the market, large companies may start acquiring small pioneering firms, and profits are healthy.

horizontal conflict Channel conflict that occurs among channel members on the same level.

hypermarket Retail store that combines a supermarket and full-line discount store in a space ranging from 200,000 to 300,000 square feet.

ideal self-image The way an individual would like to be.

IMC. *See* **integrated marketing communications.**

implementation The process that turns marketing plans into action assignments and ensures that these assignments are executed in a way that accomplishes the plans' objectives.

implied warranty An unwritten guarantee that the good or service is fit for the purpose for which it was sold.

independent retailers Retailers owned by a single person or partnership and not operated as part of a larger retail institution.

individual branding Using different brand names for different products.

industrializing society The fourth stage of economic development when technology spreads from sectors of the economy that powered the takeoff to the rest of the nation.

inelastic demand Situation in which an increase or a decrease in price will not significantly affect demand for the product.

inflation A general rise in prices without a corresponding increase in wages, which results in decreased purchasing power.

infomercial Thirty-minute or longer advertisement that looks more like a TV talk show than a sales pitch.

informational labeling Labeling designed to help consumers make proper product selections and lower their cognitive dissonance after the purchase.

InfoScan A scanner-based sales-tracking service for the consumer packaged-goods industry.

innovation A product perceived as new by a potential adopter.

institutional advertising Form of advertising designed to enhance a company's image rather than promote a particular product.

intangibility Characteristic of services that cannot be touched, seen, tasted, heard, or felt in the same manner in which goods can be sensed.

integrated marketing communications (IMC) The careful coordination of all promotional messages for a product of service to assure the consistency of messages at every contact point where a company meets the customer.

intensive distribution Form of distribution aimed at having a product available in every outlet at which target customers might want to buy it.

internal information search Process of recalling past information stored in the memory.

interpersonal communication Direct, fact-to-face communication between two or more people.

introductory stage The full-scale launch of a new product into the marketplace.

inventory control system Method of developing and maintaining an adequate assortment of products to meet customer demand.

involvement Amount of time and effort a buyer invests in the search, evaluation, and decision processes of consumer behavior.

JIT. *See* **just-in-time production.**

joint demand The demand for two or more items used together in a final product.

joint venture A venture in which a domestic firm buys part of a foreign company or joins with a foreign company to create a new entity.

just-in-time production (JIT) Redefining and simplifying manufacturing by reducing inventory levels and delivering raw materials just when they are needed on the production line.

keiretsu A network of interlocking corporate affiliates.

lead generation (prospecting) Identification of those firms and people most likely to buy the seller's offerings.

lead qualification Determination of a sales prospect's (1) recognized need, (2) buying power, and (3) receptivity and accessibility.

leader pricing (loss-leader pricing) A price tactic in which a product is sold near or even below cost in the hope that shoppers will buy other items once they are in the store.

learning Process that creates changes in behavior, immediate or expected, through experience and practice.

licensing The legal process whereby a licensor agrees to let another firm use its manufacturing process, trademarks, patents, trade secrets, or other proprietary knowledge.

lifestyle Mode of living as identified by a person's activities, interests, and opinions.

limited decision making Type of decision making that requires a moderate amount of time for gathering information and deliberating about an unfamiliar brand in a familiar product category.

logistics The process of strategically managing the efficient flow and storage of raw materials, in-process inventory, and finished goods from point of origin to point of consumption.

logistics information system Information technology that integrates and links all of the logistics functions of the supply chain.

loyalty marketing programs Promotional program designed to build long-term, mutually beneficial relationships between a company and its key customers.

Maastricht Treaty Agreement among twelve countries of the European Community to pursue economic, monetary, and political union.

major equipment (installations) Capital goods such as large or expensive machines, mainframe computers, blast furnaces, generators, airplanes, and buildings.

mall intercept interview Survey research method that involves interviewing people in the common areas of shopping malls.

management decision problem Broad-based problem that requires marketing research in order for managers to take proper actions.

manufacturers' brand The brand name of a manufacturer.

market People or organizations with needs or wants and the ability and willingness to buy.

market opportunity analysis The description and estimation of the size and sales potential of market segments that are of interest to the firm and the assessment of key competitors in these market segments.

market orientation Philosophy that assumes that a sale does not depend on an aggressive sales force but rather on a customer's decision to purchase a product.

market segment A subgroup of people or organizations sharing one or more characteristics that cause them to have similar product needs.

market segmentation The process of dividing a market into meaningful, relatively similar, and identifiable segments or groups.

market share A company's product sales as a percentage of total sales for that industry.

marketing The process of planning and executing the conception, pricing, promotion, and distribution of ideas, goods, and services to create exchanges that satisfy individual and organizational goals.

marketing channel (channel of distribution) Set of interdependent organizations that ease the transfer of ownership as products move from producer to business user or consumer.

marketing concept The idea that the social and economic justification for an organization's existence is the satisfaction of customer wants and needs while meeting organizational objectives.

marketing-controlled information source Product information source that originates with marketers promoting the product.

marketing information Everyday information about developments in the marketing environment that managers use to prepare and adjust marketing plans.

marketing mix A unique blend of product, distribution, promotion, and pricing strategies designed to produce mutually satisfying exchanges with a target market.

marketing objective A statement of what is to be accomplished through marketing activities.

marketing research The process of planning, collecting, and analyzing data relevant to a marketing decision.

marketing research objective Specific information needed to solve a market research prob-lem; the objective should provide insightful, decision-making information.

marketing research problem Determining what information is needed and how that information can be obtained efficiently and effectively.

marketing strategy The activity of selecting and describing one or more target markets and developing and maintaining a marketing mix that will produce mutually satisfying exchanges with target markets.

markup pricing Cost of buying the product from the producer plus amounts for profit and for expenses not otherwise accounted for.

Maslow's hierarchy of needs Method of clas-sifying human needs and motivations into five categories in ascending order of importance: physiological, safety, social, esteem, and self-actualization.

mass communication Communication of a concept or message to a large audience.

mass customization (build-to-order) Production method whereby products are not made until an order is placed by the customer; also a strategy that uses technology to deliver customized services on a mass basis, with products being made according to customer specifications.

mass merchandising Retailing strategy using moderate to low prices on large quantities of merchandise and lower service to stimulate high turnover of products.

materials-handling system Method of moving inventory into, within, and out of the warehouse.

materials requirement planning (MRP) Inventory control system that manages the replenishment of raw materials, supplies, and components from the supplier to the manufacturer.

maturity stage A period during which sales increase at a decreasing rate.

measurement error Error that occurs when there is a difference between the information desired by the researcher and the information provided by the measurement process.

media mix Combination of media to be used for a promotional campaign.

media planning The series of decisions advertisers make regarding the selection and use of media, allowing the marketer to optimally and cost-effectively communicate the message to the target audience.

media schedule Designation of the media, the specific publications or programs, and the insertion dates of advertising.

medium Channel used to convey a message to a target market.

merchant wholesaler Institution that buys goods from manufacturers and resells them to businesses, government agencies, and other whole-salers or retailers and that receives and takes title to goods, stores them in its own warehouses, and later ships them.

Mercosur The largest new trade agreement, which includes Brazil, Argentina, Uruguay, and Paraguay.

modified rebuy Situation in which the purchaser wants some change in the original good or service.

morals The rules people develop as a result of cultural values and norms.

motive Driving force that causes a person to take action to satisfy specific needs.

MRP. *See* **materials requirement plan.**

multiculturalism A situation in which all major ethnic groups in an area-such as a city, county, or census tract-are roughly equally represented.

multinational corporation A company that is heavily engaged in international trade, beyond exporting and importing.

multiplier effect (accelerator principle) Phenomenon in which a small increase or decrease in consumer demand can produce a much larger change in demand for the facilities and equipment needed to make the consumer product.

multisegment targeting strategy A strategy that chooses two or more well-defined market segments and develops a distinct marketing mix for each.

mystery shoppers Researchers posing as customers who gather observational data about a store.

NAICS. *See* **North American Industry Classification System.**

need recognition Result of an imbalance between actual and desired states.

needs assessment Determination of the customer's specific needs and wants and the range of options a customer has for satisfying them.

negotiation Process of both the salesperson and the prospect offering special concessions in an attempt to arrive at a sales agreement.

networking Process of finding out about potential clients from friends, business contacts, coworkers, acquaintances, and fellow members in professional and civic organizations.

new buy A situation requiring the purchase of a product for the first time.

new product Product new to the world, the market, the producer, the seller, or some combination of these.

new-product strategy Linking the new-product development process with the objectives of the marketing department, the business unit, and the corporation.

newsgroups Function like bulletin boards on the Internet. They are established to focus on a particular topic.

niche One segment of a market.

noise Anything that interferes with, distorts, or slows down the transmission of information.

nonaspirational reference group Group with which an individual does not want to associate.

noncumulative quantity discount A deduction from list price that applies to a single order rather than to the total volume of orders placed during a certain period.

nonmarketing-controlled information source Product information source that is not associated with advertising or promotion.

nonprobability sample Any sample in which little or no attempt is made to get a representative cross section of the population.

nonstore retailing Shopping without visiting a store.

norm Value or attitude deemed acceptable by a group.

North American Free Trade Agreement (NAFTA) An agreement between Canada, the United States, and Mexico that created the world's largest free-trade zone.

North American Industry Classification System (NAICS) A detailed numbering system developed by the United States, Canada, and Mexico to classify North American business establishments by their main production processes.

observation research Research method that relies on three types of observation: people watching people, people watching activity, and machines watching people.

odd–even pricing (psychological pricing) Price tactic that uses odd-numbered prices to connote bargains and even-numbered prices to imply quality.

OEM The acronym OEM stands for original equipment manufacturer. OEM's buy business goods that they incorporate into the products that they produce for eventual sale to other producers or to consumers.

off-price retailer Retailer that sells at prices 25 percent or more below traditional department store prices because it pays cash for its stock and usually doesn't ask for return privileges.

on-line retailing A type of shopping available to consumers with personal computers and access to the Internet.

open-ended question An interview question that encourages an answer phrased in the respondent's own words.

opinion leader Individual who influences the opinions of others.

optimizer Type of business customer that considers numerous suppliers, both familiar and unfamiliar, solicits bids, and studies all proposals carefully before selecting one.

order processing system System whereby orders are entered into the supply chain and filled.

outsourcing (contract logistics) Manufacturer's or supplier's use of an independent third party to manage an entire function of the logistics system, such as transportation, warehousing, or order processing.

penetration pricing Pricing policy whereby a firm charges a relatively low price for a product initially as a way to reach the mass market.

perception Process by which people select, organize, and interpret stimuli into a meaningful and coherent picture.

perceptual mapping A means of displaying or graphing, in two or more dimensions, the location of products, brands, or groups of products in customers' minds.

personal selling A purchase situation in which two people communicate in an attempt to influence each other.

personality Way of organizing and grouping the consistencies of an individual's reactions to situations.

personalized economy Delivering goods and services at a good value on demand.

persuasive labeling Labeling that focuses on a promotional theme or logo with consumer information being secondary.

pioneering advertising Form of advertising designed to stimulate primary demand for a new product or product category.

planned obsolescence The practice of modifying products so those that have already been sold become obsolete before they actually need replacement.

PLC *See* **product life cycle.**

point-of-purchase display Promotional display set up at the retailer's location to build traffic, advertise the product, or induce impulse buying.

position The place a product, brand, or group of products occupies in consumers' minds relative to competing offerings.

positioning Developing a specific marketing mix to influence potential customers' overall perception of a brand, product line, or organization in general.

poverty of time Lack of time to do anything but work, commute to work, handle family situations, do housework, shop, sleep, and eat.

preapproach A process that describes the "homework" that must be done by the salesperson before he or she contacts the prospect.

predatory pricing The practice of charging a very low price for a product with the intent of driving competitors out of business or out of a market.

preindustrial society A society in the second stage of economic development, involving economic and social change and the emergence of a middle class with an entrepreneurial spirit.

premium Extra item offered to the consumer, usually in exchange for some proof of purchase of the promoted product.

prestige pricing Charging a high price to help promote a high-quality image.

price That which is given up in an exchange to acquire a good or service.

price bundling Marketing two or more products in a single package for a special price.

price fixing An agreement between two or more firms on the price they will charge for a product.

price skimming Pricing policy whereby a firm charges a high introductory price, often coupled with heavy promotion.

price strategy Basic, long-term pricing framework, which establishes the initial price for a product and the intended direction for price movements over the product life cycle.

primary data Information collected for the first time; can be used for solving the particular problem under investigation.

primary membership group Reference group with which people interact regularly in an informal, face-to-face manner, such as family, friends, or fellow employees.

private brand A brand name owned by a wholesaler or a retailer.

probability sample A sample in which every element in the population has a known statistical likelihood of being selected.

processed materials Products used directly in manufacturing other products.

product Everything, both favorable and unfavorable, that a person receives in an exchange.

product advertising Form of advertising that touts the benefits of a specific good or service.

product category All brands that satisfy a particular type of need.

product development Marketing strategy that entails the creation of new products for present markets; process of converting applications for new technologies into marketable products.

product differentiation A positioning strategy that some firms use to distinguish their products from those of competitors.

product item A specific version of a product that can be designated as a distinct offering among an organization's products.

product life cycle (PLC) A concept that provides a way to trace the stages of a product's acceptance, from its introduction (birth) to its decline (death).

product line A group of closely related product items.

product line depth The number of product items in a product line.

product line extension Adding additional products to an existing product line in order to compete more broadly in the industry.

product mix All products an organization sells.

product mix width The number of product lines an organization offers.

product modification Changing one or more of a product's characteristics.

product offering The mix of products offered to the consumer by the retailer, also called the product assortment or merchandise mix.

production orientation A philosophy that focuses on the internal capabilities of the firm rather than on the desires and needs of the marketplace.

profit Revenue minus expenses.

promotion Communication by marketers that informs, persuades, and reminds potential buyers of a product in order to influence an opinion or elicit a response.

promotional allowance (trade allowance) Payment to a dealer for promoting the manufacturer's products.

promotional mix Combination of promotion tools—including advertising, public relations, personal selling, and sales promotion—used to reach the target market and fulfill the organization's overall goals.

promotional strategy Plan for the optimal use of the elements of promotion: advertising, public relations, personal selling, and sales promotion.

psychographic segmentation Market segmentation on the basis of personality, motives, lifestyles, and geodemographics.

public relations Marketing function that evaluates public attitudes, identifies areas within the organization that the public may be interested in, and executes a program of action to earn public understanding and acceptance.

publicity Public information about a company, good, or service appearing in the mass media as a news item.

pull strategy Marketing strategy that stimulates consumer demand to obtain product distribution.

pulsing media schedule Media scheduling strategy that uses continuous scheduling throughout the year coupled with a flighted schedule during the best sales periods.

push strategy Marketing strategy that uses aggressive personal selling and trade advertising to convince a wholesaler or a retailer to carry and sell particular merchandise.

pyramid of corporate social responsibility A model that suggests corporate social respon-sibility is composed of economic, legal, ethical, and philanthropic responsibilities and that firm's economic performance supports the entire structure.

quantity discount Price reduction offered to buyers buying in multiple units or above a specified dollar amount.

quota Statement of the individual salesperson's sales objectives, usually based on sales volume alone but sometimes including key accounts (those with greatest potential), new accounts, and specific products.

random error Error that occurs because the selected sample is an imperfect representation of the overall population.

random sample A sample arranged in such a way that every element of the population has an equal chance of being selected as part of the sample.

raw materials Unprocessed extractive or agricultural products, such as mineral ore, lumber, wheat, corn, fruits, vegetables, and fish.

real self-image The way an individual actually perceives himself or herself.

rebate Cash refund given for the purchase of a product during a specific period.

receiver Person who decodes a message.

recession A period of economic activity when income, production, and employment tend to fall—all of which reduce demand for goods and services.

reciprocity A practice in which business purchasers choose to buy from their own customers.

recruited Internet sample Sample in which respondents are prerecruited and, after qualifying to participate, are sent a questionnaire by e-mail or directed to a secure Web site to fill out a questionnaire.

reference group Group in society that influences an individual's purchasing behavior.

referral Recommendation to a salesperson from a customer or business associate.

relationship marketing A strategy that entails forging long-term partnerships with customers.

relationship selling (consultative selling) Sales practice of building, maintaining, and enhancing interactions with customers in order to develop long-term satisfaction through mutually beneficial partnerships.

repositioning Changing consumers' perceptions of a brand in relation to competing brands.

research design One that specifies which research questions must be answered, how and when the data will be gathered, and how the data will be analyzed.

retailer Channel intermediary that sells mainly to consumers.

retailing All the activities directly related to the sale of goods and services to the ultimate consumer for personal, nonbusiness use.

retailing mix Combination of the six Ps—product, place, promotion, price, personnel, and presentation—to sell goods and services to the ultimate consumer.

return on investment (ROI) Net profit after taxes divided by total assets.

revenue The price charged to customers multiplied by the number of units sold.

ROI. *See* **return on investment.**

routine response behavior Type of decision making exhibited by consumers buying frequently purchased, low-cost goods and services; requires little search and decision time.

sales orientation The idea that people will buy more goods and services if aggressive sales techniques are used and that high sales result in high profits.

sales presentation Face-to-face explanation of the sales proposal to a prospective buyer.

sales process (sales cycle) The set of steps a salesperson goes through in a particular organization to sell a particular product or service.

sales promotion Marketing activities—other than personal selling, advertising, and public relations—that stimulate consumer buying and dealer effectiveness.

sales proposal A formal written document or professional presentation that outlines how the salesperson's product or service will meet or exceed the prospect's needs.

sample A subset of a population.

sampling error Error that occurs when a sample somehow does not represent the target population.

satisficer Type of business customer that places an order with the first familiar supplier to satisfy product and delivery requirements.

scaled-response question A closed-ended question designed to measure the intensity of a respondent's answer.

scanner-based research A system for gathering information from a single group of respondents by continuously monitoring the advertising, promotion, and pricing they are exposed to and the things they buy.

scrambled merchandising The tendency to offer a wide variety of nontraditional goods and services under one roof.

screened Internet sample Internet sample with quotas based on desired sample characteristics.

screening The first filter in the product development process that eliminates ideas that are inconsistent with the organization's new-product strategy or are obviously inappropriate for some other reason.

search quality A characteristic that can be easily assessed before purchase.

seasonal discount A price reduction for buying merchandise out of season.

secondary data Data previously collected for any purpose other than the one at hand.

secondary membership group Reference group with which people associate less consistently and more formally than a primary membership group, such as a club, professional group, or religious group.

segmentation bases (variables) Characteristics of individuals, groups, or organizations.

selective distortion Process whereby a consumer changes or distorts information that conflicts with his or her feelings or beliefs.

selective distribution Form of distribution achieved by screening dealers to eliminate all but a few in any single area.

selective exposure Process whereby a consumer notices certain stimuli and ignores other stimuli.

selective retention Process whereby a consumer remembers only that information that supports his or her personal beliefs.

self-concept How a consumer perceives himself or herself in terms of attitudes, perceptions, beliefs, and self-evaluations.

sender Originator of the message in the communication process.

service The result of applying human or mechanical efforts to people or objects.

service mark Trademark for a service.

shopping product Product that requires comparison shopping, because it is usually more expensive than a convenience product and found in fewer stores.

simulated (laboratory) market testing Presentation of advertising and other promotion materials for several products, including a test product, to members of the product's target market.

simultaneous product development A team-oriented approach to new-product development.

single-price tactic Policy of offering all goods and services at the same price.

social class Group of people in a society who are considered nearly equal in status or community esteem, who regularly socialize among themselves both formally and informally, and who share behavioral norms.

socialization process Process by which cultural values and norms are passed down to children.

societal marketing orientation The idea that an organization exists not only to satisfy customer wants and needs and to meet organizational objectives but also to preserve or enhance individuals' and society's long-term best interests.

spatial discrepancy Difference between the location of the producer and the location of widely scattered markets.

specialty discount store Retail store that offers a nearly complete selection of single-line merchandise and uses self-service, discount prices, high volume, and high turnover.

specialty product A particular item that consumers search extensively for and are very reluctant to accept substitutes for.

specialty store Retail store specializing in a given type of merchandise.

status quo pricing Pricing objective that maintains existing prices or meets the competition's prices.

stimulus Any unit of input affecting one or more of the five senses: sight, smell, taste, touch, hearing.

stimulus discrimination Learned ability to differentiate among similar products.

stimulus generalization Form of learning that occurs when one response is extended to a second stimulus similar to the first.

straight commission Method of compensation in which the salesperson is paid some percentage when a sale is made.

straight rebuy Buying situation in which the purchaser reorders the same goods or services without looking for new information or investigating other suppliers.

straight salary Method of compensation in which the salesperson receives a salary regardless of sales productivity.

strategic alliance (strategic partnership) A cooperative agreement between business firms.

strategic channel alliance Cooperative agreement between business firms to use the other's already established distribution channel.

subculture Homogeneous group of people who share elements of the overall culture as well as unique elements of their own group.

supercenter Retail store that combines groceries and general merchandise goods with a wide range of services.

supermarket A large, departmentalized, self-service retailer that specializes in food and non-food items.

supplies Consumable items that do not become part of the final product.

supply The quantity of a product that will be offered to the market by a supplier at various prices for a specified period.

supply chain The connected chain of all of the business entities, both internal and external to the company, that perform or support the logistics function.

supply chain management Management system that coordinates and integrates all of the activities performed by supply chain members into a seamless process, from source to the point of consumption that results in enhanced customer and economic value.

supply chain team Entire group of individuals who orchestrate the movement of goods, services, and information from the source to the consumer.

survey research the most popular technique for gathering primary data in which a researcher interacts with people to obtain facts, opinions, and attitudes.

takeoff economy The third stage of economic development that involves a period of transition from a developing to a developed nation.

target market A group of people or organizations for which an organization designs, implements, and maintains a marketing mix intended to meet the needs of that group, resulting in mutually satisfying exchanges.

teamwork Collaborative efforts of people to accomplish common objectives.

telemarketing The use of the telephone to sell directly to consumers.

temporal discrepancy A situation that occurs when a product is produced but a customer is not ready to buy it.

test marketing The limited introduction of a product and a marketing program to determine the reactions of potential customers in a market situation.

trade allowance Price reduction offered by manufacturers to intermediaries, such as wholesalers and retailers.

trade sales promotion Sales promotion activities targeted to a channel member, such as a wholesaler or retailer.

trademark The exclusive right to use a brand or part of a brand.

traditional society A society in the earliest stages of economic development, largely agricultural, with a social structure and value system that provide little opportunity for upward mobility.

two-part pricing Price tactic that charges two separate amounts to consume a single good or service.

unbundling Reducing the bundle of services that comes with the basic product.

undifferentiated targeting strategy Marketing approach that views the market as one big market with no individual segments and thus requires a single marketing mix.

unfair trade practice acts Laws that prohibit wholesalers and retailers from selling below cost.

uniform delivered pricing Price tactic in which the seller pays the actual freight charges and bills every purchaser an identical, flat freight charge.

unique selling proposition Desirable, exclusive, and believable advertising appeal selected as the theme for a campaign.

universal product codes (UPCs) Series of thick and thin vertical lines (bar codes), readable by computerized optical scanners, that represent numbers used to track products.

universe The population from which a sample will be drawn.

unrestricted Internet sample One in which anyone with a computer and modem can fill out the questionnaire.

unsought product A product unknown to the potential buyer or a known product that the buyer does not actively seek.

UPCs. *See* **universal product codes.**

Uruguay Round An agreement to dramatically lower trade barriers worldwide.

usage-rate segmentation Dividing a market by the amount of product bought or consumed.

value Enduring belief that a specific mode of conduct is personally or socially preferable to another mode of conduct.

value-based pricing The price set at a level that seems to the customer to be a good price compared to the prices of other options.

variable costs Costs that vary with changes in the level of output.

vertical conflict Channel conflict that occurs between different levels in a marketing channel, most typically between the manufacturer and wholesaler or between the manufacturer and retailer.

want Recognition of an unfulfilled need and a product that will satisfy it.

warehouse membership clubs Limited-service merchant wholesalers that sell a limited selection of brand-name appliances, household items, and groceries on a cash-and-carry basis to members, usually small businesses and groups.

warranty Confirmation of the quality or performance of a good or service.

World Trade Organization (WTO) A new trade organization that replaces the old General Agreement on Trade and Tariffs (GATT).

WTO. *See* **World Trade Organization.**

yield management systems (YMS) A technique for adjusting prices that uses complex mathematical software to profitably fill unused capacity by discounting early purchases, limiting early sales at these discounted prices, and overbooking capacity.

zone pricing Modification of uniform delivered pricing that divides the United States (or the total market) into segments or zones and charges a flat freight rate to all customers in a given zone.

Endnotes

CHAPTER 1

1. D. M. Osborne, "Taking On Procter & Gamble," *Inc.*, October 2000, 67–73. Used with permission.
2. "About Us," American Marketing Association (on-line). Available at http://www.marketingpower.com. January 14, 2002.
3. Philip Kotler, *Marketing Management*, millennium ed. (Upper Saddle River, NJ: Prentice-Hall, 2000), 12.
4. Nora Isaacs, "Crash & Burn," http://www.upsidetoday.com, March 2001, 186–192.
5. Ibid.
6. Rekha Balu, "Listen Up," *Fast Company*, May 2000, 304–316.
7. Lucy McCauley, "Unit of One," *Fast Company*, March 2000, 94.
8. Ibid.
9. David W. Cravens, Charles W. Lamb, Jr., and Victoria L. Crittenden, *Strategic Marketing Management Cases*, 7th ed. (New York: McGraw-Hill Irwin, 2002), 2.
10. Balu, 312.
11. Cravens, Lamb, and Crittenden, 3.
12. Jerry Wind and Arvind Rangaswamy, "Customerization: The Next Revolution in Mass Customization," *Journal of Interactive Marketing* 15 (no. 1), 2001, 18.
13. Christopher J. Zane, "Creating Lifetime Customers," *The Retailing Issues Letter*, September 2000, 2.
14. "Top 10 Things That Irked Holiday Shoppers," *Business Week*, February 7, 2000, EB12.
15. Scott Thurm, "How to Drive an Express Train," *Wall Street Journal*, June 1, 2000, B1.
16. Ibid.
17. Robert Bibb and Eric Gehm, "The 360-Degree View," *Customer Relationship Management*, June 2001, 23–24.
18. "Ask Yourself, What the Hell Really Works Here?" *Fast Company*, May 2001, 82.
19. Dana Jones, "Respondez-Vous, B-to-B," *Marketing News*, May 22, 2000, 1, 9, 10.
20. Robert Levering and Milton Moskowitz, "The 100 Best Companies to Work For," *Fortune*, January 10, 2000, 81–110.
21. John Yokoyama and Jim Berg-quist, "The World Famous Pike Place Fish Story," *The Retailing Issues Letter*, November 2001, 5. Center for Retailing Studies, Texas A & M University.
22. Alessandra Galloni, "Coke to Launch Powerade Drink across Europe," *Wall Street Journal*, October 16, 2001, B11E. Used with permission.
23. Geoffrey A. Fowler, "Green Sales Pitch Isn't Moving Many Products," *Wall Street Journal*, March 6, 2002, B1, B4. Reprinted with permission of the *Wall Street Journal* ©2002 Dow Jones & Co., Inc. All rights reserved worldwide.
24. Gina Imperato, "Get Your Career in Sight," *Fast Company*, March 2000, 326.

CHAPTER 2

1. Sarah Ellison, "Levi Strauss, Losing Ground to Rivals, Is Set to Iron Wrinkles Out of Jeans Sales," *Wall Street Journal,* February 12, 2001, A23B. Used with permission.
2. Based on Edward Stevens, *Business Ethics* (New York: Paulist Press, 1979). Reprinted with permission. Used with permission of Paulist Press.
3. Anusorn Singhapakdi, Skott Vitell, and Kenneth Kraft, "Moral Intensity and Ethical Decisionmaking of Marketing Professionals," *Journal of Business Research* 36, March 1996, 245–255; Ishmael Akaah and Edward Riordan, "Judgments of Marketing Professionals about Ethical Issues in Marketing Research: A Replication and Extension," *Journal of Marketing Research*, February 1989, 112–120. See also Shelby Hung, Lawrence Chonko, and James Wilcox, "Ethical Problems of Marketing Researchers," *Journal of Marketing Research*, August 1984, 309–324; Kenneth Andrews, "Ethics in Practice," *Harvard Business Review*, September–October 1989, 99–104; Thomas Dunfee, Craig Smith, and William T. Ross, Jr., "Social Contracts and Marketing Ethics," *Journal of Marketing*, July 1999, 14–32; and Jay Handleman and Stephen Arnold, "The Role of Marketing Actions with a Social Dimension: Appeals to the Institutional Environment," *Journal of Marketing*, July 1999, 33–48.
4. O. C. Ferrell, Debbie Thorne, and Linda Ferrell, "Legal Pressure for Ethical Compliance in Marketing," *Proceedings of the American Marketing Association*, Summer 1995, 412–413.
5. "Ethics Programs Aren't Stemming Employee Misconduct," *Wall Street Journal*, May 11, 2000, A1. Used with permission.
6. This section is adapted from Archie B. Carroll, "The Pyramid of Corporate Social Responsibility: Toward the Moral Management of Organizational Stakeholders," *Business Horizons*, July–August 1991, 39–48; see also Kirk Davidson, "Marketers Must Accept Greater Responsibilities," *Marketing News*, February 2, 1998, 6.
7. "Business Ethics: Three Companies Show How Business Might Evolve Ethically in the Next Century," *PR News-wires*, November 16, 1999.
8. "The Best Corporate Reputations in America," *Wall Street Journal*, September 23, 1999, B1, B20.
9. "The Promise of the New Economy Is at Risk," *Fast Company*, March 2000, 166–167.
10. Amy Borrus, "Commerce Reweaves the Social Fabric," *Business Week*, August 28, 2000, 187–189.
11. Ibid.
12. "Survey Rates Companies' Reputations, And Many Are Found Wanting," *Wall Street Journal*, February 7, 2001, B1, B6.
13. Sankar Sen and C. B. Bhattacharya, "Does Doing Good Always Lead to Doing Better? Consumer Reactions to Corporate Responsibility," *Journal of Marketing Research*, May 2001, 225–243.
14. The "coming of age" material is adapted from Charles Schewe, Geoffrey Meredith, and Stephanie Noble, "Defining Moments: Segmenting by Cohorts," *Marketing Management,* Fall 2000, 47–53.
15. "No Place Like Home," *Wall Street Journal*, June 16, 1997, R4.
16. David Wolfe, "The Psychological Center of Gravity," *American Demographics*, April 1998, 16–19.
17. James Steinberg, "The Millennial Mind Set," *American Demographics*, January 1999, 60–64.
18. "Leisure Squeeze," *Roper Reports*, January 1999, 1.
19. Ibid.
20. "For Harried Workers in the Twenty-first Century, Six Trends to Watch," *Wall Street Journal*, December 29, 1999, B1. Used with permission.
21. "Latest Backlash against Dual Earners Ignores Some Realities," *Wall Street Journal*, May 14, 1997, B1.
22. "Sorry, Boys—Donna Reed Is Still Dead," *American Demographics*, September 1995, 13–14.
23. "Women-Owned Businesses Booming, But So Are Obstacles," *Associated Press Newswires*, April 11, 2000.
24. Gerry Myers, "Selling to Women," *American Demographics*, April 1996, 36–42.
25. Ibid.
26. Christy Harvey, "A Guide to Who Holds the Purse Strings," *Wall Street*

Journal, June 22, 2000, A14. Used with permission.

27. Ibid.

28. Shelly Branch, "Irradiated Food by Any Other Name Might Just Win Over Consumers," *Wall Street Journal,* August 14, 2001, B1, B4. Used with permission.

29. Pamela Paul, "Getting Inside Gen Y," *American Demographics,* September 2001, 43–49.

30. Rebecca Gardyn, "Swap Meet," *American Demographics,* July 2001, 51–55.

31. "Hotels Target Generation X; Young Travelers Demand High-Tech Services, Amenities," *USA Today,* February 10, 2000, 1B.

32. "Harley-Davidson's New 'Buell Blast' Roars into 18–34 Year-Old Novice Market," *PR Newswire,* March 16, 2000.

33. "Survey Sheds Light on Typical Boomer," *Marketing News,* January 31, 1994, 2.

34. Cheryl Russell, "The Master Trend," *American Demographics,* October 1993, 28–37.

35. "Booming Business," *American Demographics,* December 1999, 32–35.

36. "Boomer Havens and Young Adult Magnets," *American Demographics,* September 2001, 22–24.

37. Howard Willens and Leslie Harris, "The Mature Market . . . Is It for Real?" *Quirk's Marketing Research Review,* May 2001, 40–43. Reprinted with permission.

38. Ibid.

39. Ibid.

40. "Marketers Tweak Strategies as Age Groups Realign," *Wall Street Journal,* May 15, 2001, B1, B4. Used with permission.

41. "Work Slowdown," *American Demographics,* March 1996, 4–7.

42. William Frey, "Micro Melting Pots," *American Demographics,* June 2001, 20–23.

43. Ibid.

44. "An Almost-Invisible $1 Trillion Market," *Business Week,* June 11, 2001, 151.

45. Steve Rabin, "How to Sell across Cultures," *American Demographics,* March 1994, 56–58.

46. "P&G Reaches Out to Hispanics," *Wall Street Journal,* October 13, 2000, B1, B4. Used with permission.

47. "Diversity in the Main Stream," *Marketing News,* May 21, 2001, 1, 13.

48. "The Web Goes Multicultural," *Advertising Age,* November 29, 1999, 51, 54.

49. Ibid.

50. "Creating the Digital Dividend," *Business2.com,* March 6, 2001, 60.

51. Ibid.

52. Ibid.

53. Hassan Fattah, "The Rising Tide," *American Demographics,* April 2001, 48–53.

54. http://www.census.gov, October 12, 2001.

55. U.S. Department of Commerce: Bureau of Economic Analysis (http://www.bea.gov), October 12, 2001.

56. "How Prosperity Is Reshaping the American Economy," *Business Week,* February 14, 2000, 101–110.

57. "Masters of Innovation," *Business Week 50,* Spring 2001, 162.

58. Stacy Perman, "Automate or Die," http://www.ecompany.com, July 2001, 60–67.

59. Peter Landers, "Electronics E-Commerce in Japan Held Back by Retail Traditions," *Wall Street Journal,* March 30, 2000, A22. Used with permission.

60. The Tide story is from Katrina Brooker, "A Game of Inches," *Fortune,* February 5, 2001, 98–100.

CHAPTER 3

1. Bill Spindle, "Cowboys and Samurai: The Japanizing of Universal," *Wall Street Journal,* March 22, 2001, B1, B6. Used with permission.

2. "The Big Myth about U.S. Manufacturing," *Fortune,* October 2, 2002, 44.

3. Statistics obtained from http://www.usatradeonline.gov, October 18, 2001.

4. Ibid.

5. Ibid.

6. Ibid.

7. See http://bxa.fedworld.gov/faq.html. This is the Web site of the Bureau of Export Administration.

8. "Anti-Trade/Pro-Poverty," *Fortune,* January 10, 2000, 40.

9. Sara Terry, "Free Trade Isn't Fair," *Fast Company,* September 2000, 254–256.

10. "Anti-Trade/Pro-Poverty," 40.

11. "The Pros and Cons of Globalization," *Business Week,* April 24, 2000, 41.

12. "Globalization: What Americans Are Worried About," *Business Week,* April 24, 2000, 44.

13. "Toy Story," *Fortune,* June 26, 2000, 270.

14. "Hurting in Lockstep," *Business Week,* October 22, 2001, 30.

15. "Up the Ladder," *Business Week,* November 6, 2000, 78–85.

16. Ibid.

17. "What's at Stake," *Business Week,* October 22, 2001, 34–37.

18. Neil Jacoby, "The Multinational Corporation," *Center Magazine,* May 1970, 37.

19. "The Stateless Corporation," *Business Week,* May 14, 1990, 98–105. See also Bruce Kogut, "What Makes a Company Global?" *Harvard Business Review,* January–February 1999, 165–170; and Neil Bruce Holbert, "Worldwide Marketing Must Not Assume Imperialistic Air," *Marketing News,* February 14, 2000, 20.

20. "See the World, Erase Its Border," *Business Week,* August 28, 2000, 113–114.

21. Theodore Levitt, "The Globalization of Markets," *Harvard Business Review,* May–June 1983, 92–102.

22. Saeed Samiee and Kendall Roth, "The Influence of Global Marketing Standardization on Performance," *Journal of Marketing,* April 1992, 1–17. See also Aviv Shoham, "Global Marketing Standardization," *Journal of Global Marketing,* September 1995, 91–119.

23. "For Peruvians, Fizzy Yellow Drink Is the Real Thing," *International Herald Tribune,* December 27, 1995, 3.

24. Sherrie Zhan, "Marketing across Cultures," *World Trade,* February 1999, 80–82.

25. "Research Meaning When Giving International Gifts," *Cincinnati Business Courier,* July 28, 2000, 36.

26. "Selling Overseas Complex Endeavor," *Marketing News,* July 30, 2001, 4.

27. For an excellent article on culture and marketing, see Cheryl Nakata and K. Sivakauar, "Instituting the Marketing Concept in a Multinational Setting: The Role of National Culture," *Journal of the Academy of Marketing Science,* Summer 2001, 255–275.

28. "Portrait of the World," *Marketing News,* August 28, 1995, 20–21.

29. "Who's Free, Who's Not," *Wall Street Journal,* November 1, 2000, A26.

30. Robert Frank, "Thai Food for the World," *Wall Street Journal,* February 6, 2001, B1, B4.

31. http://www.wto.org, October 19, 2001.

32. "Beijing's Phony War on Fakes," *Fortune,* October 30, 2000, 190–199.

33. "Motorcycle Makers from Japan Discover Piracy Made in China," *Wall Street Journal,* July 25, 2001, A1, A4.

34. "NAFTA's Scorecard: So Far, So Good," *Business Week,* July 9, 2001, 54–56.

35. Material for the sections on FTAA, ASEAN, and APEC is reprinted from C. Williams, *Management,* 2nd ed. (Cincinnati, Ohio: South-Western, 2003) 274–275. Original sources for the material are provided in notes. G. Smith, E. Malkin, J. Wheatley, P. Magnusson, and M. Arndt, "Betting on Free Trade: George Bush Wants to Turn North and South America into the World's Biggest Single Market. Is It for Real or Just a Dream?" *Business Week,* April 23, 2001, 32.

36. Declaration of Principles, Summit of the Americas, "Free Trade Area of the Americas." [On-line] Available http://www.ftaa-alca.org/EnglishVersion/miami_e.htm, January 27, 1999.

37. G. Smith, E. Malkin, J. Wheatley, P. Magnusson, and M. Arndt, 32.

38. "ASEAN Free Trade Area (AFTA): An Update," Association of Southeast Asian Nations. [On-line] Available http://www.aseansec.org. September 10, 2001.

39. "Member Economies' Web sites," Asia-Pacific Economic Cooperation.

[On-line] Available http://www.apecsec. org.sg/, September 10, 2001.

40. "Trustbusting's Top Cop," *Business Week,* April 30, 2001, 88–90.

41. Tony Horwitz, "Europe's Borders Fade, And People and Goods Can Move More Freely," *Wall Street Journal,* May 18, 1993, A1, A10. Used with permission.

42. http://www.franchise.org, October 22, 2001.

43. Polly Larson, "Opening Doors to Emerging Economies," http://www. franchise.org, October 22, 2001.

44. For an excellent article on joint ventures, see Mark Houston and Shane Johnson, "Buyer-Supplier Contracts versus Joint Ventures: Determinants and Consequences of Transaction Structure," *Journal of Marketing Research,* February 2000, 1–15.

45. "Mondavi Likes the Taste of Global Joint Ventures," *The Plain Dealer,* December 15, 1999, 3F.

46. "How the Chevy Name Landed on an SUV Using Russian Technology," *Wall Street Journal,* February 20, 2001, A1, A8.

47. "Making Global Alliances Work," *Fortune,* December 17, 1990, 121–123.

48. "P&G Squabbles with Vietnamese Partner," *Wall Street Journal,* February 27, 1998, A10.

49. "How Well Does Wal-Mart Travel?" *Business Week,* September 3, 2001, 82–84.

50. "Wal-Mart's European Beachhead," *International Herald Tribune,* March 13, 2001, 11.

51. "Could Your Job Go to China?" http://CNN.com, September 7, 2001.

52. "TI Teams Up in Asia," *Dallas Morning News,* February 4, 1996, H1.

53. "Herbal Remedies Aimed at East and West," *Wall Street Journal,* January 31, 2000, A26.

54. "Can TV Save the Planet?" *American Demographics,* May 1996, 43–47.

55. "Indian Company Thrives with Simple Marketing," *Wall Street Journal,* December 1, 2000, B19A.

56. "Kiddi Just Fine in the U.K., But Here It's Binky," *Marketing News,* August 28, 1995, 8.

57. Adam Sage, "McDonald's Rebrands Itself as 100 Percent Pure French," http://www.thetimes.co.uk, March 31, 2001.

58. Phred Dvorak, "Japanese Dairy Pours on the Apologies," *Wall Street Journal,* July 12, 2000, A21. Used with permission.

59. "Exxon Centralizes New Global Campaign," *Wall Street Journal,* July 11, 2001, B6.

60. Vijay Mahajan, Marcos V. Pratini de Moraes, and Jerry Wind, "The Invisible Global Market," *Marketing Management,* Winter 2000, 31–35.

61. Ilan Greenberg, "UPS Targets Logistics Business in Asia," *Wall Street Journal,* April 26, 2001, A12.

62. "Payment System Lets Customers Choose Currency," *Information Week,* April 2, 2001, 33.

63. "In Japan, The Hub of E-Commerce Is a 7-Eleven," *Wall Street Journal,* November 1, 1999, B1, B4.

64. "In Europe, Surfing a Web of Red Tape," *Wall Street Journal,* October 29, 1999, B1, B4.

65. "E-Commerce Discovers Europe," *International Herald Tribune,* December 24, 1999, 15.

66. "Europe Defines Itself against U.S. on the Internet," *Wall Street Journal,* April 2, 2001, B9E.

67. Roger Collis, "Savvy Trekkers Map Out Routes to Career Success," *International Herald Tribune,* August 17, 2001, 7.

CHAPTER 4

1. Paul Glader, "One Industry Is Booming in the Aftermath of Attacks," *Wall Street Journal,* November 7, 2001, B1; Brian Caulfield, Matthew Maier, Ryan Tate, and Owen Thomas, "The Tipping Point," *Business 2.0,* November 2001, 42; Allison Fass, "Agencies Tread Carefully in Messages to Consumers," *New York Times,* October 18, 2001; Rick Lyman, "This Season Fewer Soldiers March Onscreen," *New York Times,* October 16, 2001; Eryn Brown, "Just Another Product Launch," *Fortune,* November 12, 2001, 102; Joseph Pereira, "Toyland Sounds a Call to Arms," *Wall Street Journal,* November 7, 2001, B1; Timothy Aeppel, "Now Is the Time to Sell 'U.S.-Made,'" *Wall Street Journal,* October 22, 2001, B1; Patricia Callahan and Amy Merrick, "Greeting-Card Firms Hasten to Serve Nation's New Mood," *Wall Street Journal,* October 4, 2001, B4; David Handelman, "In Pensive Times, Comfort Magazines Find an Audience," *New York Times,* October 29, 2001; Shelly Branch, "Campbell's Soup Shipments Rise as Buyers Stock Pantries," *Wall Street Journal,* November 15, 2001, B4.

2. Michael Totty, "Information, Please," *Wall Street Journal,* October 29, 2001, R6.

3. Emily Nelson, "P&G Checks Out Real Life," *Wall Street Journal,* May 17, 2001, B1.

4. Nancy Ann Jeffrey and Sarah Collins, "The Grandparent Industry," *Wall Street Journal,* November 2, 2001, W1.

5. "A Leg Up," *Continental,* November 2001, 22.

6. Lee Gomes, "Download, Downshift and Go: MP3 Takes to the Road," *Wall Street Journal,* February 27, 2001, B1.

7. Suzanne Bidlake, "P&G to Roll Laundry Tablet in Europe," *Advertising Age,* March 1, 1999, 18.

8. Nancy Shepherdson, "New Kids on the Lot," *American Demographics,* January 2000.

9. Ronald Alsop, "Survey Rates Companies' Reputations, And Many Are Found Wanting," *Wall Street Journal,* February 7, 2001, B1. See also Gordon Fairclough, "Philip Morris Seeks to Mold Its Image into an Altria State," *Wall Street Journal,* November 16, 2001, A3.

10. Thomas E. Weber, "To Get Expert Advice about Digital Cameras, Check Out These Sites," *Wall Street Journal,* November 5, 2001, B1.

11. Ernest Beck, "Boosting Diageo's Spirits," *Wall Street Journal,* February 23, 2001, B1.

12. David P. Hamilton, "Not an Easy Sell: TiVo, ReplayTV and Other 'PVRs' Don't Take Off," *Wall Street Journal,* February 7, 2001, B1.

13. Emily Nelson, "Too Many Choices," *Wall Street Journal,* April 20, 2001, B1.

14. Ronald Alsop, "The Best Corporate Reputations in America: Johnson & Johnson (Think Babies!) Turns Up Tops," *Wall Street Journal,* September 23, 1999, B1. See also Alsop, "Survey Rates Companies' Reputations, And Many Are Found Wanting."

15. Princeton Research Survey Associates, "Consumer Behavior, Experiences and Attitudes: A Comparison by Age Groups," *AARP,* March 1999.

16. Frederic M. Biddle, "After Years of Disdain, Korean Cars Rev Up Sales," *Wall Street Journal,* August 18, 1999, B1, B4.

17. Michael Totty, "Making the Sale," *Wall Street Journal,* September 24, 2001, R6.

18. Stephanie Thompson, "Marketers Embrace Latest Health Claims," *Advertising Age,* February 28, 2000, 20–22.

19. Ibid. See also John Urquhart, "A Health Food Hits Big Time," *Wall Street Journal,* August 3, 1999, B1, B4.

20. Dean Bonham, "Hispanic Fans Make It to Big Leagues," *Rocky Mountain News,* June 23, 2001, 5C; Rodney Ho, "Radio One Deploys an Urban Beat to Make Revenue Jump," *Wall Street Journal,* November 16, 2001, B6; Jeffrey Ball, "Chrysler's Latest Ads for Minivans Stress Multicultural over Motherly," *Wall Street Journal,* December 18, 2001, B9.

21. Cathleen Egan, "Kellogg, General Mills Battle over Bars," *Wall Street Journal,* March 26, 2001, B10.

22. Bill Stoneman, "Beyond Rocking the Ages: An Interview with J. Walker Smith," *American Demographics,* May 1998, 44–49.

23. Pamela Paul, "Getting Inside Gen Y," *American Demographics,* September 2001, 42–49. See also Pooja Bhatia, "Look Who's Reading," *Wall Street Journal,* November 9, 2001, W1.

24. Miriam Jordon, "Global Craze for Diet Drugs," *Wall Street Journal,* August 24, 2001, B1. See also Leslie Chang, "Bringing Science to Weight Loss in China," *Wall Street Journal,* August 24, 2001, B1.

25. Bill Spindle, "Cowboys and Samurai: The Japanizing of Universal," *Wall Street Journal*, March 22, 2001, B1.

26. Erla Zwingle, "A World Together," *National Geographic,* August 1999, 10–33; Hillary Mayell, "Death of the Mother Tongue," http://www.nationalgeographic.com/NEWS, February 25, 1999; Oliver Burkeman and Emma Brockes, "Trouble Brewing," *The Guardian,* December 3, 1999; "'Americanization' Fears Seem Misplaced," *Canberra Times,* October 24, 1999, 19; Swaminathan S. Ankleesaria Aiyar, "Does Globalisation Threaten Indian Culture?" *The Economic Times,* December 22, 1999; Naomi Klein, "The Tyranny of Brands," *Australian Financial Review,* February 11, 2000, 1; Sally Beatty and Carol Hymowitz, "How MTV Stays Tuned In to Teens," *Wall Street Journal,* March 21, 2000, B1, B4.

27. Joshua Harris Prager, "People with Disabilities Are Next Consumer Niche," *Wall Street Journal*, December 15, 1999, B1, B6.

28. Devon Spurgeon, "Hold the Oatmeal! Restaurants Now Court the Breakfast Burger Eater," *Wall Street Journal*, September 4, 2001, B1.

29. Eduardo Porter, "For Hispanic Marketers, Census Says It All," *Wall Street Journal*, April 24, 2001, B8. See also Bonham, "Hispanic Fans Make It to Big Leagues."

30. Heidi J. Shrager, "Closed-Circle Commerce," *Wall Street Journal*, November 19, 2001, B1.

31. Rebecca Piirto Heath, "Life on Easy Street," *American Demographics*, April 1997.

32. Elia Kacapyr, "Are You Middle Class?" *American Demographics*, October 1996.

33. Rebecca Piirto Heath, "The New Working Class," *American Demographics*, January 1998, 51–55.

34. Suein L. Hwang, "Dot-Coms Head Down-Market for Dollars," *Wall Street Journal*, July 16, 2001, B1.

35. Michael J. Weiss, "A Tale of Two Cheeses," *American Demographics*, February 1998, 16–17.

36. Bhatia, "Look Who's Reading."

37. Barbara Cooke, "Radar Fine-Tuned to 'Cool' Sets Some Teens Apart," *Chicago Tribune*, March 5, 2000, 1.

38. Erin White, "Abercrombie Seeks to Send Teeny-Boppers Packing," *Wall Street Journal*, August 30, 2001, B1.

39. Norihiko Shirouzu, "Japan's High-School Girls Excel in Art of Setting Trends," *Wall Street Journal*, April 24, 1998, B1, B6.

40. Matt Haig, "Teenage Clicks," *The Guardian*, October 25, 2001, 46.

41. Kortney Stringer, "Young and Restless," *Wall Street Journal*, September 24, 2001, R8; Nina Munk, "Peddling Cool: How Teens Buy," *Fortune*, April 13, 1998, 28–30.

42. Greg Winter, "States Try to Limit Sales of Junk Food in School Buildings," *New York Times,* September 9, 2001, 1; Betsy McKay, "Coke Finds Its Exclusive School Contracts Aren't So Easily Given Up," *Wall Street Journal,* June 26, 2001, B1; Randy Southerland, "Schools' Soda Deals Losing Fizz? Challenges Mount over Issues of Nutrition, Commercialization," *Atlanta Journal-Constitution,* September 26, 2001, JA1.

43. John Gaffney, "The Kids Are Doing It. Should You?" *Business 2.0*, November 2001, 141.

44. Jonathan Eig, "Edible Entertainment," *Wall Street Journal*, October 24, 2001, B1.

45. Janice Rosenberg, "Tweens Mesh Latest Fads, Moms & Dads," *Advertising Age*, February 14, 2000, 40.

46. Shepherdson, "New Kids on the Lot."

47. Matthew Klein, "He Shops, She Shops," *American Demographics*, March 1998, 34–35.

48. Khanh T. L. Tran, "Women Assert Computer Games Aren't Male Preserve," *Wall Street Journal*, February 26, 2001, B1. See also Meeyoung Song, "Credit-Card Companies Cater to Korean Women," *Wall Street Journal*, June 6, 2001, B4.

49. Emily Nelson, "Forget Supermodels—Revlon's New Face Gets Lipstick on Her Teeth," *Wall Street Journal*, March 30, 2001, B1.

50. Wendy Bounds and Rebecca Quick, "Men Who Shop: Retailers Target Male Shoppers as Santa's New Helpers; Gift-Wrapping Tips for Guys," *Wall Street Journal*, November 12, 1999, W1, W4.

51. Diane Crispell, "Fruit of the Boom," *Marketing Tools*, April 1998.

52. Vanessa O'Connell and Jon E. Hilsenrath, "Advertisers Are Cautious as Household Makeup Shifts," *Wall Street Journal*, May 15, 2001, B1.

53. Anita Lienert, "A More Visible Altima," *Detroit News*, September 26, 2001, 01.

54. Lisa Vickery, Kelly Greene, Shelly Branch, and Emily Nelson, "Marketers Tweak Strategies as Age Groups Realign," *Wall Street Journal*, May 15, 2001, B1.

55. Nora J. Rifon and Molly Catherine Ziske, "Using Weight Loss Products: The Roles of Involvement, Self-Efficacy and Body Image," in *1995 AMA Educators' Proceedings,* ed. Barbara B. Stern and George M. Zinkhan (Chicago: American Marketing Association, 1995), 90–98.

56. Amy Merrick, "Counting on the Census," *Wall Street Journal*, February 14, 2001, B1.

57. Sarah Hall, "What Color Is Your Cart?" *Self*, September 1999, 150.

58. Jane L. Levere, "New Campaign for Ivory Soap," *New York Times* on-line, October 25, 2001.

59. Joshua Rosenbaum, "Guitar Maker Looks for a New Key," *Wall Street Journal*, February 11, 1998, B1, B5.

60. Elizabeth J. Wilson, "Using the Dollarmetric Scale to Establish the Just Meaningful Difference in Price," in *1987 AMA Educators' Proceedings*, ed. Susan Douglas et al. (Chicago: American Marketing Association, 1987), 107.

61. Sunil Gupta and Lee G. Cooper, "The Discounting of Discounts and Promotion Thresholds," *Journal of Consumer Research*, December 1992, 401–411.

62. Mark Stiving and Russell S. Winer, "An Empirical Analysis of Price Endings with Scanner Data," *Journal of Consumer Research*, June 1997, 57–67. See also Robert M. Schindler and Patrick N. Kirby, "Patterns of Rightmost Digits Used in Advertised Price: Implications for Nine-Ending Effects," *Journal of Consumer Research*, September 1997, 192–201.

63. Sheila Muto, "What's in an Address? Sometimes, A Better Image," *Wall Street Journal*, September 5, 2001, B14.

64. Rhonda L. Rundle, "In Stores Now: Full Body Scans," *Wall Street Journal*, July 24, 2001, B1.

65. Stuart Elliot, "Growing Number of Airlines Resume Image Advertising," *New York Times* on-line, November 6, 2001.

66. Kevin Helliker, "How Hardy Are Upscale Gyms?" *Wall Street Journal*, February 9, 2001, B1.

67. Deborah Ball, "Despite Downturn, Japanese Are Still Having Fits for Luxury Goods," *Wall Street Journal*, April 24, 2001, B1.

68. Eryn Brown, "Just Another Product Launch," *Fortune*, November 12, 2001, 102.

69. Gene Del Vecchio, "Keeping It Timeless, Trendy: From Barbie to Pez, 'Ever-Cool' Kids Brands Meet Both Needs," *Advertising Age*, March 23, 1998, 24.

70. Chris Gaither, "Microsoft Explores a New Territory: Fun," *New York Times* on-line, November 4, 2001.

71. Steven Lipin, Brian Coleman, and Jeremy Mark, "Pick a Card: Visa, American Express, And MasterCard Vie in Overseas Strategies," *Wall Street Journal*, February 15, 1994, A1, A5.

72. Evan Ramstad, "Digital-Camera Makers Focus Their Attention on Printing," *Wall Street Journal*, February 8, 2001, B6.

73. Leila Jason, "Simple PCs Can Help Speed Elderly onto Net," *Wall Street Journal*, July 16, 2001, B5.

74. Jim Carlton, "Recycling Redefined," *Wall Street Journal,* March 6, 2001, B1.

75. Chang, "Bringing Science to Weight Loss in China."

76. Jack Neff, "James River Puts Muscle Behind Dixie Paper Brand," *Advertising Age*, June 16, 1997, 22.

77. Miriam Jordan, "Debut of Rival Diet Colas in India Leaves a Bitter Taste," *Wall Street Journal*, July 21, 1999, B1, B4.

CHAPTER 5

1. Gregory L. White, "In Asia, GM Pins Its Hopes on Delicate Web of Alliances," *Wall Street Journal Interactive Edition,* October 23, 2001, on-line. Used with permission.

2. For a more thorough discussion of marketing on the Internet, see Chapter 14.

3. Ward Hanson, *Internet Marketing* (Cincinnati, OH: South-Western, 2000), 6.

4. "E-Procurement Could Save Trillions," *eMarketer,* December 18, 2001, on-line.

5. "Saluting Solutions," *eMarketer,* December 19, 2001, on-line.

6. Paul C. Judge, "How I Saved $100 Million on the Web," *Fast Company,* February 2001, 174–181.

7. Ibid.

8. Ibid.

9. Alex Frangos, "Just One Word: Plastics," *Wall Street Journal,* May 21, 2001, R20.

10. Ibid.

11. David Sims, "Bringing Online Help to the B2B World," *Customer Relationship Management,* August 2001, 32–36.

12. Fara Warner and Rick Brooks, "Ford Is Hiring UPS to Track Vehicles in Transit from Factories to Dealers," *Wall Street Journal Interactive Edition,* February 2, 2000, on-line.

13. Karen L. Lundegaard, "Online Exchange of Auto's Big Three Clears Final Hurdle," *Wall Street Journal,* September 27, 2000, B10.

14. Jocelyn Parker, "As Covisint Auto Market Materializes, Concerns Arise over Smaller Suppliers," *Wall Street Journal,* September 18, 2000, B18H.

15. Karby Leggett, "In Rural China, GM Sees a Frugal but Huge Market," *Wall Street Journal,* January 16, 2001, A1. Used with permission.

16. U.S. Census Bureau, "North American Industry Classification System (NAICS)—United States," http://www.census.gov/.

17. Mark Tatge, "Caterpillar's Truck Engine Sales May Skid amid High Inventories," *Wall Street Journal Interactive Edition,* March 13, 2000, on-line.

18. "Lockheed Wins JSF Contract," *Fort Worth Star-Telegram,* December 30, 2001, 6F.

19. http://www.lockheedmartin.com/about/ethics/.

20. James W. Taylor, *The Marketing Strategy & Planning Workbook,* (South Nyack, NY: Wellington Press, 2000), 9.

CHAPTER 6

1. Thea Singer, "Little Clippers," *Inc.,* July 2001, 25–28. Used with permission.

2. Pamela Sebastian Ridge, "Chico's Scores with Its Nonjudgmental Sizes," *Wall Street Journal,* March 8, 2001, B1, B4.

3. Leslie Chang, "Bringing Science to Weight Loss in China," *Wall Street Journal,* August 21, 2001, B1, B7. Used with permission.

4. Nichole L. Torres, "It's Child's Play," *Entrepreneur,* December 2001, 24–26.

5. Kristina Feliciano, "The Kids Are Alright," *Consumer Magazines,* March 6, 2000, M8.

6. Anne D'Innocenzio, "Stores Are Catering to Tastes of Tweens," *Fort Worth Star Telegram,* September 5, 2000, 1C, 5C.

7. Torres, "It's Child's Play."

8. "Graying Boomers, Booming Teens," *Inc.,* May 15, 2001, 86–87.

9. Meg Jones, "Milking It," *Fort Worth Star Telegram,* October 29, 2001, 1F, 6F.

10. Lisa Vickery, Kelly Greene, Shelly Branch, and Emily Nelson, "Marketers Tweak Strategies as Age Groups Realign," *Wall Street Journal,* May 15, 2001, B1.

11. Ibid.

12. Dave Carpenter, "Fountain of Youth," *Fort Worth Star Telegram,* January 23, 2001, 1C, 10C.

13. Vickery, Greene, Branch, and Nelson, "Marketers Tweek Strategies."

14. "Mature Audience," *Business 2.0,* April 17, 2001, 59.

15. Kevin J. Clancy, "Getting Serious about Building Profitable Online Retail Brands," *Arthur Andersen Retailing Issues Newsletter,* Center for Retailing Studies, Texas A&M University, 12:6, November 2000, 3.

16. Khanh T. L. Tran, "Women Assert Computer Games Aren't Male Preserve," *Wall Street Journal,* February 26, 2001, B1, B8.

17. Emily Nelson, "Beauty Makers Now Go Where the Boys Are," *Wall Street Journal,* August 10, 2000, B1, B4.

18. Erin White, "Teen Mags for Guys, Not Dolls," *Wall Street Journal,* August 10, 2000, B1, B4.

19. Ann Zimmerman, "Taking Aim at Costco, Sam's Club Marshals Diamonds and Pearls," *Wall Street Journal,* August 9, 2001, A1, A4.

20. Chuck Paustian, "Anybody Can Do It," *Marketing News,* March 26, 2001, 23.

21. Chris Rooney, "Ethnic Marketing: It's the Aspiration, Stupid," *Brandweek,* September 11, 2000, 44.

22. Paustian, "Anybody Can Do It."

23. Roger O. Crockett, "Attention Must Be Paid: The African American Web Community Is Swelling and Underserved," *Business Week,* February 7, 2000, EB16.

24. Eduardo Porter, "Why the Latino Market Is So Hard to Count," *Wall Street Journal,* October 13, 2000, B1, B4.

25. Dana James, "Lingua Franca: Human Touch Translates into Better Research of Hispanic Market," *Marketing News,* January 3, 2000, 17.

26. Sonia Reyes, "Hormel Takes Herdez North of Border w/$4M," *Brandweek,* February 12, 2001, 5.

27. Joel Milliman, "U.S. Marketers Adopt Cinco de Mayo As National Fiesta," *Wall Street Journal,* May 1, 2001, B1, B4.

28. Eduardo Porter, "It's Not Easy to Bottle the Coolness and Heat of J. Lo's Decolletage," *Wall Street Journal,* August 9, 2001, A1, A6.

29. Vanessa O'Connell and Jon E. Hilsenrath, "Advertisers Are Cautious as Household Makeup Shifts," *Wall Street Journal,* May 15, 2001, B1, B4.

30. Ibid.

31. Alex Taylor III, "Porsche Slices Up Its Buyers," *Fortune,* January 16, 1995, 24.

32. Karen Benezra, "The Fragging of the American Mind," *Superbrands,* June 15, 1998, S12–19.

33. Beverly Bundy, "Central Market Says It Knows What You Want to Eat, Even If You Don't," *Fort Worth Star Telegram,* October 10, 2001, 1F, 2F.

34. Amy Merrick, "The 2000 Count: Counting on the Census—New Data Will Let Starbucks Plan Store Openings, Help Blockbuster Stock Its Videos," *Wall Street Journal,* February 14, 2001, B1.

35. "Downsizing Megamarkets: A Return to Mom-and-Pops?" *Firstlight,* March 2000, 22.

36. Jennifer Ordonez, "Cash Cows: Hamburger Joints Call Them 'Heavy Users'—But Not to Their Faces," *Wall Street Journal,* January 12, 2000, A1, A10.

37. David Armstrong, "Here's to the Net," *Wall Street Journal,* April 23, 2001, R30. Used with permission.

38. Ginger Cooper, "Centricity," *Customer Relationship Management,* December 2001, 35–40.

39. Dennis J. Chapman, "Clients, Customers and Buyers," *Customer Relationship Management,* March 2001, 65–71.

40. Anick Jesdanun, "AOL Gambit Works A-OK," *Fort Worth Star Telegram,* January 3, 2001, 1C, 3C.

41. Tricia Bisoux, "Niche Marketing Makes Its Mark," *Biz Ed,* November/December 2001, 45–47.

42. Lisa Bannon, "Let's Play Makeover Barbie," *Wall Street Journal,* February 17, 2000, B1, B4.

43. "Can Levi's Be Cool Again?" *Business Week,* March 13, 2000, 144, 148.

44. Kim T. Gordon, "Different Strokes," *Entrepreneur,* January 2002, 99.

45. Abbey Klaassen, "St. Joseph: From Babies to Boomers," *Advertising Age,* July 9, 2001, 1, 38.

46. Ian Johnson, "Herbal Remedies Aimed at East and West," *Wall Street Journal,* January 31, 2000, A26.

CHAPTER 7

1. Joseph Rydholm, "Preserving the Preservationists," *Quirk's Marketing Research Review,* March 2000, 18–19, 74–75. Reprinted by permission.

2. "Fantastic Voyage," *Fast Company*, March 2000, 178–200.

3. "Keebler Learns to Pay Attention to Research Right from the Start," *Marketing News*, March 11, 1996, 10.

4. "Why Some Customers Are More Equal Than Others," *Fortune*, September 19, 1994, 215–224.

5. Kendra Parker, "Got Questions? All You Have to Do Is Ask," *American Demographics*, November 1999, 36–39.

6. http://www.casro.org, October 29, 2001.

7. Eileen Moran, "Managing the Minefields of Global Product Development," *Quirk's Marketing Research Review*, November 2000, 24–28. Used with permission.

8. Molly Williams, "Monkey See," *Wall Street Journal*, April 23, 2001, R32. Used with permission.

9. Dana James, "The Future of Online Research," *Marketing News*, January 3, 2000, 1, 11.

10. Chris Yalonis, "The Revolution in E-research," *CASRO Journal*, 1999, 131–134.

11. Ibid.

12. Dana James, "Precision Decision," *Marketing News*, September 27, 1999, 23–24.

13. This section was adapted from James Watt, "Using the Internet for Quantitative Survey Research," *Quirk's Marketing Research Review*, June/July 1997, 67–71.

14. Carl McDaniel and Roger Gates, *Contemporary Marketing Research*, 5th ed. (Cincinnati: International Thomson Publishing, 2002).

15. Phone conversation between Kevin Bender, Information Resources, Inc., and Carl McDaniel on April 17, 2000.

16. Sheena Sharp, "New Techniques for Corporate Foresight," *Research Conference Report*, May 1998, 7–8.

CHAPTER 8

1. Stephanie Clifford, "The Grill of Their Dreams," *Business 2.0*, February 2002, 96. © 2002 Time Inc. All rights reserved.

2. Valarie A. Zeithaml and Mary Jo \Bitner, *Services Marketing* (New York: McGraw-Hill, 2000).

3. Joel Milliman, "Services May Lead U.S. to Trade Surplus," *Wall Street Journal*, December 14, 2000, A1.

4. Christina Binkley, "From Orange Shag to Pin Stripes: Sheraton Gets a Makeover," *Wall Street Journal*, April 19, 2000, B1, B10.

5. "Oral-B Unveils Age-Pegged Toothbrushes for Kids," *BusinessWeek Online*, October 4, 2001. http://www.businessweek.com/.

6. "GM Isn't Giving Up on the Pontiac Aztec Yet," *WSJ.com*, November 27, 2001, http://interactive.wsj.com.

7. Teri Agins, "Hilfiger Returns to Preppy Roots, But Sales Slump," *Wall Street Journal*, February 2, 2001, B1, B6.

8. Christine Bittar, "Shiseido Rolls Color, Light and $7M in Major Cosmetic Repositioning," *Brandweek*, October 16, 2000, 6.

9. Sonia Reyes, "Minute Maid Juices Up Calcium Fortified Line," *Brand-week*, March 13, 2000, 323.

10. Mike Beirne, "Hershey Chews on Gum, Mint Plans; Jolly Rancher Eyes Preemptive Strike," *Brandweek*, February 26, 2001, 9.

11. Katrina Brooker, "A Game of Inches," *Fortune*, February 5, 2001, 98–100.

12. Betsy McKay, "Drinks for Developing Countries," *Wall Street Journal*, November 27, 2001, B1, B6. Used with permission.

13. Steve Jarvis, "Lesson Plans," *Marketing News*, June 18, 2001, 1, 9, 10. Used with permission.

14. Gerry Khermouch, Stanley Holmes, and Moon Ihlwan, "The Best Global Brands," *Business Week*, August 6, 2001, 50–57.

15. Brian O'Keefe, "Global Brands," *Fortune*, November 26, 2001, 102–110.

16. Fara Warner, "C'Mon, Get Closer," *Fast Company*, August 2001, 129–139.

17. Lauren Gold and Michael Gold, "Change the Rules of Private-Label Packaging," *Marketing News*, November 22, 1999, 20–21.

18. Peter Galuszka and Wendy Zellner, "Soap Opera at Wal-Mart," *Business Week*, August 16, 1999, 44.

19. Mike Beirne, "Hey, Partner: Ramada Joins AmEx, Continental in Big Co-Brand Push," *Brandweek*, November 13, 2000, 18.

20. Frederic M. Biddle, "American Express, Lexus in Co-Brand Pact," *Wall Street Journal*, February 9, 2000, B12.

21. Stephanie Thompson, "The Mouse in the Food Aisle," *Advertising Age*, September 10, 2001, 73.

22. James Heckman, "Trademarks Protected through New Cyber Act," *Marketing News*, January 3, 2000, 6.

23. Sonia Reyes, "Sunsweet Updates Look, Tells Families: 'Be Good,' " *Brandweek*, February 7, 2000, 10.

24. Jonathan Eig, "Food Companies Grab Kids' Attention by Packaging Products As Toys, Games," *WSJ.com*, October 26, 2001, http://interactive.wsj.com.

25. Kenneth Hein, "Miracle-Gro Seeds TV, Radio, Print; $20M Push Targets Spring Planters," *Brandweek*, February 12, 2001, 4.

26. Gerry Khermouch, "Guinness Pours It On in Chicago," *Brandweek*, February 28, 2000, 18.

27. Herbert M. Meyers, "The Internet's Threat to Branding," *Brandweek*, December 4, 2000, 30.

CHAPTER 9

1. William J. Holstein, "DaimlerChrysler's Net Designs," *Business 2.0*, April 17, 2001, 26–28. © 2001 Time Inc. All rights reserved.

2. William J. Holstein, "Dump the Cookware," *Business 2.0*, May 1, 2001, 69–72.

3. Gary Strauss, "Squeezing New from Old," *USA Today*, January 4, 2000, B1, B2.

4. Sonia Reyes, "Groove Tube," *Brandweek*, October 16, 2000, M111.

5. David Koenig, "Product Adds Softer Touch to Tissue Issue," *Fort Worth Star-Telegram*, January 17, 2001, C1.

6. Strauss, "Squeezing New from Old."

7. Gerry Khermouch, "Beefeater Gin Sets New Bottle, First Radio Ads on Renewal Drive," *Brandweek*, December 4, 2000, 17.

8. Strauss, "Squeezing New from Old."

9. Gordon Fairclough, "A Potentially Less Toxic Cigarette Gets National Push," *Wall Street Journal*, November 5, 2001, B1, B4. Used with permission.

10. "Acquire a Taste for Lower Cholesterol," *Fort Worth Star-Telegram*, June 25, 2001, 3D.

11. Anna Muoio, "GM Has a New Model for Change," *Fortune*, December 2000, 62–64.

12. Alex Taylor III, "Kellogg Cranks Up Its Idea Machine," *Fortune*, July 5, 1999, 181–182.

13. Reyes, "Groove Tube."

14. "Phytol Products Take Market Test," *Food Ingredients News*, August 2001, online.

15. Philip Brasher, "Teens Sample Milk from Vending Machines," *Fort Worth Star-Telegram*, April 5, 2001, 10A.

16. John Gaffney, "How Do You Feel about a $44 Tooth-Bleaching Kit?" *Business 2.0*, October 2001, 125–127.

17. Ibid.

18. Roy Attaway, "Man with the Plan," *Sea Ray Living*, Summer 2001, 46–52.

19. James Daly, "Restart, Redo, Recharge," *Business 2.0*, May 1, 2001, 11.

20. Holstein, "DaimlerChrysler's Net Designs."

CHAPTER 10

1. Jeffery A. Tannenbaum, "Beverage Marketers See Refreshing Distribution Possibilities," *Wall Street Journal*, May 29, 2001, B2. Used with permission.

2. "Dell Seizes No. 1 Market Position in U.S. Corporate Desktop PC Sales," September 10, 1997, Dell Computer Corporation press release, http://www.dell.com.

3. Nicole Harris, " 'Private Exchanges' May Allow B-to-B Commerce to Thrive After All," *Wall Street Journal*, March 16, 2001, B1; Michael Totty, "The Next Phase," *Wall Street Journal*, May 21, 2001, R8.

4. Amy Merrick and Emily Nelson, "Sears Says Stores Won't Sell Makeup, A Setback for Avon's New Line," *Wall Street Journal*, July 11, 2001, B1.

5. Gary McWilliams and Kortney Stringer, "Dell Tries Selling in Kiosks, On

TV as PC Sales Drop," *Wall Street Journal*, December 20, 2001, B1.

6. Wade Lambert, "Publisher Puts Story Machines in London Tube," *Wall Street Journal*, February 22, 2001, B1.

7. Nick Wingfield, "Amazon Links with Circuit City to Boost Its Electronic Business," *Wall Street Journal*, August 21, 2001, B4; Wingfield and Amy Merrick, "Amazon Sets Citibank Deal, Expands Target Pact," *Wall Street Journal*, November 6, 2001, B8.

8. Matthew Schifrin, "Partner or Perish," *Forbes Best of the Web*, May 21, 2001, 26; Jonathan Eig, "H.J. Heinz, Japan's Kagome Agree to Investments as Part of Alliance," *Wall Street Journal*, July 26, 2001, B11.

9. Jonathan Welsh, "Auto Makers Now 'Slam' Cars Right in the Factory," *Wall Street Journal*, October 30, 2001, B1.

10. David Frederick Ross, *Competing Through Supply Chain Management: Creating Market-Winning Strategies Through Supply Chain Partnerships* (New York: Chapman & Hall, 1998), 9–12.

11. Matthew Boyle, "Supply Chains Get Sexy," *Fortune*, December 12, 2001, 272.

12. Owen Keates, "Flow Control," *Management*, March 2001, 28.

13. Rob Wherry, "Ice Cream Wars: Dreyer's Conquered Supermarket Freezers. Now It's Going After the Corner Store," *Forbes*, May 28, 2001, 160.

14. Karen Lundegaard, "Bumpy Ride," *Wall Street Journal*, May 21, 2001, R21.

15. Leigh Muzslay, "Shoes That Morph from Sneakers to Skates Are Flying Out of Stores," *Wall Street Journal*, July 26, 2001, B1.

16. Shelly Branch, "P&G Buys Iams: Will Pet-Food Fight Follow?" *Wall Street Journal*, August 12, 1999, B1, B4.

17. Evan Ramstad, "Inside Radio Shack's Surprising Turnaround," *Wall Street Journal*, June 8, 1999, B1, B16.

18. Daniel Machalba, "High-speed Grain Terminals Bode Change for Rural U.S.," *Wall Street Journal*, December 26, 2001, B2.

19. G. Bruce Knecht, "Independent Bookstores Are Suing Borders Group and Barnes & Noble," *Wall Street Journal*, March 19, 1998, B10.

20. Leslie Kaufman, "Luxury's Old Guard, Battered by New Realities," *New York Times* on-line, December 16, 2001.

21. Ellen Neuborne, "Big Brands (Small Companies)," *Business Week*, August 13, 2001, 12.

22. Laura M. Holson, "Military Contractors Set to Begin Rare Experiment in Cooperation," *New York Times* on-line, December 17, 2001.

23. Faith Keenan, "The Marines Learn New Tactics—From Wal-Mart," *Business Week*, December 24, 2001, 74.

24. Norihiko Shirouzu, "Fickle Consumers Force Auto Makers to Be More Flexible," *Wall Street Journal*, September 10, 2001, B8.

25. Carlita Vitzthum, "Just-in-Time Fashion," *Wall Street Journal*, May 18, 2001, B1; Julie Creswell, "Confessions of a Fashion Victim," *Fortune*, December 10, 2001, 48.

26. Thomas A. Foster, "3PL's Serve Up Supply Chain Innovation," *Logistics Management & Distribution Report*, November 1999.

27. Nick Wingfield, "In the Beginning . . . ," *Wall Street Journal*, May 21, 2001, R18.

28. Stephanie Strom, "A Brighter Holiday (If the Goods Hold Out)," *New York Times* on-line, December 9, 2001.

29. Ross, *Competing Through Supply Chain Management*, 232.

30. Russ Dixon, "Tomorrow's Warehouse," *Snack Food & Wholesale Bakery*, May 2000, TD10.

31. Anna Wilde Mathews, "Cargo in Ships Offers Clues to What Will Go under Tree," *Wall Street Journal*, August 6, 1997, B1.

32. Greg Ip, "As Security Worries Intensify, Companies See Efficiencies Erode," *Wall Street Journal*, October 24, 2001, A1.

33. James Aaron Cooke, "Clicks and Mortar," *Logistics Management & Distribution Report*, January 31, 2000.

34. James Aaron Cooke, "Making the Global Connection," *Logistics Management & Distribution Report*, June 1999.

35. Caitlin Kelly, "Rolling Onward," *Supply Chain Management* on-line, September 30, 2001.

36. Renee Boucher Ferguson, "Outsourcing Supply Chains," *eWeek*, April 2, 2001, 17.

37. "Ford Hands Off Vehicle Delivery to Third Party," *Logistics Management & Distribution Report*, March 2000.

38. Michael Selz, "Outsourcing Firms Venture Beyond Primary Functions," *Wall Street Journal*, June 26, 2001, B2.

39. Don Clark, "Canceled Programs: Software Is Becoming an Online Service, Shaking Up an Industry," *Wall Street Journal*, July 21, 1999, A1, A6.

40. George Anders, "Ebay, E-Stamp in Tie-Up to Market Online Postage," *Wall Street Journal*, January 12, 2000, B6.

41. Rhonda L. Rundle, "New Battlefield for E-Tickets: Home Printers," *Wall Street Journal*, February 17, 2000, B1, B4; Bruce Orwall, "Six Theater Chains Will Join in Venture to Sell Movie Tickets via Web, Phone," *Wall Street Journal*, March 3, 2000, B4.

42. Martin Peers, "Video on Demand Arrives—Sort Of," *Wall Street Journal*, January 29, 2001, B1.

43. Nick Wingfield, "Digital Video Recorders Stir Up a New Battle," *Wall Street Journal*, December 17, 2001, B4; Jon Healy, "Studios Spur Measures to Thwart Digital Piracy," *Los Angeles Times*, January 18, 2002, C1; Amy Harmon, "A Wave of Video Piracy," *San Diego Union-Tribune*, February 11, 2002; Scott Wooley, "Steal This Movie," *Forbes*, February 18, 2001, 66.

44. Ken Bensinger, "Can You Spot the Fake?" *Wall Street Journal*, February 16, 2001, W1; Todd Zaun and Karby Leggett, "Motorcycle Makers from Japan Discover Piracy Made in China," *Wall Street Journal*, July 25, 2001, A1.

45. Alejandro Reyes, "Against a World of Giants," *AsiaWeek* wire report, February 2, 2001; Zaun and Leggett, "Motorcycle Makers from Japan Discover Piracy Made in China;" "Meeting of the Minds," *Supply Chain Management Review* on-line, September 30, 2001; Andrew Tanzer, "Chinese Walls," *Forbes*, November 12, 2001, 74.

46. Louis Uchitelle, "Globalization Marches On, As U.S. Eases Up on the Reins," *New York Times* on-line, December 17, 2001.

47. Jon E. Hilsenrath, "Globalization Persists in Precarious New Age," *Wall Street Journal*, December 31, 2001, A1.

48. Kevin Hogan, "Borderline Savings," *Business 2.0*, May 17, 2001, 34. © 2001 Time Inc. All rights reserved.

49. Richard Gibson, "Merchants Mull the Long and the Short of Lines," *Wall Street Journal*, September 3, 1998, B1, B4.

50. Neal Templin, "Electronic Kiosks Check In Guests at More Hotels," *Wall Street Journal*, February 16, 1999, B1, B4.

51. Martha Brannigan, "Cruise Lines Go Online—To Tout Travel Agents," *Wall Street Journal*, August 23, 2001, B1.

52. Deborah Lohse, "Allstate Plans Direct Insurance Sales by Phone, Internet," *Wall Street Journal*, November 11, 1999, B12

53. Patrick Barta, "Home Rules," *Wall Street Journal*, October 29, 2001, R12.

54. Chuck Martin, "Oprah Fans Scoop Up Graeter's," *Cincinnati Enquirer*, June 4, 2002, on-line.

CHAPTER 11

1. Vivian Chu, "Hip Goods, Enticing Stores: How Target Beat Kmart," *Reuters* on-line, February 4, 2002; Lee Clifford, "Getting Malled," *Fortune*, December 10, 2001, 114; Alice Z. Cuneo, "On Target," *Advertising Age*, December 11, 2000; http://www.target.com.

2. Karen J. Sack, "Massive Retail Industry Propels U.S. Economy," *Standard & Poor's Industry Surveys,* November 25, 1999, 5.

3. U.S. Census Bureau, Monthly Retail Trade Report, 2001.

4. David Schulz, "The Nation's Biggest Retail Companies," *Stores* on-line, July 1, 2001.

5. Ibid.

6. David Schultz, "The Definitive Ranking of the Nation's Biggest Specialty Chains," *Stores* on-line, August 2001.

7. Pamela Sebastian Ridge, "Chico's Scores Big with Its 'Nonjudgmental' Sizes," *Wall Street Journal*, March 8, 2001, B1.

8. Leigh Gallagher, "Rebound," *Forbes*, May 3, 1999, 60.

9. Maureen C. Carini, "Retailing: Supermarkets and Drugstores," *Standard & Poor's Industry Surveys*, vol. 166, no. 14, sec. 1, April 2, 1998, 12–13.

10. Joel A. Baglole, "Loblaw Supermarkets Add Fitness Clubs to Offerings," *Wall Street Journal*, December 27, 1999, B4.

11. Alexei Barrionuevo and Ann Zimmerman, "Lastest Supermarket Special —Gasoline," *Wall Street Journal*, April 30, 2001, B1.

12. Carini, "Retailing."

13. Matt Nannery, "Pigging Out," *Chain Store Age*, July 1999, 77.

14. Carini, "Retailing."

15. Wal-Mart Web site, http://www.walmart.com.

16. Emily Nelson, "Overhauling Its Web Site, Wal-Mart Will Push Toys and Electronics," *Wall Street Journal*, October 1, 1999, B1, B4.

17. Schulz, "The Nation's Biggest Retail Companies."

18. Tony Lisanti, "Extreme Segment, Extreme Growth," *Discount Store News*, July 26, 1999, 13.

19. Company News Release, "Toys "R" Us Reports Fourth Quarter and 2000 Fiscal Year Results," March 7, 2001.

20. Ann Zimmerman, "Taking Aim at Costco, Sam's Club Marshals Diamonds and Pearls," *Wall Street Journal*, August 9, 2001, A1.

21. Ray A. Smith, "Outlet Centers Go Upmarket with Amenities," *Wall Street Journal*, June 6, 2001, B12.

22. National Restaurant Association, "Industry at a Glance," January 24, 2002.

23. Eatzi's Market and Bakery Web site at http://www.eatzis.com.

24. Rodney Ho, "Vending Machines Make Change," *Wall Street Journal*, July 7, 1999, B1, B4.

25. Cathleen Egan, "Vending-Machine Technology Matures, Offering Branded Foods, Convenience," *Wall Street Journal*, December 13, 2001, B13.

26. Ibid.; Dow Jones Newswire, "Pepsi Plans to Launch New Vending Machines That Take Credit Cards," December 13, 2001.

27. Nigel Powell, "PC Salesmen Go Door to Door," *The Times* (London), July 16, 1997, 6; "Reaching Out to Small-Town USA: Move Over Amway, PC Sales Firm Hand Technologies Adds Hi-Tech Touch," *South China Morning Post*, May 12, 1998, 8; Barbara Carton, "PCs Replace Lettuce Tubs at Sales Parties," *Wall Street Journal*, March 26, 1997, B1; "Hand Technologies: Background Information," *M2 Presswire*, May 2, 1997; Chad Kaydo, "Are PCs Like Tupperware? *Sales & Marketing Management*, June 1998, 20.

28. Elizabeth Lee, "Parties That Sell," *Atlanta Journal-Constitution*, September 6, 2001, BE12.

29. Dennis Berman, "Is the Bell Tolling for Door-to-Door Selling? *Business Week*, November 1, 1999, 58–60; Rachel Beck, "Amway Puts Direct Selling Model Online," *Marketing News*, March 29, 1999, 12.

30. Amy Lo, "Selling Dreams the Mary Kay Way," *AsiaWeek*, June 29, 2001.

31. Dell Computer Web site, http://www.dell.com/us/en/gen/corporate.

32. QVC Web site, http://www.qvc.com.

33. The Online Group of the National Retail Federation's Web site, http://www.shop.org/learn/stats.

34. Ibid.

35. CDNow Web site, http://www.CDNow.com.

36. Amazon.com Web site, http://www.amazon.com.

37. The Online Group of the National Retail Federation Web site, http://www.shop.org; Ernst & Young press release, "Despite Dot.com Woes, On-line Retailing Growth in 2000 Confirmed by New Ernst & Young Global Study," *Business Wire*, January 15, 2002; "Amazon.com: The First Global Cyber-Brand," *Ernst & Young Global Online Retail Report* at Stores on-line, January 2000, 24; Amazon.com press release, "Amazon.com Announces 4th Quarter Profit," http://www.amazon.com, January 22, 2002.

38. Timothy Henderson, "Multi-Channel Retailers Increasingly Rely on Internet-Based Kiosk to Bridge Gap Between Channels," *Stores* on-line, October 1, 2001.

39. Alexandra Peers and Nick Wingfield, "Sotheby's, eBay Team Up to Sell Fine Art Online," *Wall Street Journal*, January 31, 2002, B8.

40. McDonald's Corporation, Inside the U.S. Franchising Fact Sheet, http://www.mcdonalds.com/corporate/franchise/.

41. International Franchise Association Web site, http://www.franchise.org.

42. Domino's Pizza Web site, http://www.dominos.com/.

43. Brian O'Keefe, "Global Brands," *Fortune*, November 26, 2001, 104.

44. Louise Lee, "Gap: Missing That Ol' Mickey Magic," *Business Week*, October 29, 2001, 86–88.

45. Michael Totty, "Making the Sale," *Wall Street Journal*, September 24, 2001, R6.

46. Rebecca Quick, "Ann Taylor Gets Its Groove Back," *Wall Street Journal*, February 16, 1999, B1, B4.

47. Patrick McGuire, "The Analytics Divide," *Stores* on-line, October 2001.

48. Eleena De Lisser, "Online Retailers Slice and Dice Niches Thinner Than Julienne Fries," *Wall Street Journal*, November 29, 1999, B1, B6.

49. "An Exclusive Club," *Chain Store Age*, October 1998.

50. Jack Neff, "Wal-Mart Stores Go Private (Label)," *Advertising Age*, November 29, 1999, 1, 34–38; Emily Nelson, "For Wal-Mart, A Soap War Looms against Mighty P&G," *Wall Street Journal*, August 6, 1999, B1, B3.

51. Alice Z. Cuneo, "On Target," *Advertising Age*, December 11, 2000, 1.

52. Dean Starkman, "Mall Developers Envision Shopping Paradise, And It's Called Las Vegas," *Wall Street Journal*, July 11, 2001, B1.

53. Dean Starkman, "The Mall, Without the Haul," *Wall Street Journal*, July 25, 2001, B1.

54. Calmetta Y. Coleman, "Making Malls (Gasp!) Convenient," *Wall Street Journal*, February 8, 2000, B1, B4.

55. Anne Faircloth, "Value Retailers Go Dollar for Dollar," *Fortune*, July 6, 1998, 164–166.

56. Calmetta Cloeman, "Kohl's Retail Racetrack," *Wall Street Journal*, March 13, 2001, B1.

57. Emily Nelson, "Why Wal-Mart Sings, 'Yes, We Have Bananas!'" *Wall Street Journal*, October 6, 1998, B1, B4.

58. James Lardner, "Branching Out," *Business 2.0*, November 2001, 137.

59. Kate Murphy, "A Sales Pitch Right Under Your Nose," *New York Times*, September 13, 1998, 8.

60. "Playful Touches Dress Up the Box," *Chain Store Age*, June 1998, 110–111.

61. Timothy P. Henderson, "Perception That Some Merchants Practice Racial Profiling Generates Debate," *Stores* on-line, June 2001; Tanya Eiserer, "A Question of Security," *Fort Worth Star-Telegram*, October 28, 2001, 1; Associated Press Newswires, "Protesters Rally outside Store Where Accused Shoplifter Died," *Associated Press*, on-line, February 18, 2001.

62. Chad Terhune, "Home Depot's Home Improvement," *Wall Street Journal*, March 8, 2001, B1.

63. Totty, "Making the Sale."

64. John C. Koopman, "Successful Global Retailers: A Rare Breed," *Canadian Manager*, Spring 2000, 22.

65. Teri Agins, "Brooks Brothers Wines, Dines Potential New Customers," *Wall Street Journal*, September 7, 2001, B4; Agins, "Trunk Show Chic," *Wall Street Journal*, February 5, 2001, B1.

66. "More Consumers Shopping at Super Centers," *Chain Store Age* on-line, February 4, 2002.

67. Susan Reda, "On-line Retail Grows Up," *Stores* on-line, February 2002.

68. Jack Neff, "Dawn of the Online Icebox," *Advertising Age*, March 15, 1999, 7.

CHAPTER 12

1. Dale Buss, "The British Are Coming!" *Sales & Marketing Management*, August 2001, 32–40; Verne Gray, "Newsstand Seductress," *Brandweek*, October 23, 2000, M80; Jill Feiwell and Bill Higgins, "Maxim Maxed," *Daily Variety*, August 14, 2000, 20; http://www.maximonline.com.

2. Betsy McKay, "Gatorade Seeks to Dominate Sports-Drink Realm with Ads," *Wall Street Journal*, June 11, 2002, B4.

3. Frank G. Bingham, Jr., Charles J. Quigley, Jr., and Elaine M. Notarantonio, "The Use of Communication Style in a Buyer–Seller Dyad: Improving Buyer–Seller Relationships," *Proceedings: Association of Marketing Theory and Practice, 1996 Annual Meeting, Hilton Head, South Carolina, March 1996*, 188–195.

4. Michael Beverland, "Relationship Selling and the Selling Dyad," *Journal of Personal Selling & Sales Management*, Summer 2001, 207.

5. Frank Witsil, "Spam I Am," *Tampa Tribune*, February 9, 2002, 1; Frances Katz, "Putting the Lid on SPAM: Almost Everybody Hates the Kudzu of E-mail, But There's No Magic Formula," *Atlanta Journal and Constitution*, August 5, 2001, Q1; "Privacy Action," *Advertising Age*, October 15, 2001, 14; Donna Gillin, "Privacy Issues Take Center Stage in 2001," *Marketing Research*, Spring 2001, 36; William M. Savino and Stephen J. Smirti, Jr., "Privacy Please!" *Marketing Management*, Winter 2000, 46.

6. Jack Neff, "Male Mystique Rises a Degree," *Advertising Age*, December 31, 2001, 3.

7. Sally Beatty, "HBO Marches into Battle," *Wall Street Journal*, July 18, 2001, B1, B4; "Brothers Roll Out," *Broadcasting & Cable*, September 17, 2001, 24.

8. Stephanie Thompson, "Marketers Embrace Latest Health Claims," *Advertising Age*, February 28, 2000, 20–22.

9. Ibid.

10. "Promo Shorts," *Marketing Magazine*, September 3, 2001, P4.

11. Kate Fitzgerald, "Branding Face to Face," *Advertising Age*, October 21, 2002, 46.

12. Bill Adams, "Talking about Integrated Communications," *Public Relations Tactics*, February 2001, 26.

13. Sharon Waxman, "Spidey Toys, Yes." *Washington Post*, May 2, 2002, C4; John Lippman, "Record Debut for 'Spider-Man' Signals Hollywood's New Rules," *Wall Street Journal*, May 6, 2002, A1.

14. Lynne Eagle, Philip Kitchen, Ken Hyde, Wina Fourie, and Mani Padisetti, "Perceptions of Integrated Marketing Communications among Marketers and Ad Agency Executives in New Zealand," *International Journal of Advertising*, February 1999, 79–94.

15. Karen Raugust, "Marketing 1000: Nestlé Crunch," *Advertising Age*, October 8, 2001, S10–S30.

16. Philip J. Kitchen, "Marketing Communications Renaissance," *Internal Journal of Advertising*, 12 (1993), 367–386.

17. Amy Shipley, "Extreme Winter Games: Olympics Targeting a Younger Audience," *Washington Post*, November 25, 2001, A01.

18. Ibid.

19. Kitchen, "Marketing Communications Renaissance," 372.

20. Kellie Searle, "The Brown Trucks Are Coming! The Brown Trucks Are Coming! UPS Joins the Global Revolution," *Sales, Advertising & Marketing*, November 1, 2001, on line; Allyson L. Stewart-Allen, "Sense of Identity Crucial for Fast Food Worldwide," *Marketing News*, November 19, 2001, 12; Thomas T. Semon, "Cutting Corners in Language Risky Business," *Marketing News*, 9; Thomas J. Madden, Kelly H. Hewett, and Martin S. Roth, "Managing Images in Different Cultures: A Cross-National Study of Color Meanings and Preferences," *Journal of International MKT*, vol. 8, no. 4, 2000; Yumiko Ono, "U.S. Superstores Find Japanese Are a Hard Sell," *Wall Street Journal*, February 14, 2000, B1, B4.

21. The AIDA concept is based on the classic research of E. K. Strong, Jr., as theorized in *The Psychology of Selling and Advertising* (New York: McGraw-Hill, 1925) and "Theories of Selling," *Journal of Applied Psychology*, 9 (1925), 75–86.

22. Thomas E. Barry and Daniel J. Howard, "A Review and Critique of the Hierarchy of Effects in Advertising," *International Journal of Advertising* 9 (1990), 121–135.

23. Kim Cleland, "Marketing 1000: Poo-Chi," *Advertising Age*, October 8, 2001, S10–S30.

24. "New Loyalty Program Earns 'Grocery Miles,'" *MMR*, May 8, 2000, 58.

25. Jeffery A. Trachtenberg, "Marketing Tactics Help Canny Writer Push His Thrillers," *Wall Street Journal*, May 14, 2002, A1.

26. Hilary Chura "Marketing 1000: Smirnoff Ice," *Advertising Age*, October 8, 2001, S10–S30.

27. Elana Harris, "Standing Tall," *Sales & Marketing Management*, December 2000, 84.

28. Michael Beverland, "Contextual Influences and the Adoption and Practice of Relationship Selling in a Business-to-Business Setting: An Exploratory Study," *Journal of Personal Selling & Sales Management*, Summer 2001, 207.

29. Richard Morrison, "The Business Process of Customer Retention and Loyalty," *Customer Interaction Solutions*, October 2001, 4.

30. "The Right Questions and Attitudes Can Beef Up Your Sales, Improve Customer Retention," *Selling*, June 2001, 3.

31. Andy Cohen, "Copy Cats," *Sales & Marketing Management*, August 2000, 50–58.

32. Erika Rasmusson, "How to Manage Long Term Leads," *Sales & Marketing Management*, January 1998, 77.

33. Roger Brooksbank, "The New Model of Personal Selling: Micro-Marketing," *Journal of Personal Selling & Sales Management*, Spring 1995, 61–66; Donald W. Jackson, Jr., "Relationship Selling: The Personalization of Relationship Marketing," *Asia-Australia Marketing Journal*, August 1994, 45–54.

34. Jean Halliday, "Ford Finds E-Leads Productive," *Advertising Age*, January 22, 2001, 28.

35. Sarah Lorge, "The Best Way to Prospect," *Sales & Marketing Management*, January 1988, 80; Tricia Campbell, "What's a Referral Worth to You?" *Sales & Marketing Management*, September 1997, 103.

36. Alf Nucifora, "Need Leads? Try a Networking Group," *Business News New Jersey*, November 14, 2000, 22.

37. Mike Grebb, "The Customer Connection: Living Up to Your Sales Pitch," March 1, 2001.

38. "Leads Are a Terrible Thing to Waste," *Sales & Marketing Management*, August 1997, 108; Center for Strategic Communication.

39. Marvin A. Jolson and Thomas R. Wortruba, "Selling and Sales Management in Action: Prospecting: A New Look at This Old Challenge," *Journal of Personal Selling & Sales Management*, Fall 1992, 59–66.

40. Janelle Rice, "Show and Sell: Filling the Sales Manager's Shoes," *Sales, Advertising, and Marketing*, July 2001.

41. Robyn Griggs, "Qualifying Leads Online," *Sales & Marketing Management*, July 1997, 68.

42. Marvin A. Jolson, "Broadening the Scope of Relationship Selling," *Journal of Personal Selling and Sales Management*, Fall 1997, 75.

43. Jeff Bailey, "Tapping Local Markets Can Pay Off," *Wall Street Journal*, May 14, 2002, B4.

44. Adapted from Bob Kimball, *Successful Selling* (Chicago: American Marketing Association, 1994).

45. "Five Steps to Wrapping Up a Sales Call," *Sales & Marketing Management*, January 1998, 75.

46. Jolson, "Broadening the Scope of Relationship Selling."

47. Scott Cressman, "Eight Tips for Highly Effective Presentations," *Sales, Advertising, and Marketing*, May 1, 2001.

48. Colleen Cooper, "Overcoming Last Minute Objections," *Sales & Marketing Management*, March 1997, 32; Sarah

Lorge, "How to Close a Deal," *Sales & Marketing Management*, April 1998, 84.

49. Julia Chang, "Negotiating Tip," *Sales & Marketing Management*, 30.

50. Michelle Marchetti, "Hey Buddy, Can You Spare $113.25?" *Sales & Marketing Management*, August 1997, 69–77.

51. Cliff Ennico, "Cynical? Insecure? Ruthless? You're Hired. Essential Characteristics for Sales Success," *Sales, Advertising, and Marketing*, May 1, 2001.

52. "Can Your Reps Sell Overseas?" *Sales & Marketing Management*, February 1998, 110.

53. David Garfinkel, "The E-Vangelist: Autoresponse Marketing," *Sales & Marketing Management*, May 2001, 27.

54. Anna Wilde Mathews, "Clear Channel Pushes One-Stop Buys," *Wall Street Journal*, May 22, 2002, B6.

55. Erika Rasmusson, "The 10 Traits of Top Salespeople," *Sales & Marketing Management*, August 1999, 34–37.

56. America's 25 Best Sales Forces: Best at Sales Training," *Sales & Marketing Management*, July 2000, 68.

57. Gabriel Landriault, "In Class, Online," *Computing Canada*, March 1, 2001, 11.

58. Arun Sharma, Customer Satisfaction–Based Incentive Systems: Some Managerial and Salesperson Considerations," *Journal of Personal Selling & Sales Management*, April 1997, 61.

59. Cohen, "The Traits of Great Sales Forces."

60. Cliff Ennico, "Ideas@work: Thanks for Your Service, Now Go Away," *Sales, Advertising, and Marketing*, May 1, 2001.

61. Libby Estelle, "Rewarding and Improving Performance Motivate Employees and Customers to Grab the Brass Ring," *Sales & Marketing Manage-ment*, October 2001, S1–S4.

62. James Champy, "Waiting for Change," *Sales & Marketing Manage-ment*, August 2001, 30.

63. Kathleen Cholewka, "E-Market Stats," *Sales & Marketing Management*, September 2001, 21.

64. "Success One Account at a Time," *Business 2.0*, April 2001, http://www. business2.com/archives.

65. Jim Kirk, "Boise Taking Its Business Personally, But Technology Vital in Catering to Customers," January 6, 2002, C1.

CHAPTER 13

1. Kenneth Hein, "A Bull's Market," *Brandweek*, May 28, 2001, 21; Hein, "Red Bull Charges Ahead," *Brandweek*, October 15, 2001, M38; Rebecca Flass and Jack Feuer, "Red Bull Hands Media to Lunch, Its Creative Shop," *Adweek Western Edition*, September 10, 2001, 5; "Turn Up the Juice," *Drug Store News*, July 23, 2001, 37; Hillary Chura, "Grabbing Bull by Tail," *Advertising Age*, June 11, 2001, 4; David Noonan and Kevin Peraino, "Red Bull's Good Buzz, *Newsweek*, May 14, 2001, 39.

2. "Domestic Advertising Spending Totals by Media Bought in 2001 and 2000," http://www.adage.com/datacenter/ marketing, 2002.

3. U.S. Department of Commerce. Bureau of the Census, *Statistical Abstract of the United States* (Washington DC: Government Printing Office, December 2000), 420.

4. "Advertising to Sales Ratios by Industry: Year 2001 Data," http://www. adage.com/datacenter/marketing, 2002.

5. Betsy McKay, "Pepsi Readies Kickoff for Sierra Mist," *Wall Street Journal*, January 7, 2003, 50.

6. Tom Reichert, "Sexy Ads Target Young Adults," *USA Today Magazine*, May 2001, 50.

7. Amitava Chattaopadhyay and Kunal Basu, "Humor in Advertising: The Moderating Role of Prior Brand Evaluation," *Journal of Marketing Research*, November 1990, 466–476.

8. Rajiv Grover and V. Srinivasan, "Evaluating the Multiple Effects of Retail Promotions on Brand Loyalty and Brand Switching Segments," *Journal of Marketing Research*, February 1992, 76–89; see also S. P. Raj, "The Effects of Advertising on High and Low Loyalty Consumer Segments," *Journal of Consumer Research*, June 1982, 77–89.

9. Piu-Wing Tam, "H-P Launches Ads to Repair Image," *Wall Street Journal*, November 18, 2002, B3.

10. Jennifer Ordonoz, "Harrah's Focuses on Responsibility," *Wall Street Journal*, May 23, 2002, B2.

11. Gordon Fairclough, "Philip Morris Tells Smokers 'Light' Cigarettes Aren't Safer," *Wall Street Journal*, November 20, 2002, B1.

12. Tobi Elkin, "Microsoft to Focus on Experience," *Advertising Age*, February 26, 2001, 26.

13. Tobi Elkin, "Window XP's $200 Million Launch Kicks Off," *AdAge.com*, October 11, 2001.

14. Piu-Wing Tam, "New Apple Campaign Targets Windows User," *Wall Street Journal*, June 1, 2002, B1.

15. Sarah Ellison and John Carrey-rou, "An Unlikely Rival Challenges L'Oreal in Beauty Market," *Wall Street Journal*, January 9, 2003, A1.

16. Amy Merrick, "Target and Kmart Both Claim Victory in Spat over Ads," *Wall Street Journal*, September 4, 2001, B6.

17. Daniel Golden and Suzanne Vranica, "Duracell's Duck Ad will Carry Disclaimer," *Wall Street Journal*, February 7, 2002, B7.

18. http://www.adageglobal.com, "Absolut Vodka Must Pull Campaign in Italy," February 2, 2001.

19. http://www.adageglobal.com, "Yahoo! Korea Complains about Comparative Ads," September 21, 2001.

20. Fahad S. Al-Olyan and Kiran Karade, *Journal of Advertising*, Fall 2000, 69.

21. Jorge A. Monjara, "Wal-Mart Quits Retailers Group," *Advertising Age*, October 21, 2002, 16.

22. Betsy McKay and Suzanne Vranica, "New Coke Ads with Celebrities Will Bow Today," *Wall Street Journal*, January 9, 2003, B1.

23. Don Clark, "Intel and AMD Switch Themes with New Ads," *Wall Street Journal*, September 19, 2002, B8; Tobi Elkin, "Intel Rolls Out Lifestyle Effort," *Advertising Age*, September 16, 2002, 3.

24. Sarah Ellison, "Reckitt Hopes Product Gels in U.S.," *Wall Street Journal*, January 1, 2003, B6.

25. Ibid.

26. Ibid.

27. Laura Q. Hughes and Wendy Davis, "Revival of the Fittest," *Advertising Age*, March 12, 2001, 18–19.

28. Suzanne Vranica and Vanessa O'Connell, "Super Bowl Ads Go for the Laughs," *Wall Street Journal*, January 9, 2003, B7.

29. Roger Thurow, "Shtick Ball: In Global Drive, Nike Finds Its Brash Ways Don't Always Pay Off," *Wall Street Journal*, May 5, 1997, A1, A10.

30. Erin White, "German Ads Get More Daring, But Some Firms Aren't Pleased" *Wall Street Journal*, B6.

31. Russell Abratt and Deanna Cowan, "Client Agency Perspectives of Information Needs for Media Planning," *Journal of Advertising Research*, November 1999, 37.

32. "Domestic Advertising Spending Totals," and "Coen's Spending Totals for 2001," http://www.AdAge.com/datacenter.

33. "The 'A' List," *Advertising Age*, October 21, 2002, S2.

34. "Radio: No Longer an Advertising Afterthought," *Standard & Poor's Industry Surveys*, July 20, 1995, M36; Rebecca Pirto, "Why Radio Thrives," *American Demographics*, May 1994, 40–46.

35. Edmund O. Lawler, "B-to-B Skewed Cable Now Mainstream Buy," *Advertising Age*, May 7, 2001, 32.

36. "Ad Age's Fall 2002 Prime-Time Pricing Survey," *Advertising Age*, September 30, 2002, 58.

37. Vranica and O'Connell, "Super Bowl Ads."

38. Jim Edwards, "The Art of the Infomercial," *Brandweek*, September 3, 2001, 14.

39. Barbara Martinez, "City Sight: Giant Ads Spring from Holes in the Ground," *Wall Street Journal*, August 18, 1999, B1, B10.

40 News release, "FBI Using Billboard Campaign for Recruiting New Agents," *Outdoor Advertising Association of America*, July 22, 2002.

41. "Top 10 Advertising Categories in 2000," *Outdoor Advertising Association of America*.

42. Erin White, "Clear Channel Poland Battles Harsh Climate for Outdoor Ads," *Wall Street Journal*, July 10, 2002, B5.

43. Erin White, "Outdoor Ads May Get Indoor Rival," *Wall Street Journal*, July 17, 2002.

44. *Absolut Collectors Society Newsletter* issue 237, July 31, 2000.

45. "Internet Advertising Revenue Holds Steady As All Ad Sectors Decline," http://www.iab.com, December 4, 2001.

46. Vanessa O'Connell, "E-mail Ads Just Don't Click with Customers," *Wall Street Journal*, July 2, 2002, B2.

47. Tobi Elkin, "IAB Moves Away from the Online Banner," http://www.AdAge.com, December 11, 2002.

48. Erin White, "Marketers Tap Interactive DVDs," *Wall Street Journal*, December 27, 2002, B2; Wayne Friedman, "Coming to a Theater near You: Targeted, Digital Ad Buying," *Advertising Age*, October 21, 2002, 4.

49. Lenore Skenazy, "No Escape from Ads, Even in the Backseat," *New York Daily News*, January 1, 2003, 23.

50. Cara Beardi, "Video Venue Joins the Line for Gas-Pump Advertising," *Advertising Age*, April 23, 2001, 8.

51. Suzanne Vranica, "Think Graffiti Is All That's Hanging in Subway Tunnels? Look Again," *Wall Street Journal*, April 4, 2001, B1, B4.

52. Skenazy, "No Escape from Ads."

53. Suzy Bashford, "Sorry Ladies, This Bit of Scots Beef Is Already Taken," *Marketing*, November 1, 2001, 56; Maryann Lorusso, "Sex and Sensibility," *Footwear News*, June 11, 2001, 6; Barbara Lippert, "Kinky R Us," *Adweek*, April 2, 2001, 20; David Hakala, "Mind Your Manners, Ad Writers," *Sm@rt Partner*, March 19, 2001; Michael Miller, "The Ploy of Sex," *Pittsburgh Business Times*, April 28, 2001, 22; Tom Reichert, "Sexy Ads Target Young Adults," *USA Today Magazine*, May 2001, 50; Lauren Booth, "I Have Become Lynda LeePotter, Reactionary and Scared of a Little Innuendo," *New Statesman*, July 16, 2001, 63; Alessandra Galloni, "Clampdown on 'Porno-Chic' Ads Is Pushed by French Authorities," *Wall Street Journal*, October 25, 2001, B4; Hillary Chura, "Spirited Sex," *Advertising Age*, July 9, 2001, 1.

54. Sara Teasdale, "Study Challenges Three-Plus Viewing Rule," *Business Marketing*, December 1995, 5; Hugh M. Cannon and Edward A. Riordan, "Effective Reach and Frequency: Does It Really Make Sense?" *Journal of Advertising Research*, March 1994, 19.

55. Cannon and Riordan, "Effective Reach and Frequency," 19; Erwin Ephron, "A New Media-Mix Strategy: As Advertisers Eye Obvious Decline of TV, Agencies Expand Options," *Advertising Age*, February 28, 2000, s10.

56. Kate Lynch and Horst Stripp, "Examination of Qualitative Viewing Factors for Optimal Advertising Strategies," *Journal of Advertising Research*, May 1999, 7.

57. Sally Beatty, "Ogilvy's TV-Ad Study Stresses 'Holding Power' Instead of Ratings," *Wall Street Journal*, June 4, 1999, B2.

58. Chuck Ross, "Study Finds Continuity vs. Flights," *Advertising Age*, April 19, 1999, B2.

59. Erwin Ephron, "Recency Planning: A New Media Approach," *Advertising Age*, July 1, 1999, 21.

60. Suzanne Vranica and Vaness O'Connell, " For Immediate Release!" *Wall Street Journal*, January 21, 2003, B1.

61. Jean Sherman Chatzky, "Whose Name Here? It Seems No Event Is Too Personal to Have a Corporate Sponsor," *Money*, October 1, 2001, 196.

62. Erik Battenberg, "Bronze Anvil 2002 Winners," *Tactics*, September 2002, 16.

63. Richard Linnett, "So Many Product Placements, Fox Calls It 'Immersion,'" http://www.AdAge.com, January 20, 2003; Wayne Friedman, "Product Placements Rise at CBS," *Advertising Age*, September 23, 2002.

64. Jeff Neff, "Norelco Joins James Bond Product Placement Stampede," http://www.AdAge.com, November 11, 2002.

65. Teri Agins, "Armani Touts Urban Chic with 'Shaft,'" *Wall Street Journal*, June 19, 2002, 16.

66. Michael Waldholz, "A Push for Diabetes Awareness," *Wall Street Journal*, November 14, 2002, D3.

67. Gabriel Kahn, "Soccer's FIFA Cries Foul As Ambushers Crash World Cup," *Wall Street Journal*, June 20, 2002, B1; Christopher Lawton, "Coors, Miller Try End Run on Bud's Ad, Block Super Bowl," *Wall Street Journal*, January 24, 2003, B1.

68. Peter Wonacott, "Chinese TV Discovers Product Placement," *Wall Street Journal*, January 26, 2000, B12, used with permission; Normandy Madden, "Sponsors Follow Twists of Chinese Soap Operas," *Advertising Age International*, January 1, 2000, 9.

69. Suzanne Vranica, "New Beetle Takes on a Bug Problem," *Wall Street Journal*, October 31, 2002, B8.

70. Christopher Lawton, "Brown-Forman Returns to Its Roots," *Wall Street Journal*, July 29, 2002, B10.

71. Michael Jay Polonsky, "Reevaluating Green Marketing: A Strategic Approach," *Business Horizons*, September/October 2001, 21.

72. Kathleen Cholewka, "The 5 Best E-Marketing Campaigns," *Sales & Marketing Management*, January 2001, 53.

73. Ibid.

74. Chris Barnett, "Crisis Communications Now: Three Views," *Tactics,* January 2003, 15.

75. George Anders, "eBay to Refund Millions after Outrage," *Wall Street Journal*, June 14, 1999, B8; George Anders, "eBay Scrambles to Repair Image after Big Crash," *Wall Street Journal*, June 14, 1999, B1, B4.

76. "2001 Annual Report: Industry Report 2001," *PROMO Magazine*.

77. Annual Report "Coupons: Wing Clipping," http://www.promomagazine. com, June 1, 2002.

78. Ibid.

79. "2001 Annual Report: Industry Report 2001."

80. Shelly Branch, "Crooner May Find New Audience in Barter Deal with Earth's Best," *Wall Street Journal*, January 25, 2001, B9.

81. Anne Kandra, "Bait and Rebate," *PC World*, September 2001, 45.

82. "Right Up Their Alley; McDonald's, Toys 'R' Us Share a Holiday Happy Meal," *PROMO Magazine*, December 1, 2001, 11.

83. Mark Lacek, "Loyalty Marketing No Ad Budget Threat," *Advertising Age*, October 23, 1995, 20.

84. Ginger Conlon, "True Romance," *Sales & Marketing Management*, May 1996, 85–90.

85. Liz Mullen, "NBA Teams Reward Fans with Loyalty Programs," *Washington Business Journal*, December 10, 1999, 22.

86. Amanda Beeler, "Heady Rewards for Loyalty: Cars, Trips and Hot Tickets Expand Offerings Beyond Store Merchandise for Retailers in Touch with Rich," *Advertising Age*, August 14, 2000, S8.

87. Vincent Alonzo, "Money Isn't Everything," *Sales & Marketing Management*, April 2000, 47–48.

88. "HGTV, Sears, Join Forces for House Giveaways," *Advertising Age*, February 7, 2000, 30.

89. "2001 Annual Report: Industry Report 2001."

90. Lafayette Jones, "Ethnic Product Sampling: The Hidden Opportunity," *Retail Merchandiser*, August 2001, 45.

91. Stephanie Fagnani, "A Taste of Success: The Practice of Product Sampling Combines Favorable Location, Product Innovation, Thorough Promotion and Timely Execution," *Supermarket News*, August 27, 2001, 33.

92. Tobi Elkin, "Free Samples to the First 300 Million," http://www.AdAge.com, December 4, 2002.

93. Miriam Jordan, "Fuel and Freebies," *Wall Street Journal*, June 10, 2002, B1.

94. Andy Cohen, "A Marketing Touchdown," *Sales & Marketing Management*, October 2001, 16.

95. Geoffrey A. Fowler, "When Free Samples Become Saviors," *Wall Street Journal*, August 14, 2001, B1, B4.

96. "Point-of-Purchase: $17 Billion," *PROMO Magazine,* October 29, 2001, 3.

97. Erin Strout, "Doctoring Sales," *Sales & Marketing Management*, May 2001, 53–60; Joseph P. Shapiro and Stacey Schultz, "Prescriptions: How Your Doctor Makes the Choice," *U.S. News & World Report*, February 19, 2001, 58; Bill Brubaker, "Drug Firms Still Lavish Pricey Gifts on Doctors; Ethics Debated as Freebies Flow," *Washington Post*, January 19, 2002, E01; Ed Susman, "U.S. Doctors Touchy on Topic of Pharmaceutical Gifts," *Medical Post,* July 17, 2001.

98. "MasterCard Unwraps Priceless Holiday Prizes," *PROMO Xtra,* November 5, 2001, 22.

99. Annual Report, "Interactive Marketing: The Tempo Slows," http://www.promomagazine.com, June 1, 2002.

100. Stephanie Thompson, "Frito-Lay Reports Doritos Online Ad Success." http://www.AdAge.com, November 18, 2002.

101. Roger O. Crocket, "Penny-Pinchers' Paradise," *Business Week*, January 22, 2001, EB12.

102. Deborah Cohen, "Burger King First to Serve Up Hamburger Miles," *Reuters Business Report*, January 13, 2002, 1.

103. Libby Estell, "Economic Incentives," *Sales & Marketing Manage-ment*, October 2001, S2–S4.

104. Ben Chapman, "The Trade Show Must Go On," *Sales & Marketing Management*, June 2001, 22.

CHAPTER 14

Notes for chapter 14 can be found with the chapter itself at http://lamb.swlearning.com.

CHAPTER 15

1. Christopher T. Heun, "Log Me On to the Ball Game—For a Price," *Informationweek.com,* April 2, 2001, 33. Used with permission.

2. "Cost-Conscious Shoppers Seek Secondhand," *USA Today*, March 14, 1996, B1.

3. "Retailers Are Giving Profits Away," *American Demographics*, June 1994, 14.

4. Ramaro Desuaju and Steven Shugan, "Strategic Service Pricing and Yield Management," *Journal of Marketing*, January 1999, 44–56.

5. Michael Mendano, "Priced to Perfection," *Business2.com*, March 6, 2001, 40–41.

6. "Your Room Costs $250 . . . No! $200 . . . No," *Wall Street Journal*, May 5, 1999, B1, B16.

7. Gordon Fairclough, "Governments Can Be Addicted to Cigarettes," *Wall Street Journal*, October 2, 2000, A1. Used with permission.

8. See Joseph Cannon and Christian Homburg, "Buyer-Supplier Relationships and Customer Firm Costs," *Journal of Marketing*, January 2001, 29–43.

9. Most of this section is taken from David Hamilton, "The Price Isn't Right," *Wall Street Journal*, February 12, 2001, R8, R10. Used with permission.

10. Ibid.

11. Ibid.

12. Ibid.

13. Gary Hamel, "Edison's Curse," *Fortune*, March 5, 2001, 175–178. See also Florian Zettlemeyer, "Expanding to the Internet: Pricing and Communications Strategies When Firms Compete on Multiple Channels," *Journal of Marketing Research*, August 2000, 292–308; and Subir Bandyopadhyay, Guang Bo Lin, and Yan Zhong, "Under the Gavel," *Marketing Management*, November/December 2001, 25–28.

14. "Price Buster," *Wall Street Journal*, July 17, 2000, R12.

15. "Value Driven," *Fortune*, May 1, 2000, 74.

16. "Stores' Demands Squeeze Apparel Companies," *Wall Street Journal*, July 15,

1997, B1, B12; Timothy Matanovicy, Gary Lilien, and Arvind Rangaswamy, "Engineering the Price-Value Relationship," *Marketing Management*, Spring 1999, 48–53.

17. Daniel Michaels, "No-Frills Irish Airline Flies High," *Wall Street Journal,* September 6, 2000, B1, B4 Used with permission.

18. "Sotheby's Chief Is Convicted of Price-Fixing," *Wall Street Journal*, December 6, 2001, B1, B4.

19. Charles Quigley and Elaine Notarantonio, "An Exploratory Investigation of Perceptions of Odd and Even Pricing," in *Developments in Marketing Science,* ed. Victoria Crittenden (Miami: Academy of Marketing Science, 1992), 306–309.

20. "Nine Cents of Separation," *American Demographics*, May 1998, 41.

21. "Three-for-$3 and Other Numerical Pitches Work Magic in Stores," *Wall Street Journal*, March 12, 1998, A1. See also Herman Simon and Robert Dolan, "Price Customization," *Marketing Management,* Fall 1998, 11–17; and Margaret Campbell, "Perceptions of Price Unfairness: Antecedents and Consequences," *Journal of Marketing Research*, May 1999, 187–199.

22. Vicki Morwitz, Eric Greenleaf, and Eric Johnson, "Divide and Prosper: Consumers' Reactions to Partitioned Prices," *Journal of Marketing Research*, November 1998, 453–463.

23. This material on price penalties is from Eugene Fram and Micheal McCarthy, "The True Price of Penalties," *Marketing Management,* Fall 1999, 49–54.

24. "Going, Going, Gone," *Business Week*, April 12, 1999, 30.

Bibliographies

CHAPTER 1

Try It

Joyceann Cooney-Curran, "All About 'Me': Noodé Provides a Fun Yet Effective Skin-Care Line to the 'Generation Me' Demographic," *Global Cosmetic Industry,* November 2000, 62; Andrea Grossman, "It's a Noodé for Skin Care," *WWD,* January 5, 2001, 13; ———, "Noodé Aims to Shield Sun's Rays," *WWD,* January 4, 2002, 10; ———, "Small Firms Win with Samples, Moxie," *WWD,* January 11, 2002, 10; "Noodé for the Me Generation," *Soap & Cosmetics*, November 2000, 72.

CHAPTER 2

Try It

Joseph J. Atick, *Business Week*, 14 January 2002, 75; "Why Visionics Is Flying Higher," *Business Week*, 14 January 2002, 42; "Mobile Recognition Device to Be Utilised by Winter Olympics Police," *Telecomworldwire*, 12 February 2002; C. A. Mangis, "It's Written All Over Your Face," *PC Magazine*, 15 January 2002, 25; M. Edmunds, "Biometrics Still in Its Infancy," *Financial Times*, 13 March 2002, 11; http://www.visionics.com.

CHAPTER 3

Try It

David Greenfield, "Israeli Entrepreneurs Go Optical: The Market Downturn Hasn't Stopped Several Israeli Start-ups from Chasing the Optical Dream," *Lightwave* 19, issue 2, February 2002, 103–104. Portions reprinted with permission from *Lightwave*, February 2002, © 2002 IEEE.

Marketing Miscues

http://www.bluelight.com
Scott Carlson, "Expert Says Wal-Mart, Target Likely to Benefit from Kmart Bankruptcy," *Knight Ridder Tribune Business News,* January 23, 2002, 1; Sudeep Reddy and Steve Quinn, "Kmart Faces Short-Term, Long-Term Challenges," *Knight Ridder Tribune Business News,* January 23, 2002, 1.

Critical Thinking Case

http://www.hp.com
"Hewlett-Packard Laboratories Tests Total Web Environment," *Philadelphia Inquirer,* August 3, 2000, on-line, Gale Group, March 20, 2002; Brian Milner, "Fiorina Claims Victory in Fight of Her Life," *The Globe and Mail Metro,* March 20, 2002, A1; Sam Omatseye, "HP Serves Up Initiatives for Increasingly Mobile World," *RCR Wireless News,* October 15, 2001, 10s; Neil Orman, "Hewlett-Packard Seeks Livelier Image through 'Net Tech,'" *Sacramento Business Journal,* July 13, 2001, 24.

CHAPTER 4

Try It

Kevin Coupe, "A Theme Retailing Failure and Some Views on Restaurant and Pub Trends," *Store Equipment & Design*, January 2001, 24; Danielle Furfaro, "Entrepreneur Opens Family-Centered Restaurant in Albany, N.Y.," *Knight-Ridder Tribune Business News*, February 18, 2002; "McDonald's Launches World's First 'Town Center' Restaurant: New Restaurant Is Second Largest in U.S., Features Family 'Edu-Tainment,'" PR *Newswire*, April 30, 2002; "New Amex Seminars Focus on Consumer Dining Trends," *Nation's Restaurant News*, May 20, 2002, 200; Richard L. Papiernik, "Industry Sales for 2002 Projected to Hit $407 B," *Nation's Restaurant News*, January 7, 2002, 1.

CHAPTER 5

Try It

Alicia Neumann, "How It Works—A Better Mousetrap Catalog" *Business 2.0*, February 2000, 117–118; Aaron Baar, "Grainger Targets Purchasers," *Adweek*, May 31, 1999, 6; Peter Girard, "The Spin-off Payoff," *Catalog Age New Canaan*, March 15, 2000, 1, 18–21; Melanie Warner, Daniel Roth, Erick Schonfeld, and Marc Gunther, "Ten Companies That Get It," *Fortune*, Novembr 8, 1999, 115–117.

CHAPTER 6

Try It

Kipp Cheng, "eBay Best Viral Marketing," *Adweek*, June 28, 1999, IQ42; Claire Tristram, "Takin' It to the Street," *MC Technology Marketing Intelligence,* February 1999, 22–28; eBay Web site: http://www.ebay.com/community/aboutebay/overview/index.html.

CHAPTER 7

Try It

C. Pappas, "Pop Culture—Where It's At: Cool and How to Find It," *Advertising Age,* May 10, 2002, 16; R. A. Jones, "L.A. Duo Serves Fresh Trends Fast," *WWD,* December, 14, 2000, 11; T. Coffey, "Researchers Review Youth Buying Trends," *San Diego Business Journal,* November 13, 2000, 55.

Marketing Miscues

"A Review of the Ricochet Wireless Internet Service," 2002, on-line at http://www.wherry.com/gadgets/ricochet/; Peter Benesh, "Did Marketing Miscues Doom Metricom's Ricochet?" *Investor's Business Daily*, August 10, 2001, A6; Corey Grice, "Metricom Feels the Need for Wireless Speed," *CNET News.com* on-line, December 20, 1999; Margo McCall, "Wireless Pioneer Files Bankruptcy," *Wireless Week*, July 9, 2001, 1; Dan Meyer, "Metricom Seeks Financing as Rising Star Crashes," *RCR Wireless News*, February 12, 2001, 3.

Critical Thinking Case

Liz Consavage, "Square Two Gains with Women's Lines," *Golf World,* May 18, 2001, S6; ———, "Golf Company Shifts Focus to Women Players," *Marketing to Women: Addressing Women and Women's Sensibilities,* May 2001, 5; E. Michael Johnson, "The Total Package," *Golf World Business,* August 2000, 30; ———, "Women's Business Square Two's Focus," *Golf World,* July 14, 2000, S6; ———, "Women Wanted," *Golf World,* August 10, 2001, S2; http://www.womensgolf-unlimited.com.

CHAPTER 8

Try It

Stephanie Stoughton, "Path to Success," *Boston Globe,* June 17, 2000, C1–C2; "Topozone Launches Interactive Topographic Map Size, Revolutionizes Topographic Map Industry," *PR Newswire,* November 30, 1999, on-line; http://www.topozone.com.

CHAPTER 9

Try It

Risa Brim, "Lexington, Ky.-Based Motor Oil Producer Steps Out of Mold," *Lexington Herald-Leader*, November 5, 2001; Lucy May, "Ashland Launches Spirit 3-D Foam," *Business Courier Serving Cincinnati-Northern Kentucky*, October 12, 2001, 13.

CHAPTER 10

Try It

CarsDirect.com Web site at http://www.carsdirect.com; Robert Elder, Jr., and Jonathan Weil, "To Sell Cars in Texas, Online Firms Are Forced to Enter the Real World," *Wall Street Journal*, January 26, 2000, T1, T4; Maynard M. Gordon, "Battle Lines Forming in the Wild World of the Automotive Web Sites," *Ward's Dealer Business*, June 1, 2000, 12; Chris Knap, "Online Car Sales Will Rise, Analysts Say," *KRTBN Knight-Ridder Tribune Business News: The Orange County Register—California*, September 19, 1999; Jennifer Montgomery, "Texas State Law Bars Residents from Buying Cars Online," *KRTBN Knight-Ridder Tribune Business News: Houston Chronicle—Texas*, March 19, 2000; Fara Warner, "Racing for Slice of a $350 Billion Pie, Online Auto-Sales Sites Retool," *Wall Street Journal*, January 24, 2000, B1, B6; ———, "New Tactics Shake Up Online Auto Retailing," *Wall Street Journal*, October 18, 1999, B1; ———, "CarsDirect.com Bets on One-Stop, Desktop Showroom," *Wall Street Journal*, May 17, 1999, B4; Scott Woolley, "A Car Dealer by Any Other Name," *Forbes*, November 29, 1999, 113–116.

CHAPTER 11

Try It

Soozhana Choi, "Funky Fashions for Teen-Age Girls," *Gannett News Service*, March 16, 1999; Becky Ebenkamp, "Stephen Kahn," *Brandweek*, November 8, 1999, 32; Laura Keating, "The In Crowd: Retail Rushes to Keep Pace with Generation Y," *Shopping Center World*, May 30, 2000; Melanie Kletter, "Catalogs Lose Teen Appeal," *WWD*, March 2, 2000, 11; Paul Miller, "Apparel: Trends Analysis," *Catalog Age*, March 15, 2000, 65–69; David S. Murphy, "Delia's Next Big Step," *Fortune*, February 15, 1999, 192[C]–192[H]; Vicki M. Young, "Playing the Junior Game," *WWD*, October 27, 1999, 20; ———, "Teen Shopping Heats Up Online," *WWD*, February 3, 2000, 26B.

Marketing Miscues

"Kraus Gains Super Bowl Airtime via Mail Boxes Promo," *Brandweek*, January 8, 1999, 8; "Jeremy's MicroBatch Ice Creams," *Frozen Food Age*, January 2000, 42; "Dip Shops Part of New Management's Plans at Jeremy's," *Ice Cream Reporter*, September 20, 2000, 1; "Obits," *Inc.*, February 1, 2001, 33.

Critical Thinking Case

http://www.dekaresearch.com; http://www.segway.com; "Mystery Project Revealed," *Design Engineering*, January 2002, 7; Gareth Cook and Nicholas Thompson, "Ginger's Rough Ride," *Boston Globe*, February 5, 2002, C1–C3; "'Ginger' Revealed to be Electric Scooter," *Electric Vehicle Online Today*, December 4, 2001, on-line; Karl Greenberg, "The 'IT' Girl," *Brandweek*, November 12, 2001, 37; John Heileman, "Here 'IT' Is: The Inside Story of the Secret Invention That So Many Are Buzzing About," *Time*, December 10, 2001, 76.

CHAPTER 12

Try It

VarsityBooks.com Web site at http://www.varsitybooks.com; Jeff Gottlieb, "Internet Vendors Test College Textbook Market," *Los Angeles Times*, June 25, 2000, B-1; Ann M. Mack, "Textbook Case," *Brandweek*, August 7, 2000, IQ30; Karen Solomon, "College Bound," *Business 2.0*, April 1999; Jeffrey A. Tannenbaum, "Marketers on Campus: A New Bag of Tricks," *Wall Street Journal*, January 31, 2000, B1, B8; "Varsity Nears Breakeven on Lower Revenues," *Publishers Weekly*, April 8, 2002, 14; "Varsity Year Ends with New Business Model," *Educational Marketer*, April 15, 2002; Steven M. Zeitchik, "Capitalism on Campus," *Business 2.0*, May 2000; http://www.publishers.org.

CHAPTER 13

Try It

Bill Carter, "Will This Machine Change Television?" *New York Times*, 5 July 1999, 1; Jim Cooper, "Inside the Box," *Brandweek*, 8 May 2000, C32; Marla Matzer Rose, "TV Advertisers Worry About Growth of New PVRs," *Chicago Tribune*, 14 April 2000, 4; Erin Strout, "The End of TV Advertising?" *Sales & Marketing Management*, January 2000, 15; TiVo Web site at http://www.tivo.com; "TiVo Signs Showtime," *Advertising Age*, 16 May 2000.

CHAPTER 14

Bibliography for Chapter 14 Try It available on-line at http://lamb.swlearning.com

CHAPTER 15

Try It

Angela Lo, "Young Entrepreneurs' Dream Is to Become Mercer Island's Sole Internet Provider," *Seattle Times*, February 13, 2002; http://www.mercerislandchamber.org.

Marketing Miscues

http://www.gillette.com; "The Gillette Co.," *Drug Store News-Newsfirst*, February 13, 2002, 1; Ann Davin, "Duracell Launches New Advertising for America's Favorite Battery," Company press release, November 19, 2001, 1; Daniel Golden and Suzanne Vranica, "Advertising: Duracell's Duck Ad Will Carry Disclaimer," *Wall Street Journal*, February 7, 2002, B7; Jack Neff, "Energizing Their Bases: Duracell and Energizer Focus Ads on Flagships," *Advertising Age*, June 4, 2001, 4.

Critical Thinking Case

"iTunes Music Store Hits Five Million Downloads: Apple to Ship One Millionth iPod This Week," *M2 Presswire*, June 24, 2003; "Leaked iTunes Info Gives Insight into Apple's Success," *TV Meets the Web*, June 11, 2003; Chris Marlowe, "Apple Jams with Music Service: iTunes Music Store Offers 200,000 from All Major Labels," *Hollywood Reporter*, April 29, 2003, 4; Melinda Newman and Brian Garrity, "Apple's Service Tests Music Biz: Can Artists, Industry Capitalize on Digital Bid?" *Billboard*, May 10, 2003, 1; Justin Oppelaar, "Will Apple For-Pay Keep Doldrums Away?" *Variety*, May 12, 2003, 42; Randall Rothenberg, "Plenty to Learn from Apple's 'Near-Perfect' iTunes Store," *Advertising Age*, June 9, 2003, 22.

Index

Daimler Chrysler	http://www.chrysler.com
Deaf Resources.Com	http://www.deafresources.com
Delia*s Corp.	http://www.delias.com
Debeers	http://www.debeers.com
Dell Computer Corporation	http://www.dell.com
Delta Airlines	http://www.delta.com
Design 4 Packaging	http://www.design4packaging.com
Direct Marketing Association	http://www.the-dma.org
DirectTV	http://www.directtv.com
Disney	http://www.disney.go.com
Dun & Bradstreet	http://www.dnb.com
Easy Analytic Software, Inc.	http://www.easidemographics.com
eBay, Inc.	http://www.ebay.com
eCampus	http://www.ecampus.com
EconData	http://www.econdata.com
Economy.com, Inc.	http://www.dismal.com
Electric Library	http://wwws.elibrary.com
Electronic Gadget Depot.com	http://www.electronicgadetdepot.com
eMarketer	http://www.emarketer.com
Equifax	http://www.equifax.com/biz/index.shtml
ESRI BIS	http://www.escribis.com
European Union	http://europa.cu.int/index-en.htm
Exhibitor Magazine Group	http://www.exhibitornet.com
Expert Hotline	http://www.experthotline.com
Export-Import Bank of the United States	http://www.exim.gov
Federal Communications Commission	http://www.fcc.gov
Federal Trade Commission (FTC)	http://www.ftc.gov
Federation of International Trade Association	http://www.fita.org
Find/SVP	http://www.findsvp.com
Flash Banner Design	http://www.flash-banner-design.com
411 Direct	http://www.411direct.com/domainnamereg.htm
4Kids Entertainment, Inc.	http://www.4kidsentertainmentinc.com
Fox Network	http://www.fox.com
Fragrance Net.Com, Inc.	http://www.fragrancenet.com
Free Samples.com	http://www.FreeSamples.com
Free Trade Area of the Americas	http://www.ftaa-alca.org
Frito Lay	http://www.fritolay.com
Fuld and Company	http://www.fuld.com/i3/index.html
Game Girlz	http://www.gamegirlz.com
Gap	http://www.gap.com
Gardenburger	http://www.gardenburger.com
GE Polymerland	http://www.gepolymerland.com
General Motors Corporation	http://www.gm.com
Georgia Tech College of Computing	http://www.cc.gatech.edu/gvu/user_surveys
Godiva	http://www.godiva.com
GoLeads	http://www.goleads.com
Good Housekeeping	http://www.goodhousekeeping.com
Go2net.com	http://www.go2net.com
Government Bids.com	http://www.governmentbids.com
Grateful Dead	http://www.dead.net
Guerilla Marketing	http://www.gmarketing.com
HandSpeak	http://www.handspeak.com
Harris Info Source	http://www.harrisinfo.com
Hasbro, Inc.	http://www.monopoly.com
H.E. Butt Grocery Company	http://www.heb.com
Hershey Foods Corporation	http://www.hersheys.com
Hewlett-Packard	http://www.compaq.com
Home Depot, Inc.	http://www.homedepot.com
Home Office Association of America	http://www.hoaa.com
Hoover's Online	http://www.hoovers.com
IDEO	http://www.ideo.com
Independent Community Bankers of America	http://www.icba.org
Insight Express	http://www.insightexpress.com
Institute of Textile Technology	http://www.iit.edu/departments/csep/publicwww/codes
Inter-commerce Corporation	http://www.survey.net
International Franchise Association	http://www.franchise.org
Internet Public Library	http://www.ipl.org
Intuit, Inc.	http://www.intuit.com
itools	http://www.iTools.com/research-it/research-it.html
J. Crew	http://www.jcrew.com
Johnson & Johnson	http://www.jnj.com
Jupitermedia Corporation	http://thelist.internet.com
Klik-Klok Productions	http://www.klik-klok.com
Kraft Foods, Inc.	http://postcereal.com
Kroger Company	http://www.kroger.com/operations_manufacturing_about.htm
Lending Tree, Inc.	http://lendingtree.com
Let's Buy It.Com	http://www.letsbuyit.com

Levesque Design
Levi Strauss & Co.
Loctite Corporation
Look-Look.Com
Looksmart, Ltd.

Lycos, Inc.
Mall of America
Maps a la carte, Inc.
Marketing Research Association, Inc.
Martha Stewart Living
Matte Elsbernd
Mattel, Scrabble
Maxim Magazine

McDonald's
Media Director
MediaFinder
Mediamark Research, Inc.
Menlo Logistics
Mercosur
Michael H. Birnbaum

Micropatent
Microsoft
Monster.com
Movie Tickets.Com
Mysimon
Nabisco
Nash Finch Company
National Amusements.com
National Association of Purchasing Managers
Netnoir
Net Ratings
New Product Works
New York.Com Internet Holdings, Inc.
New York.Org
Nomina
Office.Com
Office of Nafta & Inter-American Affairs
Online Clothing Stores.com
Overture Services, Inc.
Palo Alto Software, Inc.
Papa John's
Paramount Pictures
Pizza Hut
Population Reference Bureau
Post Cereal
Power Images
Precision Machined Parts Association
Pricescan.com, Inc.
Princess Cruises
Procter & Gamble
Quaker Oats
Quicken

Radio Shack
RadioGuide
Rail Pass Express, Inc.
RCA
Real-World PR
Red Bull
Red Envelope
Rolex
Rubbermaid
Sales and Marketing Executives International, Inc.
Sears, Roebuck
Service Intelligence, Inc.
Sheraton
Sherwin-Williams Company
Smart Draw
Snip-Its Corporation
SoapWorks
Society of Competitive Intelligence Professionals
Sprint
Start Sampling, Inc.
Stop Junk Mail

http://www.levesquedesign.com
http://www.levi.com
http://loctite.com
http://www.look-look.com
http://www.looksmart.com/aboutus/media
http://www.looksmart.com
http://www.companiesonline.com
http://www.mallofamerica.com
http://www.topozone.com
http://www.MRA-net.org
http://www.marthastewart.com
http://www.firmlist.com/main.shtml
http://www.mattelscrabble.com
http://www.maximonline.com
http://www.maxim_magazine.co.uk
http://www.mcdonalds.com
http://www.mediadirector.com
http://www.mediafinder.com
http://www.mediamark.com/mri/docs/toplinereports.html
http://www.menlolog.com
http://mercosur.org/english/default.htm
http://psych.fullerton.edu/mbirnbaum/programs/surveywiz.htm
http://www.micropat.com
http://www.bcentral.com
http://www.monster.com
http://www.movietickets.com
http://www.mysimon.com
http://www.nabiscoworld.com
http://www.nashfinch.com
http://www.nationalamusements.com
http://www.napm.org
http://www.netnoir.com
http://www.nielsen-netratings.com
http://www.newproductworks.com
http://www.newyork.com
http://www.newyork.org
http://www.nomina.net
http://office.com
http://www.mac.doc.gov/nafta
http://www.onlineclothingstores.com
http://www.alltheweb.com
http://www.bplans.com
http://www.papajohns.com
http://www.paramount.com
http://www.pizzahut.com
http://www.prb.org
http://www.postcereal.com
http://pwr.com/creative
http://www.pmpa.org
http://www.pricescan.com
http://www.princesscruises.com
http://www.pg.com
http://www.quakeroats.com
http://www.quicken.com/small-business
http://www.quicken.com
http://www.radioshack.com
http://www.radioguide.com
http://railpass.com
http://www.rca.com
http://aboutpr.com
http://www.redbull.com
http://www.redenvelope.com
http://www.rolex.com
http://www.rubbermaid.com
http://www.smei.org
http://www.sears.com
http://serviceintelligence.com
http://www.sheraton.com
http://www.sherwinwilliams.com
http://www.smartdraw.com
http://www.snipits.com
http://www.soapworks.com
http://www.scip.org
http://www.sprint.com
http://www.StartSampling.com
http://www.stopjunkmail.com